Veronika Thanner, Joseph Vogl, Dorothea Walzer (Hg.)

Die Wirklichkeit des Realismus

Veronika Thanner, Joseph Vogl,
Dorothea Walzer (Hg.)

Die Wirklichkeit des Realismus

Wilhelm Fink

Gedruckt mit freundlicher Unterstützung des DAAD und des BMBF

DAAD

GEFÖRDERT VOM

Bundesministerium
für Bildung
und Forschung

Umschlagabbildung:
Artwork: *from* Coastal Scenes and Shipping, Boats at Sea, after c.1830,
Joseph Mallord William Turner (1775-1851)
Photo: ©Tate, London 2016

Bibliografische Information der Deutschen Nationalbibliothek

Die Deutsche Nationalbibliothek verzeichnet diese Publikation in der Deutschen Nationalbibliografie; detaillierte bibliografische Daten sind im Internet über http://dnb.d-nb.de abrufbar.

Internet: www.fink.de

Lektorat und Satz: Margret Westerwinter
www.lektorat-westerwinter.de
Einbandgestaltung: Evelyn Ziegler, München
Herstellung: Brill Deutschland GmbH, Paderborn

ISBN 978-3-7705-6169-8

Inhalt

Veronika Thanner, Joseph Vogl, Dorothea Walzer

Die Wirklichkeit des Realismus. Einleitung

Verschwimmende Sicht, Nebel und dubiose Flecken im Blickfeld des Erzählers: Joseph Conrads Erzählung *Heart of Darkness* führt eine Schreibweise vor, die – nicht untypisch für den zeitgenössischen literarischen Realismus des 19. und frühen 20. Jahrhunderts – ein besonderes Interesse an Unschärfen und *blind spots* zeigt, ja mehr noch: solche „bedeutungslose Flecken"[1] erzähltechnisch produziert. Das Wirkliche wird bei Conrad dort aufgesucht, wo es sich ‚gleißend' und ‚glitzernd' der Anschauung – und damit auch der Darstellung – entzieht. Zugleich führt seine Erzählung an eine Brechung oder genauer Verdoppelung des Wirklichen heran:

> Now and then a boat from the shore gave one a momentary contact with reality. It was paddled by black fellows. You could see from afar the white of their eyeballs glistening. [...] They wanted no excuse for being there. They were a great comfort to look at. For a time I would feel I belonged still to a world of straightforward facts; but the feeling would not last long. Something would turn up to scare it away.[2]

Dass eine in die symbolische Ordnung eingebettete Wirklichkeit der ‚ehrlichen Fakten' zurückweichen muss vor einem genauso verlockenden wie bedrohlichen Realen, verweist auf eine grundlegende Problematisierung von Referenzialität, die – über die epochale Lokalisierung von ‚Realismen' hinweg – Repräsentationsweisen des Wirklichen in Literatur und Kunst bis heute bestimmt.

Bereits die frühen Realismusdebatten, wie sie im deutschsprachigen Raum Mitte des 19. Jahrhunderts etwa von Julian Schmidt, Gustav Freytag oder Karl Gutzkow geführt werden, machen nachdrücklich nicht nur realistische Darstellungsformen, sondern vor allem die „sogenannte [...] Wirklichkeit"[3] selbst zum Problem. So wurde dabei die literarische Bezugnahme auf eine „handgreifliche Realität [...], die uns Widerstand leistet"[4], auf unberechenbare Subjekte oder generell der strittige Status des Irrationalen, Zufälligen und „Nebelhaften"[5] bei Autoren wie Georg Büchner, Friedrich Hebbel oder Erich Auerbach von den Vertretern des Poetischen Realismus aufs Schärfste angegriffen. Abseits der Positionen des programmatischen (*Grenzboten*-)Realismus entstehen dabei (früh-)realistische Schreibweisen, die, wie

1 Roland Barthes, *Das Rauschen der Sprache. Kritische Essays IV*, Frankfurt/M., 2006, S. 166.

2 Joseph Conrad, *The Heart of Darkness*, New York, NY, London, 2006, S. 13 f.

3 Julian Schmidt, „Der neueste englische Roman und das Princip des Realismus", in: *Die Grenzboten. Zeitschrift für Politik und Literatur* 15, 4 (1856), S. 466-474: 468.

4 Ebd., S. 470.

5 Theodor Fontane, „Unsere lyrische und epische Poesie seit 1848", in: *Deutsche Annalen zur Kenntniß der Gegenwart und Erinnerung an die Vergangenheit*, Band 1, 1853, S. 353-377: 359.

bei Gutzkow, die Wirklichkeit als „einhüllendes Gespinnst“[6] darstellen oder die mit der narrativen Aufhebung der geordneten Struktur von Form und Grund experimentieren wie bei Adalbert Stifter. Im literarischen Realismus des 19. Jahrhunderts findet sich somit eine radikale Infragestellung der Wirklichkeit vorformuliert, die wir als signifikant für realistische Darstellungsformen behaupten.

Gerade dort, wo die Existenz von Wirklichkeit als Referenzpunkt künstlerischer Auseinandersetzung auf den ersten Blick ungebrochen scheint, macht sich eine Verschiebung, ein Stocken, eine minimale Abweichung in den Darstellungsweisen bemerkbar: Die emphatische Bezugnahme auf die wirkliche Welt geht hier Hand in Hand mit der Häufung von darstellerischen Unschärfen, (Wahrnehmungs-)Störungen oder pararealistischen Einschüben, mit denen der Status der erzählten oder beschriebenen Wirklichkeit fragwürdig geworden ist. Hier wird ein prekärer Bezug zur Wirklichkeit offengelegt, der im vorliegenden Band als Indikator des Realistischen in Literatur, Film und Kunst verstanden werden soll. Denn im „Fleck“ („*tache*“)[7] und im Flimmern des Bildes manifestiert sich, wie Jacques Lacan erläutert hat, ein Reales: die Funktion des Blicks, der sich dem Sehen selbst entzieht und dennoch wirkt, weil das Subjekt ihn „auf dem Feld des Andern“ imaginiert und damit an den Abgrund seiner Weltverhältnisse gerät.[8]

Realismus als die Verhandlungsform eines nicht selbstverständlich festgestellten Realen zu interpretieren, heißt also einerseits, systematisch eine „konstitutive Nicht-Feststellbarkeit des Realen“[9] im Angesicht einer zunehmend komplexen Wirklichkeit zu detektieren. Es heißt aber auch, nach den epistemischen, den medialen und politischen Dimensionen einer solchen Undarstellbarkeits- bzw. Unschärferelation zu fragen. Was also sind die Medien und Wahrheitspraktiken realistischen Schreibens und Darstellens? Worin korrespondieren oder divergieren institutionelle Wissensbestände (Recht, Geschichte, Wissenschaft usw.) einerseits und literarische, künstlerische Verwirklichungspraktiken andererseits? Und inwiefern lässt sich das skizzierte Darstellungsproblem, wie im Rahmen einer marxistisch informierten Realismusdebatte von Georg Lukács über Bertolt Brecht bis zu Fredric Jameson vorgeschlagen, als Effekt einer kapitalistischen Moderne interpretieren? Realismus, ausdrücklich nicht im Sinne einer literaturhistorischen Epochenbeschreibung verstanden, sondern als spezifische Schreibweise der Erzeugung, Erprobung und Ver(un)sicherung von Wirklichkeit, formiert sich in dieser Hinsicht sowohl als ästhetisches, wie auch als epistemologisches und politisches

---

6 Karl Ferdinand Gutzkow, *Die Ritter vom Geiste*. Roman in neun Büchern, hg. von Thomas Neumann, nach dem Text der Erstausgabe von 1850/1851, Frankfurt/M., 1998, S. 12.

7 Jacques Lacan, *Das Seminar XI (1964). Die vier Grundbegriffe der Psychoanalyse*, hg. von Norbert Haas und Hans-Joachim Metzger, Berlin, 1996, S. 80 f.

8 Ebd., S. 90.

9 Albrecht Koschorke, „Das Mysterium des Realen in der Moderne“, in: Helmut Lethen/Ludwig Jäger/Albrecht Koschorke (Hg.), *Auf die Wirklichkeit zeigen. Zum Problem der Evidenz in den Kulturwissenschaften. Ein Reader*, Frankfurt/M., New York, NY, 2015, S. 13-38: 16.

Problem, das der vorliegende Band entlang von vier thematischen Fluchtlinien untersuchen will.

I. Legen wir den Fokus auf die epistemische Fassung des Wirklichen, so gerät zunächst eine Realität der wissenschaftlich induzierten „Verdatung"[10] in den Blick, die aufs Engste an die Entwicklung spezifischer Medientechniken (Fotografie, Film und digitale Medien) und der ihnen zugehörigen Verfahren und Institutionen der Objektivierung (z. B. Experiment, Reportage oder die von Ulrike Vedder untersuchte (Welt-)Ausstellung) gebunden ist. Dass der Zugriff auf Wirklichkeit gerade im Realismus nie unvermittelt ist, sondern mit einem medien- bzw. apparatbedingten Überschuss gleichsam eine zweite Dimension des Wirklichen eröffnet, ist im literarischen Realismus – etwa, in dem von Elisabeth Strowick behandelten ‚Szenischen Realismus' Adalbert Stifters – ebenso deutlich geworden wie in den von Volker Pantenburg beschriebenen Konzepten des filmischen Realismus. Gleiches gilt für die diskursive Durchdringung der Wirklichkeit. Wo realistische Literatur, filmischer Realismus oder Realismen in der Kunst auf multiple Wirklichkeiten Bezug nehmen, beziehen sie sich bereits auf eine durch juristisches, medizinisches, historisches oder soziologisches Wissen produzierte Realität. Umgekehrt setzen solche Spezialdiskurse wiederum spezifische Praktiken der ‚poietischen' Verfertigung von Wirklichkeit voraus, wie Chenxi Tang entlang der Parallelen zwischen realistisch-naturalistischem Rechtsverständnis und literarischem Realismus aufzeigt. Ob der literarische ‚historische Realismus' Bilder von solchen Spezialdiskursen voraussetzt, simuliert oder zitiert (z. B. in Émile Zolas *Lourdes* oder Fjodor M. Dostojevskijs *Die Brüder Karamasov*), ihre diskursive Verfasstheit ausstellt (wie Veronika Thanners Beitrag das am Beispiel von Wilhelm Raabes *Abu Telfan* demonstriert), sie parodiert oder überbietet (etwa in Gustave Flauberts *Salambo*) – er produziert hierbei seinerseits Bilder von wissenschaftlichen Diskursen, die einer eigenen Logik folgen oder die zitierten Diskurse gleichsam mit verstörender Varianz verdoppeln, mithin auf einem inhärenten Verfremdungseffekt beruhen. So zeigt etwa Christian Begemann anhand von Paul Heyse und Theodor Storm auf, wie realistisches Erzählen genau dort den Konsens über das Wirkliche zersetzt, wo (natur-)wissenschaftlich bestimmte Wirklichkeitskonzepte einer narrativen Ordnung des Phantastischen begegnen und damit etablierte Erzählordnungen gleichsam unterwandern.

II. Den Nexus von Literatur und Geschichte als zweiten zentralen Problemhorizont realistischer Darstellungspraxis zu interpretieren, legt eine Beobachtung von Roland Barthes nahe: „[Z]eitgleich zur Herrschaft der ‚objektiven' Geschichte" entstehen demnach unter dem Namen des literarischen Realismus Erzählungen, die „bereit sind, die Zwischenräume zwischen ihren Funktionen mit struktural über-

---

10 Jürgen Link, „‚Wiederkehr des Realismus' – aber welches? Mit besonderem Bezug auf Jonathan Littell", in: *kultuRRevolution*, 54 (2008), S. 6-24: 9.

flüssigen Eintragungen auszufüllen", solange diese denotieren, „was stattgefunden hat".[11] In der von Barthes konstatierten Brechung des Erzählflusses durch eingeschobene Elemente und referenzlose Details ohne strukturelle Funktion, formiert sich Wirklichkeit als Effekt einer dem Kunstwerk inhärenten Differenz von Erzählung und Beschreibung.[12] Mit dieser internen Verschiebung rückt zugleich die Frage nach dem Status von Wahrscheinlichkeit im literarischen Realismus in den Blick. Denn wenn Wirklichkeit als Verteilung möglicher, mehr oder weniger wahrscheinlicher Zustände begriffen wird, wie Niklaus Largier anhand einer Problematisierung von Geschichtlichkeit und Möglichkeitsdimensionen im figuralen Realismus diskutiert, dann erscheint das Detail innerhalb der Darstellung als das, was sich der Wahrscheinlichkeit narrativer Formen entzieht. So kann die „zitternde Oberwelt in der schmutzigen Pfütze"[13] für Siegfried Kracauer zum Signum eines der Signifikation entzogenen Realen des Films werden, wie Friedrich Balke in seinem Beitrag zum Rohmaterialaspekt nachzeichnet.

Nehmen wir also an, dass die spezifische Wahrscheinlichkeit des Realismus – Gegenstand der Debatten um Nachahmung und Mimesis –„nur vom Referenten beglaubigt wird"[14], dann kann realistische Darstellung einerseits auf die immanenten Verfahren und Geschichte(n) der Objektivierung, kurz auf die in ihr produzierten „Realitätseffekte" (Barthes) hin befragt werden. Gleichzeitig steht mit der Narrativierung kontingenter Prozesse, die Jacques Rancière als „große Parataxe" (*„grande parataxe"*)[15] bezeichnet hat, die politische Dimension eines Realismus im Raum, der die Vermutung nahelegt, das „Reale [müsse] zur Dichtung werden, damit es gedacht werden kann"[16]. Zur materiellen Trope gewordene Details – „feine Stäubchen, die in der Sonne glänzen, ein Tropfen geschmolzenen Schnees, der auf den changierenden Moiréstoff eines Schirms fällt, ein Fetzen Laub an der Schnauze eines Esels"[17] bei Flaubert oder „Berge von Gemüse, Wurstwaren, Fischen und Käse"[18] bei Zola – beziehen ihre Wirklichkeit Rancière zufolge daraus, dass sie dem System der Ursachen die Vernunftlosigkeit der Dinge eintragen. Darin geht die Mimesis des von Rancière sogenannten „ästhetischen Regimes der Künste", wie Maria Muhle in ihrem Text über *Mimesis und Aisthesis* argumentiert, über Auerbachs Mimesis hinaus, bleibt letztere doch einem wissenschaftlichen Paradigma der Kritik verhaftet, das Reinhart Koselleck als Unterordnung der Ge-

---

11 Barthes (2006), *Das Rauschen der Sprache*, S. 170.

12 Ebd., S. 165 f. und S. 169.

13 Siegfried Kracauer, *Theorie des Films. Die Errettung der äußeren Wirklichkeit*, übers. von Friedrich Walter und Ruth Zellschan, Frankfurt/M., 1979, S. 14.

14 Barthes (2006), *Das Rauschen der Sprache*, S. 171.

15 Jacques Rancière, *Les destin des images*, Paris, 2003, S. 55-64.

16 Jacques Rancière, *Die Aufteilung des Sinnlichen. Die Politik der Kunst und ihre Paradoxien*, übers. von Maria Muhle, Berlin, 2006, S. 61.

17 Rancière (2003), *Les destin des images*, S. 61.

18 Ebd.

schichten unter die notwendige Verlaufsform der „Geschichte selbst"[19] bezeichnet hatte.

III. Ist es richtig, dass in realistischen Darstellungsweisen systematisch eine Krise des Realitätszugriffs aufscheint, dann geht diese nicht nur mit einer Fragwürdigkeit des Referenten, sondern auch mit einer Infragestellung des wahrnehmenden Subjekts und der damit zusammenhängenden gesellschaftlichen Selbstwahrnehmung einher. Verstehen wir Wirklichkeit – in Abgrenzung von einem ‚Spekulativen Realismus'[20], der auf eine Rückgewinnung zweifelsfreier Realitäten ‚spekuliert' (vgl. die Beiträge von Joseph Vogl und Jenny Nachtigall) – als eine durch unzuverlässige Wahrnehmungsereignisse determinierte, eröffnet dies also drittens die Frage nach neuen Konstitutionsformen des wahrnehmenden und/oder erzählenden Subjekts.[21] Die fortschreitende Erosion souveräner Erzählinstanzen bei Raabe, Stifter oder Storm, genau wie die kontinuierliche Auflösung der ‚holistischen' und ‚organischen' Sinn-Geschlossenheit des realistischen Figurenarsenals des 19. Jahrhunderts in Männer und Frauen ohne Eigenschaften, die Devin Fore in *Realism after Modernism* mit Blick auf die künstlerischen Avantgarden beschrieben hat,[22] und sogar noch der von ihm in diesem Band behandelte deverbative Sprachgebrauch der sowjetischen Faktografie erscheinen in dieser Hinsicht als literarische Reflexion einer epistemologischen Verunsicherung des Subjekts.

Schon in Conrads eingangs zitierter Erzählung *Heart of Darkness* wird der Leser Zeuge des spektakulären Zusammenbrechens eines Kolonialsubjekts, das Fakten sucht, um Angst bzw. „horror" zu finden. Wo die Realität der Fakten („straightforward facts") dem Schrecken eines irreduziblen „Etwas" („something") weichen muss, wird Angst zum „Signal des Realen"[23]. Noch auf der basalen Ebene des Sprechens lässt die dialektal-artikulatorische Verunreinigung, wie von Natalie Binczek an Riccaut de la Marliniéres ‚Kauderwelsch' belegt, das Lachen zum Effekt des Realen werden. Jameson hat das Auftauchen eines Subjekts, das nicht mehr empfindet (fühlt), sondern erfährt (affiziert ist) sogar als Gründungsakt realistischen Schreibens, den „Realitätseffekt" mithin als eine Art Realitäts*affekt* reinterpretiert.[24]

---

19 Reinhart Koselleck, *Vergangene Zukunft. Zur Semantik geschichtlicher Zeiten*, Frankfurt/M., 2015, S. 50.

20 Vgl. Armen Avenassian (Hg.), *Realismus Jetzt. Spekulative Philosophie und Metaphysik für das 21. Jahrhundert*, Berlin, 2013; Quentin Meillassoux, *Nach der Endlichkeit – Versuch über die Notwendigkeit der Kontingenz*, Berlin, Zürich, 2014 [frz. OA 2006].

21 Vgl. hierzu Elisabeth Strowick, „‚Und schon konnte ich nicht mehr mit Sicherheit die Hufen meines Pferdes erkennen.' Erosion der Wahrnehmung in Theodor Storms *Der Schimmelreiter*", in: Christiane Arndt/Silke Brodersen (Hg.), *Organismus und Gesellschaft: Der Körper in der deutschsprachigen Literatur des Realismus (1830-1930)*, Bielefeld, 2011, S. 93-122.

22 Devin Fore, *Realism after Modernism*, Cambridge, MA, 2012.

23 Jacques Lacan, *Die Angst. Seminar X*, Wien, Berlin, 2010, S. 197.

24 Fredric Jameson, *Antinomies of Realism*, London, 2013, S. 27.

IV. Schließlich gerät die systematische und methodische Funktion eines Realen der ‚Krise' selbst in den Blick. Denn als „realistätssteigernde Anomalie"[25] erscheinen krisenhafte Ereignisse und Katastrophen in der vermeintlichen Unmittelbarkeit ihres ‚Hereinbrechens' und ihrer beängstigenden Überwältigungswirkung prädestiniert, eine Wirklichkeit zu fassen, die sich scheinbar ihrer konventionsbedingten Konstruiertheit und ihrer medialen Filter entledigt hat. Realismen profitieren damit offenbar von einem Krisenwissen der Moderne, erscheinen (ökonomische) Krisen mit der zunehmenden Verkürzung ihrer zyklischen Wiederkehr doch ganz offenbar als „epistemologische Glücksfälle"[26], welche die Kanäle und Elemente des Systems sowie die fatale Effizienz seines Funktionierens offenlegen. Bereits für Zola wurde die Störung als Indikator der Funktionsweise des physiologischen Systems zum Ausgangspunkt des *Roman expérimental*;[27] Samo Tomšič spitzt diese These in seinem Beitrag in methodologischer Hinsicht zu, wenn er zeigt, dass die Wirklichkeit des Experimentierens mit Lacan (und im Anschluss an Alexandre Koyré) als „immanentes Hindernis" und das Reale als „Unmögliches" zu denken ist. Ähnlich zielt Lukács darauf ab, die Krisenhaftigkeit des kapitalistischen Reproduktionsprozesses als epistemologisches Vehikel für seine Realismustheorie fruchtbar zu machen, indem er die Krise, wie Ulrich Plass am Beispiel von Christian Krachts *Imperium* und W. G. Sebalds *Ringe des Saturn* aufzeigt, als Manifestation der verborgenen Ganzheit oder Totalität eines prinzipiell desintegrativen Systems begreift.[28] Aber auch filmische Techniken wie die Montage können als Einsatzpunkt eines Realismus fungieren, der die Widersprüche des wirklichen Lebens oder die Logik des Klassenkampfes hervortreiben will – Dorothea Walzers Beitrag stellt dies anhand von Sergej Eisensteins filmischen, John Heartfields fotografischen und Kurt Tucholskys publizistischen Karikaturen bzw. ‚Realsatiren' aus.

Tatsächlich spricht einiges dafür, im Krisenhaften selbst eine epistemologische wie ästhetische Urszene des Realismus zu erkennen und – damit zusammenhängend – nach spezifischen Schreibweisen seiner Artikulation zu fragen, wie sie Till Breyer am Beispiel politischer und ökonomischer Krisenszenerien des Jahres 1918 bei Hermann Broch untersucht. Ganz in diesem Sinne erfährt die Anrufung des Krisenhaften in Joe Clearys Begriff eines „peripheral realism"[29] neue Aufmerksamkeit. So lautet Clearys Vorschlag, den Realismus von den Peripherien her, oder genauer, aus dem krisenhaften Verhältnis von Peripherie und Zentrum – und das heißt auch: zwischen der Ersten Welt und ihren Kolonien, ihrem Außen – zu bestimmen.[30] Wenn nun das Paradigma eines „traumatic realism"[31], wie Hal Foster in

25 Koschorke (2015), Das Mysterium des Realen in der Moderne, S. 36.

26 Joseph Vogl, „Gezähmte Zeit. Finanzialisierungsprozesse und ihre Medien", in: David Unterholzner/Eva Lanquièze/Marianne Kubaczek/Peter Berz (Hg.), *Spielregeln. 25 Aufstellungen. Eine Festschrift für Wolfgang Pircher*, Zürich, 2012, S. 61-71: 68.

27 Emile Zola, *Der Experimentalroman. Eine Studie*, Leipzig, 1904.

28 Vgl. auch Georg Lukács, „Realism in Balance", in: *Aesthetics and Politics*, London, 1977, S. 32.

29 Joe Cleary, „Realism after Modernism and the Literary World-System", in: *Modern Language Quarterly* 73, 3 (2012), S. 255-268: 267.

30 Ebd., S. 268.

seinem Beitrag argumentiert, in der zeitgenössischen Kunst und Literatur durch den Realismus einer „forensic architecture" ersetzt wird, wenn also die Realität weder als Texteffekt noch als traumatischer Affekt, sondern als *reenactment* von Wirklichkeit konzeptualisiert wird, dann wird die Evokation eines Bruchs oder Sprungs zukunftsträchtig: Sie erlaubt es, eine andere Realität zu erahnen.

---

[31] Hal Foster, *The Return of the Real*, Cambridge, MA, 1996, insbes. S. 130-136; ders., „Object, Abject, Traumatic", in: *October*, 78 (1996), S. 106-124: 122.

Hal Foster

Real Fictions

1. Despite rumors of its disappearance, the real remains with us. The labor of its production is "obstinate," Alexander Kluge and Oskar Negt argue; it persists in the overlooked furniture of our everyday lives. The real is as intractable as history, Fredric Jameson adds; neither can be transcended. If these formulations seem right, then the question of the real is not its presence but its position—where it is located, how, by whom, and for what reasons. One way to come to terms with some criticism, art, and literature is through these framings.[1]

2. We say that modern critique took its bearings from Marx, Freud, and Nietzsche, but what did these thinkers have in common? Little more than a "hermeneutics of suspicion" (as Paul Ricoeur termed it), the operative assumption that the real is hidden or buried and the critic must hunt it out or dig it up.[2] Of course, for Marx the unacknowledged truth of history is class struggle; that is the occluded narrative that must be extracted from all other accounts. For Freud, the unconscious reality of subjective life is psychic conflict; such is the latent content to limn that must be teased from the manifest confusions of our dreams, symptoms, and slip-ups. And, for Nietzsche, the unspoken force behind any system of thought is a will to power, which is to be challenged or celebrated as one sees fit. The Frankfurt School drew on all three approaches, and a key instance of its caustic critique remains the assessment of New Objectivity photography delivered by Brecht by way of Benjamin: "A photograph of the Krupp works or the AEG tells us next to nothing about these institutions," Brecht remarked with the steel manufacturer and the electric utility in mind. "The reification of human relations – the factory, say—means that they are no longer explicit. So something must in fact be *built up*, something artificial, posed. [Emphasis in the original.]"[3] This statement captures

---

1 See Alexander Kluge and Oskar Negt, *History & Obstinacy*, trans. by Richard Langston et al., ed. by Devin Fore, New York, NY: Zone Books, 2014, passim, and Fredric Jameson, *The Political Unconscious: Narrative as Socially Symbolic Act*, Ithaca, NY: Cornell University Press, 1981, p. 82 and p. 102. There are other framings of the real (such as speculative realism) that I do not take up here, and more overlap in the ones I do discuss than a chronological review such as this can address. This text was originally published in *Artforum* (April 2017).

2 See Paul Ricoeur, *Freud & Philosophy: An Essay on Interpretation*, trans. by Denis Savage, New Haven, CT: Yale University Press, 1970, p. 34. Ricouer uses the exact phrase only later, in a retrospect on this text. See, also, Rita Felski, *The Limits of Critique*, Chicago, IL: University of Chicago Press, 2015.

3 Brecht quoted in Walter Benjamin, "Little History of Photography" (1931), in: Michael W. Jennings et al. (eds.), *Selected Writings, Volume 2, Part 2: 1931-1934*, trans. by Rodney Livingstone et al., Cambridge, MA: Belknap Press, 1999, pp. 507-530: here p. 526. Benjamin doubles down on this attack in

the characteristic move of ideology critique: to expose the real behind the representations that conceal it or otherwise shore it up. As Brecht indicated, one way to attempt this exposé in art is via an image or text (or, from John Heartfield to Barbara Kruger, a combination of the two) that is "built up," montaged.

3. A late epitome of ideology critique is *Mythologies* (1957), in which, with a mix of old Brechtian estrangement and new Structuralist decoding, Roland Barthes read various manifestations of middle-brow culture (e.g., "The Family of Man" exhibition staged by Edward Steichen in 1955, the Blue Guide travel books) as so many class-bound myths that present specific beliefs as general truths. *Mythologies* was a first manual of critical suspicion for many artists and critics; its influence was especially strong in conceptual and feminist practices that employed image appropriation (e.g., Victor Burgin and Sherrie Levine). However, in the wake of 1968, Barthes already had second thoughts: "Any student can and does denounce the bourgeois or petit-bourgeois character of such and such a form," he wrote in 1971. "It is no longer the myths which need to be unmasked (the doxa now takes care of that), it is the sign itself which must be shaken."[4] What could be more radical than this quasi-Maoist call for a "semioclasm" that passed beyond demystification to attack representation as such? The signs that stitch the real together were to be not merely exposed but torn utterly asunder.

4. In the event, however, the real was only repositioned: No longer hidden or buried, it was now thought to lie, overlooked but in plain sight, on the surface of things. One signal of this shift, soon to be associated with poststructuralist theory, was another Barthes essay, "*L'effet de réel*" (The Reality Effect, 1968), which considered the function of the detail in nineteenth-century narrative, both fictional and historical (his test cases were Flaubert and Michelet, respectively).[5] In such narrative, Barthes argued, everything is expected to mean; even incidental details that seem not to signify do so nonetheless, for what they thus signify is *in*significance, and the apparent meaninglessness of the mere facts of the contingent world helps to clinch the realist evocation of the real. In this account, nothing escapes the "empire of signs," and so it was but a short step to see realism *in toto* as a system of conventions, as Barthes did in *S/Z* (1970), his painstaking analysis of the Balzac short story "Sarrasine" (1830). There he demonstrated, line by line, how Balzac referred "not from a language to a referent but from one code to another"—that is, how the narrative consisted "not in copying the real but in copying a (depicted)

"The Author as Producer" (1934). In both cases, the main target is Albert Renger-Patzsch, but his work is more differentiated than either Benjamin or Brecht allows. See Jennings, "Agriculture, Industry, and the Birth of the Photo-Essay in the Early Weimar Republic," in: *October* 93 (Summer 2000): pp. 23-56.

4 Roland Barthes, "Change the Object Itself" (1971), in: *Image-Music-Text*, trans. by Stephen Heath, New York, NY: Hill and Wang, 1977, pp. 166-167.

5 Roland Barthes, "The Reality Effect" (1968), in: *The Rustle of Language*, trans. by Richard Howard, New York, NY: Hill and Wang, 1986, pp. 141-148.

copy of the real." "This is why realism cannot be designated a 'copier'," Barthes concluded, "but rather a 'pasticheur' (through secondary mimesis, it copies what is already a copy)."[6] A decade later this figure of the pasticheur became the dominant avatar of the postmodernist artist, in the guise of both the Neo-Expressionist painter who mixed historical and pop motifs and the critical appropriationist who held up media stereotypes for our scrutiny. Semiotically speaking, these ideological opponents played on the same team.

5. If Barthes contributed to the first two framings of the real, he exemplified yet a third. Here the real was still attached to the detail that resists meaning, but it was now located in the subject as much as in the object. This detail is the famous *punctum*, the term Barthes used in *Camera Lucida* (1980) to describe the inadvertent point in a particular photograph that pricks the unconscious of the viewer: "It is this element which rises from the scene, shoots out of it like an arrow, and pierces me."[7] Inflected by Lacan, this third positioning of the real, which we might call traumatophilic, differs from the first two in key ways. In the ideology-critical framing, the critic exposes the real, whereas here the real exposes the subject; and in the poststructuralist framing, the subject is displaced, and the real subsumed, by conventions and codes, whereas here the subject is called back as witness to a real now understood as traumatic.[8] What could be more real than a real that resists all symbolization? Gradually, however, it became clear that this real could be codified too; in fact, it could count as a realism of its own. This was the case with abject art and fiction in the 1990s, exemplified in the work of Mike Kelley and Dennis Cooper, once their tropes of bodily disfiguration and psychic damage were established.

6. In one way or another, all the aforementioned framings of the real rejected the naïve notion that the realist work is a mirror of the world, yet a reflectionist assumption sneaks back in when we refer cultural outlooks too directly to economic processes. Nonetheless, a few connections between the two registers might be hazarded here if only to underscore that they do in fact exist. Jameson saw the transition to postmodernism in terms of a crackup of the sign under advanced

---

6 Roland Barthes, *S/Z*, trans. by Richard Howard, New York, NY: Hill and Wang, 1974, p. 55.

7 Roland Barthes, *Camera Lucida*, trans. by Richard Howard, New York, NY: Hill and Wang, 1981, p. 26.

8 See the title essay of my *The Return of the Real: The Avant-Garde at the End of the Century*, Cambridge, MA: MIT Press, 1996. For good and bad, *Camera Lucida* long dominated theoretical reflection on photography; certainly its emphasis on medium specificity and traumatic subjectivity distracted many of us from the social-historical field of photography. Barthes acknowledges this field, which he calls the *studium*, but his heart belongs to the *punctum* (he sees the *studium* as an array of conventional signs). So, too, his traumatophilic reading of photography restricts its temporality to the past, one that affects us but which we cannot affect in turn. This view limits photography as a means of historical reflection; it also reduces its potential for critique as well as for construction—both of which were foregrounded in the photo debates in interwar Europe, not to mention in the recent work of the late Allan Sekula.

capitalism. In the modernist epoch, he argued, "reification 'liberated' the sign from its referent," as evidenced in the abstraction that pervaded its arts. Yet this "dissolution" only deepened in the postmodernist era: Now internal to the sign, reification worked to liberate "the signifier from the signified, or from the meaning proper."[9] Here our second framing of the real, the real as a textual effect, was suddenly repositioned, for such semioclasm was now taken to do the cultural work of a capitalist order that thrives on "floating signifiers." In part, the third framing of the real—the real as traumatic affect—stemmed from a recognition that the postmodernist crackup of the sign was not as resistant to advanced capitalism as it purported to be, that it might even be structurally consonant with that order. Of course, other forces were also at work in this shift from the textual to the traumatic—the AIDS crisis, systemic poverty, racism, and sexism, a broken welfare state, a wounded body politic.[10] Nevertheless, to some degree, "the body in pain" emerged as a protest against the empire of signs.

7. The last decade has seen yet another turn in the framing of the real, one that bespeaks a frustration with the three positionings that preceded it. First, ideology critique was already under attack on account of the authority that it appeared to arrogate. Like most poststructuralist theory, much postmodernist art had questioned such authority, but this challenge was soon understood to erode the very ability to claim a truth or to posit a reality at all, and so it came to be questioned as a species of nihilism. (The critique of representation, central to both poststructuralism and postmodernism, was also tainted when the Right later appropriated it for its own ends, as in the assertion that global warming is a "mere construction.") Lastly, the traumatophilic framing of the real brought authority back into play, in the strong guise of the subject as witness (even as survivor), yet this development came with a problem of its own—for how is such authority to be questioned in turn? Bruno Latour emerged as a prominent skeptic of all three framings of the real, especially with regard to the negativity that each appeared to advance in its own way. Against this destructive critic, he offered his own benevolent figure:

> The critic is not the one who debunks, but the one who assembles. The critic is not the one who lifts the rugs from under the feet of the naïve believers, but the one who offers the participants arenas in which to gather. The critic is not the one who alternates haphazardly between antifetishism and positivism like the drunk iconoclast drawn by Goya, but the one for whom, if something is constructed, then it means it is fragile and thus in need of great care and caution.[11]

---

9 Fredric Jameson, "Periodizing the '60s," in: *The 60s Without Apology*, ed. by Sohnya Sayres et al., Minneapolis, MN: University of Minnesota Press, 1984, p. 200.

10 Again, it is this condition that abject art and fiction evoked with their own version of realism.

11 Bruno Latour, "Why Has Critique Run Out of Steam? From Matters of Fact to Matters of Concern," in: *Critical Inquiry* 30, 2 (Winter 2004): pp. 225-248: here p. 246. Also see my "Post-Critical?" in: *Bad New Days: Art, Criticism, Emergency*, New York, NY: Verso, 2015.

8. This shift, with the real now viewed as a fragile construction to tend with care and caution, is evident in recent documentary practices—a category that was often a bad object for both ideology critique and postmodernist art (not to mention poststructuralist theory). Brecht can represent the former position—again, "a photograph of the Krupp works or the AEG tells us next to nothing about these institutions"—while Martha Rosler can stand in for the latter with her framing of documentary photography as an "inadequate descriptive system." Today, however, this critique of the document is largely assimilated, and many artists have passed from a posture of deconstruction to one of reconstruction—that is, to the use of artifice to rehabilitate the documentary mode as an effective critical system, if not an adequate descriptive one. (Roughly speaking, this is the epistemological posture of Harun Farocki, Hito Steyerl, and Trevor Paglen, among others.) In large part, this shift was a response to the increased control by corporations and governments, through satellite imaging and information mining, of what is given to us as the real in the first place—what can be represented, known, disputed, proven—at all scales from the individual pixel to the vast agglomerations of big data. With such control, events that are criminal and/or catastrophic (secret wars, genocidal campaigns, territorial occupations, environmental disasters, refugee abuses, detention centers, drone strikes, and so on) can be partially or totally blocked from view.[12] It becomes imperative, then, to reconstruct these events as cogently as possible by means of media both new and old (some of which were questioned in the initial critique of the documentary). Eyal Weizman has termed this modeling of the real "forensic architecture," and he points to a turn from a politics of the witness, based on "individual testimony" and aimed at "empathy with victims" (which corresponds to our traumatophilic framing of the real), to a politics of human-rights advocacy undertaken as "a process of materialization and mediatization."[13] Such forensic practice salvages, assembles, and sequences fragmentary representations in order both to image and to narrate disputed events; these scripts can then be offered as evidence in courts of law as well as in courts of opinion. (As Latour speaks of "arenas," so Weizman speaks of "forums," which can include art institutions, too, and he reminds us that *forensis* is Latin for "pertaining to the forum".) At first glance, this turn might be interpreted as neo-Brechtian ("something must in fact be *built up*, something artificial, posed"), but the relevant work here (again, Farocki, Steyerl, Paglen, et al.) is concerned less to expose a

12 The historians of science Robert N. Proctor and Jimena Canales have argued that *agnotology*—the analysis of how it is we do not know or, better, how we are prevented from knowing—is a necessary complement to epistemology.

13 See Yve-Alain Bois, Michel Feher, and Hal Foster, "On Forensic Architecture: A Conversation with Eyal Weizman," in: *October* 156 (Spring 2016): pp. 120-121. Also see Eyal Weizman, *Forensic Architecture: Violence at the Threshold of Detectability*, New York, NY: Zone Books, 2017. This shift from testimony is only partial, as evidenced by a recent project of Forensic Architecture that models, with the aid of survivors, the Saydnaya Prison, a "black hole" site where, according to a new Amnesty International report, the Syrian government has tortured or murdered c. 13,000 Syrians since 2011. See http://www.forensic-architecture.org/case/saydnaya/.

given reality behind representation than to reconstruct an occluded reality, or to point to an absented one, by means of representation.[14]

9. This epistemological recalibration is also active in recent literature. The fiction in question does not express a "reality hunger," as proclaimed by David Shields—that is, it does not conscript real experience to reanimate novel writing in an attempt to overcome the old binary of life versus art. Rather, it too deploys great artifice, not to demystify or to disrupt the real but to make the real real again, which is to say, effective again, felt again, as such. Consider the 2005 novel *Remainder* by Tom McCarthy. The unnamed narrator is struck by an unknown object fallen from the sky, and receives a large settlement from an insurance company as a consequence. He then spends this vast sum in repeated attempts to hire reenactors to perform his fragmentary memories of scenes that seem relevant to the event. Affectively blocked by his trauma, he stages these episodes to experience them for the first time, and in his desperation to do so, his enactments become ever more violent. On the one hand, *Remainder* circles around the real as a traumatic remainder; in Lacanian terms, it narrates a "missed encounter" with the real that, because it is missed, can only be repeated.[15] On the other hand, the repetition of the scenes is dedicated to realize them, not to simulate them, much less to derealize them. The film adaptation of *Remainder* captures this repetition-compulsion perfectly; its director, the artist Omer Fast, explores this mixed framing of the real, which oscillates between the traumatophilic and the reconstructive, in his other work as well.[16]

10. Thomas Demand has also advanced this mixed positioning of the real. As is well known, he builds his photographs from models based on found images—news sources, postcards, and the like—in a way that complicates the discursive opposition between indexical and constructed representations. Demand treats the imagistic mediation of the world as given, and he assumes that we do as well; here, too, the aim is not to demystify or to deconstruct the real but to activate it. Consider a familiar work, *Bathroom*, 1997, which shows an oblique view down on a porcelain tub set in blue tile. In 1987, the premier of the German state of Schleswig-Holstein, Uwe Barschel, was found dead in a hotel bath like this one; in fact, Demand based his image on the tabloid photo taken by the journalist who discovered the body. A rising star in the Christian Democratic Union, Barschel was involved in a secret investigation of a political opponent, and the cause of his death—originally ruled

---

14 Paglen calls his practice "experimental geography." A cousin of "forensic architecture," it involves the indexing of space that cannot be documented positively, or that is otherwise removed from representation; often, in his photographs, it is registered in the (non)form of a blur.

15 See Jacques Lacan, *The Four Fundamental Concepts of Psychoanalysis*, trans. by Alan Sheridan, ed. by Jacques-Alain Miller, New York, NY: Norton, 1978, p. 55. Also see Tom McCarthy and Simon Critchley, "The Manifesto of the Necronautical Society," in: *The Times* (London), December 14, 1999, p. 1.

16 For more on reenactments in contemporary art, see the coda to *Bad New Days*.

a suicide—remains undetermined. This information alters our response to the image: Suddenly, the open door, the rustled curtain, the creased mat, and the undrained bathwater read as possible signs of foul play. Yet *Bathroom* is also true to the utter banality of its source. "What is decisive," Demand has remarked, "are the blurred traces left in the media by the incidents [that they relay]." On the one hand, this blurring produces a distraction in us, "a very diffuse sense of dullness;" on the other, it allows these traces of incidents to "lodge in the memory," one that Demand regards as collective as well as individual. Such are the blurred traces of the real that he is able to evoke in the blunted details of his photographs. Here, *contra* Barthes, the *punctum* is not inadvertent: It must be constructed (again, "built up") if the real is to be made effective as such.[17]

11. Repetition takes on a new valence in this epistemological recalibration. From Pop paintings to Pictures photographs, serial images typically evinced a world of spectacle become simulacral, where representations appear to float free, through repetition, from referents and signifieds alike. This view changed with the traumatophilic framing; there repetition was rededicated to the real, now understood in a Lacanian sense. Lately, however, a further shift has occurred in fiction and art: Repetition is not on the side of simulation, but neither does it circle around a traumatic past. Rather, its purpose is to produce an interruption, a crack or a gap, that might allow a different reality to be glimpsed. Consider *10:04* (2014) by Ben Lerner, who places his novel under the epigraphic sign of Benjamin: "The Hassidim tell a story about the world to come that says everything will be just as it is.... Everything will be as it is now, just a little different."[18] The narrator, who is Lerner but just a little different, replays episodes from his life in this way, too, "a little changed, a little charged," charged as real through repetition—or, perhaps better, through coincidence.[19] Intermittently, as the narrator does this, he also reflects on how such coincidence can be transformative. For example, of the partially transparent hand of an otherwise embodied saint in a nineteenth-century painting by Julien Bastian Lepage, he remarks, "It's as if the tension between the metaphysical

17 See "A Conversation between Alexander Kluge and Thomas Demand," in: *Thomas Demand*, exh. cat., London: Serpentine Gallery, 2006, n. p. Sometimes with Demand, as often with Gerhard Richter, it is the blank or the blur, not the detail, that takes on a punctal quality. In his *sui generis* writing Kluge can be counted as an early practitioner of the real fictions at issue here. On this point see Alexander Kluger and Ben Lerner, "Angels and Administration," https://www.theparisreview.org/blog/2017/02/02/an-interview-with-alexander-kluge/.

18 Walter Benjamin, "In the Sun" (1932), in: Michael W. Jennings et al. (eds.), *Selected Writings, Volume 2, Part 2: 1931-1934*, trans. by Rodney Livingstone et al., Cambridge, MA: Belknap Press, 1999, pp. 662-665: here p. 664. See, also, the final thesis in his "Theses on the Philosophy of History" (1940), in: *Illuminations*, trans. by Harry Zohn, ed. by Hannah Arendt, New York, NY: Schocken, 2007, pp. 253-264: here p. 264.

19 Ben Lerner, *10:04*, New York, NY: Macmillan, 2014, p. 18. Lerner is a practitioner of autofiction, but like some others in this genre, such as Rachel Cusk and Jenny Offill, he puts the autobiography in autofiction under erasure; the ego is refracted, splintered, even dispersed by fictional pressure. In my view, for all the transformations they undergo, other subjects in autofiction sometimes remain more egonauts than argonauts.

and physical worlds, between two orders of temporality, produces a glitch in the pictorial matrix."[20] Yet his exemplum of these folds in space-time is Christian Marclay's *The Clock* (2010) which proceeds through twenty-four hours of film clips, each keyed to a precise moment, which is almost always registered on the face of a timepiece depicted in the found footage. Lerner takes the title of his novel from the clip that represents 10:04 pm, the moment at which lightning strikes the clock tower in *Back to the Future* (1985). The narrator draws his own lesson here:

> I'd heard *The Clock* described as the ultimate collapse of fictional time into real time, a word designed to obliterate the distance between art and life, fantasy and reality. But . . . that distance hadn't been collapsed for me at all; while the duration of a real minute and *The Clock*'s minute were mathematically indistinguishable, they were nevertheless minutes from different worlds. . . . I felt acutely how many different days could be built out of a day, felt more possibility than determinism, the utopian glimmer of fiction.[21]

12. Tacita Dean also produces a glitch in the matrix in her film *Event for a Stage* (2015). A man paces a stage as people wander into an auditorium; we surmise that he is an actor and they are an audience. He speaks of a great storm; the lines, from *The Tempest*, cue us that illusion will be one subject of this event. Yet the film lays bare not only its setting but also its production: There are abrupt shifts from one camera to another (which the actor calls out) as well as from one staging to another. (Dean edited her film from four performances, each marked by different costumes and hairstyles.) Sometimes, too, the actor interacts with an audience member who prompts him with notes (it is Dean); at other times he leaves the stage altogether. At such moments, the fourth wall (which the actor calls "a membrane") is not broken so much as stretched: Life does not intrude on art so much as art expands to comprehend actions, thoughts, and feelings that lie beyond the usual ambit of theater. These moments include confusions that seem genuine ("I don't know what this is," the actor proclaims at one point), as well as statements that sound autobiographical (the line between the lived and the performed is blurred too). The actor tells us about the dementia of his mother (she repeats things) and the "unconventional relationship" of his father with "characters in a TV series," but then we realize that the actor shares in mental uncertainties and unconventional relationships, and that we do too (especially in our viewing of *Event*). Here, again, life does not break into art, nor does all the world become a stage; rather, the imbrication of the two is explored as a condition that is as common as it is complex. If, near the beginning, *Event for a Stage* quotes *The Tempest*, toward the end it cites "On the Marionette Theater" (1810), the great Heinrich von Kleist story that ponders the equal and opposite "grace" achieved by God and marionettes, the former

---

20 Ibid., 9.

21 Ibid., 54. The Surrealists were interested in this "ultimate collapse" too; in fact, André Breton defined "the marvelous" in these very terms. Yet the narrator of *10:04* is concerned to detach the "convulsive beauty" of the Surrealists from the uncanny with which it was bound up, that is, to redirect coincidence away from a traumatic past and toward an unforeseen future.

through total consciousness, the latter through its utter lack. What is his relation to self-awareness?, Dean asks the actor. Does he ever experience stage fright? Can he ever forget the gaze of the audience upon him? He responds ambiguously that, like all actors, he becomes real only through a "great text," but that, like "good parents," good actors can provide a space-time for make-believe that is actual.

13. "The lie described my life better than the truth," the narrator says (or imagines he says) in *10:04*. "Art is what makes life more interesting than art," the actor declaims (perhaps on behalf of the artist) in *Event for a Stage*.[22] These are not witticisms à la Oscar Wilde that delight in paradox and advocate style so much as they are proposals about how artifice, the utopian glimmer of fiction, can be placed in the service of the real. Two questions linger, however. First, what prepares this latest shift in the framing of the real? Might the desire to open up alternative futures be, in part, a response to the dominance of financial futures—that is, to the way in which, in a world governed by finance capitalism, present time is always mortgaged to time to come (a time that never actually arrives)?[23] Second, what relation do the real fictions reviewed here have to "alternative facts," and might the former be deployed to challenge the latter in a way that avoids a simple retrenchment to a positivistic framing of the real?

---

22 This line is a quotation from Robert Filliou.

23 Joseph Vogl has called this development a "raid by the future on the rest of time;" see *The Specter of Capital*, trans. by Joachim Redner and Robert Savage, Stanford, CA: Stanford University Press, 2015, p. 3.

Maria Muhle

Mimesis und *Aisthesis*. Realismus und Geschichte bei Auerbach und Rancière

Zu Beginn seiner 1992 unter dem Titel *Die Wörter der Geschichte*[1] veröffentlichten Studie macht Jacques Rancière auf die Doppeldeutigkeit von Geschichte aufmerksam, die einerseits die historischen Ereignisse und ihre Akteure bezeichnet, andererseits aber auch den Bericht oder die Erzählung dieser historischen Ereignisse und Subjekte meint. Eine Doppeldeutigkeit, die das Englische durch den Unterschied von *history* und *story*, das Deutsche durch denjenigen von Historie und Geschichte löse. Darüber hinaus unterscheidet Rancière eine „Geschichte im üblichen Sinne" als „eine Reihe von Ereignissen, die im Allgemeinen mit Eigennamen bezeichneten Subjekten zustoßen"[2] und eine *moderne* Geschichte, die jene Namen und Ereignisse durch die Namenlosen oder Anonymen und die berühmt gewordene *lange Dauer* ersetzt. Dabei sind jedoch beide – die Ereignisgeschichte oder Chronik der Könige und großen Taten und die moderne Geschichte der anonymen Massen – mit ihrem problematischen Wahrheitsstatus befasst, insofern sie eben jener Tatsache Rechnung tragen müssen, dass die historischen Ereignisse berichtet, also erzählt werden müssen: Der Ungewissheit, die sich in dem Abstand zwischen den Wörtern der Geschichte und den Ereignissen und historischen Akteuren auftut, begegnen die Anhänger der „alten" Geschichte bekanntermaßen mit strenger Quellenkritik und kritischer Prüfung der Dokumente, die modernen Historiker suchen sie mit den Methoden der Statistik, der Geografie und der Demografie auszuräumen.

Gleichwohl vergisst diese statistisch informierte Geschichte jedoch, dass auch die „neuen" Subjekte – „das Königtum statt des Königs, die sozialen Klassen, das

[1] Den Spekulationen über den Wechsel von dem Titel *Die Namen der Geschichte* (der zweiten französischen Ausgabe bei Seuil von 1993 sowie der ersten deutschen Übersetzung bei Fischer 1994) zu dem Titel *Die Wörter der Geschichte* (der französischen Erstausgabe ebenfalls bei Seuil von 1992) entgegnet Rancière im Vorwort zur Neuausgabe der deutschen Übersetzung von 2015: „Ich nutze die Gelegenheit, um klarzustellen: Die Übersetzung des Titels der vorliegenden deutschen Neuausgabe entspricht genau dem der französischen Erstausgabe: *Les Mots de l'histoire*. Dieser Titel musste später modifiziert werden, weil bereits ein anderes Buch mit diesem Namen existierte. Auch die Übersetzungen mussten dieser Änderung folgen. Aufgrund neuer Umstände kann das Buch heute wieder seinen ursprünglichen Titel tragen, der dem Seminar entlehnt war, dem es seine Entstehung verdankte. Es macht also wenig Sinn, den Wechsel von den „Namen" zu den „Wörtern" als – ästhetische oder sonstige – Wende im Denken des Autors zu lesen. Es handelt sich dabei um eine rein juristische Angelegenheit." Jacques Rancière, *Die Wörter der Geschichte. Versuch einer Poetik des Wissens*, Berlin, 2015, S. 14.

[2] Ebd., S. 17.

Mittelmeer oder de[r] Atlantik statt der Generäle und Feldherren"[3] – *benannt* und Ereignissen zugeordnet werden müssen und dass für diese historische Tätigkeit die klassische Quellenkritik letztendlich viel eher geeignet scheint als die neuen Methoden der statistischen Berechnung: Denn während die Prüfung von Quellen und Dokumenten zumindest zu einem „hinreichenden Grad von Gewissheit" führen könne, kann

> die Strenge der statistischen Reihen den Historiker [nicht] in die Lage versetzen, gefahrlos die These zu verfechten, dass das Bürgertum diesen oder jenen Zustand erreichte, das Proletariat diese oder jene Entwicklung nahm oder der Mittelmeerraum dieses oder jenes Ereignis erlebte.[4]

Will die neue Geschichte also tatsächlich ihre kopernikanische Wende vollbringen und sich von der klassischen Geschichtsschreibung mit ihren Chroniken, Ereignissen und großen Männern emanzipieren, so muss sie mehr tun, so scheint Rancière hier sagen zu wollen, als allein die hohen Subjekte gegen die minderen auszutauschen sowie gegen die statistischen Serien die Kritik der Dokumente und Quellen; denn obgleich sie all dies tut, teilt die gelehrte moderne Geschichtsschreibung mit der alten Geschichte weiterhin die (immer wieder enttäuschte) Hoffnung, den Wahrheitsgehalt ihrer Erzählung, also ihrer Geschichtsschreibung zu gewährleisten – und damit auch die Hoffnung darauf, die lästige Tatsache zu überwinden, dass Geschichte auch immer eine erzählte und damit fiktive Geschichte ist.

Eine neue Geschichte, die sich auf einem rein quantifizierenden Umgang mit den im 19. Jahrhundert auftretenden und von den Sozialwissenschaften eingefassten anonymen Massen und ihrer *longue durée* begründet, wäre folglich nichts anderes als ‚eine' Sozialwissenschaft unter anderen; denn, das ist hier das Hauptargument Rancières, sie würde gerade den besonderen Status von Geschichte verfehlen, der darin begründet liegt, dass sie die Homonymie ihres eigenen Namens *nicht* zu überwinden trachtet. Die *wirklich* neue Geschichte steht damit nicht nur der klassischen Chronik und ihrer Ereignisgeschichte entgegen, sondern zugleich auch einer modernen wissenschaftlichen Geschichtsschreibung, deren Ideal es ist, „von der Unbestimmtheit der Wörter und Sätze der Geschichte"[5] befreit zu sein. Denn sie unterscheidet sich von diesen *beiden* Spielarten darin, dass sie die Unbestimmtheit der Wörter, die zuallererst ihren eigenen Namen betrifft, *nicht* aufzulösen sucht:

> Das Besondere an der Umwälzung der Historie besteht also nicht einfach darin, dass es ihr gelungen ist, die neuen Gegenstände der langen Dauer, der materiellen Zivilisation und des Lebens der Massen zu definieren und ihnen die neuen Instrumente der Sprache der Zahlen anzupassen, sondern darin, im Sirenengesang des szientistischen Zeitalters die Drohung ihres Untergangs zu entziffern, das hinter den Vorschlägen zu ihrer Verwissenschaftlichung verborgene Dilemma: *entweder* Erzählung *oder* Wissenschaft. Sie hat es verstanden, als Antwort darauf das Spiel der Homony-

[3] Ebd., S. 18.
[4] Ebd., S. 19.
[5] Ebd., S. 23.

> mie beizubehalten, weil es als einziges geeignet war, die Disjunktion in Konjunktion zu verwandeln: *sowohl* Wissenschaft *als auch* Erzählung, das heißt: Nicht-Geschichte und Geschichte, die Fähigkeit, Namen und Ereignisse miteinander zu verschränken, eine Fähigkeit, die zwar mit der ontologischen Unbestimmtheit der Erzählung zusammenhängt, aber die Spezifizität einer *historischen* Wissenschaft im Allgemeinen zu bewahren vermag [Herv. i. O.].[6]

Dieses „Spiel der Homonymie" betrifft jedoch nicht nur wie zu Anfangs bereits gesagt den Namen der Geschichte selbst, sondern setzt sich ebenfalls auf der Ebene der Sujets der Geschichtsschreibung fort und betrifft damit jene anonymen Massen, die den Platz der Könige eingenommen haben und die nun ebenfalls ansetzen zu reden und Wörter zu produzieren. Auch hier muss Geschichte das Prinzip des ‚Sowohl-als-auch' durchsetzen, um sich zu dieser exzessiven Sprache, zu den massenhaften Wörtern der neuen Sujets in ein Verhältnis zu setzen, das eben gerade nicht jenes der Statistiker ist. Denn diese zielen darauf ab, den Exzess der neuen Massen in Serien zu organisieren, um ihn so handhabbar zu machen – ein durch und durch gouvernementales Anliegen, so wie Michel Foucault es in seinen Vorlesungen zur Geschichte der Gouvernementalität besonders hinsichtlich der Frage der Bevölkerung erläutert hat.[7] Neue Geschichtsschreibung im anspruchsvollen Sinne wird also nicht nur durch ihr minderes Sujet bestimmt – die Armen, die Massen oder das Mittelmeer –, denn das ist ebenfalls für die moderne gelehrte, statistisch und sozialwissenschaftlich informierte Geschichte der Fall; vielmehr ist sie auf besondere Weise mit jenem Exzess der Wörter befasst, der diesen neuen Sujets eigen ist und aus dem Verschwinden des „legitimen" Sprechens des Königs resultiert: Entgegen des historiografisch-gouvernementalen Versuchs, diesen Exzess soziologisch-statistisch-demografisch einzuhegen, avanciert er vielmehr in seiner Exzessivität zum zentralen Element der neuen Geschichte.[8]

---

6 Ebd., S. 24 f.

7 Vgl. hierzu Michel Foucault, *Sicherheit, Territorium, Bevölkerung, Geschichte der Gouvernementalität I*, Frankfurt/M., 2006, bes. die Vorlesungen 2 und 3, S. 52-133.

8 Neben ihrem zentralen Einsatz in seinem politischen Denken („Aber das Politische arbeitet genau an der Homonymie und am Ununterscheidbaren." Jacques Rancière, „Gibt es eine politische Philosophie?", in: Alain Badiou und ders., *Politik der Wahrheit*, Wien, 1997, S. 79-118: 115) verhandelt Rancière die Frage der Homonymie, also der Mehrdeutigkeit der Wörter, auch in den politisch-ästhetischen Überlegungen, und zwar hier unter dem Begriff der „Literarizität", die eben jene Fliehkraft der Wörter meint, die es ihnen erlaubt, überallhin und zu jedem zu wandern: „Literarizität ist gleichzeitig Ursache und Wirkung der Zirkulation von im ‚wortwörtlichen Sinne' literarischen Aussagen. Aber diese Aussagen besetzen die Körper und lenken sie in dem Maße von ihrer Bestimmung ab, in dem sie selbst keine Körper – im Sinne von Organismen –, sondern Quasi-Körper – Wortblöcke – sind, die ohne legitimen Vater, der sie bis zu einem adäquaten Adressaten begleiten würde, zirkulieren. [...] Es ist richtig, dass die Verbreitung dieser Quasi-Körper die sinnliche Wahrnehmung des Gemeinsamen der Sprache und der sinnlichen Aufteilung der Räume und Betätigungen verändert. [...] Die Wege der politischen Subjektbildung sind nicht die der imaginären Identifikation, sondern der ‚literarischen' Entkörperung." Jacques Rancière, *Die Aufteilung des Sinnlichen*, Berlin, 2006, S. 63.

1. Homonymie: „Der Exzess der Wörter“

Im dritten Kapitel der *Wörter der Geschichte*, „Der Exzess der Wörter“, erörtert Rancière diese besondere Zirkulationsfähigkeit der Wörter unter dem Begriff eines „parole hors lieu“, eines „außerhalb seines Orts gesprochene[n] Wort[s]“.[9] Hierfür rekonstruiert er einerseits einen klassischen historiografischen Umgang mit diesem skandalösen Sprechen anhand der *Annalen* von Tacitus, sowie andererseits den Zugriff der gelehrten Geschichtsschreibung anhand von Alfred Cobbans *The Social Interpretation of the French Revolution*. Ich möchte mich hier auf Rancières Lektüre des 16. Kapitels von Tacitus' *Annalen* beschränken, in dem es, so Rancière, um ein „subversives Ereignis“ geht, nämlich „die Meuterei der in Pannonien stehenden Legionen, die kurz nach dem Tod des Augustus von einem obskuren Agitator namens Percennius aufgestachelt wurden“.[10] Bekanntermaßen – und Rancière erinnert hieran – steht die Rede des Percennius ebenfalls im Mittelpunkt des zweiten Kapitels von Erich Auerbachs Hauptwerk *Mimesis. Dargestellte Wirklichkeit in der abendländischen Literatur*, in dem Auerbach sie der Geschichte der Verleugnung des Petrus im Markus-Evangelium entgegensetzt. Auerbach zeigt auf, dass Percennius Rede zwar ein Sprechen *hors lieu* ist, insofern Percennius, der einfache Soldat, ein Wort ergreift, das ihm nicht zusteht; zugleich zeigt er aber auch, inwiefern Tacitus dieses exzessive Sprechen von Anfang an wieder neutralisiert, indem er einen *non-lieu* feststellt. Percennius, der nicht zu sprechen hatte, spricht, weil wir uns in einem Machtvakuum befinden, in einer Art karnevalesker Zeit: Augustus ist gerade gestorben, Tiberius noch nicht gekrönt, die militärischen Übungen sind unterbrochen, die Disziplin verfällt stehenden Fußes und in den Mittelpunkt rücken Figuren wie „ein gewisser Percennius, der früher Chef einer Theaterclaque gewesen war, jetzt gemeiner Soldat“.[11] Diese Umkehrung der Zeiten hat zur Folge, dass auch die einfachen Soldaten sprechen dürfen; und zwar dürfen sie sprechen, weil ihre Sprache folgenlos bleibt, insofern sie nicht über das Ende des eröffneten Ausnahmezustands hinaus reicht.

Die Rede des Percennius findet damit im aristotelischen Sinne *kein Gehör*; jedoch ist sie nicht, wie bei Aristoteles, nur Stimme, reiner Lärm, der ausschließlich Lust und Leiden anzeigt, aber nicht den Unterschied zwischen Gutem und Schlechten markiert, der das politische, sprachbegabte Tier auszeichnet. Vielmehr ist die Rede des Percennius insofern delegitimiert, weil sie, so Auerbach, „vor allem Rhetorik“ ist bzw. weil Tacitus' Gründe, diese „Forderungen der Soldaten, für die er sich überhaupt nicht interessiert, in der Rede des Percennius so lebendig zum Ausdruck zu bringen [...] rein ästhetisch“ sind.[12] Denn zum Stil der großen Geschichtsschreibung gehören die großen, zumeist fingierten Reden, die „der anschaulichen Darstellung (*illustratio*) des Vorgangs“ dienen und „die rhetorischen Glanzstücke

---

9 Rancière (2015), *Die Wörter der Geschichte*, S. 51.

10 Ebd., S. 51 f.

11 Erich Auerbach, *Mimesis. Dargestellte Wirklichkeit in der abendländischen Literatur*, Bern, 2001, S. 38.

12 Ebd., S. 42.

der Darstellung sein" sollen.[13] Insofern diese Einschübe also „vor allem Rhetorik" sind, also auf den Rhetorenschulen eingeübte Exerzitien, geht es hier in keinster Weise um Percennius und dessen aufrührerischen Aufruf an die einfachen Soldaten, sondern um Tacitus, der seine Meisterschaft darin vorführt, seine Reden „mit dem Charakter und der Lage des Menschen, der als redend fingiert wird", zu erfüllen. Folglich, so Auerbach, redet „Percennius nicht seine eigene Sprache, sondern taciteisch".[14]

Diese Aussage wird vor allem vor dem Hintergrund der im ersten Kapitel von Auerbachs *Mimesis*, „Die Narbe des Odysseus", am Unterschied von homerischer und alttestamentarischer Darstellung erläuterten Stiltrennungsregel virulent: Anhand der Schlussepisode der *Odyssee*, in der die alte Magd den heimkehrenden Odysseus an seiner Narbe am Fuß erkennt, zeigt Auerbach, dass zwar auch in den homerischen Gedichten das Alltäglich-Realistische, die Szene der Fußwaschung, in das Erhaben-Tragische, die Heimkehr des Helden, hineinspielt. Zugleich vollziehen sich die erhabenen Vorgänge bei Homer fast ausschließlich unter den Angehörigen der Herrenschicht, die eine intakte und abgeschlossene soziale Welt darstellen; andersherum bleibt die Darstellung des alltäglichen Lebens, der „häusliche Realismus", stets im „Idyllisch-Friedlichen" und folgt somit der klassischen Trennung der Gattungen, die besagt, dass alltägliche, mindere Ereignisse und Personen allein in den niederen Gattungen darstellbar sind. Nicht so in den Erzählungen des Alten Testaments, in denen sich das „Erhabene, Tragische und Problematische" – paradigmatisch die „erhabene Wirkung Gottes" – „gerade im Häuslichen und Alltäglichen gestaltet" und zwar derart, „daß die beiden Bezirke des Erhabenen und Alltäglichen nicht nur tatsächlich ungetrennt, sondern grundsätzlich untrennbar sind".[15] Diesen Gegensatz der beiden als Ausgangspunkte der Untersuchung eingeführten Stilarten buchstabiert Auerbach auch hinsichtlich ihrer historiografischen Relevanz aus, insofern die „Beschränkung im Geschichtlich-Entwickelnden und im Menschlich-Problematischen" der homerischen Gedichte dem „weltgeschichtliche[n] Anspruch, [der] Ausbildung der Vorstellung vom geschichtlich Werdenden und Vertiefung des Problematischen" im Alten Testament entgegensteht.[16]

Eine ähnliche Entgegensetzung kommt auch in der taciteischen Entmachtung des Percennius zum Tragen, der als einfacher Soldat scheinbar in den Rang der ernsthaften Darstellung erhoben wird – obgleich derlei Personen eigentlich nur in den niederen Genres der Komödie oder der Satire auftreten dürfen. Zugleich wird dieser Auftritt des Percennius von Tacitus gleich wieder für null und nichtig erklärt, insofern seine Rede reine Rhetorik sei – und damit auch kein wirklicher Bruch der Stiltrennungsregel, die bestimmt, was wie gesagt werden darf. Als Gegensatz zu dieser „rhetorischen Annullierung" führt Auerbach hier nun die Ver-

13 Ebd.
14 Ebd., S. 43.
15 Ebd., S. 25 f.
16 Ebd., S. 26.

leugnung des Petrus im Markus-Evangelium an, in der eine tatsächlich Vermischung der Genres zum Tragen kommt, die Tacitus verstellt ist:

> Auf den ersten Blick erkennt man, dass von der Stiltrennungsregel – in der besagten Verleugnungsszene des Petrus mit ihrer Beschreibung des Hofes mit den Knechten am Feuer, der Magd, die ihn erkennt und der Erwähnung seines eigenen galiläischen Dialekts – keine Rede sein kann. Die nach Schauplatz und handelnden Personen – man beachte insbesondere ihren niedrigen sozialen Rang – durchaus realistische Szene ist von tiefer Problematik und Tragik. Petrus ist nicht eine zur ‚illustratio' dienende Staffagefigur wie die Soldaten Vibulenus und Percennius, die als bloße Lumpen und Schwindler hingestellt werden, sondern im höchsten und tiefsten, im tragischsten Sinne ein Bild des Menschen.[17]

2. Mimetischer Realismus

Rancière deutet diese Aussage Auerbachs als eine „Bereicherung" des Verhältnisses „zwischen einer Politik des Wissens und einer Poetik des Berichts" um die – politisch brisante – „Frage der Darstellung des Anderen", also des Anonymen, Namenlosen, Ungenannten: Tacitus kann hierauf keine befriedigende Antwort geben, weil er „das Wort eines einfachen Mannes nicht ernst nehmen kann und weil er in den Kategorien der Einteilung in hohe und niedere Gattungen denkt", was zugleich bedeutet, dass „er diesseits der Möglichkeitsbedingungen eines literarischen Realismus [bleibt], die der Bericht des Evangelisten dagegen eröffnet", wie Rancière im Anschluss an Auerbach festhält.[18] Literarischer Realismus ist also, mit Auerbach gesprochen, *erstens* ein Realismus jenseits der Stiltrennungsregel, der *zweitens* das Wort des einfachen Mannes, des Minderen, Nicht-Darstellungswürdigen, *ernst nimmt*, indem er es nicht in die minderen Genres verbannt, sondern im erhaben-tragischen Modus zur Darstellung bringt. Literarischer Realismus ist also in gewisser Weise eine erhabene und erhebende Darstellung dieses Minderen, die in ihm „das Entstehen einer Tiefenbewegung, das Sichentfalten geschichtlicher Kräfte" sieht; „daß dabei beliebige Personen in großer Zahl auftreten, ist sehr wesentlich; denn nur an vielen beliebigen Personen können solche geschichtlichen Kräfte in ihrer hin- und herflutenden Wirksamkeit lebendig gemacht werden".[19]

Wenn also der literarische Realismus bei Auerbach aus zwei Aspekten besteht – der Überwindung der Stiltrennungsregel und damit einhergehend der Darstellung des Minderen im erhabenen Modus, die allein der Tatsache gerecht wird, dass sich die geschichtlichen Kräfte tatsächlich in diesem Minderen, Kleinen, Anonymen entfalten –, schließt Rancière in unterschiedlicher Weise an diese beiden Aspekte an: Einerseits nimmt er die Rede von der Überwindung der Stiltrennungsregel

---

17 Ebd., S. 44.
18 Rancière (2015), *Die Wörter der Geschichte*, S. 55 f.
19 Auerbach (2001), *Mimesis*, S. 47.

bzw. der Trennung der Gattungen auf und verortet sie, wie Auerbach das in einem späteren Kapitel ebenfalls tut, im literarischen Realismus des 19. Jahrhunderts – besonders in Flauberts „demokratischen" Romanen *malgré eux*. Zugleich, und darin unterscheidet Rancière sich grundlegend von Auerbach, führt ihn der Bruch mit der Stiltrennungsregel *nicht* zu der Annahme einer realen historischen Kraft, die in den minderen Sujets verdeckt läge und nun entschleiert würde. Denn mit diesem zweiten Aspekt seines literarischen Realismus-Verständnisses verbleibt Auerbach, so könnte man die historiografische Diskussion wieder aufnehmen, einer Auffassung von Geschichte verhaftet, die von der Eindeutigkeit ihres Begriffs oder Namens ausgeht und damit dessen Homonymie verkennt.

„Geschichte" vollzieht sich bei Auerbach als Entfaltung „geschichtlicher Kräfte", deren Sujet zwar hier „vermindert" wird – von den Herren zu den Sklaven, von den außergewöhnlichen Ereignissen zu den alltäglichen Handlungen –, deren geschichtliche (Fortschritts-)Logik dabei aber unangetastet bleibt. Ebenso wie Rancière bereits die sogenannte kopernikanische Wende der Ecole des Annales hin zu den nicht-geschichtswürdigen Gegenständen, den Serien und der langen Dauer dahingehend infrage gestellt hatte, dass diese neue Methode ebenso wenig wie die traditionelle Chronik der Mehrdeutigkeit des historiografischen Unterfangens gerecht würde – also der Tatsache, dass Geschichte immer zugleich die Geschichten (Literatur) und die Historie (Geschichtswissenschaft) umfasst –, so scheint auch die Auerbach'sche Erhebung der kleinen Geste oder des kleinen Wortes in den erhaben-tragischen Modus eine Art Einhegung dieser Kleinheit zu vollziehen. Mit dem grundlegenden Unterschied natürlich, dass sich diese historiografische Ästhetisierung in und durch die Literatur vollzieht – dass also auch die fiktionalisierende Darstellung Geschichtswert zugesprochen bekommt und die Literatur hier zur Quelle einer historiografischen Wende, wie sie im Alten Testament vollzogen wird, avanciert – also letztendlich auch das literarische Wort seines Exzesses entkleidet wird.

In diesem Sinne bleibt Auerbachs Realismus des Minderen trotz seiner Überwindung der Hierarchien der Stiltrennungsregel in einem repräsentativen Schema verhaftet, insofern er von der Eindeutigkeit geschichtlicher Darstellung ausgeht, die eben nur zu ihren wahren – minderen – Sujets geführt werden muss. An die Stelle der klassischen Stiltrennungsregel wird damit eine neue Stiltrennungsregel gesetzt, der zufolge historische Ereignisse sich *qua* historischer Notwendigkeit im alttestamentarischen Alltag des kleinen Volkes oder im modernen Arbeitsalltag des Proletariats ereignen – die Umkehrung der normativen Hierarchien ist damit keinesfalls als deren Überwindung zu verstehen. Rancière hingegen nimmt die Rede von der Überwindung der Stiltrennungsregel – er spricht selbst von den Hierarchien der Darstellung – zum Anlass, einem derart verstandenen repräsentativen oder mimetischen Realismus einen ästhetischen Realismus entgegenzusetzen.

3. Ästhetischer Realismus

Bekanntermaßen hat Rancière den Bruch mit den Hierarchien der Darstellung und die daraus resultierende allgemeine Darstellbarkeit in seiner ästhetischen Theorie im Übergang eines repräsentativen Regimes zu einem ästhetischen Regime der Künste gefasst.[20] In Absetzung zu tradierten kunsthistorischen Periodisierungen bestimmt Rancière die moderne Ästhetik derart nicht über die Abstraktion, also als Abschied von der Gegenständlichkeit, sondern vielmehr als eine *andere Politik der Darstellung*: Innerhalb des repräsentativen Regimes wird Realismus in Anlehnung an den aristotelischen Mimesis-Begriff als Repräsentation einer nicht notwendig stattgefundenen, aber wahrscheinlichen (also: realistischen) Handlung gedacht, in der man etwas Allgemeines über den Gegenstand der Darstellung erfahren kann. Denn Darstellung entspricht hier einem geordneten normativen System, das, wie Aristoteles in der *Poetik* zeigt, festlegt, was wie und wo dargestellt werden darf: Mimesis funktioniert im repräsentativen Regime folglich als normativer Begriff. Von diesem repräsentativen Realismus unterscheidet sich ein in Anlehnung an die Rede vom ästhetischen Regime verstandener ästhetischer Realismus, der sich durch die radikale Beliebigkeit seiner Gegenstände und Darstellungsformen auszeichnet. Zugleich erfährt die klassische Entgrenzung der Künste im ästhetischen Realismus eine spezifische Ausformulierung, insofern dessen Strategien nicht nur die gängigen Darstellungsnormen unterbrechen, sondern gleichsam als Konsequenz daraus die Darstellungsrelation als solche hinterfragen. Dies geschieht, indem sie die Trennung zwischen der dargestellten Wirklichkeit und der wirklichen Wirklichkeit suspendieren, d. h. diese Relation unbestimmt oder in der Schwebe halten. Dieses In-der-Schwebe-Halten ermöglicht eine Reflexion auf die allgemeinen Bedingungen, unter denen Realität überhaupt erst erscheinen und zugänglich sein kann, d. h. auf die Bedingungen des Erscheinens von etwas als etwas. Diese Bedingungen sind mit Rancière als eine Aufteilung des Sinnlichen zu denken, als ein Regime oder System von Normen, die implizit die Wahrnehmung der gemeinschaftlichen Welt bestimmen. Wahrnehmung steht dabei für eine Topologie, die in Abhängigkeit von den Plätzen, die die Individuen in Raum und Zeit einnehmen, ihnen bestimmte Funktionen, Tätigkeits- oder Sprachformen zuordnet und ihnen so einen bestimmten Erscheinungsraum zugesteht.

Rancières „ästhetischer" Realismus bezieht sich, im Gegensatz zu Auerbachs „repräsentativem" Realismus, auf eben jene historisch-apriorische Ebene, die Realität allererst erscheinen lässt, d. h. diese „aufschließt" als eine Realität, die nur als auf bestimmte Weise aufgeteilte und als irgendwie bestimmte erscheinen kann. Der ästhetische Realismus muss an diesen Aufteilungen ansetzen, die von Anfang an in jede Darstellung eingelassen sind, und gibt dabei der Einsicht statt, dass jedes Erscheinen von Realität an eine vorausgegangene Aufteilung des Sinnlichen gekoppelt ist. Diese Reflexion auf die historisch-apriorischen Formen der sinnli-

---

20 Rancière (2006), *Die Aufteilung des Sinnlichen*, bes. S. 35-49.

chen Erfahrung – die keine thematische ist, sondern eine „ästhetische“ – eröffnet einen neuen Sinn von Wirklichkeit, der sich vom mimetisch-repräsentativen Wirklichkeitsbegriff unterscheidet. Oder, um es noch einmal mit den *Wörtern der Geschichte* zu sagen, ist der ästhetische Realismus einer, der die Homonymie von Sprache und Darstellung ernstnimmt, was eben nicht nur für historiografische Fragen wichtig ist, sondern ebenso für ästhetische und politische.

Denn Homonymie wird von Rancière sowohl in den *Wörtern der Geschichte* als auch in der politischen Ästhetik der *Aufteilung des Sinnlichen* mit dem Begriff der Literarizität in Verbindung gebracht, also mit der in Abwandlung von der aristotelischen Rede vom politischen Tier verstandenen Tatsache, dass der Mensch ein „literarisches Tier“ sei, d. h. ein Wesen, dessen Weltbezug von Darstellungsmedien bestimmt wird, die ihn von seiner „natürlichen“ oder „gewohnten“ Bestimmung abweichen lassen, weil er sich in seinen Artikulationen von der an-archischen Macht von Wörtern, Bildern und Gesten leiten lässt. Diese Macht bezeichnet sowohl die Fähigkeit der Worte, Bilder und Gesten immer mehr und anderes auszusagen und zu bezeichnen, weil sie ohne vorgängige Ordnung und Legitimität „zirkulieren“, als auch die daraus folgende Feststellung, dass ihr Sinn nicht von einem oder wenigen festgestellt werden kann, sondern stets diesen potenziellen Überschuss mit sich trägt und von anderen anderes verwendet werden kann. Und damit bezeichnet diese doppelte „Macht“ der Wörter auch die ästhetisch-politische Dimension des Bezugs auf die Wirklichkeit, die vor dem Hintergrund des ästhetischen Regimes der Künste vollzogen wird: Denn gerade der ästhetische Realismus bezeichnet diesen Bezug auf die Wirklichkeit, der, insofern er ästhetisch ist, d. h. die Aufteilung des Sichtbaren und Sagbaren betrifft, immer zugleich auch politisch zu nennen ist. Diese Rede von der Literarizität (Literarität), also die „unselige Eigenschaft des Menschen, ein literarisches Tier zu sein“, die das ästhetische Regime der Künste begründet, ist jedoch zugleich auch dasjenige, was „die Geschichte möglich und die Geschichtswissenschaft unmöglich macht“[21] – also jener entscheidende Einsatz, der es ermöglicht, eine Geschichte zu denken, die sich von der Ereignisgeschichte gelöst hat, ohne in die Falle der szientistischen sozialwissenschaftlichen Geschichtsschreibung zu gehen.

4. Appropriativer Realismus

Ein solcherart verstandener *ästhetischer* Realismus unterscheidet sich folglich grundlegend von einem mimetischen Realismus im Sinne Auerbachs und es ist daher auch nicht verwunderlich, dass Rancière ihn in seiner Auerbach-Lektüre gerade an jener Sprechsituation festmacht, die von Auerbach verworfen wurde, nämlich an der taciteischen Rede des Percennius, die Rancière als einen *ästhetischen Gebrauch von Mimesis* versteht. Denn obgleich Tacitus Percennius' Sprechakt als reine Rhetorik neutralisiert, lässt er ihn doch sprechen und produziert da-

[21] Rancière (2015), *Die Wörter der Geschichte*, S. 91.

mit ein Modell für andere, die nach der Sprache greifen, ähnlich wie im Falle jener Plebejer auf dem Aventin, die im *Unvernehmen* die Patrizier im Sinne einer emanzipatorischen Mimesis *nach-ahmen*, um sich als deren „Gleiche" zu konstituieren, indem sie sich eine politische Ordnung und damit eine politische Sichtbarkeit geben.[22] Denn was Tacitus nicht versteht, genauso wenig wie es die Patrizier auf dem Aventin verstehen, ist, dass die Sprache, derer sie sich bedienen, um Plebejern oder einfachen Soldaten ihre Ungleichheit zu signalisieren, nach dem Prinzip des einschließenden Ausschlusses funktioniert: Es handelt sich um ein „Sprachspiel", das

> in der Person des Percennius denjenigen einschließt, der mit keiner Sprache zu spielen hat. Die Sprache, auf die dieser kein Recht hat, schließt ihn dadurch, dass sie sich das Recht nimmt, ihn sprechen zu lassen, in ihre Gemeinschaft ein. Die Disqualifizierung, die ihn trifft, wird kompensiert durch das Vertrauen in die Sprache, in die Fähigkeiten des sprechenden Wesens, die keine Unterschiede kennen. [...] Percennius hat nichts gesagt, was die öffentliche Meinung im Gedächtnis behalten hätte. Bleibt allerdings die zusammenführende Macht der Sprache und der Spiele, die sie erlaubt, die Macht einer Rede, die stets imstande ist, diejenigen zu ihrer Gemeinschaft zuzulassen, die ihre Grenzziehung ausschließt.[23]

Derart kehrt dieses Sprachspiel die Vereinnahmung der Sprache um: Es ist nicht mehr Tacitus, der Percennius vereinnahmt und seine Sprache der Folgenlosigkeit überführt, vielmehr schafft Tacitus ein „Modell subversiver Eloquenz", das allen Perceniussen von nun an zur Verfügung steht und das diese sich aneignen können: Die gemeinen Soldaten „werden fortan nicht Percennius wiederholen, dessen Stimme verhallt ist, sondern Tacitus, der die Gründe aller Percenniusse besser artikuliert als sie".[24]

Die Auseinandersetzung mit einem Sprechen des Anderen kann also weder in historiografischer noch in ästhetischer oder politischer Hinsicht allein darin bestehen, jenen das Wort zu erteilen, die unter normalen oder ‚natürlichen' Umständen – also den Umständen der Beherrschung – nicht sprechen dürfen. Vielmehr geht es darum, dass das Sprechen des Anderen – die Wörter der Anonymen, die ‚Papierberge der Armen' – dasjenige, was Rancière später als den Anteil der Anteillosen benennen wird, zugleich die gesamte Aufteilung des Sinnlichen infrage stellt und neuverteilt. Konkret heißt das, dass es nicht allein darum gehen kann, den Nicht-Gehörten das Wort zu erteilen, den Minderen ihre Darstellbarkeit zu vermitteln – gerade dies entspräche dem Verständnis jenes aufgeklärten Intellektuellen, das Rancière seit seiner kritischen Auseinandersetzung mit Althussers Gegensatz von Wissenschaft und Ideologie und Bourdieus kritischer Soziologie immer wieder kritisiert. Vielmehr muss das unklare Bedeutungsspektrum der Wörter ausgeschöpft werden, ihre Literarizität oder Homonymie, also die Tatsache, dass sie immer auch anders und von anderen in anderen Kontexten benutzt

---

22 Vgl. Jacques Rancière, *Das Unvernehmen. Philosophie und Politik*, Frankfurt/M., 2002, bes. S. 33-54.
23 Rancière (2015), *Die Wörter der Geschichte*, S. 58.
24 Ebd., S. 59.

und angeeignet werden können. Bereits in den *Wörtern der Geschichte* spricht Rancière in diesem Sinne von

> einer Aneignung ‚außerhalb der Wahrheit' des Worts des Anderen (Formeln der Souveränität, des alten Texts, des heiligen Worts), die es auf andere Weise bezeichnen lässt […]. Das Ereignis gewinnt seine paradoxe Neuheit daraus, dass es mit Wieder-Gesagtem (*du re-dit*) verbunden ist, mit außerhalb des Kontexts, an unrechter Stelle Gesagtem […]. Das Ereignis besitzt die Neuheit des Anachronistischen.[25]

Diese irreduzible Mehrdeutigkeit der Sprache, die Rancière als Grundprinzip des Unvernehmens[26] politisch reformulieren wird, rückt die Rede von der „zusammenführende[n] Macht der Sprache"[27] in ein spezifisches Licht: Denn es geht Rancière nicht darum, in der geteilten Sprache ein zugrunde liegendes und verdecktes Prinzip freizulegen, die Tatsache, dass alle Menschen *qua* Sprachbegabtheit (strukturgleich zum wie wohl anders gelagerten Rekurs auf Menschenrechte) gleich sind, vielmehr ist die Rede von der axiomatischen oder leeren Gleichheit operativ zu verstehen, d. h. im Sinne einer Gleich*setzung*: Percennius und die Percenniusse konstituieren sich als Gleiche, genauso wie die Plebejer auf dem Aventin, indem sie die homonymische Macht der Sprache für ihren Einschluss nutzen. Ein Einschluss, der niemals universal ist, sondern immer andere Ausschlüsse unangetastet lässt.

Während Auerbachs Realismus dem Wort des Anderen einen Ort gibt und es als historisch wertvoll und bedeutsam herausstellt, gar als ‚de"' Ort der historischen Entwicklung, und sich damit in einem repräsentativen oder mimetischen Verständnis von Geschichte bewegt, ‚ästhetisiert' Rancière diese Mimesis, insofern er ein emanzipatorisches Modell der Nachahmung entwirft, das zugleich nachahmt und enteignet, dessen Wiederholung also stets mit einer Verfremdung einhergeht, die der homonymischen Fähigkeit der Wörter Rechnung trägt. Oder, anders gesprochen: Der Auerbach'schen *Mimesis des Minderen* setzt Rancière eine *mindere Mimesis* entgegen. Das hieße ganz konkret hinsichtlich der von Tacitus erzählten Geschichte des Percennius, dass diese letztlich keine Frage der Rhetorik ist, wie Auerbach es mit Tacitus hervorhebt, und damit auch keine Frage der repräsentativen Mimesis, sondern eine Frage der Poetik, „die die sowohl wahre wie falsche Sprache der Geschichten als Sprache der Wahrheit konstituiert[e]".[28] Percennius' Geschichte wäre in dieser Lesart dann (auch) eine Frage des ästhetischen Regimes und ihrer politisch-ästhetischen Neuformulierung von Mimesis im Sinne der Potenzialität einer emanzipatorischen Nachahmung, die vom Imperativ der Ähnlichkeit abrückt, so wie Rancière sie im *Unvernehmen* ausformulieren und in seinen ästhetischen Arbeiten in unterschiedlichen medialen Kontexten verorten wird.

---

25 Ebd., S. 60.

26 Vgl. Rancière (2015), *Die Wörter der Geschichte*, S. 13: „*Die Wörter der Geschichte* analysierte die politischen Implikationen des wissenschaftlichen Willens, den Exzess der Wörter einzuhegen. *Das Unvernehmen* sollte später zeigen, dass in der Reduktion der Demokratie auf den Konsens derselbe Wille am Werk war."

27 Ebd., S. 58.

28 Ebd., S. 28.

5. Anachronie: Wiederholung als Aneignung

Das Modell dieser spezifischen Art der Wiederholung, die mit dem Bereits-Gesagten, dem Wieder- und Anders-Gesagtem in Beziehung steht, und die den Übergang von einer repräsentativen zu einer ästhetisch-politischen Nachahmung zu vollziehen ermöglicht, ist, so möchte ich abschließend kurz skizzieren, eine genuin historische Figur, nämlich diejenige des Anachronismus. So zeigt Rancière in den *Wörtern der Geschichte*, dass die Revolution der Geschichte nicht nur darin besteht, die Homonymie ihres eigenen Namens und davon ausgehend die Homonymie, die das Sprechen im Allgemeinen kennzeichnet, anzunehmen und als zentrales Element von Geschichte auszustellen. Diese Revolution besteht auch darin, zu verstehen, inwiefern Geschichte von einem zweiten zentralen Element, dem des Anachronischen, gekennzeichnet wird: Auch hier geht es um die Einsicht, dass der Anachronismus nicht überwunden werden muss, sondern vielmehr Geschichte grundlegend bestimmt.

In dem Text „Der Begriff des Anachronismus und die Wahrheit des Historikers"[29] nimmt Rancière diese Diskussion wieder auf, schlägt allerdings den Anachronismus jener chronologistisch-kontinuistischen Geschichtsschreibung zu, die von einem linearen Geschichtsverlauf ausgeht und eine normative Ordnung der Zeiten und Orte voraussetzt. Am Beispiel von Lucien Febvres *Rabelais* kritisiert Rancière ein Verständnis von Geschichte, das den Menschen vollkommen mit seiner Epoche – man könnte auch sagen: mit seiner Aufteilung des Sinnlichen – identifiziert und Anachronismus rein normativ versteht als die Frage danach, ob etwas zu einem Zeitpunkt x habe existieren *können*: „Der Vorwurf des Anachronismus ist nicht die Behauptung, dass etwas zu einem gegebenen Datum nicht existiert habe, sondern die Behauptung, dass es zu diesem Datum *nicht habe existieren können.*"[30] Der moderne Historiker unterscheidet sich zwar vom klassischen Historiker, insofern er nicht fragt, ob etwas wahr ist, sondern vielmehr „ob es möglich ist, dass es nicht gewesen sei"; zugleich teilt er wiederum mit diesem ein rein negatives Verständnis von Anachronismus, den es, so wie im Falle der Homonymie, um jeden Preis zu umgehen gilt. Und, wie im Falle der Homonymie, ist die Geschichte, auf die Rancière abzielt, wiederum eine, die den Anachronismus nicht versucht zu beseitigen, sondern vielmehr ein positives Verständnis desselben entwickelt, das er hier als „Anachronie" reformuliert:

> Eine Anachronie, das ist ein Wort, ein Ereignis, eine signifikante Sequenz, die ‚ihre' Zeit verlassen haben, zugleich ausgestattet mit dem Vermögen, noch nie da gewese-

[29] Jacques Rancière, „Der Begriff des Anachronismus und die Wahrheit des Historikers", in: Eva Kernbauer (Hg.), *Kunstgeschichtlichkeit. Historizität und Anachronie in der Gegenwartskunst*, München, 2015, S. 33-50. Vgl. zum Begriff der Anachronie ausführlicher Maria Muhle, „‚Aufteilung der Zeiten'. Die Anachronie der Geschichte", in: ebd., S. 51-66.

[30] Rancière (2015), Der Begriff des Anachronismus, S. 39.

> ne zeitliche Weichenstellungen zu definieren und den Sprung oder die Verbindung von einer Linie der Zeitlichkeit zu einer anderen zu gewährleisten.[31]

Wenn die Homonymie ein Sprechen außerhalb seines Ortes bezeichnet, das zugleich die Möglichkeit von Geschichte überhaupt erst begründet, ist die Anachronie ein Sprechen außerhalb der Zeit, das ebenfalls „ein Vermögen, die Geschichte ‚zu machen'" bedeutet, insofern

> die Mannigfaltigkeit von Linien der Zeitlichkeit und sogar von Bedeutungen der Zeit, die in einer ‚selben' Zeit enthalten ist, die Bedingung des geschichtlichen Handelns [sind]. Und ihre tatsächliche Berücksichtigung müsste der Ausgangspunkt für eine Geschichtswissenschaft sein, die sich weniger um ihren ‚wissenschaftlichen' Ruf und mehr um das kümmert, was ‚Geschichte' sagen will.[32]

Zugleich, so kann man abschließend hinzufügen, ist diese doppelte Berücksichtigung von Homonymie und Anachronie auch der Ausgangspunkt für eine politische Ästhetik, die sich über die Neuaufteilung von Sicht- und Sagbarkeiten definiert, d. h. über die Neuverhandlung der Zuteilung von Orten und Zeiten, deren natürliche Ordnung durch das Auftreten eines Anteils der Anteillosen subvertiert wird, und deren zentraler Einsatz ein ästhetisch reformulierter Realismus ist.

---

[31] Ebd., S. 50.
[32] Ebd.

Niklaus Largier

Die Figur des Realen. Zur Konvergenz von Realität und Möglichkeit

„Etwas wie eine Geschichte des europäischen Realismus", notiert Erich Auerbach im Schlusskapitel seines *Mimesis*-Buches,

> hätte ich niemals schreiben können; ich wäre im Stoff ertrunken, ich hätte mich in die hoffnungslosen Diskussionen über die Abgrenzung der verschiedenen Epochen, über die Zuordnung der einzelnen Schriftsteller zu ihnen, vor allem aber über die Definition des Begriffs Realismus einlassen müssen.[1]

Dass er Letzteres nicht getan und auch nie zu tun versucht hat, frustriert viele seiner Leser, doch es drückt sich darin aus, was Auerbach nicht nur als das Charakteristikum der „modernen Schriftsteller"[2] sieht, sondern als wichtigstes Merkmal seines eigenen Verfahrens. Was im Verzicht auf die umfassende Geschichte und die Definition des Realismus in den Blick kommt, ist daher zunächst die spezifische Modernität, die Auerbach mit Texten von Marcel Proust, Virginia Woolf, Knut Hamsun, Thomas Mann und James Joyce beschreibt. Das Zusammenbrechen großer narrativer Aktions- und Ereigniszusammenhänge im modernen Roman, das er dabei in den Vordergrund rückt und das Georg Lukács bekanntlich einer scharfen Kritik unterzieht,[3] sieht Auerbach indes nicht nur als „Durcheinanderwirbeln der europäischen Tradition" und als „grellen und schmerzhaften Zynismus"[4], sondern gleichzeitig als Genese einer neuen Form und „Meisterschaft" der Wirklichkeitsdarstellung. Diese privilegiert den „beliebigen Vorgang", ohne ihn „im Dienst eines planvollen Handlungszusammenhangs auszuwerten". Doch dabei, betont er, „erscheinen Bezirke des Vorgangs und Verbindungen zu anderen Vorgängen, die vordem kaum geahnt, nie gesehen und beachtet wurden – und die doch bestimmend sind für unser wirkliches Leben."[5] Mit anderen Worten, die Literatur wird in ihrer modernen Gestalt nicht (bloß) als Verlustgeschichte beschrieben, sondern es artikuliert sich in der Krise eine neue Form realistischer Darstellung, die mit all ihren älteren Formen in einem Korrespondenzverhältnis

---

1 Erich Auerbach, *Mimesis*, Berlin, Leipzig, 1988 [schw. OA 1947], S. 509.

2 Ebd., S. 510.

3 Vgl. Georg Lukács, *Der historische Roman*, Berlin, 1955 [russ. OA 1938]; Joe Cleary, „Realism after Modernism and the Literary World-System", in: *Modern Language Quarterly* 73 (2012), S. 255-268. Im Unterschied zu Cleary sehe ich nicht, wie Auerbach und Lukács hier parallel gelesen werden können. Auerbach macht deutlich, dass seine eigene Methode unter denselben historischen Bedingungen entsteht wie der moderne Roman und in ihrer Eigenart diese historische Bedingung reflektiert.

4 Auerbach (1988), *Mimesis*, S. 512.

5 Ebd., S. 513.

steht. Erst diese Beobachtung macht Auerbachs historischen Blick und seinen Zugang zur Figur des Realen verständlich, in der dieses nicht einen Bereich determinierter Wirklichkeit als solche fasst, sondern immer neu ein Moment sinnlich-konkreter Intensität zum Ausdruck kommt. Darin wird Geschichtlichkeit konkret als Erfahrung am Text greifbar – und als Erfahrung von Möglichem, das sich in einer narrativ und diskursiv überbestimmten Wirklichkeit gegen die Bestimmungsmacht der Geschichte einnistet.

Den Leser hier zunächst verblüffend, schreibt Auerbach im besagten Kapitel weiter:

> Der gewaltige Roman von James Joyce, ein enzyklopädisches Werk, Spiegel Dublins, Irlands, Spiegel auch Europas und seiner Jahrtausende, hat als Rahmen den äußerlich unbedeutenden Tagesverlauf eines Gymnasiallehrers und eines Annoncenaquisiteurs; er umfaßt weniger als vierundzwanzig Stunden aus ihrem Leben, ähnlich wie der Leuchtturmroman Virginia Woolfs, der Teile von zwei zeitlich weitauseinanderliegenden Tagen schildert – vergleichbar aber auch, wie man nicht umhin kann, hier festzustellen, der Komödie Dantes.[6]

Dieser überraschende Schritt zu Dante Alighieri, dem Auerbachs stärkstes Interesse schon in seinem frühen Werk gilt, bringt nochmals in den Blick, was gleichzeitig Auerbachs eigene Methode und die Verfahren moderner Literatur prägt, die sich „gerade in den Jahrzehnten um den Ersten Weltkrieg und nach diesem gebildet"[7] haben. Es ist eine quasi-monadologische Hinwendung zum einzelnen Moment, zum partikularen Geschehen, das keiner Totalität und großen Erzählung mehr subsumiert werden kann, das indes in der Darstellung – und in Auerbachs historischer Beschreibung[8] – zum konstitutiven Kern einer Entfaltung möglicher Welten, Geschichtlichkeiten und Wirklichkeitsschichten wird. Sichtbar wird in der Artikulation des partikularen Moments etwas „ganz Neues und Elementares", nämlich die „Wirklichkeitsfülle und Lebenstiefe eines jeden Augenblicks, dem man sich absichtslos hingibt."[9] Gemeint ist hier indes keine Verklärung des Augenblicks als Ort transzendenter Wirklichkeit, sondern, darin ist Auerbachs Position derjenigen Robert Musils vergleichbar,[10] die elementare Wirkung partikularer Momente poetisch amplifizierter Intensität, aus denen Linien geschichtlicher Formung je neu entfaltet werden können. „Denn", so Auerbach,

---

6 Ebd., S. 508.

7 Ebd., S. 511.

8 Zum Problem der Beschreibung vgl. Sharon Marcus/Heather Love/Stephen Best, „Building a Better Description", in: *Representations* 135 (2016), S. 1-21; Cannon Schmidt, „Interpret or Describe?", in: *Representations* 135 (2016), S. 102-118; Klaus Scherpe, *Beschreiben, nicht Erzählen! Beispiele zu einer ästhetischen Opposition: von Döblin und Musil bis zu Darstellungen des Holocaust*, Berlin, 1995 (Öffentliche Vorlesungen 44).

9 Auerbach (1988), *Mimesis*, S. 513.

10 Vgl. Robert Musils „Theorem der menschlichen Gestaltlosigkeit" („Der deutsche Mensch als Symptom", in: ders., *Gesammelte Werke in neun Bänden*, Band 8, hg. von Adolf Frisé, Reinbek bei Hamburg, 1978, S. 1353-1400: besonders S. 1369-1371). Dazu: Niklaus Largier, *Zeit der Möglichkeit. Robert Musil, Georg Lukács und die Kunst des Essays*, Hannover, 2016, S. 83-97.

> es vollzieht sich in uns unablässig ein Formungs- und Deutungsprozeß, dessen Gegenstand wir selbst sind: unser Leben mit Vergangenheit, Gegenwart und Zukunft, unsere Umgebung, die Welt, in der wir leben, versuchen wir unablässig deutend zu ordnen, so daß es für uns eine Gesamtgestalt gewinnt, die freilich, je nachdem wir genötigt, geneigt und fähig sind, neu sich aufdrängende Erfahrungen aufzunehmen, sich ständig mehr oder weniger schnell und radikal wandelt.[11]

Damit tritt eine Spannung in den Blick zwischen gestaltbildenden Momenten, die in der modernen Literatur oft scheinbar zusammenhangslos in den Vordergrund rücken, und dem „synthetischen Deutungswillen des Lesers", der narrative Totalität intendiert und immer wieder an der formbildenden Kraft solch partikularer Momente scheitert. In der Krise der Moderne tritt deutlicher denn je ein Verständnis des „Realen" und „Wirklichen" in den Vordergrund, das die deskriptiven oder evokativen Momente als Intensitätskerne in ihren gestaltbildenden Effekten erscheinen lässt, statt diese einem sinntragenden Ganzen zu subsumieren. Damit eröffnen sie, als Bruchstellen einer diskursiv verwalteten Welt, neue Möglichkeitsräume, die narrativ nicht bewältigt werden können.[12] Gleichzeitig verweist das „realistische" Moment auf eine irreduzible Spannung zwischen „Ausdruck" und „Deutung", „Formungs- und Deutungsprozess", Effekt und Hermeneutik, die nicht nur die Moderne bestimmt, sondern als ‚Realismus' historisch je neu Gestalt anzunehmen vermag. Dies ist denn auch schon in Auerbachs früher Beschäftigung mit Dantes literarischer Sprache sichtbar. Realistisch, so schreibt er in *Dante als Dichter der irdischen Welt*, ist Dantes Liebesdichtung nicht, weil diese einen größtmöglichen Grad von Ähnlichkeit mit einem dargestellten Geschehen produziert, sondern weil sie in ihrer plastischen Intensität den Leser formt und verstrickt – und damit den Augenblick konstituiert, in dem der Leser, vor aller Deutung, das Sinnlich-Konkrete gleichzeitig als Moment irreduzibler Geschichtlichkeit und als bisher ungekannte Möglichkeit erfährt. Auerbach wird seine Methode denn auch später – durchaus in ironischer Abgrenzung von Ernst Robert Curtius – als „historische Topologie" bezeichnen, die nicht Topoi in ihrer kulturellen Tradierung, sondern als intensive Figuren mit ihren Geschichtlichkeit reflektierenden und möglichkeitskonstituierenden Effekten fasst.[13]

---

11 Auerbach (1988), *Mimesis*, S. 510.

12 Mit Hans Blumenberg, „Wirklichkeitsbegriff und Möglichkeit des Romans" (in: ders., *Ästhetische und metaphorologische Schriften*, hg. von Anselm Haverkamp, Frankfurt/M., 2001, S. 47-73) kann dies als Endpunkt einer Entwicklungslinie gesehen werden, die ich hier indes weniger in ihrer historisch-genealogischen als in ihrer systematischen Dimension der Analyse von Möglichkeitsbedingungen verschiedener Formen des Romans in Anschlag bringen möchte.

13 Erich Auerbach, *Vier Untersuchungen zur Geschichte der französischen Bildung*, Bern, 1951, S. 7: „Das Gemeinsame in diesen wie in meinen sonstigen Arbeiten ist die Bemühung, zu einer historischen Topologie zu gelangen; wobei es also nicht so sehr darauf abgesehen ist, die Eigentümlichkeit der Erscheinungen überhaupt zu erläutern, als die Bedingungen ihres Entstehens und die Richtung ihrer Wirksamkeit."

Damit wird Realismus auf eine Art verstanden, die ich figural nennen möchte[14] und die immer eine prekäre Stelle der Resistenz zwischen formgebendem Ausdruck und hermeneutischer Kontrolle markiert. Deutlich wird dies in Auerbachs *Figura*-Essay von 1938,[15] in dem nicht so sehr die Genealogie eines rhetorischen Begriffs rekonstruiert als vielmehr die Spannung zwischen Ausdruck und Bedeutung exploriert wird. In diesem Essay hat er auf eine bemerkenswerte Differenz zwischen Figur und Allegorie aufmerksam gemacht, in der die Figur zum Kippmoment wird. Figuration ist nicht einfach als Grundlage allegorischer und sinnstiftender Rede zu denken, sondern zunächst als rhetorisches Verfahren, das jeder Abstraktion und Spekulation Widerstand entgegensetzt. Es ist die materielle, sinnliche und plastische Qualität der Figur, in der diese gegenüber Allegorese und Hermeneutik, auch gegenüber Abstraktion und Spekulation, zumindest partiell resistent ist. Wie Auerbach zu verstehen gibt, ist die Allegorie ein sekundäres Phänomen, ein hermeneutischer und interpretativer Gestus, der die konkreten, sinnlichen, plastischen, das heißt die realistischen Aspekte des Figuralen überschattet und verdrängt. Damit wird auch die Möglichkeit, die das Figurale als realistisch-kritischer Schnitt in eine hermeneutisch und diskursiv verwaltete Wirklichkeit produziert, als solche immer neu in determinierte Formen abstrakter Bedeutung und einen normativen Realismus gebunden (und reterritorialisiert, um mit Gilles Deleuze zu sprechen). Im Unterschied dazu weist Auerbachs figuraler Realismus solch idealistische Hypostasierung des Realen zurück. Durch figurale Produktivität wird keine normative Wirklichkeit reproduziert, sondern es bilden sich Emergenzpunkte als Möglichkeitsdimensionen (noch) nicht begriffener Faktizität, die vor aller Deutung wahrnehmungsformend wirken – und darin die Konkretheit des geschichtlichen Moments ‚spiegeln'. Das ‚noch' ist indes hier ähnlich zu qualifizieren wie oben der Augenblick. Es verweist nicht auf eine verborgene Essenz, sondern bloß auf die – ich möchte sagen: haptotrope – Resistenz der realistischen Figur als geschichtliches Intensitätsmoment gegenüber dem hermeneutischen und diskursiven Zugriff. Als Zusammenbruch der Deutungsordnungen ist sie Affirmation des Augenblicks in ihrer endlose Verknüpfungsmöglichkeiten eröffnenden Position; aber auch radikale Affirmation einer Geschichtlichkeit, die immer nur aus dem partikularen Moment rekonstruiert werden kann.[16]

---

14 Im Unterschied zu Hayden White („Auerbach's Literary History. Figural Causation and Modernist Historicism", in: ders., *Figural Realism. Studies in the Mimesis Effect*, Baltimore, MA, London, 1999, S. 92-97), der ebenfalls von einem figuralen Realismus spricht, lege ich das Gewicht nicht auf Fragen der Historiografie und Geschichtsphilosophie, sondern auf die epistemologische Dimension, die den Begriff des Figuralen mit seinem Fokus auf „Wirksamkeit" von realistischer Ontologie und Identitätsmetaphysik unterscheidet.

15 Erich Auerbach, *„Figura"*, in: ders., *Gesammelte Aufsätze zur Romanischen Philologie*, Bern, München, 1967, S. 55-92.

16 Vgl. White (1999), Auerbach's Literary History, S. 96: „Auerbach posits a form of modernist historicism so radically different from its nineteenth-century prototype as to appear to consist of a repudiation of history itself." Vgl. auch Timothy Bahti, „Auerbach's *Mimesis*", in: ders., *Allegories of History. Literary Historiography after Hegel*, Baltimore, MA, London, 1992, S. 154 f.; Luiz Costa Lima,

In diesem Beitrag werde ich zunächst zeigen, wie Auerbach diesen Begriff der Figur entwickelt. In einem zweiten Abschnitt werde ich darauf eingehen, inwiefern Giambattista Vicos Denken (und damit auch ein barock-rhetorisches Erbe) für Auerbach in diesem Zusammenhang neue Bedeutung erlangt. Und in einem dritten Teil werde ich ausführen, inwiefern Auerbachs Verständnis der Figur es ermöglicht, rhetorische Praktiken der Figuration als Exploration von Möglichkeiten und als einen experimentellen Empirismus zu verstehen, der nicht beim Realen und der Referenz als normativen Ebenen der Wirklichkeitsdarstellung, sondern bei Realitätseffekten als rhetorisch und poetisch produzierten Intensitätsmomenten einsetzt.[17]

I. *Figura*

Was Auerbach betont und worauf er sich in seinen Textlektüren immer wieder bezieht, ist das „Konkrete", das „Realistische" als etwas, das sich mit partikularen Momenten nicht der Referenz, sondern der Attraktion und der Absorption im Akt des Lesens verbindet. Diese Sichtweise tritt schon 1929 in *Dante als Dichter der irdischen Welt* in den Vordergrund. Bereits auf den ersten Seiten dieses Buches wird sichtbar, dass Auerbachs Interesse einem spezifischen Aspekt des literarischen Textes gilt, nämlich der Form und dem Stil, in dem der Text Ereignisse als „unmittelbar evident" gegenwärtig macht, und zwar so, „dass die Frage nach ihrer Wahrscheinlichkeit erst bei nachträglicher Reflexion auftauchen kann."[18] Damit ist der Leser gezwungen, das vom Text Präsentierte wahrzunehmen,[19] bevor er darüber nachzudenken beginnt oder das Wahrgenommene zum Anlass einer hermeneutischen Deutung nimmt. Die Kraft des Textes liegt also Auerbach zufolge im Einbruch des Realen in „Gestalt" der rhetorischen Figur – nicht in ihrem Inhalt oder dem Faktum, dass sie einen hermeneutischen Prozess auslöst. Die Kraft liegt im evokativen Charakter, in der lebendigen Gegenwart, die der Text mit der Produktion des Geschehens oder Ereignisses durch die Darstellung herstellt. „Ausdruck"[20], nicht Repräsentation oder mimetische Referenzialität, ist der Schlüsselbegriff. Wie Auerbach weiter ausführt, sind es die folgenden Momente, die die Form dieses Ausdrucks charakterisieren, durch die die Aufmerksamkeit des Lesers fokussiert und seine Erfahrung geformt wird: Konkretheit, Intensität, Sinnlichkeit, Affekt, Partikularität, irreduzible Vielheit. Dies heißt indes gerade nicht, dass der

---

„Between Realism and Figuration: Auerbach's Decentered Realism", in: *Diacritics* 2 (2008), S. 133-140.

[17] Vgl. die Diskussion des Barthes'schen Begriffes bei Fredric Jameson, *Antinomies of Realism*, London, New York, NY, 2015, S. 35-37, zu Auerbach: S. 141-143.

[18] Erich Auerbach, *Dante als Dichter der irdischen Welt*, 2. Aufl., hg. von Kurt Flasch, Berlin, 2001 [1929], S. 6. Schon hier spricht Auerbach methodologisch von seiner „Entschlossenheit", „das Wirkliche nicht durch Spekulation abzutun und sich in die Transzendenz zu flüchten" (S. 25).

[19] Ebd., S. 42-44.

[20] Ebd., S. 57.

Text – in einer gewissermaßen naiven Form realistischer Mimesis – außertextuelle Ereignisse zur Darstellung bringen und damit dem Leser ein Gefühl des Gefallens oder Erstaunens angesichts der Ähnlichkeit von Text und sogenannter Realität vermitteln würde. Nach Auerbach ist es vielmehr die gemachte Form des Textes, in der ein Ereignis Gestalt, Konkretheit und sinnliche Intensität erhält und damit den Leser in einem partikular-geschichtlichen Moment absorbiert. Bei Dante, schreibt Auerbach, erscheint das Reale mit solcher Intensität, dass es in unserer Einbildungskraft „ungedeutet"[21] wahrgenommen wird – oder, vielleicht besser, dass es unmittelbar zum formbildenden Prinzip wird, das der Einbildungskraft, den Sinnen und den Affekten Gestalt verleiht.

Diese „Konkretheit"[22], eine Konkretheit, die auf der intensiven Kraft rhetorischer Mittel beruht – bei Aristoteles also der *energeia*[23] –, ist nach Auerbach im Gegensatz zu zwei „Tendenzen" der mittelalterlichen Literatur und Hermeneutik zu sehen: einerseits der „didaktischen Allegorie", andererseits dem „neuplatonischen Spiritualismus", die in einen Bereich der „Transzendenz" und „Spekulation [...] flüchten".[24] Beides führt zum Verlust der „sinnliche[n] Gestalt"; beides zerstört die „sinnliche Gestaltungskraft"[25] und dämpft die Wahrnehmung des Textes, indem es diese durch Prozesse allegorisierender Hermeneutik, Abstraktion und Spiritualisierung überlagert. Dabei verschwinden die gestaltgebenden Effekte der poetischen Sprache hinter der Deutung.

In seiner Arbeit mit literarischen Texten – so später auch im *Mimesis*-Buch – versucht Auerbach, diese Momente zu rekonstruieren und ihrer Kraft die gebührende Aufmerksamkeit zu schenken, ohne dabei die semantische und hermeneutische Ebene ganz außer Acht zu lassen. Dennoch bleibt immer der Fokus auf einem Verständnis der Figur im Vordergrund, die gewissermaßen die experientielle Seite des Texts in den Blick nimmt und diese in der Lektüre amplifizierend darstellt. Auerbach tut dies im Bezug auf Textstellen – *topoi* im Rahmen seiner „historischen Topologie" –, an denen die Konkretheit fassbar wird und die vor-allegorischen und nicht-spirituellen Effekte der Texte deutlich werden. Man kann hier durchaus von einer Phänomenologie rhetorischer Effekte sprechen,[26] tritt doch

---

21 Ebd., S. 77.

22 Ebd., S. 21.

23 Ich folge hier meinen Ausführungen in „Zwischen Sinnlichkeit, Rhetorik und Hermeneutik. Erich Auerbachs *Figura* und das Konzept der ‚historischen Topologie'", in: *Figura. Dynamiken von Zeichen und Zeiten*, hg. von Katharina Mertens Fleury und Christian Kiening, Würzburg, 2013, S. 51-70. Zum Verhältnis von *energeia* und *enargeia* vgl. Rüdiger Campe, „Aktualität des Bildes. Die Zeit rhetorischer Figuration", in: *Figur und Figuration. Studien zu Wahrnehmung und Wissen*, hg. von Gottfried Boehm, München, 2007, S. 163-18: 170. Zu Vico vgl. Diane Meur, „Auerbach und Vico. Die unausgesprochene Auseinandersetzung", in: *Erich Auerbach. Geschichte und Aktualität eines europäischen Philologen*, hg. von Karlheinz Barck und Martin Treml, Berlin, 2007, S. 57-70, besonders S. 65-67.

24 Auerbach (2001), *Dante*, S. 23-26.

25 Ebd., S. 26 f.

26 Vgl. Niklaus Largier, „Die Applikation der Sinne. Mittelalterliche Ästhetik als Phänomenologie rhetorischer Effekte", in: *Das fremde Schöne. Dimensionen des Ästhetischen in der Literatur des Mittelalters*, hg. von Manuel Braun und Christopher Young, Berlin, 2007, S. 43-60.

das in den Vordergrund, was der Leser als „intensiv", „bezaubernd", manchmal auch „verstrickend" erfährt,[27] also immer als intensive Wirkung spezifischer Figuren im Blick auf sinnliche und affektive Wahrnehmungsmomente. So begegnet hier eine Phänomenologie des Lesens als Charakterisierung spezifischer Lektüremomente, die den Text reartikulieren. Vielleicht kann man, ich komme darauf zurück, hier auch von einem experimentellen Empirismus sprechen, und zwar im Blick auf sinnliche, affektive und kognitive Wahrnehmungskomplexe, die sich in der Lektüre entfalten und dem Leser die Erfahrung konkreter geschichtlicher Momente vermitteln. Dies ist einerseits als Differenzmoment zu fassen, in dem die realistische Figur determinierte Wirklichkeit in ihrer geschichtlichen Konkretheit aufbricht und zur Möglichkeit werden lässt, andererseits als experimentelle Gestaltung von Wahrnehmungsmomenten, die sich zunächst der Deutung entziehen und im Geschichtlich-Konkreten einnisten.

Immer wieder begegnet dabei das Schlüsselwort „konkret" oder auch „konkrete Unmittelbarkeit". Auerbach versteht diese als Produkt poetischen Könnens, also als Artefakt, das ein Ereignis entstehen lässt, welches nichts als „Ausdruck" innerhalb der geschichtlichen Welt ist. „Der Eindruck", schreibt er über Dantes expressiven Stil in dieser Hinsicht, „ist rein sinnlich", und darin gelingt Dante „das Ereignishafte"[28], das den Leser sinnlich, affektiv und kognitiv absorbiert, bevor dieser zu reflektieren beginnt. Es muss betont werden, dass dabei keine Metaphysik des Ereignisses, keine hypostasierte reine Präsenz, auch kein ‚eigentliches' Reales als Referenzebene postuliert wird. Im Blick steht allein die Mechanik der rhetorischen und poetischen Form spezifischer Textstellen und ihrer wahrnehmungsformenden Effekte. Absorption bedeutet hier nichts anderes als eine Verschiebung von *agency*, in der die Figur und ihr prägender Effekt als das ‚Reale' einbricht und damit Möglichkeiten des Denkens und Fühlens produziert, die in der diskursiv und hermeneutisch geordneten Welt (noch) nicht gefasst werden können. Figuraler Realismus, so darf man sagen, produziert das Reale nicht als Feld historischer Determiniertheit, sondern der faktischen Möglichkeiten, die sich der Bestimmung, also der etablierten und damit abstrakten Wirklichkeit entziehen.

Um dies genauer zu verstehen, müssen wir uns zunächst nochmals kurz dem *Figura*-Aufsatz zuwenden, den Auerbach zehn Jahre nach dem *Dante*-Buch publiziert hat und in dem er gewissermaßen die Erklärung nachliefert, wie die dort wegweisenden Begriffe des Konkreten und der sinnlichen Intensität zu verstehen sind.

Nach Auerbach wird der Begriff *figura* von frühen christlichen Autoren – seine wichtigste Quelle ist hier Tertullian – auf eine dezidiert anti-allegorische und anti-spiritualistische Weise verwendet. Das heißt, dass dabei nicht zunächst auf eine Bewegung von der literalen Bedeutung der Heiligen Schrift zu einer geistigen Bedeutung des Wortes abgehoben wird, sondern auf die irreduzible geschichtliche Gestalt. Damit wird der Leser in eine Literalität einbezogen, die im Akt des Lesens

---

27 Auerbach (2001), *Dante*, S. 46.
28 Ebd., S. 58 f.

als Exposition an die nackte Faktizität des Geschichtlichen ihren Ort hat und zunächst alle Exegese und Spiritualisierung zurückweist. Um dieses Verständnis von *figura* herauszuarbeiten, rekonstruiert Auerbach die Benutzung des Wortes. Dabei zeigt er, dass *figura* sich nicht auf die Bedeutung der Wörter bezieht, sondern auf das, was er an anderer Stelle als „Ausdrucksformen" bezeichnet[29]; und vor allem, dass *figura* in der lateinischen Literatur „nach seiner Herkunft ‚plastisches Gebilde'" bedeute und sich in der „besonderen Bildung des Wortes etwas Lebend-Bewegtes, Unvollendetes und Spielendes" ausdrücke, in der „eine hohe Eleganz der lautlichen Erscheinung" liege, die „viele Dichter bezaubert" habe.[30] Obwohl sich dies unter dem Einfluss stärker wissenschaftlich-rhetorischen Denkens abgeschwächt und einer abstrakteren Bedeutung Platz gemacht habe, sei die „ursprüngliche Bedeutung des Plastischen nicht ganz verloren gegangen".[31] *Figura* ist, was als Ereignis zunächst die unaufgeregte Erwartung bricht und als Sinnliches in die Wahrnehmung tritt, nicht etwas, was schon Bedeutung besitzt. Als plastische Formung der Wahrnehmung, gewissermaßen als *adaequatio rei et perceptionis*, ist es Teil einer Welt von Wahrnehmungsereignissen, die sich (noch) nicht hermeneutisch erschließen. Seit Quintilian hat *figura* als *terminus technicus* bekanntlich auch eine wichtige Bedeutung im rhetorischen Diskurs, und zwar ist sie „jede Formung der Rede, die vom gewöhnlichen und nächstliegenden Gebrauch abweicht."[32] Nach Auerbach ist es die „raffinierte Technik [...] etwas auszudrücken oder zu insinuieren, ohne es auszusprechen, und zwar natürlich etwas, was aus politischen oder aus taktischen Gründen oder einfach um der größeren Wirkung willen verborgen oder wenigstens unausgesprochen bleiben sollte."[33] Im Vordergrund stehen damit zunächst drei Aspekte der *figura*: primär der „plastisch-sinnliche"[34], dann eine unmittelbare Verbindung zur Bildhaftigkeit, und als Drittes die rhetorische Bedeutung, die kunstvolle Zurichtung und ein Moment wirkungsvoll-strategischen Verbergens beinhaltet.

Eine „eigentümlich neue Bedeutung des Wortes" tritt nun nach Auerbach bei den Kirchenvätern auf, wo – nach ihm erstmals bei Tertullian – *figura* eine „Realprophetie oder vorausdeutende Gestalt des Zukünftigen" bezeichnet, und zwar als „etwas Wirkliches, Geschichtliches, welches etwas anderes, ebenfalls Wirkliches und Geschichtliches darstellt und ankündigt."[35] Damit wird *figura* zum Begriff der Sakral- oder Heilsgeschichte. Er ist dies jedoch nicht als Allegorie und generell nicht als Bedeutungsträger, sondern in seiner Gestalthaftigkeit, die den plastisch-sinnlichen Aspekt geschichtlicher Ereignisse – gegen alle Geschichtsnarrative – im Vordergrund hält.

---

29 Erich Auerbach, *Literatursprache und Publikum in der lateinischen Spätantike und im Mittelalter*, Bern, 1958, S. 12.

30 Auerbach (1967), *Figura*, S. 55.

31 Ebd., S. 57.

32 Ebd., S. 63.

33 Ebd., S. 63 f.

34 Ebd., S. 62.

35 Ebd., S. 65.

Es ist wichtig zu sehen, dass Auerbach, um dem *figura*-Begriff klarere Konturen zu verleihen, auf das Vokabular zurückgreift, das er eingangs etymologisch entwickelt hat und das er nun auf den Begriff der „geschichtlichen Wirklichkeit" bezieht. Nach ihm wendet sich Tertullian in seiner Verwendung des *figura*-Begriffs „gegen etwaige Übergriffe des Spiritualismus", und dies drückt sich darin aus, dass das Alte Testament „überall [...] wörtlichen Wirklichkeitssinn" behalte und jede Figur vor aller Deutung „geschichtliche Wirklichkeit", „sinnlich-geschichtliche Tatsache" ist, die auf andere „sinnlich-geschichtliche Tatsachen" bezogen ist.[36] Das eine Ereignis ist als Ereignis – nicht als Allegorie – Figur (und Versprechen), das andere als Ereignis Figur (und Erfüllung). Beides ist „sinnlich", und es wird getragen von dem, was Auerbach als Tertullians „lebendige Sätze" und seinen „energische[n] Realismus" bezeichnet.[37] Im Sinne dieses ‚Realismus' ist denn auch die *figura* nicht einfach bildhafte Bedeutung oder Abbildung eines vergangenen wirklichen Ereignisses, sondern durchaus, wie Auerbach schreibt, „ein Teil der Substanz" des „sinnlich wirkliche[n] Gegenstand[es] oder Vorgang[s]", oder auch eine rhetorische Textur, eine Sprachwirklichkeit, die auf Formen der gestalthaften Ähnlichkeit abhebt und zunächst ästhetisch-sinnliche Erfahrung geschichtlicher Faktizität ist.

Entscheidend ist dabei, dass die Wirkung des Figuralen nicht auf einzelne Momente beschränkt bleibt, sondern immer die Bildung von Texturen, Verbindungen und Vernetzungen beinhaltet – unter anderem auch diejenige Verbindung, die hermeneutisch als heilsgeschichtliche Typologie gelesen werden kann. „Geistig daran" ist indes nicht die Verbindung, sondern „nur die Deutung".[38] Gerade diese Unterscheidung ist entscheidend. Mit einer Reihe von Begriffen sucht Auerbach deutlich zu machen, dass nicht die Interpretation der Schrift in den Vordergrund rückt, nicht das geistige Deuten („*spiritaliter interpretari*"), sondern die innergeschichtliche, konkrete, wirklichkeitsgesättigte, fleischliche Ebene, auf der Figuren in ihrer wechselseitigen Beziehung stehen, bevor sie einer spiritualisierenden Allegorese unterzogen werden. Mit anderen Worten: Figuren produzieren in ihrer plastischen Wirkung Möglichkeitsfelder und Verbindungen, die nicht von einem interpretierenden Zugriff abhängen, also weder Abstraktion noch Spekulation oder allegorisierende Hermeneutik voraussetzen, sondern als solche der Wahrnehmung Gestalt verleihen. Sie durchbrechen die diskursive Ordnung in ihrer geschichtlichen Konkretheit und fungieren als Emergenzpunkte, die zunächst differenziell als intensive Attraktoren fungieren und gleichzeitig in ihrer konkreten Sättigung Bezüge mit anderen Emergenzpunkten ausbilden. Die *agency* liegt dabei, wenn man so will, in den realistischen Figuren, die den geschichtlichen Moment in Wahrnehmung überführen. Ihre ‚realistische' Form ist eins mit dieser Funktion.

---

36 Ebd., S. 66.

37 Ebd.

38 Ebd., S. 67.

II. Vicos Imagination

Ein anderer Denker hat Auerbachs Figurbegriff wesentlich mitgeprägt, freilich ohne dass er dies im *Figura*-Essay explizit gemacht hätte. Es handelt sich um Vico und seine *Scienza nuova*. Vico ist, neben Dante, eine weitere Faszinationsgestalt in Auerbachs Schriften. Auerbach schreibt in seiner Einleitung zu *Literatursprache und Publikum*, Vico und sein Verständnis der menschlichen Natur als einer grundsätzlich historischen Natur, die sich durch poetische Mittel der Imagination forme, bilde den Hintergrund seines Verständnisses philologischer Arbeit. Die Praktiken der Imagination, von denen Vico spricht, sind Auerbach zufolge wiederum zunächst als Praktiken der Figuration zu verstehen, nicht als hermeneutische Praktiken der Sinn- und Bedeutungsfindung. Wenn etwa der (hypothetische) archaische Mensch angesichts drohender Blitze ein apotropäisches Monument erstellt, handelt es sich dabei nicht um „Deutung", sondern um ein Artefakt, dessen Effekt gleichzeitig die Abschreckung des dämonischen Gewitters und die Beruhigung des Gemüts ist. Mit der Produktion des bannenden Elements geht eine Rekonfiguration sinnlicher, affektiver und kognitiver Wahrnehmungsbestände, also eine Modifikation der ‚Natur' des Menschen einher, lebt dieser doch nun ohne Angst. Wenn das Artefakt so gleichzeitig zum Teil der materiellen Kulturgeschichte und der Geschichte der menschlichen Wahrnehmungsformen wird, muss es zunächst in dieser effektiven Kraft verstanden werden, in der es als figuraler Akteur konstitutives Moment der Naturgeschichte des menschlichen Gemüts ist. Gerade dies hat nach Auerbach der „Philologe" nachzuvollziehen, wenn er mit historischen Artefakten und Texten arbeitet. Um geschichtlich zu ‚verstehen', hat er sich einer Erfahrung am Text auszusetzen, die zunächst auf Abstraktion verzichtet und der figuralen, partikularen, gestaltgebenden Kraft in ihrem Ausdruck gerecht wird. Konkret bedeutet dies, in Auerbachs humanistischer Formulierung, in der Erfahrung am Text sich den ungefassten Möglichkeiten auszusetzen, welche die Figuren produzieren:

> Eigene Erfahrung, Diskretion und eine auf Grund sehr genauer Kenntnis des Materials erworbene Großzügigkeit sind erforderlich, um Leben und Werk in die richtige Beziehung zu setzen. Jedenfalls aber ist das, was wir an einem Werk verstehen und lieben, das Dasein eines Menschen, eine Möglichkeit von uns selbst.[39]

Dies meint wiederum nicht eine abstrakte Fassung der Möglichkeiten, von denen hier die Rede ist, sondern es bezieht sich auf Akte, in denen sich der Leser den Figuren aussetzt und darin ihre geschichtsbildende Kraft an sich selbst als Möglichkeitsform erfährt, da es keine „andere Natur des Menschen gebe als seine Geschichte."[40]

Dabei spricht Auerbach von einem doppelten historischen Relativismus; doppelt, insofern er sich auf den Leser ebenso bezieht wie auf den Text (und alle kul-

---

[39] Auerbach (1958), *Literatursprache*, S. 14.
[40] Ebd., S. 12.

turellen Artefakte). Es ist zunächst ein Relativismus, insofern der Leser sich von der Versuchung verabschiedet, von der konkreten Ebene des Textes zu einer Abstraktion überzugehen und damit Realitätseffekte in ihrem partikularen Charakter gewissermaßen zu neutralisieren; und es ist zweitens ein Relativismus, insofern der Leser sich in diesem Prozess selbst dramatisiert, dem Effekt der realistischen Figuration und den bisher ungefassten Möglichkeiten aussetzt.

Wie man unschwer erkennen kann, rekapituliert Auerbach in diesen Überlegungen zu seiner eigenen Methode und zu Vicos Geschichtsverständnis die Unterscheidung zwischen Figur und spiritualisierender Abstraktion, die er im *Figura*-Aufsatz entwickelt. Historische Philologie ist demnach zunächst dramatisierende Exposition des Lesers (mit Michel Foucault: kritische Analyse der die Gegenwart determinierenden Faktoren[41]), in der dieser den figuralen Effekten, also den konkreten, geschichtlichen Momenten der Texte Raum gibt. Was Vico dabei vor Augen führt, ist einerseits die Kreativität figuraler Produktion (sie produziert das, was wir als menschliche Natur verstehen), andererseits die Funktion der Imagination in diesem Prozess. Zudem macht der Rekurs auf Vico deutlich, dass die Rhetorik als Technik und Theorie kulturformender Ausdrucksformen den Schlüssel zum Verständnis der Produktivität der Imagination bildet. Auerbach schreibt über Vico:

> Er entwickelt seine Ideen nicht wie die Späteren aus dem Gegensatz zur neuklassischen Rhetorik, sondern im Gegenteil unmittelbar aus dieser heraus. Er war ja selbst den größten Teil seines Lebens Professor der Rhetorik. Er sieht in den rhetorischen Figuren des Schulbetriebes Reste des ursprünglichen, konkret sinnlichen Denkens, das die Dinge selbst zu fassen meinte.[42]

Mit anderen Worten: Vicos rhetorische Figuren sind „konkret vorgestellte, körperlich gestaltete Synthesen [nicht Symbole oder Zeichen; N. L.], die aus einer vor Chaos schützenden, ritual formelhaft gerichteten Einbildungskraft hervorgehen“[43], und insofern als Medien die menschliche Natur in ihrer Geschichtlichkeit konstituieren.

Was Auerbach hier beschreibt, ist eine spezifische Form, in der der Historiker, der Philologe, ja der Leser überhaupt sich selbst als *realiter* geschichtlich geformt erfährt, und zwar so, dass er sich dem Effekt der Figuren exponiert, um wahrzunehmen, wie diese Figuren dem Leben Gestalt verleihen und es modifizieren. Auch den Begriff der Modifikation des Lebens übernimmt Auerbach von Vico, der angesichts der historischen Produktion der menschlichen Natur von *modificazioni della mente umana* spricht. Vicos „wichtigste [...] Entdeckung“, so Auerbach in seinem Aufsatz „Giambattista Vico und die Idee der Philologie“, ist „die Entdeckung des Menschen in den Frühzeiten seines gesellschaftlichen Zustandes“, die „zwar

---

41 Vgl. Michel Foucault, „Qu'est-ce-que les Lumières?“, in: ders., *Dits et écrits 1954-1988*, Band 4, hg. von Daniel Defert und François Ewald, Paris, 1994, S. 562-567.

42 Auerbach (1958), *Literatursprache*, S. 16.

43 Ebd.

ganz arm war an logischen Verstandeskräften, aber umso reicher an sinnlicher Erschütterungsfähigkeit, Formkraft und Phantasie."[44] Und er fährt fort:

> Aus der Kraft ihrer ungeheuren Phantasie belebten die Urmenschen die sie umgebende Natur, personifizierten ihre Kräfte, erforschten ihren Willen, schufen sich daraus ihre völlig phantastische, aber strenge und sakral-formelhafte Welt- und Lebensordnung. In dieser Entdeckung liegt der Kern des ganzen vichianischen Werkes.[45]

Um für uns, die wir hier nicht mehr von der Phantasie der Urmenschen ausgehen wollen, diese Sphäre freizulegen, müssen wir uns auf den „radikale[n] Relativismus" einlassen, der nicht zu „fürchten"[46] ist.

Nun sind es in Auerbachs Vico-Lektüre wiederum die Aspekte der Konkretheit und der Sinnlichkeit, welche die Brücke bilden zum frühen *Dante*-Buch und zum *Figura*-Essay. Sie lassen erkennen, worin nach Auerbach gleichzeitig die Sensibilität des aufmerksamen Lesers wie des Philologen bestehen soll. Dabei ist durchaus ein Stück Ideologiekritik mitzudenken. So formuliert Auerbach diese Position gegen Linien ideologischer Literaturgeschichtsschreibung und Geschichtsnarrative, denen er die ‚relativistische' Aufmerksamkeit für den Moment entgegensetzt. Wichtiger aber ist mir hier die spezifische Kontur, die der Rekurs auf die *figura* im Licht der Beschäftigung Auerbachs mit Vico gewinnt. Die Figur ist damit nicht nur als Kristallisationspunkt der Aufmerksamkeit des Lesers zu sehen, sondern als Ansatzpunkt einer Analyse der kontinuierlichen Modifikation des Lebens und ihrer literarischen Reflexion. Letztere wird dort realistisch, wo sie rhetorisch die Effekte produziert, die den Idealisierungsversuchen entgegenstehen, diese am Konkreten zerbrechen lassen, und damit den Figuren der Produktion der Naturgeschichte des Menschen in ihrer sinnlich-konkreten Gestalt zum Ausdruck verhelfen. Was der Umweg über Vicos Vorstellung der imaginativen Produktion des archaischen Menschens zu denken erlaubt, ist ein Zugang zur Geschichtlichkeit des Lebens, der immer neu bei der Praxis, den konstitutiven Momenten und ihrer partikularen, lebensformenden Kraft ansetzt, die im figuralen Realismus kritisch greifbar werden.

III. Experimenteller Realismus

Um diese Praxis etwas genauer zu umreißen, komme ich nochmals auf Auerbachs scharfe Unterscheidung von realistischer Figur und idealistischer Allegorie zurück. Es ist offensichtlich, dass sich eine solche Trennung nicht einfach aufrecht erhalten lässt. Selbst dort, wo Auerbach die Wirkung und Form von Dantes Poesie beschreibt, kommt er natürlich nicht umhin, semantische Momente aufzugreifen, Hermeneutik zu betreiben und gelegentlich dem Allegorischen Raum zuzugeste-

---

44 Erich Auerbach, „Giambattista Vico und die Idee der Philologie", in: ders., *Gesammelte Aufsätze zur Romanischen Philologie*, Bern, München, 1967, S. 233-241: 235.

45 Ebd.

46 Auerbach (1958), *Literatursprache*, S. 15.

hen. Deshalb ist die Entgegensetzung von „energischem Realismus" der Figur und spekulativem Gebäude der Allegorie auch als Kritik zu denken. Dies ist bei Auerbach in Form methodischer Entscheidungen greifbar, die bei spezifischen Textpassagen und ihren konkreten, realistisch-figuralen Differenzmomenten ansetzen. Noch besser als in den von Auerbach gewählten modernen Texten, lässt sich dies am Beispiel von Robert Musils *Der Mann ohne Eigenschaften* beschreiben, der den „Möglichkeitssinn" dem „Wirklichkeitssinn" entgegensetzt und die Spannung zwischen beiden mittels einer kritischen Analyse der gestaltbildenden Kraft realistisch-figuraler Arrangements exploriert. Deutlich wird dies aber auch in einer Reihe mittelalterlicher Texte aus dem zeitlichen Umfeld Dantes, die Auerbach selbst nirgends eingehend bespricht. Es handelt sich dabei um mittelalterliche Gebetstexte und Gebetsanleitungen, die auf exemplarische Weise den gleichzeitig kritischen und experimentellen Charakter des figuralen Realismus vor Augen führen.

Ich habe oben bereits den Begriff einer „Phänomenologie rhetorischer Effekte" benutzt, die im figuralen Realismus mitzudenken ist. Was ich damit meine, lässt sich am Beispiel etwa von Hugo von Sankt Victors Gebetstheorie in *De virtute orandi* einfach darstellen.[47] Ihm zufolge hat das meditative Gebet die Funktion, bestimmte Elemente aus einem umfassenden Text- und Erinnerungsarchiv so verfügbar zu machen, dass diese eine affektiv-sinnliche Wirkung entfalten und so auf ihren rhetorischen, figural-realistischen Effekt abgehoben wird. Damit wird scheinbar zunächst ein spiritueller Sinn der Schrift hervorgehoben, der im Rahmen der mittelalterlichen Hermeneutik semantisch entfaltet werden kann. Davon setzt sich Hugo indes unmittelbar ab, wenn er nicht die hermeneutische Ebene, sondern in kritischer Absetzung davon die literalen Effekte figuraler Momente und so eine Ebene quasi-empirischer Experimente mit der Wirkung rhetorischer Effekte in den Vordergrund rückt. Gebetspraxis setzt mit der hermeneutischen Lektüre, also durchaus auch dem „Deutungswillen" ein, führt indes in einer permanenten Kritik daran zurück zur wahrnehmungsformenden Funktion sprachlicher Figuren in ihrer sinnlichen Konkretheit, also zum figuralen Realismus. Und sie tut dies, wie ich im Folgenden kurz zeigen will, indem sie mit den dabei erzeugten Realitätseffekten und Wahrnehmungsmomenten experimentiert.

Bei Hugo wird die Affektgestalt und eine mit Affekten und Sinnlichkeit Hand in Hand gehende kritische Neuformung der Wahrnehmung zum eigentlich charakteristischen Aspekt der Gebetsübung. Diese ist weder Bittstellung noch Wissensform, sondern kritische Absetzung von diskursiven Wissensbeständen, also Reflexion auf die konstitutiven Aspekte des historischen Moments. Eine historisch bestimmte Wahrnehmungsform soll dabei dekonstruiert und im rhetorisch-figuralen Realismus experimentell gleichzeitig unterlaufen und neu gestaltet werden. Dabei führt der kritische Übergang vom Lesen (*lectio*) zur Kontemplation

---

47 Hugo von Sankt Victor, „De virtute orandi", in: *L'Oeuvre de Hugues de Saint-Victor*, hg. von Hugh B. Feiss und Patrice Siccard, Turnhout, 1997, S. 126-171 (Verweise auf diesen Text mit den Nummern der Kapitelzählung).

(*contemplatio*), von der sachlichen Lektüre des Textes zur Intensität realistischer Figuration, dann zur affektiv aufgeladenen Perzeption, zur Fokussierung des Affekts und schließlich zur Absorption im Habitus einer neuen Leidenschaft, die in der absoluten Figur, wenn man so will: im irreduziblen Realismus des elend leidenden Gott-Menschen,[48] als radikalste Form alle Wahrnehmung und alles Denken in die *compassio* und die Immanenz einer absorbierenden Liebe eingehen lässt.

Wichtig ist mir hier indes nicht dieses Programm monastischer Kontemplation, sondern seine Logik, auf die auch Auerbach im Begriff der Konkretheit abhebt. Getragen wird die geforderte Praxis, und dies ist ausschlaggebend, von einem schon im Mittelalter auch medientheoretisch komplex erörterten figuralen Realismus, der – Musils Verfahren vergleichbar[49] – bewusst experimentell eingesetzt wird. Die Praxis führt von der kritischen Analyse einer idealisierten Wirklichkeit zum Experiment mit den Möglichkeiten des Erlebens, die mittels eines figuralen Realismus produziert und gleichzeitig in ihren Erfahrungsdimensionen experimentell ausgelotet werden. Die Ebene der Abstraktion und Spiritualisierung, also eine auf Transzendenz und Wissen abhebende Diskursivierung, wird einerseits kritisch dekonstruiert, andererseits im Blick auf die Möglichkeiten neuer Wahrnehmungsformen befreit. Dabei werden die den geschichtlichen Moment formenden Kräfte erfahrbar, ohne dass eine abstrakte Ebene der Transzendenz eingezogen würde. Der figurale Realismus verweist vielmehr, als koextensive Entfaltung von Kritik und Konstruktion, beides in eine Ebene der Immanenz geschichtlicher Kräfte, die nur in der Erfahrung des Partikularen und im Experiment diese Gestalt anzunehmen vermag.

Masticare, ruminare, aber auch *frequens cogitatio* (Kauen, Wiederkäuen, reiteratives Vorstellen) sind bei den mittelalterlichen Autoren Kennworte für den Prozess der kritischen Absetzung von der abstrakten Perspektive und einer programmatischen Verkörperung des Wortes, die dabei gefordert wird. Dies weist auch hier von der Hermeneutik zurück in die Rhetorik als einer Technik, die mit der Mobilisierung plastischer Effekte sprachlicher Figuren eine diskursive Wissensordnung punktuell zu durchbrechen vermag – und darin realistisch wird.

Nach Hugo von Sankt Victor bedeutet dies zunächst, dass der Mensch sich darin übt, aufgrund der eigenen Lebenserfahrung, der Erinnerung, der Heiligen Schrift und anderer Texte sinnlich-konkrete Listen von Worten, Bildern und Textstellen zu erstellen, die gleichzeitig die abstrakte Ordnung auflösen und affektiv-sinnliche Wahrnehmungsmomente produzieren. Dies tut der Betende etwa dadurch, dass er alle möglichen Aspekte der Vergänglichkeit und Gebrechlichkeit

---

48 Vgl. Auerbach (2001), Dante, S. 18-23; Niklaus Largier, „Bare Figure. The Poetics of the Image in Late Medieval Mysticism", in: *Image and Incarnation: The Early Modern Doctrine of the Pictorial Image*, hg. von Lee Palmer Wandel und Walter S. Melion, Leiden, Boston, MA, 2015, S. 173-186.

49 Vgl. Susanne Reichlin/Robert Leucht, „Ein Gleichgewicht ohne festen Widerhalt, für das wir noch keine rechte Beschreibung gefunden haben.' Robert Musils ‚anderer Zustand' als Ort der Wissensübertragung", in: *Medien, Technik, Wissenschaft. Wissensübertragung bei Robert Musil und in seiner Zeit*, hg. von Ulrich J. Beil, Michael Gamper und Karl Wagner, Zürich, 2011, S. 289-322.

der Welt und allen Übels bedenkt, aufzählt und bildhaft gestaltet. Je mehr er dies tut, desto mehr „stöhnt und seufzt er"[50] und verstärkt dadurch dramatisch sein affektiv-sinnliches Erleben. Als Gegengewicht mag der Mensch, wie Hugo schreibt, in einem nächsten Schritt dieser experimentellen Poetik der Wahrnehmung alles Gute und die künftige Herrlichkeit bildhaft-imaginativ vor sein inneres Auge führen und dies den Torturen der ewigen Verdammnis gegenüberstellen. Auch hier stehen Momente der Lebenserfahrung, Erinnerung und Schriftstellen als Quellen rhetorischer *inventio* nebeneinander, wobei wiederum der Affekt im Zentrum des Verfahrens steht. Dieses zielt, gerade in der agonalen Gegenüberstellung, darauf ab, aus einer Serie von Betrachtungen anhand der hergestellten Listen, also mittels gezielt eingesetzter Realitätseffekte und des Spiels ihrer Amplifikation, die Absetzung von der ‚natürlich' gegebenen Welt zu leisten, die Wahrnehmung neu zu gestalten und mit den Gestaltungsmöglichkeiten zu experimentieren. Die *meditatio* ist so als Resonanzraum zu sehen, in dem die erzeugten Realitätseffekte sich verstärken und die Intensität des Affekts und der Sinne einen absoluten Realismus produzieren, der keine transzendente Ebene der Deutung mehr zulässt.

Dabei tritt nochmals vor Augen, was Auerbach wichtig ist, aber den scharfen Gegensatz zwischen Figur und Allegorie zumindest punktuell immer wieder unterläuft. Das von Hugo vorgeschlagene Verfahren ist denn auch geradezu paradox, produziert es doch – da die deutungslose Intensität und die radikale Kritik unhaltbar sind – in der Sedimentierung der Realitätseffekte permanent wiederum hermeneutische Allegoresen. Das Verfahren tut dies indes nur, um in der endlos wiederholten Kritik dieser Sedimentierung neue Figuren zu gewinnen und je neu von der Abstraktion in die Literalität der Figur, von der Transzendenz in die Immanenz, vom totalisierenden Geschichtsnarrativ in den geschichtlichen Moment zurückzulaufen. Erst wo die Figur immer neu mit der Hermeneutik bricht, wird sie realistisch, erst darin entfaltet sie die Effekte, die den Affekten, Sinnen und dem Denken neu Gestalt verleihen. Um es mit Auerbach oder noch etwas abstrakter zu sagen: Wenn sich im Lesen die allegorische Bildlichkeit und die Abstraktion an der sinnlich-konkreten Intensität der Sprache brechen, wird der figurale Effekt, der „Ausdruck" gleichzeitig zur Kritik der historischen Welt und zur „Gestalt" des Lebens. Darin erschließt sich nach Auerbach indes auch, worin die konkrete Geschichtlichkeit der menschlichen Natur, die Sedimentierung der Figuraleffekte, je neu entsteht und mit welchen Möglichkeiten des Lebens der Mensch zu experimentieren vermag.

Das heißt, dass wir es bei Sankt Victor wie bei Auerbach mit einer experimentellen Phänomenologie zu tun haben, in der Affekte mit rhetorischen Mitteln – neben der Ebene intellektueller und sinnlicher Wahrnehmungsgestaltung – als Form geschichtlich-konkreter empirischer Evidenz produziert, erfahren und exploriert werden. Dabei zielt die Gebetsübung nicht darauf ab, eine punktuelle Erfahrung des Göttlichen oder einen punktuellen Dialog mit dem Göttlichen zu produzieren, sondern die Wahrnehmung in ihrer alltäglichen Form zu modifizieren.

---

50 Hugo von Sankt Victor (1997), De virtute orandi, n. 3.

Als Technik vollzieht das Gebet einen Bruch mit der diskursiv verwalteten, sogenannten natürlichen Wahrnehmungsordnung, um in einem zweiten Schritt eine – kraft der im Medium des Gebets mobilisierten Figuren – neu geordnete Wahrnehmungsordnung zu produzieren und zu explorieren. Dabei wird das diskursive Weltwissen nicht einfach preisgegeben und vom Licht des Schriftwissens gewissermaßen überblendet. Es ist vielmehr die Funktion des Gebets, das Weltwissen in seiner geschichtlichen Konstituiertheit zum Ausdruck zu bringen, es in Formen der Dramatisierung zu dekonstruieren, und in der Preisgabe von Welt und Selbst die Spannung zwischen Position und Negation, Bild und Bildlosigkeit, instrumenteller Aktivität und expansiver Rezeptivität experimentell zu dramatisieren. Steht dabei, wie etwa bei Hugo, der Affekt im Zentrum, so nicht deshalb, weil er ein erotisches Gegenstück zum diskursiven Verstehen und der damit korrelierten negativen Theologie, also der radikalen Bildlosigkeit darstellt, sondern weil sich an ihm das positive Wissen um Welt und Selbst immer wieder am Partikularen bricht. Diesen Effekt zu produzieren ist der Kern von Hugos Verfahren im Gebet, das damit gewissermaßen zum privilegierten Ort des Experiments eines figuralen Realismus wird.

Insofern diese Figuren dem Archiv der Geschichte entnommen sind, impliziert diese Praxis natürlich immer ein analytisch-kritisches Verhältnis zum geschichtlich Gewordenen, das als *narratio* sinnvoll entfaltet werden kann. Sie produziert indes gleichzeitig ein anderes Verhältnis zur Geschichte, da die *narratio* an der Konkretheit der Figur bricht. Über die Momente figural-realistischer Wirkung werden so einerseits die – hermeneutisch, also ideologisch überblendeten – geschichtsbildenden Kräfte erfahren, exponiert und kritisch unterlaufen, andererseits experimentell affektive, sinnliche und kognitive Felder unbegriffener Möglichkeiten exploriert.

Friedrich Balke

Zwischen Medusa und *Family of Man*. Zum Realismus filmischer Darstellung bei Siegfried Kracauer

1. Darstellen und Enthüllen

In Siegfried Kracauers *Theorie des Films* hat es zunächst den Anschein, als ließen sich Filme problemlos in der Weise klassifizieren, dass sie entweder (in der Tradition der Brüder Lumière) die physische Realität wiedergeben oder enthüllen (und damit zugleich ‚erretten') oder (in der Nachfolge Georges Méliès') der künstlerischen Phantasie „freien Lauf"[1] lassen. Aus dieser Perspektive würde man die „psychologische Geschichte des deutschen Films", die Kracauer in *Von Caligari zu Hitler* schreibt[2], als eine umfassende Kritik, ja gelegentlich als eine regelrechte Denunziation eines filmischen *Expressionismus* lesen, der auf breiter Front den Film seiner realistischen Grundtendenz und damit seiner medialen „Grundeigenschaft"[3] zu entfremden versucht. Statt Geschichten zu erzählen, soll die Kamera sich im Sinne der Lumières „auf die Welt" richten. Um die „realistische Tendenz" als mediale Grundform des Films festzuschreiben, verweist Kracauer zunächst, medienhistorisch korrekt, auf das technische Analogmedium der Fotografie. Der Film übernimmt von der Fotografie die Ontologie des Indexikalischen[4] und schränkt auf diese Weise die *künstlerische* Freiheit des Mediums ein, eine Einschränkung, die seinem spezifischen Realismus zugutekommt. Kracauer lobt die „Realisten" des 19. Jahrhunderts, die die Fotografie nicht als ein *per se* unkünstlerisches Medium verwarfen, dafür, dass sie diese technisch auferlegte Einschränkung begrüßen (statt sie als Fesselung ihrer *Einbildungskraft* zu beklagen).[5]

Der filmische Realismus geht aber über das fotografische Moment insofern hinaus, als er die Wirklichkeit *in Bewegung* zeigt und damit einen unübersehbar vita-

---

1 Siegfried Kracauer, *Theorie des Films. Die Errettung der äußeren Wirklichkeit*, übers. von Friedrich Walter und Ruth Zellschan, Frankfurt/M., 1985 [amerik. OA 1960], S. 57.

2 Siegfried Kracauer, *Von Caligari zu Hitler. Eine psychologische Geschichte des deutschen Films*, Frankfurt/M., 1984 [amerik. OA 1947].

3 Kracauer (1985), *Theorie des Films*, S. 55.

4 Zu den Aspekten und Problematiken, die die Konzeptionen der Fotografie als Abdruck, Spur und Index aufwerfen, vgl. Peter Geimer, *Theorien der Fotografie zur Einführung*, Hamburg, 2014, S. 13-69. Alle berechtigte Kritik an der Vorstellung einer Wirklichkeitsübertragung vom Ding auf das fotografische Bild hat nicht dazu geführt, dass sich das Motiv eines physischen Kontakts zwischen Gegenstand und Empfängermedium erschöpft hätte. Zur fortgesetzten Virulenz des Spur-Realismus im Hinblick auf aktuelle *consumer*-basierte (Laien-)Filmproduktion vgl. Simon Rothöhler, *Amateur der Weltgeschichte. Historiographische Praktiken im Kino der Gegenwart*, Zürich, 2011, S. 13.

5 Vgl. Kracauer (1985), *Theorie des Films*, S. 27 f.

listisch konnotierten Bezug zu dem unterhält, was Kracauer immer wieder das *Leben* nennt, genauer: *ein* Leben, denn die Kamera-Realität ist durch ein Moment der technisch bedingten *Gleichstellung* der abgebildeten Phänomene definiert und bringt damit die etablierten Ordnungen und Hierarchien ins Wanken, die darüber befinden, was darstellungswürdig ist und was nicht: „Der Film ist die Dynamik des Lebens, der Natur und ihrer Manifestationen, der Menschenmengen und ihrer Bewegungen. Alles, was sich durch Bewegung kundgibt, ist ihm verwandt und zugehörig."[6] Der Film vollbringt bei Kracauer allerdings eine doppelte Leistung, er *stellt* Wirklichkeit nicht nur *dar*, sondern *enthüllt* sie zugleich. Filmische Sichtbarmachung tritt damit in ein Spannungsverhältnis zu Konzepten der Repräsentation. Die Wirklichkeit, um die es Kracauer geht, teilt mit der *enthüllenden* Leistung bestimmter Formen der Fotografie (insbesondere der Chronofotografie) die Eigenschaft, „Leben in seinen unkontrollierbarsten und unbewußtesten Augenblicken, ein Durcheinander kurzlebiger, sich ständig auflösender Formen, wie es nur der Kamera zugänglich ist"[7], vorzuführen. Seine posthum erschienenen Überlegungen zur *Geschichte – Vor den letzten Dingen* vorwegnehmend, qualifiziert Kracauer diese Realität auch als das Ergebnis „detachierter Feststellungen" – also als Feststellungen oder Beobachtungen, die von einem bestimmten Darstellungs- oder Formungs*willen* losgelöst sind und die Realität als „physische" zeigen bzw. mit einem Begriff, den er vielfach verwendet und den man als Chiffre filmischer Komplexität, um deren *Rettung* es ihm geht, begreifen kann, als „Rohmaterial"[8].

2. Der vierfache Sinn des „Rohmaterials"

Kracauers Filmtheorie, die im Untertitel die „Errettung der äußeren Wirklichkeit" verspricht (im amerikanischen Original heißt es allerdings: „*physical* reality", eine Formulierung, die über eine bloße *res extensa* hinausweist), ist im Kern eine Rohmaterialtheorie. Wenn ich Kracauers Position über den Realismus hinaus als eine *materialistische* bezeichnen würde, dann im Sinne eines Materialismus des (ungeformten) Materials, das eben die spezifische Rohheit dieses Materialismus definiert. Von einer materialistischen Parteinahme des Films hatte bereits Erwin Panofsky gesprochen, der die filmischen Verfahrensweisen kategorisch von denen „aller früheren bildenden Künste" unterschied, die „mehr oder weniger, einem idealistischen Weltbild"[9] entsprechen. Kracauer übernimmt von Panofsky die topologische Vorstellung, der zufolge der Film von unten nach oben agiert und sich jeder *Stilisierung* enthält: „Der Stoff des Films ist die äußere Realität als solche"[10]. Wie bei Kracauer werden auch von Panofsky die „expressionistischen De-

[6] Ebd., S. 58.
[7] Ebd.
[8] Ebd., S. 62.
[9] Erwin Panofsky, *Stil und Medium im Film & Die ideologischen Vorläufer des Rolls-Royce-Kühlers*, übers. von Rainer Grundman und Helmut Färber, Frankfurt/M., 1999, S. 19-57.
[10] Ebd., S. 54.

kors" des *Caligari* als Paradigma einer gegenläufigen Tendenz der Filmkunst behandelt, die darauf abzielt, das Medium den traditionellen bildenden Künsten zu unterwerfen. Während die formgebenden Tendenzen des Films (das *storytelling* und die frei erfundenen Gebilde, aber auch die Belehrung in sogenannten *Tatsachenfilmen*) komplexe filmtechnische Verfahren (Schnitt, Montage, vom Theater abgeborgte Bühneneffekte etc.) aufbieten, um über diese niedere Abkunft des Films (dessen Emblem für Kracauer das Spiegelbild einer schmutzigen Pfütze ist) hinwegzutäuschen, verlangt die *rohe* Materialität der realistischen Tendenz eine spezifische Einfachheit oder Selbstbeschränkung in der Handhabung dieser technischen Mittel. Das „Rohe" bzw. die „Rohheit" des Materials exponiert Kracauer in *vierfacher* Hinsicht:

1. Als *technische Mangelhaftigkeit* gerät das Rohe in den Blick einer Filmtheorie, die die gezeigte Realität vom technischen Stand der Aufzeichnungsapparate und Beleuchtungstechnik ebenso wie vom Überlieferungszustand des filmischen Trägermaterials abhängig macht. Die durchweg antiidealistische Zuspitzung des *Rohen* beginnt *niedrig* auch insofern, als sie die Effekte technischer Unzulänglichkeiten der filmischen Aufzeichnung ausdrücklich zum Begriffsinhalt der physischen Realität rechnet. So sehr Kracauer im Übrigen die technischen Möglichkeiten des Films (von Schnitt und Montage bis hin zu den Spezialeffekten) würdigt, so ist die realistische Tendenz ausdrücklich nicht von der Mobilisierung des Standes der filmtechnischen Verfahrensweisen abhängig. *Das Realistische ist für Kracauer das technisch Frugale*:

> Man stelle sich einen Film vor, der in Übereinstimmung mit den Grundeigenschaften interessante Aspekte physischer Realität auf technisch unzulängliche Art wiedergibt; vielleicht ist er ungeschickt belichtet oder fantasielos geschnitten. Dennoch ist solch ein Film in spezifischerem Sinne ein Film als einer, der sämtliche technischen Hilfsmittel und Tricks virtuos zu einer Darbietung verwendet, die der Kamera-Realität keinerlei Rechnung trägt.[11]

2. Nicht das Atelier, nicht der Schneideraum, sondern die *Kamera* ist daher für Kracauer die zentrale Größe, die über den Realismus eines Films entscheidet. Auch hier allerdings nicht die Kamera als ein Aufnahmegerät, das sich in ständiger technischer Entwicklung befindet, sondern die Kamera als Apparat, der spezifische Möglichkeiten seiner (*unauffälligen*) *Positionierung* zulässt, und zwar mitten in einem Geschehen, das nicht eigens *für* die Kamera angeordnet ist: „Die Kamera, die an jeder Straßenecke stehen könnte"[12], ist das Emblem der Filmästhetik Kracauers. Nicht ihre technische Komplexität, sondern die Einfachheit ihrer Einfügung in das Geschehen, das sie aufzeichnet, ihre Unauffälligkeit, wie sie heute Webcams ermöglichen, die das Geschehen in einem immer gleichen Bildausschnitt registrieren, fasziniert Kracauer an der Kamera. In seinen Berliner Straßenszenen hat Kracauer den Effekt einer permanent an einem bestimmten Ort platzierten Kamera im Medium der Literatur nachzuahmen versucht, wenn er „Stra-

---

[11] Kracauer (1985), *Theorie des Films*, S. 56.

[12] Siegfried Kracauer, *Das Ornament der Masse. Essays*, Frankfurt/M., 1977, S. 296.

ßen ohne Erinnerung“ beschreibt, also solche, in denen sich *über Nacht* abrupte, aber für das Auge des Passanten nicht wahrnehmbare Veränderungen vollziehen, die aber für ein Kameraauge, das dort permanent positioniert wäre, dokumentierbar würden: Läden und Betriebe kommen und verschwinden, alte machen neuen Platz, der Zeitpunkt aber,

> zu dem diese Lokalitäten jeweils auf der Bildfläche erscheinen, ist grundsätzlich nicht zu ermitteln. Genug, daß sie von irgendeinem Termin an vorhanden sind, aus dem Nichts entstandene Restaurants, Cafés, Barinterieurs, Pensionen und Geschäfte, die sich durchweg so gebärden, als existierten sie wirklich.[13]

Die Kamera zeichnet auf, was keine Erinnerung zu bewahren vermag, weil es gar nicht erst in den flüchtigen Blick von Menschenaugen gerät:

> Sonst bleibt das Vergangene an den Orten haften, an denen es zu Lebzeiten hauste; auf dem Kurfürstendamm tritt es ab, ohne Spuren zu hinterlassen [...] Was einmal war, ist auf Nimmerwiedersehen dahin, und was sich gerade behauptet, beschlagnahmt das Heute hundertprozentig.[14]

3. Das „Rohe“ bringt sich, *drittens*, in einer bestimmten *Bevorzugung der Dinge und Objekte vor den Personen und Figuren* zur Geltung.[15] So wie Kracauer die realitätsverbürgende Macht des Films zwar dem Medium als „Grundeigenschaft“[16] zuschreibt, die Besonderheit dieser Realität aber zugleich (über eine Auseinandersetzung mit Erich Auerbach) durch die Bezugnahme auf literarische Verfahren erläutert, wird im Hinblick auf die „leblosen Gegenstände“ ausgerechnet ein Maler zum Verteidiger des Films: Scharfsinnig betont Fernand Léger, „daß einzig der Film dazu befähigt sei, uns mit Hilfe von Großaufnahmen für die Möglichkeiten empfänglich zu machen, die in einem Hut, einem Stuhl, einer Hand und einem Fuße beschlossen liegen“[17]. Der filmische Realismus, wie ihn Kracauer denkt, steht in einem Spannungsverhältnis zur wesentlichen Anthropozentrik des Theaters: „Bühnenbilder rücken unvermeidlicherweise den Schauspieler in den Mittelpunkt, während es dem Film freisteht, bei Teilen seiner Erscheinung und seiner Umwelt zu verweilen.“[18] Die enthüllende Funktion des Films kulminiert bei Kracauer in spezifischen „Ausfallserscheinungen“[19], zu denen er u. a. *Abfälle* rechnet. Anders als der menschliche Blick, der zahlreiche Dinge nicht bemerkt, weil er sie ignoriert („Die meisten Menschen vermeiden den Anblick von Mülleimern, von Schmutz zu

---

13 Siegfried Kracauer, *Straßen in Berlin und anderswo*, Frankfurt/M., 2009, S. 21.
14 Ebd., S. 24.
15 Für eine filmwissenschaftliche Methodik, die sich dem Kinematografischen aus der Perspektive der Objekte nähert, vgl. Marius Böttcher et al. (Hg.), *Wörterbuch kinematografischer Objekte*, Berlin, 2014.
16 Kracauer (1985), *Theorie des Films*, S. 55.
17 Ebd., S. 76.
18 Ebd.
19 Ebd., S. 86.

ihren Füßen, von all dem Abfall, den sie hinter sich lassen"[20]), kennen Filme „dergleichen Hemmungen"[21] nicht.

4. Eine *vierte* und letzte Dimension des „Rohen" bzw. des „Rohmaterials" (besser: des *rohen Materials*, das der Film liefert) verstärkt den Eindruck, dass die Wirklichkeit, um die es Kracauer geht, weit davon entfernt ist, einen vorbildlichen Charakter aufzuweisen oder einer Idee zum Ausdruck zu verhelfen. Das Rohe weist neben dem technisch Defizienten, ästhetisch Reduzierten und dem Abjekten die Eigenschaft des *moralisch Verwerflichen* auf, dessen filmische Darstellung von einer eigentümlichen *Hemmungslosigkeit* gekennzeichnet ist. Naturkatastrophen, Pornografie und exzessive Gewalt haben dem Film den „Vorwurf billiger Sensationshascherei"[22] eingebracht, aber dieser Vorwurf geht am zugleich ethischen und politischen Einsatz dieser *Rohheiten* im Film vorbei. Die „blutigen Gladiatorenkämpfe in der antiken Arena", die schon bei Auerbach Vorbild des „Rohen" waren,[23] ahme der Film nicht einfach nur nach, er füge ihnen vielmehr „etwas Neues und ungemein Wichtiges" hinzu: „[E]s ist ihm um die Sichtbarmachung dessen zu tun, was sonst in innerer Erregung untergehen würde".[24] Die Art, wie der Film *das Rohe* exponiert, dient dazu, „den innerlich aufgewühlten Zeugen in einen bewußten Beobachter umzuwandeln"[25]. Und Kracauer unterstreicht den Rationalismus dieses Arguments noch durch den Zusatz: „Nichts könnte legitimer sein als sein Mangel an Hemmungen bei der Darstellung von Vorgängen, die uns außer Fassung bringen."[26]

3. Nachleben der Medusa

Unter der Überschrift „Materielle Evidenz" nimmt Kracauer im Epilog zu seiner *Theorie des Films* die ethisch-politische Problematik des *Rohmaterials* zum Anlass, sie mithilfe eines klassischen Mythos zu explizieren. Weil uns das Kino „Auge in Auge mit Dingen" bringt, „die wir fürchten"[27], stellt sich die Frage, zu welchem Zweck es das tut und ob eine Antwort auf diese Frage, die sich im ästhetischen Rahmen bewegt, ausreicht. Der Abschnitt, in dem Kracauer diese Frage angeht, ist mit „Das Haupt der Medusa" überschrieben. Kracauer erzählt den Mythos noch

---

20 Ebd., S. 87.
21 Ebd.
22 Ebd., S. 92.
23 Erich Auerbach, *Mimesis. Dargestellte Wirklichkeit in der abendländischen Literatur*, Tübingen, Basel, 2001, S. 70. „Sadismus, Blutrausch, und das Überwiegen des Magisch-Sinnlichen über das Rationale und Ethische" benennt Auerbach im Anschluss an eine ausführlich interpretierte Szene aus den *Bekenntnissen* des Augustinus die Wirkung der Gladiatorenkämpfe auf den Zuschauer.
24 Vgl. Kracauer (1985), *Theorie des Films*, S. 92.
25 Ebd.
26 Ebd., S. 93.
27 Ebd., S. 395.

einmal[28], wobei er nicht vergisst, den Ort anzugeben, an dem die Geschichte „gelernt“ wurde, nämlich die Schule, um sie dann einer komplexen Neuauslegung zu unterziehen. Die Geschichte vom Haupt der Medusa, das Perseus auf Befehl Athenes abzuschlagen hatte, wird von Kracauer unmittelbar auf die *große* Geschichte des 20. Jahrhunderts und ihre kollektiven Gräuel bezogen, weil der Mythos für die Bewältigung dieser Geschichte eine Lektion bereithält. Der Mythos wirft nicht nur die vordergründige Frage nach der Darstellbarkeit historischen Schreckens auf, sondern zugleich auch die nach der Möglichkeit von Handlungsmacht angesichts des dargestellten Grauens.

Bei genauerem Hinsehen stellt man fest, dass Kracauer in seiner Einschätzung des Verhältnisses zwischen der Darstellungsfunktion und der Funktion der Handlungsaktivierung schwankt. Dieses Schwanken, so meine These, hängt mit der spezifischen *politischen Rahmung* des im Mythos erzählten Geschehens zusammen, wie sie exemplarisch etwa in den *Metamorphosen* Ovids erkennbar ist. Denn es ist keineswegs so, als sei Perseus durch die unmittelbare Konfrontation mit dem Ungeheuer gezwungen worden, sich seiner in einem Kampf auf Leben und Tod zu erwehren. Athene, die spätere Schutzgöttin der Stadt, in der die Demokratie erfunden wird, erteilt Perseus nicht nur den Auftrag zur Vernichtung des Ungeheuers, sie händigt ihm auch das Medium, den „blanken Schild“, die „kleine optische Maschine“[29], wie sie Louis Marin genannt hat, aus – samt der Gebrauchsanweisung, deren Befolgung allein den Sieg über den entsetzlichen Blick des Ungeheuers gewährleistet: „Perseus folgte dem Rat der Athene und enthauptete die Medusa mit der Sichel, die Hermes zu seiner Ausrüstung beigesteuert hatte.“[30]

Das Schild ist nicht nur eine Abwehrwaffe, sondern zugleich ein bilderzeugendes Medium. Die eigens präparierte Oberfläche erzeugt „Spiegelbilder“[31], so Kracauer, in denen er die Bilder des Kinos präfiguriert sieht. Das Kino ermögliche „die ‚Reflexion‘ von Ereignissen [...], die uns versteinern würden, träfen wir sie im wirklichen Leben an. Die Filmleinwand ist Athenes blanker Schild.“[32] Damit ist Kracauers Lektüre des Mythos allerdings noch nicht abgeschlossen. Denn mit dem Vollzug des Befehls durch Perseus ist die Wirkung des Schreckens, dessen Träger das Haupt der Medusa ist, keineswegs erschöpft. Kracauer spricht den Sachverhalt unmissverständlich aus, dass die heroische Tat, die Befreiung der Menschen vom Terror der Medusa, kein „Selbstzweck“ ist, so wie auch die Bilder auf dem Schild kein Selbstzweck sind. Diese mildern den Schrecken des Hauptes, das den Be-

---

28 Da der Mythos nicht auf einen ursprünglichen, philologisch zu rekonstruierenden Text zu beziehen ist, sondern in seinen Varianten und Wiederaufnahmen *fortlebt*, gilt für Kracauers Adaption, was Hans Blumenberg in methodischer Hinsicht so formuliert hat: „Der Reiz des Neuen geht in den Genuß des Verstehens dadurch über, daß es als Kühnheit gegenüber dem Alten und als beziehbar auf dieses verstanden wird.“ Ders., „Wirklichkeitsbegriff und Wirkungspotential des Mythos“, in: ders./Anselm Haverkamp (Hg.), *Ästhetische und metaphorologische Schriften*, Frankfurt/M., 2001 S. 327-405: 351.

29 Louis Marin, *Die Malerei zerstören*, übers. von Bernhard Nessler, Berlin, 2003 [frz. OA 1977], S. 201.

30 Kracauer (1985), *Theorie des Films*, S. 395.

31 Ebd.

32 Ebd.

trachter versteinert, gerade so weit, dass ihre Wahrnehmbarkeit sich nicht zu einem ästhetischen Vergnügen abschwächt, einem *interesselosen Wohlgefallen*, dem die Existenz des Abgebildeten völlig gleichgültig ist. Die Bilder auf dem Schirm sind, wie Kracauer ausdrücklich sagt, „Mittel zu einem Zweck": „[S]ie sollen den Zuschauer befähigen – mehr noch: dazu antreiben –, das Grauen zu köpfen, das sie spiegeln".[33] In der Enthauptung des Ungeheuers kommt der staatlich-polizeiliche Charakter der Maßnahme zum Ausdruck, die Athene anordnet, denn die Enthauptung ist nicht nur ein kriegerischer Akt, sondern zugleich auch eine Hinrichtungstechnik. Der Auftrag zur Exekution der Medusa, die spezifische Handhabung des Schildes, in die die Göttin Perseus einführt, damit er seinen Auftrag erfolgreich ausführen kann, schließlich die Art der angeordneten Exekution, vor allem aber die *weitere Verwendung* des abgeschlagenen Medusenhauptes verweisen allesamt auf die Bedeutung der politischen Rahmung des heroischen Geschehens. Kracauer stellt mit der Reaktivierung des Medusa-Mythos Film und Zuschauer erneut vor die (vermeintlich schon längst gelöste) Aufgabe, die Welt von den Ungeheuern zu befreien. Der Mythos entspricht Hans Blumenberg zufolge „dem Bedürfnis" des ihm zuhörenden Menschen, „in der Welt heimisch zu sein"[34], einen Vorgang, den der Film für die moderne Welt, wie Kracauer ausdrücklich feststellt, zu wiederholen versucht.

Worin besteht Athenes Plan für die weitere Verwendung des abgeschlagenen Kopfes der Medusa? Kracauers Antwort: „Athene, so wird uns berichtet, befestigte den entsetzlichen Kopf an ihrer Ägis, um ihren Feinden Schrecken einzujagen. Perseus, dem Betrachter des Spiegelbilds, gelang es nicht, das Gespenst für immer zu bannen."[35] Caravaggios berühmte Medusa trägt diesem Aspekt insofern Rechnung, als er das Bild des abgeschlagenen Kopfes auf ein Schild, die *rotella*, aufträgt und damit durch die Wahl des Formats das flüchtige Bild im Bronzeschild des Perseus in eine dauerhafte Institution verwandelt, anders gesagt: in eine Waffe, die auch über den Tod der Dargestellten hinaus deren Stärke *kapitalisiert*.[36] Die Ägis ist das Schild der griechischen Götter Zeus und Athene. Das Schild übernimmt im

---

33 Ebd., S. 394.

34 Hans Blumenberg, *Arbeit am Mythos*, Frankfurt/M., 2006, S. 127.

35 Kracauer (1985), *Theorie des Films*, S. 395.

36 „Das Haupt also, das ich sehe, ist nicht das Bild, das sich im Bronzespiegel gespiegelt hat", sondern die (dem Herzog der Toscana, Cosimo, übereignete) „Repräsentation des Schildes von Perseus, der nach dem Kampf mit dem furchterregenden Haupt geschmückt ist, weshalb das Haupt auch eine Art Vorsprung bildet – im Relief –, nach vorne auf der Oberfläche der *rotella*" (Blumenberg (2006), *Arbeit am Mythos*, S. 164). Marin treibt in seiner Lektüre des Caravaggio-Bildes „die List des Perseus auf die Spitze: Medusa medusiert sich im Spiegel des Schildes selbst" (ebd., S. 160), der Schild des Perseus wäre also nicht ein Medium, das den Anblick des Ungeheuers für den Helden erträglich macht, indem er die direkte Wahrnehmung des Gesichts der Medusa zur Wahrnehmung eines Bildes ermäßigt; es wäre vielmehr so, dass Perseus an der Medusa vollzieht, was diese an allen anderen vollzieht, auf die ihr Blick trifft und die sie zu Stein erstarren lässt. Das Problem dieser Interpretation besteht nicht nur darin, dass (bei Ovid) die Medusa von Perseus im Schlaf überrascht wird und daher von ihren Augen gar keine Gefahr ausgeht; selbst wenn die äußerste List gelänge und die Medusa von ihrem eigenen Blick versteinert würde, bleibt die Frage, wie sich anschließend das Haupt vom Rumpf trennen ließe, wenn ihr Körper bereits zu Marmor erstarrt wäre.

Mythos und bei Kracauer also eine *doppelte* Funktion: die des Spiegelbildes bzw. der Leinwand, auf der sich der Schrecken (für einen Moment) zeigt, ohne dass er den Betrachter erstarren lässt, allerdings auch, ohne ihn dauerhaft festhalten zu können; und die einer Schutz- oder Kampfvorrichtung, an die sich das abgeschlagene Haupt und damit: der *Ab-fall* des Ungeheuers befestigen lässt, um fortan eine apotropäische Funktion auszuüben. Die Handlungsmacht der Medusa wird durch die Instrumentalisierung ihres abgeschlagenen Kopfes aufs Äußerste gesteigert, denn sie löst sich von dem Ort, an dem sie zu Lebzeiten des Ungeheuers ausgeübt wurde und auf den sie begrenzt war. Die Macht der Versteinerung wird gewissermaßen mobil und verwandelt sich in eine beliebig einsetzbare „Zauberwaffe"[37], wie es bei Ovid heißt, dessen epische Ausgestaltung des Medusa-Mythos Kracauer zweifellos vor Augen stand.

4. *Family of Man*: Du und ich und der Rest der Menschheit

Kracauers Auslegung des Medusa-Mythos folgt unmittelbar auf einen Abschnitt, der die Funktion des Films in der Darstellung von „Momenten des täglichen Lebens" verankert. Hier entwickelt er seine Überlegungen nicht zufällig in explizitem Rückgriff auf Auerbachs *Mimesis*. Die titelgebende *physical reality*, die der Film zu retten habe, wird in äußerster Distanz zu „artikulierten Glaubensinhalten, ideologischen Zielen, besonderen Unternehmungen und dergleichen" bestimmt – wobei der Mythos und seine Großkonflikte ebenfalls in diese Reihe von *außeralltäglichen* Geschehnissen (Kracauer nennt Kriege, Epidemien, Erdbeben) gehören:

> Auerbachs beiläufiger Hinweis auf das ‚alltägliche Leben' enthält einen wichtigen Fingerzeig. Von den kleinen Zufalls-Momenten, die dir und mir und dem Rest der Menschheit gemeinsame Dinge betreffen, kann in der Tat gesagt werden, daß sie die Dimension des Alltagslebens konstituieren, dieser Matrize aller anderen Formen der Realität. Es ist eine sehr substantielle Dimension. Wenn man für einen Augenblick artikulierte Glaubensinhalte, ideologische Ziele, besondere Unternehmungen und dergleichen beiseite läßt, so bleiben immer noch die Sorgen und Befriedigungen, Zwiste und Feste, Bedürfnisse und Bestrebungen, die jeder Tag mit sich bringt. Als Produkte von Gewohnheiten und mikroskopisch kleinen Wechselwirkungen bilden sie ein elastisches Gewebe, das sich nur langsam ändert, das Kriege, Epidemien und Revolutionen überlebt. Filme tendieren dazu, dieses Gewebe des täglichen Lebens zu entfalten.[38]

Weil Kracauer und Auerbach den Alltag zu einem normativen (und zugleich auch geschichtsphilosophischen) Bezugspunkt ihrer Theorie der literarischen bzw. filmischen Darstellung von Wirklichkeit erheben[39], endet die *Theorie des Films*

---

[37] Ovid, *Metamorphosen*, übers. von Erich Rösch, München, 1997, S. 197.

[38] Kracauer (1985), *Theorie des Films*, S. 394.

[39] Vgl. Friedrich Balke, „Erich Auerbachs niederer Materialismus", in: ders./Hanna Engelmeier, *Mimesis und Figura. Mit einer Neuausgabe des ‚Figura'-Aufsatzes von Erich Auerbach*, Paderborn, 2016, S. 13-88.

auch nicht mit dem Schreckenshaupt der Medusa, denn diese Episode aus dem Arsenal des Mythos ist nur nötig, weil sie an die Existenz von Ungeheuern erinnert, die uns noch vom Zustand der vereinten Menschheit trennen mögen. Die *Theorie des Films* endet nicht einmal mit der Analyse eines Films, dem die Darstellung des Alltags exemplarisch gelungen wäre, sondern mit einer Eloge auf eine berühmte *Ausstellung*, deren Titel das ethische und geschichtsphilosophische Programm der beiden Realismen, des Auerbach'schen wie des Kracauer'schen, einlöst: *The Family of Man.*

„Unterhalb der Kämpfe und auch durch sie vollzieht sich ein wirtschaftlicher und kultureller Ausgleichsprozeß", hatte Auerbach in *Mimesis* festgestellt, dessen noch fernes, aber schon sichtbares Ziel das „gemeinsame Leben der Menschen"[40] sei. Die Menschheit soll eine Familie sein, auch wenn sie weiter in Staaten, Völker und soziale Gruppierungen differenziert ist. Die fotografischen Medien sind nach Kracauer prädestiniert, der physischen Realität, die sie zeigen, eine *Spiritualität* abzugewinnen, wie sie ungefähr zur selben Zeit Marshall McLuhan für die elektronischen Medien und ihre Herbeiführung eines *global village* reklamieren wird. Kracauer schreibt über diese Medien:

> [S]ie allein sind in der Lage, die materiellen Aspekte gemeinsamen täglichen Lebens an vielen Orten wiederzugeben. Es ist kein Zufall, daß die Idee der Ausstellung *The Family of Man* von einem geborenen Fotografen stammt. [Frage: Was ist ein ‚geborener' Fotograf?; F. B.] Und einer der Gründe für den Welterfolg von Edward Steichens Ausstellung muß eben der Tatsache zugeschrieben werden, daß sie aus Fotografien besteht – Bildern, in deren Natur es liegt, die Realität der von ihnen gemeinten Vision zu beglaubigen. Ihres fotografischen Charakters wegen sind Filme dazu prädestiniert, eben dieses Thema aufzugreifen.[41]

Der Alltag gerät in der Ausstellung *The Family of Man* zu einer pathetischen Figur, der der Realismus des Rohen und des Rohmaterials vollständig ausgetrieben ist, auf die Kracauer ansonsten das Filmbild, wie wir gesehen haben, rigoros festzulegen versucht. *The Family of Man* kennt keine Pfützen, in denen sich „unsichtbare Hausfassaden und ein Stück Himmel spiegel[n]", die zu schwanken beginnen, als eine Brise aufkommt.[42] Dieses Bild, erinnert sich Kracauer im Vorwort zur *Theorie des Films*, war für ihn aber der Inbegriff dessen, was der Film als „Entdecker der Schönheiten des alltäglichen Lebens"[43] leisten konnte.

Was bewegt Kracauer, das Bild der bewegten Pfütze gegen die Vision vom Alltag mit seinen „Sorgen und Befriedigungen, Zwisten und Festen, Bedürfnissen und Bestrebungen"[44], die auch der Bezugspunkt von *The Family of Man* sind, auszutauschen? Kurz gesagt: politische Ökonomie oder Kapitalismus. Wir werden diese beiden nicht los! Was bei Kracauer wie bei Auerbach zu schön klingt, um wahr zu sein, nämlich, dass Medien dabei mitwirken, die Zone des Alltags immer mehr

---

40 Auerbach (2001), *Mimesis*, S. 401.
41 Ebd., S. 401 f.
42 Vgl. Kracauer (1985), *Theorie des Films*, S. 14.
43 Ebd.
44 Ebd., S. 394.

auszuweiten und den Menschen die *großen Schicksalskonflikte* zu ersparen, ist bloß, wie schon Roland Barthes in seiner Kritik der Ausstellung auf den Punkt gebracht hatte, die Figur eines durchsichtigen Humanismus. Die morphologischen Unterschiede der Menschen werden zugunsten nicht eines politischen, sondern eines *bequemen*, nämlich anthropologischen Universalismus relativiert: „Der Mensch wird geboren, arbeitet, lacht und stirbt überall auf die gleiche Weise."[45] Dieser Humanismus, der die „Universalität menschlicher Gesten im Alltag sämtlicher Länder der Welt"[46] ins Bild setzt (nicht zuletzt auch unter Zuhilfenahme von allerlei Sprichwörtern und Versen, die den Bildern beigegeben werden), ist eben der *Mythos des Alltags* schlechthin, mit dem die *Theorie des Films* schließt, um nicht dem sehr anderen Mythos der Medusa das letzte Wort zu lassen. Der Mythos der Ausstellung schließt die Menschheit in der genealogischen Fiktion der *Familie* zusammen, um über alles hinwegzutäuschen, was diese Einheit (die wir heute *Weltgemeinschaft* nennen) in ihrer Gewaltsamkeit sichtbar zu machen erlauben würde. Deshalb musste es, worauf Allan Sekula so hartnäckig hingewiesen hat[47], Edward Steichen sein, der eine derartige Ausstellung konzipierte, nachdem er im Ersten Weltkrieg die Fotografie als Medium der militärischen Feindaufklärung kennen und schätzen gelernt hatte. Wirft man nur einen kursorischen Blick in den Katalog der von Kracauer gepriesenen Ausstellung, wird klar, in welchem Maße ihr *creator* nach dem Krieg die Fotografie einer sehr anderen formgebenden Tendenz auslieferte, die allerdings mit der Kriegsfotografie zu Aufklärungszwecken eine bestimmte Konzeption der *automatischen Wiedererkennbarkeit* teilte. Die militärische Aufklärungsfotografie gehorcht nicht der von Kracauer formulierten Alternative von realistischer und formgebender Tendenz, denn diese Fotografie stellt die physische Wirklichkeit nicht um ihrer selbst willen dar, sondern um in spezifischer, nämlich destruktiver Weise auf sie *einzuwirken*. Die Formgebung vollzieht sich im Falle operativer Bilder allerdings nicht durch ästhetische Gestaltung, sondern durch die rigorose Codierung dessen, was sie zu sehen geben, wodurch diese Bilder so weit wie möglich jeden Interpretationsspielraum unterbinden, um automatisierte Reaktionen auf die fotografisch präsentierte Lage zu ermöglichen. Steichen hielt nach dem Krieg gegen alle piktorialistischen Versuchungen der Fotografie an ihrer *Beglaubigungsfunktion* fest, um sie jetzt allerdings für die Darstellung eines Daseinsbereichs nutzbar zu machen, den Auerbach als das „Unterhalb der Kämpfe" bezeichnet: „Steichen, the liberal technician, was able to condemn war while recovering its beneficial technical fallout"[48], kommentiert Sekula diese Wendung. Fotografie wird von Steichen, ob im Krieg oder im Frieden, immer „against the grain", also gegen die Körnigkeit des Mediums, die seine Opa-

---

45 Roland Barthes, *Mythen des Alltags*, Berlin, 2010, S. 226.

46 Ebd.

47 Vgl. Allan Sekula, „The Instrumental Image: Steichen at War", in: ders., *Photography against the Grain*, Halifax, 1984, S. 32-51.

48 Ebd., S. 49.

zität stört, gewendet, damit, wie für die militärische Aufklärungsfotografie entscheidend, möglichst kein Zweifel am repräsentierten Gegenstand übrig bleibt.[49]

Kracauer macht im „Epilog" zu seiner *Theorie des Films* unmissverständlich klar, dass die *filmischen Filme*, wie er unter Inkaufnahme eines Pleonasmus sagt, uns dabei helfen, „unsere gegebene materielle Umwelt nicht nur zu würdigen, *sondern überall hin auszudehnen*. Sie machen aus der Welt virtuell unser Zuhause [Herv. i. O.]."[50] Dass diese Ausdehnung die Ausdehnung eines spezifischen politisch-ökonomischen Lebensmodells ist, das „unser Zuhause" im Weltmaßstab nur werden kann, wenn andere Daseinsformen beschädigt, zurückgedrängt oder gar zerstört werden, ist der Grund, warum zwischen der Anerkennung des Alltags als der letzten ontologischen Bezugsgröße des Films und der Eloge auf die Ausstellung Steichens der Mythos vom Haupt der Medusa und damit die Insistenz eines Realen eingefügt ist, dessen Schrecken nicht zufällig instrumenteller Natur ist. Den Bildern einer Ausstellung, die ein blühendes globales Leben zeigen, stellt Kracauer das explizit mythische Bild voran, das tötet. Die Bilder der Ausstellung, Kracauer spricht es unmissverständlich aus, „*beglaubigen* [Herv. i. O.]" die Realität der von ihnen „gemeinten Vision"[51]. Im Begriff der Vision verbergen sich jene Abstraktionen, die im Album visuelles Fleisch annehmen müssen, Abstraktionen, von denen Kracauer ja ausdrücklich die Fotografie und erst recht den Film freihalten wollte. Der Schluss der *Theorie des Films* widerruft daher ihren Beginn. Die Reaktionen der Besucher auf die Ausstellung, wie sie Steichen beschreibt oder auch nur imaginiert, bestätigen, was man nach allem ahnt und was Kracauer entgangen war: *The Family of Man* ist das Ornament der Masse, das sich aus den Stadien in die Museen und Ausstellungsräume verlagert. Auch hier gibt es die Regelmäßigkeit von Mustern zu bejubeln, in denen sich die Zuschauer wiederzuerkennen haben, ohne dass sie, jedenfalls in der Erinnerung des Ausstellungsmachers, das Ornament, das sie auf den Fotografien zustande bringen, mitdenken würden[52]: „Regardless of the place", schreibt Steichen rückblickend, „the response was always the same [...] [T]he people in the audience looked at the pictures and the people in the pictures looked back at them. They recognized each other."[53] Aber sie erkennen nicht die Anordnung, deren Teil sie geworden sind. Es ist genau dieser Effekt der Wiedererkennung, den Kracauer mit der Funktion der Beglaubigung beschreibt. Dieser fundamentale Effekt einer Art fotografischen Spiegelstadiums tritt am Ende der *Theorie*

---

49 *Grain*, das Korn, steht bei Sekula also für die mediale Opazität, die das militärische Transparenzbegehren des fotografischen Realismus irritiert und daher im Bild *wegretuschiert* werden muss: „The quest for transparency led to the use of large photographic plates to minimize the effect of grain. Cameras were mounted on springs to reduce the blurring that resulted from airframe vibration; high speed shutters were developed to eleminate the distortions caused by the coincidence of airplaine and shutter movement." (Ebd., S. 36.)

50 Kracauer (1985), *Theorie des Films*, S. 394.

51 Ebd., S. 402.

52 Kracauer (1977), *Das Ornament der Masse*, S. 52. „Das Ornament wird von den Massen, die es zustandebringen, nicht mitgedacht." Es wird aber miterlebt, ja sogar bejubelt: „Der Regelmäßigkeit ihrer Muster jubelt die durch die Tribünen gegliederte Menge zu." (Ebd.)

53 Allan Sekula, „The Traffic in Photographs", in: *Art Journal* 41, 1 (1981), S. 15-25: 21.

des Films an die Stelle des Schildes der Medusa: Es ist die Ägis, der man für die Dauer einer Ausstellung die Trophäe des Hauptes der Medusa abgenommen hat, damit kein anderer in die imaginäre Beziehung von abgebildeten und anblickenden Menschen eindringt.

Volker Pantenburg

Neo-, Sur-, Super-, Hyper-. Realismuskonzepte im Kino

1.

Wie andere Konzepte in den Film- und Medienwissenschaften existiert auch ‚Realismus' nicht im Singular, sondern nur als Bindestrich-Phänomen. Um produktiv davon sprechen zu können, ist daher zunächst zu spezifizieren, was damit gemeint sein soll. Noch dazu hat der Begriff in der Philosophie, in der Literaturgeschichte, in den Kunstwissenschaften und der Filmtheorie sehr unterschiedliche und zum Teil miteinander inkompatible Bedeutungen angenommen. Was Karl Kraus allgemein bemerkt hat, gilt für den Begriff ‚Realismus' erst recht: Je näher man das Wort ansieht, desto ferner blickt es zurück.[1]

Auffällig ist dabei, dass der Begriff in seiner wechselhaften Geschichte häufig vehemente Reaktionen provoziert hat. Das mag bei einem eher unscheinbar wirkenden Wort wie ‚Realismus' überraschen. Tatsächlich jedoch ist Realismus selten nüchtern und sachlich beschrieben worden, sondern war meist eingebunden in kunstpolitische und ideologisch aufgeladene Debatten. Mal ist als abwertender Vorwurf gemeint, etwas sei ‚nur' realistisch und gebe sich mit der Reproduktion und Repräsentation der Wirklichkeit zufrieden, ohne über sie hinaus zu deuten. In anderen Fällen liegt gerade im Realismus das Versprechen, die meist politisch oder sozial interpretierte Wirklichkeit vergleichsweise direkt und ohne die üblichen Vermittlungsschritte in die künstlerische Artikulation hineinzuholen. Sogleich ist damit die Frage gestellt, ob es sich beim Realismus eher um ein politisches oder ein ästhetisches Projekt handelt, oder – dialektischer –, ob nicht im Problem des Realismus ästhetische und politische Zugriffe auf die Wirklichkeit miteinander interagieren und sich wechselseitig durchdringen.

Ich will im Folgenden zunächst einige Eingrenzungen vornehmen. Die erste besteht darin, dass es um das *Kino* gehen soll, oder etwas allgemeiner: um Bewegtbilder, auch wenn es unvermeidlich sein wird, dabei auf die Fotografie als Referenzmedium einzugehen. Die zweite Eingrenzung ist, dass ich paradigmatisch einige film- und theoriegeschichtlich relevante Momente – gewissermaßen: Standardsituationen der Problemstellung – herausgreifen werde, um Kriterien und Hinsichten des Realismus an ihnen zu diskutieren. Dies soll aus zwei unterschiedlichen Perspektiven geschehen, im Wechsel zwischen konkreten Beispielanalysen

---

1 Einen Einblick in die Komplexität und Vielfältigkeit des Konzepts gab jüngst der Band *Seien wir realistisch. Neue Realismen und Dokumentarismen in Philosophie und Kunst*, hg. von Dieter Mersch und Magdalena Marszałek, Zürich, 2016.

und dem Versuch, zu allgemeineren Bestimmungen einzelner Realismusvarianten zu kommen. Zunächst aber noch eine Vorbemerkung: Der Titel meines Textes ist von Frieda Grafe geborgt, die es auf beispielhafte Weise verstanden hat, ihr Schreiben zwischen Filmkritik, -analyse und -theorie zu verorten. Ihr Zeitungsartikel über eine Retrospektive neorealistischer Filme in Wien im Jahr 1979 trägt den programmatischen Titel: „Realismus ist immer Neo-, Sur-, Super-, Hyper-". Im Untertitel fügt sie hinzu: „Sehen mit fotografischen Apparaten"[2]. Eine erste wichtige These: Beim unvermittelten Zugriff auf die Wirklichkeit, der im Begriff des Realismus in Aussicht gestellt wird, handelt es sich, wie Grafe andeutet, um eine komplexe Konstruktion. Die Erscheinungen, die wir als vermeintliche Abweichungen und Weiterentwicklungen von einem vorausgesetzten Grundkonzept des Realismus (als ‚Neo-', ‚Sur-' etc.) zu definieren gewohnt sind, sind in Wirklichkeit integraler Bestandteil des Konzepts selbst. Von Realismus als ‚Konstruktion' zu sprechen impliziert jedoch keineswegs, dass die Realität damit geleugnet oder als völlig unzugänglich eingeklammert wäre, wie der in den 1980er Jahren populäre Begriff ‚Simulation' oder der radikale Konstruktivismus programmatisch behauptete. Es meint eher, dass uns realistische Darstellungsweisen *Hinsichten* und *Perspektiven* auf die Welt vorschlagen. Man könnte sagen: Jeder ‚realistische' Weltbezug verfehlt die Welt auf produktive Weise. Dieses Verfehlen ist kein Mangel, sondern generiert einen Überschuss, der sich den Instrumenten – wie Grafe schreibt: „fotografischen Apparaten" – verdankt. Durch den apparativen Blick auf die Wirklichkeit entsteht eine eigentümliche zweite Welt, deren Charakter und Eigenschaften auf komplizierte und je andere Weise mit ersterer verknüpft sind.

2.

Es ist unabdingbar, eine historische Diskussion des filmischen Realismus mit den Lumière-Brüdern beginnen zu lassen. Zahlreiche mythische Erzählungen beschwören die Drastik, mit der die ersten Vorführungen des Kinematografen auf die Zuschauer/innen gewirkt haben. Auch wenn viele dieser Berichte das Erschrecken ausschmücken und übertreiben – niemand ist vor dem einfahrenden Zug aus dem Saal geflohen –, bleibt die grundsätzliche Wirkung unwidersprochen. Zeitzeugen sprechen im Dezember 1895, nach der ersten öffentlichen Vorführung des Kinematografen, von „Szenen von erstaunlichem Realismus"[3], und ein Jahr später schreibt ein Dichter über einen Lumière-Film: „Man hört weder den einen weinen noch den anderen lachen, aber die Gesten und die Mimik sind mit einer solchen Genauigkeit eingefangen, dass ein Gefühl der Realität vom Zuschauer Besitz ergreift und diesen ganz beherrscht."[4] Bereits an dieser Urszene des filmischen Rea-

---

2 Frieda Grafe, „Realismus ist immer neo-, sur-, super-, hyper-. Sehen mit fotografischen Apparaten", in: dies., *Film/Geschichte. Wie Film Geschichte anders schreibt*, Berlin, 2004, S. 45-53.

3 So ein Besucher der ersten öffentlichen Vorstellung des Kinematografen am 28. Dezember 1895, zitiert bei Guido Kirsten, *Filmischer Realismus*, Marburg, 2013, S. 13.

4 Luiz Gonzaga Urbina, ebenfalls zitiert in ebd.

lismus lassen sich zwei Strategien erkennen, die zwar eng ineinander greifen, aber auf deutlich unterschiedlichen Ebenen ansetzen: Während „Szenen von erstaunlichem Realismus" auf innerfilmische Qualitäten hinweisen, auf die vormals nie gesehene mimetische Ähnlichkeit von Darstellung und Bewegung, hebt das „Gefühl der Realität" auf die Wirkung der Bilder ab, die im Zuschauer entsteht. Als ‚Realismus' wird also im ersten Fall ein bestimmbares Repertoire an Verfahren und Qualitäten auf der Ebene des filmischen Textes bestimmt, im zweiten ein Effekt und eine wirkungsästhetische Größe, die am Übergang von der Leinwand in den Zuschauerraum lokalisiert ist. Auf diese Differenz wird später zurückzukommen sein, weil sie die filmtheoretische Beschäftigung mit Realismus kontinuierlich prägt. Zunächst aber ein Blick auf einen Lumière-Film von 1897, *Barque sortant du port*[5]:

In den 50 Sekunden, die den Kameraleuten der Lumières zur Verfügung standen, sehen wir drei Männer in einem Boot. Zwei davon rudern, einer sitzt leicht erhöht im Bug. Einmal blickt er kurz in die Kamera, während die Gesichter der anderen beiden im Schatten des Gegenlichts nicht zu erkennen sind. Vom Rand des nahegelegenen Piers aus verfolgen zwei Frauen in eleganter Kleidung das Manöver. Sie haben ein Kind dabei, und an einer Stelle winken sie den Männern im Ruderboot zu und stellen auf diese Weise eine punktuelle Verbindung zwischen den beiden Orten und narrativen Zellen dar. So weit, so unspektakulär, zumindest für unsere Augen, die dies mehr als 120 Jahre nach der Aufnahme sehen. Der britische Cutter und Autor Dai Vaughan hat diesem Film und dem Kino der Lumières einige aufschlussreiche Seiten gewidmet. In seinem Kommentar hebt er besonders den Beginn und das Ende des kurzen Films hervor: „*A Boat Leaving Harbour* begins without purpose and ends without conclusion, its actors drawn into the contin-

5 Der erhaltene und heute unter diesem Titel kursierende Film (*Vue No. 678*) ist laut Catalogue Lumière im Sommer 1897 gedreht worden. Wahrscheinlich handelt es sich um das Remake eines nur noch als Fragment erhaltenen früheren Films von 1895 (*Vue No. 9*). Die Frauen auf dem Steg sind Marguerite Lumière und Jeanne-Joséphine Lumière. Vgl. https://catalogue-lumiere.com/barque-sortant-du-port/, (zuletzt aufgerufen am 31.03.2017).

gency of events."[6] Ein Anfang ohne Absicht, ein Ende ohne Schließung; stattdessen strukturiert den Film eine unvorhersehbare Spannung zwischen der Absicht der Protagonisten und der Kontingenz der Elemente. Das Ausschnitthafte, Fragmentarische ist für Vaughan entscheidend. Der Film beginnt ansatzlos und abrupt, ohne die Leere des Bildes, die in anderen Lumière-Filmen oft zu finden ist und die Bildfläche wie für einen Auftritt vorbereitet. Stattdessen geht es gleich in die rudimentäre Handlung hinein. Ebenso überraschend wie der Beginn ist das Ende, denn zum wahrscheinlich geplanten Verschwinden des Boots hinter der Kaimauer (zum im Titel versprochenen „Verlassen" des Hafens) kommt es aufgrund des unruhigen Seegangs nicht. Die hier beschriebenen Elemente erzeugen einen erstaunlichen Effekt. „Successive viewings serve only to stress its pathetic brevity as a fragment of human experience", schreibt Vaughan. „It survives as a reminder of that moment when the question of spontaneity was posed and not yet found to be insoluble: when cinema seemed free, not only of its proper connotations, but of the threat of its absorption into meaning beyond it."[7] Der kurze und scheinbar beiläufige *Barque sortant du port* birgt in dieser Beschreibung beinahe utopische Züge, weil er das Kino in einem Modus vorführt, in dem noch alle Optionen offen sind und die später einsetzende Kanalisierung hin auf Erzählung, Sinn und Bedeutungsproduktion noch nicht eingesetzt hat. Was hier vorliegt, ist filmisches Material im Modus des wirklichkeitsgesättigten Rohstoffs, ein kinematografisches *objet trouvé*, ein Dokument im engen Wortsinn.

Zugleich sollte die Rede vom Realismus dieser Szene jedoch nicht dazu verleiten, die radikale und unhintergehbare Grenze zwischen der Wirklichkeit und ihrer Aufzeichnung zu vergessen. Auch hier gibt uns Vaughan einen Hinweis, wenn er die „distinction between film and reality" auf ebenso simple wie verblüffende Weise beschreibt: „[F]ilm is about something, whereas reality is not."[8] Anders gesagt: Filmische (und, so darf man extrapolieren, jede künstlerische, wissenschaftliche, diskursive) Auseinandersetzung ist exakt das, was am Umschlagpunkt beider Ebenen entsteht. Ein Sachverhalt, der einfach *ist*, ohne *über* etwas zu sein oder *von* etwas zu handeln, bekommt in seiner medialen Verdopplung einen perspektivischen Index. Aus dem Rohmaterial der Wirklichkeit wird die Artikulation einer Einstellung.

3.

Schon in den Filmen der Lumières ist also nicht die Realität zu beobachten, sondern die Begegnung zwischen einem kontingenten Ausschnitt der Welt und einem Aufzeichnungsapparat, der dieser Kontingenz eine vorübergehend stabile Form

---

6 Dai Vaughan, „Let There Be Lumière" [1981], in: ders., *For Documentary. Twelve Essays*, Berkeley, CA, 1999, S. 1-8: 8.

7 Ebd.

8 Dai Vaughan, „The Space between Shots", in: ders., *For Documentary. Twelve Essays*, Berkeley, CA, 1999, S. 9-28.

verleiht. Alles, was in den darauffolgenden 120 Jahren Filmgeschichte folgt, lässt sich auf der damit etablierten Skala zwischen vorfilmischer Realität und kinematografischer Aufzeichnung anordnen. ‚Realistische' Zugriffe versuchen dabei den Einfluss des Apparats soweit wie möglich einzuklammern, um die Wirklichkeit möglichst unbeeinflusst wiederzugeben. Andy Warhols *Empire* (1964) wäre nach dieser Definition einer der realistischsten Filme überhaupt, und dieses Paradigma setzt sich fort in den autorlosen, anonymen Überwachungskameras und Live-Webcams von heute.[9] Aber schon an Warhol lässt sich die Kurzschlüssigkeit einer solchen Einschätzung gut erläutern. Denn bei genauerem Hinsehen ist keineswegs klar, über welche Realität wir etwas erfahren, wenn wir acht Stunden lang das Empire State Building aus dem 44. Stock des Time-Life Buildings in einer 16-mm-Projektion anschauen. Über die geschichtliche Wirklichkeit der Metropole New York in der Nacht vom 25. auf den 26. Juni 1964? Über die ästhetische Faszination von Dauer und Langsamkeit, die Warhol durch die verlangsamte Projektion des Materials zusätzlich betonte? Über die avantgardistische Geste, das Banale und Alltägliche aufzuwerten und zum legitimen Gegenstand der Kunst zu machen?[10]

In der nachrevolutionären Sowjetunion der 1920er Jahre lässt sich beobachten, wie sich das Denken des Realismus offensiv mit einem Denken der Maschine verbindet und beides unter konstruktivistischen Vorzeichen eine enge Allianz eingeht. Dziga Vertov, Theoretiker und Praktiker dieser Symbiose, spricht nicht von ‚Realismus', sein Begriff für ein verwandtes Phänomen ist „Faktographie".[11] Schon in den Manifesten und theoretischen Texten seit 1922 geht es Vertov und seinen Mitstreitern darum, nicht die menschliche Wahrnehmung als Maßstab zu setzen, sondern den genuin neuen Modus der filmischen Aufzeichnung:

> Ich lasse den Zuschauer so sehen, wie es mir für dieses oder jenes visuelle Phänomen am geeignetsten scheint. Das Auge unterwirft sich dem Willen der Kamera und wird von ihr auf jene folgerichtigen Momente eingestellt, die auf knappstem und deutlichstem Wege die Filmphrase zur Höhe oder Tiefe ihrer Lösung führen.[12]

Anhand eines Boxkampfs und eines Balletts spezifiziert er, was er damit meint: „Aufnahme eines Boxkampfs nicht aus dem Blickwinkel eines Zuschauers, der

---

9 In seinem Film *Arbeiter verlassen die Fabrik* hat Harun Farocki 1995 diesen Bezug hergestellt, wenn er darauf hinweist, dass am Ort, an dem sich der Kameramann der Lumières vor dem Fabriktor aufstellte, heute zahlreiche Überwachungskameras montiert sind.

10 David E. James hat beschrieben, wie *Empire* einerseits formalistisch als „primarily a device by which to present the full range of tones from black to white" (so Gregory Battock), andererseits als Anlass „to construct a documentarian Warhol" (James) aufgefasst wurde. Vgl. David E. James, *Allegories of Cinema. American Film in the Sixties*, Princeton, CA, 1989, S. 66.

11 Vgl. zur Faktografie als „gekurbeltem Sozialismus" Margarete Vöhringer, *Avantgarde und Psychotechnik. Wissenschaft, Kunst und Technik der Wahrnehmungsexperimente in der frühen Sowjetunion*, Göttingen, 2007, S. 149-160.

12 Dziga Vertov, „Kinoki – Umsturz" [1922], in: *Texte zur Theorie des Films*, 3. Aufl., hg. von Franz-Josef Albersmeier, Stuttgart, 1998, S. 36-50: 42.

dem Wettkampf beiwohnt, sondern Aufnahme der aufeinanderfolgenden Bewegungen (Verfahren) der Boxenden."[13]

Vertov beabsichtigt die vehemente Steuerung des Zuschauerblicks, der mit den Mitteln von Aufnahme und Schnitt von Eindruck zu Eindruck geschleudert wird.

> Das System der aufeinanderfolgenden Bewegungen erfordert eine Aufnahme der Tanzenden oder Boxenden in der Ordnung der einander ablösenden festgelegten Verfahren mit einer *gewaltsamen* Verlagerung der Augen des Zuschauers auf jene Abfolge von Details, die man unbedingt sehen muß. *Die Kamera bugsiert die Augen des Filmzuschauers* von den Händchen zu den Beinchen, von den Beinchen zu den Äuglein in der vorteilhaftesten Ordnung und organisiert die Details zu einer gesetzmäßigen Montageetüde [Herv. i. O.].[14]

In diesem hochgradig komponierten und konstruierten Vorgang geht es, anders als man denken könnte, nicht um eine Abkehr vom Ideal des Realismus, sondern um seine radikale Umformulierung nach Maßgabe der Technik und der gefilmten Objekte. Die angemessene, adäquate Erscheinungs- und Darstellungsform der Wirklichkeit bemisst sich nicht an den vermeintlichen Vorgaben und Anforderungen eines Zuschauerblicks, sondern an der unübersichtlichen, oft chaotischen und bewegten Welt der Dinge einerseits, an den immensen Möglichkeiten von Kamera und Schnitt andererseits. Sechs Jahre nach dem zitierten Manifest „Kinoki – Umsturz", zeigt uns Vertov in *Der Mann mit der Kamera* (1929), wie ein solches Ideal in der praktisch-filmischen Umsetzung aussehen könnte.

Festzuhalten ist an dieser Stelle zweierlei: (1) Zum einen wechselt der Referenzpunkt für Realismus bei Vertov kontinuierlich zwischen zwei Seiten: Zwischen der vorfilmischen Ebene dessen, was abgebildet wird – alle denkbaren Alltagsphänomene von Verkehr über Arbeit hin zum Haareschneiden und Freizeitvergnügen – und der Ebene der Verknüpfungen, der Montage, der Herstellung einer genuin eigenen, mit keinen anderen Mitteln als denen des Films herstellbaren Wirklichkeit. Vertov und sein Kameramann gehen von einer durch und durch medial durchwirkten, elektrifizierten und technischen Welt aus, so dass konsequenter-

[13] Ebd.

[14] Ebd., S. 43.

weise diese mediale Ebene mitverfilmt werden muss, um ein adäquates Bild der Gegenwart zu entwerfen. Die Kamera kommt deshalb – ebenso wie der Schneidetisch – notwendigerweise auf beiden Seiten der Unterscheidung vor: Sie ist Gegenstand der Abbildung und abbildendes Werkzeug, zugleich Subjekt und Objekt einer ‚realistischen' Konstruktion der Welt. Einerseits charakterisiert den Film die dokumentarische Transparenz und Durchlässigkeit auf das, was den Alltag sowjetischer Städte zum Ende der 1920er Jahre ausmachte, andererseits ist der Blick stets mit dem selbstreflexiven Hinweis versehen, dass dies eben *gefilmte* Realität ist und damit etwas, das überhaupt erst mit den Mitteln von Kamera und Schnitt hergestellt wird. (2) Zweitens definiert sich diese Ausprägung des Realismus nicht durch die Reproduktion der Wirklichkeit, sondern durch ihre aktive Veränderung. Dazu noch ein letztes Zitat von Vertov, erneut aus dem Kinoki-Text von 1923, in dem er tatsächlich aus der Perspektive der Kamera formuliert:

> Ich, die Maschine, zeige euch die Welt so, wie nur ich sie sehen kann. [...] *Ich bin in ununterbrochener Bewegung*, ich nähere mich Gegenständen und entferne mich von ihnen, ich krieche unter sie, ich klettere auf sie, ich bewege mich neben dem Maul eines galoppierenden Pferdes, ich rase in voller Fahrt in die Menge, ich renne vor angreifenden Soldaten her, ich werfe mich auf den Rücken, ich erhebe mich zusammen mit Flugzeugen, ich falle und steige zusammen mit fallenden und aufsteigenden Körpern [Herv. i. O.].[15]

Und schließlich: „Dies ist mein Weg zur Schaffung einer neuen Wahrnehmung der Welt. So dechiffriere ich aufs neue die euch unbekannte Welt."[16] Verständlich wird die Euphorie und Begeisterung, die Vertovs Manifeste und auch noch *Der Mann mit der Kamera* durchziehen, wenn man sich erinnert, dass die „Schaffung einer neuen Wahrnehmung der Welt" an das politische Projekt einer sozialistischen Gesellschaft gekoppelt war.

So unterschiedlich die kulturellen und politischen Kontexte sind, führt von hier aus eine recht gerade Linie zu Bertolt Brecht und seiner Auffassung von Realismus, die Anfang der 1930er Jahre – also schon im Zeitalter des Tonfilms – mit einer harschen Kritik am simplen Abbilden einsetzt. Brecht richtet seinen viel zitierten Einwand gegen die vermeintlich exakte Reproduktion der Wirklichkeit durch Fotografien, aber das Argument gilt ebenso sehr für das Medium Film:

> Die Lage wird dadurch so kompliziert, daß weniger denn je eine einfache ‚Wiedergabe der Realität' etwas über die Realität aussagt. Eine Photographie der Krupp-Werke oder der AEG ergibt beinahe nichts über diese Institute. Die eigentliche Realität ist in die Funktionale gerutscht. Die Verdinglichung der menschlichen Beziehungen, also etwa die Fabrik, gibt die letzteren nicht mehr heraus. Es ist also tatsächlich ‚etwas aufzubauen', etwas ‚Künstliches', etwas ‚Gestelltes'.[17]

---

[15] Ebd., S. 46.

[16] Ebd.

[17] Bertolt Brecht, „Der Dreigroschenprozess", in: ders., *Werke. Große kommentierte Berliner und Frankfurter Ausgabe*, Band 21, hg. von Werner Hecht et al., Berlin, Frankfurt/M., 1992, S. 448-514: 469.

Wollte man dieser Ausprägung des Realismus einen Namen geben, könnte man von einem ‚synthetischen' oder ‚konstruktiven' Realismus sprechen. Häufig, wenn auch nicht immer, verbindet sich das Konzept mit einer Bevorzugung von Montage und Schnitt gegenüber der ungeschnittenen Plansequenz, so im Kontext des modernen Kinos seit den 1960er Jahren bei Alexander Kluge oder Jean-Luc Godard. In der Gegenüberstellung mit dem Beispiel der Lumière-Brüder ist zudem der normative Gehalt dieses Typus von Realismus hervorzuheben. Für Vertov und Brecht, später auch für Godard oder Kluge essenziell ist die Einbindung des Realismus in ein politisches Projekt. Nicht die neutrale, möglichst zurückhaltende Aufzeichnung, sondern die aktive Setzung einer kinematografischen Wirklichkeit, die zu einem neuen Blick, und damit zu einem neuen Menschen führt.

4.

Keine Diskussion über den filmischen Realismus kommt an André Bazin vorbei. Gemeinsam mit Siegfried Kracauer und Stanley Cavell gehört Bazin zu den zentralen Theoretikern des Realismus im 20. Jahrhundert.[18] In je eigentümlicher Ausprägung und mit je unterschiedlichen Begrifflichkeiten basieren die Kinokonzepte der drei genannten Autoren auf dem Axiom, dass *qua* Kamera die materielle Wirklichkeit auf eine automatisierte, nüchtern registrierende Weise abzubilden ist – ein Gedanke, der uns schon bei den Lumières begegnet ist. In seiner *Theorie des Films* spricht Kracauer 1960 von der „Errettung der äußerlichen Wirklichkeit", in *The World Viewed* beschreibt Cavell das Vermögen des Films zur „automatic world projection"[19].

In einer Reihe von Texten, bei denen Kritiken einzelner Filme mit theoretisch inspirierten Grundsatztexten abwechseln, entwickelt auch Bazin eine umfassende Idee des Kinos, in deren Mittelpunkt der Realismus steht. ‚Realismus' verweist dabei auf zwei grundsätzlich unterschiedliche Ebenen, die sich zumindest in einem ersten Zugriff gut voneinander trennen lassen. Der Übersichtlichkeit halber werde ich sie vorübergehend mit ‚Realismus I' und ‚Realismus II' bezeichnen. ‚Realismus I' ist ein medientheoretischer Begriff, der fotografische Medien grundsätzlich kennzeichnet. Hier geht es darum, auf welche Weise das Bild erzeugt wurde. Ohne expliziten Rekurs, aber in einer gedanklich verwandten Figur wie der Zeichentheoretiker Charles Sanders Peirce im 19. Jahrhundert, betont Bazin das Verursachungsverhältnis zwischen der Wirklichkeit und deren Abbild in Fotografie und Film. Der *locus classicus* dieses Arguments ist sein Text zur „Ontologie des

---

[18] Ich orientiere mich im Folgenden eng an Kirsten (2013), *Filmischer Realismus*, S. 90-111. Bazin ist in den letzten Jahren wieder verstärkt rezipiert worden. Vgl. unter anderem den Band *Opening Bazin. Postwar Film Theory and Its Afterlife*, hg. von Dudley Andrew und Hervé Joubert-Laurencin, Oxford, 2011 und im deutschsprachigen Raum das Themenheft von *montage/AV* 18, 1 (2009) [Themenheft „Warum Bazin", hg. von Guido Kirsten].

[19] Stanley Cavell, *The World Viewed. Reflections on the Ontology of Film*, enlarged Edition, Cambridge, MA, London, 1979, S. 105.

photographischen Bildes“ von 1945. Bazin hebt hier die technische Komponente der fotografischen Repräsentation hervor, aber er gibt ihr interessanterweise eine psychologische, wenn nicht sogar anthropologische Wendung: „Unseren Hunger nach Illusion befriedigt vollständig nur eine mechanische Reproduktion, in der der Mensch keinerlei Rolle spielt.“[20] Die Fotografie, und in ihrem Gefolge der Film docken an dieses Bedürfnis nach automatisierter, einflussloser Verdopplung der Welt an. Vor dieser grundsätzlichen Eigenschaft, die übergreifend alle je besonderen Ausfertigungen von Fotografie und Film kennzeichnet, verblassen individuelle Unterschiede.

> Welche kritischen Einwände wir auch haben mögen, wir sind gezwungen, an die Existenz des wiedergegebenen Gegenstands zu glauben, der ja tatsächlich wiedergegeben, das heißt in Raum und Zeit wieder gegenwärtig gemacht wird. Die Photographie profitiert von einer Wirklichkeitsübertragung vom Ding auf seine Reproduktion.[21]

Es ist zugleich heikel und interessant, dass Bazin hier von „Wirklichkeitsübertragung“ – im Original: *transfert de réalité* – spricht und das fotografische Phänomen damit dem religiösen Konzept der Transsubstantation annähert.[22] In fotografischen Abbildungen begegnet uns, so suggeriert der Begriff, weitaus mehr als nur eine Repräsentation oder Reproduktion. Uns begegnet, wie im Falle der Reliquie, die Wirklichkeit selbst. Folgerichtig beginnt Bazin seinen Text damit, die Geschichte der Künste dem „Mumienkomplex“ zuzuordnen und als Kampf gegen die Vergänglichkeit zu interpretieren.

‚Realismus II‘ ist demgegenüber eher ein Stilbegriff, der ästhetische Besonderheiten einzelner Filme oder Strömungen kennzeichnet. In seiner umfassenden Untersuchung zum filmischen Realismus bringt Guido Kirsten dies auf die griffige Formulierung, dass es zum einen den „Realismus *des* Films“ – sprich, eine medientheoretische Bestimmung gibt, die ganz unabhängig von den jeweiligen Inhalten gemeint ist, und zum anderen den „Realismus *im* Film“, sprich: eine benennbare Ausprägung von Verfahren und Techniken innerhalb einzelner Filme und Strömungen. Wie sich beide Komponenten von Bazins Realismusbegriff zueinander verhalten, ist dabei keineswegs ausgemacht und durchaus problematisch.[23]

Eine Möglichkeit, die Verbindung beider Realismen zu denken, wäre, den ‚Realismus I‘ als medientheoretisches Apriori zu verstehen, auf dessen Fundament die Besonderheiten einzelner Beispiele für ‚Realismus II‘ dann aufbauen können. Ein Film, dem dies nach Bazins Meinung in besonders frappierender Weise gelingt, ist Vittorio de Sicas *Umberto D.* Entscheidend für Bazin ist das besondere Verhältnis, das dieser Film zu Handlung, Erzählung und Zeit ausbildet. Bazin schreibt:

---

20 André Bazin, „Ontologie des photographischen Bildes“, in: ders., *Was ist Film?*, hg. von Robert Fischer, Berlin, 2004, S. 33-42: 36.

21 Ebd., S. 37.

22 Vgl. dazu Vinzenz Hediger, „Das Wunder des Realismus. Transsubstantiation als medientheoretische Kategorie bei André Bazin“, in: *montage AV* 18, 1 (2009), S. 75-107.

23 Vgl. Kirsten (2013), *Filmischer* Realismus, S. 109-111.

> Die erzählerische Einheit des Films ist nicht die Episode, das Ereignis, der Theatercoup, der Charakter der Protagonisten, sondern die Aufeinanderfolge der konkreten Augenblicke des Lebens, von denen keiner den Anspruch erheben kann, wichtiger zu sein als der andere: Ihre ontologische Gleichwertigkeit löst schon vom Prinzip her jede dramatische Kategorie auf.[24]

Zugespitzt ist dies in einer Sequenz zu beobachten, die nach Bazin „einer der bleibenden Höhepunkte des Kinos überhaupt" ist.[25] Etwas mehr als vier Minuten lang begleiten wir das Dienstmädchen dabei, wie sie nach dem Aufwachen eine Abfolge von Alltagsverrichtungen durchläuft. Zunächst bleibt sie auf der Bettkante sitzen und vergräbt das Gesicht in den Händen, dann steht sie auf und geht langsam den Gang entlang, während sie sich den Morgenmantel überstreift; sie betritt die Küche, reibt sich die Augen, entfacht nach einigen vergeblichen Versuchen mit einem Streichholz den Herd, geht herüber zum Fenster und blickt über die Dächer, holt eine Kanne aus dem Schrank und füllt sie mit Wasser, räumt im Vorbeigehen einige Dinge vom Tisch, stellt die Kanne auf den Herd, fährt mit ihrer Hand ihren Körper entlang, zwinkert mit den Augen, nimmt die Kaffeemühle vom Tisch und setzt sich, um einige Bohnen zu mahlen. In ihrem Gesicht sind Tränen zu erkennen. Mit einem lang gestreckten Fuß tippt sie die Tür an, um sie zu schließen. Telefonklingeln unterbricht sie und sie verlässt die Küche.

Bazin erläutert an dieser Szene eines der Prinzipien des Neo-Realismus: „Im klassischen Film hieße die Ereigniseinheit ‚das Aufstehen des Dienstmädchens': Zwei oder drei kurze Einstellungen würden genügen, es zu illustrieren."[26] Im schroffen Gegensatz dazu verfährt de Sica anti-elliptisch und zeigt die vergehende Zeit als Abfolge kleiner, diskreter und folgenloser Handlungen. Anders als bei den Lumières und Vertov wird Realismus hier also als Abweichung von einer *erzählerischen* Konvention beschrieben, an der zweierlei entscheidend ist: zum einen die Nivellierung von narrativen Verdichtungen und üblicher Dramaturgie, die den Zuschauer auf

[24] André Bazin, „Ein großes Werk: Umberto D." [1952], in: ders., *Was ist Film?*, hg. von Robert Fischer, Berlin, 2004, S. 375-379: 377.

[25] Ebd.

[26] Ebd.

dem kürzesten Weg von Plotpoint zu Plotpoint schicken würde; zum anderen die zeitliche Integrität dessen, was gezeigt wird. Zwar ist die Sequenz geschnitten, aber dennoch kann der Eindruck entstehen, als seien erzählte Zeit und Erzählzeit deckungsgleich.

5.

Man sieht: In Bazins Auffassung von Realismus verbindet sich eine medientheoretische mit einer stilanalytischen Komponente, eine ontologische Zuschreibung mit erzähl- und zeitökonomischen Aspekten. Zugleich hat sein Realismus eine deutlich religiöse Färbung und impliziert einen ‚Glauben' an die wirklichkeitsübertragende Kraft des Kinos. Es wundert daher nicht, dass diese Einschätzung seit den 1960er Jahren vehement kritisiert worden ist und für einige Jahrzehnte einen schweren Stand hatte.

Einer der Schlüsseltexte, der die Realismusdebatte nach 1968 bestimmt und in semiotischer Terminologie reformuliert, ist Roland Barthes' kurzer Essay zum „Realitätseffekt". Barthes spricht darin vor allem über die Literatur des 19. Jahrhunderts und insbesondere über Gustave Flaubert, aber seine Überlegungen lassen sich übertragen und sind in der Filmtheorie adaptiert worden. In den Aufzählungen und Beschreibungen Flauberts – insbesondere in der Erwähnung des berühmt gewordenen Barometers in Flauberts Erzählung *Un cœur simple* – erkennt Barthes „bedeutungslose Eintragungen", die sich weder in symbolische noch in andere Modi einer strukturalen Erzählanalyse einpassen lassen.

> Das Barometer Flauberts, die kleine Tür Michelets sagen nichts anderes als: *wir sind das Wirkliche*; bedeutet wird dann die Kategorie des ‚Wirklichen' (und nicht ihre kontingenten Inhalte); anders ausgedrückt, wird das Fehlen des Signifikats zugunsten des Referenten zum Signifikat des Realismus [Herv. i. O.].[27]

Bei Barthes geht es somit nicht um eine Ontologie, sondern um eine sprachliche Operation, mittels derer durch ein Übermaß an erzählerisch ungebundenen, frei flottierenden Details der Eindruck von Realität erzeugt wird. Die Differenzen und Verbindungen zwischen Barthes Konzept und der „impression de réalité", wie sie in der Filmtheorie der 1970er Jahre bestimmend ist, müssten kleinteiliger rekonstruiert werden, als dies hier möglich ist. Wichtig ist in diesem Kontext, dass der Effekt, den Barthes an Flaubert und Michelet beschreibt, im Film in verzeitlichter Form wiederkehrt. Wie Kirsten schreibt: „Die Wirklichkeitseffekte verdanken sich dann filmisch inszenierten Einzelhandlungen, die ohne unmittelbare Bedeutung für die erzählte Geschichte bleiben: funktionslose Details in temporalisierter Form."[28] Auch was Bazin an *Umberto D.* hervorhebt und als ‚Realismus' feiert, ist problemlos – und nüchterner – als ein gelungener Einsatz des Realitätseffekts zu

---

[27] Roland Barthes, „Der Wirklichkeitseffekt" [1968], in: ders., *Das Rauschen der Sprache. Kritische Essays IV*, Frankfurt/M., 2006, S. 164-172: 171.

[28] Kirsten (2013), *Filmischer* Realismus, S. 169-170.

beschreiben. Von hier aus verläuft auch eine Linie hin zu dem, was Jacques Rancière a-signifikante Details nennt und etwa in Humphrey Jennings' *Listen to Britain* hervorhebt.[29]

6.

Ich mache an dieser Stelle einen Sprung in die Gegenwart, will aber darauf hinweisen, dass das neorealistische Projekt in der Zwischenzeit zahlreiche Modifikationen und Aktualisierungen erfahren hat. Stand seit den 1970er Jahren vor allem die harsche Kritik am Humanismus und der vermeintlichen Naivität realistischer Projekte und Theorien im Vordergrund, ist seit dem 1990er Jahren in vielfacher Hinsicht an realistische Positionen angeschlossen worden. Es ist auffällig, dass diese neueren Realismen sich verstärkt an den vermeintlichen Peripherien des Kinos antreffen lassen. Zu denken ist an die Filme Abbas Kiarostamis, denen Jean-Luc Nancy ein Buch gewidmet hat, das den Begriff der „Evidenz" ins Zentrum stellt,[30] an realistische Wellen im rumänischen, argentinischen oder ostasiatischen Kino, für die Namen wie Lisandro Alonso oder Jia Zhang Ke stehen können. Aber auch im US-amerikanischen und europäischen Kino, etwa in Rumänien, haben sich realistische Positionen verstärkt zurückgemeldet. Die Filme von Ramin Bahrani, Kelly Reichardt und anderen haben in der Publizistik den Begriff „Neo-neo-realism" provoziert.[31] Und tatsächlich docken einige der Genannten an die Praktiken des Neo-Realismus an – Arbeit an realen Schauplätzen, Bevorzugung von Laien vor professionellen Schauspielern, Entschleunigung der Erzählung. Ich betone das auch deshalb, um die Frage des Realismus nicht unzulässig auf Probleme des Dokumentarischen zu verkürzen. Ganz im Gegenteil wird Realismus in der überwiegenden Zahl von Untersuchungen auf das fiktionale Kino bezogen und daran diskutiert – ein deutliches Zeichen dafür, dass die Protokolle realistischer Verfahren und Rezeptionsmodi übergreifend sind und mit der problematischen Differenz zwischen dokumentarischem und fiktionalem Kino nicht angemessen zu beschreiben sind.

Nichtsdestotrotz möchte ich zuletzt auf zwei aktuelle Filme eingehen, die erneut eher dem dokumentarischen Pol des Kinos zuzurechnen sind. Beide Filme stammen aus dem „Sensory Ethnography Lab" der Harvard University, an der sich um Lucien Castaing-Taylor herum eine Gruppe von Ethnologen und Filmemacherinnen versammelt hat, die seit geraumer Zeit in wechselnden Teams produzieren, aber vor allem in den letzten fünf bis sechs Jahren verstärkt Aufmerksamkeit auf Festivals, in akademischen Zirkeln und in der zeitgenössischen Kunst erhalten

---

[29] Vgl. Jacques Rancière, „Die Geschichtlichkeit des Films", in: *Kunst Fortschritt Geschichte*, hg. von Christoph Menke und Juliane Rebentisch, Berlin, 2006, S. 69-86.

[30] Vgl. Jean-Luc Nancy, *L'Evidence du film / The Evidence of Film. Abbas Kiarostami*, Paris, 2001.

[31] Scott, A. O., „Neo-Neo-Realism", in: *The New York Times* vom 17. März 2009 sowie Richard Brody, „About Neo-Neo-Realism", in: *The New Yorker* vom 20. März 2009.

haben.[32] Der Film, der die bislang stärksten Reaktionen hervorgerufen hat, ist *Leviathan*.[33]

Es wäre absurd, diesen Film über sein Thema charakterisieren zu wollen, auch wenn *Leviathan* vom Fischfang vor der Küste Neuenglands handelt, in den Gewässern, in denen *Moby Dick* spielt. Eine solche Inhaltsangabe geht aber an der Bildästhetik sowie an der drastischen Wirkung des Films vollständig vorbei. Seinen Grund hat dies vor allem in der Verwendung zahlreicher GoPro-Kameras, handelsüblicher, nicht besonders teurer HD-Consumer-Kameras, die ansonsten vor allem von Extremsportlern – Mountainbikern, Climbern, Fallschirmspringern – benutzt werden. Castaing-Taylor und Véréna Paravel haben diese sucherlosen, weitwinkligen Kameras an Ketten und Netzen befestigt, an die Arbeiter an Bord des Schiffs angeheftet, ober- und unterhalb der Wasseroberfläche filmen lassen und daraus eine gewalttätige, an die Grenzen des Erträglichen gehende Bild- und Tonsinfonie bzw. -kakofonie hergestellt.

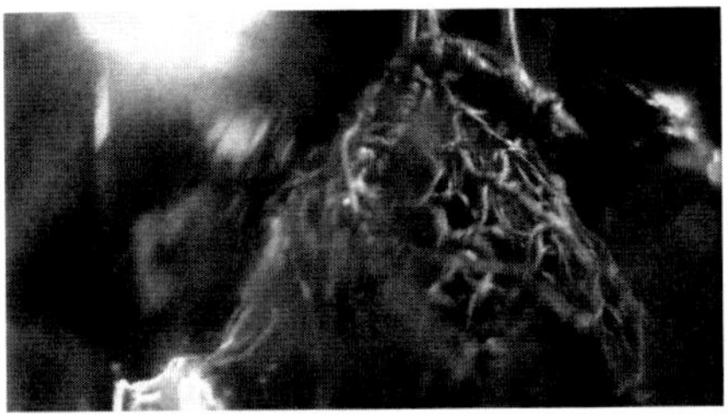

Es wundert nicht, dass zur Beschreibung des Films Begriffe wie „digital hyperrealism"[34] ebenso wie „surrealism" ins Feld geführt wurden. Auf besonders zugespitzte Weise handelt es sich um den „Neo-, Sur-, Super-, Hyperrealismus", den Frieda Grafe in ihrem Titel beschwört. Es liegt nahe, in *Leviathan* die digitale Wiederkehr des Vertov-Paradigmas zu erkennen. Auch hier gibt es eine Kamera, die sich mit allem, was sich bewegt, verbinden kann, die in die Tiefen des Meers und die Körper der toten Fische vordringt, sich an die Arbeitsprozesse der Fischer und die Rhythmen der Maschinen anschmiegt und eine zersplitterte, maschinelle Kamera-

---

32 Vgl. das Kapitel „Lucien Castaing-Taylor and Sensory Ethnography", in: Scott MacDonald, *American Ethnographic Film and Personal Documentary. The Cambridge Turn*, Berkeley, CA, 2013, S. 314-338 sowie Simon Rothöhler, „Zum Sensory Ethnography Lab der Harvard University", in: *MERKUR* 67, 771 (2013), S. 720-725.

33 Für eine filmhistorische Kontextualisierung von „Leviathan" und eine Beschreibung seiner ästhetischen Strategien vgl. Sabine Nessel, „Die (experimentelle) Filmkamera im Forschungslab. Am Beispiel ‚Leviathan' (2012) von Lucien Castaing-Taylor und Véréna Paravel", in: *Seien wir realistisch. Neue Realismen und Dokumentarismen in Philosophie und Kunst*, hg. von Dieter Mersch und Magdalena Marszałek, Zürich, 2016, S. 231-245.

34 Leo Goldsmith, „The Violence of Sensation," in: *Reverse Shot* vom 25. Februar 2013, online unter: http://reverseshot.org/reviews/entry/1682/leviathan, zuletzt aufgerufen am 31.03.2017: „The viscera, scales, and blood of the captured sea-life come violently and directly at us in all their rich, gory detail, but they do so through a process of digitization, through a digital hyperrealism, which allows for a kind of extension of vision and the body, or even vision through the body."

und Tonwirklichkeit zeigt. Es wäre wohl angemessen, hier von einem *sensorischen* Realismus zu sprechen, der den klassisch-realistischen Kategorien einer nachvollziehbaren räumlichen und zeitlichen Ordnung zuwiderläuft, wie Simon Rothöhler dies beschrieben hat:

> Das digitalkinetisch entfesselte Flux-Bild verunmöglicht nicht nur die rezeptionsästhetische Erfahrung von Dauer, sondern jede konventionelle Form dokumentarischer Lesbarkeit, die als anthropologisches Wissen semantisier- und speicherbar wäre.[35]

Am anderen Ende dessen, was unter dem Label „Sensory Ethnography" produziert wird, befindet sich Stephanie Sprays und Pacho Velez' *Manakamana*, der 2013 auf diversen Festivals von sich reden machte.

Zu sehen (und hören) sind elf ungeschnittene Einstellungen von jeweils gut zehn Minuten Länge, aufgenommen von einer statischen Kamera, die in der Gondel einer Seilbahn postiert ist und deren Insassen auf dem Hin- und Rückweg zum „Manakamana"-Heiligtum in Nepal begleitet. Die Länge der Einstellungen entspricht der Dauer der Fahrt, und gleichzeitig bemisst sie sich an der Länge einer 16-mm-Filmrolle. „Manakamana" beerbt zwei einflussreiche Strömungen der Filmgeschichte: Den strukturellen Film der 1970er Jahre, der über konzeptuelle und materialbezogene Vorentscheidungen eine Zurücknahme des Autorenprinzips anstrebte einerseits, das ethnografische Kino Robert Gardners, der als graue Eminenz im Kontext Harvards hinter dem Gesamtprojekt des „Sensory Ethnography Lab" steht, andererseits. Tatsächlich haben Spray und Velez den Film mit derselben – nicht der gleichen, derselben – 16-mm-Kamera gedreht, mit der Gardner 1986 *Forest of Bliss* in Benares drehte.

Was den Realismus dieses Films angeht, führt er uns, nach den reflexiven Schleifen der Filmgeschichte gewissermaßen zurück zum Lumière-Paradigma: Zum Einströmen einer kontinuierlichen, diversen Kontingenzen ausgesetzten Wirklichkeit durch die Kameralinse.[36]

---

[35] Simon Rothöhler, *High Definition. Digitale Filmästhetik*, Berlin, 2012, S. 67.

[36] Jüngst hat Diedrich Diederichsen den Vorschlag gemacht, die Verfahren und Wirkungen der „nachpopulären Künste" seit ca. 1960 als verschiedene Umgangsweisen auf den „Index-Effekt" aufzeichnender Medien zu beziehen: „Konstitutiv für den Index-Effekt ist also, dass er der künstlerischen Konstruktion entgeht. Doch genau dies wird nun die entscheidende Herausforderung für künstlerisches Handeln, obwohl sich gerade stärkere Index-Effekte kaum gezielt beabsichtigen lassen. Allerdings gibt es Strategien, die ihr Eintreten begünstigen (Cinéma vérité), sowie andere,

7.

Nach diesem kurzen Durchgang durch eine lange Geschichte unterschiedlich konfigurierter Realismen drängt sich die Frage nach der heutigen Relevanz und Konjunktur des Realismusbegriffs auf. Ich will dazu abschließend einige Hypothesen formulieren:

(1) Zunächst ist zu bemerken, dass Realismus sich in den unterschiedlichen filmhistorischen und mediengeschichtlichen Konstellationen meist als Gegenbewegung zum Autonomiekonzept der Kunst versteht. ‚Realistische' Filmpraktiken versprechen einen Durchstoß auf die *‚physical reality'*, die materielle Substanz der Welt, auf die als eine Art Asymptote immer wieder zugesteuert wird, um sie zu verfehlen. „Bei aller Zeichenhaftigkeit führte eine Nabelschnur in die Wirklichkeit"[37], schreibt Grafe einmal über den Vorteil fotografischer Weltzugriffe gegenüber dem Medium Text.

(2) In diesem unterschiedlich stark gebrochenen Wirklichkeitsbezug lässt sich wohl auch ein vielleicht schwacher, aber doch deutlich spürbarer Nachhall politischer Konzepte des Filmemachens vernehmen. Zu diskutieren wäre dabei, wie belastbar die Allianz zwischen ‚Realismus' und ‚politischem Film' im Einzelnen ist.

(3) Auf der Produktionsebene des Filmens implizieren realistische Ansätze, dass an die Stelle starker Hierarchien und Asymmetrien zwischen den Filmschaffenden und ihren Objekten eher Modelle von Komplizenschaft, Miteinander und Gemeinschaft treten. Gerade in neueren Beispielen realistischer Filme entsteht eine Nähe und Intimität mit dem Gegenstand dadurch, dass der Film das Produkt eines Zusammenlebens ist. Hier berühren sich Realismus und die Methoden der ethnografischen Feldforschung, wie es bei Pedro Costa und anderen zu beobachten ist.[38] In *Leviathan*, in dessen Abspann zuallererst (und etwas ostentativ) Bruno Latour gedankt wird, betrifft das auch und insbesondere die *non-human actors*, die Dinge und Tiere, kurz: den Menschen als Teil einer umfassenden Verschaltung von unterschiedlichen Akteuren. Ganz gleich, ob dies im Einzelnen gelingt oder nicht: *Leviathan* versucht sich daran, eine Art *‚object orientation'* im Filmemachen zu etablieren.

(4) Meine vierte und letzte Anmerkung betrifft die technikgeschichtlichen Neuerungen der letzten 15 Jahre. Durch den Wegfall zeitlicher und ökonomischer Schranken im Modus digitaler Bildaufzeichnung, -bearbeitung und -zirkulation ist ein bestimmter Aufzeichnungsmodus des ‚Realen' zum Standardmodus der Selbsttechnologien geworden. Der Gedanke liegt nahe, dass sich eine Geschichte der Realismen auch als Mediengeschichte der immer mobiler und versatiler geworde-

---

die sie zu unterdrücken beabsichtigen (MGM-Musical)." Ders., *Körpertreffer. Zur Ästhetik der nachpopulären Künste*, Berlin, 2017, S. 46.

37 Frieda Grafe, „‚Das Bild: Der Text'. Bilder illustrieren", in: dies., *Film/Geschichte. Wie Film Geschichte anders schreibt, Schriften*, 5. Band, Berlin, 2004, S. 54-61: 58.

38 Vgl. zu Costas spezifischen Verfahren Verf., „Digitaler Realismus. Pedro Costas dokumentarische Fiktionen", in: *Realismus in den Künsten der Gegenwart*, hg. von Dirck Linck, Michael Lüthy, Brigitte Obermayr und Martin Vöhler, Zürich, 2010, S. 107-120.

nen Bildaufzeichnungsmedien schreiben ließe. Hinzu kommt, dass in den diversen Dokumentarismen, die auf YouTube-Kanälen oder in Facebook-Clips zirkulieren, die vormals institutionell und technisch etablierte Grenze zwischen Rezipienten und Produzenten zunehmend porös wird. Die am Beginn des Textes geschilderte Beobachtung, dass der ‚Realismus' des bewegten Bildes im frühen Kino mal auf der Produktions-, mal auf der Rezeptionsseite lokalisiert wurde, findet in der gegenwärtigen Konstellation ihr Pendant.

Aus den diskutierten Beispielen ergibt sich ein vielleicht trügerisch symmetrisches Modell, in dem die beiden ersten Stationen am italienischen Neo-Realismus und Bazin punktgespiegelt werden und in den zeitgenössischen Positionen des SEL wiederkehren.[39] Es mag Zufall sein, aber fast scheint es so, als fänden wir mit *Leviathan* und *Manakamana* – mit 120 Jahren Nachdenken über die Realismen des bewegten Bildes im Rücken – auf komplizierte Weise zu den Brüdern Lumière und Vertov zurück.

[39] Selbstverständlich ist die Filmgeschichte seit jeher dicht bevölkert von Filmemachern und Filmemacherinnen, die offensiv Mischformen diverser Realismen propagieren. Abkürzend sei hier auf Jean-Pierre Gorins „Beispiele eines essayistischen Kinos 1909-2004" verwiesen, das er mit einem Konzept Manny Farbers 2007 bei der Retrospektive der Viennale vorgestellt hat. Zum Kanon des dort versammelten „termitischen" Kinos gehören Chris Marker, Jean-Luc Godard, Alexander Kluge, Agnes Varda, Thom Andersen, Patrick Keiller und viele andere. Vgl. *Der Weg der Termiten. Beispiele eines essayistischen Kinos 1909-2004. Eine Filmschau kuratiert von Jean-Pierre Gorin*, hg. von Astrid Ofner, Wien, 2007.

CHENXI TANG

LEGAL REALISM AND LITERARY REALISM

In the late nineteenth century, the concepts of realism and naturalism—already widely debated in literary criticism—entered jurisprudence. With the publication of Karl Llewellyn's programmatic and provocative essay "A Realistic Jurisprudence – The Next Step" in the *Columbia Law Review* in 1930, "realism" became a keyword in legal thought. Legal historians speak of "realist" or "naturalist" conceptions of law in the period roughly from the 1870s to the 1930s.[1] Jurists of the time noted the origin of the concept of realism in literary and art criticism. For instance, Roscoe Pound, the doyen of American jurisprudence in the early twentieth century, states in his reply to Llewellyn:

> As I read them, the new juristic realists hardly use realism in a technical philosophical sense. They use it rather in the sense which it bears in art. By realism they mean fidelity to nature, accurate recordings of things as they are, as contrasted with things as they are imagined to be, or wished to be, or as one feels they ought to be.[2]

Writing in 1933, a young jurist by the name of James Hopkins observed a parallel development of realism in law and literature during the past half century:

> In literature, of course, the development of realism has had a more obvious course, owing undoubtedly to the fact that the term was first affixed to its manifestations in fiction. In law, though its path has been more obscure; nevertheless, the common signs lie imprinted on modern legal theory. The realistic influence has affected both law and literature with virtually the same result. The parallel development in point of time is astounding in the face of the apparent cultural lag in the law.[3]

The present essay investigates the remarkable parallels between the realist-naturalist conception of law and literary realism-naturalism in the late nineteenth and early twentieth centuries. In the first part, the essay reconstructs the radical re-orientation of jurisprudence in Rudolf von Jhering (1818-1892) and Oliver Wendell Holmes (1841-1935), which led to the rise of legal realism. Realist jurispru-

---

1 For instance, Franz Wieacker stresses the "juristic naturalism" in private law around 1900: *Privatrechtsgeschichte der Neuzeit*, second edition, Göttingen: Vandenhoeck und Ruprecht, 1967, pp. 558-586 (§ 29, "Die Entartung des Positivimus und der juristische Naturalismus"); Michael Stolleis identifies a similar tendency in public law: *Geschichte des öffentlichen Rechts in Deutschland. Volume 2*, Munich: Beck, 1992, pp. 435-447 ("Die realistische Staatsauffassung"). Morton Horwitz claims that American legal history in the century after 1870 revolves around legal realism: *The Transformation of American Law, 1870-1960*, New York, NY, Oxford: Oxford University Press, 1992.

2 Roscoe Pound, "The Call for a Realist Jurisprudence," in: *Harvard Law Review*, 44 (1931), pp. 697-711: here p. 697.

3 James D. Hopkins, "The Development of Realism in Law and Literature During the Period 1883-1933: The Cultural Resemblance," in: *Pace Law Review*, 4 (1983), pp. 29-60: here p. 33.

dence, as we shall see, offers a theoretical model of the origin of legal norms in facts and actual behaviors. The second part of this essay then explains the poetics of literary realism as a theoretical model of the origin of poetic fiction in factual, non-normative reality. The parallel between legal realism and literary realism indicates a structural as well as functional equivalence between legal norm and poetic fiction. This equivalence, in turn, provides a unique perspective from which to think about realism.[4]

1.

In the preface to his last book *Der Besitzwille*, Rudolf von Jhrering, arguably the greatest jurist in the second half of the nineteenth century, postulates a diametric opposition between two methods in jurisprudence: "the formalist" and "the realist."[5] By means of a kind of Augustinian confessional narrative, Jhering laments his adherence to the formalist method in the early stage of his career as youthful folly in order to affirm an unshakable faith in the realist method.

The formalist method is associated with the so-called *Begriffsjurisprudenz* or jurisprudence of concepts. A polemical term coined by Jhering to designate the systematic study of civil law in pandectism (*Pandektistik*)[6], *Begriffsjurisprudenz* connotes the theoretical position that "the given law can be traced back to a logically organized system of concepts ('pyramid of concepts'), [and that] new law can be logically deduced from superordinate legal concepts, which themselves are found inductively ('method of inversion')."[7] *Begriffsjurisprudenz* may not have existed in any pure form in the nineteenth century[8], but the term does capture the prevailing conception of the nature and source of law up to Jhering's time—the conception that a legal norm is derived from other legal norms, and that all norms make up a logically consistent whole. For instance, for Friedrich Carl von Savigny (1779-1861), the founder of the historical school and of pandectism, law grows out of the spirit of the people as an organic whole. Statute is no arbitrary will of the legislator, but the pronouncement of the common conviction of the people through the legislator. With the progress of culture, the formation of law devolves upon jurists who are academically trained representatives of the people. The so-

4 For the purposes of this essay, I make no distinction between realism and naturalism in either jurisprudence or literary criticism, treating naturalism as an offshoot of realism.

5 Rudolf von Jhering, *Der Besitzwille. Zugleich eine Kritik der herrschenden juristischen Methode*, Jena: Fischer, 1889, p. IX.

6 Rudolf von Jhering, *Scherz und Ernst in der Jurisprudenz*, Leipzig: Breitkopf und Härtel, 1884, p. 337.

7 Hans-Peter Haferkamp, "Begriffsjurisprudenz/Jurisprudence of Concepts," http://www.enzyklopaedie-rechtsphilosophie.net/inhaltsverzeichnis/19-beitraege/96-begriffsjurisprudenz (retrieved 30/1/2017).

8 Cf. Hans-Peter Haferkamp, *Georg Friedrich Puchta und die Begriffsjurisprudenz*, Frankfurt/M.: Vittorio Klostermann, 2004.

called "jurists' law" (*Juristenrecht*) operates with concepts, elaborating and ordering them logically and systematically.[9]

Initially, Jhering fully subscribed to the logical and systematic ordering of legal material as advocated by Savigny and his followers, developing it into what he called "juristic construction" according to the "method of natural history."[10] But then a radical re-orientation took place in the early 1860s.[11] His lecture *Der Kampf um's Recht*, published in 1872, begins with the assertion that "the concept of law is known to be a practical one, i.e. a concept of purpose (*Zweckbegriff*)."[12] He proceeds to argue that "law is no logical concept, but a concept of force."[13] Such attempts at redefinition serve to develop a new theory of the genesis of law: law is not merely a product of purely conceptual operations according to formal-logical criteria, but is produced by physical as well as social forces—the keyword is struggle, *der Kampf*—for specific practical purposes. "As a concept of purpose, law is caught up right in the chaotic gears of human purposes, aspirations, and interests. It must continuously grope and search for its way, and once it finds its way, it has to struggle and apply force to really walk along it."[14] Statutes, for instance, come about through the assertion of the practical interests of certain social groups by the state power. Law, both as a single legal norm and as a system of norms or a legal order, arises, often by violent means, from a field of forces that is decidedly non-normative. Having come into being, law reacts upon this field of forces, realigning and refashioning it. In so doing, law itself cannot help being modified, reshaped, or even destroyed—only to give rise to a new law. For this reason, law is always in the making, is an "eternal becoming."[15] This non-normative field of forces that both gives rise to legal norm and is subsequently refashioned by legal norm is called, in Jhering's words, the "raw reality," *die rauhe Wirklichkeit*.[16] The study of law in terms of this "raw reality" is realist jurisprudence.

In Jhering, the realist method pertained mostly to the making of law. Soon after him, it also extended to the interpretation of law, as the so-called *Interessenjurisprudenz* or jurisprudence of interests attested to. Interpretation, as Philip Heck puts it in *Gesetzesauslegung und Interessenjurisprudenz* (1914), consists in "a historical research of interests." It ascertains the ideas that come to the fore in the process of legislation, but it must go beyond these ideas to find out the "interests causative for the law." According to Heck: "The old formula 'the will of the legisla-

9 See Friedrich Carl von Savigny, *System des heutigen römischen Rechts. Volume 1*, Berlin: Veit, 1840, pp. 6-66 ("Allgemeine Natur der Rechtsquellen").

10 Rudolf von Jhering, *Geist des römischen Rechts auf den verschiedenen Stufen seiner Entwicklung, zweiter Theil, zweite Abteilung*, second edition, Leipzig: Breitkopf und Härtel, 1869, pp. 340-372.

11 See Jhering (1884), *Scherz und Ernst in der Jurisprudenz*, p. 338; Okko Behrends, "Rudolf von Jhering (1818 – 1892) – Der Durchbruch zum Zweck des Rechts," in: Fritz Loos (ed.), *Rechtswissenschaft in Göttingen*, Göttingen: Vandenhoeck und Ruprecht, 1987, pp. 229-269.

12 Rudolf von Jhering, *Der Kampf um's Recht*, Vienna: Manz, 1872, p. 7.

13 Ibid., p. 9.

14 Ibid., p. 16.

15 Ibid.

16 Ibid., p. 18.

tor' has a real content (*Realgehalt*). But the concept of the will is [...] a concept of interests. The 'legislator' is no phantom, but a summary name for the causative interests."[17] The task of the judge is thus far from the formal application of a given law in order to deduce from it another norm, i.e. a judgment. It is rather to lay bare the practical interests underlying a given law in order to create a new norm that does justice to these interests. Juridical interpretation retraces the legislative movement from interest to norm only to repeat it on another level.

Jhrering's realist jurisprudence was by no means one of a kind. On the other side of the Atlantic, Oliver Wendell Holmes reached similar insights, which, in part due to the difference between common law and civil law systems, and in part due to his heightened sensitivity to social and economic developments on the bench, added new dimensions to the realist method. At least two arguments of Holmes's are worth mentioning in this regard. First, like Jhering, Holmes noted the purposiveness of law: "A body of law is more rational and more civilized when every rule it contains is referred articulately and definitely to an end which it subserves, and when the grounds for desiring that end are stated or are ready to be stated in words."[18] But Holmes went a step further in noting that in order to state clearly the grounds for desiring a certain end, it was not enough to refer to socio-economic reality in general terms. Rather, one would need scientific knowledge of, and quantitative data about, socio-economic reality: "For the rational study of law [...] the man of the future is the man of statistics and the master of economics."[19] Second, Holmes emphasized the concrete circumstances, contingent factors, and all the imponderables in the juridical decision-making process. In his now famous "bad-man" account of law, he pointed out that neither moral principles nor existing legal norms really mattered:

> [I]f we take the view of our friend the bad man we shall find that he does not care two straws for the axioms or deductions, but that he does want to know what the Massachusetts or English courts are likely to do in fact. I am much of his mind. The prophecies of what the courts will do in fact, and nothing more pretentious, are what I mean by the law.[20]

This statement lies at the origin of the realist quip that the court decision depends on what the judge has had for breakfast.

Drawing on Jhering and Holmes, and in a gesture reminiscent of the literary-artistic avant-garde of the early twentieth century, Karl Llewellyn published a manifesto of legal realism entitled "A Realistic Jurisprudence – The Next Step" in 1930, followed by a more substantial second manifesto "Some Realism About Realism – Responding to Dean Pound" in the following year. A jurist versed in German

---

17 Philip Heck, "Gesetzesauslegung und Interessenjurisprudenz," in: *Archiv für die civilistische Praxis*, 112 (1914), pp. 1-318: here p. 8.

18 Oliver Wendell Holmes, "The Path of Law," in: David Kennedy and William W. Fisher III (eds.), *The Canon of American Legal Thought*, Princeton, NJ: Princeton University Press, 2006, pp. 29-43: here p. 36.

19 Ibid., p. 37.

20 Ibid., p. 31.

culture, Llewellyn found the motto for legal realism in Goethe's *Faust*: "In the beginning was not a Word, but a Doing."[21] The use to which he puts this Faustian rendition of the biblical statement, however, has little to do with either Faust or the Bible, serving as it does to theorize juridical decision-making in the American legal system. What matters in juridical decision-making, for Llewellyn, is not "verbal formulae and verbalized [...] conceptual pictures," but what the judge actually does, "such as element of practices, of habits and techniques of action, of behavior."[22] This distinction between word and deed encapsulates the core claim of legal realism: court decisions are reached through the judges' response to the stimulus of the facts of the case at hand, rather than through the application of received rules and concepts such as statutes, precedents, doctrines and the like. Decisions come about under the "fact-pressures of the cases,"[23] and rules are invoked retrospectively as rationalizations, "intended to make the decision seem plausible, legally decent, legally right, to make it seem, indeed, legally inevitable."[24] In contrast to formalism, which emphasizes legal reasons for a court decision and conceives of it as derived from or built upon other legal norms, legal realism provides a theoretical model of the non-legal origin of legal norms. This model features a number of interlinked arguments. First, legal norms are not deduced from other norms, but are created on the basis of facts or non-normative data. Realist legal scholars see their main task in describing how facts, usually in the form of data culled from social scientific research, contribute to the making of court decisions as well as legislative regulations. Second, created out of the non-normative space of facts—a space also known as social reality—legal norms are artifices meant to have an effect on this space. Legal realists are not only interested in "describing or predicting the action of officials—be they appellate courts, trial courts, legislators, administrators," but also in "describing and predicting the effects of their actions on the laymen of the community."[25] Third, created out of, and meant to impinge on, the non-normative space of facts, legal norms do not form a contiguous body of rules, but are full of gaps and always in flux.

2.

In one of his manifestos of legal realism, Llewellyn calls the law the most "fiction-ridden of disciplines."[26] Law is not only full of the so-called legal fictions. As arti-

---

21 Karl Llewellyn, "Some Realism about Realism – Responding to Dean Pound," in: David Kennedy and William W. Fisher III (eds.), *The Canon of American Legal Thought*, Princeton, NJ: Princeton University Press, 2006, pp. 141-162: here p. 141.

22 Karl Llewellyn, "A Realist Jurisprudence – The Next Step," in: *Columbia Law Review*, 30 (1930), pp. 431-465: here p. 434.

23 Llewellyn (2006), Some Realism about Realism, p. 154.

24 Ibid., p. 151.

25 Ibid., p. 57.

26 Llewellyn (1930), A Realist Jurisprudence – The Next Step, p. 454.

fices created out of the non-normative space of facts, law consists, in a certain sense, of nothing other than fictions. Perhaps not surprisingly, then, the rise of legal realism from Jhering to Llewellyn went hand in hand with a specific model of fiction known as literary realism.

While realist jurisprudence dismissed the formalist emphasis on preexistent concepts and rules, literary realism demanded that writers break with established poetic norms. Both called for a turn towards "the chaotic gears of human purposes, aspirations, and interests" (Jhering). For instance, William Dean Howells (1837-1920), Holmes's contemporary and a major representative of literary realism in America, wrote in 1891: "The time is coming, I hope, when each new author, each new artist, will be considered, not in his proportion to any other author or artist, but in his relation to the human nature." With regard to the portrayal of literary personages, what matters is "life-likeness" rather than "book-likeness."[27] That is to say, verisimilitude of poetic fiction is to be measured in relation to facts rather than to the standards set by great works of the past. This turn to "human nature," to "life" as it actually is, i.e. to what is generally called "reality," does not mean that realists are uninterested in norms. On the contrary, common to various programs of literary realism is the attempt to determine how things ought to be, and how poetic writing ought to be. To be sure, it is of paramount importance for realists to represent social reality in as precise detail as possible. But just as the jurist invokes social reality in order to demonstrate how it gives rise to legal norms, theorists of literary realism seek to expound how the representation of social reality generates aesthetic as well as other social norms. Such norms are usually called ideals. Julian Schmitt, an important theorist of realism in the mid nineteenth century, claimed: "If literature merely provided a duplicate of reality, one would wonder why it existed at all. It is supposed to edify, to move, and to entertain; it can do so only through ideals."[28] Towards the end of the nineteenth century, in the heated debates about naturalism as a radical form of realism, the norms or ideals that a literary work is supposed to produce came to be located in the reader. With regard to Emile Zola's novels and Gerhardt Hauptmann's dramas, the critic Wilhelm Bölsche wrote: "Even the fiercest artistic realism does not go without ideals. It is just that it does not really inscribe these ideals in the picture of life that it paints, but lets them emerge only through a kind of reaction in the audience."[29] This shift towards the judgment of the reader as the ground of norms seemed to correspond to the rise of jurisdiction as a main source of law—the so-called judges' law (*Rich-*

27 William Dean Howells, *Criticism and Fiction and Other Essays*, ed. by Clara Kirk and Rudolf Kirk, New York, NY: New York University Press, 1959, pp. 11 f.

28 Julian Schmitt, "Georg Büchner," in: *Die Grenzboten: Zeitschrift für Politik und Literatur* 10, 1 (1851), pp. 121-128: here p. 123.

29 Wilhelm Bölsche, "Die soziale Grundlagen der modernen Dichtung," in: *Sozialistische Monatshefte*, 1 (1897), pp. 100-105: here p. 101.

terrecht)—in the late nineteenth and early twentieth centuries.[30] In literature as in law, registering facts and collecting data became a key concern, and it was by evaluating facts and data—i.e. in the act of judging—that norms were supposed to be produced.

More important than any particular social norms that a literary work may produce, however, is the work's status as a meaningful construct. Literary realism from the mid nineteenth century onwards provided a specific model of the nature and function of such a meaningful construct. It was especially in this sense that it demonstrated some striking resemblances to legal realism. With its professed aim of representing reality, literary realism was often associated with the idea of mimesis. But in fact, it marked a radical departure from traditional theories of mimesis and poetic fiction. Up to the eighteenth century, within a more or less Aristotelian framework, poetic fiction was said to be the imitation of nature. Its meaningfulness and truth-claim depended, to a great extent, on the normativity of nature. For nature was seen as meaningfully, normatively ordered in and by itself, informed by laws that were either inscribed in the heart of humankind (according to the ancient natural-law theory) or could be discovered and deduced by reason (according to the modern natural-law theory).[31] Representing the inherently normative nature, poetic fiction was supposed to bring to light the truth that would otherwise have remained hidden, as well as to achieve certain effects through rhetorical devices. In the literary and intellectual ferment often loosely termed romanticism, as literary historians know, the conception of poetic fiction as imitation of nature was eclipsed by a conception of poetic fiction as expression—expression of the individual self, expression of the people or nation, expression of a vibrant, living nature.[32] Against this broad literary historical background, realism marked a new departure in two important senses: first, it broke with the romantic idea of expression; and second, it conceived of poetic fiction as depicting reality without, however, regarding reality as already meaningful or normatively ordered in itself. Rather, it saw reality as something given, as facts, as data. Accordingly, poetic fiction did not so much represent as transmute the factual reality into a meaningful structure.

As to the realist break with the idea of expression, one needs to look no further than Gustave Flaubert and Émile Zola. Both stressed, time and again, the impersonality of literary writing. "Art," Flaubert insisted, "ought [...] to rise above personal feelings and nervous susceptibilities! It is time to give it the precision of the

30 On the rise of jurisdiction as a source of law around 1900, see Jan Schröder, *Recht als Wissenschaft. Geschichte der juristischen Methodenlehre in der Neuzeit (1500–1933)*, Munich: Beck, 2012, pp. 305-310.

31 See Merio Scattola, "Models in History of Natural Law," in: *Ius Commune. Zeitschrift für europäische Rechtsgeschichte*, XXVIII (2001), pp. 91-160.

32 For the transition from representation to expression, see M. H. Abrahms's classic *The Mirror and the Lamp: Romantic Theory and the Critical Tradition*, New York, NY: Oxford University Press, 1953; for a more recent account see Jacques Rancière, *Mute Speech: Literature, Critical Theory, and Politics*, trans. by James Swenson, New York, NY: Columbia University Press, 2011, pp. 41-51.

physical sciences, by means of a pitiless method."[33] With regard to *Madame Bovary*, he said:

> I have put into it nothing of my feelings or of my experience. The illusion (if there is one) comes, on the contrary, from the *impersonality* of the work. It is one of my principles that you must not *write yourself*. The artist ought to be in his work like God in creation, invisible and omnipotent. He should be felt everywhere but not be seen [emphasis in the original].[34]

In his *Le roman expérimental*, Zola argues that "what it is necessary to emphasize above all is the impersonal nature of the method." Comparing himself to the great physiologist Claude Bernard, he states: "I was simply trying, in my novels and criticism, to apply the scientific method, which has been in use for a long time."[35]

This emphatic rejection of the conception of literary writing as personal expression went hand in hand with the insistence on the importance of meticulous, precise depictions of reality in all its factual details. Flaubert spoke of "attentive observation of the dullest details," reporting how his eyes were "fixed on the spores of mildew growing on the soul."[36] Poetic literature, in his view, should emulate the natural scientific treatment of facts:

> That's what is so fine about the natural sciences: they don't wish to prove anything. Therefore what breadth of fact and what an immensity for thought! We must treat men like mastodons and crocodiles. Does anyone fly into a passion about the horns of the former and the jaws of the latter? Show them, stuff them, and put them in solution, that's enough, but appreciate them, no.[37]

Zola, as is well known, went even further in praising the natural sciences as the model for poetic literature, developing a theory of the novel as the ultimate laboratory for testing out the experimental method:

> The novelist is both observer and experimenter. The observer in him presents data as he has observed them, determines the point of departure, establishes the solid ground on which his characters will stand and his phenomena take place. Then the experimenter appears and institutes the experiment, that is, sets the characters of a particular story in motion, in order to show that the series of events therein will be those demanded by the determinism of the phenomena under study.[38]

For the realist, then, reality means facts and data. It is, as Flaubert put it, "ignoble,"[39] evacuated of any normative content, quite the opposite of the normative nature worthy of poetic imitation in the traditional theory of mimesis up to the eighteenth century.

---

33 George J. Becker (ed.), *Documents of Modern Literary Realism*, Princeton, NJ: Princeton University Press, 1963, p. 95.
34 Ibid., p. 94.
35 Ibid., p. 188.
36 Ibid., p. 91.
37 Ibid., p. 92 f.
38 Ibid., p. 166.
39 Ibid., p. 94.

Yet it is precisely the minute depiction of the "ignoble," even ugly and repugnant reality—observation of facts and presentation of data—that is supposed to bring about a poetic work of art. Such a poetic work of art would, in Flaubert's words, "hold together by itself through the internal force of its style." It is a meaningful construct abiding by its own laws, "the indefinable Beautiful," "the splendor of Truth."[40] Zola spoke of the "complete knowledge of a truth" achieved by the experimental novel.[41] In short, a realist poetic work of art is normative. It embodies aesthetic norms liable to evaluation and criticism. It also embodies epistemological norms, insofar as it claims to reveal truths about human nature and society. The poetics of realism thus revolves around two opposing poles: the one pole is the factual, non-normative reality, and the other is the fictional, normative poetic work of art. It aims to connect these two poles, providing a theoretical model of the origin of poetic fiction in facts, of the normative in the non-normative.

3.

Literary realism and legal realism emerged almost simultaneously in the second half of the nineteenth century and continued into the early twentieth century. The one was concerned with the making of poetic fiction, and the other with the making of legal norms. But they made the same discovery: the non-normative space of facts and data was the ground and origin of both poetic fiction and legal norms. Literary realism saw the poetic work of art arise from the most ordinary of lives, while legal realism saw legal norms arise from chaotic human actions. What are the implications of the parallel between literary and legal realism?

First of all, this parallel raises the fundamental theoretical question about the commonality between poetic fiction and legal norm. Both poetic fiction and legal norm are artifices that exceed the real, creating a distance from and an alternative to the factual world, yet at the same time having the potential of intervening in the factual world by guiding conduct and serving as a basis for evaluation.[42] This commonality may well be the foundation of the many resemblances and correspondences between law and literature.

Second, juxtaposed, literary realism and legal realism illuminate each other. In particular, realist jurisprudence affords us new perspectives on realist literature. In terms of historical periodization, Jhering's distinction between formalist and realist jurisprudence corresponds to the literary historical transition from romanticism to realism. More importantly perhaps, literary writing and reception could now be analogized to lawmaking and adjudication. Lawmaking, according to realist jurisprudence, consists in the process of creating a norm to regulate the raw

---

40 Ibid., p. 90 and p. 95.

41 Ibid., p. 169.

42 See Christoph Möllers, *Die Möglichkeit der Normen. Über eine Praxis jenseits von Moralität und Kausalität*, Berlin: Suhrkamp, 2015, pp. 239-246.

reality of conflicting "purposes, aspirations, and interests" (Jhering). Jhering stressed the struggle, the contest of social power involved in such a process, while Holmes and the American legal realists in his wake stressed the knowledge or data produced by the nascent social sciences such as economics and statistics. But their arguments actually converge, for power operates through knowledge, while knowledge exercises power. As Jhering's and Holmes's contemporary Friedrich Nietzsche never tired of pointing out, power and knowledge at once presuppose and produce each other. Indeed, explaining the ways in which the will to power and to knowledge produces legal norms, the realist account of lawmaking is hardly different from Nietzsche's genealogy.[43] In the realist view, literary writing looks similar to lawmaking, consisting in the process of transmuting the raw reality of conflicting "purposes, aspirations, and interests" into the beauty and truth of poetic fiction. Characterized by Flaubert mystifyingly as "marvelous chemistry,"[44] this process actually involves the contest of power through knowledge production and the harnessing of knowledge to exercise power. In the early phase of literary realism in the nineteenth century, it mainly took the form of staging and managing the varying perceptions of characters and narrators.[45] Later on, especially in its naturalist phase, realist writing deployed and even generated scientific knowledge or data in its depiction of social struggle. The naturalist movement spearheaded by Zola made the processing of the knowledge produced by contemporary social as well as natural sciences about human life and society the core task of literary writing. Even realist writers usually not classified as naturalists, for example Theodor Fontane, drew on technical and scientific knowledge in narrating the social reality of conflicting purposes and interests.[46] When realism staged, after the intermezzo of the avant-garde and modernism, a comeback in the second and third decades of the twentieth century, incidentally at precisely the same time as realism swelled to a mighty current in jurisprudence, technical and scientific data became the only material out of which human figures were constructed.[47] In sum, just as in lawmaking, literary writing first prepares social conflicts into knowledge and data, in order then to use this knowledge and data as the basis for imposing a norm—with the only difference that the norm is now called literary form. By the same token, literary reception may now be understood in terms of adjudication. With the realist method, adjudication means identifying the practical purposes and interests underlying a case and then creating a norm—a judgment—to do justice to them.

---

43 Franz Wieacker, "So gibt es etwa für Jhering – schon vor Nietzsches Genealogie der Moral – eine Genealogie des Rechts," in: *Privatrechtsgeschichte der Neuzeit*, second edition, Göttingen: Vandenhoeck und Ruprecht, 1967, p. 565.

44 Becker (1963.), *Documents of Modern Literary Realism*, p. 93.

45 Perception belongs to one of the issues addressed in recent research on literary realism. See for example Elisabeth Strowick and Ulrike Vedder (eds.), *Wirklichkeit und Wahrnehmung. Neue Perspektiven auf Theodor Storm*, Bern et al.: Peter Lang, 2013.

46 See Stephan Braese and Anne-Kathrin Reulicke (eds.), *Realien des Realismus. Wissenschaft – Technik – Medien in Theodor Fontanes Erzählprosa*, Berlin: Vorwerk 8, 2010.

47 See Devin Fore, *Realism after Modernism: The Rehumanization of Art and Literature*, Cambridge, MA: MIT Press, 2012.

In doing so, the judge may need to make use of the relevant social scientific knowledge and data, as Holmes and Llewellyn pointed out. Similarly, realist literary criticism tends to focus on uncovering the purposes and interests of poetic characters, as well as the social forces at work in the plot. It reaches an aesthetic judgment based on the analysis of these social purposes, interests, and forces, often drawing on knowledge gathered by means of social scientific methods. The title of an 1897 critical piece by Wilhelm Bölsche—"Soziale Grundlagen der modernen Dichtung" ("Social Foundations of Modern Literature")—epitomizes the general tenor of realist literary criticism.

Finally, the parallel between realist jurisprudence and literary realism raises the question of why 'realism' became a rallying call in both law and literature. Such a question necessitates an overarching explanation of the social functions of law and those of literature. The rise of realism in jurisprudence has certainly something to do with the fact that the rapid and profound transformation of European and American society in the age of industrial capitalism made all pre-existing norms appear either implausible or inappropriate. In the face of the widening chasm between *Sein* and *Sollen*, between Is and Ought, it dawned on jurists that law derives neither from preexisting legal norms nor from any kind of transcendental norm, but arises from pressing social problems, from facts. Given this realization, law has to be seen as a social force itself, something that arises from social reality, and that also impinges upon social reality. The juridical apparatus becomes, whether one likes it or not, an item in the toolbox of social engineering, a part of governmentality. In terms of disciplinary knowledge, realist jurisprudence marks the beginning of the study of legislation, jurisdiction, and law enforcement as social phenomena, i.e. of legal sociology. The rise of realism in literature may be traced back to the same socio-historical transformation. In the face of the same widening chasm between Is and Ought, writers and readers conceive of poetic fiction no longer in relation to existing aesthetic norms nor to an unchanging, normative nature, but as a possible alternative to Is, as a symbolic practice that holds a mirror up to society. This practice is supposed to issue from social reality and at the same time intervene in social reality. Poetic fiction or literature thus becomes a social force as well. Literary realism marks the beginning of the social study of literary production and reception, i.e. of literary sociology.

CHRISTIAN BEGEMANN

REALISMUS UND PHANTASTIK

Die notorisch unscharfe Kategorie der Phantastik ist, so scheint es, auf einen Kontrastbegriff angewiesen und nur als die eine Seite eines Oppositionspaars denkbar. ‚Phantastik' beinhaltet die Vorstellung von Überschreitung oder Normverletzung. Traditionellerweise hat man sie als verstörenden Einbruch eines Unerklärlichen „gegenüber den kulturellen Leitdiskursen des Rationalen und Logischen in der Moderne" bestimmt, als einen unaufgelösten „Ordnungskonflikt zwischen einer Welt des Wunderbaren und des Normalen"[1], als einen Bruch mit den bekannten Naturgesetzen, den Konventionen der Wahrnehmung oder der bürgerlichen Lebensordnung. Immer jedenfalls scheint das Phantastische nur als Gegenbegriff zu einem Anderen und in der Abgrenzung gegen dieses definierbar – wobei sein Begriff irreführend ist, sofern er präjudiziert, die entsprechenden Phänomene seien Produkte der Phantasie. Gerade das aber bleibt einem nahezu flächendeckenden Konsens zufolge in der Schwebe, der von Tzvetan Todorovs Kategorie der *hésitation*, der Unschlüssigkeit der erzählten Figuren wie des Lesers über den ontologischen Status der phantastischen Erscheinungen, ausgeht.[2]

Der verbreitetste Gegenbegriff zu ‚Phantastik' ist der des ‚Realismus', der in seinen Konturen kaum weniger unscharf ist als jener. Wie auch immer man ‚Realismus' begreifen mag, ob als mimetische Referenz von Literatur auf eine vorgängige Realität, als Simulation einer solchen Referenz durch einen *effet de réel*[3] oder als Rekurs auf diskursive *Konzepte* von Realität – sein Verhältnis zur Phantastik scheint man nur als einen Gegensatz begreifen zu können. So, wie auf der Ebene der *histoire* ein Unerklärliches das geläufige Wirklichkeitsverständnis der Figuren erschüttere, so stehe der phantastische Text selbst quer zu realistischen Erzählkonventionen. In diesem Sinne hat man Phantastik im Kern als eine Form nichtmimetischer Literatur bezeichnet[4], und auch in historischer Hinsicht gilt der Gegensatz: Als Hochkonjunkturen der Phantastik zeigen sich gerade die tendenziell ‚nicht-mimetischen' Epochen der Romantik und der Frühen Moderne, nicht aber die dazwischen liegende Phase des Realismus. Hier sei, folgt man der Forschung, eine Minimierung der Phantastik zu beobachten. Marianne Wünsch hat das Phan-

---

1 Hans Richard Brittnacher/Markus May, „Phantastik-Theorien", in: dies. (Hg.), *Phantastik. Ein interdisziplinäres Handbuch*, Stuttgart, Weimar, 2013, S. 189-197: 189.

2 Tzvetan Todorov, *Einführung in die fantastische Literatur*, München, 1992 [1970], S. 31-33.

3 Roland Barthes, „L'effet de réel", in: *Communications* 11 (1968), S. 84-89.

4 Marianne Wünsch, *Die Fantastische Literatur der Frühen Moderne*, München, 1991, S. 17, differenzierend dazu S. 23.

tastische „an den Grenzen des Realismus"[5] verortet, und Uwe Durst gesteht dem Realismus überhaupt nur ein „begrenztes Wunderbares"[6] zu. Der Einbruch unerklärlicher und unheimlicher Phänomene in die bürgerliche Normalwelt könne in den literarischen Texten das realistische Realitätssystem nicht ernsthaft erschüttern, denn er werde narrativ entmächtigt, relativiert und marginalisiert.[7]

In der Tat kann sich eine solche Auffassung auf programmatische Texte des Realismus stützen. In einem Zeitalter, in dem „die erfahrungsmäßig erkannte Wirklichkeit, also die schlechthin nicht mehr mythische, die wunderlose Welt"[8], allgemeine Geltung erlangt hat, wie der linkshegelianische Ästhetiker Friedrich Theodor Vischer in seiner seit 1846 erscheinenden *Aesthetik* schreibt, im Zeitalter also der Ausdifferenzierung der Naturwissenschaften, des Empirismus und Säkularismus scheint es keinen literarischen Ort mehr für ‚wunderbare' oder ‚übernatürliche' Phänomene zu geben, da sie im Raum der nachzuahmenden Natur nicht mehr anerkannt werden. Diese Auffassung ist prägend für die realistische Literaturprogrammatik.[9]

Noch 1887, am Ende der realistischen Ära, affirmiert Wilhelm Bölsche in seinem Buch über *Die naturwissenschaftlichen Grundlagen der Poesie* diesen Standpunkt. Die Poesie des „Realismus" habe sich in dem Rahmen zu bewegen, den ihr die Wissenschaft stecke: „Die Basis unseres gesammten modernen Denkens bilden die Naturwissenschaften. Wir hören täglich mehr auf, die Welt und die Menschen nach metaphysischen Gesichtspuncten zu betrachten"[10]. Diese Grundüberzeugung hat auch die Dichtung zu teilen, und exemplarisch ist es hier das Gespenst, das

---

5 Marianne Wünsch, „Experimente Storms an den Grenzen des Realismus: neue Realitäten in ‚Schweigen' und ‚Ein Bekenntnis'", in: *Schriften der Theodor-Storm-Gesellschaft* 41 (1992), S. 3-23. Vgl. Gregor Reichelt, *Phantastik im Realismus. Literarische und gesellschaftliche Einbildungskraft bei Keller, Storm und Fontane*, Stuttgart, Weimar, 2001, S. 10 f.

6 Uwe Durst, *Das begrenzte Wunderbare. Zur Theorie wunderbarer Episoden in realistischen Erzähltexten und in Texten des ‚Magischen Realismus'*, Berlin, 2008.

7 Dieser Deutungslinie folgt auch Julia Neu, für die es zwei Erzählstrategien gibt, phantastische Elemente in den Text zu integrieren, ohne dessen „realistische[n] Status" zu gefährden: Zum einen würden die phantastischen Aspekte dem „Diskurs der Figuren" zugeschrieben, zum anderen sorge eine „Strategie des konnotativen Überschusses" dafür, dass „die Frage nach einer anderen Realität [...] nicht in solchem Ausmaß gestellt [werde], dass diese als ontologische Frage zentral wird." Julia Neu, „‚Das klingt ja sonderbar, als ob es doch möglich wäre.' Fantastik als Herausforderung für den Realismus", in: Moritz Baßler (Hg.), *Entsagung und Routines. Aporien des Spätrealismus und Verfahren der frühen Moderne*, Berlin, 2013, S. 130-150: 133 und 136. Allerdings bleibe das für den Realismus dann doch nicht ohne Folgen, denn auf diese Weise lege das „fantastische Element das Strukturprinzip der [kulturellen] Codierung offen", wobei „die natürliche Referenz der übrigen, realitätsbeherrschenden kulturellen Codes potenziell ins Wanken" gerate (ebd., S. 137). So werde etwa in Storms *Schimmelreiter* „der selbstverständliche Nexus zwischen Rationalität, Realismus und Empirie" aufgehoben" (ebd., S. 147).

8 Friedrich Theodor Vischer, *Aesthetik oder Wissenschaft des Schönen*, Band 6, hg. von Robert Fischer, Hildesheim (u. a.), 1996 [ND der Ausgabe München, 1923], § 879, S. 176.

9 Zur Opposition der realistischen Literaturprogrammatik gegen das ‚Übernatürliche' und ihren Verwerfungen vgl. Christian Begemann, „Spiegelscherben, Möwengeflatter. Poetik und Epistemologie des Realismus, bodenlose Mimesis und das Gespenst", in: *Poetica* 46 (2014), S. 412-438: 418-428.

10 Wilhelm Bölsche, *Die naturwissenschaftlichen Grundlagen der Poesie. Prolegomena einer realistischen Poetik*, hg. von Johannes Braakenburg, Tübingen, 1976 [1887], S. 4.

zum Inbild wissenschaftlicher wie poetischer Unmöglichkeit wird. Nach wissenschaftlichem Ermessen gebe es keine Gespenster, und die Poesie werde zum bloßen „Fabuliren für Kinder", wenn sie trotzdem welche auftreten lässt.

> Es kann ihr, was Jedermann einsieht, von dem Puncte ab, wo das Dasein von Gespenstern wissenschaftlich widerlegt ist, nicht mehr gestattet werden, dass sie [...] einen Geist aus dem Jenseits erscheinen lässt, weil sie sich sonst durchaus lächerlich und verächtlich machen würde.[11]

Die Literatur selbst allerdings hat sich solchen Imperativen gegenüber höchst zweideutig verhalten, sie gelegentlich stillschweigend unterlaufen, aber auch ihre Voraussetzungen infrage gestellt. Selbst wenn man zugesteht, dass das Phantastische in vielen realistischen Texten eine eingeschränktere Rolle spielt als in romantischen, bleibt doch das auffällige Interesse erklärungsbedürftig, das ihm entgegengebracht wird, obwohl es mit den Maximen der Realismusprogrammatiker zu kollidieren scheint. So viele ‚realistische' Texte sind von Spuk, Gespenstern, prophetischen Ahnungen oder zumindest ‚abergläubischen' Anwandlungen der Figuren durchzogen, dass es angebracht scheint, die Polarisierung von Realismus und Phantastik neu zu beleuchten. Mit Blick auf die Realismusproblematik sind dabei vor allem epistemologische und psychologische Aspekte zu akzentuieren.

1. Phantastik und Epistemologie: Paul Heyse

Zu den aufschlussreichen literarischen Fällen gehören insbesondere jene, die die diskursiven Bedingungen von Einschluss oder Ausschluss des Phantastischen selbst auf den Prüfstand stellen. Das ist etwa in Paul Heyses metapoetischer Sammlung *In der Geisterstunde* von 1892 der Fall, in der anlässlich der Erzählung von Spukgeschichten in einem geselligen Kreis eine ganze Palette weltanschaulicher und epistemologischer Positionen vorgeführt wird. Sie steht in der Tradition der großen Erzählungssammlungen insbesondere der Romantik, doch anders als in Tiecks *Phantasus* oder Hoffmanns *Serapions-Brüdern* drehen sich die Rahmengespräche bezeichnenderweise weniger um eine ästhetische Evaluation des Erzählten als um die Fragen nach dessen möglichem Realitätsgehalt. Die Teilnehmer der nachmitternächtlichen Runde sind Repräsentanten konkurrierender Realitätskonzepte im gebildeten Bürgertum des 19. Jahrhunderts und formieren ein Tableau zeitgenössischer Problemstellungen, das Heyse als gut informierten Beobachter zeigt. Erzählt und diskutiert werden überwiegend Spukgeschichten, die die Erzähler selbst erlebt haben. Seinen Ausgang nimmt der Abend von der „Entlarvung eines spiritistischen Gauklers, die gerade vor wenigen Tagen gelungen war"[12]. Das ist auch topografisch signifikant, war doch München, Heyses Wohnsitz,

---

[11] Ebd., S. 5.

[12] Paul Heyse, „In der Geisterstunde", in: ders., *Gesammelte Werke*, 3. Reihe, Band IV, Stuttgart, Berlin, o.J. [1924], S. 3-92: 3.

bereits seit Längerem ein Zentrum des Okkultismus und Spiritismus.[13] Allgemein anerkannt, so scheint es, werden im Gesprächskreis demgegenüber Phänomene „auf der helldunklen Grenze zwischen Seelen- und Nervenleben", wie „Suggestion, Telepathie, Autohypnose", die „selbst von der hochmütigsten Wissenschaft nicht länger mit Schweigen und Achselzucken abzufertigen sind"[14], weil sie „durch tausend Tatsachen bestätigt" seien[15] – Phänomene also, die seit einem Artikel Max Dessoirs von 1889 unter ‚Parapsychologie' verbucht werden.[16] Uneinigkeit entsteht dagegen vor allem beim Thema Gespenst, das ein Leben nach dem Tode zu indizieren scheint, eine Abtrennung des Seelischen vom Körperlichen und damit einen Dualismus, der zum weltanschaulichen Streitfall werden muss, weil er einem Hauptstrang der Wissenschaftsentwicklung widerspricht.

Verteidiger des Glaubens an die Wahrheit der erzählten Gespenstergeschichten haben es schwer in diesem Kreis. Sie argumentieren zwar mit Erfahrung, können das aber argumentativ kaum einholen, weil eine Verallgemeinerbarkeit fehlt. Am deutlichsten wird das bei der älteren Tante Julie in Heyses Textsammlung, die „steif und fest" daran glaubt, „daß ein abgeschiedener Geist wieder erscheinen kann, wenn er was Wichtiges auf der Erde zu tun oder zu bestellen vergessen hat", und sich darin von ihrer eigenen Erfahrung bestätigt sieht.[17] Diesem Schema folgen in der Tat die Erzählungen: Immer ist es etwas Versäumtes, das die Wiederkehr bedingt, ein (An)Trieb, der über das Grab hinaus wirkt. Dem Glauben an die erzählten und durch die Erfahrung der Erzähler – aber eben auch nur durch diese – beglaubigten Geschichten neigen auch die Hausfrau[18] und die Frau eines anwesenden Arztes zu, die selbst den zweiten Teil der Spukgeschichte vom *Waldlachen* vorträgt. Die Annahme, die Haltung zu Spukphänomenen sei ‚gegendert', trügt allerdings. Zum einen ist auch die Schwester der Hausfrau bei aller Liebe zum literarischen Schauer „vom Aufklärungsfieber unseres klugen Jahrhunderts angesteckt"[19], zum anderen sind es zwei Männer, die die ersten unheimlichen Geschichten vortragen. Ein pensionierter Oberst gibt die Vampirgeschichte von der *Schönen Abigail* zum Besten, und ein Geschichtsprofessor berichtet vom *Mittagszauber* der Erscheinung einer längst Verstorbenen. „Meine Studien haben mich zu manchen rätselhaften Erscheinungen im Menschen- und Völkerleben geführt, die aller nüchternen historisch-kritischen Erklärung spotten"[20], so beschreibt er seinen ideologisch nicht fest definierten Erkenntnishorizont. Als Historiker geht er von

---

13 Vgl. Diethard Sawicki, *Leben mit den Toten. Geisterglauben und die Entstehung des Spiritismus in Deutschland 1770-1900*, 2. Aufl., Paderborn, 2016, S. 203-217, S. 252 und S. 348. Vgl. Priska Pytlik (Hg.), *Spiritismus und ästhetische Moderne: Berlin und München um 1900. Dokumente und Kommentare*, Tübingen, 2006, S. 251-452.

14 Heyse (o.J.), In der Geisterstunde, S. 3.

15 Ebd., S. 5.

16 Wieder abgedruckt in: Pytlik (2006), *Spiritismus und ästhetische Moderne*, S. 30-34.

17 Heyse (o.J.), In der Geisterstunde, S. 55 f.

18 Ebd., S. 88 f.

19 Ebd., S. 55.

20 Ebd., S. 34.

Einzelfällen, das heißt vom Besonderen aus, und das ‚Wissen' von Gespenstern ist in aller Regel Wissen vom Einzelfall – genau das ist ja seine Crux.

Mit dem Auftreten eines Geisteswissenschaftlers deutet sich an, dass der Konflikt zwischen Glauben und Nicht-Glauben von Spukerscheinungen nicht einfach eine individuelle Angelegenheit ist. In Heyses Text wird er mit einer paradigmatischen Dimension in Beziehung gesetzt, nämlich dem zunehmenden Auseinandertreten der *two cultures* (C. P. Snow) im 19. Jahrhundert. Einen dominanten Strang der modernen Naturwissenschaften repräsentiert der skeptische Hausherr, ein „hartgesottene[r] Naturforscher"[21] und „Vertreter der exacten Forschung": „[W]as sich der Natur mit Hebeln und mit Schrauben nicht abgewinnen läßt, negirt er frischweg, weil es ihm unbequem ist"[22], bemerkt seine Frau spöttisch. An seiner Seite stehen im Prinzip der Arzt sowie der Ich-Erzähler des Rahmens. Die Basis ihres Denkens ist ein tendenziell materialistischer Monismus, der mit seiner Opposition gegen die idealistische Philosophie und insbesondere die romantische Naturphilosophie eine treibende Kraft beim Aufstieg der Naturwissenschaften im 19. Jahrhundert darstellte. Obwohl es um die Mitte des 19. Jahrhunderts zu einem erbitterten Streit zwischen materialistischen und idealistischen Strömungen kommt[23], dominiert doch unter Naturwissenschaftlern ein skeptischer Agnostizismus[24], der von avancierten religionsphilosophischen Entwicklungen gestützt wird (Schopenhauer, Strauß, Feuerbach, Marx, Nietzsche), die in Richtung Säkularisierung und „Entchristianisierung" gehen.[25]

Die Konstellation in Heyses Sammlung ist signifikant, weil sie zeigt, wie das phantastische Erzählen den Finger auf ein grundsätzliches Problem kultureller Selbstverständigung im 19. Jahrhundert legt. Die Gespenstergeschichten tragen ein mysteriöses und unerklärliches Geschehen in einen geselligen Kreis hinein, dessen Meinungsführer mit großer Selbstsicherheit am Paradigma der materialistischen Naturwissenschaft und ihrem prinzipiellen Erklärungsanspruch festhalten, nun aber mit der Problematik einer Erklärungslücke und ihren weitreichenden Implikationen konfrontiert sind. Bereits Auguste Comte hatte 1844 auf die „relative Natur des positiven Geistes" hingewiesen, der „weit davon entfernt [sei], irgendeine wirkliche Existenz vollständig erforschen zu können"[26]. Breitenwirksamkeit erhält diese Einsicht im sogenannten Ignorabimus-Streit, der von einem 1872 gehaltenen Vortrag des angesehenen Physiologen Emil Du Bois-Reymond *Über die Grenzen des Naturerkennens* seinen Ausgang nahm und von Zeitgenossen als „Ab-

---

21 Ebd., S. 33.

22 Ebd., S. 87.

23 Vgl. Kurt Bayertz/MyriamGerhard/Walter Jaeschke (Hg.), *Der Materialismus-Streit*, Hamburg, 2012.

24 Vgl. Thomas Nipperdey, *Deutsche Geschichte 1800-1866. Bürgerwelt und starker Staat*, 3. Aufl., München, 1985, S. 497. Hier auch ein Überblick über die Wissenschaftsentwicklung, S. 484-498. Vgl. für die Folgezeit ders., *Deutsche Geschichte 1866-1918*, Band 1: *Arbeitswelt und Bürgergeist*, München, 1990, S. 602-691.

25 Nipperdey (1985), *Deutsche Geschichte 1800-1866*, S. 440-451. Vgl. Rudolf Schlögl, *Alter Glaube und moderne Welt. Europäisches Christentum im Umbruch. 1750-1850*, Frankfurt/M., 2013.

26 Auguste Comte, *Discours sur l'Esprit Positif/Rede über den Geist des Positivismus* [1844], hg. von Iring Fetscher, Hamburg, 1979, S. 29.

gesang auf den ‚Materialismus'" und als Infragestellung der weltanschaulichen Autorität der Naturwissenschaften wahrgenommen wurde.[27] Was Heyses Naturwissenschaftler gegen die Existenz von Gespenstern vorbringen, kann man als ein natur- und humanwissenschaftlich informiertes Update der aufklärerischen Aberglaubensbekämpfung ansehen. Die vermeintlich gespenstischen Phänomene sprechen für die Naturwissenschaftler dezidiert nicht für eine „Fortdauer nach dem Tode"[28] und ein „Hereinragen einer übersinnlichen Welt in die unsere"[29] – übrigens ein ungefähres Zitat aus *Kraft und Stoff*, dem materialistischen Hauptwerk Ludwig Büchners von 1855[30] –, sie gehen aber auch nicht bloß auf Betrug zurück. Sollte ein Spukphänomen als wirklich gelten können, so könnte es kein ‚übernatürliches', sondern nur ein immanentes, also ein zumindest potenziell ‚natürlich' erklärbares Phänomen sein; vor allem aber müsste es verallgemeinerbar, wenigstens intersubjektiv beobachtbar sein, und das ist nicht der Fall. Daher wird zwar durchaus eingeräumt, dass die Erzähler ihre Geschichten „erlebt" haben, „nur eben mit ihren inneren Sinnen, deren von Hirn oder Herz oder Nervenzentrum ausgehende Eindrücke durch einen Selbstbetrug der Phantasie in äußere Wahrnehmungen verwandelt worden sind" – um „reale Tatsachen" jedenfalls handle es sich nicht.[31] Das Erlebte basiert demnach auf mentalen und psychischen Mechanismen, für deren Erklärung die ganze mehr oder weniger neue Forschung in Anspruch genommen wird: Mit dem Stichwort von der „Schwelle des Bewußtseins"[32] beispielsweise – es entstammt Johann Friedrich Herbarts schon betagterem Werk *Psychologie als Wissenschaft* von 1824/1825 – rückt explizit die Kategorie des Unbewussten ins Blickfeld, die im 19. Jahrhundert einen kontinuierlichen Aufstieg erfährt. Weiterhin werden, wo der Ich-Erzähler die „Psychophysik"[33] ins Feld führt, Gustav Theodor Fechners *Elemente der Psychophysik*, immerhin auch schon von 1860, eingespielt, doch mit den Mechanismen der „Suggestion" und Autosuggestion[34], der Projektion[35] und nicht zuletzt der Hysterie[36] geraten aktuelle Erklärungsmodelle in den Blick.

Doch die Problematik der Erkenntnislücke hat über das Konkrete hinaus einen grundsätzlichen Charakter, indem sie die Grundlagen der naturwissenschaftlichen Arbeit selbst, vor allem aber die ‚letzten Dinge' betrifft, für die den Naturwissen-

---

27 Einen sehr guten Überblick über die Debatte geben Kurt Bayertz/Myriam Gerhard/Walter Jaeschke (Hg.), *Der Ignorabimus-Streit*, Hamburg, 2012, hier die Einleitung, S. VII-XXXVII, v. a. S. XV-XVIII; darin auch Du Bois-Reymond, S. 153-186.

28 Heyse (o.J.), In der Geisterstunde, S. 90.

29 Ebd., S. 34.

30 Ludwig Büchner, *Kraft und Stoff oder Grundzüge der natürlichen Weltordnung* [1855], 19. Aufl., Leipzig, 1898, S. 335.

31 Heyse (o.J.), In der Geisterstunde, S. 89, vgl. S. 92.

32 Ebd., S. 91 f.

33 Ebd., S. 89.

34 Ebd., S. 3.

35 „Mein Mann hat mir ausreden wollen, daß es etwas anderes gewesen sei, als eine innere Empfindung, die ich in meiner Erregung […] nach außen projiziert hätte" (ebd., S. 82).

36 Ebd., S. 88.

schaften – anders als ein dezidierter Materialismus es implizieren musste – Zuständigkeit und Kompetenz abgesprochen wurden.[37] Die Fragen nach Seele, Tod und Fortleben nach dem Tod bleiben damit so ungesichert wie je – und damit auch der Status des Gespenstischen. Es ist eben gerade nicht so, wie Bölsche fünf Jahre zuvor suggerieren wollte, dass nämlich „das Dasein von Gespenstern wissenschaftlich widerlegt“[38] sei. Selbst Heyses agnostischer Hausarzt muss mit Blick auf die Wiederkehr des verstorbenen kleinen Lisabethle einräumen: „Das letzte Wort über diese wundersamen Phänomene wird ohnehin wohl schwerlich, solange die Welt steht, gesprochen werden“[39]. Die szientistische Erkenntniserwartung wird damit auf die lange Bank verschoben und ernüchtert. Der Doktor folgt damit Lessing, der in der *Hamburgischen Dramaturgie* bemerkt hatte, da sich die „Unmöglichkeit“ von Gespenstern faktisch nicht erweisen lasse, könne der Satz „Wir glauben itzt keine Gespenster [...] also nur so viel heißen: in dieser Sache, über die sich fast eben so viel dafür als darwider sagen läßt, hat die gegenwärtig herrschende Art zu denken den Gründen darwider das Übergewicht gegeben“[40]. Lessing deutet damit den Konstruktionscharakter des Wissens als sozialer Übereinkunft an.

Der Szientismus des 19. Jahrhunderts hat „den Gründen darwider“ ganz entschieden das Übergewicht gegeben, aber die „hochmütigste Wissenschaft“[41] steht auf dünnem Eis. Denn die Erklärungslücke ist nicht nur ein unbefriedigendes Faktum, sondern macht das System anfällig für das Fortleben bzw. die Wiederkehr älterer Erklärungsmodelle. Auguste Comte, Ludwig Büchner und andere bemerken die Neigung moderner Wissenschaften wie Gesellschaften zu „[v]orübergehende[n] Rückfälle[n] in den Aberglauben“[42], zu obsoleten „theologischen Erklärungen“[43] oder zu weltanschaulichen ‚Atavismen‘[44]. Der Ethnologe Edward Burnett Tylor, obwohl Anhänger eines ausgeprägten Glaubens an den Fortschritt der Menschheit, entwickelt in seinem Werk *Primitive Culture* von 1871 seine prominente Theorie der „survivals“, der „Ueberlebsel“. Es handelt sich hier um Reste früherer Kulturzustände, Fälle, „wo Anschauungen mitten in Zuständen der Gesellschaft fortleben, welche sich ihnen allmählich mehr und mehr entfremden und sie schließlich gänzlich zu unterdrücken streben“[45], allerdings erfolglos. Eine Variante

---

37 Vgl. Bayertz/Gerhard/Jaeschke (2012), *Ignorabimus-Streit*, S. XXVI-XXXIV, hier v. a. zu Hartmann, Dilthey, Wittgenstein und Carnap.

38 Bölsche (1976), *Die naturwissenschaftlichen Grundlagen*, S. 5.

39 Heyse (o.J.), In der Geisterstunde, S. 64.

40 Gotthold Ephraim Lessing, „Hamburgische Dramaturgie“, in: ders., *Werke*, Band IV, hg. von Herbert G. Göpfert, Darmstadt, 1996, 11. Stück, S. 229-720: 282.

41 Heyse (o.J.), In der Geisterstunde, S. 3.

42 Carus Sterne (= Ernst Krause), *Die Naturgeschichte der Gespenster. Physikalisch-physiologisch-psychologische Studien*, Weimar, 1863, S. IV.

43 Comte (1979), *Discours*, S. 11.

44 Büchner (1898), *Kraft und Stoff*, S. 332.

45 Edward B. Tylor, *Die Anfänge der Cultur. Untersuchungen über die Entwicklung der Mythologie, Philosophie, Religion, Kunst und Sitte* [1871], 2 Bände, Leipzig, 1873, Band 1, S. 111. Zu diesem Konzept und seinem diskursiven Umfeld vgl. Michael C. Frank, „Überlebsel. Das Primitive in Anthropologie und Evolutionstheorie des 19. Jahrhunderts“, in: Nicola Gess (Hg.), *Literarischer Primitivismus*, Berlin, Boston, MA, 2013, S. 159-187.

stellt das „Wiederaufleben“[46] dar, das ein latentes Überleben voraussetzt. Das hervorstechende Beispiel solcher Beharrungskraft von erratischen Partikeln einer älteren Kulturstufe ist für Tylor der Aberglaube, dem er auch den modernen Spiritismus zurechnet.[47] Schon sein (englischer) Begriff zeigt diese ‚Unzugehörigkeit‘ an: „Das Wort ‚superstition‘ selbst drückt vielleicht in seinem ursprünglichen Sinne eines ‚Ueberstehens‘ aus alten Zeiten, den Begriff des Ueberlebens aus“[48]. Die Beharrungskraft bzw. die Wiederkehr vermeintlich obsoleter und ‚dysfunktionaler‘ Elemente ist nicht zuletzt darum so hartnäckig, weil die materialistisch-monistische Wissenschaft zwar ‚Weltanschauung‘ zu sein beansprucht, dabei aber ältere Sinngebungskonzepte destruiert hat, ohne sie durch neue ersetzen zu können.[49] Viele Zeitgenossen deuten daher gerade den Spiritismus als Kompensation der Säkularisierung: Er trete in die Lücke, die der Verlust der Religion gelassen habe.[50] So kommt es zu Diskontinuitäten und Ungleichzeitigkeiten, zu temporalen Gemengelagen, Brüchen, Verwerfungen und Überlagerungen nicht nur von weltanschaulichen Konzepten, sondern von „Zeitschichten“[51], denen diese sich zuordnen lassen, auch wenn die Überlebsel nicht mehr dem ‚Alten‘ allein zugehören, sondern auch in ihren neuen Kontexten Funktionen erfüllen. Das szientifische – und nicht minder das technologische und ökonomische – Fortschrittsdenken bringt eine eigene Zeitform mit sich, die sich progredient in die Zukunft erstreckt, während sie die Vergangenheit hinter sich zu lassen meint. Sie setzt stärker auf ein produktives Vergessen[52] als auf eine systematische Erinnerungskultur, wie sie der gleichzeitige Historismus praktiziert. In den Atavismen, Rückfällen und Überlebseln aber, so stellt sich die Epoche selbst ihren Befund, kehren die Vergangenheit und gerade diejenigen ihrer Aspekte zurück, die die Moderne aus sich ausschließen zu müssen meinte: Irrationales, Mythisches, Animistisches und ‚Abergläubisches‘. Der Prozess der Modernisierung von Gesellschaft und Bewusstsein erweist sich als begrenzt und durchsetzt mit widerständigen und gegenläufigen Aspekten. Es ist daher kein Zufall, dass gerade das Gespenst zur Reflexionsfigur solcher Strukturen werden kann, ist es doch in einem doppelten Sinn die paradigmatische Figur der Wiederkehr: Zum einen ist es, weil es noch etwas zu erledigen hat, *als Figur* der Wiedergänger *par excellence*, in dem sich *per se* die lineare Zeitfolge auflöst, zum anderen entstammt es dem Reich des vermeintlich obsoleten mythi-

46 Tylor (1873), *Anfänge der Cultur*, S. 17.

47 Ebd., S. 142-159.

48 Ebd., S. 72.

49 Vgl. Hartmut Böhme, *Fetischismus und Kultur. Eine andere Theorie der Moderne*, Reinbek bei Hamburg, 2006, S. 22.

50 So etwa Paul Heyse in seiner Erzählung *Das Haus ‚Zum unglaubigen Thomas‘ oder Des Spirits Rache* (Heyse [o.J.], *Gesammelte Werke*, S. 103) oder Wilhelm Bölsche in seinem Spiritismus-Roman *Die Mittagsgöttin* von 1891. I. d. S. auch Helmut Zander, *Geschichte der Seelenwanderung in Europa. Alternative religiöse Traditionen von der Antike bis heute*, Darmstadt, 1999, S. 472. Grundsätzlich Marco Frenschkowski, „Phantastik und Religion“, in: Hans Richard Brittnacher/Markus May (Hg.), *Phantastik. Ein interdisziplinäres Handbuch*, Stuttgart, Weimar, 2013, S. 553-561.

51 Reinhart Koselleck, *Zeitschichten. Studien zur Historik*, Frankfurt/M., 2003.

52 Vgl. Aleida Assmann, *Formen des Vergessens*, Göttingen, 2016.

schen Denkens, dessen Relikte man selbst in der Ära seiner Entzauberung nicht los wird, weil sie längst schon Teil des kulturellen Imaginären geworden sind.

Das phantastische Erzählen, so ließe sich sagen, verhilft Überlebseln zu einer ‚unzeitgemäßen' literarischen Existenz, ja einem Existenzrecht, eben weil sie noch etwas Unabgegoltenes an sich haben. Joachim Metzner hat die „Wiederkehr des Verdrängten" als die narrative Grundfigur der Phantastik ausgemacht[53], und diese These lässt sich auch über ihre enge psychoanalytische Fassung hinaus festhalten. In diesem Sinne hat Renate Lachmann festgestellt, dass in der phantastischen Literatur „die Kehrseite einer Kultur, ihr Anderes, Verleugnetes, Verbotenes, Begehrtes" wiederkehre. Sie hole zurück, „was den Ausgrenzungen zum Opfer gefallen ist", durch die sich Kulturen von ihrem Anderen abgrenzen.[54] Die phantastische Literatur verweist so auf Ungleichzeitigkeiten und Widersprüche in der Konstitutionsgeschichte der Moderne. Heyses Textsammlung sieht diesen Prozessen der Wiederkehr zu. *Indem* sie davon erzählen lässt, führt sie auf einer ersten Ebene intentional den Ausschluss des Phantastischen vor. Sie reflektiert die epistemologische und ‚weltanschauliche' Situation ihrer Epoche, indem sie Erzählungen über wissenschaftlich inkompatible Phänomene buchstäblich zur Diskussion stellt und mit heterogenen Wirklichkeitskonzepten abgleicht, die unterschiedlichen paradigmatischen Modellen zugehören. Reflektiert wird dabei gerade die umstrittene Frage, was Wirklichkeit eigentlich sei und mit welchen Mitteln sie zu erkennen ist, und diese Reflexion geschieht quasi in Form einer diskursiven Bestandsaufnahme. Nicht nur der Ich-Erzähler des Rahmens, auch der Text insgesamt – einschließlich der hinter dem Rücken der jeweiligen Binnenerzähler angeordneten Relativierungen ihrer Selbstdeutungen – arbeitet daran, das Erzählte ‚natürlich' zu erklären, und in dieser Hinsicht behalten die Naturwissenschaftler zumindest das letzte Wort. Die Überlebsel werden, kaum dass sie die Bühne betreten haben, sozusagen gleich wieder mortifiziert, und damit scheint das realistische Paradigma mit seinem Fluchtpunkt der „realen Thatsachen"[55] rehabilitiert. Diese dreifache Konstellation – Bilanzierung der Diskursvielfalt, Diskussion der Realitätsproblematik, Ausschluss des Phantastischen – markiert Heyses Nähe zum Realismus.

Zweierlei allerdings gibt zu denken. *Erstens* wird im Text eine kleine Theorie der phantastischen Literatur mit nicht unerheblicher Widerstandskraft entfaltet, die mit der realistischen Poetik des Rahmens kollidiert. Die Pointe ist, dass ihre Vertreterin, die süffisante Schwester der Hausfrau, dezidiert nicht an Gespenster glaubt, ihnen aber gerade darum literarische Lizenz einräumt. Was sie verlangt, sind „echte und rechte Gespenstergeschichten" ohne „prosaische Aufklärung"[56]. Sie

---

[53] Joachim Metzner, „Die Vieldeutigkeit der Wiederkehr. Literaturpsychologische Überlegungen zur Phantastik", in: Christian W. Thomsen/Jens Malte Fischer (Hg.), *Phantastik in Literatur und Kunst*, Darmstadt, 1980, S. 79-108: 108.

[54] Renate Lachmann, „Literatur der Phantastik als Gegen-Anthropologie", in: Aleida Assmann/Ulrich Gaier/Gisela Trommsdorff (Hg.), *Positionen der Kulturanthropologie*, Frankfurt/M., 2004, S. 44-60: 46.

[55] Heyse (o.J.), In der Geisterstunde, S. 89 und S. 92.

[56] Ebd., S. 3 f.

glaube zwar nicht an Spukerscheinungen, trotzdem könne sie sich bei guter Präsentation

> eines angenehmen Gruselns nicht erwehren [...] und nichts hab' ich lieber, als wenn mir [...] die Haut ein bißchen schaudert und das Haar zu Berge steht. Gerade daß man weiß, es ist alles Unsinn, und doch hat es diesen wunderlichen Effekt, ist das Hübsche daran, wie man es ja auch bei allem Poetischen erfährt, das uns mit fortreißt, obwohl wir wissen, es ist ein Spuk der Phantasie.[57]

Vordergründig scheint sich dies komplementär zu den Entmächtigungsstrategien der Naturwissenschaftler zu verhalten und deren Wirklichkeitskonzept nicht zu erschüttern, zumal im Text das phantastische Erzählen nur die Binnenerzählungen prägt, nicht aber den realistischen Rahmen, in den diese eingebettet sind und durch den sie relativiert werden. Was man nicht glaubt, kann ästhetisch umcodiert und risikolos fiktionalisiert werden. Zum einen ließe sich sagen, dass phantastische Phänomene damit frei werden für vielfältige Metaphorisierungen: Insbesondere das Gespenst wird in der realistischen Literatur zur Reflexionsfigur unter anderem der Erinnerung, des Unbewussten, des sozialen Imaginären oder des Geldes.[58] Das gilt auch hier für die Binnenerzählungen: In fast allen ist eine Deutungslinie angelegt, die das Unheimliche als Effekt des Unbewussten, Verdrängten oder Vergessenen, einer erotischen Angstlust oder eines Schuldgefühls aufseiten der jeweiligen Erzähler ‚natürlich' interpretierbar macht. Damit aber würde das Phantastische im Sinne des minimalistischen Kriteriums der Unschlüssigkeit (*hésitation*) ausgehebelt. Zum anderen aber kommt mit dem Gefühl des Schauers nun doch ein gegenläufiges Moment ins Spiel. Denn wenn etwas „unglaublich ist und uns doch gruseln macht"[59], dann gibt es im Inneren eine Sphäre, die hier mit der „Phantasie" identifiziert wird, die das Gruseln sehr viel ernster nimmt als der urteilende Verstand – sonst gäbe es ja keines. Faktisch also erfolgt damit eine Spaltung der Person in verschiedene Instanzen, und diese begründet eine Variante der phantastischen Unschlüssigkeit, die ja auch sonst im Normalfall nicht als rationales Abwägen zwischen zwei Optionen zu denken ist, sondern ‚irrationale' Anteile haben muss, also ein latentes Bezweifeln des rational-szientifischen Konsenses und seiner Definitionsmacht. Dass diese Ebenen der Person hierarchisiert werden, indem der Widerstand der Phantasie nicht ganz ernst genommen und, wenn er es zu weit treiben sollte, pathologisiert wird, bestätigt allenfalls die diskursiven Machtverhältnisse, muss aber in der Sache gerade nichts entscheiden. So bleibt letztlich ein unaufgelöster Widerstreit, den Heyses Textsammlung im Bemühen, am Ende mehr oder weniger realistischen Klartext zu erzeugen, allenfalls verschleiert.

---

[57] Ebd., S. 3.

[58] Vgl. Christian Begemann, „Figuren der Wiederkehr. Gespenster, Erinnerung, Tradition und Vererbung bei Theodor Storm", in: Elisabeth Strowick/Ulrike Vedder (Hg.), *Wirklichkeit und Wahrnehmung. Neue Perspektiven auf Theodor Storm*, Bern (u. a.), 2013, S. 13-37; ders., „Erkundungen im ‚inneren Afrika'. Adalbert Stifter und das Unbewusste", in: *Jahrbuch des Adalbert-Stifter-Instituts des Landes Oberösterreich* 18 (2011), S. 11-29.

[59] Heyse (o.J.), In der Geisterstunde, S. 5.

Bestätigt wird dies – *zweitens* – dadurch, dass es selbst diesseits des Lagers der „spiritistischen Geisterbanner“[60] nicht möglich ist, Einigkeit über die Beschaffenheit der Wirklichkeit herzustellen. Im Sinne Lessings ist und bleibt es unmöglich, die Nicht-Existenz des Gespenstischen zu beweisen. Unter diesen diffusen Bedingungen ist es schwierig zu sagen, wogegen Phantastik eigentlich genau verstoßen soll. In Erweiterung des Todorov'schen Arguments der Unschlüssigkeit hat Marianne Wünsch festgehalten, phantastische Literatur müsse eine spezifische Erklärungsstruktur aufweisen, aus der hervorgehe, dass die dargestellten phantastischen Ereignisse mit dem kulturellen Wissen und dem Realitätskonzept der „kulturell vorherrschenden Gruppe(n)“ nicht kompatibel sei[61] – wogegen Monika Schmitz-Emans mit dem Argument Widerspruch eingelegt hat, „unter den Mitgliedern einer Kommunikationsgemeinschaft [bestehe] kaum je ein Konsens über das ‚Realitätskompatible‘“[62]. In der Tat zeigt Heyse genau das, auch wenn er für eine bestimmte Position parteiisch zu sein scheint. Man könnte sagen, die Unschlüssigkeit gehöre selbst schon zur diskursiven Situation, die der Text abbildet, und münde, wenngleich *contre cœur*, in einen „Zweifel an der Möglichkeit, sich überhaupt ‚richtige Begriffe‘ von der Welt zu machen.“[63] So zersetzt gerade das ‚realistische‘ Erzählen einen Konsens über das Wirkliche und arbeitet damit einer Grundstruktur des Phantastischen zu, wie umgekehrt dieses beansprucht, die von den Wissenschaften eruierten Seiten des Wirklichen durch andere Aspekte zu ergänzen, seien es noch unentdeckte ‚natürliche‘ oder ‚okkulte‘. ‚Realismus‘ und ‚Phantastik‘ konvergieren hier im Effekt, eine Debatte über die ‚Ordnungen‘ des Wirklichen in Gang zu setzen.

2. Gespaltene Moderne: Theodor Storm

Was bei Heyse einerseits auf verschiedene Figuren verteilt ist, andererseits aber auch ansatzweise eine Spaltung in vernünftige Einsicht und Phantasie beim Rezipienten der Erzählungen bewirkt, zeigt sich in Theodor Storms Erzählung *Ein Bekenntnis* von 1887 als innerer Konflikt des Protagonisten, wiederum der Figur eines Wissenschaftlers. Von Schuldgefühlen bedrückt, berichtet der Mediziner Franz Jebe seinem Jugendfreund, dem Rahmenerzähler der Novelle, dass er seine an Unterleibskrebs erkrankte Ehefrau auf deren eigenen Wunsch vergiftet habe, um ihr schweres Leiden zu ersparen. Kurz darauf stellt er jedoch bei der Lektüre eines Zeitschriftenartikels fest, dass er die Möglichkeit einer Operation mit guten Heilungschancen übersehen hat. Im Gefolge dieser Thematik hat man die Erzählung lange Zeit als Auseinandersetzung mit dem ethischen Problem der aktiven Sterbehilfe gelesen. Schon Paul Heyse, der langjährige Brieffreund Storms, der sich

---

60 Ebd., S. 88.

61 Wünsch (1991), *Fantastische Literatur der Frühen Moderne*, S. 54.

62 Monika Schmitz-Emans, „Phantastische Literatur. Ein denkwürdiger Problemfall“, in: *Neohelicon* 22 (1995), S. 53-116: 65 f.

63 Ebd., S. 107.

in seiner Erzählung *Auf Tod und Leben* gleichfalls mit dieser Frage befasst hatte, moniert etliche Punkte, die ihm vom Thema abzulenken scheinen, wogegen Storm darauf insistiert, es sei ihm um einen sehr viel spezielleren Aspekt gegangen, nämlich um die Frage, wie jemand dazu komme, „sein Geliebtestes zu tödten"[64]. Im Gegensatz zu Heyse eröffnet sich damit unter der ethischen Schicht des Textes eine psychodynamische Problematik.

Jebes Weltbild ist einerseits geprägt vom modernen Szientismus, speziell der pathologischen Anatomie, dem Materialismus und einer metaphysiklosen Immanenz. Das Verhalten des schnellen Diagnostikers ist bestimmt von Professionalismus, intellektuellem Hochmut und sozialen Defiziten. Andererseits eignet ihm ein „phantastischer Zug"[65], der ihn mit den epochentypischen Tendenzen des Okkultismus und Spiritismus verbindet und ihm offenbar nur teilweise bewusst ist. Heyse hat auch daran Anstoß genommen, was angesichts der Wissenschaftlerfiguren in der *Geisterstunde* nicht verblüfft: „[D]as visionäre Element" sollte „dem Charakter des hellblickenden Naturkundigen fremd sein [...], zumal es mit dem Verlauf der Geschichte nichts Wesentliches zu schaffen hat"[66]. Diese Sicht verfehlt in mehrfacher Hinsicht die Pointen der Erzählung, denn sie geht von einer homogenen Anlage von Figuren (und Personen überhaupt) aus, die Storm gerade unterläuft.

Der „phantastische Zug" des Wissenschaftlers Jebe äußert sich nicht nur in der Lektüre der einschlägigen Autoren Maximilian Perty und Georg Friedrich Daumer[67], die dem Spiritismus und Okkultismus nahestanden.[68] Vor allem zeigt er sich im Verhältnis zu seiner Frau Elsi. Sein „Bekenntnis" beginnt Jebe mit dem Rückblick auf ein „Nachtgesicht"[69], das eine ambivalente Begehrensstruktur enthüllt: Noch während seiner Gymnasialzeit war ihm im Traum das gleichermaßen faszinierende wie unheimliche Bild eines von seuchentoten Knaben umstandenen Mädchens erschienen, das ihn nicht mehr loslässt. In ihm glaubt der Jugendliche „das Geheimnis des Weibes" zu erkennen, das sich ihm mit dem „Genius des Todes" amalgamiert.[70] Jahre später begegnet Jebe, der mittlerweile ein bekannter Gynäkologe geworden ist, der feenartigen Elsi Füßli, einer Großnichte des Malers Johann Heinrich Füssli, dem, wie mit Anspielung auf das Gemälde *Die Nachtmahr* gesagt wird, „zuerst die Darstellung des Unheimlichen in der deutschen Kunst

---

64 Theodor Storm, *Sämtliche Werke in vier Bänden*, Band 3, hg. von Karl Ernst Laage und Dieter Lohmeier, Frankfurt/M., 1988, S. 580-633, hier Anhang S. 1039.

65 Ebd., S. 581.

66 Ebd., S. 1038.

67 Ebd., S. 581.

68 Vgl. z. B. Maximilian Perty, *Die mystischen Erscheinungen in der menschlichen Natur*, Leipzig, 1861; ders., *Der jetzige Spiritualismus und verwandte Erfahrungen der Vergangenheit und Gegenwart*, Leipzig, Heidelberg, 1877. Georg Friedrich Daumer, *Das Geisterreich in Glauben, Vorstellung, Sage und Wirklichkeit*, Dresden, 1867; ders., *Das Reich des Wundersamen und Geheimnisvollen. Thatsache und Theorie*, Regensburg, 1872.

69 Storm (1988), *Sämtliche Werke*, S. 587.

70 Ebd., S. 589.

gelang“[71]. In der derart vorbelasteten Elsi glaubt Jebe sein „Nachtgesicht“[72] wiederzuerkennen und heiratet sie. Sobald die reale Elsi in Jebes Leben tritt, wird sie von ihm, seinen Neigungen zum ‚Phantastischen‘ folgend, mit allen mythischen Imagines des Weiblichen im Gefolge der Romantik besetzt und zum reinen Projektionsschirm – bereits die Verbindung von ‚Weib‘ und ‚Tod‘ gehörte in diesen für das 19. Jahrhundert signifikanten genderhistorischen Zusammenhang.[73] Jebe stilisiert Elsi zu einem „Märchenbild“, einer „Undine, eine[r] Elbe, eine[r] Fee“[74], d. h. zur Verkörperung einer elementaren ‚Natur‘, die dem wissenschaftlich sozialisierten, auf Intellekt und Ratio fixierten Mann abhanden gekommen ist. Die Phantasie des aufgeklärten Wissenschaftlers ist ganz und gar von mythischen Elementen durchdrungen[75], Überlebseln eines für den Szientisten ‚eigentlich‘ obsoleten Denkens. Schon diese Alterisierung der Frau schlägt fast zwangsläufig ins Unheimliche um: Jebe betont das „Eigene, Fremdartige an ihr“[76], das „aus anderen Existenzen“ zu stammen scheint[77], und nachdem ihm unter ihren Blicken zunehmend „unheimlich“ wird[78], wird er noch deutlicher: „Deine Augen sind so gespenstisch, Elsi“[79]. Diese Unheimlichkeit geht nicht nur auf die mythisierenden Elemente zurück, sondern vor allem darauf, dass Elsi – schon ganz im Sinne Freuds – als ein projizierter Anteil von Jebe selbst wahrgenommen wird, sein eigenes Anderes. Auf seine Frage „Was bist du eigentlich?“, antwortet sie denn auch doppelsinnig: „Dein bin ich; nichts als dein!“[80], und die Erzählperspektive, die ja niemals Jebes *point of view* verlässt, bestätigt dies zwangsläufig. Von Elsi wissen wir ausschließlich, was Jebe von ihr sagt bzw. aus ihr macht. Am deutlichsten wird das, wenn Jebe, wiederum „fast wie traumredend“, bemerkt: „Ich hatte nun mein Nachtgespenst geheiratet“[81]. Schon das stete Aschgrau ihrer Kleidung, aber auch ihre Todesnähe, Lebensschwäche und Krankhaftigkeit verbinden Elsi mit dem Traumgesicht. Sein eigener Traum tritt Jebe als fremde Gestalt gegenüber, aber genau das macht auch seine Ambivalenz aus.

Hochgradig ambivalent – definitive Wunscherfüllung und äußerste Infragestellung der eigenen Person in einem – ist insbesondere die von Jebe ständig umkreiste Frage nach einer Identität Elsis mit der nächtlichen Vision, die, wäre sie der Fall, das immanent-materialistische Weltbild in Richtung einer anderen Dimension aufbrechen müsste: sei es einer metaphysischen Sphäre oder einer immanenten

---

71 Ebd., S. 592.
72 Ebd., S. 587.
73 Vgl. Elisabeth Bronfen, *Nur über ihre Leiche. Tod, Weiblichkeit und Ästhetik*, München, 1994.
74 Storm (1988), *Sämtliche Werke*, S. 595.
75 Vgl. auch Peter Küng, *Die Krise der liberalen Anthropologie in der Literatur des Bürgerlichen Realismus. Männlichkeit, Bürgerlichkeit und Individualität bei Theodor Storm, Theodor Fontane und Paul Heyse*, Würzburg, 2015, S. 87 f.
76 Storm (1988), *Sämtliche Werke*, S. 594.
77 Ebd., S. 601.
78 Ebd., S. 605.
79 Ebd., S. 606.
80 Ebd., S. 595.
81 Ebd., S. 594.

Transzendenz, jedenfalls aber der Existenz einer vom Körper unterschiedenen Seele, die telepathisch kommunizieren oder sogar den leiblichen Tod überdauern kann.[82] Seinen Eindruck, Elsi könne vielleicht gar „nicht sterben", zensiert Jebe umgehend als eine Art von „Irrsinn"[83]. In einer charakteristischen Szene kommt es fast zur Aussprache zwischen den Ehepartnern. Elsi selbst äußert das Gefühl, Jebe früher schon gesehen zu haben, „vielleicht im Traum nur", doch statt die Gelegenheit einer Klärung seines lebensbestimmenden Problems zu ergreifen, wiegelt dieser ab und entwertet ihre Traumerinnerung, die seine eigene bestätigen könnte. Er verdrängt mit ‚rationalen' Argumenten genau das, woran er doch zugleich zu glauben scheint[84], so dass die Situation im Text ungeklärt bleibt – ganz im Sinne der Todorov'schen *hésitation*.[85]

Zum einen also markiert Jebes Geschichte Defizite der materialistischen Wissenschaft. Sein „phantastischer Zug" tritt in eine Lücke, die sein szientistisches Denken offen lässt und füllt ein „Vakuum [...], das die institutionalisierte Religion des Christentums hinterließ"[86]. Es sind vor allem die Fragen nach den ‚letzten Dingen', nach dem Tod und der Seele, auf die die Naturwissenschaft dezidiert keine Antwort geben kann und will. Die implizite Kritik des „Nichtchristen" Storm[87] am Agnostizismus der Naturwissenschaft reicht darüber jedoch hinaus. Die eigentlich dem Leben verpflichtete Medizin nämlich zeigt sich auf den Tod fixiert. Sie teilt die Objektivierung, die radikale Verdinglichung ihrer menschlichen ‚Gegenstände' mit den materialistischen Naturwissenschaften, und der Text sieht darin eine Neigung zur Mortifizierung. Der jugendliche Jebe macht sich auf die Suche nach dem „Geheimnis des Weibes", das er schon einmal mit dem Tod identifiziert hatte, und wird – Gynäkologe. Mit Blick auf seine pathologische Ausbildung resümiert er sarkastisch: „[A]n Leichnamen hatte ich den inneren Menschen kennen gelernt, so daß mir Alles klar vor Augen lag, und wie mit solchen rechnete ich mit den Lebendigen; was war da Großes zu bedenken!"[88] Retrospektiv erscheint diese pervertierte Ausrichtung der Lebenswissenschaft auf den Tod nicht nur in der moralischen Kategorie des „Frevels[s]"[89], sondern auch als pathologi-

---

82 Vgl. ebd., S. 633.

83 Ebd., S. 610.

84 Ebd., S. 606.

85 Gegen Wünsch (1992), Experimente Storms, S. 20-22, hat Küng (2015), *Krise der liberalen Anthropologie*, S. 32 f. u. ö., die Nähe der Erzählung zur Phantastik herausgestellt.

86 Yahya A. Elsaghe, „Sterbehilfe, Glaubensverlust und Religionsersatz in Theodor Storms ‚Bekenntnis'", in: *Zeitschrift für Religions- und Geistesgeschichte* 63, 1 (2011), S. 23-44: 36. Bestätigt wird die kompensatorische Funktion der „phantastischen Neigung" noch einmal am Ende von Jebes Leben. In seinem letzten Brief an den Rahmenerzähler kommt seine Hoffnung auf die Fortdauer der Seele zur Sprache, die seiner Vorstellung von einem „leeren Himmelsraum" widerspricht (Storm [1988], *Sämtliche Werke*, S. 629): „‚Die Kräfte sinken rasch [...] zugleich aber sehe ich vor mir das Tor zur Freiheit von anderer, ich weiß nicht von welcher Hand geöffnet – – o, meine Elsi! möchte es die deine sein!'" (Ebd., S. 633.)

87 Zur Auseinandersetzung um Storms religiöse Position vgl. Christian Demandt, *Religion und Religionskritik bei Theodor Storm*, Berlin, 2010, hier S. 18.

88 Storm (1988), *Sämtliche Werke*, S. 591.

89 Ebd.

scher Sachverhalt: Sie führt bildlogisch zur Fortpflanzungsunfähigkeit des kinderlosen Paars und schließlich zur todbringenden Krankheit. Der „heilige Keim", den das „Nachtgesicht" in Jebe bildet[90], wächst sich gleichsam im Leib der Frau aus, aber nicht zu einem Baby, sondern zu einem Karzinom am Uterus, dem Differenzorgan „des Weibes". Diese intrikate und mehrdeutige Konstellation ist in mancher Hinsicht nicht weniger ‚phantastisch' als die Wiederkehr eines Gespensts als Ehefrau. Sie zeigt gerade die Zukunftsunfähigkeit dessen, was sich „hochmütig"[91] als Fortschritt geriert, und auch darin mag eine Tendenz zur Wiederkehr des Vergangenen begründet sein.

Zum anderen produziert Jebes „phantastischer Zug" zugleich einen inneren Widerspruch, der seine gesamte Identität, und insbesondere die als aufgeklärter Wissenschaftler, bedroht. Das Phantastische lockt mit der Ergänzung des Eigenen und bedroht dieses zugleich mit Untergang und Selbstverlust. In diesem Licht nun muss die Frage, wie jemand dazu kommt, „sein Geliebtestes zu tödten", noch einmal neu gesehen werden. Es ist festzuhalten, dass der Text keinen Anlass zum Zweifel an Jebes Liebe zu seiner Frau, seinem Leiden an ihrem Tod und seinen Schuldgefühlen lässt. Zugleich aber gehorcht die Sterbehilfe untergründig derselben Verdrängungslogik wie Jebes Weigerung, Elsis Version der gemeinsamen Traumgeschichte an sich heranzulassen. Bezeichnenderweise erfolgen das ‚Übersehen' des wissenschaftlichen Artikels mit der Beschreibung der rettenden Operation[92], das Heraussuchen des Giftes[93] und schließlich dessen Verabreichung[94] in einem fast tranceartigen Zustand auf der Bewusstseinsschwelle: „ohne eine Absicht [...]. [I]ch kann nicht sagen, ob gedankenvoll oder gedankenlos"[95]. Auf der Ebene unbewusster Regungen, um deren Exploration es dem Text ganz offenkundig geht[96], lassen sich für die Tötung Elsis Motivationen feststellen, die etwas weniger altruistisch anmuten als der Wunsch, ihr Leiden abzukürzen. Offenbar geht es zugleich um den Ausschluss des gerade als solchen lockenden Fremden, Anderen, mythisch Naturhaften und „Phantastischen", das unmittelbar vor seiner Bewahrheitung zu stehen scheint und als etwas, das mehr ist als ein bloßes Gedankenexperiment, die eigene Identität fundamental bedroht.[97] In mancher Hinsicht realisiert Jebe mit Elsis Tötung nur, was er dem Bild des Weiblichen als dem Anderen immer schon beigelegt hatte, und darin begegnen sich die epochale Faszination von der weiblichen Leiche und die materialistische Mortifikationsneigung.

---

90 Ebd.
91 Ebd., S. 582.
92 Ebd., S. 608.
93 Ebd., S. 612.
94 Ebd., S. 614.
95 Ebd., S. 612.
96 Vgl. dazu auch Küng (2015), *Krise der liberalen Anthropologie*, S. 76-79 u. ö.
97 Verschiedene Varianten solcher Ausschlüsse bei Wünsch (1992), Experimente Storms, S. 22; Bernadette Malinowski, „Mimesis als Transgression. Gattungsdiskursive Untersuchungen zu Theodor Storms Bekenntnisnovelle ‚Ein Bekenntnis'", in: *Jahrbuch der Raabe-Gesellschaft*, 2003, S. 77-116: 102 f.; Küng (2015), *Krise der liberalen Anthropologie*, S. 78, S. 83 und S. 88.

Storms Erzählung stellt, so ließe sich ohne größere Übertreibung sagen, ihrer Epoche die Diagnose, und zwar mit den Mitteln der Phantastik. Zeigt Heyse einen zeittypischen Konflikt von Wirklichkeitskonzepten zwischen den verschiedenen Figuren seines Gesprächskreises, so hat sich dieser Konflikt bei Storm in den Protagonisten selbst verschoben, der als eine paradigmatische Gestalt der Moderne die ‚Nachtseiten' einer Wissenschaft vor Augen führt, die von dem träumt, was sie von sich abspaltet. Auf die angeblich flächendeckende „Entzauberung der Welt" (Max Weber) antworten Momente einer Wiederverzauberung, einer Fortdauer ‚archaischer' Überlebsel und eine Rückkehr von Magie und Mythos. „Keine Theorie der Moderne", schreibt Hartmut Böhme, „könnte falscher sein als die, welche Modernisierung mit linearem Rationalitätszuwachs identifiziert"[98]. Die Wissenschaft und der „phantastische Zug" gehören ebenso zusammen, wie sie sich ausschließen. Anders als Heyse interessiert sich Storm in erster Linie für die Widersprüche seiner Figur und den Eigen-Sinn ihres Unbewussten, ohne aber das Geschehen ganz ins Psychische auflösen zu wollen. Die Pathologisierung, die die Forschung gegenüber Storms Figur praktiziert hat[99], greift deshalb zu kurz, solange sie nicht die epochalen Züge ihres Befunds berücksichtigt. Der Realismus, der sich – in welcher Form auch immer – der Darstellung der ‚Wirklichkeit' seiner Zeit verschreibt, zeigt zunächst gerade diese Situation in ihren inneren Spannungen und unter Einschluss des kulturellen Imaginären, zu dem das Unheimliche und Gespenstische als mehr oder minder misstrauisch beäugte Überlebsel gehören. Zugleich findet in dieser Verhandlung von Konzepten des Wirklichen eine poetologische Selbstreflexion statt, insofern der Realismus hier gewissermaßen seine eigene Geschäftsgrundlage zur Debatte stellt. Während Heyse genau das in Szene setzt, dabei aber den Weltanschauungskonflikt zu vereindeutigen sucht – was bezeichnenderweise nicht vollständig gelingen will –, zieht Storm die literarische Konsequenz aus der epistemologischen Unsicherheit, indem er die verschiedenen Deutungsoptionen und Wirklichkeitskonzepte in der Schwebe lässt. Im Psychogramm des aufgeklärten Szientisten kommt nicht nur das Begehren nach einem ‚Romantisch'-Mythischen zum Vorschein, sondern auch die Frage, ob diesem nicht eine spezifische ‚Realität' zukomme. Der Text, der davon erzählt, hält diese Frage als unentschieden und unentscheidbar offen: „[W]as wissen wir denn auch von diesen Dingen!"[100] Wenn die phantastische Erzählliteratur Renate Lachmann zufolge das Verdrängte, Vergessene und Unbewusste einer Kultur artikuliert, dann tut Storms Novelle genau das, ja sie führt den Prozess von Verdrängung und Wiederkehr selbst noch vor und reagiert zudem in ihrer strukturellen Anlage auf die Problematik, die sie an ihrem Protagonisten analysiert. Das spricht nicht gegen den ‚Realismus' des Textes – im Gegenteil. Vielmehr ließe sich sagen, Storm greife die zeitgenössische Debatte um Konzepte von ‚Realität' auf und betreibe dabei eine

98 Böhme (2006), *Fetischismus und Kultur*, S. 24 f.

99 Z. B. David Jackson, „‚Ein Bekenntnis' – Theodor Storms frauenfreundliche Abrechnung mit einem mörderischen romantischen Liebesideal", in: *Schriften der Theodor-Storm-Gesellschaft* 50 (2001), S. 37-63: 40; Küng (2015), *Krise der liberalen Anthropologie*, S. 88 u. ö.

100 Storm (1988), *Sämtliche Werke*, S. 594.

Art tentativer Komplettierung eines sich dominant setzenden Verständnisses von ‚Wirklichkeit' um abweichende und ausgegrenzte Facetten. ‚Mimetisch-realistische' und ‚phantastische' Momente lassen sich in dieser Konstellation nicht mehr scharf voneinander trennen. Von der Wirklichkeit lässt sich vielleicht nicht anders erzählen als im Rückgriff auf das, was sie scheinbar aus sich ausschließt.

ELISABETH STROWICK

SZENISCHER REALISMUS: ZU STIFTERS *NARRENBURG*

Beginnen wir mit einer Szene aus Stifters *Narrenburg*, die – so peripher sie daherkommt – gleichwohl die Struktur und Dynamik von Stifters Realismus, wie ihn die Erzählung entwickelt, *in nuce* enthält. Es ist der schwindelerregende Auftritt Pias – des rätselhaften Kindes, das gemeinsam mit dem Greis Ruprecht in dem verwilderten Schlossgelände lebt –, welcher sich den Besuchern Heinrich und Robert wie folgt darstellt:

> „Ich falle nicht, siehe nur, ich falle nicht." Die Freunde blickten empor, und auf dem höchsten der vielen Balkone des zerfallenden Schlosses, auf einem Balkone, der so in der Luft draußen hing, als klebe er nur an einem einzigen Steine, war ein Kind – ja sogar nicht einmal auf dem Balkone, sondern auf dem Steingeländer desselben war es, halb sitzend, halb reitend, es schien ein Mädchen; [...] am äußersten Geländer saß sie und jauchzte, [...] sie stand auf, und schwebte nun stehend auf dem unsichtbar schmalen Stege des Geländers, und ging vorwärts und ging rückwärts, und neigte sich und beugte sich über, daß den Männern unten ein Schwindel und Grauen ankam, und daß ihnen die Augen vergingen.[1]

Erweckt die Passage zunächst den Anschein, es handele sich um den Auftritt eines handelnden Subjekts auf einem umgrenzten Schauplatz, das sich der Beobachtung durch eine Gruppe von Zuschauern darbietet, zeigt ein genauer Blick auf die Struktur der Szene diese weniger als Inszenierung von Sichtbarkeit und Präsenz denn als Apparatur von Transformation, Entgrenzung und Defiguration – ein Geschehen, das jegliche Beobachtung übersteigt. Die Betrachter erfasst „Schwindel und Grauen", die Augen vergehen ihnen. Eigentümlich eingerichtet erscheint hingegen das Kind in dem, was dem Betrachter als prekärer Balanceakt erscheinen muss – als wäre es selbst der Schwerkraft enthoben: „Ich falle nicht, [...] ich falle nicht." Und mit ihm untersteht auch die Szene nicht dem Gesetz der Gravitation, welche vielmehr als schwebender Schauplatz erscheint und entsprechend bewegliche Perspektiven generiert: Pia „schwebte nun stehend [...] und ging vorwärts und ging rückwärts, und neigte sich und beugte sich über": „‚Ich sehe hierhin, und dorthin, und sehe alle Mauern, alle Bäume und die ganze Welt.'" (372) – Der Auftritt Pias lässt nicht nur die Augen der Schlossbesucher vergehen, er vollzieht sich als sukzessive Verrückung der Szene auch vor den Augen der Leserin/des Lesers, nämlich im Medium der Schrift: Die fortwährende Verschiebung der Szene ge-

[1] Adalbert Stifter, *Die Narrenburg*, in: *Werke und Briefe. Historisch-Kritische Gesamtausgabe*, Band 1.4: *Studien. Buchfassungen 1*, hg. von Helmut Bergner und Ulrich Dittmann, Stuttgart (u. a.): Kohlhammer, 1980, S. 319-436: 372. Im Folgenden im laufenden Text zitiert.

schieht mittels der spezifischen Syntax des Satzes – eines einzigen Satzes wohlbemerkt. In der seriellen Syntax zweier ineinander geflochtener Stränge schraubt sich der Satz – einer doppelten Spirale gleich – vom Äußeren ins immer weiter Äußere und generiert damit die Szene als serielle Randstruktur. Hier der erste Strang:

> [...] auf dem höchsten der vielen Balkone des zerfallenden Schlosses – auf einem Balkone, der so in der Luft draußen hing, als klebe er nur an einem einzigen Steine – ja sogar nicht einmal auf dem Balkone, sondern auf dem Steingeländer desselben – am äußersten Geländer – auf dem unsichtbar schmalen Stege des Geländers [...]. (372)

In serieller Supplementierung und Korrektur strebt der Satz – und mit ihm die Szene – weiter und weiter in die Peripherie: vom höchsten Balkon über den im Außen hängenden Balkon zum Steingeländer desselben, weiter zum äußersten Geländer und hin zum „unsichtbar schmalen Stege des Geländers". Mit der Entfaltung der Szene vollzieht sich zugleich ihre sukzessive Entgründung. Keine Bühne, sondern schwindelerregende Haltlosigkeit stellt sich als privilegierter ‚Ort' des Auftritts dar, mit welchem die Figur konsequent in bzw. als Bewegung erscheint. Diesen Auftritt und die dynamische Figuration/Defiguration inszeniert der zweite Strang des Satzes – ein Auftritt, der sich entsprechend seriell vollzieht: „[...] war ein Kind – war es, halb sitzend, halb reitend – es schien ein Mädchen – saß sie und jauchzte – sie stand auf, und schwebte nun stehend – und ging vorwärts und ging rückwärts, und neigte sich und beugte sich über [...]" (372).

In der wechselseitig-seriellen Unterbrechung der zwei Stränge des Satzes entfaltet sich ein Schauplatz in Bewegung, die *Szene als abyme*, proliferierende Randstruktur ohne verankerndes Zentrum. Der Schauplatz, der sich hier eröffnet, ist ein *Schauplatz der Schrift* – erzeugt in der seriellen Dynamik der Schrift, die – von Intervall zu Intervall fortschreitend – keine fixe Perspektive, keine stabile Beobachterposition generiert, sondern den Blick, wo sie ihn in die multiple Randstruktur verlegt, dynamisiert, serialisiert. Was ein solcher Schauplatz/eine solche Szene hervorbringt, sind nicht Handlungen von Personen auf einer Bühne, sondern Erscheinungen. Wirkliches generiert sich in der Dynamik von Erscheinen/Verschwinden, wie sie auch der folgende Auftritt Pias in Szene setzt: „[...] – endlich verschwand sie plötzlich oben, [...] – und fast in dem nämlichen Augenblicke wurde sie unten auf dem Rasen sichtbar, wie sie durch eine kleine Bresche neben dem Himbeergesträuche heraustrat." (373)

Welchen Einsatz hat das Szenische, das Stifters *Narrenburg* durchzieht, für die Darstellung bzw. Konstitution des Wirklichen? Handelt es sich bei diesem schwindelerregenden, diesem *anderen* Schauplatz, den Stifter kreiert, um eine ‚Urszene' des Realismus, auf der sich Wirkliches als szenischer Effekt generiert? Und welcherart wäre dieses Wirkliche bzw. Reale? In der Tat fällt der Signifikant „wirklich" kurz vor der oben besprochenen Szene. Nicht erst durch Pias Auftritt, sondern schon durch seinen Eintritt in den Schlosskomplex mit seinen unzähligen und „närrischen" Gebäuden fühlt sich Heinrich der Wirklichkeit auf sonderbare Weise entrückt. Gegen diese Ent- bzw. Verrückung des Wirklichen verlangt es Heinrich nach „Umsicht", sprich: einem festen Standpunkt, welcher Wahrnehmung und Wirklichkeit in festen Koordinaten verankert.

> „Das ist ja ganz herrlich und närrisch," rief Heinrich, „wer hätte gedacht, daß eine solche Menge von Gebäuden auf diesem Berge Platz haben sollte, und daß noch die schönste Landschaftsdichtung zwischen ihnen und um sie liege. Mir ist es wie in einem uralten Märchen, alles so wunderlich, als läge die Fichtau gar nicht unten, in der ich doch gestern noch war. Komm, laß uns auf die äußerste Spitze dieser Zunge vorgehen, dort muß die schönste Umsicht sein, und ehe wir in all das Mauerwerk kriechen, wollen wir hintersehen auf das Land; ob es denn auch wirklich noch ist, wie gestern." (368)

Wie „närrisch" und „Landschaftsdichtung", so findet sich auch der Ausdruck „wirklich" nur in der Studienfassung, nicht in der Journalfassung[2] der *Narrenburg*. Im Vergleich zur Journalfassung – so ließe sich sagen – arbeitet Stifter in der Studienfassung die Epistemologie seines närrischen Realismus weiter aus. Wenn „wirklich" in der Formulierung „ob es denn auch *wirklich* noch ist, wie gestern [Herv. E. S.]" zweifellos Heinrichs Intention zum Ausdruck bringt, sich eines vertrauten Wirklichen zu vergewissern, so scheint in der Betonung des Wirklichen zum Zeitpunkt größter Verunsicherung zugleich ein *anderes Wirkliches* auf – ein Wirkliches, das sich dezidiert im Entschwinden eines (vertrauten) Wirklichen ein-, als Wirklichkeitsverlust darstellt – und wohl darum als närrisch, unvertraut, ja, *unheimlich* bezeichnet werden kann. In der Tat weisen die Szenen/Schauplätze eines solch *anderen Wirklichen*, wie sie Stifters *Narrenburg* durchziehen, die strukturelle Dynamik auf, welche Freud dem Unheimlichen attestieren wird: „Das Unheimliche", so Freud, „wäre eigentlich immer etwas, worin man sich sozusagen nicht auskennt."[3] „[E]s sei etwas eben darum schreckhaft, weil es *nicht* bekannt und vertraut ist. [Herv. i. O.]"[4] Allerdings ist nicht jedes Unvertraute unheimlich: „Zum Neuen und Nichtvertrauten muß erst etwas hinzukommen, was es zum Unheimlichen macht."[5] Das Supplement – und man kann getrost sagen: das ‚gefährliche Supplement' (Derrida) – das „hinzukommen" muss, um das Nichtvertraute zum Unheimlichen – zum *Unheimlich-Wirklichen* – zu machen, ist nichts anderes als ein szenisches Moment: „Unheimlich sei alles, was [...] im Verborgenen bleiben sollte und hervorgetreten ist."[6] Freud bezieht sich in dieser Beschreibung des Unheimlichen auf Schelling. Der Akt des Hervortretens ist von besonderer szenischer Qualität: Nicht um einen Auftritt *auf* einer Szene handelt es sich, sondern um die „*emergence of the scene as such*"[7], genauer: um das Hervortreten der

---

2 Adalbert Sifter, *Die Narrenburg*, in: *Werke und Briefe. Historisch-Kritische Gesamtausgabe*, Band 1.1: *Studien. Journalfassungen 1*, hg. von Helmut Bergner und Ulrich Dittmann. Stuttgart (u. a.): Kohlhammer, 1978, S. 301-403. Im Folgenden im laufenden Text mit der Sigle NJ zitiert.

3 Sigmund Freud, *Das Unheimliche*, in: *Studienausgabe*, Band IV, Frankfurt/M.: Fischer, 1970, S. 241-274: 244.

4 Ebd.

5 Ebd.

6 Ebd., S. 249.

7 So Samuel Weber über die Urszene in: ders., *The Legend of Freud*, Palo Alto, CA: Stanford University Press, 2000, S. 10.

Szene im Modus der „Entstellung“ (153), als *anderer Schauplatz*, Schauplatz eines *Unheimlich-Wirklichen*.[8]

Das *Szenisch-Wirkliche*, das in Stifters *Narrenburg* am Werk ist, ist von spezifischer Zeitlichkeit – auch diesbezüglich findet sich eine Korrespondenz zu Freuds *Unheimlichem*. Wenn Freud vom Unheimlichen als „ehemals Heimische[n], Altvertraute[n]“[9] spricht, „was im Verborgenen hätte bleiben sollen und hervorgetreten ist“[10], so charakterisiert er das *Unheimlich-Wirkliche* als Wiederkehr eines Vergangenen. Die intrikate Beziehung von Vergangenheit und Gegenwart kennzeichnet auch Stifters Szenisches. Die Szene, in welcher es Heinrich nach „Umsicht“ und Vertrautem verlangt, ist dezidiert zeitlicher Art: Nicht nur die Verunsicherung, in der es Heinrich ist „wie in einem uralten Märchen, alles so wunderlich, als läge die Fichtau gar nicht unten, in der [...] [er; E. S.] doch gestern noch war“ (368), auch die Vergewisserung trägt einen zeitlichen Index: „Wohl war das Land noch, wie gestern: grün und weich und ruhig lag die Fichtau [...] – alles bekannt und vertraut, eine holde Gegenwart, herumliegend um die unklare Vergangenheit, auf der sie standen.“ (368 f.) „Gegenwart“ und „Vergangenheit“ gewinnen hier eine szenische Dimension („Gegenwart, herumliegend“, „Vergangenheit, auf der sie standen“), sprich: die Szene verschaltet Gegenwart und Vergangenheit. Wenn Heinrichs Vergewisserung („alles bekannt und vertraut“) mit der feinsäuberlichen Trennung von Gegenwart und Vergangenheit einhergeht, so lässt die Szene doch keinen Zweifel daran, dass es sich hier nur um eine temporäre Trennung und Vergewisserung handelt: Das „noch“ in der Formulierung „[w]ohl war das Land noch“ (368)[11] hält den Schauplatz in ambivalenter Schwebe, kündigt es doch die Verschiebung des Verhältnisses zwischen Gegenwart und Vergangenheit und mit dieser eine entsprechend andere Konfiguration der Szene an. Das Unklare, Verworrene, das in Heinrichs Perspektive der Vergangenheit zugeschlagen wird („unklare Vergangenheit“), trägt die Erzählung konsequent in das Verhältnis von Gegenwart und Vergangenheit ein, womit jegliche „holde Gegenwart“ obsolet ist, und Gegenwart nurmehr noch als unheimliche erscheint. Emblematisch hierfür ist die sonderbare ‚Figur‘ Ruprechts, des Schloss-Kastellans, dessen Gegenwart in der Studienfassung explizit als „unheimlich“ beschrieben wird: „[M]ir wird es unheimlich in der Gegenwart dieses alten Mannes“ (378), so Heinrich zu seinem Begleiter. „Gegenwart“ ist hier durchaus auch zeitlich, als Präsens, zu lesen, denn „der Alte“ (391) scheint in anderen, längst vergangenen Zeiten zu leben. In solch zeitlicher (statt figurativer) Lesart nimmt die ‚Gegenwart des Alten‘ dezidiert Züge von Freuds Unheimlichem an. Wenn im Gegenwärtigen das Alte wiederkehrt, sprich: Gegenwärtiges zur Wiederkehr wird, stellt sich Gegenwart nicht als Präsenz, sondern

---

8 In anderem Zusammenhang spricht Freud auch von einer „Wirklichkeit von etwas Unbekanntem“ (Sigmund Freud, *Aus der Geschichte einer infantilen Neurose* [„Der Wolfsmann“], in: *Studienausgabe*, Band VIII, Frankfurt/M.: Fischer, 1969, S. 125-231: 153).

9 Freud (1970), *Das Unheimliche*, S. 267.

10 Ebd., S. 264.

11 Die Journalfassung zeigt keinen epistemischen Zweifel, lautet die Passage dort doch: „Freilich lag das Land unten wie gestern.“ (NJ 352)

vielmehr als heterochroner Schauplatz der Genese eines Unheimlich-Wirklichen dar.

Die folgende Lektüre geht Stifters szenischem Realismus und seinen unheimlichen Wirklichkeitseffekten in verschiedenen Hinsichten nach: mit Blick auf die erratischen Präsentationen des Alten, dem gespenstischen Performativ der Schrift[12] sowie dem szenischen Erzählverfahren der *Narrenburg*, wie es u. a. in der Rahmentechnik zur Geltung kommt. Welche ‚Schauplätze der Schrift' entwickelt die Erzählung und welche Wirklichkeitseffekte generieren diese? Wenn das Wirkliche, das sich dabei abzeichnet, als Närrisches, Gespenstisch-Unheimliches, kurz: Szenisches erscheint, dann ist es eben diese epistemische Unsicherheit, der Wirklichkeits‚verlust', die/der es allererst zum Wirklichen macht.

1. Szenische Bild-Akte – szenische Sprech-Akte: Wiederkehr und Ent-setzung

Die augenfälligste szenische Darstellung findet sich zweifellos in der Führung durch die Ahnengalerie, den „grünen Saal" (382), welche der Schloss-Kastellan den Besuchern Heinrich und Robert gibt. Die Gemälde – in für Stifter charakteristischer Reihung („[...] – – und andere und wieder andere – eine ganze Reihe" [383]), lassen sich nicht von ihrer Inszenierung trennen, die der Alte mit großer Geschicklichkeit auszuführen weiß. Auch der Saal dient einzig dem Zweck der Präsentation der Bilder, ist mit anderen Worten wesentlich Bühnenraum, in dem die Gemälde zur Wirkung kommen:

> [D]aß der Gründer dieser Anstalt nicht die Bilder des Saales wegen aufgestellt, sondern daß dieser in seiner ungeheuren Größe und einfachen Pracht nur zur Verherrli-

12 Insbesondere mit Blick auf das Performativ der Schrift schließt meine Lektüre an Christian Begemanns Arbeiten an, welche die Inszenierung von Genealogie in der *Narrenburg* dezidiert an das Medium, die „Kulturtechnik" Schrift, knüpfen (Christian Begemann, „Das Verhängnis der Schrift", in: *Adalbert Stifter, Die Narrenburg*, Salzburg, Wien: Residenz Verlag, 1996, S. 121-143; ders., *Die Welt der Zeichen: Stifter-Lektüre*, Stuttgart, Weimar: Metzler, 1995, bes. S. 242-259). Stimmt meine Lektüre mit der Charakterisierung der Schrift als Medium von Übertragung und Genealogie wie auch mit Begemanns Beobachtung überein, dass in der *Narrenburg* „die verrückten Urheber und Referenten der Schrift als Untote, als Wiedergänger und Dämonen" (Begemann (1995), *Welt der Zeichen*, S. 244) erscheinen, so schlägt sie im Vergleich zu Begemanns strukturalistischem Schriftbegriff und den ihn grundierenden Oppositionen wie auch zu der am Bildungsideal ausgerichteten Konzeption von Wirklichkeit einen entschieden anderen Weg ein. Nicht soll im Folgenden die Inszenierung der Schrift in der *Narrrenburg* einem normativen Bildungsideal unterworfen oder an einem diesem verpflichteten Wirklichkeitsbegriff gemessen werden, vielmehr dient sie als Ausgangspunkt zur Eruierung von Stifters Epistemologie des Wirklichen. – Zur Genealogie in Stifters *Narrenburg* vgl. auch Sigrid Weigel, „Zur Dialektik von Generation und Geschlecht um 1800. Stifters *Narrenburg* als Schauplatz von Umbrüchen im genealogischen Denken", in: Ohad Parnes/Ulrike Vedder/Sigrid Weigel/Stefan Willer (Hg.), *Generation: Zur Genealogie des Konzepts – Konzepte von Genealogie*, München: Fink, 2005, S. 109-124, welche Begemanns „Entgegensetzung von Biologie und Schrift" in „Das Verhängnis der Schrift" kritisiert (S. 111) und den Akzent stattdessen auf das „subtile[] Zusammenspiel von leiblicher Reproduktion und verschiedenen Kulturtechniken wie Schrift, Bild und Architektur" (ebd.) in Stifters Text legt.

> chung jener dienen sollte. So war auch im ganzen wüsten Zimmer nicht ein einziges Geräthstück; bloß an Fenstervorhängen waren die mannigfaltigsten behutsamsten Vorrichtungen, um theils die verschiedensten Lichterspiele auf die Gemälde wirken lassen zu können, theils dieselben vor unmitttelbarer Sonne zu schützen. Und wie sehr Ruprecht mit der Sache vertraut war, und sie liebte, zeigte der Umstand, daß er oft durch unbedeutende gelegentliche Züge an Schnüren oder Federn ganze entfernte Bilderreihen plötzlich in das zarteste Licht legte, da sie vorher in ungünstiger Dämmerung geschwebt hatten. (383 f.)

Neben dem Saal als Bühne umfasst Stifters theatrale Apparatur Vorhänge und Vorrichtungen, mit denen sich Lichtspiele erzeugen und derart Betrachtungseffekte generieren lassen, in denen die Bilder abwechselnd erscheinen und verschwinden. Auch als der Greis schließlich das Bild Sixtus II. präsentiert, liegt der Schwerpunkt ganz auf der Herstellung szenischer Effekte: Er „drückte gegen eine Feder, und zum Erstaunen der Männer sprang der Serpentin los – [...] Sie sahen nun, daß der Stein bloß auf eine Kupfertafel gemalt war, daß sich diese völlig umlege, und noch ein Bild entblöße, das sie vorher gedeckt hatte [...] ‚Sixtus II.'" (390 f.) Mit der Präsentation des Bildes tritt zugleich die frappierende Ähnlichkeit oder präziser: unheimliche Doppelung – von Sixtus II. und Heinrich als szenischer Effekt hervor: „Allein das Bild war das Heinrichs Zug für Zug, nur in fremden Kleidern." (391)

Zeigt sich schon an der Präsentation der Bilder, dass Stifters *Narrenburg,* insofern sie unheimliche Verdoppelungen sowie eine Dynamik von Erscheinen/Verschwinden in Szene setzt, mit der Logik von Repräsentation bricht, so hat auch die Konzeption der Bilder nichts mit der Logik von Repräsentation gemein[13], ja, lädt vielmehr dazu ein, Bild als szenische Apparatur/Dynamik zu denken: „Vorzügliche Gemälde waren alle, obwohl sie augenscheinlich viel später gemalt wurden, als die Urbilder lebten, aber wahrscheinlich nach vorhandenen, wenn auch schlechten Originalen, denn dafür sprach der in allen Gesichtern der Männer fortgehende Familienzug." (383)

Unmissverständlich streicht diese Passage jegliches der Darstellung vorgängiges Wirkliche oder Leben aus. Zugleich erweist sich Darstellung als seriell gestaffelt, Abbildung von Abbildung: Keiner der porträtierten Vorfahren hat hier Modell gesessen; die „vorzüglichen Gemälde" sind vielmehr nach anderen Gemälden, „schlechten Originalen", gemalt, und zwar posthum in einem spezifischen Sinne, „viel später [...] als die Urbilder lebten". Das Bild referiert nicht auf Leben, sondern ist als Urbild selbst mit Leben ausgestattet. Leben ist in Darstellung eingetragen, womit diese gespenstische Züge annimmt und sich zugleich Leben – im Reigen serieller Darstellung – ins Untote transformiert. Über die Ausstreichung von Referenz und Ausrichtung von Bildlichkeit auf serielle Darstellung – Abbild von Abbild – wird (dargestellte) Wirklichkeit zum Simulakrum, zum gespenstisch-szenischen Wirklichkeitseffekt. Dieser zeigt sich auch im szenisch-unheimlichen Hervortreten der Doppelfiguration Sixtus II./Heinrich, angesichts derer sich nicht sagen lässt, ob

---

13 Zur Performativität der Bilder in Stifters *Narrenburg* vgl. auch Tove Holmes, *Literary Images: Viewing and Visuality in German Realism* (unveröff. Dissertation, Johns Hopkins University, Baltimore, MD, 2011), S. 107-148.

Heinrich der Nachkomme von Sixtus II. ist oder umgekehrt. Bezeichnet bereits der Erzähler das Bild Sixtus II. als dasjenige Heinrichs: „Allein das Bild war das Heinrichs Zug für Zug, nur in fremden Kleidern“ (391), so betont auch Heinrich später die unheimliche, heterochrone Alterität des Bildes resp. Ichs: „[W]ie ich auf jenem Bilde in längst verschollenen Kleidern stehe“ (399). Die szenische Präsentation lässt sich präzise als Bild-Akt im performativen Sinne bezeichnen: „So, jetzt ist Alles geschehen, und gesehen, sagte er [der Alte; E. S.] und trat zurück.“ (393) Sehen ist Geschehen, Bild ist Akt/Vollzug: Mit dem szenischen Doppel Sixtus II./Heinrich, das die Unterscheidung von Bild und Betrachter unterläuft, hat man eine Art gespenstisches Spiegelstadium vor sich: zweifellos ein transformatorischer Akt – nicht jedoch im Sinne einer jubilatorischen Setzung eines vorgeblich integren Ichs, sondern einer unheimlichen Ent-setzung, gespenstischen Defiguration, über die sich Nachkommen als einander wechselseitig vorgängig/nachträgliche Wiedergänger generieren.

So verwirrend diese Szene für Heinrich und Robert ist, so bemerkenswert klar ist der Alte. Wenn „der wahnwitzige Greis“, der „einzige“ ist, „der völlig klar“ (391) ist, dann weil die szenische Darstellung und die durch sie generierte spektrale Wirklichkeit in nichts der Logik des „Wahnwitze[s]“ (380) nachstehen, die der Greis verkörpert. Strukturell und in den Worten des Alten heißt dies: Wiederkehr und Ent-setzung. Als sich die Freunde noch vor der Enthüllung des Bildes Sixtus II. zum Gehen wenden wollen, interveniert der Alte mit scharfen Worten: „‚Aber wie seid ihr denn?‘ rief er mit heftiger Stimme, ‚wozu habe ich euch denn hergeführt? Wozu seid ihr denn zurückgekehrt?‘“ (390) Mit seinem Einwurf benennt der Alte Heinrich als „zurückgekehrt“, sprich: *revenant.* Die Position des Zurückkehrenden wird noch genauer markiert. Es ist die des Verworfenen:

> Alle sind sie da [...] nur *einer* war verworfen, – ich habe ihn immer sehr geliebt, und dachte, es soll nicht so sein – seht nun: ich war es, der es machte, daß ihr schon im Saale standet, als er [Jodok; E. S.] noch lebte, aber er wußte es nicht, er ging hinüber und wußte es nicht. – – [Herv. i. O.]“ (390).

Noch mit einer anderen Formulierung des Alten lässt sich das szenische Geschehen beschreiben. Die Worte der Warnung Ruprechts an Heinrich, bevor er diesem das Bild Chelions zeigt: „[I]hr werdet euch entsetzen“ (386), lassen sich als präzise Beschreibung der strukturellen Dynamik des Bild-Aktes lesen – eine Ent-setzung, in der nicht nur das Subjekt *sich ent-setzt,* sondern die auch die transformative Kraft der *Szene als ent-setzte* markiert. Die Führung durch den „grünen Saal“ ist nicht interessierte Bildbetrachtung, sondern szenische Transformation, aus der Heinrich als Nachkomme hervorgeht. Wenn er den „grünen Saal“ verlässt, dann *in sich ent-setzt,* der Reihe der Nachkommen wie der Welt der Simulakren einverleibt, ein Untoter, ein Wiedergänger. Auch dies kann den Alten in keinster Weise erschüttern, sind doch die ver-rückten Koordinaten der *Narrenburg* eben diese, wie auch die folgende Passage zeigt:

> Heinrich trat einige Schritte weg, aber der wahnwitzige Kastellan folgte ihm sachte mit glänzenden Augen: „Er hätte euch über den Stein hinabgestürzt – ihr seid aber

> auch viel schöner, als er es je gewesen [...] ihr waret fort – – es ist sehr gut, daß ihr fort waret – – [...] alle sind gestorben, die arme Chelion starb, mein Weib Bertha starb, ihr starbet, und wie er das Schloss angezündet hatte, und unten im Häuschen auch todt lag [...] Alle sind todt – – ...“ (388).

Dass alle, inklusive Sixtus II./Heinrich tot sind, heißt im selben Zuge: ‚Alle sind untot.‘ Stifters *Narrenburg* gebiert eine Welt von Wiedergängern. Die konsequente Adressierung Heinrichs als Sixtus II. im Sprechen des Alten evoziert die nämliche Doppelung/Wiederkehr/Ent-setzung, die sich auch im szenischen Bild-Akt Sixtus II./Heinrich zeigt; und so lassen sich auch die Sprechakte des Greises als szenisch bezeichnen.

Hatte Robert den Alten zunächst für harmlos gehalten („er ist ja übrigens ganz harmlos“ [378]), so gewinnt das Gefühl des Unheimlichen bald die Oberhand. Wie bereits zitiert, ist es Heinrich „unheimlich in der Gegenwart dieses alten Mannes“ (378), und auch die Freude, mit der der Alte die Vorrichtungen zur szenischen Präsentation der Bilder bedient, ist als „unheimliche Freude“ (390) beschrieben. Dass der Zeitsprung, die wechselseitige Durchdringung von bzw. der bruchlose Wechsel zwischen Vergangenheit und Gegenwart, dafür grundlegend ist, sagt der Text explizit. So heißt es über Heinrichs Reaktion auf den Alten:

> [Heinrich; E. S.] zitterte fast, nur um ein Haar breit in der verdunkelten Seele des Andern weiter zu forschen, um sie nicht noch tiefer zu zerrütten. Die Verrückung jener Gesetze, auf deren Dasein im Haupte jedes Andern man mit Zuversicht baut, [...] trägt etwas so Grauenhaftes an sich, daß man sich nicht getraut, das fremdartige Uhrwerk zu berühren, daß es nicht noch grellere Töne gebe, und uns an dem eigenen irre mache. (380)

Als „fremdartiges Uhrwerk“ bezeichnet die Passage die „aberwitzige Vermittlung“ (386) des Alten, die – wie anhand seines Sprechens und der Präsentation der Gemälde gesehen – eine grundsätzlich szenische ist. Die „Verrückung“ der Zeit, der Zeitsprung als buchstäbliches Zerspringen der Zeit, ist mit anderen Worten *das* Charakteristikum des Szenischen in Stifters Realismus. Mit der närrisch-szenischen Darstellung setzt Stifters Realismus nicht auf Verstehen, sondern auf Performanz: auf die Erzeugung unheimlicher Wirklichkeitseffekte, mit denen sich Gegenwart/Wirklichkeit als Wiederkehr darstellt. Und so steht zu erwarten, dass sich die närrische Szenografie nicht in Ruprechts Auftritten erschöpft, sondern auch in Stifters Erzählverfahren am Werk ist, dessen szenischer Beschaffenheit ich im Folgenden nachgehen will. In der Tat ist die *Narrenburg* durchzogen von Akten des Ein-, Auf- und Hervortretens, installiert sie wiedergängernde Szenen als Träger des Erzählens und produziert *qua* komplexer Rahmentechnik serielle Szenen.

2. Eintreten: Szenische Randstruktur

Die Frage des Eintritts in die Szene könnte nicht prominenter inszeniert sein. Fast wähnt man sich in Kafkas Welt, mit dem labyrinthischen, durch fortwährendes

Graben veränderten Bau, den seriellen Fluchten des Schlosskomplexes und einem sonderbar agierenden Türhüter: „‚Ich werde öffnen‘, so der Alte zu den Schloßbesuchern, ‚denn ich halte immer gesperrt.‘ Und er drehte große Schlüssel in dem knarrenden Schlosse – aber es war lächerlich, zu schließen, wo nichts zu verschließen war; denn alle Mauern klaften“ (373 f.).

Das Szenische des Schlosskomplexes ist deutlich markiert: Dieser ist aus der „übrigen Welt heraus[geschnitten]“, „umfangen“ durch eine „graue Eisenmauer“ (367), an der kein Eingang zu finden ist. Der „Eintritt“ (361) in das Schloss, das „weder Thor noch Eingang hat“ (332), gestaltet sich entsprechend sonderbar:

> Vergeblich rief Robert: „He, Holla! *ich* bin es, der Sindikus, den du einzulassen versprochen.“ Es erfolgte keine Antwort. Nur sah Heinrich, da er zufällig emporblickte, am Mauerrande ein Haupt: Gesicht und Haare so grau, wie daneben die uralte Steinmetzarbeit. [...] Nach einer Weile verschwand es, und kurz darauf hörte man ein seltsames Aechzen und Knarren in der Mauer, und zum Erstaunen des Wanderers schob sich ein Stück derselben gleichsam ineinander, und es wurde die dunkle Mündung eines Pförtchens sichtbar, darinnen, wie in einem Rahmen, eine große Gestalt stand, dieselben steingrauen Gesichtszüge tragend, die Heinrich auf der Mauer gesehen hatte, nur ein Lächeln war jetzt auf ihnen, so seltsam, wie wenn im Spätherbste ein einsamer Lichtstrahl über Felsen gleitet. [Herv. i. O.] (364)

Kein Akteur – und zweifellos kein menschliches Wesen – steht hinter dem Akt des Öffnens, den das Sichineinanderschieben bzw. die Einfaltung der Mauer bewirkt. Die Schließung erfolgt gleichfalls durch den „Mechanismus der Mauer. Es hob wie eine ablaufende Turmuhr zu schnarren an, schwenkte herum, und schloss sich, so dass der Ort kaum zu erkennen war, durch den sie hereingekommen.“ (364 f.) Die als Grenze figurierte Mauer stellt sich als Dynamik von Öffnung/Schließung dar; die erzählheoretische Formulierung folgt auf dem Fuße: Die Mauer erscheint als Rahmen („wie in einem Rahmen“) – ein Schwellenort, eine Randstruktur, in der die *agency* des Szenischen liegt. So wenig sich Ein- und Ausgang konturieren, so prekär ist der Akt der Figuration, der sich – gleichfalls am „Mauer*rande*“ – abzeichnet: ein „Haupt“ so „grau“ wie der Stein, das bald wieder verschwindet, eine „Gestalt“, „dieselben steingrauen Gesichtszüge tragend, die Heinrich auf der Mauer gesehen hatte, nur ein Lächeln war jetzt auf ihnen, [...] wie wenn im Spätherbste ein einsamer Lichtstrahl über Felsen gleitet.“ Mit diesen Formulierungen bleibt ambivalent, ob Gesichtszüge und Lächeln dem Stein zukommen oder der Gestalt, die sich nur unvollständig aus diesem löst. Die steinernen Züge („versteinerten Züge“ [366]) – Schriftzüge zweifellos – lassen keine klare Figur-Grund-Unterscheidung zu, sondern operieren im Modus von Mimikry[14], d. h. von Defiguration.

---

14 Ich beziehe mich hier auf Roger Caillois' *Mimicry and Legendary Psychasthenia* (1935), der – entgegen der These, es handle sich bei der Mimikry um eine Abwehrreaktion und Form der Selbsterhaltung – selbige als einen „gefährlichen Luxus“ (ders., „Mimese und legendäre Psychasthenie“, in: ders., *Méduse & Cie*, aus dem Französischen von Peter Geble, Berlin: Brinkmann & Bose, 2007, S. 25-43: 33), eine „*Versuchung durch den Raum* [Herv. i. O.]“ (ebd., S. 35), als eine „*Angleichung an die Umgebung* [Herv. i. O.]“ (ebd.), „des Belebten an das Unbelebte“ (ebd., S. 38) konzipiert. Mit Bezug auf Caillois bezeichnet Lacan Mimikry als „the derealizing effect of an obsession with space“ (Jacques Lacan, „The

Nicht weniger unheimlich stellt sich der Akt des Eintretens dar, der nicht nur vom Erklingen der Töne des Untoten begleitet ist, sondern zudem auf eine Szene führt, die von der ‚Präsenz' von Niemandem zeugt:

> Sie traten ein, und in demselben Augenblicke ging ein fürchterlicher, ein zärtlich gewaltiger Ton über ihren Häuptern durch die Luft. „Es ist nur die Geige des Prokopus," sagte der alte Mann, „schreitet herein, Erlaucht, in die Stadt des alten Geschlechts." Bei diesen Worten verbeugte er sich gegen Stellen, wo Niemand stand – (364).

Überdies überrascht die räumliche Beschaffenheit der Szene. Kein Schlossplatz – also in szenischer Lesart: kein(e) zentrale(r) Schauplatz/Bühne – findet sich; stattdessen führt der Eintritt erneut in ein Außen, in welchem sich der Schloss*komplex* als Labyrinth und proliferierende Randstruktur darbietet.

> Die Freunde standen aber nun innerhalb der Mauer nicht etwa auf einem Schloßplatze oder dergleichen, sondern wieder im Freien, und vor ihnen stieg der Berg sachte weiter hinan, nur war seiner Senkung ein breites, weites rätselhaftes Vieleck abgewonnen, auf dem sie sich eben befanden; es war mit Quadersteinen gepflastert, aber aus den Fugen trieb üppiges Gras hervor [...] [A]us den Randsimsen quollen Halme und dürre Blümchen (365).
> Es war Alles viel [...] weiter, und auch verworrener, als er gedacht hatte. Ein ganzes Geschlecht mußte durch Jahrhunderte hindurch auf diesem Berge gehauset, gegraben und gebaut haben. Abgesonderte Bauwerke, gleichsam selber wieder Schlösser, standen auf verschiedenen Punkten (366 f.).
> [V]on dem eigentlichen Schlosse aber war nichts zu erblicken als graues Dachwerk, [...] von kreisenden Mauerschwalben umflogen (365).

Die Szene hat kein Zentrum, sondern strebt in die Peripherie: ein „Vieleck", zerstreute Schlösser an „verschiedenen Punkten", eine durch unablässiges Graben und Bauen erzeugte Weite und Verwirrung, die auf kein Ende angelegt scheint, die kreisende Bewegung von Mauerschwalben. In diesem dynamischen Geschehen kommt den Rändern und Fugen besondere Produktivität zu: „[A]us den Randsimsen" *quellen* Halme und Blumen, „aus den Fugen" *treibt* üppiges Gras. Mit ‚Quellen' und ‚Treiben' ist die szenische Kraft benannt, die sich als proliferierende Randstruktur fortzeugt – eine serielle Szene, die wie die Zeit buchstäblich aus den Fugen ist (*the scene*/„the time is out of joint"[15]). Die Perspektive, die sich mit dieser dynamischen (Schreib-)Szene eröffnet, ist keine „Umsicht" (368), nach der es Heinrich verlangt hatte, sondern die multiple Perspektive partialisierter („wovon

---

Mirror Stage as Formative of the *I* Function as Revealed in Psychoanalytic Experience", in: *Écrits*, übers. von Bruce Fink, New York, NY, London: W. W. Norton, 2006, S. 75-81: 77). Was Mimikry betreibt, ist m. a. W. eine radikale Destabilisierung der Figur-Grund-Unterscheidung – mit Rosalind Krauss gesprochen: „an effacement of the figure. Ground on ground." (Rosalind Krauss, *The Optical Unconscious*, Cambridge, MA: MIT Press, 1994, S. 155).

[15] Vgl. Jacques Derrida, *Marx' Gespenster. Der Staat der Schuld, die Trauerarbeit und die neue Internationale*, aus dem Französischen von Susanne Lüdemann, Frankfurt/M.: Fischer Taschenbuch Verlag, 1996, bes. S. 45-55.

er nur einen Theil gesehen" [367]), beweglicher Blicke. Was sich darbietet, ist eine in räumlicher wie zeitlicher Hinsicht zersplitterte, multiple Szene.

Ich arbeite hier die Lesart des Schlosskomplexes als Schriftkomplex, wie sie sich auch bei Christian Begemann findet[16], hin auf die Frage des Szenischen – was heißt: eines Dynamisch-Szenischen – aus. Schauplatz der Schrift, ist die Szene eine dezidiert literarische Szene: Wenn die Studienfassung von „Landschaftsdichtung" spricht, so benennt sie die Szene explizit als literarische. Auch die Journalfassung tut dies, welche anstelle von „Landschaftsdichtung" von „Dichterchaos" spricht und überdies das „Wirken", welches man mit Nietzsche als das „Wesen der Wirklichkeit"[17] ansehen mag, als Charakteristikum des Literarisch-Szenischen hervorhebt:

> [E]in unabsehliches Feld von Wirken und Schaffen that sich auf, und von Genießen und Schwärmen für seine [Heinrichs; E. S.] arbeitende, närrrische Phantasie, der ein solches Dichtungschaos, wie dieser Berg, gerade willkomen war. Er mußte von der Platte weggehen: denn ein Wirrsal und ein Getümmel von Plänen und Gedanken kam schon in sein Haupt, die sich schoben und drehten und noch keine Gestalt hatten. (NJ 350 f.)

Die Szene als bewegter Schauplatz, Schreib-Szene, wie sie der Schlosskomplex darstellt, findet ihre Allgorie in einer weiteren Szene – der unermüdlichen Tätigkeit des Wabenbaus der Bienen im Sixtusbau:

> [A]us einigen zerbrochenen Scheiben desselben wogte es von Bienen aus und ein, und so viel man durch das trübe Glas erkennen mochte, war der Gang, insbesondere die Nischen abenteuerlich mit riesenhaften Waben bebaut, und die allergrößte Thätigkeit herrschte fort, daß es einem ordentlich im Kopfe wirrte und schwirrte, je länger man dem Treiben dieses Knäuels [...] zusah (378).

Permanente Bewegung, Tätigkeit, Wirken, findet das Bauen und Treiben des Geschlechtes der Scharnasts im Bauen und Treiben der Bienen seine Korrespondenz, und wie *jene* Szene (der Schlosskomplex) versetzt auch *diese* (Bienenstock) die Betrachung in ein Wirren und Schwirren. Dabei ist kein Ende je in Sicht: „[A]ber ich lasse sie fortbauen, und es sind schon manche Schwärme in die Fichtau hinausgeflogen" (378). So wenig wie die Bienen oder das Geschlecht der Scharnasts wird die Erzählung müde, die Szene *in actio* zu zeigen – denn, wie gesagt: kein Mensch ist hier Träger von Handlung („Auf dem ganzen Weg erblickten sie kein einziges menschliches Wesen. [...] Aber nirgends war ein Mensch."[366]), sondern das Szenische selbst, dessen seriell-dämonischen Taten des Erzählens ich im Folgenden nachgehen will.

---

16 Begemann bezeichnet „die ganze Anlage" als „ein überdimensionales Aufzeichnungssystem, eine Schrift der Steine" (Begemann (1995), *Welt der Zeichen*, S. 224).

17 „[D]aß das ganze Wesen der Wirklichkeit eben nur Wirken ist" (Friedrich Nietzsche, *Die Philosophie im tragischen Zeitalter der Griechen*, Fragment 1873, in: *Kritische Studienausgabe*, Band 1, München, Berlin, New York, NY: de Gruyter, 1999, S. 824).

2.1 *„Dämon der Thaten" – szenische Wiederkehr*

Es ist eine spezifische Konzeption von Tat/Handlung, welche die *Narrenburg* entwickelt und überdies in ihrem szenischen Erzählverfahren praktiziert. Begründet wird dieses Performativ von dem „lächerliche[n] Fideikommiß" (321) Hanns von Scharnasts, das alle Nachkommen auf die Schrift verpflichtet. Der Erbe, so verfügt es das Fideikommiss, habe nicht nur sämtliche Lebensbeschreibungen seiner Vorfahren zu lesen, überdies ist das eigene Leben vollständig in Schrift zu überführen („von der Zeit seiner ersten Erinnerung an bis zu jener, da er nur noch die Feder zu halten im Stande war" [321]) und „Heft für Heft" (321) im Archiv zu hinterlegen. Nachkommenschaft wird derart zum komplexen Aufschreibesystem: Mit dem Eintritt in selbiges wird Leben zum Akt des Lesens und Schreibens. Nicht zu trennen ist dabei der Akt des Lesens von dem des Schreibens, ja, es ist eben in der Überführung vom Lesen (anderer Leben) ins Schreiben (des eigenen), dass die Schrift Nachkommenschaften generiert:

> [S]elbst die, welche bisher ein stilles und manierliches Leben geführt hatten, schlugen in dem Augenblicke um, als sie in den Besitz der verwetterten Burg kamen, und die Sache wurde immer ärger, je mehr Besitzer bereits gewesen waren, und mit je mehr Wust sich der Kopf anfüllen mußte (322 f.).

Der Stiftungsakt – die Verpflichtung auf Lesen und Schreiben – setzt eine proliferierende Dynamik der Schrift in Gang, welche das/die Leben affiziert und entsprechend närrische Nachkommen hervorbringt.

Qua Untrennbarkeit von Lesen und Schreiben schleust das Fideikommiss vergangene Leben in das ‚eigene' ein, das sich mithin als heimgesuchtes, gespenstisches erfährt, wie es zugleich vergangene Taten je wieder neu belebt/wiederholt. Jodoks Aufzeichnungen geben eine präzise Analyse dieser gespenstischen Implikationen der Schrift: Nicht nur sind die Taten nicht die eigenen, das Leben weicht zudem dem Untoten: „Was ich hier schreibe, bin nicht ich – mich kann ich nicht schreiben, sondern nur, was es durch mich that." (410) Deutlicher kann der Bruch mit dem Autobiografischen nicht artikuliert werden. Was die Lebensbeschreibung eruiert, ist, „was es durch mich that". Das Schreibprojekt gilt nicht dem Ich, sondern der Tat/dem Tun, die/das nicht die/das ‚eigene' ist, sondern jeglichen ‚Thäter' „hinter dem Thun, Wirken, Werden"[18] zugunsten von – mit Deleuze gesprochen – „unpersönlichen und präindividuellen Singularitäten, das *man* des reinen Ereignisses, in dem *es* stirbt wie *es* regnet"[19] suspendiert: „[W]as *es* durch mich that. [Herv. E. S.]" Das Fideikommiss generiert einen „Dämon der Thaten" – Taten mit kollektiver Urheberschaft und seriellem Fortgang, welche sich im Bereich des Un-

---

[18] „[E]s giebt kein ‚Sein' hinter dem Thun, Wirken, Werden; der ‚Thäter' ist zum Thun bloss hinzugedichtet, – das Thun ist Alles." (Friedrich Nietzsche, *Zur Genealogie der Moral*, in: *Kritische Studienausgabe*, Band 5, München, Berlin, New York; NY: de Gruyter, 1999, S. 245-412: 279.)

[19] Gilles Deleuze, *Logik des Sinns*, aus dem Französischen von Bernhard Dieckmann, Frankfurt/M.: Suhrkamp, 1993, S. 190.

toten ansiedeln und sowohl die früheren wie die nachfolgenden Leben ins Untote einrücken: „[I]ch gehe dem Engel meiner schwersten That entgegen", so Jodok,

> und aus den Pergamenten des rothen Felsensaales kam dieser Engel zu mir. Dort liegen die Schläfer, von ihrem Ahnherrn verurtheilt, daß sie nicht sterben können; eine schauderhaft durcheinanderredende Gesellschaft liegt dort, vor jedem Ankömmling müssen sie ihre Thaten wieder neu thun, sie seien groß oder klein; – diese Thaten, genug, sie waren ihr Leben, und verzehrten dieses Leben. (411)

Wie die stets zu wiederholenden Taten die Toten nicht zur Ruhe kommen lassen, so ist auch das Leben der Nachkommen „getrübt von dem *nach*ziehenden *After*leben eines Gestorbenen [Herv. E. S.]". (411) Ja, es lässt sich wohl sagen, dass die Nachkommmenschaft der Schrift Leben grundsätzlich in „*After*leben" verwandelt – *Nach*kommen von daher auch im Sinne der strukturellen Nachträglichkeit des Lebens, welches Stiters *Narrenburg* als untotes, gespenstisches inszeniert. Noch der „Stifter", so heißt es, „würde sich im Grabe umgekehrt haben" (323), hätte er von den Effekten des Fideikommiss in Gestalt der Narrenburg Kenntnis erhalten; was mit dem ‚untoten Stifter' hinter den Kulissen spukt, ist mithin ein Kollektiv untoter Ahnen/Nachkommen, die, ohne je Urheber ihrer Taten zu sein, selbige „vor jedem Ankömmling" immer „wieder neu thun", d. h. auf- und ausführen müssen. Die Narrenburg ist ein Theater nicht von Akteuren, sondern von sich differenziell wiederholenden Taten/Handlungen – ein sich permanent rekonfigurierender Schauplatz sich seriell fortpflanzender Stiftungsakte.

Wie nun ist das Performativ der Schrift im szenischen Erzählen der *Narrenburg* wirksam? Wie agiert der „Dämon der Thaten" (410) im Stifter'schen Text? Welche gespenstische Tat treibt die Erzählung voran, ja, wird zum seriellen Akt des Erzählens selbst?

Der „Engel" seiner „schwersten That" kommt Jodok aus der Schrift zu, und so ist es weniger Jodok, der handelt, als dass eine Tat geschieht, die – wo sie die Dimension des Subjekts übersteigt –, dieses gleichwohl grundlegend affiziert. „Ich hörte die Stimmen nicht, bis es zu spät war, und eine That geschah, die Alles, Alles endete. – –" (416) Nicht zu sagen ist, was, noch wie und wann es geschah; die einzige Signatur der Tat ist zeitlicher Art, ein „zu spät", womit die Tat niemals wieder gutzumachen ist. „Jodok, du willst mich tödten." „Ich dich tödten, Chelion?" „Ja, du bist so furchtbar." (421) Dass Jodok hierauf das Zimmer verlässt und das Fläschchen mit Gift in den Abgrund schleudert, vermag an der Tat nichts mehr zu ändern:

> Aber es war nicht mehr auszutilgen. Sie hatte mich einmal mit dem Mörderauge an dem Bette stehen gesehen, und dieß war nicht mehr aus ihrer Seele zu nehmen. [...] Wer einmal den Arm erhob zum Todtschlage eines seiner Mitgeschöpfe, wenn er ihn auch wieder zurückzog, dem kann man nicht mehr trauen; er steht jenseits des Gesetzes [...] Ich habe jahrelang das Uebermenschliche versucht, daß Alles wieder sei, wie früher, allein es war vergebens (424 f.).
>
> Nie mehr seit jener Nacht ist die Röthe der Gesundheit wieder in ihr Angesicht gekommen – und so starb sie [...]; die brechenden Augen noch auf mich gerichtet, wie

> das arme Thier den Mörder anschaut, der ihm die Kugel in das furchtsame Herz gejagt hatte. (425)

Entgegen der Suggestion des Textes, geht es hier nicht um Mord*intention*. „Dämon"/„Engel" der Tat heißt, dass Jodok Mörderauge und Tat aus den Pergamenten zukommen, ihn heimsuchen, sich ihm anheften. Die gespenstische Tat macht das Subjekt handeln, ohne dass es weiß, was es tut, rückt es „jenseits des Gesetzes", an den Ab-Ort des Verworfenen (das bereits mit Sixtus II. begegnet war: „[N]ur *einer* war verworfen [Herv. E. S.]" [390]), von dem her es – als Wiedergänger – einen wiedergängernden Akt vollzieht.

Zeitlich aus den Fugen (*out of joint*) ereignet sich die Tat als Heimsuchung und Wiederkehr. Im Modus von Nachträglichkeit (*zu spät*) hat sie sich immer schon vollzogen, wie sie gleichwohl je noch aussteht, verknüpft die Tat ein irreduzibel Vergangenes mit einem Zukünftigen, zwischen denen die *Nach*kommen als Überträger agieren. Es ist diese seriell-gespenstische Übertragung der Tat von einem Nachkommen auf den nächsten, die Stifters *Narrenburg* im Erzählakt – seinerseits ein serieller Akt, Akt der Wiederholung – mobilisiert.

Jodoks Beschwörung seines Lesers, die Schrift auszulöschen oder doch wenigstens „das Gelesene" „augenblicklich" wieder zu vergessen, auf dass „sich die Gespenster all ihres Thuns nicht in dein Leben mischen und es trüben" (412), vermag Heinrich nicht nachzukommen. Vielmehr sieht er „überall die Gestalt des Jodokus" (427) und kann auch auf seiner Hochzeit mit Anna nur an Chelion denken. Vom Lesen affiziert, mischen sich auch in seine Handlungen die „Gespenster" (427) – nicht nur der „schwersten That" Jodoks, sondern auch die Dämonen, welche schon Jodoks Tat spektralisiert und derart bewirkt hatten. Welches Geschehen dies freisetzt, zeigt sich in signifikanter Weise in einem weiteren performativen Akt: der Trauung von Heinrich und Anna. Bemerkenswerterweise wird der Akt der Trauung selbst nicht erzählt, ja es starrt eine unmarkierte Leerstelle zwischen der beschriebenen Fahrt zur Trauung und dem Satz: „Als die Trauung vorüber war" (432). Wo der Akt der Trauung ausgespart bleibt, erscheint die Stiftung der ehelichen Bindung zwischen Heinrich und Anna verschoben – hin auf die Fahrt zur Trauung und die damit einhergehende sonderbare Szene:

> [A]ls er mit ihr bis zu dem Wagen gekommen war, sah man, daß von der Hand, bei der er sie führte, kaum zwei Finger die seine berührten, und daß diese Finger zitterten. Auch der Schleier [...] bebte an ihren schlagenden Pulsen [...] Auch Anna schien von Ehrfurcht überkommen zu sein; denn dieselben Augen, die ihn sonst [...] so freundlich angeblickt hatten, schlugen sich auch während des Fahrens nicht ein einziges Mal zu ihm auf – sondern sie weinten nun fast unablässig fort. Er redete ihr nicht zu, sondern er dachte an Chelion, wie sie kaum so rein, so schön, so schuldlos gewesen sei, als wie die an seiner Seite, und er bezähmte sein Herz, daß es nur nicht breche vor Freude und vor Glück. Als die Trauung vorüber war und die Wagen wieder zurückkehrten [...] (431 f.).

Wenn sich diese Szene in der Tat als Trauung lesen lässt, dann im Sinne eines närrischen Performativs, mit dem sich eine spezifische Konstellation und Nachkommenschaft eröffnet. Die hoch affektive Szene mag weniger in der Beziehung zwischen Anna und Heinrich gründen, die hier einander vielmehr entfremdet scheinen, als dass sie eine andere Szene aktualisiert/wiederholt – in die Nachkommenschaft der schweren Tat und unglücklichen Liebe zwischen Chelion und Jodok eintritt. Weder der Text noch Heinrich unternehmen einen Versuch, Annas rätselhafte, nicht zu stillende Tränen zu deuten. „[S]chien von Ehrfurcht überkommen" kann als Erklärung nicht wirklich herhalten. Zugleich wandern Heinrichs Gedanken zu Chelion, deren tragisches Schicksal Jodoks Lebensbeschreibung in sein Herz inskribiert hatte. Die Hochzeitsszene stellt sich als Wiederholungsszene dar: Die Trauung wird zur Artikulation einer unvordenklichen Trauer. Als würde die tragische Liebesgeschichte von Chelion und Jodok – um nicht zu sagen: die „schwerste That" – im Akt der Eheschließung von Anna und Heinrich, d. h. im Modus von Nachträglichkeit/Wiederholung vollzogen, als ‚erfüllte' sie sich einzig in dieser gespenstisch-närrischen Differenz und schriebe sich *qua* dieser als zukünftige fort. Annas unablässig „fort"dauernde Tränen kennen keine Gegenwart, sondern sind Siegel einer solchen nachträglichen Zukünftigkeit. – Bemerkenswert ambivalent ist in diesem Kontext auch die Formulierung, die sich an die von Heinrich wahrgenommene Ähnlichkeit zwischen Anna und Chelion anschließt: „[U]nd er bezähmte sein Herz, daß es nur nicht breche" – war es doch das Brechen des Herzens, das Chelion und Jodok geschehen war. Und wenn der Satz in einem gleichsam syntaktischen Nachtrag endet mit den Worten „vor Freude und vor Glück", so wirkt dieses *happy ending* des Satzes wie ein Kontrast zur restlichen Szene und ebenso angefügt wie das *happy ending* der Erzählung, über welches noch zu sprechen sein wird.

Stifters närrisches Erzählperformativ zeugt (Ur-)Szenen einer Ehe *qua* gespenstischer Doppelbelichtung: Im selben Zuge, wie sich Jodoks „schwerste That" konstitutiv nachträglich, d. h. als immer schon andere vollzieht, wird – in der unheimlichen Doppelfiguration – die Bindung zwischen Heinrich und Anna im Modus der Entfremdung gestiftet. Ganz im Sinne des Fideikommiss richtet Stifter Erzählen hin auf Akte der Wiederholung aus, Szenen auf Wiederkehr, Figuren auf Doppelfigurationen. Wenn gesagt war, dass das Fideikommiss die Subjekte zu seriellen Überträgern von Taten macht, so mobilisiert Sifter diese Serialität für die Performanz des Erzählens. Das Szenische ist von der Dynamik der Nachkommenschaft. Strukturell nachträglich, seriell, Ur-Szene, ist die Szene zugleich Ein- und Ausfaltung anderer Szenen. Erzählen vollzieht sich *qua* szenischer Wiederkehr, und es ist eben das Serielle der Szene, in dem die szenische *agency* liegt. Wie anhand von Jodoks „schwerster That" und Annas rätselhaften Tränen gesehen, ist Stifters szenischem Erzählen ein Nicht-Erzählen, ein Nicht-Wissen inhärent. So wenig wie die Figuren, weiß der Text, was er tut. Das Erratische, das die szenischen Präsentationen des Alten charakterisiert hatte, kennzeichnet auch Sifters szenisches Erzählen: Im Ausfall des Erzählens artikuliert sich ein zugleich Unvergessliches wie Unerinnerliches, ein Trauma, das, obgleich es keinen anderen Schauplatz als die Wiederholung hat, doch in keiner Wiederholung abgeglichen werden kann, und mithin das Proliferieren des Szenischen bewirkt. Kein Motiv, kein Inhalt lässt sich diesen szenischen Akten attestieren. Leerstellen/verworfene Stellen im Text fungieren gerade dadurch als Scharniere serieller Übertragung, welche die Erzählung vorantreibt und gespenstische Wirklichkeitseffekte – seien es dämonische Taten oder Tränen – zeitigt.

Die Tränen bei der Hochzeit mögen noch eine andere Quelle haben – oder ist es vielleicht doch dieselbe? Denn Schrift und Akt des Lesens sind hierbei ebenfalls grundlegend: „Es war fast närrisch, wie sehr ich euch gut ward", so Anna zu Heinrich, „[d]ie Bücher, welche mir die Thrine immer schickte – – sagt, habt ihr auch schon einmal bei einem Buche geweint?" „Wohl, Anna, wohl." „Seht, ich hab' es gleich gedacht, daß ihr das gethan habt" (346 f.). Affektproduktion ist auch hier an Schrift, genauer: Literatur, gebunden: „[A]ch", so Anna weiter über die Bücher, „da standen auch Dinge darinnen, daß mir oft das Herz zerspringen mochte vor lauter Schmerz und Sehnsucht" (345). Damit nicht genug, vollzieht der Text noch eine weitere – dezidiert szenische – Wendung im Verhältnis von Leben und Schrift, wie es das Fideikommiss installiert: Sind Leben und Liebe Heinrichs und Annas gespenstisch gespeist aus der Lektüre von Jodoks Aufzeichnungen, erweisen sich Literatur und Schrift hier zudem als konstitutiv für die Figurenkonzeption. Auf Heinrichs Frage, wie es denn kam, dass sie ihm gut wurde, antwortet Anna, dass es ihr gewesen sei, als wäre Heinrich aus der Literatur herausgetreten: „– – – und da kamet *ihr* [Herv. i. O.]" (346). „Es war mir öfters, als seid ihr in einem solchen Buche gestanden, und daraus in unsern Garten getreten" (347). Der szenische Auftritt – ein Heraustreten aus der Schrift – ist im Schriftbild selbst markiert: „– – –" – eine Auslassung, die nicht nur den Liebesaffekt als Schrifteffekt markiert, sondern mit dem sich die Szene/der Schauplatz der Schrift in eine *mise en abyme* transformiert. Heraustreten (des Lebens) aus der Schrift [Heinrich] und Eintreten (des Lebens) in die Schrift [Fideikommiss] fallen im irreduzibel doppelten, szenisch-unheimlichen Akt des Lesen zusammen. Ja, es ist eben diese seriell-rhythmische Dynamik von *Heraus- und Eintreten der Schrift aus der/in die Schrift*, welche die *Narrenburg* erzähltechnisch installiert – ein abysmales Szenario, das Simulakren produziert.

2.2 *Serielle Rahmen: Offene Szenen*

Die Randstruktur des Szenischen wurde vielfach angesprochen – im Kontext von Pias Auftritt, des Eintritts in den Schlosskomplex oder des Schlosskomplexes selbst, dessen Szenenhaftigkeit sich als seriell proliferierende Randstruktur darstellt –, und so gilt es abschließend, das spezifische Erzählverfahren Stifters in den Blick zu nehmen, welche die Randstruktur des Textes generiert: die Rahmentechnik, wie sie in der *Narrenburg* am Werk ist. Die vorangegangenen Ausführungen lassen keinen einfachen Rahmen erwarten, und in der Tat wartet Stifters Erzählung mit vielfältigen Rahmungen auf – Rahmen, die sich in den Text einfalten, ihn seriell durchziehen und derart szenische Randstrukturen kreieren.

Die Rahmenstruktur, die die Studienfassung entwickelt, könnte kaum komplexer sein: Da ist – zwischen Titel und erstem Teil der Erzählung („Die grüne Fichtau") – zunächst das Motto: „Sieh nur, welch düstere Geschichte diese Trümmer reden. *Altes Buch* [Herv. i. O.]" (320). Eine wesentlich zeitliche (alt) und mediale Rahmung (Trümmer, Buch, Schrift), wirft das Motto seinen düsteren Schatten voraus. In deutlichem Kontrast dazu steht, was als unmittelbar anschließende Rahmung gelten kann: Die ins Absurde gesteigerte, närrische Beschreibung des Fideikommiss und seiner Bedingungen, in der Stifters Komik voll zur Geltung kommt. Auf die Darstellung des Verfalls der Scharnast-Burg und die schalkhaft vorgetragene „lächerliche Rechtsfrage, ob nun auch der Fiscus seine Lebensbeschreibung werde schreiben müssen" (323), findet sich der diesen Rahmen schließende Satz, welcher in die Erzählung der Geschichte Heinrichs überleitet: „So standen actenmäßig die Sachen, als sich das zutrug, was wir in den folgenden Blättern erzählen wollen." (323) Mit dem Eingang in die ‚Binnenerzählung' erschöpft sich die Rahmenbildung allerdings nicht; vielmehr bildet die Binnenerzählung in sich einen weiteren Rahmen, faltet sich in sich selbst ein. Dies geschieht im zweiten Abschnitt der Erzählung („Das graue Schloss"), in Vorbereitung des Eintritts Heinrichs und Roberts in den Schlosskomplex. Die Worte des Erzählers lauten:

> [U]nd nun fuhr Alles der grünen Fichtau zu. Wir aber müsssen hier von derselben scheiden, so gerne unsre Feder noch bei dem klaren, freien, heiteren Fichtauer Leben verweilen möchte. Allein der Zweck der vorliegenden Blätter führt uns aus dieser harmlosen Gegenwart, die wir mit Vorliebe beschrieben haben, einer dunklen schwermüthigen Vergangenheit entgegen [...]. Zu Ende versprechen wir wieder in die Gegenwart einzulenken, und so ein dämmerndes, düsteres Bild in einen heitern freundlichen Rahmen gestellt zur Ansicht zu bringen. (361)

Explizit spricht der Text hier von Rahmung („Rahmen"), welche er zugleich zeitlich bestimmt: Die „harmlose Gegenwart" wird hin auf eine „dunkle schwermüthige Vergangenheit" verlassen, deren „düsteres Bild" am Ende durch Wiedereinlenken in die „Gegenwart" in einen „heitern [...] Rahmen" gestellt werden soll. Unzweifelhaft stellt das „düstere Bild" der Vergangenheit ein Echo auf das Motto („düstere Geschichten") dar, kehrt mit anderen Worten das rahmende Motto in der Einfaltung der Binnengeschichte wieder, schlägt sich ein Rahmen in den anderen ein. (Auf die Zeitlichkeit des Rahmens wird insbesondere mit Blick auf das Szenische zurückzukommen sein.) Hier sei zunächst bemerkt, dass sich der Szenenwechsel von der „harmlosen Gegenwart" der Fichtau zur dunklen Vergangenheit des Schlosskomplexes zögerlich vollzieht: Gleichsam ausgestattet mit einem sich sukzessive schließenden Vorhang tritt die Szene der Fichtau nur allmählich aus dem Blick. So lauten die Worte des Erzählers: „Ehe wir sie nun auf den alten Berg und in das alte Schloß geleiten, ist es uns noch vergönnt, den letzten Rückblick in das Fichtauer Thal zu thun" (362). Und eine weitere Seite später heißt es: „Und somit war dieß unser letzter Blick in die Fichtau [...] so versank hinter ihm und auch hinter uns die ganze liebe grüne Fichtau" (363). Auf die Schließung des Rahmens folgt das Eintreten in den Schlosskomplex, dessen Rand- und Rahmenstruktur oben bereits ausführlich diskutiert wurde. Auch dort war – mit Bezug auf die sich selbst öffnende/schließende Mauer – die Rede vom „Rahmen" (364), in dem die Gestalt des Alten erscheint und, insofern sich ihre steingrauen Züge mit denen der Mauer verbinden, wieder verschwindet. – Einen weiteren Rahmen bilden die szenischen Präsentationen des Alten, die die Geschichte der Vorfahren auf so närrische Weise darbieten und Figuren (Sixtus II./Heinrich) und Geschehen in eine unheimliche Zweizeitigkeit ent-setzen – eine perforierte Rahmung, die mit ihren notorischen Zeitsprüngen jegliche Trennung zwischen Gegenwart und Vergangenheit, Rahmen- und Binnenerzählung desavouiert. Eine stabilere Rahmung zwischen der Geschichte Heinrichs und der düsteren Vergangenheit der Burg Scharnast verspricht zunächst Heinrichs Lektüre der Aufzeichnungen Jodoks im dritten Teil der Erzählung („Der rothe Stein“): „Auf dem hohen Stuhle sitzend, die Papiere vor sich auf dem Tische, schlug er die ersten Blätter um, bis er zu einem eingelegten Zeichen kam, dann sein Haupt sachte vorwärts neigend, las er weiter, wie folgt“ (41). Wie allerdings gezeigt, agieren auch hier Schrift und Lektüre rahmenübergreifend, suchen Heinrichs Leben gespenstisch heim, speisen Vergangenes ins Gegenwärtige ein, womit Letzteres konstitutiv als Wiederkehr erscheint.

Die Zeitlichkeit der Rahmen in der *Narrenburg* könnte nicht prekärer sein. Ja, Stifters Rahmen nehmen – darin den szenischen Präsentationen des Greises verwandt – die fröhlich-unheimliche Verkreuzung der Zeiten vor, generieren ein Heterochron-Szenisches. Die Verschaltung von Vergangenheit und Gegenwart war – man erinnere sich – auch schon bestimmend für das Szenische: In der Szene, in der Heinrich „Umsicht“ zu erlangen sucht, lässt sich die umliegende „holde Gegenwart“ der Fichtau durchaus nicht klar von der „unklare[n] Vergangenheit, auf der sie standen“ (369), unterscheiden; vielmehr emergiert Wirkliches (als Unheimlich-Szenisches) allererst aus der zeitlichen wie räumlichen Ent-setzung/Verschiebung der Szene hin zum *anderen Schauplatz*. Es ist *qua* Heterochronie, dass die multiplen Rahmen der *Narrenburg* serielle Szenen zeitigen, wie sich zugleich das Szenische als serielle Rahmenstruktur generiert.

Wie gestaltet sich in Anbetracht dieser heterochronen Rahmenstruktur von Stifters szenischem Realismus nun die versprochene Wiedereinlenkung in die „Gegenwart“, um derart am Ende das „dämmernde[], düstere[] Bild [der Vergangenheit; E. S.] in einen heitern freundlichen Rahmen gestellt zur Ansicht zu bringen“ (361)? Wie vollzieht sich die Rahmung, die sich der zeitlichen Diskrepanz zwischen Bild und Rahmen wohl bewusst ist, ja, aus eben dieser Diskrepanz ihre spezifische Perspektive gewinnt? Denn es geht ja ausdrücklich um ein „zur Ansicht bringen“, sprich: auch hier wieder um einen szenischen Akt. Bezüglich des Endes der Erzählung besteht wohl der signifikanteste Unterschied zwischen Studien- und Journalfassung: Während die Journalfassung mit einem „Lebe wohl“ an das „glückliche Paar“ (NJ 403) endet, hält die Studienfassung eine Reihe schließender Rahmungen bereit.

Wo Düster-Vergangenes im Heiter-Gegenwärtigen ‚zur Ansicht gebracht‘ wird, steht nicht notwendigerweise ein Ungetrübtes, ein *happy ending*, ein – wie es in der Journalfassung heißt – „unsägliche[s] Glück“ (NJ 403) zu erwarten. Strukturell ließe sich eine spektrale Perspektive, eine gebrochen-doppelte Szene vermuten, in der Düsteres und Heiteres so wenig voneinander zu trennen wären wie Vergangenheit und Gegenwart, die sich immer schon ineinander eingelagert und wechselseitig verschoben hätten. Was also tut, wie endet die Studienfassung? Der Tenor des Glücks ist zweifellos auch hier vorherrschend, und doch lohnt ein genauerer Blick auf die Sprechakte, mit denen der Text schließt bzw. nicht schließt. Den „heitern [...] Rahmen" (361) aus dem Versprechen zitierend lautet die erste Schließung wie folgt: „Wir [...] beschließen unsere Erzählung mit diesem heitern Ausgange der trüben Geschichten des Rothensteins, und wünschen dem Paare, daß es so glücklich fortlebe, wie ihre Ehe glücklich begonnen." (434) Zwei Momente lassen innehalten: Zum einen handelt es sich um einen Wunsch, der als solcher Offenheit produziert; zum anderen ist es durchaus nicht ausgemacht, dass die Ehe zwischen Anna und Heinrich glücklich begonnen hatte. Man denke nur an die unstillbaren, gespenstischen Tränen Annas anlässlich ihrer Trauung – Tränen, die sich wiederum nur in der Studienfassung finden. Mischt sich der durch die Tränen getrübte Blick hier in die „Ansicht" der „trüben Geschichten" der Vergangenheit durch den heitern Rahmen der Gegenwart – und wäre mithin die glückliche Szene konstitutiv getrübt?

Besorgt um die Dauer des Glücks, fügt der Erzähler einen *Nach*trag hinzu, ein im Präsens gehaltenes Postscriptum, welches die Leserin/den Leser des noch anhaltenden Glückes vergewissert: „Ein Anfang dazu ist gemacht; denn die einigen Jahre, die seitdem, was wir eben erzählten, bis auf heute verflossen, sind ganz glücklich gewesen." (435) Das „noch", das bereits im Zusammenhang mit Heinrichs Vergewisserung ob der Fichtau begegnet war („[w]ohl war das Land noch, wie gestern" [368]) und dort einen epistemischen Zweifel artikuliert hatte, klingt hier erneut an. Auch lässt sich sagen, dass ein *happy ending* in Serie, wie es die *Narrenburg* in unnachahmlich Stifter'scher Manier entwickelt, eine durchaus prekäre Dynamik in Gang setzt. Die schließende Rahmung, die das *happy ending* gemeinhin verbürgt, wird von einem *happy ending* in Serie unterlaufen, in ein *nach* und *nach*, einen Aufschub, eine Zwischenzeitlichkeit/Nachträglichkeit überführt. Mit der durch die Rahmentechnik installierten seriellen Schließung/Öffnung wird die Szene in Offenheit, Ambivalenz, Ungewissheit gehalten – und mag eben darin Schauplatz des Stifter'schen Glücks sein: serielles Fortdauern. Wenn der Erzähler mit dem Nachtrag um die Dauer des Glücks besorgt erscheint, so ist er es wohl in der Tat: nicht jedoch im Sinne einer Sorge um die allzu große Flüchtigkeit des Glücks, das nur den Augenblick kennt, sondern im dezidierten Sinne einer Konzeption von Glück als Dauer. Wie bei Kierkegaard das Glück in der Wiederholung liegt, so bei Stifter im Seriellen, in der gepenstischen Trübung des *nach.*

Und so mag es nicht verwundern, dass sich am Ende der *Narrenburg* noch ein weiterer schließender Rahmen auftut: Auf das aus der Journalfassung bekannte Lebewohl an das glückliche Paar („Und so, du glückliches Paar, lebe wohl!" [436]) folgt in der Studienfassung ein weiterer Abschnitt, der die Erzählung beschließt bzw. wieder neu eröffnet: „Wenn von den andern Schriften des rothen Felsensaales von Julian, Christoph, Prokop, etwas bekannt wird, so wird es dereinst vorgelegt werden." (436) Mit diesem, ihrem letzten Satz ruft die Erzählung die Gespenster der Schrift erneut auf den Plan. Kein einfaches Wiedereinlenken also nimmt die Rahmung am Ende der *Narrenburg* vor, sondern ein doppeltes: Nicht nur bringt sie das „düstere[] Bild“ der Vergangenheit im „heitern [...] Rahmen“ der Gegenwart „zur Ansicht“ (361), letzterer wird erneut durch die Schrift gerahmt, sprich: in den vergangen-zukünftigen Blick des Gespenstischen genommen. Vergangenes bleibt in Latenz und wird als Zukünftiges wiederkehren („so wird es dereinst vorgelegt werden“). Weit davon entfernt, eine Auflösung des Düsteren ins Heitere zu betreiben, installiert die serielle Rahmung der *Narrenburg* die wechselseitige Heimsuchung von Vergangenheit und Gegenwart und generiert damit eine spezifische „Ansicht“ bzw. Szene: ein spektrales Perspektiv, eine doppelte Szene, welche Wirklichkeitseffekte als Simulakrum, *déjà vu*, produziert.

Wenn die *Narrenburg* an einer Sache keinen Zweifel lässt, dann an ihrem Fortgang: Der letzte Satz impliziert die Fortsetzung des Erzählens[20] – garantiert von den Gespenstern der Schrift. Stifters szenischer Realismus und serielle Rahmentechnik produzieren keine geschlossenen, sondern offene Szenen, und so endet die *Narrenburg* weniger, als dass sie sich szenisch fortsetzt – oder um es mit den Worten des Alten zu sagen: „– – Alles ist nicht zu Ende; Alles ist falsch“ (395).

[20] Eine dieser Fortsetzungen ist Stifters Erzählung *Prokopus* (1847). Zudem ist die in enger zeitlicher Nähe zur *Narrenburg* entstandene *Mappe meines Urgroßvaters* diesem Kontext zuzurechnen. In der Journalfassung der *Mappe* trägt der Obrist noch den Namen Julius Scharnast, welcher der Urgroßvater Heinrichs ist. Zum Verhältnis zwischen *Narrenburg* und *Mappe meines Urgroßvaters* vgl. auch Begemann (1995), *Die Welt der Zeichen*, S. 242-259.

Till Breyer

Form des Zerfalls. Zur politischen Ökonomie von Hermann Brochs *Die Schlafwandler*

1. Einleitung

Hermann Brochs Romantrilogie *Die Schlafwandler*, die zwischen 1928 und 1931 in Wien entsteht, scheint kaum als ein realistischer Roman lesbar zu sein. Von Beginn an vermischen sich äußere und innere, materielle und seelische Wirklichkeiten und verdichten sich in Motiven und Figuren, die, wie Broch in einem Brief schreibt, „am Rande der Wirklichkeit“[1] stehen und im dritten Roman, *Huguenau oder die Sachlichkeit*, in disparate Stimmen, Perspektiven, Textgattungen und diegetische Ebenen auseinanderfallen. *Die Schlafwandler* sind durch eine Hermeneutik der Gegenwart motiviert, deren Scheitern sie zugleich leitmotivisch durchzieht: Das Dunkle und Verschwommene, das Nicht-Wissen und die Paralyse des Denkens umgeben die Romanfiguren und machen sie als jene ‚Schlafwandler' erkennbar, die sich im Zwielicht brüchiger Wertsysteme bewegen. Am Ende der 1920er Jahre, als sich eine Krise der liberalen Gesellschaft, der parlamentarischen Systeme und nicht zuletzt der europäischen Wirtschafts- und Währungsordnung zuspitzt, macht Brochs Romantrilogie den historischen Prozess einer Destabilisierung von Wirklichkeitsbezügen zu seinem zentralen Gegenstand.

Dabei hat Broch mit den zehn Essays, die zusammen den Titel *Zerfall der Werte* tragen, einen theoretisch-begrifflichen Deutungsrahmen in den dritten Roman eingefügt, der teils explizit auf die Romanhandlung referiert und sie in jene geschichtsphilosophische These vom Zerfall des mittelalterlichen, ‚geschlossenen' Weltbildes einfügt, durch den der Glaube an den christlichen Gott als das „ideale Wertzentrum“ und als zentraler „Plausibilitätspunkt“[2] abhanden gekommen sei. Sowohl epistemisch (Was hält man für wahr?) als auch ethisch (Was soll man tun?) und ästhetisch (Wie betrachtet man die Wirklichkeit?)[3] habe sich ein jahrhundertelanger „Prozeß des Wertzerfalls“ vollzogen, als dessen Endphase die moderne Gesellschaft auf das „tonlose Vakuum einer grausamen Absolutheit“[4] zulau-

1 Hermann Broch, „Problemkreis, Inhalt, Methode der *Schlafwandler*“, in: *Kommentierte Werkausgabe*, Band 1, hg. von Paul Michael Lützeler (im Folgenden: *KW*), Frankfurt/M., 1978, S. 723-725: 724.

2 Hermann Broch, *Die Schlafwandler*, in: *KW* 1, S. 9-716: 496 f. (im Folgenden: SW).

3 Zur begrifflichen Architektonik von Brochs Wertkonzeption siehe Friedrich Vollhardt, *Hermann Brochs geschichtliche Stellung. Studien zum philosophischen Frühwerk und zur Romantrilogie „Die Schlafwandler“ (1914-1932)*, Tübingen, 1986.

4 SW, S. 703 und S. 705.

fe. Sowohl der anti-metaphysische Positivismus als auch die Schrecken des Ersten Weltkriegs werden in den Essays als Symptome dieses sukzessiven Zerfalls gesellschaftlich gültiger Wertbezüge gedeutet.

Wird diese idealistisch-geschichtsphilosophische Konzeption des ‚Wertzerfalls' in der Broch-Forschung häufig als zentraler ‚Plausibilitätspunkt' des Romans selbst aufgefasst, etwa als „Enzyklopädie, die den Zugang zu den [...] dunklen Stellen des Romans erschließt"[5], so gehe ich im Folgenden davon aus, dass mit den Essays eine nur relative Deutungsposition bezeichnet ist.[6] Nicht nur, dass diese einer intradiegetischen Erzählerfigur zugeschrieben werden, dem Intellektuellen Dr. Bertrand Müller, ein ‚unzuverlässiger Theoretiker', dem seine eigenen Erfahrungen als „ein Fremdes, in das ich niemals eindringen werde"[7] erscheinen; wichtiger ist, dass sich die dominante Selbstdeutung des Romans mittels des geschichtsphilosophischen Konzepts des ‚Wertzerfalls' an einer gegenläufigen, ökonomischen Semantik des Werts bricht, die auf ein kritisches Wissen der politischen Ökonomie verweist.[8] Durch ihre Analyse lässt sich die ambivalente Realismuskonzeption der *Schlafwandler*-Trilogie, die Broch einer „Heraushebung der tieferen Schichten [...] des Lebens"[9] verpflichtet sah, genauer beleuchten. Brochs Roman verknüpft den Zerfall der diegetischen Welt, in dem sich die ‚Krise' des Romans reflektiert und vollzieht, mit dem Prozess ihrer ökonomischen Formierung. Dadurch wird die geschichtsphilosophische Theorie der Essays und ihre Fokussierung auf „die Mentalitäten, die Denkstile"[10] gleichsam materialistisch unterspült. Die durch Marx geprägte Verknüpfung von Geschichtsprozess und ökonomischer Wertbildung, von der Broch sich in seinen theoretischen Arbeiten zum ‚Wertzerfall' explizit abgrenzt[11], insistiert in der Motivstruktur des Romans und geht in eine literarische Problematisierung gesellschaftlicher Wirklichkeit ein, die letztlich auf die Frage nach der Ökonomie des ‚Wertzerfalls' selbst zuläuft.

---

5 Vollhardt (1986), *Stellung*, S. 253; siehe bereits Richard Brinkmann, „Werttheorie und Romanform bei Hermann Broch", in: *Deutsche Vierteljahrsschrift* 31 (1957), S. 169-197.

6 Vgl. Thomas Sebastian, *Der Gang der Geschichte. Rhetorik der Zeitlichkeit in Hermann Brochs Romantrilogie „Die Schlafwandler"*, Würzburg, 1995, S. 40.

7 SW, S. 617.

8 Vgl. Christoph Zeller, „‚Annäherung an die Unsterblichkeit'. Ökonomie und Religion in Hermann Brochs *Die Schlafwandler*", in: *Internationales Archiv für Sozialgeschichte der Literatur* 38, 1 (2013), S. 31-63.

9 Hermann Broch, „Über die Grundlagen des Romans *Die Schlafwandler*", in: *KW* 1, S. 728-733: 733.

10 Paul Michael Lützeler, *Die Entropie des Menschen. Studien zum Werk Hermann Brochs*, Würzburg, 2000, S. 41.

11 Siehe die Einleitung des 1931 entstandenen Essays „Logik einer zerfallenden Welt", in: *KW* 10/2, Frankfurt/M., 1977, S. 156-172.

2. Krise und Roman

Wenn Broch mit den *Schlafwandlern* „die Möglichkeit einer neuen Form des Romans"[12] anvisiert, so reagiert er darin nicht nur auf einen zeitdiagnostischen, sondern auch auf einen poetologischen Krisenbefund, der seit den frühen 1920er Jahren als ‚Krise des Romans' formuliert wird.[13] Der realistische Roman des 19. Jahrhunderts sei heute, so schreibt Otto Flake in seinem Essay „Die Krise des Romans" (1922), obsolet geworden, indem „Ordnung und Zustände in Fluß geraten" seien. Die „bürgerliche Ordnung", die im 19. Jahrhundert noch gegeben gewesen sei, habe sich verflüchtigt, und der „Ansturm aller wechselnden Gesichtspunkte" mache die Prämisse einer „darstellbare[n] Welt" zur „Fiktion"[14].

Die *Schlafwandler* lassen sich als Intensivierung dieses Krisenbefunds lesen. Ihre Form lässt sich nicht mehr durch einen qualitativen Begriff des Lebens bestimmen, wie es von Georg Lukács – den Broch 1920 in Wien kennenlernt[15] – in der *Theorie des Romans* (1916) für den modernen Roman versucht worden war. Auf der einen Seite bewegen sich die unterschiedlich fokalisierten Reflexionen der *Schlafwandler* in einem motivischen Resonanzverhältnis zu Lukács' geschichtsphilosophischen Thesen.[16] Auf der anderen Seite aber hat das „Leben des problematischen Individuums", das Lukács als Quelle einer immanenten „Pseudoorganik des Romanstoffes"[17] bestimmt, bei Broch seine formästhetische Gültigkeit verloren. Wird bei Lukács die notorische gattungspoetische Unbestimmtheit der Romanform in eine ebenso positive wie dynamische Bestimmung gewendet, der zufolge die „literarische Form im Roman [...] zuletzt die Form des Lebens selbst"[18] ist, so bewegen sich die *Schlafwandler* entlang eines Zerfalls dieses Entsprechungsverhältnisses. „Hat dieses verzerrte Leben noch Wirklichkeit? hat (sic!) diese hypertrophische Wirklichkeit noch Leben?"[19], so heißt es am Beginn des ersten Essays über den ‚Zerfall der Werte'.

Das ‚Leben' verliert hier seine Funktion als primäres romanpoetisches Erschließungsmedium des Wirklichen; es ist „weitgehend aller Substanz entleert" und wird „belangloses Leben".[20] Während das „verzerrte Leben" seine Organik eingebüßt hat, kehrt die ‚hypertrophische', sich ins Überdimensionale ausdehnende Wirk-

12 Broch (1978), Problemkreis, S. 725.

13 Zur Diskussion um die ‚Krise des Romans' siehe Helmuth Kiesel, *Geschichte der literarischen Moderne. Sprache, Ästhetik, Dichtung im zwanzigsten Jahrhundert*, München, 2004, S. 315-320.

14 Otto Flake, „Die Krise des Romans", in: *Die Neue Bücherschau* 4, 2 (1922), S. 87-94: 90-92.

15 Paul Michael Lützeler, „Broch, Lukács und die Folgen", in: *Modern Austrian Literature* 13, 4 (1980), S. 99-120: 101.

16 Vgl. Paul Michael Lützeler, „Lukács' ‚Theorie des Romans' und Brochs ‚Schlafwandler'", in: Richard Thieberger (Hg.), *Hermann Broch und seine Zeit*, Bern (u. a.), 1980, S. 47-59.

17 Georg Lukács, *Die Theorie des Romans. Ein geschichtsphilosophischer Versuch über die Formen der großen Epik*, München, 1994, S. 67 und S. 65.

18 Rüdiger Campe, „Form und Leben in der Theorie des Romans", in: Armen Avanessian/Winfried Menninghaus/Jan Völker (Hg.), *Vita aesthetica. Szenarien ästhetischer Lebendigkeit*, Zürich, Berlin, 2009, S. 193-211: 210.

19 SW, S. 418.

20 SW, S. 422.

lichkeit Signaturen des Todes hervor: Die Subjekte tragen „den Stempel des Todes in ihren Gesichtern"[21]. In diesem Riss zwischen Leben und Wirklichkeit, „in dem die Zeit zerfallen ist"[22], vollzieht sich die Krise der Gegenwart. Wurde bereits bei Lukács das Moment der Krise als konstitutiver Teil eines modernen Romans hervorgehoben, dessen „erstrebte[] Organik" stets „gefährdete Form"[23] bleibt, so ist bei Broch nicht mehr der Begriff des Lebens, sondern der Begriff der Krise ausschlaggebend für die Form des Romans: Zerfällt die Kohärenz des Lebens, so wird der Roman zur Form ihres Zerfalls.

3. Zerfall der Perspektive

Der Formaspekt des Zerfalls schreibt sich von Beginn an als Dislozierung der Narration in die *Schlafwandler* ein.[24] Wie bei Flake der moderne Roman in einer ‚in Fluß geratenen' Wirklichkeit keine stabile Beobachterposition mehr ausbilden kann, so verwischt sich in den *Schlafwandlern* immer wieder das Verhältnis der Rede zur Figurenebene. Die Lokalisierung erlebter Rede oder innerer Monologe wird angetäuscht, um in ein wechselseitiges ‚Ansteckungsverhältnis' mit anderen Figuren, intradiegetischen Erzählern (wie dem Autor der Essays) oder jener Instanz einzutreten, die als Rest eines auktorialen Erzählers bleibt.[25] So beginnen etwa die Passagen über das „Problem der Uniform"[26] mit einer Zuordnung von Diskurs und Subjekt, die zugleich in den Konjunktiv zurückgenommen wird: „Bertrand könnte zum Thema der Uniform etwa sagen [...]", „So mochte Bertrand sprechen [...]". Es folgen Reflexionen über die Funktion der Uniform nach dem Bedeutungsverlust der Kirche: Die Gesellschaft müsse nun „irdische Hierarchien [...] an die Stelle des Glaubens" setzen, so dass die „eigentliche Romantik dieses Zeitalters die der Uniform"[27] sei. Wer spricht hier? Ist es Joachim von Pasenow, in dessen Gedanken auch an anderer Stelle regelmäßig die Ansichten des Freundes nachklingen? Ist es bereits jener Dr. Bertrand Müller, der im *Huguenau*-Roman das Verhältnis von Romantik, Kirche, Glaube und Wertzerfall theoretisieren wird? Ist es – dem Konjunktiv zum Trotz – der analytisch denkende Eduard v. Bertrand? Oder schließlich ein heterodiegetischer Erzähler? All diese Lesarten erweisen sich als inkohärent, denn die Passage enthält sowohl Elemente, die jeweils über das Bewusstsein der einzelnen Figuren hinausweisen, als auch solche, die eine schein-

21 SW, S. 366.

22 SW, S. 464.

23 Lukács (1994), *Theorie des Romans*, S. 66 und S. 62.

24 Vgl. Ulf Eisele, *Die Struktur des modernen deutschen Romans*, Tübingen, 1984, S. 64-66; Brinkmann (1954), Werttheorie und Romanform, S. 173-176.

25 Vgl. Gunther Martens, *Beobachtungen der Moderne in Hermann Brochs* Die Schlafwandler *und Robert Musils* Der Mann ohne Eigenschaften. *Rhetorische und narratologische Aspekte von Interdiskursivität*, München, 2006, S. 75-89.

26 SW, S. 26.

27 SW, S. 23 f.

bare Eindeutigkeit herstellen.[28] Die Narration umspielt die Konsistenz der Fiktion in einem weder personalen noch auktorialen, sondern vielmehr einem ‚depersonalen' Erzählen: einem Erzählen, das sich von der realistischen Perspektivkonstruktion herschreibt, diese imitiert und doch die Kopplung von Perspektive und Diskurs immer wieder überschreitet.

Diese Momente einer zerfallenden Perspektive, die in unterschiedlichen Graden den Erzählfluss irritieren, korrespondieren auf der Figurenebene mit einem Zerfall der wahrgenommenen Wirklichkeit. Die Romanfiguren werden mit einem Konturverlust ihrer Wirklichkeit konfrontiert, der auf einen Schwund der Urteilskraft im kantischen Sinn hindeutet, etwa wenn Joachim „erschrocken gewahr wurde, daß er der verschwimmenden und verfließenden Masse des Lebens nicht mehr habhaft zu werden vermochte"[29], oder wenn es über Huguenau heißt, in seiner „luzideren Realität [...] zerfielen die Dinge, rückten auseinander"[30]. Und Esch scheint regelrecht die Erzählform des Textes zu kommentieren, wenn es im Modus der erlebten Rede heißt: „Von neuem begannen die Dinge und Standpunkte sich in der ärgerlichsten Weise zu verschieben und zu vermischen"[31]. In diesen Zerfalls- und Vermischungsphänomenen depersonalisieren sich auch die Subjekte: Immer wieder wird eine Form von negativer Prosopopöie, ein Entzug des Gesichts vorgeführt. Als Joachim seine spätere Verlobte Elisabeth auf dem Land besucht, verfließen ihre Konturen zu einer „Landschaft des Gesichts", die mit ihrer Umgebung in „seltsam Einheitliches und nicht mehr Unterscheidbares verschmolz"[32]. Auch Ruzenas „Antlitz" lässt Joachim in seiner Erinnerung „ins Unbestimmte verdämmern, bis hart an die Grenze, wo es ins Unmenschliche umzukippen drohte und das Gesicht gesichtslos wurde."[33] Und nach dem Duelltod des Bruders Helmuth erzählt man, „daß das Gesicht des Toten durch die Schußwunde entstellt sei."[34] Wenn die Romanfiguren, wie der Autor in einem Brief schreibt, „manchmal ins Undeutliche abgeschliffen"[35] werden, dann korrespondiert dieses Verschleifen mit einer Dissoziation erzählter Perzeptionen und, auf der formästhetischen Ebene, mit einem latenten Zerfall der Perspektive.

Diese formästhetische Signatur des Romans ist in der Forschung entlang jener Werttheorie erläutert worden, die der Autor selbst unter anderem in dem zeitgleich zum Roman entstehenden Essay „Logik einer zerfallenden Welt" darlegt. In der Optik der Broch'schen Werttheorie ist jede „Kultur" als die „Gesamtheit von Wertsetzungen eines bestimmten Wertkreises"[36] zu verstehen, deren jede aus

---

28 So heißt es etwa, „der Uniform wahre Aufgabe" sei es, „das Weichliche und Verschwimmende des Menschenkörpers" (SW, S. 24) zu verbergen: eine Diskursprobe der ängstlichen, neurotisch anmutenden Wirklichkeitsdeutung des Joachim von Pasenow.

29 SW, S. 128.

30 SW, S. 408.

31 SW, S. 300.

32 SW, S. 119.

33 SW, S. 127.

34 SW, S. 47.

35 Broch (1978), Problemkreis, S. 724.

36 Broch (1977), Logik einer zerfallenden Welt, S. 163.

einem „wertsetzenden Akt“ und einem „geformte[n] Wert“[37] besteht. Dieser ‚Wertkreis‘, deren Höhepunkt die Etablierung einer dominanten Religion darstellt, ist bei Broch einem historischen „Phasenwechsel“ oder einer „Wellenbewegung der Geistesgeschichte“[38] unterworfen, die den ‚Zerfall der Werte‘ als Teil einer zwingenden Logik kenntlich macht. Orientiert man sich an dieser gleichsam ‚auktorialen‘ Theorie aus dem begrifflichen und werkbiografischen Kontext des Romans, so lassen sich beispielsweise die „engeren Fokalisationen“ als „Ausfluss der Differenzierung der Wertbereiche“ deuten, während die auktorialen Erzählmomente das Chaos „wieder ins rechte Licht zu rücken“[39] versuchen.

Demgegenüber lässt sich zeigen, dass die Motivstrukturen und Figurenkonstellationen des Romans konsequent mit ökonomischen Codierungen verknüpft sind, die die Romanfiguren nicht nur „in ihrem jeweiligen Verhältnis zum marktwirtschaftlichen Dogma“[40], sondern auch im Verhältnis zur kapitalistischen Wertbildung selbst situieren. Auf der Ebene der politischen Ökonomie tritt dabei in den drei Romanen eine je eigene Problemkonfiguration hervor: Substitution, Fetischismus, Akkumulation.

4. Dämon der Substitution

Das Motiv der Uniform lässt sich als strukturierende Metapher des *Pasenow*-Romans lesen.[41] Wie auf der formalen Ebene die Erzählperspektive, so stellt die Uniform als kulturelles Artefakt die Begrenzung und die Adressierbarkeit der Subjekte sicher. Dass die Uniform das „Verfließende des Lebens aufzuheben“ bestimmt sei, dass sie „eine zweite und dichtere Haut“ darstelle, die dazu dient, „den Dingen nicht mehr verbunden“[42] sein zu müssen, deutet darauf hin, dass das Subjekt Pasenow sich auf der Grenzscheide eines zweiseitigen Spannungsfeldes situiert, das in eine ‚uniformierte‘ und eine ‚zivile‘, eine ‚geordnete‘ und eine ‚verfließende‘ Seite auseinanderstrebt.[43] Die beiden Sphären knüpfen sich an die beiden Frauen Ruzena und Elisabeth. Ruzena ist als Animiermädchen eines Berliner Kasinos bereits metonymisch mit dem der spekulativen und unbeherrschbaren Seite der Geldzirkulation verknüpft. Im Laufe eines Abends, den Joachim gemeinsam mit seinem Vater und einigen Kameraden in dem Kasino verbringt, spitzt sich die Situation zu: Ruzena, das böhmische Animiermädchen, flirtet mit Vater und Sohn zugleich, bis Ruzena vom Vater „fünfzig Mark in die Hand gedrückt bekommt und

37 Ebd., S. 160.
38 Ebd., S. 167.
39 Martens (2006), *Beobachtungen*, S. 228.
40 Zeller (2013), Annäherung, S. 35.
41 Vgl. Lützeler (2000), *Entropie*, S. 41 f.
42 SW, S. 24 f.
43 Vgl. Peter v. Zima, *Roman und Ideologie. Zur Sozialgeschichte des modernen Romans*, München, 1986, S. 99-135.

sie sogar fröhlich einsteckt: „‚Danke, Pappa', sagt sie, ‚Schwiegerpappa', bessert sie sich aus und zwinkert zu Joachim."[44]

Dieses ökonomische Spiel wird im weiteren Handlungsverlauf die Grenzen der Familie und des Familiären überschreiten und immer neue trianguläre Konstellationen eröffnen. Wurden Joachim und sein Vater durch die Geldzahlung gegenüber Ruzena in ein Verhältnis der wechselseitigen Vertretung gebracht, in welchem der eine stellvertretend zahlt, der andere stellvertretend genießen soll, so kehrt das Phantasma der Vertretung wieder, als Joachim am Berliner Alexanderplatz einen unbekannten Passanten zu verfolgen beginnt, der in seiner Vorstellung „sehr sonderbar dem Bild" gleicht, „das er sich stets von Bertrands Vertreter gemacht hatte"[45]. Kurz darauf mutmaßt er, dass der Verfolgte ein „Geschäftsfreund" Bertrands sei: „Wahrscheinlich sind die beiden im Jägerkasino gesessen, und der Mann hat Ruzena fünfzig Mark zugesteckt."[46] Spätestens hier wird deutlich, dass die Logik der Substitution eine eigenartige Hermeneutik des Verdachts angestoßen hat: „[E]s mochte schon sein", so mutmaßt Joachim, während er den unbekannten Passanten betrachtet, „daß er darauf wartete, Joachim werde ihm jetzt die fünfzig Mark zurückgeben."[47] In Joachims Vorstellung wird also der Vater durch den Geschäftsfreund vertreten, der selbst der Vertreter Bertrands ist. Diese Reihung wird durch den Umlauf eines imaginären Geldbetrags konstituiert, der die ursprüngliche Position des Vaters ständig umbesetzt und die Subjekte miteinander vertauscht. Als der Unbekannte schließlich im Gebäude der Berliner Börse verschwindet, drängt sich Joachim der Gedanke auf, dass „dies der Ort der Verwandlung" sei: „Würde nun Bertrand selbst herauskommen?"[48]

Der ambivalente und ironische Bertrand, der in regelmäßigen Abständen mit seinem alten Freund Joachim zusammentrifft, lässt sich als Agent des Handelskapitals lesen.[49] Als Unternehmer in der Baumwollbranche mit Handelssitzen in Bremen und Liverpool betreibt er in Form von „weltumspannenden Geschäften"[50] jene grenzüberschreitenden Verknüpfungen, die das Gegenprinzip zur Pasenow'schen Uniform bilden. Vermittelt über Joachims Empfindungstexturen wird dabei der Topos einer dämonischen Ökonomie reinszeniert, der von der mephistophelischen Papiergeldschöpfung in Goethes *Faust* über Balzacs *Melmoth réconcilié* bis zu Wilhelm Raabes diabolischer Gläubigerfigur in *Zum wilden Mann* reicht.[51] „Man soll bekanntlich immer das tun, wozu einen der Dämon treibt"[52], sagt Bertrand einmal in Bezug auf seine Geschäftsreisen und treibt damit die Hermeneutik des Dämonischen an, die Joachims dualistische Weltdeutung zu imprägnieren be-

44 SW, S. 22.
45 SW, S. 55.
46 Ebd.
47 SW, S. 56.
48 SW, S. 58.
49 Vgl. Zeller (2013), Annäherung, S. 37.
50 SW, S. 100, siehe auch S. 30 f.
51 Zum *Faust* als Prätext des *Pasenow*-Romans vgl. Lützeler (1980), Lukács' ‚Theorie des Romans', S. 41.
52 SW, S. 32.

ginnt: Er argwöhnt, dass Bertrand „gleich Mephisto alles vernichten und selbst Ruzena nicht schonen wollte.“[53]

Die Funktion des Dämonischen im *Pasenow*-Roman lässt sich als Verschiebung des Dämoniebegriffs in Lukács' *Theorie des Romans* lesen. Dort bildet das Dämonische gleichsam den Rest eines ohnmächtigen Göttlichen in der Moderne: Die „Macht“ der Dämonen, so Lukács, „durchdringt die Welt nicht mehr oder noch nicht: die Welt hat einen Sinneszusammenhang und eine Kausalverknüpftheit erhalten, die der lebendig wirkenden Kraft des zum Dämon gewordenen Gottes unverständlich ist“.[54] Der ‚Sinneszusammenhang' und die Verknüpftheit einer Welt, deren Ordnungsmodelle sich zu parzellieren beginnen, und die nicht zuletzt deswegen des Supplements der Uniformen bedarf, stellt sich im *Pasenow*-Roman als eine Dämonie der Substitution her, die durch die Figur des Bertrand regelrecht vollzogen wird, wenn dieser sich sukzessive als Substitut innerhalb anderer Figurenverhältnisse etabliert.[55] Zunächst in Bezug auf Joachim: Als weibliche Figur – „blond und beinahe mädchenhaft“[56] – hat Bertrand Ähnlichkeit mit Elisabeth, während er als Teufelsfigur dem zwielichtigen Bereich der Ruzena zuzuordnen ist. Zugleich vertritt er Joachim beiden gegenüber, wenn er an dessen Stelle Ruzena in ihrer Wohnung aufsucht und dort im Streit von ihr verletzt wird, und wenn er kurz darauf Elisabeth ein Liebesgeständnis macht.[57] Der alte Pasenow wiederum deutet an, Bertrand anstelle von Joachim als Erben seines Landgutes einsetzen zu wollen.[58] In dieser Funktion eines Zielpunktes heterogener Wünsche, die Bertrand zum teils temporären, teils nur latenten Substitut der anderen Figuren werden lässt, erscheint er „weniger als eine reale Person als vielmehr als Personifikation des Begehrens der Hauptfiguren“[59].

Auf der Ebene der Handlungs- und Motivstruktur erscheint Bertrand damit als Figuration jener „allgemeinen Äquivalentform“, wie sie in Marx' *Kapital* entwickelt wird.[60] Die ‚allgemeine Äquivalentform', durch die eine bestimmte Ware die Funktion des Geldes zugewiesen bekommt, bildet „die gemeinsame Wertgestalt dieser Welt“, in deren Medium alle Waren sich auszutauschen vermögen und erst dadurch auch „einander als Tauschwerte erscheinen“.[61] Der Einbruch eines Spiels der Substitutionen, das sich als Dämonie in den *Pasenow*-Roman einschreibt, rein-

53 SW, S. 78.

54 Lukács (1994), *Theorie des Romans*, S. 79.

55 Sigrid Schmid-Bortenschlager, „Noch einmal: Die Figur Bertrand in den *Schlafwandlern*“, in: *German Life and Letters* 40 (1987), S. 177-185.

56 SW, S. 163.

57 SW, S. 136 f., S. 153 und S. 156.

58 SW, S. 103.

59 Schmid-Bortenschlager (1987), Figur Bertrand, S. 178.

60 Das Verhältnis des Broch'schen Tauschbegriffs zu Marx diskutiert Claus Caesar, *Poetik der Wiederholung. Ethische Dichtung und ökonomisches „Spiel“ in Hermann Brochs Romanen „Der Tod des Vergil“ und „Die Schuldlosen“*, Würzburg, 2001, S. 25-46.

61 Karl Marx, *Das Kapital. Kritik der politischen Ökonomie. Erster Band*, in: ders./Friedrich Engels, *Werke*, Band 23, Berlin, 1973, S. 80 f.

szeniert jene „allgemeine gesellschaftliche Verpuppung"[62], die durch die Zirkulation des allgemeinen Äquivalents in Gang gesetzt wird. Wie bei Marx einer bestimmten Warenart (etwa dem Gold) nur deshalb die „allgemeine Äquivalentform" zukommt, „weil und insofern sie durch alle andern Waren als Äquivalent ausgeschlossen wird"[63] – insofern sie also selbst nicht mehr als Ware, sondern als Maßstab aller übrigen Warenrelationen gehandhabt wird –, so wird auch Bertrand, nachdem er alle Funktionsstellen fremder Affekte und Begehren durchlaufen hat, von Joachim und Elisabeth in dem Moment ausgeschlossen, in dem sie ihr Verlobungsverhältnis arretieren. Der Ausschluss des Freundes, der als ihr wechselseitiges Substitut ihr gesellschaftlich codiertes Verlobungsverhältnis buchstäblich ‚relativiert' hatte, verläuft über eine Reihe surrealer und aggressiver Markierungen – „[s]ein Dämon treibt ihn fort", „[e]r ist fremd", „[s]ein Tod wird einsam sein"[64] –, um schließlich den Entschluss der Verlobung mit dem imaginären Tod des Freundes zu verbinden.

5. Erweiterter Fetischismus

Verzeichnet der *Pasenow*-Roman den Einbruch der Zirkulation, so ist im zweiten Roman, *1903. Esch oder die Anarchie*, die Zirkulation der Subjekte und des Begehrens bereits vorausgesetzt und in der wechselseitigen Wahrnehmung der Figuren in unterschiedlichen Graden verankert.[65] Was den Protagonisten antreibt, ist nicht, wie im *Pasenow*-Roman, die Bedrohung stabiler Identität durch das Spiel der Substitution, sondern das Verhältnis von Zirkulation und Täuschung, das als imaginäre Buchführung seine Interpretation des Wirklichen strukturiert. Es ist das Phantasma einer täuschenden oder korrupten Rechnungslegung des Wirklichen, die den Protagonisten zu einem quichottesken und anarchischen Furor der globalen Richtigstellung von Recht und Unrecht, zu einem „Kampf um die akribe Evidenz der Welt"[66] antreibt.

Wenn bei Broch der moderne Roman „zur Hermeneutik der Erfahrungswelt"[67] wird, so trifft diese Hermeneutik hier auf weitere, ‚intradiegetische' Hermeneutiken, die die Wirklichkeit des Romans strukturieren und im Sinne Nietzsches als „fortgesetzte Zeichen-Kette von immer neuen Interpretationen und Zurechtmachungen"[68] erscheinen lassen. Soziale Verhältnisse treten Esch in Form von „komplizierten Buchungen" gegenüber, buchhalterisch berechnet er die „Anzahl Mäd-

62 Ebd., S. 81
63 Ebd., S. 83.
64 SW, S. 160.
65 Vgl. Anjeana K. Hans, „Broch's *1903: Esch oder die Anarchie*: Desiring the Abject Outside", in: *The German Quarterly* 81, 1 (2008), S. 86-109.
66 SW, S. 415.
67 Vollhardt (1986), *Stellung*, S. 241.
68 Friedrich Nietzsche, *Zur Genealogie der Moral*, in: *Sämtliche Werke. Kritische Studienausgabe in 15 Bänden*, Band 5, hg. von Giorgio Colli und Mazzino Montinari, München, 1999, S. 245-412: 314.

chen, mit denen er in den letzten Jahren geschlafen hatte", während seine Innenwelt einer enigmatischen „Buchhaltung seiner Seele"[69] unterworfen wird. Wenn Esch gleich zu Beginn des Romans wegen eines angeblichen Buchungsfehlers aus seiner Position in einer Weingroßhandlung entlassen wird, so ist mit seiner Figur zugleich eine hermeneutische Bewegung freigesetzt, die zwischen den wirklichen Ereignissen und der Logik ökonomischer Buchhaltung eine neue Lesbarkeit der Welt generiert, die darauf zielt, all die „Buchungsfehler [zu] durchschauen [...], die so tückisch in die Welt geraten sind, daß nur einer, der genau zu rechnen versteht, den Erlösertod sterben darf."[70]

Diese Verquickung der ökonomischen Praxis der Buchhaltung mit dem theologischen Begriff der Erlösung strukturiert die ‚Anarchie' des Protagonisten und treibt ihn in eine Verschränkung von Verschwörungswahn und messianischen Phantasien.[71] Auf chaotische Weise verzeichnet Esch von ihm empfundene Ungerechtigkeiten – moralisch-metaphysische ‚Buchungsfehler' –, die von der Tatsache, dass sein ehemaliger Chef Nentwig ihn straflos hat entlassen können, über die polizeiliche Inhaftierung des Gewerkschafters Martin Geyring, die in Eschs Augen skandalöse Arbeit der Künstlerin Ilona als Partnerin eines Messerwerfers bis hin zur ‚verwerflichen' Homosexualität des Präsidenten der ‚Mittelrheinischen Reederei-A.G.' reichen, der niemand anderes ist als Eduard v. Bertrand.

> Und ohne Ordnung in den Büchern gab es auch keine Ordnung in der Welt, und solange keine Ordnung war, würde Ilona weiter den Messern ausgeliefert sein, würde Nentwig sich weiterhin frech und gleisnerisch der Sühne entziehen und Martin würde ewig im Kerker schmachten.[72]

Eschs Überzeugung, die Welt müsse von Personen wie Nentwig und Bertrand, bei dessen Firma in Mannheim er Anstellung findet, „erlöst werden"[73], ergibt sich dabei keinesfalls daraus, dass beide „Vertreter des Tauschwertes" seien, „dessen Ambivalenzen [...] von der Ideologie [Eschs] negiert werden."[74] Vielmehr ist es der Buchhalter Esch selbst, der die Ideologie des Tauschwerts vertritt, und der gerade deshalb zu Bertrand eine ambivalente Beziehung aufbaut.[75] Bertrand erscheint ihm in einer doppelten Codierung: zum einen als „etwas Besseres", „etwas Größeres", das er „gerne einmal zu Gesicht bekommen"[76] hätte. Hier ist die Figur des Bertrand von der Funktion allgemeiner Substituierbarkeit, in der er im *Pasenow*-Roman auftritt – dort für Elisabeth noch „ein unruhiger und deshalb [...] beunruhigender Mensch"[77] –, zum ruhenden Pol aufgestiegen, der „in den oberen Stock-

---

69 SW, S. 319, S. 233 und S. 199.

70 SW, S. 183 und S. 319.

71 Vgl. Martens (2006), *Beobachtungen*, S. 200-203.

72 SW, S. 243.

73 SW, S. 237.

74 Zima (1986), *Ideologie*, S. 109.

75 Zum von Ressentiment und Begehren widersprüchlich strukturierten Verhältnis Esch/Bertrand siehe Hans (2008), Abject Outside, S. 90-92.

76 SW, S. 211, S. 237 und S. 245.

77 SW, S. 158.

werken des Bürohauses“[78] residiert und von Esch zu einer beinah sakralen Figur erhoben wird: nicht Äquivalentform, sondern Verkörperung des abstrakten ‚Werts‘ selbst. Zum anderen mutmaßt Esch, derselbe Bertrand könnte der „Sitz des Giftes“[79] sein, das die Buchungsfehler in die Welt bringt. Als Esch das Hauptgebäude der Reederei-A.G. aufsucht, um seine Stellung zu kündigen, vermutet er sogleich, dass „unter dem Schein schöner Ordnung, glatter Gänge, schöner glatter Buchungen“ nichts als „Infamien“, ja „lauter Nentwigs“[80] verborgen seien. Gegen diesen janusköpfigen, zugleich verehrten und verdächtigten Fetisch tritt Esch als Vertreter einer verlorenen Tauschgesellschaft an, deren universale Äquivalenzen er überprüfen und restituieren will.[81]

Esch, der im Namen bereits die Schwundstufe einer heilsgeschichtlichen Weltauslegung anzeigt, steht für eine ins Eschatologische gesteigerte Opposition von falschem und richtigem Tauschwert, von manipulierter und wahrer Äquivalenz. Damit wird im *Esch*-Roman der Problembezug auf den Marx'schen Wertbegriff fortgeschrieben: Anhand von Esch inszeniert der Roman parodistisch eine Universalisierung jener Wirklichkeitsschicht, die bei Marx als „Zirkulationssphäre“ die Tiefenstruktur des Sozialen verdeckt: „Diese geräuschvolle, auf der Oberfläche hausende und aller Augen zugängliche Sphäre“, die als Spiel freier und äquivalenter Tauschakte „in der Tat ein wahres Eden der angebornen Menschenrechte“ ist, kann das notorische „Geheimnis der Plusmacherei“[82] nicht erklären. Während „der Freihändler vulgaris“ aus jener „Sphäre der einfachen Zirkulation [...] Begriffe und Maßstab für sein Urteil über die Gesellschaft des Kapitals und der Lohnarbeit entlehnt“, hat die *Kritik der politischen Ökonomie* vom Wechselspiel der Warenwerte und Geldbeträge zur „verborgne[n] Stätte der Produktion“[83] vorzudringen. Das ‚wahre Eden‘, als das Marx eine um ihre Produktionsverhältnisse bereinigte Zirkulationssphäre gleichsam an die Nationalökonomie seiner Zeit zurückgibt, ist in den *Schlafwandlern* zu Eschs Leitprinzip geworden: „Leistung erforderte Gegenleistung und Ware wollte Bezahlung.“[84]

Wenn die Essays im dritten Roman der Trilogie einen ‚Wertzerfall‘ als geschichtsphilosophisches Postulat setzen, so produziert der *Esch*-Roman durch die parodistische Offenlegung des Äquivalenzprinzips zugleich selbst einen Zerfall spezifisch ökonomischer Wertkonstruktionen, denen zufolge, wie es in einem Grundlagenwerk der neoklassischen Wirtschaftstheorie heißt, „die unzähligen Tauschakte [...] in ihrer Gesamtheit die äußere Form [bilden], in der der Kreislauf des wirtschaftlichen Lebens dahinströmt.“[85] In den *Schlafwandlern* vollzieht sich die narrative Abnutzung dieser Semantik entlang der Figur des Esch nicht zuletzt

78 SW, S. 244.

79 SW, S. 237.

80 SW, S. 244.

81 Vgl. Sebastian (1995), *Gang der Geschichte*, S. 95 f.

82 Marx (1973), *Kapital I*, S. 189.

83 Ebd., S. 190 f. und S. 189.

84 SW, S. 199.

85 Joseph Schumpeter, *Theorie der wirtschaftlichen Entwicklung*, Berlin [1912], 2006, S. 63.

in der Form einer Ausweitung und Dislozierung jener sozialen Praxis, die Marx als ‚Fetischismus' bezeichnet hat: Wenn der ‚Tauschwert' darin seine eigentümliche Wirkungsmacht besitzt, dass das „gesellschaftliche Verhältnis der Menschen", wie es im *Kapital* heißt, „für sie die phantasmagorische Form eines Verhältnisses von Dingen annimmt"[86], wenn die Ware demnach als „eine gesellschaftliche Hieroglyphe" bezeichnet werden muss, die nur eine Kritik der politischen Ökonomie „zu entziffern"[87] vermag, so schießt der Furor von Eschs Tauschprinzip gleichsam über das Feld des Geldes und der Waren, d. h. der bereits gesellschaftlich fetischisierten Gegenstände, hinaus. Alles erscheint als Ware, jede Handlung als Bezahlung, jede Irritation als Buchungsfehler, und noch die zwischenmenschliche Entfremdung soll den Geschäftsweg nehmen: Esch will „seine ganze Fremdheit" in Mutter Hentjen „aufgehen lassen", um „auch all ihre Fremdheit [...] sozusagen im Tauschwege zu erwerben"[88].

So deterritorialisiert Esch den Marx'schen Fetischismus und schafft damit gleichsam eine doppelte Textur, Hieroglyphen von Hieroglyphen, die, wie Esch selbst, aus dem Bereich der Arbeitsprodukte und ihrer Märkte auf das ganze Ereignisfeld der Gesellschaft ‚entlassen' wird. Damit beobachtet der Roman einen Kollaps der Unterscheidung zwischen Wert und Wirklichkeit: Esch fungiert als Operator, der überall die Differenz zwischen Tausch und Gebrauch, zwischen Fetisch und Materialität aufhebt. So schlägt die Brüchigkeit der Pasenow'schen Erfahrungswelt um in eine durchgehende Verzerrung des Wirklichen.

6. Zerfall und Akkumulation

Wenn für den Buchhalter Esch die Wirklichkeit „geteilt" ist „in Soll und Haben" und sich auf diese Weise in Form von Bilanzen „symbolisiert"[89], so umspielt der *Esch*-Roman darin implizit die Leerstelle einer Wirklichkeit, die dieser Symbolik von Soll und Haben entgeht, und die sich im toten Winkel der imaginär-eschatologischen Buchhaltung zusammenfügt. Diese gleichsam profane Wirklichkeit, die sowohl die Dämonie der Zirkulation als auch den Fetischismus von Soll und Haben unterläuft, tritt – so meine These – im dritten Roman *1918. Huguenau oder die Sachlichkeit* in den Vordergrund.

Als „wertfreier Mensch"[90] ist Huguenau eine Gegenfigur zu Esch, der Wirklichkeit ausschließlich im Zerrbild einer imaginären Buchhaltung wahrzunehmen vermag. Huguenau handelt in einer Kleinstadt nahe Trier, in die er nach seiner Desertion von der belgischen Front geflüchtet ist, unreflektiert und gleichsam unschuldig nach dem Prinzip eines radikalen Eigeninteresses, in dessen Rahmen selbst ökonomischen Werten und ihrer Notation nur eine verminderte Signifikanz

86 Marx (1973), *Kapital I*, S. 86.
87 Ebd., S. 88.
88 SW, S. 359.
89 SW, S. 479 und S. 412.
90 SW, S. 693.

zukommt. Hat es zum einen „seit seiner Knabenzeit keine andern Inhalte des Redens und Denkens gegeben [...] als Geld und Geschäft“[91], so hat Huguenaus Egoismus doch mit der liberalwirtschaftlichen Ideologie von Marktpreisen und Interessenausgleich nicht viel zu tun. Das Profil des Geschäftsmanns ist für ihn nur ein temporäres und lästiges Format der Machtausübung, die ökonomische Charaktermaske selbst eine Maske dessen, was Broch als „Durchbruch des Irrationalen“[92] bezeichnet.

Der Vertragsabschluss zwischen August Esch, der mittlerweile Chefredakteur des Zeitungsverlags ‚Kurtrierscher Bote‘ geworden ist, und Huguenau, der die Zeitung zu einer Kapitalgesellschaft umzuformen gedenkt, ist weder eine juristische noch eine ökonomische Szene, sondern die Szene einer beinah komödiantischen Machtausübung. Ausgerechnet Esch, der Anarchist einer radikalen Buchhaltung, wird von Huguenau auf platteste Weise über den Tisch gezogen. Huguenau verpflichtet sich zu einer Kapitaleinlage von 20.000 Mark, ohne über irgendeine Geldsumme zu verfügen, indem er zum einen als Vertreter einer „Gruppe lokaler Interessenten“ auftritt, die er zuvor für das patriotische Projekt des Zeitungsunternehmens gewonnen hat, zum anderen als Vertreter einer ominösen „Industriegruppe“, die Huguenau frei erfindet und deren Identität er im Vagen belässt, so „daß man in ihm tatsächlich den Exponenten der kapitalkräftigsten Industriegruppe des Reiches zu sehen hatte (Krupp).“[93] Die Verhandlungssituation wird zur Farce eines ökonomischen Interessensausgleichs: Während Huguenau sich immer wieder an Frau Esch wendet, um deren Gatten zu einem Schleuderpreis für Verlag und Druckerei zu überreden, während er die transitorische Rechtsform „Gedächtnisprotokoll“ bruchlos in den „Vertrag“ übergehen lässt und den Streit immer wieder „geschickt“ auf ein „Nebenthema“ verschiebt, wird die Auszahlungsforderung des Esch, der „von den in Aussicht stehenden komplizierten Buchungen geblendet“[94] ist, schließlich von 18.000 auf 12.000 Mark heruntergehandelt. Huguenau, der tatsächlich ohne jedes Eigenkapital ist, wird ein Gewinnanteil von 60 % zugesichert.

Das Prinzip der Vertretung hat hier alles Dämonische abgestreift und wird im Kalkül Huguenaus zur leeren Form. Die wechselseitige Substitution der Figuren im *Pasenow*-Roman ist zur Substitution realer Personen (wie der „Industriegruppe“, die Huguenau erfindet) durch Fiktionen geworden. Die Interpretation allerdings, Huguenau „allegorisier[e] das autopoietische Wesen des Kredits“, da Kredit stets „seine Deckung [...] in die Zukunft verschiebt“[95], verkehrt die konsequente Profanierung des Ökonomischen, die der *Huguenau*-Roman vornimmt. Vielmehr ist es, so legt der Roman nahe, der Begriff des Kredits selbst, der die Banalität von Enteignungsprozessen ‚allegorisiert‘: Die betriebswirtschaftliche Logik von „verspätete[r] Einzahlung“, „Ratenverzinsung“[96] usw., die im Vertragstext das Konzept des

91 SW, S. 395.
92 SW, S. 689.
93 SW, S. 457 f. und S. 439.
94 SW, S. 456-459.
95 Sebastian (1995), *Gang der Geschichte*, S. 113.
96 SW, S. 458 f.

Kredits reproduziert, wird bei Huguenau zu einer Reihe willkürlicher Setzungen, deren Fluchtpunkt nicht eine konstitutive Fiktivität des Kredits, sondern der platte Mord am Anderen darstellt: Huguenau macht sich „wenig Sorge, wie er selbst die Raten der legendären Industriegruppe aufbringen würde, [...] vielleicht würde Esch bis dahin tot sein“[97].

Wo im *Esch*-Roman eine Verdinglichung des Sozialen eskaliert, gibt es für Huguenau von vorn herein nur noch Dinge: Gegenstände, Körper, Maschinen, Geld. Jene ‚depersonalen‘ Erzählbewegungen, die in den ersten beiden Romanen einen Zerfallsprozess der Perspektive anzeigen, werden annulliert und in die Äußerlichkeit eines gleichsam ohnmächtigen Erzählers verschoben. Während Geldbeträge, Prozentsätze und montierte Vertragstexte die Narration durchsetzen, wird zugleich die reflexive Tiefe der ersten beiden Romane, und insbesondere des *Pasenow*-Romans, eingezogen und auf einer ‚flachen‘ Wirklichkeit verteilt. Diese Wirklichkeit zeigt sich im Medium immer kürzer werdender Unterkapitel als rapide Folge von Orts- und Szenenwechseln, in deren Rahmen Verträge und Morde, Tanzbälle und Vergewaltigungen, Kaffeekränzchen und Erpressungen aneinandergefügt werden und als indifferentes Ereigniskontinuum erscheinen. Es ist diese flache Wirklichkeit, die im Titel des dritten Romans mit dem Begriff der ‚Sachlichkeit‘ belegt wird, und die vom Machtinstinkt Huguenaus wie von einem Vektor durchlaufen werden kann. Dem fiktiven Autor der Essays, Bertrand Müller, bleibt diese Wirklichkeit unzugänglich: „ein Fremdes, in das ich niemals eindringen werde [...], vergehend und zerfallend“[98].

Wenn jener Bertrand Müller die Versachlichung der Wirklichkeit dennoch als „Auflösung des christlich-platonischen Weltbilds“ deutet, vor dessen Hintergrund „sogar die Probleme der Güterverteilung [...] in den Hintergrund“[99] träten, so hat der *Huguenau*-Roman die „Probleme der Güterverteilung“ längst auf das Problem der gewaltsamen Aneignung von Gütern verschoben: Huguenau ist kein Vertreter des berechenbaren *homo oeconomicus*, sondern Agent einer chaotischen Aneignungsgewalt. Anders als Pasenow und Esch ist er weder durch die Überreste eines Wertsystems noch durch die Fetische der Zirkulation gebunden. Seine „hochgradige Kurzsichtigkeit“[100] gilt auch im übertragenen Sinn für jene kulturell-ideelle Tiefenstruktur der ‚Wertsysteme‘, deren Begriff in den theoretischen Essays expliziert wird.

Daher ist die Feststellung, mit Huguenau gelange „das Kommerzielle, die Ökonomie“ und der „Profit“ zum „Sieg“[101], allzu unspezifisch, ist doch der Begriff ‚Öko-

---

97 SW, S. 458.

98 SW, S. 617.

99 SW, S. 705 und S. 703.

100 SW, S. 385.

101 Bärbel Lücke, „Hermann Brochs *1918. Huguenau oder die Sachlichkeit* (*Die Schlafwandler*) und Elfriede Jelineks *Abraumhalde*. Zwischen Zerfall und Restituierung religiöser und ökonomischer Paradigmen – eine Engführung“, in: *Weimarer Beiträge* 56, 4 (2010), S. 485-500: 491 f.; ähnlich Zeller (2013), Annäherung, S. 35, der die Problematik des Huguenau auf die „Prädominanz wirtschaftlicher Erwägungen“ reduziert.

nomie' nicht von sozialen Ordnungsfiguren, ,Kommerz' und ,Profit' nicht von institutionalisierten und normalisierten Marktmechanismen zu trennen. Im *Huguenau*-Roman bricht vielmehr die Materialität eines Prozesses hervor, als dessen „klassische Form" Marx den frühneuzeitlichen „Expropriationsprozeß"[102] gegen die englische Landbevölkerung beschrieben hat. Wie Marx das nationalökonomische ,Geheimnis' der ,ursprünglichen Akkumulation' dadurch auflöst, dass er die Verflechtung frühneuzeitlicher Staatsgewalt mit der Geschichte gewaltsamer Landnahmen als ,Genesis' der kapitalistischen Sozialformen rekonstruiert, so tritt in den *Schlafwandlern* mit Huguenau ein Trieb der Akkumulation in Erscheinung, der selbst von den Institutionen des Ökonomischen – Märkte, Preise, Äquivalenz – entbunden ist. Diese innere, intensive Fortsetzung ,ursprünglicher Akkumulation', die der Roman im Krisengeschehen am Ende des Weltkriegs aufbrechen sieht, korrespondiert mit jener Theorie ihrer extensiv-imperialen Fortsetzung, die Rosa Luxemburg kurz vor Beginn des Krieges ausgearbeitet hatte.[103]

Am Ende wird Huguenau die politischen Unruhen des Novembers 1918 dazu nutzen, Esch – spontan und gleichsam ohne Vorsatz, im Moment einer empfundenen „Erleuchtung"[104] – mit einem Bajonett hinterrücks niederzustechen. Kurz zuvor hat er dessen schutzlos zurückgebliebene Frau vergewaltigt, der gegenüber er später, nachdem er die Stadt bereits verlassen hat, brieflich 8.000 Francs für die Überlassung seiner Firmenanteile einfordern wird. Und wie bei Marx die ,ursprüngliche Akkumulation' auf der Ebene ökonomischer Kategorien nicht mehr repräsentiert werden kann und dem bürgerlichen Ökonomen als „Geheimnis" erscheint, das nachträglich entlang der „Idylle"[105] einer ursprünglichen, symmetrischen Tauschgesellschaft gedeutet wird, so wird sich für Huguenau später, wenn er „ins kaufmännische System zurückgefunden" haben wird, ein „Verdämmern und Vergessen"[106] über seine Erinnerung legen.

7. Meta-Realismus

Die Figuren der *Schlafwandler*-Trilogie bewegen sich in einer zerfallenden Ordnung, die sie zu restituieren (*Pasenow*) oder deren Schwundformen sie, wie im *Esch*-Roman, auf eigene Faust zu verabsolutieren versuchen.[107] Diese kulturtheoretische Codierung des Schlafwandelns ist es, die die Essays über den ,Wertzerfall' in den Roman selbst einlegen und dadurch eine „Introduzierung des ideellen Be-

102 Marx (1973), *Kapital I*, S. 744 und S. 756.

103 Rosa Luxemburg, *Die Akkumulation des Kapitals. Ein Beitrag zur ökonomischen Erklärung des Imperialismus* [1913], in: *Gesammelte Werke. Band 5: Ökonomische Schriften*, Berlin, 1975, S. 5-411.

104 SW, S. 677.

105 Marx (1973), *Kapital I*, S. 742.

106 SW, S. 703 und S. 698.

107 Vgl. Howard L. Kaye, „Hermann Broch's *The Sleepwalkers*: Social Theory in Literary Form", in: *Mosaic* XV, 4 (1982), S. 79-89.

obachters in das Beobachtungsfeld"[108] vornehmen, wie es im ,Erkenntnistheoretischen Exkurs' heißt. Aus der Perspektive dieses ,ideellen Beobachters' verkörpert Huguenau einen „Nullpunkt der Wertatomisierung", der auf die Utopie einer zukünftigen „ersehnteren Gemeinschaft" hoffen lässt, in welcher „die entfesselten irrationalen Kräfte sich wieder zu einem Wertsystem zusammenschließen"[109]. Demgegenüber wird durch die ökonomische Motivstruktur der Trilogie eine andere Fluchtlinie in den Roman eingeführt, die diesen ,Zusammenschluss' ungebundener und zirkulierender ,Kräfte' zu einer neuen Gemeinschaft implizit auf eine Logik des Kapitals ausrichtet und dabei nicht nur die Perspektive des ,ideellen Beobachters', sondern auch die Distanz des Autors Broch zum marxistischen Geschichts- und Gesellschaftsbegiff zu unterlaufen scheint.[110] Diese Logik kündigt sich im unheimlichen Einbruch der Substitution in den *Pasenow*-Roman an, strukturiert bei Esch die Fetischisierung der Äquivalenz, um dann im *Huguenau* als Exzess von Aneignungen die Form des Ökonomischen selbst zu überschreiten.

Entlang dieser Fluchtlinie situiert sich in den *Schlafwandlern* die Logik des Kapitals als Macht einer Entwirklichung von Wertsystemen und damit als Nährboden jener ,überwachen Schlaflosigkeit'[111], die am Ursprung der liberal-demokratischen Gesellschaftsordnung die Gestalt des Huguenau hervortreibt. Wenn der verzweifelte Werttheoretiker Dr. Bertrand Müller eine Figuration des Intellektuellen Hermann Broch darstellt[112], so verdichtet sich in der Figur des Huguenau nicht nur das Irrationale einer von ,Werten' entbundenen Zeit, sondern auch das ,Wirkliche' jener Entwirklichung, die die Subjekte als Schlafwandler erscheinen lässt. Wenn sich dabei die historisch-materialistische Tradition einer Problematisierung gesellschaftlicher Wirklichkeit in die *Schlafwandler* einschreibt, so geht es dem Roman doch weniger um ein positives Wissen von wirtschaftlichen Prozessen als vielmehr um ein Verhältnis von Darstellung und Wirklichkeit, das sich als meta-realistisch bezeichnen ließe: Brochs *Schlafwandler*-Trilogie steht gerade insofern in der Tradition realistischen Erzählens, als ihre Poetik sich an die Form zerfallender Realitätsbezüge knüpft. In diesem Zerfall analysiert der Roman die je spezifische Art und Weise, auf die die Wirklichkeit der Romanfiguren ihre Konturen verliert, auf die ihre Fetische eskalieren und ihre Tiefendimension sich verflacht und verschwindet.

An den Bruchstellen dieses Zerfalls aber wird die Signatur einer kapitalistischen Verwertung lesbar, die als das materielle und zugleich verdeckte ,Reale' des idealistischen *grand récit* vom ,Wertzerfall' erscheint. Selbst ästhetische Form des Zerfalls, stoßen die *Schlafwandler* mit der Logik des Kapitals auf eine andere gesellschaftliche Form des Zerfalls, welche die Utopie der ,ersehnteren Gemeinschaft' an eine Szenerie der Kapitalisierung zurückbindet. Dabei trägt Brochs Roman, indem er zwischen einer idealistischen Wertkonzeption und einer politischen

108 SW, S. 623.

109 SW, S. 712, S. 713 und S. 710.

110 Ernestine Schlant, „Hermann Brochs Auseinandersetzung mit dem Marxismus", in: *Modern Austrian Literature* 13 (1980), S. 121-144.

111 SW, S. 355.

112 Zeller (2013), Annäherung, S. 62.

Ökonomie des Werts oszilliert, die Brüchigkeit von Wirklichkeitsbezügen gleichsam als Doppelblick in seine eigene Erzählstruktur ein.

Ulrike Vedder

Phantastische Realien: Weltausstellung und Literatur

Begriff, Konzept und Erfolgsgeschichte des Realismus hängen mit der Geschichte der Weltausstellungen eng zusammen, wie sich an einem historischen Ereignis manifestiert. Im Jahr 1855 erklärt Gustave Courbet sein *Realistisches Manifest*, das gegen den Akademismus und Klassizismus der zeitgenössischen französischen Malerei gerichtet ist. Unmittelbarer Auslöser ist die Ablehnung seiner Gemälde durch die Jury der Pariser Weltausstellung 1855: Da die Bilder *L'Enterrement à Ornans* (1850) und *L'Atelier* (1855) mangels idealisierender Darstellung nicht zugelassen werden, errichtet Courbet daraufhin vor dem offiziellen Gebäude einen von ihm sogenannten *Pavillon du réalisme*, der nicht nur der Ausstellung und dem Verkauf seiner Gemälde dient, sondern der auch Begriff und Sache des Realismus in der Malerei erfolgreich propagiert; anders gesagt: den Durchbruch des Realismus einleitet.

Auch wenn also die innerhalb der *Exposition universelle* 1855 ausgestellten Gemälde die künstlerischen Möglichkeiten des Realismus (noch) nicht nutzen, stellen sie doch – sozusagen *contre cœur* – einen Beitrag zur Wirklichkeitskonstruktion *qua* Weltausstellung dar. Denn wenn der *Palais des Beaux-Arts* – wie der Londoner Kristallpalast 1851 aus Glas und Eisen erbaut – über 5.000 Kunstwerke präsentiert,[1] so ist diese hohe Anzahl kein Zufall, setzt doch die Weltausstellung seit ihrer ersten Realisierung auf eine synchronisierende Darstellung der Welt in Form einer überwältigenden Menge an Realien. Die Ding- bzw. Warenflut wird 1851 in London auf einer Fläche von zehn Hektar – davon sieben Hektar im Crystal Palace – präsentiert: Eine Million Exponate von 14.000 Ausstellern aus 94 Staaten, Kolonien und Fürsten- und Herzogtümern werden von über sechs Millionen Besuchern während der gut halbjährigen Ausstellungsdauer besichtigt.

Dass eine solche gigantische Exposition zugleich zum „poetischsten und weltgeschichtlichsten Ereignis der Zeit" erklärt werden kann – durch den preußischen Botschafter in London, Freiherr von Bunsen[2] –, ist für den im Folgenden darzulegenden Diskussionszusammenhang symptomatisch: Zwar prägt ein realistischer, auf materiale Objekte, funktionale Technik und Industriemoderne bezogener Zugriff auf die Welt das Ausstellungskonzept der *Great Exhibition of the Works of*

[1] Vier Jahre zuvor, bei der ersten Weltausstellung 1851 in London, fand noch keine Ausstellung von Gemälden und Skulpturen statt.

[2] Zit. nach Alexander Geppert, „Die normative Kraft des Flüchtigen. Exponierungen des Globalen in der Welt der Weltausstellungen, 1851-1900", in: Ulrike Bergermann (Hg.), *Das Planetarische. Kultur – Technik – Medien im postglobalen Zeitalter*, München, 2010, S. 81-96: 84.

Industry of All Nations, doch zugleich fungiert die Weltausstellung als „Leitmedium des neuen globalisierten Imaginären",[3] das auf unterschiedliche Weise aufgerufen wird. So ist beispielsweise eine umfassende Fetischisierung der Ware zu beobachten, wie sie auf den Weltausstellungen – Walter Benjamin nennt sie „Wallfahrtstätten zum Fetisch Ware"[4] – mit hohem inszenatorischem Aufwand betrieben wird. Dabei werden bevorzugt illusionistische und narrative Ausstellungsformen popularisiert, befördert durch die Darstellungstechniken von Diorama, Panoptikum und Panorama, also durch auf die Schaulust berechnete Vorläufer der bewegten Bilder.

Das vielfältige Spannungsverhältnis zwischen realistischen und imaginären Dimensionen soll im Folgenden zunächst anhand einiger Narrations- und Inszenierungsprinzipien der frühen Weltausstellungen seit 1851 entfaltet werden, um es anschließend in Bezug auf literarische Narrative des späten 19. und frühen 20. Jahrhunderts, die die Institution der Weltausstellung aufnehmen, zu diskutieren. Interessanterweise sind es weniger die paradigmatischen realistischen Romane oder die ‚großen Autoren' des Realismus von Émile Zola bis Wilhelm Raabe, die auf die zeitgenössischen Weltausstellungen rekurrieren, offenbar sind dafür eher tagesaktuelle Journale oder popularisierende Magazine zuständig. Im engeren Sinne literarisiert werden die Weltausstellungen hingegen in ihren geradezu mythischen Dimensionen durch beobachtungsstarke und am Imaginären interessierte Texte von Charles Baudelaire bis Arthur Schnitzler. Dieser auf den ersten Blick erstaunliche Befund – dass der literarische Realismus sich die Weltausstellung als Sujet und Kulisse überwiegend entgehen lässt – kann angesichts der bekannten „Probleme bei der Darstellung von Realität"[5] zur doppelten Frage nach den Funktionsweisen und Aporien realistischer Repräsentationsweisen sowie nach der Aussage- und Formationskraft des Imaginären der ausgestellten Dingwelten gewendet werden.[6]

---

3 Gerhart von Graevenitz, *Theodor Fontane: Ängstliche Moderne. Über das Imaginäre*, Konstanz, 2014, S. 210.

4 Walter Benjamin, „Paris, die Hauptstadt des XIX. Jahrhunderts", in: *Das Passagenwerk*, Band V.I., hg. von Rolf Tiedemann (= *Gesammelte Schriften*, hg. von Rolf Tiedemann und Herrmann Schweppenhäuser, Band V.I.), Frankfurt/M., 1982, S. 45-59: 50.

5 Vgl. den einschlägigen Buchtitel von Christiane Arndt, *Abschied von der Wirklichkeit. Probleme bei der Darstellung von Wirklichkeit im deutschsprachigen literarischen Realismus*, Freiburg i. Br., Wien, Berlin, 2009.

6 Wenn im Folgenden die Begriffe des Imaginären und der Imagination denen des Realistischen bzw. des Realismus nicht einfach entgegengestellt werden, sondern die Verflechtung zwischen beiden Dimensionen sich für die Literatur als besonders erkenntnisträchtig und kritikfähig erweist, so folge ich damit gerade nicht der Unterscheidung zwischen dem Imaginären und dem Fiktiven, die ein Gegenstand der Auseinandersetzung zwischen Wolfgang Iser und Karlheinz Stierle war. Vgl. dazu Wolfgang Iser, *Das Fiktive und das Imaginäre. Perspektiven literarischer Anthropologie*, Frankfurt/M., 1991, sowie Karlheinz Stierle, Art. „Fiktion", in: Karlheinz Barck et al. (Hg.), *Ästhetische Grundbegriffe. Historisches Wörterbuch in sieben Bänden*, Band 2, Stuttgart, Weimar, 2001, S. 380-428, v. a. S. 380 f.

1. Welt und Ausstellung: Narrations- und Inszenierungsprinzipien der Weltausstellungen

Analog zum zeitgleich entstehenden Warenhaus,[7] das, so Benjamin, „eine Stadt, ja eine Welt im kleinen"[8] darstellt, kondensiert auch die *Great Exhibition* 1851, wie all ihre Nachfolgerinnen, in ihren zeitlich und räumlich zwar begrenzten, aber zugleich aufs Unendliche zielenden Dimensionen die ‚ganze Welt': „Die Weltausstellung präsentiert, wenngleich in verkleinertem Maßstab, ein Modell von Welt, das – wie die Welt im Großen – betreten und begangen und über sämtliche Sinneswahrnehmungen erschlossen werden kann."[9] Damit ist nicht nur ein neuartiger dreidimensionaler Wahrnehmungs- und Erfahrungsraum angesprochen; auch soll sich nicht nur ein Makrokosmos in einem Mikrokosmos spiegeln: die Weltausstellung als Wunderkammer der Moderne. Vielmehr zielt sie in ihrer ökonomischen Bedingtheit darüber hinaus auf jene „umfassende Absorption der Außenwelt in einem vollständig durchgerechneten Innenraum", die Peter Sloterdijk in seinen Überlegungen zum Londoner Kristallpalast als Grundlage eines „integralen, erlebnisorientierten, populären Kapitalismus" begreift. Zugleich weist dieser Raum imaginäre Dimensionen auf, denn er verkörpert, so Sloterdijk, „die Idee eines Gehäuses [...], das geräumig genug wäre, um es vielleicht nie mehr verlassen zu müssen."[10]

Der ‚Palast' ist ein in neuer Bautechnik aus vorfabrizierten – und von vornherein für die spätere Demontage vorgesehenen – gusseisernen Elementen, Holz und Glas geschaffener monumentaler Bau, 563 Meter lang und 124 Meter breit mit einem 33 Meter hohen Glasgewölbe, um die alten Ulmen auf dem Gelände in den Bau zu integrieren. Mitsamt der in ihm ausgestellten Maschinen, Rohstoffe, Produkte und Kunstwerke tritt er als eine Art Gesamtkunstwerk auf, das „die Erfassung des ästhetischen Potentials der Industrie"[11] ermöglicht. Dabei wird der Kristallpalast selbst zur „Ikone", deren gläserne Wände „als Membran und Körper"[12] die Grenzen

---

7 1852, ein Jahr nach der Londoner Weltausstellung, entwickelt das Ehepaar Boucicaut das Warenhaus *Le Bon Marché* aus einem kleineren Unternehmen; 1855, im Jahr der Pariser *Exposition universelle*, werden die *Grands Magasins du Louvre* gegründet. Zu einigen Parallelen zwischen Warenhaus und Weltausstellung vgl. Ulrike Vedder, „Eine enzyklopädische Literatur der Dinge: Émile Zolas Warenhausroman ‚Au Bonheur des Dames'", in: *arcadia* 48, 2 (2013), S. 354-367.

8 Benjamin (1982), Paris, die Hauptstadt des XIX. Jahrhunderts, S. 45 (Benjamin zitiert hier aus „Illustrierter Pariser Führer").

9 Nicole Pöppel, „Weltausstellungen als Schreibstätten des Globalen", in: Christian Moser/Linda Simonis (Hg.), *Figuren des Globalen. Weltbezug und Welterzeugung in Literatur, Kunst und Medien*, Göttingen, 2014, S. 633-644: 633. Vgl. zum Folgenden auch: Ulrike Vedder, „Museum/Ausstellen", in: Karlheinz Barck et al. (Hg.), *Ästhetische Grundbegriffe. Historisches Wörterbuch in sieben Bänden*, Band 9, Stuttgart, Weimar, 2005, S. 148-190.

10 Peter Sloterdijk, *Im Weltinnenraum des Kapitals. Für eine philosophische Theorie der Globalisierung*, Frankfurt/M., 2005, S. 275.

11 Georg Maag, *Kunst und Industrie im Zeitalter der ersten Weltausstellungen. Synchrone Analyse einer Epochenschwelle*, Diss. Konstanz, 1982, S. 152.

12 Christoph Asendorf, *Batterien der Lebenskraft. Zur Geschichte der Dinge und ihrer Wahrnehmung im 19. Jahrhundert*, Gießen, 1984, S. 22.

zwischen Innen- und Außenraum aufzuheben und die Materialität der ausgestellten Dinge zu überwinden scheinen. Dank solcher ästhetischen Erfahrung erlangen die Waren Kultcharakter, ihr Tauschwert wird verklärt.

Allerdings ist der Ausstellungsbesuch mit Zerstreuungs- und Entfremdungserfahrungen verbunden, weil die überdimensionierte Fülle der Exponate den Betrachter zu lähmen und zu annihilieren droht.[13] Dieser Realitätsverlust gründet aber nicht nur in der Massenhaftigkeit der Exponate, sondern auch im Synkretismus der künstlich arrangierten Wirklichkeit als „Kompositwelt", die „sich vom Kunstwerk die kompositorische Gebärde, von der Wirklichkeit die handgreifliche Dreidimensionalität leiht"[14]. Dabei drohen der museale Aspekt der Weltausstellung mit ihrer retrospektiven Präsentation der Menschheitsgeschichte einerseits und der experimentelle Aspekt zukunftsweisender Entwürfe andererseits sich wechselseitig zu dementieren. Die vereinheitlichende Rahmung erfolgt dagegen sowohl durch den Glauben an Harmonie und Völkerversöhnung (1867 verfasst Victor Hugo zur Pariser Weltausstellung sein Manifest *An die Völker Europas*) als auch durch die Wahrnehmung aller Exponate – auch der präsentierten Kunstwerke – als Ware.

Mit der systematischen Katalogisierung und Bewertung industrieller Produkte, das heißt kapitalistischer Leistungsfähigkeit, betreibt die Weltausstellung seit ihren Anfängen eine „Epiphanie des Werts"[15], der als – die Ausstellungen organisierender – Inbegriff einer Darstellung und Darstellbarkeit der Welt fungiert. Konkretisiert wird dies nicht zuletzt in der viel beachteten Preisverleihung und der damit verbundenen Steigerung der Verwertbarkeit der Waren wie auch in der Synchronisierung nationaler Märkte durch den internationalen Waren- und Technologieaustausch. Was die Weltausstellung über die wachsende weltwirtschaftliche Vernetzung hinaus zeigt, ist „die Integration aller menschlichen Bereiche und Individuen in eine gemeinsame industrielle Produktivität"[16], die sich ausstellungstechnisch und -ästhetisch in Joseph Paxtons *Crystal Palace* umgesetzt findet. Auch Victor Hugo hebt zur Weltausstellung 1867 deren integrative Funktion hervor,

---

[13] Dies hält nicht erst Georg Simmel mit seiner Diagnose „Paralyse des Wahrnehmungsvermögens" anlässlich der „Berliner Gewerbe-Ausstellung" 1896 fest (in: *Die Zeit* 8/95 vom 25. Juli 1896, S. 59, hier zit. nach Geppert (2010), Die normative Kraft des Flüchtigen, S. 93), sondern auch schon ein Besucher in Paris 1855: „C'est peut-être bien parce que l'exposition universelle est la manifestation la plus éloquente de ces progrès, qu'elle plonge l'observateur dans un sentiment qui est bien plus de la stupeur que de l'admiration. L'homme, écrasé par ce qui l'entoure, se cherche et ne se trouve que pour constater son exiguité." Gustave Claudin, „L'exposition à vol d'oiseau, suivi d'une lettre à M. Maxime du Camp", Paris, 1855, S. 11. Zit. nach Maag (1982), *Kunst und Industrie im Zeitalter der ersten Weltausstellungen*, S. 89.

[14] Werner Hofmann, *Das Irdische Paradies. Kunst im neunzehnten Jahrhundert*, München, 1960, S. 152.

[15] Peter Sloterdijk, „Weltmuseum und Weltausstellung. Absolut museal", in: *Jahresring. Jahrbuch für moderne Kunst*, Band 37: „Präsentation und Re-Präsentation. Über das Ausstellbare und die Ausstellbarkeit", München, 1990, S. 183-202: 199.

[16] Gert Reising, „Die englische Museumsbewegung in der Zeit der Weltausstellung von 1862. Gedanken zur Bewertung von Kultur, Öffentlichkeit und Bildung: Das South Kensington Museum in London", in: Bernward Deneke/Rainer Kahsnitz (Hg.), *Das kunst- und kulturgeschichtliche Museum im 19. Jahrhundert*, München, 1977, S. 99-106: 99.

allerdings weniger im Sinne des industriellen Kapitalismus als vielmehr zugunsten politischer (Völker-)Verständigung: „Qu'est-ce qu'une exposition universelle? C'est le monde voisinant. On va causer un peu ensemble. On vient comparer les idéals. Confrontation de produits en apparence, confrontation d'utopies en réalité."[17] Als weiteres Mittel der Vereinheitlichung fungiert auch die Ästhetisierung der Waren, zeigt doch die Logik der Ausstellung „in einer museal abgedichteten Atmosphäre" beispielsweise die Maschinen nicht im industriellen Produktionsprozess, sondern in jenem „illusionären Schein, mit dem das Bürgertum die aus der Industrialisierung entstandene Problematik verdrängte"[18]. Auch deshalb kann Walter Benjamin von der Weltausstellung als „Phantasmagorie"[19] sprechen.

Zwischen Selbstmusealisierung und einem übermäßigen Imaginationsvermögen bewegt sich auch die Hoffnung der gigantischen *Exposition universelle* in Paris im Jahr 1900 (mit über 50 Millionen Besuchern), aus zwölf ihrer Pavillons entlang der Seine künftig Museen zu machen, darunter ein Museum für die Retrospektive aller bislang veranstalteten Weltausstellungen.[20] Hier wird die Selbstreferenzialität des Unternehmens Ausstellung als eine Konsequenz des Erfolgs und als eines seiner Prinzipien sichtbar. Zudem lässt die „behagliche Hybris" solcher Pläne erkennen, dass „die Kapitalisierung und die Inventarisierung der Welt weitgehend parallele Prozesse sind"[21].

Unverzichtbarer Teil dieser Imaginationsgeschichte sind die dreidimensionalen Präsentationen fremder Völker, das heißt ethnografischer Lebenswelten, die etwa bei der Weltausstellung 1878 in Paris so erfolgreich sind, dass kurz darauf das Musée d'Ethnographie du Trocadéro eröffnet wird. Im Zuge der Kolonialisierung und Zerstörung indigener Lebensweisen wird an ihrer systematischen Musealisierung gearbeitet, die allerdings weniger die Rettung der bedrohten Völker als vielmehr die propagandistische Entschärfung des Prozesses ihrer Kolonialisierung betreibt. Besonders aufschlussreich ist gerade in diesem Zusammenhang wiederum die Vermengung von Imagines und Realitäten, wie Timothy Mitchell sie als Hinüberziehen der zeitgenössischen Lebenswirklichkeit ins Imaginäre des Orientalismus plastisch beschreibt:

> Als der Khedive [Gouverneur] von Ägypten 1867 zum Besuch einer [...] *exposition universelle* nach Paris kam, fand er, daß der ägyptische Teil der Ausstellung als Nachbildung des mittelalterlichen Kairo in Form eines königlichen Palastes errichtet worden war. Der Khedive wohnte während seines Aufenthalts in der Palastimitation, er

---

17 So Victor Hugo in der Einleitung zum *Paris-Guide*, erschienen anlässlich der *Exposition universelle* von 1867, zit. nach Pöppel (2014), Weltausstellungen als Schreibstätten des Globalen, S. 640.

18 Maag (1982), *Kunst und Industrie im Zeitalter der ersten Weltausstellungen*, S. 137 f.

19 Benjamin (1982), Paris, die Hauptstadt des XIX. Jahrhunderts, S. 50.

20 Weitere Planungen betreffen „Museen für Erziehung, Geschichte, Sport und Handwerk, ein Friedensmuseum, ein Museum für Hygiene und Experimentalwissenschaften oder ein Kunstmuseum" (Martin Wörner, *Vergnügung und Belehrung. Volkskultur auf den Weltausstellungen 1851-1900*, Münster u. a., 1999, S. 238).

21 Sloterdijk (1990), Weltmuseum und Weltausstellung, S. 200.

> wurde zu einem Teil der Ausstellung und empfing dort mit mittelalterlicher Gastfreundlichkeit Besucher.[22]

Solche Vermengungen erzeugen wiederum Irritationen in Bezug auf die gängige Trennung zwischen der Realität einerseits und ihrer Repräsentation durch die Ausstellung andererseits:

> Die Grenzen der Ausstellung waren natürlich mit hohen Umfassungsmauern und riesigen Toren deutlich markiert, doch [...] gab es an der ‚realen Welt' außerhalb [...] vieles, was der Weltausstellung ähnelte [...]. Ungeachtet der entschlossenen Versuche, die Ausstellung als die lediglich perfekte Repräsentation einer Außenwirklichkeit zu isolieren, erwies sich die wirkliche Welt jenseits der Tore eher als eine Erweiterung der Ausstellung,[23]

etwa durch das Primat des Visuellen, der Objektbezogenheit, der vorherrschenden Blickorganisation etc. Es sind solche wechselseitigen Imaginations- und Realitätseffekte der Ausstellung, die auch die Literatur interessieren.

2. Realien als Phantasmagorie: Literarisierungen der Weltausstellung

Obwohl „der realistische Roman mit der forcierten Visualität seines Stils" als diejenige literarische Gattung gilt, „die es im neuen Geschäft des globalisierten Imaginären mit so gemischten Medien wie der großen Oper, den Weltausstellungen oder den Museen aufnehmen wollte",[24] zeigt eine Musterung einschlägiger Szenen, wie eingangs formuliert, dass der literarische Realismus in der Weltausstellung offenbar kein bevorzugtes Sujet sieht. In ihren Realien, Dingarrangements und enzyklopädischen Ansprüchen wird die Weltausstellung von dezidierten Autoren des Realismus nicht thematisiert. Stattdessen fungiert sie sporadisch als Kulisse, historische Markierung oder betonte Zeitgenossenschaft, so zum Beispiel in Wilhelm Raabes Roman *Horacker* (1876). In diesem Werk nimmt der Erzähler die realhistorische Situierung des Geschehens mithilfe einer Ereignisliste des Jahres 1867 vor, die an erster Stelle die Pariser Weltausstellung nennt; sie fungiert also als prominente Markierung eines Datums und als konkrete Bezugnahme auf Wirklichkeit. Doch kurz danach relativiert der Roman das Ereignis der Weltausstellung und führt auf diese Weise die idyllisierende Selbstbezogenheit der Provinz mit ihrer Aggression gegen ‚Andere' und mit ihrer Ignoranz gegenüber weltpolitischen Geschehnissen kritisch vor: „Die Gegend kümmerte sich nicht im geringsten um die Pariser Weltausstellung, den Kaiser Napoleon den Dritten, den Kaiser von

---

22 Timothy Mitchell, „Die Welt als Ausstellung", in: Sebastian Conrad/Shalini Randeria (Hg.), *Jenseits des Eurozentrismus. Postkoloniale Perspektiven in den Geschichts- und Kulturwissenschaften*, Frankfurt/M., 2002, S. 148-176: 152.

23 Ebd., S. 157.

24 Graevenitz (2014), *Theodor Fontane*, S. 341.

Mexiko, [...] den König Otto von Griechenland: die Gegend kümmerte sich nur um – Horacker."[25]

Ähnlich beiläufig, aber aussagekräftig, spielt auch Émile Zola auf die *Exposition universelle* von 1867 an: In seinem Roman *L'Argent* (1891) wird die spekulative Erhitzung des Börsenmarkts auch durch den Erfolg der Pariser Weltausstellung und die dadurch demonstrierte Überlegenheit über das Deutsche Reich motiviert, wohlgemerkt in der Figurenrede zwischen dem „Haussier Pilleraut" und dem „Baissier Moser":

> Pilleraut brach hier in lautes Lachen aus. „[...] Wenn Sie nach dem überwältigenden Erfolg der Ausstellung noch nicht zufrieden sind, was verlangen Sie eigentlich noch? Ja, mein Lieber, Europa gehört jetzt unser." Moser schüttelte verzweifelt den Kopf [...]. Infolge der Weltausstellung seien zu viele Unternehmungen in die Halme geschossen, alles sei in einen übermäßigen Taumel geraten, der jetzt zum reinen Wahnsinn führe.[26]

Obwohl also der durch die *Exposition universelle* erzeugte Taumel hier mit dem spekulativen Geschehen kurzgeschlossen wird, und obwohl Paris zu Zolas Lebzeiten mehrfach Veranstaltungsort von Weltausstellungen ist (1855, 1867, 1878, 1889, 1900), die er besucht, hat Zola diese weder als materiellen bzw. ökonomischen Schauplatz noch als visuelles Medium, weder als Globalisierungsphänomen noch als gesellschaftliches Ereignis ausführlicher in seine literarischen Texte aufgenommen. Seine viel zitierte Weigerung, über Weltausstellungen zu schreiben, formuliert er im Jahr 1900: „Je ne suis pas de cette Exposition, et je ne veux pas en être, par aucune manifestation."[27]

Auch Theodor Fontane, ein weiterer wichtiger Protagonist des Realismus, hat die Weltausstellung nicht als Romanschauplatz genutzt. Sie stellt jedoch ein Thema in seinen London-Reportagen der 1850er Jahre dar, die im Verhältnis zur Etablierung des poetischen Realismus zu lesen sind, dessen Programmatik Fontane zeitgleich 1853 in seinem Aufsatz *Unsere lyrische und epische Poesie seit 1848* formuliert. Darin betont er, Realismus bedeute nicht „das nackte Wiedergeben alltäglichen Lebens, am wenigsten seines Elends und seiner Schattenseiten", sondern ziele durch „die Widerspiegelung alles wirklichen Lebens" hindurch auf „das *Wahre*".[28] Wenn auch das hieraus sprechende Prinzip von „Entmischung, [...] Grenz-

---

25 Wilhelm Raabe, *Horacker*, in: *Sämtliche Werke*, Band 12 [Braunschweiger Ausgabe], 2. Aufl., hg. von Karl Hoppe, Göttingen, 1969, S. 291-454: 298.

26 Émile Zola, *Das Geld*, übers. von Leopold Rosenzweig, Frankfurt/M., Leipzig, 2001, S. 431 f.

27 Zit. nach Alke Brockmeier, „Die Pariser Weltausstellung in deutschen Kulturzeitschriften", in: Ulrich Mölk/Heinrich Detering (Hg.), *Perspektiven der Modernisierung: Die Pariser Weltausstellung, die Arbeiterbewegung, das koloniale China in europäischen und amerikanischen Kulturzeitschriften um 1900*, Göttingen, 2010, S. 25-40: 26. Nur für die russische Monatsschrift *Messager de l'Europe*, das heißt auf dem Sektor der Kulturzeitschriften, hat Zola zur Weltausstellung 1878 drei Artikel verfasst (vgl. F. W. J. Hemmings, „Émile Zola devant l'Exposition universelle de 1878", in: *Cahiers de l'Association internationale des études francaises* 24, 1 (1972), S. 131-153).

28 Theodor Fontane, „Unsere lyrische und epische Poesie seit 1848", in: ders., *Werke, Schriften und Briefe*, hg. von Walter Keitel, 3. Abt., Band I, hg. von Jürgen Kolbe, München, Wien, 1969, S. 236-260: 240 und 242.

ziehung und Ausschluss alles Problematischen"[29] im Sinne eines poetischen Realismus, den dieser Aufsatz postuliert, in der ja erst 25 Jahre später erfolgenden Romanproduktion Fontanes keineswegs als Leitprinzip fungiert, so stellt es doch für Fontanes Überlegungen zur Londoner Weltausstellung eine entscheidende Folie dar. Denn hier hebt er vor allem die Erfahrung der Notwendigkeit hervor, jener „Zerfahrenheit unserer Zeit"[30], für die der Crystal Palace stehe, Maß und Bündelung entgegenzusetzen.

So beschreibt Fontane in seiner Reportage mit dem Titel „Kristallpalast-Bedenken" (im Mai 1856 in der *Vossischen Zeitung*) die Verwirrung, die die Versammlung bis dato vereinzelter Ausstellungsinstitutionen in einem einzigen Raum mit dem Format der Weltausstellung produziere:

> Gewerbeausstellungen sind gut, Kunstausstellungen sind gut, zoologische und botanische Gärten, Museen und Galerien, Kunst- und Rüstkammern, alles ist gut und alles ist lobenswert, aber ein furchtbares Durcheinander aller dieser Dinge ist eine geistige Parforce-Kur, durch die einige Universalgenies aus dem Volk zu Zierden der Nation geweckt und gebildet werden mögen, während die große Masse nichts davon hat als – Begriffsverwirrung.[31]

Jenseits seiner deutlichen „Kritik"[32] am Topos der (Volks-)Bildung *qua* Weltausstellung stellt Fontane die ambivalente Faszination durch Dingmassen und Fortschrittsfuror einerseits, durch Orientierungsverlust und Entfremdung andererseits hier zur Diskussion. Er diagnostiziert mithin Phänomene und Diskurse der Moderne, in die er damit zugleich interveniert.

Besonders plakativ formuliert Fontane diese Spannung in dem kurzen Prosatext „Ein Gang durch den leeren Glaspalast" (in *Ein Sommer in London*, 1854), der der eben genannten Reizüberflutung nun den *horror vacui* an die Seite stellt. Der aufgelassene Crystal Palace, spektakuläres Sinnbild technischer Herrschaft und industrieller Ästhetik, erscheint nach dem Ende der Ausstellung nurmehr als Körper, dessen Seele und Geist verloren seien:

> Wie eine Riesenleiche streckt sich dieser Glasleib aus, dessen Seele mit jenen farbenreichen Shawls und Teppichen entflohn, die einst wie Phantasien ihn durchglühten und dessen geistiges Leben mit jenen tausend Meß- und Rechenkräften dahin ist, die eisern und unbeirrt ihr Urteil fällten.[33]

Die vermeintlich allein übrig gebliebene Materialität des ‚Glasleibs' ist allerdings weiterhin durch Phantasmen gekennzeichnet: Das spricht nicht nur aus dem grotesken Bild der „Riesenleiche", sondern auch aus der Beschreibung, wie die Natur –

---

29 Gustav Frank, „Auf dem Weg zum Realismus", in: Christian Begemann (Hg.), *Realismus. Epoche – Autoren – Werke*, Darmstadt, 2007, S. 27-44: 43.

30 Theodor Fontane, „Kristallpalast-Bedenken", in: ders., *Aus England und Schottland*, hg. von Charlotte Jolles, München, 1963, S. 587-591: 591.

31 Ebd., S. 589.

32 Ebd., S. 587.

33 Theodor Fontane, „Ein Gang durch den leeren Glaspalast", in: ders., *Aus England und Schottland*, hg. von Charlotte Jolles, München, 1963, S. 10-11: 10.

die doch durch die Ausstellung industriellen, wissenschaftlichen und kulturellen Fortschritts überwunden werden sollte – ihre Herrschaft wieder übernimmt:

> Unsere Zeit eilt schnell: sie ist rasch im Schaffen wie im Zerstören; noch ein Winter und – das Glashaus ist eine Ruine. Schon dringen Wind und Staub durch hundert zerbrochene Scheiben, [...] schon findet die Spinne sich ein und webt ihre grauen Schleier, die alten Fahnen der Zerstörung.[34]

Hierbei handelt es sich weniger um vertraute (und damit depotenzierende) Bilder des Zerfalls als vielmehr um eine Steigerung jenes „Wahrnehmungsschocks",[35] den der Glasbau dank seiner extremen Dimensionierung und blendenden Lichtstärke – wodurch Raumorientierung und Selbstverortung erschwert werden – schon während der Ausstellung provoziert hat. Im nunmehr ausgeräumten Kristallpalast, „die bloße Macht des Raumes"[36] demonstrierend, bedeutet die Leere einen umso größeren Schock, einen

> *horror vacui* in einem Gebäude, das ein Museum der menschlichen Zivilisation war. Dieses Museum ist leer. [...] Die beängstigende Leere – sie ist nicht nur ein ‚Abdruck' dieser Zivilisation, sie steht geradezu unter Verdacht, das zu sein, was von dieser Zivilisation ‚bleibt'.[37]

Auch im Umfeld seines frühen Realismusprogramms also, das (noch) ungebrochen die viel beschworene „Verklärung" als probates Verfahren eines poetischen Realismus zur Vermittlung von Wirklichkeit und Bedeutung, von Kontingenz und Repräsentanz propagiert, zeigt sich – bei aller Faszination auch für die „Globalisierung und Generalisierung des Imaginären"[38] – Fontanes Skepsis sowohl gegenüber technisch-globalisiertem Fortschritt wie auch gegenüber kultureller Kohärenzstiftung und Kontingenzbeherrschung.

Trotz solcher eher sporadischen Auftritte in literarischen Texten von verschiedenen Autoren des Realismus stellt die Weltausstellung ein umfassendes gesellschaftliches Faszinosum dar: Gustave Flauberts entsprechender Eintrag im *Dictionnaire des idées reçues*, das die bürgerlichen Phrasen seiner Epoche festhält, lautet „Exposition. Sujet de délire du XIXe siècle". Die Ausstellung bietet also einen Schauplatz sowohl für literarische Gesellschafts- und Kulturkritik als auch für Fragen der Ästhetik und Aisthesis. Entsprechende Auseinandersetzungen lassen sich im Zuge der *Exposition universelle* 1855 in Paris in der französischen Literatur-

---

34 Ebd., S. 11.

35 Philipp Frank, *Theodor Fontane und die Technik*, Würzburg, 2005, S. 82.

36 Fontane (1963), Ein Gang durch den leeren Glaspalast, S. 10.

37 Stephan Braese, „Im Labyrinth des Fortschritts. Fontanes ‚Ein Sommer in London'", in: ders./Anne-Kathrin Reulecke (Hg.), *Realien des Realismus. Wissenschaft – Technik – Medien in Theodor Fontanes Erzählprosa*, Berlin, 2010, S. 27-52: 37.

38 Graevenitz (2014), *Theodor Fontane*, S. 185. Graevenitz hebt hervor, es sei Fontane und seinen Freunden um „die Fragen nach den Stellungen und Funktionen des neuen Imaginären in der Gesellschaft und Kultur der Moderne" (ebd.) gegangen, und betont, das *Deutsche Kunstblatt* (mit Fontane als Beiträger) habe „auf seine eigene Weise im Rauschen der kulturellen *faits divers* [darunter 1851 die Londoner Weltausstellung] seine *éclats* der Kunst- und Kulturentwicklung gestaltet" (S. 187).

szene beobachten. Wie eingangs bemerkt, ist die achte von acht Hallen, der *Palais des Beaux-Arts*, der Kunst vorbehalten (allerdings einem ‚Rückblick' auf die Kunst, ohne den aktuellen Realismus eines Gustave Courbet), während Technik und Industrie in den sieben vorhergehenden Abteilungen ihr Publikum begeistern. Dass die Industrieobjekte wie künstlerische Artefakte inszeniert werden – das heißt aus dem Produktionskontext herausgelöst und dem bewundernden Blick des bürgerlichen Publikums präsentiert werden –, führt zu einer Überbietung der Kunst, die Félix Belly pointiert formuliert: „La réalité là écrasait la fiction."[39] Darauf reagieren die zeitgenössischen Autoren in gegenläufiger Weise: Während die einen eine Kunst fordern, die an Technik bzw. Industrie orientiert ist, und den menschlichen/männlichen Genius bewundern, der sowohl ästhetische als auch technische Objekte erschafft, geht es den anderen um eine Kunst, die dem Ideal des industriellen Fortschritts entgegentritt.

Zu Letzteren gehört Charles Baudelaire, der die Weltausstellung zum Anlass seines Nachdenkens über eine notwendige Modernisierung der Kunst nimmt. Wie er in seiner Kritik „Exposition universelle" von 1855 festhält, soll die Kunst ein Gegengewicht gegen die Herrschaft der Technik bilden, wobei sie die Vitalität anderer Kulturen als produktive Irritation (als ‚das Bizarre') zur Kenntnis zu nehmen hat:

> Für Baudelaire war die erste Pariser Weltausstellung zu einem aufreizenden Symbol der modernen – und fatalen – europäischen Fortschrittsidee und zugleich eine stupende Demonstration der Verlagerung künstlerischer Vitalität in andere Weltregionen [...]. Gegen eine Ordnung oder gar von Autoritäten auferlegte Hierarchie der Kulturen setzt Baudelaire stattdessen die Varietät der Welt und die Vielfalt ihrer Erscheinungen, die sich gerade im ‚Bizarren' und damit auch im Vitalismus der fremden, großenteils kolonialisierten, doch eigensinnigen Kulturen und jenseits von Verlusterfahrungen der europäischen Moderne ausdrücken.[40]

Für Baudelaires Ästhetik der Moderne ist seine berühmte Formulierung „*Le beau est toujours bizarre* [Herv. i. O.]"[41] von großer Bedeutung: Sie verdankt sich seiner Erfahrung der Weltausstellung und begreift das Bizarre – jeder realistischen Programmatik entgegengesetzt – als nicht aufzulösende Fremdartigkeit, irritierend

---

[39] Félix Belly, „La poésie de l'Exposition", in: *Revue contemporaine*, Dezember 1855, S. 162, zit. nach Marta Caraion, *„Les philosophes de la vapeur et des allumettes chimiques". Littérature, sciences et industrie en 1855*, Genève, 2008, S. 27. Vgl. zudem Marta Caraions Überlegungen ebd.: „La halle des machines, centre vital de l'exposition, devient un lieu de contemplation béate, d'admiration fascinée, qui procure des sensations comparables auf plus intenses émotions esthétiques [...]. Cependant, les objets d'art sont introduits dans la taxinomie encyclopédique et indifférencié des produits de l'activité humaine: un tableau, une machine, un meuble, un livre: autant de produits fabriqués par l'homme."

[40] Walburga Hülk, „Baudelaire: Die Erfindung der *modernité*", in: dies., *Bewegung als Mythologie der Moderne. Vier Studien zu Baudelaire, Flaubert, Taine, Valéry*, Bielefeld, 2012, S. 15-54: 23.

[41] Charles Baudelaire, „Exposition universelle", in: *Œuvres complètes*, Band 2, S. 575-597: 578.

und unerwartet, an die Wahrnehmung des Betrachters gekoppelt. In diesem Sinne bestimmt sie auch seine Modernekonzepte der Großstadt und der Flanerie.[42]

Dass die Weltausstellungen neuartige ästhetische Erfahrungen ermöglichen, ja erzwingen, thematisiert auch Hans Christian Andersen. Sein Märchen „Die Dryade" (1868) macht einen Besuch der Pariser Ausstellung 1867 zur Lebenssehnsucht einer Dryade, also eines Baumgeistes. In ihrem Kastanienbaum in einem Dorf hört die Dryade von der großen Ausstellung, während sie die vielen Eisenbahnen mit Abertausenden von Besuchern Richtung Paris fahren sieht. Ihre Sehnsucht nach Paris scheint zunächst befriedigt, als ihr Baum in die Stadt verpflanzt wird. Doch um sich endlich frei durch die Großstadt bewegen und die Weltausstellung besuchen zu können, ist die Dryade bereit, ihr langes Baumleben gegen eine kurze Lebensspanne einzutauschen. Die märchenhaften Elemente dieser Metamorphose werden mit dem Märchencharakter der Weltausstellung parallelisiert. Zwar betont der Textbeginn das Profane der zeitgenössischen Verkehrstechnik, die keine Zauberei sei: „Wir reisen nach Paris zur Ausstellung. Nun sind wir da. Das war eine Fahrt, ein Fliegen ohne Zauber. Wir fuhren mit Dampf über das Meer und durch die Länder." Doch lautet der folgende Satz: „Ja, unsere Zeit ist die Zeit des Märchens."[43] Kein zeitloses Märchen also, sondern eine Konkretion der eigenen historischen Verortung in der Zeit der Weltausstellung, die eine „quasi in einer einzigen Bewegung stattfindende Ent- und Wiederverzauberung der Welt"[44] bewerkstelligt.

Die Idee der Metamorphose als Bewältigungsstrategie zeigt sich beispielsweise in der Darstellung der Überdimensioniertheit der Ausstellung, die die Wahrnehmungsmöglichkeiten der Besucher herausfordert, ja übersteigt:

> Der überwältigend große, bunte Anblick muß in kleine Teile zerlegt, muß zu einem Spielzeug zusammengedrängt werden, damit man ihn wiedergeben und in seiner Gesamtheit erfassen kann. Wie ein großer Weihnachtstisch trug das Marsfeld ein Aladinschloß der Industrie und der Kunst, und rundherum waren Nippes aus allen Ländern ausgestellt.[45]

Doch eine solche Spielzeugwelt fungiert nicht nur als Bewältigungsstrategie, sondern auch als kritische Vorführung: Der Nippes-Charakter der Exponate, beliebig austauschbar und verfügbar gemacht, wird ebenso offengelegt wie die bloße Parataxe der Objekte, deren Raumkontext – wie Nippes im bürgerlichen Interieur – einen Sinnzusammenhang nur suggeriert, aber nicht realisiert.

---

42 Vgl. beispielsweise: „Quelles bizarreries ne trouve-t-on pas dans une grande ville quand on sait se promener et regarder?" (Charles Baudelaire, „Mademoiselle Bistouri", in: *Œuvres complètes*, Band 1, S. 355.)

43 Hans Christian Andersen, „Die Dryade", in: ders., *Sämtliche Märchen und Geschichten*, Band 2, hg. von Leopold Magon, Leipzig, Weimar, 1985, S. 395-417: 395.

44 Friederike Felcht, „‚Die Straßenbahnen und Omnibusse sind gestopft und gepfropft und mit Menschen garniert'. Überlegungen zur Aufhebung des Anthropozentrismus von Mensch-Ding-Beziehungen", in: Elisabeth Tietmeyer/Claudia Hirschberger/Caroline Noack/Jane Redlin (Hg.), *Die Sprache der Dinge. Kulturwissenschaftliche Perspektiven auf die materielle Kultur*, Münster, New York, NY, 2010, S. 43-52: 45.

45 Andersen (1985), Die Dryade, S. 400.

Das gilt auch für das Bild der Blume, das sowohl von der Pariser Weltausstellung als auch von Andersens Märchen eingesetzt wird. Bedenkt man, dass die Ausstellung 1867 ihren enzyklopädischen Anspruch auch architektonisch, nämlich in Form ihres ovalen segmentierten Baus manifestiert,[46] so stellt das Bild der Blume in Andersens Märchen zunächst eine treffende Analogie dar: „Eine Prachtblüte der Kunst und der Industrie [...]; eine riesengroße Sonnenblume, aus deren Blättern man Geographie und Statistik lernen, [...] zur Kunst und Poesie sich erheben und die Größe und Macht der Länder erkennen kann."[47] Doch das Bild endet mit dem Vergehen der Blume, „die Herbststürme werden sie fortwehen, daß kein Blatt, keine Wurzel übrigbleibt."[48] Kein harmloses Märchen- und Naturbild also, sondern eine durchaus frappierende Ankündigung des Endes – die sich am Märchenschluss im bevorstehenden Tod der Dryade spiegelt, wenn sie das sprudelnde Wasser um Erquickung bittet, dieses aber bekennt, „keine lebendige Quelle", sondern von einer „Maschine" abhängig zu sein, oder wenn sie den Wind bittet, ihr einen „Lebenskuß" zu geben, und dieser darauf „Alles nur Staub!" antwortet.[49] Andersens Märchen zielt demnach nicht auf eine Überhöhung oder Allegorisierung der Weltausstellung „als disparater Mikrokosmos"[50]. Vielmehr erzählt es von der attraktiven Macht ihres imaginären Potenzials, während es ihre märchenhaften Versprechen zugleich ‚ent-täuscht'.

Abschließend sei ein literarisches Verfahren angeführt, das keine ausgestellten Realien, sondern auf Weltausstellungen exponierte Menschen thematisiert. In Form einer ironischen Realisierung zielt es auf eine groteske Verkörperung phantasmatischer, ja rassistischer Projektionen.

> Der Neger, der von der Weltausstellung nachhause gebracht wird und, irrsinnig geworden von Heimweh, mitten in seinem Dorf unter dem Wehklagen des Stammes mit ernstestem Gesicht als Überlieferung und Pflicht die Späße aufführt, welche das europäische Publikum als Sitten und Gebräuche Afrikas entzückten.[51]

Was Franz Kafka in einer Notiz im Oktavheft G (1917/1918) festhält, ist eine ebenso verzweifelte wie ironische Antwort auf das ungeheure Projektionspotenzial der

[46] Vgl.: „Der im Grundriss ovale, aus konzentrischen Galerien bestehende Bau lud den Besucher zu einer imaginären Weltreise ein, die sich zugleich als eine Art virtueller Gang durch die Zivilisationsgeschichte gestaltete. [...] Über Radialgänge waren diese Galerien nochmals unterteilt; jedes der so entstandenen Segmente wiesen die Organisatoren einer beteiligten Nation zu. Auf diese Weise konnte der Besucher sowohl einen länderübergreifenden Rundgang durch Sektionen wie Rohstoffe, Nahrungsmittel, Maschinen, Hausgeräte und Kunstwerke vornehmen als auch die Errungenschaften eines einzelnen Staates erkunden, indem er die radialen Wege abschritt." (Roland Prügel, „Die Welt als Vitrine. Weltausstellungen im 19. Jahrhundert", in: Jutta Zander-Seidel/ders. (Hg.), *Wege in die Moderne. Weltausstellungen, Medien und Musik im 19. Jahrhundert*, Nürnberg, 2014, S. 18-33: 19.)

[47] Andersen (1985), Die Dryade, S. 399.

[48] Ebd.

[49] Ebd., S. 416.

[50] Pöppel (2014), Weltausstellungen als Schreibstätten des Globalen, S. 637.

[51] Franz Kafka, *Beim Bau der chinesischen Mauer und andere Schriften aus dem Nachlaß*, hg. von Hans-Gerd Koch, Frankfurt/M., 1994, S. 188.

Weltausstellungen mit ihren Authentizitätsbehauptungen und auf ihren ebenso vereinnahmenden wie exkludierenden Umgang mit dem ‚Anderen' der europäischen Moderne. Die Verkörperung solcher Projektionen durch das ‚Ausstellungsobjekt' macht *qua* Realisierung diese destruktiven Zuschreibungen sichtbar.

Ähnlich verfährt Arthur Schnitzlers Erzählung *Andreas Thameyers letzter Brief* (1902). Darin rechtfertigt Thameyer die Tatsache, dass seine Frau ein dunkelhäutiges Kind zur Welt gebracht hat, mithilfe der Idee mütterlicher Impression („das Versehen der Schwangeren"[52]), da sie bei einer Weltausstellung ein inszeniertes Dorf mit afrikanischen Bewohnern gesehen habe. Historischer Bezugspunkt ist die Weltausstellung 1896 in Wien, die den Schaulustigen im Prater drei Monate lang 70 Westafrikaner vorführte. Die Treue seiner Ehefrau wird von Thameyer so ausdrücklich beschworen, dass sie immer unwahrscheinlicher wird. Für Thameyer ist aber eine sexuelle Beziehung zwischen seiner Frau und einem der ausgestellten Afrikaner dermaßen undenkbar, dass er bereit ist, die Glaubwürdigkeit seiner Frau durch seinen eigenen Suizid wiederherzustellen. Damit treten zum einen die krisenhafte Disposition und Unzuverlässigkeit des Erzählers hervor, die wiederum auf die in der Erzählung inszenierte Krise von Männlichkeit und *whiteness* verweisen. Zum anderen werden die einander überkreuzenden – wissenschaftlichen und populären – Geschlechter- und ‚Rasse'-Diskurse erkennbar, die auch die zeitgenössischen Ausstellungspraktiken prägen.

Es sind solche und andere am kulturellen und gesellschaftlichen Imaginären der Weltausstellungen interessierte Texte, die – auch jenseits programmatischer Realismen – an der Formierung und Darstellung literarischer Wirklichkeiten und Dingwelten arbeiten und dabei die Aporien realistischer Repräsentationsweisen reflektieren.

---

52 Arthur Schnitzler, *Andreas Thameyers letzter Brief*, in: ders., *Gesammelte Werke. Erzählende Schriften*, Band 1, Frankfurt/M., 1981, S. 514-520: 516. Vgl. dazu Achim Aurnhammer, *Arthur Schnitzlers intertextuelles Erzählen*, Berlin, Boston, MA, 2013, S. 103-131.

Veronika Thanner

Stottern, Stocken, Stammeln. Wilhelm Raabes diskontinuierliches Erzählen

Am Ausgang meiner Überlegungen zu Wilhelm Raabes poetischen Verfahren realistischer Darstellung steht die Beobachtung einiger wiederkehrender Auffälligkeiten auf Ebene des Schriftbildes, die Texte durch alle Schaffensperioden Raabes hinweg auszeichnen.[1] Die Seiten sind durchzogen von exzessiv eingesetzten Gedankenstrichen oder zeilenlangen Auslassungspunkten, durch die der Text gleichsam zerlöchert wird und der Lesefluss ins Stocken gerät:

> Auch dieses Haus grenzt mit seinem Gärtchen an den Paddenauer See, und der Schimmer von zwei Lichtern, die im ersten Stockwerk brennen, zieht uns bedeutend an. Das erste flimmert hinter den Fenstern des Rektors Gustav Fischarth und das andere in der Wohnstube der Frau Agnes Fischarth, des ehelichen Weibes des Rektors von Paddenau –
> *Drillinge!* . . . .
> . . . .[2]

Ein solches Stocken der Erzählung durch Mittel der Typografie und Interpunktion lässt zunächst an großflächige Streichungen[3] oder Leerstellen mit Platzhalterfunktion denken und kommt bei Raabe unter anderem zum Einsatz, um einen Abbruch des Erzählens anzuzeigen, bedeutende Inhalte oder Ereignisse gleichsam zu ‚unterstreichen', wie im ersten Zitat, oder um einem Affekt Raum im Text zu geben, der sich der sprachlichen Beschreibung in der Figuren- oder Erzählerrede zu entziehen scheint:

1 Hier kann naturgemäß nicht Raum für eine werkumfassende Analyse der beschriebenen Formaspekte bei Raabe sein. Korrespondierende Befunde lassen sich indes in Werken aus der frühen (*Die Chroniken der Sperlingsgasse*) und der mittleren Schaffenszeit (*Abu Telfan*, *Christoph Pechlin*, *Der Dräumling* u. a.), genau wie in den Spätwerken *Kloster Lugau* (1894), in reduzierterem Umfang in den *Akten des Vogelsangs* (1886), *Gutmanns Reisen* (1891) oder in Raabes letztem, Fragment gebliebenen Werk *Altershausen* (1902) nachweisen.

2 Wilhelm Raabe, *Der Dräumling*, in: *Sämtliche Werke: Braunschweiger Ausgabe*, Band 10, hg. von Karl Hoppe, Göttingen, 1968, S. 9-201: 11.

3 So wird der Gedankenstrich von Raabe mitunter auch in der Funktion einer Materialstreichung eingesetzt, wenn beispielsweise in *Gutmanns Reisen* der Erzähler „einen Strich durch den Reichtum unseres diesmaligen Quellenmaterials" zieht (Wilhelm Raabe, *Gutmanns Reisen*, in: *Sämtliche Werke: Braunschweiger Ausgabe*, Band 18, hg. von Karl Hoppe, Göttingen, 1969, S. 208-415: 258) und die angesetzte historische Anekdote mit fünf Gedankenstrichen aus dem Text tilgt („– – – – –") (S. 257 f.).

> „Herr Rektor, Feyerabend ist unrein!“
>
> ....
>
> Diese Punkte bedeuten das Erschrecken und Erstarren, das Zusammen-, Auf- und Auseinanderfahren im Festsaal [...].[4]

Die Hinweise auf ein gesteigertes Interesse Raabes an unterbrochenen Rede- und Erzählformen verdichten sich durch einen zweiten Blick auf die diegetische Textebene, in der das Sprechen der Figuren auf die Abbrüche und Stockungen der Schriftebene Bezug nimmt: Angefangen bei der einfachsten Form, die das Sprechen einer Figur schlicht als „stotterte er“, „stockte“ oder „stammelte“[5] beschreibt, ohne dass dies weitere gestalterische Konsequenzen im Text hat, bis hin zur sprachlich-phonetischen Abbildung solcher Redequalitäten in ihrer Lautgestalt. Beispiele für stotternde Figurenrede, die mit den Mitteln der Lautmalerei, Silbentrennung, -dehnung und -wiederholung arbeitet, finden sich zahlreich bei Raabe: „Holla - ä - ä - häh - bäh!“[6], „Carmabis – bis – bis – ein wenig hart. Atmen schwer – des Königs Sklaven atmen schwer!“[7], „‚Ah – oh – hm – ei – rrrr – hmmhmm – oh – ah! ... Bravo!‘“[8] oder „‚Ah – o – uh!‘ stöhnte der Vetter“[9], sind nur einige Beispiele hierfür. Häufig kommt bei Raabe auch eine extreme Dehnung und Verzögerung in der direkten Figurenrede zum Einsatz: „Der Freiherr sah mit verlegenem Lächeln und höchst nervös die Hände reibend auf den Studiengenossen. ‚Mit gro – ßem Ver – gnü – gen – sogleich – willst du die Gü – te – haben – einzu – tre – ten? Aber lieber Freund‘ – und er sah ihn kläglich genug an [...].“[10]

An diese Kategorie stotternder und stockender Schreibverfahren schließen rhetorische Figuren an, die Sprache im Text auf syntaktischer Ebene stocken lassen. Hier sei etwa auf die vielfältige Verwendung von Aposiopesen und Ellipsen verwiesen, die bei Raabe ebenfalls besonders häufig und prägnant in der direkten Figurenrede verwendet werden: „‚Ja, der wird bald rot, bald bleich und hat geschworen, nur über seine Leiche ginge der Weg, nach – zu – zur –‘“.[11] Oder: „‚Ah!‘ sagte er erst: dann sagte er: ‚Wundervoll! Wundervoll!‘ *Und dann – dann* trat er sechs Schritte zurück und stammelte: ‚Getroffen – wunderbar getroffen – herrlich – aber – aber, du lieber Himmel, das – ist – sie – ja selber!‘ [Herv. V. T.]“[12]

---

4 Wilhelm Raabe, *Altershausen*, in: *Sämtliche Werke: Braunschweiger Ausgabe*, Band 20, hg. von Karl Hoppe, Göttingen, 1968, S. 201-312: 220.

5 Vgl. beispielsweise Wilhelm Raabe, *Abu Telfan oder die Heimkehr vom Mondgebirge*, in: *Sämtliche Werke: Braunschweiger Ausgabe*, Band 7, hg. von Karl Hoppe, Göttingen, 1952, S. 3-382: 191 f.; ders. (1968), *Der Dräumling*, S. 130 und ders., *Christoph Pechlin*, in: *Sämtliche Werke: Braunschweiger Ausgabe*, Band 10, hg. von Karl Hoppe, Göttingen, 1968, S. 202-449: 362 und 439.

6 Raabe (1968), *Der Dräumling*, S. 12.

7 Ebd., S. 13.

8 Raabe (1969), *Gutmanns Reisen* S. 315.

9 Raabe (1968), *Der Dräumling*, S. 171.

10 Raabe (1968), *Christoph Pechlin*, S. 214.

11 Raabe (1969), *Gutmanns Reisen* S. 351.

12 Raabe (1968), *Der Dräumling*, S. 130.

Ein solches Stocken der Rede verweist bei Raabe zum einen auf Sprünge in der Erzählzeit[13] oder Erzählebene, wenn sich das Stammeln der Figur wie im zweiten Textbeispiel von der Figuren- auf die Erzählerstimme überträgt („Und dann – dann trat er sechs Schritte zurück“), zum anderen auf einen Überschuss des Affekts, der auf körperlicher Ebene in die Rede interveniert,[14] und dem auf rhetorischer Ebene die asyndetische (unverbundene) Aufzählung entspricht. Eine dermaßen unvermittelte, stockende Akkumulation von Substantiven, darauf hat Corinna Sauter hingewiesen, fungiert bei Raabe unter anderem als narratives Mittel der Assoziation von unterschiedlichen Ideen, Vorstellungen und Eindrücken oder mitunter auch als Vehikel für Intertextualität,[15] wenn sich – wie in einer beispielhaften Traumsequenz in *Gutmanns Reisen* – Jean-Paul-Referenzen unauflöslich mit Erinnerungssequenzen des Protagonisten vermischen: „‚... Puh, der Onkel Poltermann mit seinem albernen Jean Paul! Wunsiedel – Liane – der hohe Albano – Pärnreuther – Klotilde – Katzenbergers Badereise – Gutmanns Reisen – o Fräulein – Fräulein Klotilde Blume! ...‘“.[16]

In welchem Verhältnis stehen solche Formen des unsouveränen Sprechens in Gestalt von Stottern und Stammeln, Unterbrechung und Einschub zu Raabes Strategie der Wirklichkeitsdarstellung? Dient das Stottern und Stammeln der Figuren, vergleichbar mit Raabes häufiger Verwendung von Umgangs- oder Dialektsprache in der direkten Figurenrede, in erster Linie der Inszenierung von Authentizität oder nur als humoristische Einlage? Oder verweisen die Auslassungspunkte und Gedankenstriche im Schriftbild in erster Line auf Affekte[17] der dargestellten Figuren, wie es Raabe mitunter selbst nahezulegen scheint?

Zunächst einmal gilt es hier auf den scheinbar einfachen, aber unstrittigen Ausgangsbefund zurückzukommen, dass die besagten Erzählverfahren und Gestaltungselemente Kommunikationssituationen auf Figurenebene stören, Unterbrechungen im Erzählfluss markieren und zugleich auf Seite der Rezipienten den Lesefluss hemmen. Sie zeigen damit auf intra-, extradiegetischer und rezeptiver Ebene nicht anderes an als ein Unvermögen, einen Unwillen oder ein Zögern, etwas mit den Mitteln der Sprache kohärent und linear auszudrücken. Dass diese Momente des Stockens, Anhaltens und Auslassens dabei zugleich unterschiedliche Relevanzgrade markieren, lässt Raabe seine Erzähler gerne selbst betonen: „– – – Drei Gedankenstriche, eine Fermate, eine Pause und ein Paukenschlag werden genügen, die Welt unserer Zuschauer und Zuhörer auf die Wichtigkeit des Momentes aufmerksam zu machen.“[18]

---

13 Markante Zeitraffereffekte z. B. in Raabe (1968), *Christoph Pechlin*, S. 448.

14 Bernhard Siegert, [...] *Auslassungspunkte*, Vortrag an der Hochschule für Grafik und Buchkunst Leipzig, Leipzig, 2003, S. 11.

15 Vgl. Corinna Sauter, „Wilhelm Raabe Meisterdieb. Plagiarismus in ‚Gutmanns Reisen‘“, in: *Jahrbuch der Raabe-Gesellschaft* 57, (2016), S. 124-149: 147.

16 Raabe (1969), *Gutmanns Reisen*, S. 287.

17 Johann Christoph Adelung, *Vollständige Anweisung zur Deutschen Orthographie, nebst einem kleinen Wörterbuche für die Aussprache, Orthographie, Biegung und Ableitung*, Frankfurt/M., 1788, S. 390 f.

18 Raabe (1968), *Christoph Pechlin*, S. 385.

Der hier von Raabe in der Erzählung *Christoph Pechlin* verwendete musiktheoretische Begriff der Fermate[19], ein musikalischer Freiraum zur individuellen Gestaltung durch den Solisten, gibt bereits den wichtigen Hinweis, dass mit dem Stocken der Rede, der Auslassung und dem Gedankenstrich[20] ein nicht festgestellter, offener Raum in die realistische Darstellung ‚wirklicher Welt' eingeschrieben wird. Einer solchen Kopplung von Hinweis- und Platzhalterfunktion der stotternden, unterbrochenen Rede einer Figur oder der Erzählstimme lohnt es sich bei Raabe auf erzählstruktureller Ebene nachzugehen. Als wesentlich vielschichtiger und Teil eines komplexeren diskontinuierlichen Erzählverfahrens entpuppen sich die genannten Verfahren vor allem in Raabes Roman *Abu Telfan* von 1867: Hier spielen Auslassungen, Redeabbrüche, inhaltliche und formale Leerstellen eine zentrale erzählerische Rolle und problematisieren damit, wie in einer kursorischen Lektüre zu erweisen sein wird, systematisch und explizit das der Darstellung zugrunde liegende Konzept von Wirklichkeit.

1. Entgleiste Existenzen, prekäre Erzählinstanzen

In *Abu Telfan* erzählt Raabe die überraschende Rückkehr des einst in Afrika verschollenen Leonhard Hagebuchers. Die Thematik der Verschollenheit hat im Roman indes nicht nur motivische, sondern auch signifikante poetologische Konsequenzen und verweist ihrerseits wieder auf die Problematik der Sprach- und Kommunikationsstörung: So bedeutet Verschollenheit dem Wortsinne nach eine Unterbrechung oder Störung von Kommunikation – verschollen ist derjenige, von dem es keine Nachricht gibt, dessen Stimme „verschallt"[21] ist. In Gestalt des verstummenden, stotternden und abbrechenden Protagonisten Hagebucher stellt Raabe in *Abu Telfan* damit systematisch die Möglichkeiten und Bedingungen des Erzählens überhaupt infrage: „Mit Stottern sprach Leonhard Hagebucher gleich einem, welcher sich mühsam in einer fremden, ungewohnten Sprache auszudrücken hat."[22] Oder:

---

19 Der Begriff „Fermate" wird aus dem Italienischen „anhalten" abgeleitet: „Ein solcher Ruhepunkt in dem Verfolge eines Tonstückes, bey welchem die Bewegung des Taktes dadurch auf einige Zeit mit Vorsatz unterbrochen wird, daß man den Ton auf einer Note viel länger aushält, oder bey einer kleinen Pause länger verweilt, als es die Dauer derselben erfordert. [...] Die Zeit, wie lange durch die auf die Pause fallende Fermate die Taktbewegung unterbrochen werden soll, hängt von dem Geschmacke des Ausführers der Hauptstimme, oder auch von dem Anführer des Orchesters ab." Heinrich Christoph Koch, *Musikalisches Lexikon, welches die theoretische und praktische Tonkunst, encyclopedisch bearbeitet, alle alten und neuen Kunstwörter erklärt, und die alten und neuen Instrumente beschrieben, enthält*, Frankfurt/M., 1802, S. 562 f.

20 In diesem Sinne ordnet auch Joseph Vogl den Gedankenstrich als „Auslassung, eine Lücke im Text" ein, die den Text fragmentiert und gleichzeitig öffnet. Ders., „Der Gedankenstrich bei Adalbert Stifter", in: Alexander Nebrig/Carlos Spoerhase (Hg.), *Die Poesie der Zeichensetzung. Studien zur Stilistik und Interpunktion*, Publikation zur *Zeitschrift für Germanistik*, Band 25, Bern, 2012, S. 275-294: 277.

21 Vgl. Ulrike Vedder, „Figur des Verschollenen in der Literatur des 20. Jahrhunderts (Kafka, Burger, Treichel)", in: *Zeitschrift für Germanistik* 21, 3 (2011), S. 548-562: 550.

22 Raabe (1952), *Abu Telfan*, S. 45.

> Noch einmal versuchte [Hagebucher] seinen Faden wieder zu finden; aber er gab es schnell auf und schloss mit der konfus und undeutlich hervorgestotterten Versicherung, daß er in acht Tagen, wenn das Schicksal es erlaube, da fortfahren werde, wo er jetzt endige.[23]

Dem stotternden Subjekt wird von Raabe damit nachdrücklich eine dezentralisierte, instabile Position zugewiesen. Ein Sprecher, der sich in einer von fremden, ‚andersartigen' Tönen durchzogenen Sprache verloren hat. Auf die Tradition der diskriminierenden Engführung von Stottern und tierischem ‚Sprechen' bzw. Tiergeräuschen ist von Marc Shell hingewiesen worden.[24]

Hagebucher, der dem Erzähler übrigens schon zu Beginn des Romans gleich nach seinem überraschenden Wiederauftauchen erneut im „dicksten Nebel"[25] verloren geht, wird damit von Anfang an als prekäre Erzählinstanz und Assistent eines nicht minder unzuverlässigen Erzählers[26] eingeführt. Erzählerische Leerstellen und Unterbrechungen prägen dabei in *Abu Telfan* nicht nur die einzelne Figurenrede, sondern werden von Raabe mitten ins strukturelle Zentrum seines Romans gerückt. Abenteuerliche Reiseberichte des Heimkehrers, für die die Erwartung auf Seiten der erzählten Zuhörerschaft wie auf Seiten von Raabes Leser zunächst geschürt werden, brechen wiederholt ab, werden vom Erzähler unterschlagen oder enden regelmäßig genau an ihrem Höhepunkt in einem nebulösen „Nichts":

> Mit offenem Munde, mit zurückgehaltenem Atem saß sie da, den Erzähler anstarrend, und als sie wieder fähig war zu sprechen, rief sie: „Und dann, und dann, o Gott, und dann?" „Nichts!" sagte der Afrikaner mit einer Ruhe, die in der Tat etwas gespensterhaft Unheimliches hatte.[27]

Solche Effekte der Auslassung prägen auch die Romanstruktur als Ganzes, denn Hagebuchers große öffentliche Vorlesung „über das innere Afrika und das Verhältnis des europäischen Menschen zu demselben"[28], der „sowohl formell wie auch dem Inhalte nach den Mittelpunkt der wahrhaften und merkwürdigen Geschichte, die Spitze der Pyramide [bildet], auf welcher der afrikanische Redner sitzt, seine schöne Seele aufknöpft"[29], bleibt bis auf ein „Bruchstück des Schlusses"[30] eine ebensolche Leerstelle, ein trügerischer Schein, eine „Fata Morgana"[31] des Romans. Alle wesentlichen Stellen der vom Erzähler als besonders spektakulär und skanda-

---

23 Ebd., S. 192.

24 Marc Shell, „Animals That Talk; or, Stutter", in: *differences* 15, 1 (2004), S. 84-107.

25 Raabe (1952), *Abu Telfan*, S. 14.

26 Eine Erzählstrategien, die bei Raabe häufig zum Einsatz kommt, besonders prägnant im Roman *Stopfkuchen*. Vgl. hierzu Johannes Graf/Gunnar Kwisinski, „Heinrich Schaumann, ein Lügenbaron? Zur Erzählstruktur in Raabes Stopfkuchen", in: *Jahrbuch der Raabe Gesellschaft*, Band 33, Berlin, New York, NY, 1992, S. 194-213. Allgemein hierzu: Wayne C. Booth, *Rhetoric of Fiction*, 2. Aufl., Chicago, IL, 1983, S. 149 f. und S. 158.

27 Raabe (1952), *Abu Telfan*, S. 28.

28 Ebd., S. 175.

29 Ebd., S. 183 f.

30 Ebd., S. 190.

31 Ebd., S. 188.

lös angekündigten Rede spart Raabe aus und überlässt dem Leser stattdessen nur Kenntnis einiger nebulöser Phrasen – mithin den „Spuk“[32] einer Rede, die elliptisch bleibt und in zwei Gedankenstrichen abbricht:

> „[I]ch aber habe jetzt nur den *einen* Wunsch, daß Sie alle Ihre Rechnungen – –“ [...] Der Redner stockte im besten Flusse seiner Rede und starrte in den Saal, als tauche nunmehr ihm selbst in den Reihen seiner Zuhörer ein Gespenst auf, ein Geist, welchen er in diesem Augenblicke nicht gerufen hatte [Herv. i. O.].[33]

In solchen diskontinuierlichen Erzählverfahren Raabes, in den Ellipsen, Aposiopesen und Auslassungspunkten, die das Sprechen der zwischen Afrika und Europa kulturell „entgleisten Existenz“[34] Hagebucher gleichsam durchlöchern, manifestiert sich ein fragmentarisiertes Ich, das „von der Erfahrung der Entfremdung geprägt“[35] ist, wie Ulrich Adolph mit Bezug auf Raabes Spätwerk *Altershausen* proklamiert hat. Bernhard Siegert hat eine solche „Irritation des Subjekts“[36] im Stocken der Sprache mit dem Argument verbunden, dass Auslassungszeichen historisch auf das „Andere fremder Texte“ verweisen und somit „Effekt kultureller Diskontinuität“[37] seien. So sind es auch in *Abu Telfan* nicht zufällig gerade die Rückkehrer aus der Fremde, Hagebucher und der ‚verrückte Schneider‘ Täubrich Pascha, die unter dem Eindruck von Depersonalisation und Derealisierung (im Sinne eines Geltungsverlustes von Wirklichkeitskonventionen) stehen und mit ihren „unartikulierten Laute[n], gedehnten Verbindungen, gewaltsamen Beschleunigungen und Verzögerungen“[38] ein Fremd-Werden in der eigenen Sprache mitteilen. An den wenigen Stellen, an denen Hagebuchers Rede in freien Fluss kommt, tut sie es in Form der asyndetischen Aufzählung, die das Stocken gleichsam in ein Stolpern der Sprache überführt. Raabe lässt hier nicht nur syntaktischen Zusammenhalt, sondern auch die Grenzen zwischen Zeit-, Bild- und akustischen Formaten implodieren:

> – ein unendliches, wühlendes, staubaufrührendes, brüllendes, plärrendes, kreischendes, quiekendes, rasselndes, klapperndes, hinten und vorn ausschlagendes, purzelbaumschlagendes Gefolge von Arabern und Affen, Nubiern, Abyssiniern, Schilluks, Baggaras und Dschournegern, von Büffeln, Eseln, Lasttieren aller Art, Käfigen mit jungen Löwen und Tigern, Kasten (sic!) mit Krokodilen und Schlangen und bunten Vögeln! Halt des Zuges an der Barriere von Abu Telfan; exaltiertestes Verhandeln der Parlamentäre und Dolmetscher – allgemeine Verständigung und wahnsinnigster Ju-

---

32 Ebd., S. 191 f.

33 Ebd., S. 191.

34 Ebd., S. 42.

35 Ulrich Adolphs, „Schreibakt als Suche nach Identität. Wilhelm Raabes ‚Altershausen‘“, in: *Jahrbuch der Wilhelm Raabe Gesellschaft*, Band 26, Berlin, New York, NY, 1985, S. 92-106: 104. „Das Bewußtsein Feyerabends ist, wie gezeigt wurde, von der Erfahrung der Entfremdung geprägt. Diese Erfahrung findet formal ihren Ausdruck in zahlreichen Auslassungen und Brüchen. Der Erzählfluß gerät immer wieder durch Gedankenstriche und Auslassungspunkte ins Stocken, die teilweise eine ganze Zeile einnehmen.“

36 Siegert (2003), [...] *Auslassungspunkte*, S. 33.

37 Ebd., S. 10.

38 Gilles Deleuze, „Stotterte er ...“, in: ders., *Kritik und Klinik*, Frankfurt/M., 2015, S. 145-154: 148.

> bel! Große gegenseitige Vorstellung von Altengland und Tumurkieland, Mrs. Lavinia Drawboddy und Madam Kulla Gulla; – der Gorilla am Bratspieß und Mr. Augustus Montague Drawboddy in tiefsinniger Betrachtung des Gorillas – Herr Kornelius van der Mook und Herr Leonhard Hagebucher aus Nippenburg, Grand-Duchy of ***, German Confederation! – –[39]

Die assoziative Aneinanderreihung von Erinnerungsbildern von Hagebuchers Befreiung aus der afrikanischen Gefangenschaft, wiedergegeben in Form von indirekter Rede, funktioniert hier als protomodernes Erzählverfahren eines Bewusstseinsstroms. Gedanken und Wahrnehmungsbruchstücke der subjektiven und diskontinuierlichen Erinnerung des Protagonisten werden unvermittelt und ohne Erzählerintervention wiedergegeben. Wirklichkeit kommt hier in einer Dimension des höchst instabilen inneren Erlebens zum Ausdruck, in der sich reale Erfahrung und traumhafte/traumatische Illusion vermengen: „Mit der Innensicht ist zugleich ein subjektiver Wirklichkeitsraum abgesteckt, in den die Erfahrung der Außenwelt nur über das Bewußtsein vermittelt eindringt."[40]

2. Wirklichkeit des Sprechens

Welche Implikationen ergeben sich nun aus Raabes diskontinuierlichen Erzählverfahren für sein Konzept der Formation und literarischen Darstellbarkeit von Wirklichkeit? Hier gibt die zentrale Rolle, die der (wörtlichen) Figurenrede in seinen Texten zukommt, den entscheidenden Hinweis darauf, dass Wirklichkeit bei Raabe zuallererst eine diskursiv verfertigte ist.[41] Prägnant wird das unter anderem dort, wo Raabe über längere Passagen die Erzählinstanz zugunsten „wörtliche[r] Reden, denen weder Gesicht noch Adresse zugewiesen werden"[42], zurücknimmt. Uwe Steiner hat anhand der Erzählung *Unruhige Gäste* überzeugend dargelegt, dass bei Raabe das Geschehen oft nur aus den kommunikativen Situationen, mithin aus den einander überlagernden Diskursen erschlossen werden kann:[43] „Er reflektiert die Wirklichkeit des Redens, und er beschreibt Wirklichkeit als eine beredete, im Reden potentiell immer auch verfehlte Wirklichkeit".[44] Diese kommunikativen Fehlleistungen, Missverständnisse und blinden Flecken bilden den narrative Clou der Erzählung. Die diskursive Wirklichkeitsstruktur wird durch die beschriebenen Erzählstörungen sichtbar gemacht und als Praktik problematisiert, wenn die geglättete Oberfläche von Raabes Erzählungen immer wieder un-

---

39 Raabe (1952), *Abu Telfan*, S. 86.

40 Adolphs (1985), Schreibakt als Suche nach Identität, S. 105.

41 Ich folge hier zum Teil meinen Ausführungen in *‚Tückische Oberflächen' und ‚Höllische Gestade' im Inneren. Topologien der Gefahr im 19. Jahrhundert*, Würzburg, 2016, S. 186 f.

42 Uwe C. Steiner, „Das Rauschen der Unterhaltung und der Schrecken im Bade. Wilhelm Raabes ‚Unruhige Gäste' und die Kulturgeschichte des Hörens", in: *Jahrbuch der Wilhelm Raabe Gesellschaft*, Band 57, Berlin, New York, NY, 2016, S. 3-22: 18.

43 Ebd., S. 17.

44 Ebd., S. 18.

terbrochen wird durch scheiternde oder stockende Sprech- bzw. Erzählakte: „Denn Stottern bedeutet ja, dass der Sprecher aus seiner Rolle fällt bzw. den Situationsrahmen thematisiert".[45]

Die Darstellung des zeitgenössischen Afrika-Diskurses[46] in *Abu Telfan* führt dieses Prinzip der poetischen Auseinandersetzung mit (gesellschaftlich-kultureller) Wirklichkeit symptomatisch vor. Tatsächlich wird der Schauplatz trotz der prägnanten Setzung im Titel nie betreten oder erzählerisch konkretisiert, stattdessen nimmt der geografische Ort Dar Fur ausschließlich als Effekt konkurrierender Stimmen, Medien und Diskurse[47] ständig changierende, perspektivische Kontur an. Die herausragende Rolle, die Formen der mündlichen Rede in der Erzählung spielen, verweist darauf, dass Raabe damit das Gerücht als Erzähl- bzw. Strukturmuster von Wirklichkeit einführt. So sabotieren die mündlichen Berichte der Heimkehrerfiguren im Roman durch Verschweigen, Auslassung oder Verkehrungen systematisch den gängigen zeitgenössischen (imperialistischen) Afrika-Diskurs, wie er in Zeitschriften, Kolonialliteratur oder Ausstellungen transportiert und sowohl vom impliziten Leser als auch von der Figurenwelt des Romans vorausgesetzt wird: Nicht durch den sanktionierten Bericht eines souveränen Erzählers, sondern in einer Kakofonie heterogener, stotternder und plötzlich versagender Stimmen erfährt der Leser von Afrika. Die Handlung von *Abu Telfan* dreht sich zu einem wichtigen Teil um die Kollision dieser Redeordnungen und Inhaltsprojektionen. Es geht Raabe damit vorrangig um die epistemologische und sprachliche Verfasstheit eines Diskurses, „den Akt des Sprechens über koloniale Themen"[48] und ein Spiel mit der Erwartungshaltung seines Publikums an Inhalt und Gesetzmäßigkeiten eines vorgeblich exotischen Reise- oder Abenteuerromans, welches Raabe seinerseits bereits mit seiner Titelwahl „Abu Telfan" eröffnet.

Den authentischen, linear erzählten Bericht über das ‚wirkliche Afrika' kann es unter diesen Bedingungen nicht geben. Die Leerstelle, die in Hagebuchers Bericht

---

45 Kathrin Röggla, *das stottern des realismus: fiktion und fingiertes, ironie und kritik*, Paderborn, 2011, S. 13.

46 Um die Aktualität des Topos Afrika zur Zeit der Romanentstehung 1867 zu verdeutlichen, sei an dieser Stelle zum einen auf die Fertigstellung des Suezkanals 1869 verwiesen, zum anderen auf die erfolglose aber medienwirksame Suche nach den Quellen des Nils durch Livingston 1866. Relevant ist auch die Erstveröffentlichung von *Abu Telfan* in der Zeitschrift *Über Land und Meer*, in der literarische Texte sich in direkter Nachbarschaft zu populärwissenschaftlichen Darstellungen aus dem Bereich der „Länder- und Völkerkunde" befanden. Auch Leonhard Hagebuchers Bericht über das kuriose Ehepaar Drawboddy ist als Referenz auf ein beliebtes Motiv der zeitgenössischen Berichterstattung über fremde Kontinente zu verstehen: Expeditionen von berühmten Entdecker-Ehepaaren wie das Forscherpaar Baker, das Duo Eduard und Cecilie Seler oder auch Margarete und Emil Selenka.

47 In *Abu Telfan* wird Afrika aus Sicht ökonomischer Interessen (Suezkanal, Elfenbeinhandel) thematisiert, als Gegenstand politischer Diskussion (europäische Kolonialpolitik), historischer Anthropologie und Sprachgeschichte (Prof. Reihenschlager) oder aus moralisch-ethischer Hinsicht (Frage der Universalität von Menschenrechten, wenn in Hagebuchers Erzählungen zeitgenössische Topoi wie die Sklaverei oder die ‚richtige' Missionierung aufgerufen werden).

48 Florian Krobb, *Erkundungen im Überseeischen: Wilhelm Raabe und die Füllung der Welt*, Würzburg, 2009, S. 116.

an die Stelle der erwarteten großen Afrika-Erzählung tritt, ist somit symptomatisch für die Verfasstheit von Wirklichkeit überhaupt. So sind es gerade die diskursiven Verwerfungen, Diskontinuitäten und Risse sowie die Turbulenzen in der Hierarchie der Wirklichkeitsinterpretation,[49] für die Raabe sich vornehmlich interessiert. Die Figur des von den Stadtbewohnern in *Abu Telfan* gemeinhin als „verrückt" oder „närrisch"[50] betrachteten Täubrich Pascha führt diesen Taumel zwischen Fiktion, fingierter Wirklichkeit und ‚Fakten' vor Augen: Zunächst verunsichert Raabe die Leser dadurch, dass er den Erzähler Täubrichs Reisen und Abenteuer im Orient mit dem Verweis auf die Figur Alexander von Humboldts als beglaubigte Fakten referieren lässt, um dieses Wissen nachträglich in der Figurenrede als traumhaft oder als Symptom seines Wahns wieder zu delegitimieren. In der Täubrich-Pascha-Episode erhalten damit „verrückte" Hirngespinste denselben narrativen Stellenwert, wie die vom Lesepublikum und der zeitgenössischen Kritik geforderte künstlerisch-poetische Idealisierung der Wirklichkeit.[51] Auf solch einen expliziten Hinweis einer dichterischen Manipulation der Grenze zwischen Fakten und Fiktion reagiert die Kleinstadt im Roman genau wie Raabes zeitgenössisches Lesepublikum[52] entsprechend ablehnend.

Indem Raabe das Problem der Darstellung von Wirklichkeit durch erzählerische Verfahren der Diskontinuität und Störung adressiert, suspendiert er indes nicht einfach Referenzialität, sondern eröffnet vielmehr die Wirklichkeitsproblematik komplexer: „Es schließt jetzt, indem es die Vermittlung gleichsam ans Erzählte delegiert, nämlich die Wirklichkeit von Vermittlung ein. [...] Real, wirklich, erscheint das Verfahren, erscheint die Vermittlung, abkünftig dagegen das Vermittelte."[53] Wo Rede ins Stottern und Stocken kommt und Signifikanten nicht mehr für die eine bezeichnete Wirklichkeit einstehen (bzw. nicht mehr hinter dieser zurücktreten), sondern in kontingenter Reihung für sich selbst stehen, kommt es zu einem „Taumel der Denotation".[54] Die weiter oben zitierte längere Passage der Befreiung Hagebuchers führt das vor. Die beliebige Aufrufung von Substantiven wie „Arabern und Affen, Nubiern, Abyssiniern, Schilluks, Baggaras und Dschournegern, [...] Käfigen mit jungen Löwen und Tigern, Kasten (sic!) mit Krokodilen"[55] destabilisieren nicht allein die Fokalisation des Erzählten, sondern unterminieren

49 Röggla (2011), *das stottern des realismus*, S. 13.

50 Raabe (1952), *Abu Telfan*, S. 93, S. 103 und S. 107.

51 Zur Auseinandersetzung Wilhelm Raabes mit dem programmatischen ‚poetischen Realismus' vgl. Ulla Heine, *Psychopathologische Phänomene im Kunstspiegel der Literatur des Realismus, dargestellt an Werken von Wilhelm Raabe*, Marburg, 1996, S. 33 f.

52 Zur negativen Aufnahme des Romans, insbesondere der Kritik an Raabes „Hang zum Absonderlichen", bei der Kritik und den Lesern vgl. Anhang zur HKA. Wilhelm Raabe, *Sämtliche Werke: Braunschweiger Ausgabe*, Band 7, hg. von Karl Hoppe, Göttingen, 1952, S. 399.

53 Steiner (2016), Das Rauschen der Unterhaltung, S. 20 f.

54 Roland Barthes, „Der Wirklichkeitseffekt", in: ders., *Das Rauschen der Sprache. Kritische Essays IV*, Frankfurt/M., 2006, S. 164-172: 168.

55 Raabe (1952), *Abu Telfan*, S. 86.

zugleich das vom Subjekt erinnerte Ereignis mit dem Vokabular von Romanphantasien.[56]

3. Raabes stotternder Realismus

Die Lektüre des Romans *Abu Telfan* hat nicht nur aufgezeigt, dass Wirklichkeit bei Raabe keinen vorgängigen Charakter hat, sondern dass sie sich darüber hinaus aus dem Diskursiven, aus der Kommunikation der Figuren heraus generiert. Realität erweist sich damit als Aushandlungsprozess mit ungewissem Ausgang. Stets nur näherungsweise, tastend und stolpernd umkreist die Erzählung eine diskursiv formierte Wirklichkeit, für die der Autor durch kontrafaktisches, diskontinuierliches oder „dualistisches Gegeneinandererzählen"[57] immer neue, diskrepante Versionen liefert. Auch die erst in der Erfahrung von Wirklichkeit sich ausbildende Identität des Subjekts wird von Raabe dementsprechend nicht als feste, kohärente Größe geführt, sondern als mehrfach gebrochene, von Erzählmustern und Medien abhängige Variable.[58] Dabei ist der Fokus auf gestörte oder scheiternde Rede alles andere als zufällig oder dekorativ-humoristisch motiviert, denn gerade in den erzählerischen, typografischen und sprachlichen Bruchstellen, Störungen und Sackgassen, die in unterschiedlicher Intensität das Gros der Raabe'schen Erzähltexte prägen, wird das dominierende Strukturprinzip der Instabilität und Brüchigkeit von Wirklichkeit manifest. Raabe führt mit seinen Verfahren des diskontinuierlichen Erzählens vor, dass sich Wirklichkeit aus unterschiedlichen Beobachter- und Redepositionen sowie den damit verbundenen Beobachtungs- und Darstellungsschwierigkeiten immer wieder neu konstituieren muss, womit „nicht nur der Transfer der Wirklichkeit in Literatur eine Schimäre ist, sondern die Wirklichkeit selbst nicht eins zu eins zu haben ist".[59] Eine realistische Poetik des diskontinuierlichen Sprechens und sabotierten Erzählens unterläuft in Raabes Texten immer wieder subversiv die präzise und zuverlässige Beschreibung sozialer Zusammen-

---

56 Vgl. hierzu: Albrecht Koschorke, „Kreisbewegung und semantische Zirkel bei Wilhelm Raabe. Eine exemplarische Analyse der Exposition seiner Erzählung ‚Vom alten Proteus'", in: *Jahrbuch der Wilhelm Raabe Gesellschaft*, Band 31, Berlin, New York, NY, 1990, S. 36-49: 46.

57 Rolf Parr, „Raabes Effekte des Realen", in: *Jahrbuch der Wilhelm Raabe Gesellschaft*, Band 52, Berlin, New York, NY, 2011, S. 21-38: 26. So löst Raabe beispielsweise die innere Einheit des Subjekts auf, indem er die Innenwelt seiner Figuren mit Gegenpositionen des Erzählers kontrastiert, ein Verfahren, das systematisch die Grenze zwischen Einbildung und Wirklichkeit verunklart und mit der Beschreibung von Wirklichkeit als Ausdruck psychisch verwirrter Wahrnehmung experimentiert.

58 Die auffällige Passivität des vermeintlichen Abenteurers Hagebucher verweist auf ein Darstellungsverfahren Raabes, mit dem die Figur als Interaktionsprozess widersprüchlicher Antriebe und Interessen darstellbar wird. Raabe lässt andere Figuren stellvertretend für Hagebucher handeln, sprechen und fühlen. Die um die Figur im Roman herum gruppierten und in ihrer Ähnlichkeit (zum Beispiel durch biografische oder physische Übereinstimmungen) auf ihn bezogenen Figuren Nikola von Einstein, Kornelius van den Mook, Vetter Wassertreter oder Täubrich wirken in Raabes Darstellung deswegen abstrakt und einseitig, weil es sich bei ihnen um potenzielle Personen bzw. um Facetten eines diskontinuierlichen Ichs, anstatt um souveräne Figuren handelt.

59 Röggla (2011), *stottern des realismus*, S. 7.

hänge (zum Beispiel der süddeutschen Kleinstadt-Gesellschaft in *Abu Telfan*, aber auch auf die Erzählung *Stopfkuchen* sei hier verwiesen).

Diesem prozesshaften und vorläufigen Charakter entspricht in *Abu Telfan* ein Zerfall der Wirklichkeit in drei Dimensionen, deren Unterscheidbarkeit bereits im Vorwort des Romans zum Taumeln gebracht wird.[60] Hier wäre zum ersten die Ebene der (deklarierten) Fiktion zu nennen: Dazu zählen unter anderem Täubrichs phantastische Reise und Rückkehr, genau wie die im Roman indirekt zitierte Abenteuerliteratur oder auch die wilden Spekulationen und Projektionen der Kleinstadtbewohner bezüglich des heimgekehrten „Menschenfressers"[61] Hagebucher. Die zweite Dimension von Wirklichkeit umfasst eine Ebene des Fingierten, der (bewussten) Täuschung und Geschichtsfälschung (sozusagen Fake-News): Hierzu zählt insbesondere die in der zweiten Romanhälfte aufgedeckte gesellschaftliche Realität der betrügerischen Manipulation in Gestalt der Lügen und Ränkespiele des Barons von Glimmern zur Vertuschung eines lange zurückliegenden Skandals. Eine dritte Wirklichkeitsdimension wird in *Abu Telfan* mit der Beschwörung einer Welt der ‚reinen Fakten' eröffnet: Hier spielt vor allem der Erzählrahmen mit seinem ironisch-legitimierenden Rekurs auf „Material"[62], „Dokument"[63] und „Archiv"[64] eine zentrale Rolle, aber auch der besondere Status, der anfänglich den afrikanischen Augenzeugenberichten Hagebuchers von den Städtern eingeräumt wird (bis zu ihrer Enttäuschung aufgrund seines erzählerischen Versagens).

Durch die permanente Überlagerung dieser drei Dimensionen im Roman wird eine Auflösung von Wirklichkeitsgrenzen in Gang gesetzt, durch die Phantasien, Träume und Lügen auf textstruktureller Ebene die gleiche Geltung beanspruchen, wie empirisch zu überprüfende ‚Wahrheiten' und die damit den zeitgenössischen, künstlerischen Realitätsbegriff systematisch verunsichert: „Hat jemals die Wirklichkeit der Phantasie ärgerlicher ein Bein gestellt? Abscheulich, abscheulich!"[65]

---

60 Die titelgebende Stadt „Abu Telfan" im Mondgebirge dürfte von Raabe daher nicht zufällig gewählt worden sein, handelte es sich bei dem Land Dar Fur noch zur Entstehungszeit des Romans 1867 um ein diffuses „Grenzgebiet, eine [...] Übergangszone zwischen der bekannten, karthographierten, mit geographischen Details ‚gefüllten' und der leeren, weißen Welt." (Krobb (2009), Erkundungen im Überseeischen, S. 107 f.) Ganz in diesem Sinne markiert Raabe im Vorwort „Abu Telfan" als Ort unsicheren Wissens und schieren „Glaubens", von dem der Autor fälschlicherweise behauptet, er sei nicht auf der Landkarte zu finden: „Ich bitte ganz gehorsamst, weder den Ort Abu Telfan noch das Tumurkienland auf der Karte von Afrika zu suchen; und was das Mondgebirge anbetrifft, so weiß ein jeder ebensogut als ich, daß die Entdecker durchaus noch nicht einig sind, ob sie dasselbe wirklich entdeckt haben. Einige wollen an der Stelle, wo ältere Geographen es notierten, einen großen Sumpf, andere eine ausgedehnte Salzwüste und wieder andere nur einen unbedeutenden Hügelzug gefunden haben, welches alles keineswegs hindert, daß ich für meinen Teil unbedingt an es glaube. –" (Raabe (1952), *Abu Telfan*, S. 5.)

61 Ebd., S. 38.

62 Ebd., S. 10.

63 Ebd., S. 9.

64 Ebd., S. 11.

65 Ebd., S. 139.

Erst die Lücke im Text, die „Fermate“, die durch das Stocken der Rede (oder der Schrift) entsteht, erlaubt es, dass Wünsche, Projektionen oder ein residuales Vergangenes Teil der realistischen Darstellung der Gegenwart werden. Mit dem verfremdenden Stottern, den Störgeräuschen der Kommunikation, überlagern sich bei Raabe gleichsam Wahrnehmungs- und Wirklichkeitsdimensionen, mischt sich ein „Rauschen der Vergangenheit“ in die Gegenwart des Erzählten, das „ein Unterscheiden von Traum und Wahrheit“[66] sabotiert. In den blinden Flecken der Narration, den Missverständnissen, Unterbrechungen, Auslassungen und variierten Wiederholungen manifestiert sich das Reale als Raum des Möglichen: Das Stottern, Stocken und Stammeln ist bei Raabe kein Authentizitätseffekt, wohl aber ein spezieller Realitätseffekt, der im Text den Raum für ein Dahinter öffnet: „Rather, its purpose is to produce an interruption, a crack or a gap, that might allow a different reality to be glimpsed.“[67] So entstehen Risse in der glatten Textur des Erzählten, die einerseits sein ‚Gemachtsein‘ offenbaren, andererseits Wirklichkeitserzählungen für den Raum des Spekulativen und Zweifelhaften einer ‚anderen Realität‘ öffnen, mithin ein realistisches Darstellungsrepertoire mit einem doppelten Boden ausstatten.

[66] Beides wörtliche Zitate aus Wilhelm Raabe, *Stopfkuchen*, in: *Sämtliche Werke: Braunschweiger Ausgabe*, Band 18, hg. von Karl Hoppe, Göttingen, 1969, S. 5-207. 25.

[67] Siehe den Beitrag „Real Fictions“ von Hal Foster im vorliegenden Band, S. 23.

Natalie Binczek

Inkorporation und Dissimulation. Der artikulatorische Akzent im 18. Jahrhundert: Riccaut de la Marlinières ‚Kauderwelsch'

1. Schibboleth

‚Schibboleth' bezeichnet ein Losungswort und dient somit als Medium der Authentifizierung. In seiner ursprünglichen Form erfolgte diese über die Aussprache. Nicht das Wissen um die Wortbedeutung, nicht das Wissen um die Schreibweise, sondern allein das Wissen um und das Vermögen der korrekten Artikulation erlaubten es nämlich den Gileaditern, zwischen sich und den anderen, das heißt zwischen Freunden und Feinden eine Unterscheidung zu treffen. Im „Buch der Richter" heißt es dazu:

> Vnd die Gileaditer namen ein die furt des Jordans fur Ephraim. Wenn nu sprachen die flüchtigen Ephraim / Las mich hin übergehen / So sprachen die Menner von Gilead zu jm / Bistu ein Ephraiter? Wenn er denn antwortet / Nein / So hiessen sie jn sprechen / Schiboleth / So sprach er / Siboleth / vnd kunds nicht recht reden / So griffen sie jn vnd schlugen jn an der furt des Jordans / Das zu der zeit von Ephraim fielen zwey vnd vierzig tausent.[1]

Der Ausdruck ‚Schibboleth' verweist auf die Artikulationsform als bedeutungstragende und distinguierende Einheit der sprachlichen Performanz, die sich im Unterschied zum Dialekt und damit einem ganzen System von lexikalischen, syntaktischen und phonetischen Elementen nur auf den Gesichtspunkt der Lautung bezieht. Einen Gesichtspunkt allerdings, der aufgrund der besonderen Nähe zum Körper die indexikalische Wirkung des Sprechens betrifft. Zum einen, so Jacques Derrida in seiner Analyse dieser biblischen Textstelle, ist es eine spezifische Disposition des „Stimmapparates", die es den Ephraimitern unmöglich macht, das ‚sch' auszusprechen. Zum anderen bekommen sie die Konsequenzen der an der phonetischen Differenz zwischen sch/s entschiedenen Identifikation „im Körper und am eigenen Leib zu spüren".[2] Indem ihnen nämlich der Zugang zu ihrem eigenen Territorium versperrt wird, sind sie Flüchtlinge geworden, die schließlich, durch das Sprechmerkmal erkannt, als Feinde erschlagen werden.

Die biblische Erzählung stellt nicht nur das Sprechen in einen engen Konnex zum Körper des Sprechenden. Sie legt diese Beziehung auch territorial fest. Denn auf dem zuvor den Ephraimitern zugehörigen Gebiet – an den Jordan-Furten – hat

---

1 Die Bibel nach der Übersetzung Martin Luthers, Stuttgart, 1984, RI 12,5-6.

2 Jacques Derrida, *Schibboleth. Für Paul Celan*, hg. von Peter Engelmann, Graz, Wien, 1986, S. 127.

eine spezifische Artikulationsnorm Geltung gehabt, welche durch die Besetzung der Gileaditer umgewertet wird. Infolge dieses Machtwechsels wird eine korrekte von einer nicht korrekten Aussprache unterschieden, mehr noch: Es wird überhaupt erst eine Unterscheidung der Aussprache eingeführt, die zwei verschiedene Sprechweisen, zwei verschiedene Akzente hervorbringt und so die Bildung eines Losungswortes ermöglicht.

Die ephraimitische, den Anfangslaut als ‚s' aussprechende Artikulationsform markiert in diesem Kontext nicht nur die Abweichung von einer seitens der Besatzer normierten Lautung, sondern erzeugt zugleich auch eine Deterritorialisierung, insofern hier ein bestimmtes Wort auf einem bestimmten Territorium gleichsam zum Fremdwort wird. An den von den Gileaditern bewachten Jordan-Furten entsteht es aus dem zuvor dort heimisch gewesenen ‚Sibboleth'. Deutlich wird daran, wie innerhalb eines Sprachsystems auf der Ebene der Aussprache bzw. des Akzents Grenzen gezogen werden können, die die Wirkung von Sprachgrenzen entfalten.[3] Am Akzent, an einer bestimmten phonetischen, idiomatischen Umsetzung des Wortes ‚Schibboleth', lassen sich Unterscheidungen ablesen, welche von territorial-politischer Relevanz sind.

In der biblischen Erzählung wird kein Hinweis auf den lexikalisch-semantischen Bezug des Wortes ‚Schibboleth', das ‚Getreideähre', aber auch ‚Strom'[4] bedeuten kann, gegeben. Diese Sinnreferenz scheint, obgleich sich von hier aus vielschichtige Lesarten des Textes entwickeln ließen, aufgehoben. Die Funktion des Wortes liegt ausschließlich in seiner Aussprache, wobei sich gleichwohl die Frage aufdrängt, ob es nicht auch andere Kandidaten für diesen Code gegeben hätte. Unterstrichen wird jedenfalls die Einsicht in die Arbitrarität sprachlicher Zeichen, wenn die phonetische Umsetzung des Signifikanten in Absehung der Signifikatseite als existenziell bedeutsam ausgestellt wird.

Mit der ephraimitischen Aussprache des ‚Schibboleth' wird keine Sprechstörung, wie sie das Stottern[5] oder das Lispeln etwa repräsentieren, bestimmt. Es handelt sich nicht um eine individuelle Beeinträchtigung des Sprechflusses, sondern

---

3 Erst im Zuge der Herausbildung der Linguistik im ausgehenden 19. Jahrhundert wird die sprachkonstitutive Bedeutung des Akzents einer systematischen Betrachtung unterzogen. Saussure unterscheidet in diesem Sinn die Funktion des Akzents als sprachbildend – im Sinne seiner ‚grammatischen' Bedeutung – von einer Funktion, die nicht unmittelbar das Sprachverstehen betrifft, sondern lediglich eine dialektale Herkunft des Sprechers andeutet, hierbei spricht er vom ‚natürlichen Akzent'. Siehe dazu: Ludwig Jäger/Mareike Buss/Lorella Ghiotti, „Notes sur l'accentuation lituanienne", in: Simon Bouquet (Hg.), *Cahier de l'Herne Ferdinand de Saussure*, Paris, 2003, S. 323-350.

4 „*Schibboleth*, dieses Wort, das ich hier als hebräisch bezeichne, findet sich, wie Sie wissen, in einer ganzen Familie von Sprachen, im Phönizischen, im Jüdisch-Aramäischen, im Syrischen. Es hat eine Vielzahl von Bedeutungen durchlaufen: Strom, Fluß, Kornähre, Ölzweig. Doch jenseits dieser Bedeutungen hat es die Bedeutung eines Losungswortes angenommen. Man gebrauchte es während des Krieges oder danach zum Passieren eines bewachten Grenzübergangs." (Derrida (1986), *Schibboleth*, S. 51.)

5 Vgl. dazu Manfred Schneider, „Den Tod buchstabieren: Stottern – Zeitlupe – Schreiben", in: *Akzente* 33, 5 (1986), S. 443-451; Kathrin Röggla, *Stottern und Stolpern. Strategien einer literarischen Gesprächsführung. Essay*, Frankfurt/M., 2013.

vielmehr um eine Distinktion, welche auf die Sprechweise eines ganzen Stammes, Volkes bzw. einer Ethnie verweist, insofern exakt diese Sprechweise ihre soziale Einheit konstituiert. Keine Störung,[6] sondern eine kulturelle Eigenart. Sie erzeugt Bedeutung, weil und indem sie die Ephraimiter, die ihrerseits, so Derrida, „sich dem diakritischen Unterschied *Schi* und *Si* gegenüber indifferent verhielten",[7] zu identifizieren erlaubt. Die Fähigkeit, den phonetischen Unterschied zu erkennen und auf ihre eigene Sprechweise anzuwenden, besaßen sie nicht, weil ihre Sprechkultur und mit ihr die sprachliche Verfasstheit ihrer sozialen Wirklichkeit sie nicht erforderte. So erzählt die Bibelgeschichte im Gegensatz zum rhetorischen Verständnis des Sprechens als einer Technik, die im Kontext der *pronuntiatio* als ein nach Bedarf verwendbares Instrument eingesetzt werden könne, von der *Inkorporation* des Sprechens, über welches die Sprecher nicht verfügten und über das sie keine Macht hatten, weil es ihnen gewissermaßen vorausging. Die Art und Weise, wie die Ephraimiter das ‚Schibboleth' aussprachen, wird nicht als eine Technik reflektiert, sondern als Bestandteil ihrer kulturellen Physiognomie. Aufgrund dieser Disposition weist die Erzählung auf das sich im 18. Jahrhundert etablierende Konzept der ‚Muttersprache' voraus, welches der Sprache, indem es sie naturalisiert, auch einen realen und eindeutig festlegbaren Herkunfts- und Sprechort zuweist. Der Akzent dient dabei als unhintergehbares Authentifizierungsmerkmal der muttersprachlichen Sprachkompetenz.

2. Muttersprache

Die ‚Muttersprache' bilde, so David Martyn, „eine Norm, die der Muttersprachler nicht nur anzuwenden befugt ist, sondern quasi *qua* Geburt – genauer, qua sprachlicher Sozialisation im Kindesalter – *verkörpert*".[8] Eine *qua* Geburt bedingte und ermöglichte sprachliche Sozialisation, die die Voraussetzung für eine nicht nur grammatische und lexikalische Sprachbeherrschung schafft, sondern sich insbesondere auch in der Fähigkeit niederschlägt, ‚akzentfrei' zu sprechen. ‚Akzentfreies' Sprechen bedeutet zunächst einmal, dass sich keine phonetisch fremd- und anderssprachige Markierung in die Aussprache mischt. Die höchste Stufe der Sprachbeherrschung liegt allerdings erst dann vor, wenn überhaupt keine als regional und das heißt als provinziell wahrnehmbare Färbung, nicht einmal mehr die muttersprachlich inkorporierte, vernehmbar ist. Hochlautung[9] ist dabei das Ergeb-

6 Dagegen schreibt Michel Serres den artikulatorischen bzw. „regionale[n] Akzent[]" – den er sogar in einem Zug mit dem „Stottern und Stammeln" nennt – dem Rauschen zu, womit er als eine Störung, zugleich jedoch auch als „*wesentliches* Moment der Kommunikation [Herv. i. O.]" bestimmt wird. (Michel Serres, *Hermes I. Kommunikation*, hg. von Günther Rösch, Berlin, 1991, S. 49.)

7 Derrida (1986), *Schibboleth*, S. 51.

8 David Martyn, „Es gab keine Mehrsprachigkeit, bevor es nicht Einsprachigkeit gab. Ansätze zu einer Archäologie der Sprachigkeit (Herder, Luther, Tawada)", in: Till Dembeck/Georg Mein (Hg.), *Philologie und Mehrsprachigkeit*, Heidelberg, 2014, S. 39-51: 41.

9 Siehe dazu Christian Winkler, „Zur Frage der deutschen Hochlautung", in: ders., *Satz und Wort im heutigen Deutsch*, Düsseldorf, 1967, S. 202-217.

nis einer Normativität, die einen Akzent gleichsam unhörbar macht und somit das Sprechen in Bezug auf die Artikulation neutralisiert. Diese Stufe der Sprachbeherrschung lässt sich dem Register der Technik zuschreiben, gilt sie doch als eine der zentralen „Regeln für Schauspieler".

> Wenn mitten in einer tragischen Rede sich ein Provinzialismus eindrängt, so wird die schönste Dichtung verunstaltet und das Gehör des Zuschauers beleidigt. Daher ist das Erste und Notwendigste für den sich bildenden Schauspieler, daß er sich von allen Fehlern des Dialekts befreie und eine vollständige reine Aussprache zu erlangen suche. Kein Provinzialismus taugt auf die Bühne! Dort herrsche nur die reine deutsche Mundart, wie sie durch Geschmack, Kunst und Wissenschaft ausgebildet und verfeinert worden.[10]

Die Forderung nach einer ‚vollständigen reinen Aussprache' impliziert die Möglichkeit, dass sie erlernt werden könne. Insbesondere die Ausbildung zum Schauspieler[11] widmet sich zuallererst – es sei sogar „das Erste und Notwendigste" dieser Ausbildung – der Reinigung des Sprechens von dialektalen sowie damit einhergehend von den Akzent betreffenden ‚Provinzialismen'. Hochlautung im Sinne akzentfreien Sprechens wird mittels der Unterscheidung Zentrum/Provinz organisiert. Sprechweisen indizieren die Zugehörigkeit zum Zentrum oder aber den Verweis in die Provinz. Provinziell ist dabei, was einen Akzent aufweist, wohingegen im Zentrum akzentfrei gesprochen wird. Goethe spezifiziert seine Überlegungen, indem er auf das dem ‚Schibboleth' vergleichbare Problem hinweist, wonach „man sich bei dem Buchstaben b in acht nehmen (muß), welcher sehr leicht mit w verwechselt wird, wodurch der ganze Sinn der Rede verdorben und unverständlich gemacht werden kann. Zum Beispiel: Leben um Leben, nicht Lewen um Lewen".[12]

Ähnlich der den Ephraimitern attestierten Lautindifferenz zwischen ‚s' und ‚sch' wird im Kontext der deutschen Sprache die zwischen ‚b' und ‚w' markiert. Sie ‚verderbe den Sinn der Rede', womit nicht nur eine folgenreiche Fehlleistung, sondern zugleich auch die Notwendigkeit einer der grammatisch-orthografischen Regulierung des Deutschen[13] analogen Regulierung auf der Ebene der Phonetik angesprochen ist. So lässt sich dieses von Goethe an Schauspieler adressierte Regelwerk als Ausdruck einer allgemeinen Kultivierung und Normierung des Sprechens im ausgehenden 18. Jahrhundert lesen, die deutliche Hinweise auf Standards korrekter Artikulation auch außerhalb des Theaters liefert.[14]

Entscheidend ist, dass eine solche Elaboration der Aussprache keineswegs in Opposition zum Konzept der ‚Muttersprache' gedacht wird, sondern sie vielmehr voraussetzt und gewissermaßen auch vollendet.

---

10 Johann Wolfgang von Goethe, „Regeln für Schauspieler", in: ders., *Sämtliche Werke. Briefe, Tagebücher, und Gespräche. Band 18: Ästhetische Schriften 1771-1805*, hg. von Friedmar Apel, Frankfurt/M., 1998, §1, S. 860 f.

11 Irmgard Weithase, *Zur Geschichte der gesprochenen Sprache*, Tübingen, 1961, S. 357 ff.

12 Goethe (1998), Regeln für Schauspieler, §8, S. 862.

13 Siehe zur Geschichte der deutschen Orthografie u. a. Hermann Scheuringer, *Geschichte der deutschen Rechtschreibung. Ein Überblick. Mit einer Einführung zur Neuregelung ab 1998*, Wien, 1996.

14 Weithase (1961), *Zur Geschichte der gesprochenen Sprache*, S. 280.

Zedlers *Universal-Lexicon* definiert „Mutter=Sprache“ als eine Grundvoraussetzung des Sprechens überhaupt: „Alle Sprachen sind Mutter=Sprachen, aber in Ansehung einer Person ist auch nur eine Sprache dessen Mutter=Sprache. Nemlich diejenige Sprache, die an dem Ort geredet wird, wo einer geb. und erzogen worden, heisst dessen Mutter=Sprache.“[15] ‚Muttersprache‘ bildet demnach nicht nur ein konstitutives Merkmal des Sprechens, sie liegt sogar dem Verständnis der Sprache überhaupt zugrunde. Eine Sprache, die sich nicht als ‚Muttersprache‘ und mithin nach dementsprechenden Kriterien beschreiben lässt, wäre demzufolge keine. Als Muttersprache aber bildet sie eine ebenso territorial wie biologisch grundierte Kategorie, insofern sie nämlich nur dort gelernt und gesprochen werden kann, wo man – wie es dort heißt – „geboren und erzogen wird“.[16] Ferner basiert das Konzept auf der Vorstellung der Einsprachigkeit.[17] Demzufolge kann ein Mensch nur eine Sprache auf muttersprachlichem Niveau erlernen. Bilingualität im Sinne eines gleichwertigen Nebeneinanders unterschiedlicher Sprachen ist in diesem Konzept nicht vorgesehen und nicht verankerbar, weil es Sprache an eine sprachlich-homogene kulturelle Ökologie bindet. Insofern es die deutsche Sprache zum einen von andren Nationalsprachen unterscheidet, zum zweiten auch von ihnen unabhängig macht, wird deutlich, in welchem Maße das Konzept der Einsprachigkeit im 18. Jahrhundert auch politisch motiviert ist. Alle weiteren Sprachen haben nunmehr den Stellenwert von Fremd- oder Zweitsprachen, sie werden somit als Ergebnisse eines technisch gedachten Lernprozesses bestimmt und, einem Schibboleth vergleichbar, von einem primären, *qua* Geburt und Sozialisation erworbenen Sprachvermögen – das einem als natürlich *realisierten* Kulturkontext entspricht – unterschieden.

Im zwei Jahre später erschienenen 29. Band des *Universal-Lexicons* findet sich folgender Eintrag unter dem Lemma „Pronunciatio“:

> [I]n der Sprach=Kunde ein deutlich und vernehmliches Aussprechen der Worte und Buchstaben. Dieses ist das vornehmste und schwerste bey Erlernung der Sprachen, und nicht wohl möglich recht zu lernen, als in dem Lande, wo die Sprache geredet wird.[18]

---

15 Johann Heinrich Zedler, *Grosses Vollständiges Universal-Lexicon aller Wissenschaften und Künste*, Band 22, Halle, Leipzig, 1739, Sp. 1656.

16 Die Mutter gilt dabei auch als Sprachvermittlerin und maßgebliches Medium der Alphabetisierung: Siehe dazu Friedrich A. Kittler, *Aufschreibesysteme 1800/1900*, 3. vollst. überarb. Aufl., München, 1995, S. 37 ff.

17 Muttersprache wird als Einsprachigkeit gedacht. David Martyn hält fest, „dass die neue Einsprachigkeit des Menschen sich sehr gut mit einer bestimmten Art der Mehrsprachigkeit verbinden lässt. Mehrsprachigkeit und Muttersprache vertragen sich nicht nur, die beiden Begriffe setzen einander vielmehr gegenseitig voraus: Es gilt gerade jetzt, ‚fremde‘ Sprachen zu lernen. Das Kompositum ‚Fremdsprache‘ kommt bezeichnenderweise erst im 19. Jahrhundert auf und gewinnt dann rasant an Bedeutung“ (Martyn (2014), Es gab keine Mehrsprachigkeit, bevor es nicht Einsprachigkeit gab, S. 44).

18 Johann Heinrich Zedler, *Grosses Vollständiges Universal-Lexicon aller Wissenschaften und Künste*, Band 29, Halle, Leipzig, 1741, Sp. 839.

Bedeutsam ist an dieser Definition, dass auch sie den Aspekt des Territoriums als Voraussetzung der richtigen Sprechweise hervorhebt. Der Erwerb der korrekten Aussprache wird hier jedoch nicht an die für die ‚Muttersprache' konstitutiven Bedingungen der ‚Geburt und Sozialisation' gebunden. Im Begriff der ‚Pronunciation' scheint vielmehr die Möglichkeit gegeben, sie auch dort als Zweit- und Drittsprache auf muttersprachlichem Niveau erlernen zu können, wo sie muttersprachlich verortet ist. Wenn allerdings die korrekte Aussprache auf die Attribute ‚deutlich' und ‚vernehmlich' begrenzt wird, sind mit ihnen kaum jene Spezifika der Artikulation erfasst, welche eine muttersprachlich richtige von einer nicht-muttersprachlichen zu unterscheiden erlauben. Die Distinktion ‚Schibboleth' versus ‚Sibboleth', die auf verschiedene, *qua* Geburt und Sozialisation bedingte Ausspracheformen zurückgeht, vermag sie letztlich nicht abzubilden. Derjenigen zwischen deutlich/undeutlich entspricht sie jedenfalls nicht. Wenn Zedler jedoch konzediert, das „Aussprechen der Worte und Buchstaben" sei das „schwerste bey Erlernung der Sprachen" – es ist dieser Einschätzung zufolge schwieriger als die Kompetenzen im Feld der Grammatik oder Lexik –, dann verweist seine Graduierung auf das Problembewusstsein, wonach sich in einer Fremdsprache etwas, das eigentlich nur muttersprachlich inkorporiert werden kann, allenfalls mühsam erlernen lässt. Der Artikel stellt somit die Konfrontation zwischen dem Sprechvermögen als etwas, über das man nicht verfügen kann, mit dem Sprechen als einer Technik, die sich durch Übung bearbeiten und perfektionieren lässt, aus.

Bis in das späte 19. Jahrhundert hinein kann kein systematisches Bewusstsein für die linguistische Spezifik des Akzents rekonstruiert werden. Die Aussprache wird weitegehend in den Kategorien der antiken *pronunciatio* gedacht, das heißt vielfach über Merkmale der Deutlichkeit oder Lautstärke etc. beschrieben. In Johann Christoph Adelungs *Grammatisch-kritischem Wörterbuch der hochdeutschen Mundart* findet sich zwar das Lemma „Aussprache", jedoch wird diese sehr allgemein als die „Stimme und der Ton eines Sprechenden, und deren Art und Weise"[19] definiert. Vor allem die stilistische[20] Dimension wird dabei zunächst hervorgehoben, bevor der Artikel auch die sprachkonstitutive Bedeutung der Aussprache streift, wenn er eine korrekte von einer falschen unterscheidet: „Besonders das Aussprechen der Buchstaben, Sylben und Wörter. Eine falsche Aussprache, ein Fehler in der Aussprache, oder wider die Aussprache."[21] Ausgegangen wird von Standards der Artikulation, die selbst nicht im Einzelnen genannt sind, jedoch unterstellen, dass bestimmte Formen des Aussprechens eine Abweichung bilden, die das Verständnis einer Mitteilung zu beeinträchtigen drohen. Auf dialektale Unterschiede verweist hingegen die Bezeichnung „Mundart", die Adelung als „die besondere Art zu reden, wodurch sich die Einwohner einer Gegend von den Ein-

---

[19] Johann Christoph Adelung, *Grammatisch-kritisches Wörterbuch der hochdeutschen Mundart*, Band 1, Leipzig 1793-1801, Sp. 653.

[20] Siehe zur Beschreibung des Akzents gemäß der Unterscheidung von Ornament und Figur Till Dembeck, „Schibboleth/Sibboleth: Phonographie und kulturelle Kommunikation um 1900", in: *Zeitschrift für Literaturwissenschaft und Literatur* 142 (2006), S. 43-68.

[21] Adelung (1793-1801), *Grammatisch-kritisches Wörterbuch*, Sp. 653.

wohnern anderer Gegenden unterscheiden"[22], definiert und damit sprachterritorial festlegt. Erst in Joachim Heinrich Campes *Wörterbuch der deutschen Sprache* wird unter „Mundart" die jeweilige, dialektal bestimmte Sprechweise mit der jeweils regionalen Aussprache verknüpft. Demnach realisiere sich die Mundart „nicht allein durch verschiedene Aussprache, sondern auch durch Abweichungen in der Bildung, Bedeutung und im Gebrauch der Wörter".[23] Diese Formulierung verweist auf zwei Sprachebenen: auf die Differenz zwischen dialektaler Aussprache und der grammatischen sowie lexikalischen Beschaffenheit eines Dialektes. Auf der Grundlage dieser Unterscheidung erst können hybride Sprechweisen beobachtet werden, die beispielsweise eine grammatisch korrekte Sprachverwendung mit einem regionalen Akzent verbinden.

Mag er hörbar oder unhörbar sein, stets grundiert und ermöglicht er das Sprechen, ist dieses doch ohne eine bestimmte Akzentuierung nicht realisierbar, ja nicht einmal denkbar. Die Hochlautung aber bestimmt jenen Akzent, der unhörbar geworden ist und von welchem aus alle anderen Artikulationsformen als bloße Abweichungen, als Störungen der Norm erscheinen. Eine Struktur, in welcher die heterogene Vielfalt unterschiedlicher Dialekte und Akzente auf die Opposition von Zentrum und Peripherie bzw. Provinz, von Hochsprache und Dialekt verdichtet wird.[24] Mit „‚hoch' und ‚nieder'" werden indes nicht, „zwei Sprachen beschrieben, sondern zwei Gebrauchsweisen oder Funktionen der Sprache",[25] wie Gilles Deleuze und Félix Guattari festhalten. Damit verweisen sie auf den dynamischen Prozess innerhalb der Hierarchie und heben die „kontinuierliche Variation"[26] hervor, die dafür sorgt, dass ‚minoritäre' bzw. provinzielle Sprachen und ihre jeweiligen Artikulationsformen „nicht nur einfach Unter-Sprachen, Idiolekte oder Dialekte [sind], sondern Potentiale, die die Hochsprache mit all ihren Dimensionen und Elementen zu einem Minoritär-Werden bringen."[27]

---

22 Johann Christoph Adelung, *Grammatisch-kritisches Wörterbuch der hochdeutschen Mundart*, Band 3: *M-Scr*, Leipzig, 1798, Sp. 311.

23 Joachim Heinrich Campe, *Wörterbuch der deutschen Sprache*, Braunschweig, 1809, S. 363.

24 Von hier aus lässt sich eine Beziehung zum Konzept des „peripheral realism" herstellen, der in literarischen Abgrenzungsdynamiken eine mit der hier beschriebenen sprachlichen Struktur vergleichbare Konstellation beobachtet: „On other levels, the term *peripheral realism* also suggests that the whole history of realism and modernism might now be read productively from the perspectives of our current peripheries. The creation of the realist novel tradition, a process in which *Don Quixote* functioned as a decisive pivot, helped what we now call Western Europe claim social and cultural modernity and loosen itself from its earlier peripheral literary and philosophical indebtedness to the Mediterranean and North African worlds." (Joe Cleary, „Realism after Modernism and the Literary World-System", in: *Modern Language Quarterly* 73 (2012), S. 255-268: 267.) Für diesen Hinweis danke ich Dorothea Walzer.

25 Gilles Deleuze und Félix Guattari, *Tausend Plateaus: Kapitalismus und Schizophrenie*, Berlin, 1992, S. 145.

26 Ebd., S. 148.

27 Ebd.

3. Kauderwelsch

In der biblischen Erzählung wird an der spezifischen Aussprache, also an der Akzentuierung des Wortes ‚Schibboleth' die Entscheidung zwischen Leben und Tod getroffen. Im Theater entscheidet die Sprechweise über die Differenz zwischen Simulation und Dissimulation und damit über das Ernstnehmen und Verlachtwerden.

> Eine solche [vollständige reine Aussprache; N. B.] suche sich der Schauspieler anzueignen, indem er wohl beherzige, wie ein verschluckter Buchstabe oder ein undeutlich ausgesprochenes Wort oft den ganzen Satz zweideutig macht, wodurch denn das Publikum aus der Täuschung gerissen und oft, selbst in den ernsthaftesten Szenen, zum Lachen gereizt wird.[28]

Auch Goethe bezieht sich, indem er das Szenario eines theatralen Desasters entwirft, auf die ‚deutliche', also die unzweideutige Aussprache. Damit „das Publikum" nicht „aus der Täuschung gerissen" werde und gar „in den ernsthaftesten Szenen" zu lachen anfange, müsse der Schauspieler artikulatorische Zwei- und Uneindeutigkeiten vermeiden. Er müsse die im Rauschen der Aussprache mögliche Polyvalenz unterbinden, um so die performative Dissimulation des Ausdrucks und theatralen Spiels zu vermeiden. Die aufgestellten Regeln beugen aber auch einer Entwicklung vor, die es den minoritären, provinziellen (Aus-)Sprachen ermöglichen würde, sich gegen die Hochlautung des Zentrums aufzulehnen und dessen vermeintlich unmarkierte Norm in ihrer spezifischen Markierung vorzuführen.

Die ‚deutliche Aussprache', ein Kriterium, auf welches Goethe sich dabei bezieht, knüpft zwar unmittelbar an das Regelwerk der antiken Rhetorik an. Ähnlich fordert auch Quintilian unter Berufung auf die ‚deutliche' *pronunciatio*, dass etwa „die Wörter ihre vollen Ausgänge erhalten, die ja gewöhnlich teils verschluckt, teils entstellt werden"[29]. Jedoch geht in Goethes – nach Paragrafen durchgezählten – Argumentationsordnung der Forderung nach ‚deutlicher' Aussprache die Forderung nach ‚reiner deutscher Mundart' voraus. Diese bildet die artikulatorische Voraussetzung der ‚deutlichen' Aussprache. Demnach müsse sich der Schauspieler zunächst „von allen Fehlern des Dialekts befreie[n] und eine vollständige reine Aussprache zu erlangen suche[n]." Auf dieser Grundlage erst hat das Kriterium der ‚deutlichen' Artikulation seine Relevanz. Was deutlich und unzweideutig ist, hängt nämlich überhaupt erst von dem jeweiligen artikulatorischen Standard ab. Gegenüber dem Primat der akzentfreien, das heißt den Akzent unhörbar machenden, ‚reinen deutschen Mundart' – dies geht aus der argumentativen Gesamtarchitek-

---

[28] Goethe (1998), Regeln für Schauspieler, §6, S. 862.

[29] Quintilian schreibt zu „Pronunciatio": „Deutlich nun ist der Vortrag [...] dann, wenn die Wörter ihre vollen Ausgänge erhalten, die ja gewöhnlich teils verschluckt, teils entstellt werden, da die meisten die Schlußsilben nicht voll bringen, während sie im Ton der vorangehenden Silben schwelgen." (Marcus Fabius Quintilian, *Institutionis Oratoriae. Ausbildung des Redners.* Band 2, hg. und übers. von Helmut Rahn, Darmstadt 1995, S. 621.)

tur des Textes hervor – haben die Kategorien ‚deutlich' und ‚eindeutig' einen lediglich supplementären Charakter.

Wenn aber die Bühnensprache „von allen Fehlern des Dialekts" und allen artikulatorischen ‚Zweideutigkeiten', vom kommunikativen Rauschen gereinigt werden müsse, damit das Tragische nicht ins Lächerliche umkippt, dann kann umgekehrt die dialektal-artikulatorische Verunreinigung auch als Medium der Komik eingesetzt werden. In diesem Sinn wird in Lessings *Minna von Barnhelm* gerade die ‚unvollständige, unreine Aussprache' zum wichtigen Akteur des Spiels. So kennzeichnet Riccaut de la Marlinières Sprechweise[30] ihn als jemanden, dem die muttersprachliche Sprechkompetenz fehlt, der radebrecht und dabei sowohl die Grenzen des Französischen als auch und vor allem die des Deutschen verletzt, indem er ein durch und durch ‚unreines' Hybrid spricht, ein Kauderwelsch,[31] in welchem sich die beiden Sprachen ebenso wenig versöhnen wollen wie über weite Strecken die beiden Figuren Minna und der Major von Tellheim. In der teilweisen Unverständlichkeit seiner Sprechweise verweist Riccaut auf die Löcher im Realismus, den das theatrale Sprechen inszeniert, indem es durch den französischen Akzent die territoriale Herkunft des Sprechers zu authentifizieren scheint. Überdies reflektiert er das zwischen den Protagonisten des Stücks bestehende Kommunikationsproblem[32] im konfliktuellen Aufeinandertreffen der Sprachen Französisch und Deutsch, womit es zugleich in einen anderen Zusammenhang verschoben wird. An der Sprechweise Riccauts lässt sich nämlich auch das Minoritärwerden des Französischen erkennen. Die Konstellation des Stücks ist indes komplexer, bedenkt man, dass die Handlung in Berlin kurz nach Beendigung des Siebenjährigen Krieges spielt, in dem auch Riccaut für die preußische Armee und damit für einen König tätig war, dessen bevorzugte Sprache nicht Deutsch, sondern Französisch gewesen ist.[33]

---

30 Siehe zur typenkomödiantischen Bestimmung Riccauts exemplarisch: Walter Hinck, *Das deutsche Lustspiel des 17. und 18. Jahrhunderts und die italienische Komödie. Commedia dell'arte und Théâtre italien*, Stuttgart, 1965, S. 216. Zur Kritik an dieser die Lessing'sche Figur in die Tradition der europäischen Komödie und ihrer Typen einschreibenden Forschung siehe: Claude D. Conter, „Fremdsprachen in der Komödie. Komiktheoretische Aspekte der Multilingualität am Beispiel von Lessings *Minna von Barnhelm oder das Soldatenglück* (1767) und Dicks' *D'Kirmesgèscht* (1856)", in: *Philologie und Mehrsprachigkeit* (2014), S. 253-273, hier insb. S. 256-258.

31 „KAUDERWELSCH, *oder* kauderwälsch, *früher auch* kauterwelsch *und* kuderwelsch (*so noch* STIELER 2423, *schweiz.* STALDER 2, 431), *adj., adv. und subst. n. von unverständlicher sprache, von gänzlich fremder sowol wie besonders von solcher die durch schlechte aussprache, falsche formen, vermengung mit fremdem unverständlich wird*" (Jacob und Wilhelm Grimm, *Deutsches Wörterbuch*, Band 11, Leipzig, 1873, Sp. 308-315: 308).

32 Siehe zur Streitkultur in diesem Text: Günter Saße, „Der Streit um die rechte Beziehung. Zur verborgenen Organisation von Lessings Minna von Barnhelm", in: Wolfram Mauser/Günter Saße (Hg.), *Streitkultur. Strategien des Überzeugens im Werk Lessings*, Tübingen, 1993, S. 38-55.

33 Siehe dazu Nicola Kaminski, „‚Vis-à-vis du rien' oder Wie in einer Partie Karten mit dem Fräulein von Barnhelm und dem Chevalier de la Marlinière der Major von Tellheim das große Los zieht", in: Jürgen Stenzel/Roman Lach (Hg.), *Lessings Skandale*, Tübingen, 2005, S. 161-178: 168.

Der erste von ihm in dem Lustspiel ausgesprochene Satz ist fremdsprachig: „Riccaut (*noch innerhalb der Szene*): Est-il permis, Monsieur le Major?"[34] Das Französische ist Mitte des 18. Jahrhunderts in vielfacher Hinsicht codiert. Vor allem natürlich als Sprache der Aristokratie,[35] aber auch als Sprache einer klassizistischen Dramenpoetik. Beide Referenzen dienen in Lessings Drama dazu, sie einer Demontage zu unterziehen. Vollzogen wird diese anhand des Sprechens, das bereits im nächsten Satz seine Einsprachigkeit in den Zustand einer sprachlichen Deterritorialisierung[36] übergehen lässt. Denn das Französische wird hier in gewisser Weise, indem es sich mit dem Deutschen vernetzt, provinzialisiert und in dem Sinn ‚minoritär', als es seinen Status als Sprache des Hochadels und damit einer sozialen Normativität verloren hat.

Riccaut möchte den Major von Tellheim sprechen, findet aber nicht ihn, sondern Minna von Barnhelm in dessen ehemaligem Zimmer im Gasthof vor: „Riccaut: Parbleu! Ik bin unriktig. – Mais non – Ik bin nit unriktig – C'est sa chambre."[37] Bedeutsam ist an dieser Textpassage, dass ihr eine Vertreibung vorausgeht, da der Major sein Zimmer für Minna verlassen musste.[38] Er ist obdachlos geworden, weil er aufgrund seiner ‚Großmut' zahlungsunfähig geworden ist.[39] Ohne Adresse aber ist er nicht erreichbar. Bedeutsam ist an dieser Textpassage allerdings auch, dass sie Deutsch und Französisch miteinander vermischt, dabei jedoch das Französische, orthografisch und phonetisch korrekt darstellt, die deutsche Sprache hingegen als eine phonetische Deformation, als Kauderwelsch, auftreten lässt, für das es keine Standards schriftlicher Repräsentation gibt. So dokumentieren die Redeteile Riccauts das grundsätzliche Problem der Schreibung sprachlicher Merkmale, für die es keine orthografischen Regeln gibt.[40] – Als muttersprachlich sozialisierter Franzose wird Riccaut durch die Unfähigkeit charakterisiert, das „ch", etwa im ‚ich' oder ‚richtig', zu artikulieren. Es ist somit seine Muttersprache, das Französische, die Riccaut an einer „reine[n] Aussprache" der „deutsche[n] Mundart" hindert. Indem er sie mit französischer Akzentuierung ausspricht, werden die

---

34 Gotthold Ephraim Lessing, „Minna von Barnhelm", in: ders., *Sämtliche Schriften*. Band 2, hg. von Karl Lachmann, Stuttgart, 1886, S. 227.

35 Siehe Peter von Polenz, *Deutsche Sprachgeschichte vom Spätmittelalter bis zur Gegenwart*, Band 2, Berlin, Boston, MA, 1994; Ulrich Hoinkes, *Französisch und Franzosen im Deutschland des 18. Jahrhunderts*, in: Michael Elmentaler (Hg.), *Deutsch und seine Nachbarn*, Frankfurt/M., 2009, S. 169-184.

36 Eine Deterritorialisierung, die zugleich auch das „Machtvakuum" spiegelt „zwischen Nicht-mehr-Krieg und Noch-nicht-Frieden" (Kaminski (2005), „Vis-à-vis du rien", S. 164).

37 Lessing (1886), Minna von Barnhelm, S. 227.

38 „Einem Manne, wie meinem Herrn, der Jahr und Tag bei ihm gewohnt, von dem Er schon so manchen schönen Taler gezogen, der in seinem Leben keinen Heller schuldig geblieben ist; weil er ein paar Monate her nicht prompt bezahlt, weil er nicht mehr so viel aufgehen läßt, – in der Abwesenheit das Zimmer auszuräumen!" (Ebd., S. 175.)

39 Siehe dazu Heiner Weidmann, „Ökonomie der ‚Großmut'. Geldwirtschaft in Lessings *Minna von Barnhelm* und *Nathan dem Weisen*", in: *DVjS* 68 (1994), S. 447-461.

40 „Daß sie den Akzent und die Inflexion nicht zu transkribieren vermag, isoliert oder analysiert die Misere einer Schrift, die sich mit ihren eigenen Mitteln bescheiden muß. [...] Die Differenz zwischen dem Akzent und den Akzenten trennt somit die Rede und die Schrift" (Jacques Derrida, *Grammatologie*, Frankfurt/M., 1983, S. 390 f.).

deutschsprachigen Ausdrücke gleichsam entfremdet, französisiert und ausschließlich über den Satzkontext als deutschsprachige Wörter identifizierbar. Seine Sprechweise spiegelt Riccauts Status als Entwurzelter wider. In zweifacher, nämlich in kulturell-topografischer und in sozialer Hinsicht ist auch er, in dieser Hinsicht Tellheim korrespondierend, heimatlos geworden.

Anstelle des eigentlichen Adressaten nimmt Minna die Nachricht Riccauts entgegen, die sie jenem, also dem Major von Tellheim, unter dessen Adresse sie sich vorübergehend niedergelassen hat, weiterzugeben verspricht. Eine Nachricht, die auf eine umständliche Übertragungskette hindeutet, da der Informant sich im Deutschen eben nicht verständlich auszudrücken vermag und Minna, die Botin, den Major ebenfalls nicht auffinden kann. Wie Riccaut weiß auch sie nicht, wo Tellheim zu erreichen ist. Dabei spricht sie einen Satz aus, den das Drama im Folgenden einer Prüfung unterzieht: „Ist es gleichviel, aus wessen Munde er diese gute Nachricht erfährt, so erbiete ich mich, mein Herr".[41] Die Unterstellung, es spiele keine Rolle, von wem die Nachricht überbracht und ausgesprochen werde, ist recht besehen, das heißt ihrer grammatischen Form nach, eine Frage: „Ist es gleichviel, aus wessen Munde er diese gute Nachricht erfährt"? Nur in dem Fall, dass sie bejaht wird – was zugleich impliziert, dass sie auch verneint werden könnte –, ist die Bedingung des Folgesatzes erfüllt und Minna kann als Botin eingesetzt werden. Dass Botschaften jedoch unabhängig von den Boten bestehen,[42] wird hier aber als Frage und damit letztlich auch infrage gestellt. Ist es nicht vielmehr Riccauts spezifische sprachliche Performanz, die eine unübersetzbare Botschaft generiert?

> Riccaut: […] Mademoiselle parle français? […]
> Das Fräulein: Mein Herr –
> Riccaut: Nit? Sie sprek nit Französisch, Ihro Gnad?
> Das Fräulein: Mein Herr, in Frankreich würde ich es zu sprechen suchen. Aber warum hier? Ich höre ja, daß Sie mich verstehen, mein Herr. Und ich, mein Herr, werde Sie gewiß auch verstehen; sprechen Sie, wie es Ihnen beliebt.[43]

Dieser Dialog weist zunächst einmal die Wirkmächtigkeit des Französischen in seine Schranken. Er zeugt von der ‚Minorisierung' seiner kommunikativen Relevanz. Minnas Forderung hat somit eine politische Implikation. Es ist das deutsche Sprachterritorium, dessen Verteidigung als Raum einer spezifischen Einsprachigkeit sie somit unternimmt. Aus Thüringen kommend, in dem wenig später sich die ‚Weimarer Klassik' herausbilden wird, weist sie auch auf eine literarische Dimension der deutschen Sprache voraus. In Berlin, wo sie sich derzeit aufhält, muss das Deutsche noch vehement gegen das Französische eingefordert werden. Während Minna zuvor die unmittelbare Beziehung zwischen dem „Mund", aus dem eine Nachricht kommt, und der Nachricht selbst zu lösen versuchte, so insistiert sie

---

41 Lessing (1886), Minna von Barnhelm, S. 228.

42 Vgl. dazu Sybille Krämer, *Medium, Bote, Übertragung. Kleine Metaphysik der Medialität*, Frankfurt/M., 2008.

43 Lessing (1886), Minna von Barnhelm, S. 228.

nun auf der Beziehung des Sprechens zu einer an den Sprachraum gebundenen Mundart.

Die Mundart, die Riccaut spricht, führt allerdings die Instabilität der Ordnung der Einsprachigkeit vor. Im Zuge seiner Ausführungen entgleitet ihm die deutsche Sprache zunehmend, womit er eine Verletzung der geforderten Sprachgrenzen begeht. Die Botschaft, wonach von Tellheim nach seiner unehrenhaften Entlassung aus dem Militärdienst rehabilitiert werden solle, übermittelt Riccaut buchstäblich im Modus eines Kauderwelsches, welches darauf verweist, dass hier ein Zwischenhandel mit Informationen betrieben wird. Unter „kaudern" wird nämlich *„zwischenhandel treiben"* verstanden, etwa wenn *„man dem bauern, der schon auf dem markt steht, seine frücht abkaudere und dann diese frucht auf eben demselben markte wieder verkaudere"*[44]. Tatsächlich hat Riccaut die Nachricht nicht, wie er Minna glauben lassen will, von einem befreundeten Minister erhalten, der sich auf Riccauts Veranlassung hin beim König für den Major eingesetzt habe. Er hat sie vielmehr dem Feldjäger entwendet, der Tellheim den Brief des Königs überbringen soll. Auch in diesem Sinne, dass der Bote sich für die Botschaft letztlich auszahlen lässt, spielt es durchaus eine Rolle, wer er ist, mithin wer sie überbringt. Seine Glaubwürdigkeit, die immer auch die Kreditwürdigkeit des Boten meint, soll die Wahrheit der Botschaft verbürgen:

> Das Fräulein: Gewiß mein Herr, diese Nachricht wird dem Major von Tellheim höchst angenehm sein. Ich wünschte nur, ihm den Freund zugleich mit Namen nennen zu können, der so viel Anteil an seinem Glücke nimmt –
> Riccaut: Mein Namen wünscht Ihro Gnad? – Vous voyez en moi – Ihro Gnad seh in mik le Chevalier Riccaut de la Marlinière, Seigneur de Pret-au-val, de la branche de Prens d'or. – Ihro Gnad steh verwundert, mik aus so ein groß, groß Familie zu hören, qui est véritablement du sang Royale. [...] – Ik dien von meiner elfte Jahr. Ein Affaire d'honneur makte mik fliehen.[45]

Zwar lässt sich die Figur Riccaut de la Marlinière einerseits – im Sinne der traditionellen Auffassung[46] – verstehen als Verkörperung des durch eine „Affaire d'honneur" bedingten sozialen Abstiegs vom Mitglied einer hoch angesehenen Familie „véritablement du sang Royale" zu einem heimatlosen Hasardeur und Betrüger, der gerade dabei ist, indem er Minna vermeintlich vertrauliche, mehr noch: ver-

---

44 „KAUDERN, *zwischenhandel treiben, mäkeln, dazu* abkaudern, auf-, ein-, zusammen-, verkaudern, *bair.* SCHMELLER 2, 281, *tirol.* SCHÖPF 307, *schwäb.* SCHMID 307, *s.* kauderer: dasz man dem bauern, der schon auf dem markt steht, seine frücht abkaudere und dann diese frucht auf eben demselben markte wieder verkaudere." (Jacob und Wilhelm Grimm, *Deutsches Wörterbuch*, Band 11, Leipzig, 1873, Sp. 307.)

45 Lessing (1886), Minna von Barnhelm, S. 229.

46 „Hier geriet die Typen-Tradition des Spielers, in der Riccaut ja steht, sowie der soziale Kontext – Riccauts Anstellung im preußischen, nicht im französischen Dienst – fast völlig aus dem Blickfeld. Die nationale Komponente bestimmte die meisten für Schule und Unterricht bestimmten Interpretationen. Beide, der ehrenhafte Held Tellheim und der leichtfertige Geck Riccaut, wurden zu zeitlosen Typen verschiedener Völkermentalitäten simplifiziert." (Gunter E. Grimm, „‚Riccaut de la Marlinière, Glücksritter und Franzos.' Die Rezeption einer Lustspielfigur zwischen Gallophilie und Gallophobie", in: *Euphorion* 90 (1996), S. 383-394: 392.)

meintlich abgesicherte Botschaften überbringt, auch Geld abzulisten. Er lässt sich aber zum Zweiten als „eine hochmoderne Figur“ beschreiben,[47] als ein Spekulant und Spieler,[48] der aus Nachrichten Kapital zu schlagen versucht, welches er im Glücksspiel zu vermehren sich vornimmt. Wie er Güter, präziser: zu unrecht erworbenes Insiderwissen, in Geld umwandelt, wie er also eine Botschaft in Geld übersetzt, so versucht er die französische in die deutsche Sprache zu übersetzen, was ihm allerdings nicht gelingen will. Sein Kauderwelsch führt gerade die Unübersetzbarkeit des Französischen ins Deutsche vor, und dies insbesondere dort, wo Riccaut Deutsch spricht und an der deutschen Aussprache, an ihrem Akzent scheitert. So vermag seine Sprechweise es nicht, das Problem des ‚Schibboleth‘ zu überwinden. Riccaut bleibt auf der Ebene der Akzentsetzung Franzose. Insofern schafft er durch die permanenten Sprachwechsel, die keine Übersetzungen, sondern Übergänge von einem ins andere Sprachsystem sind, eine Hybridität,[49] welche die Unterscheidungsgrenzen zwischen Zentrum und Provinz, zwischen niederer und Hochsprache zu verwischen droht. Zugleich führt er eine Hybridität auf der Ebene der Aussprache vor. Wo er Deutsch spricht, dort tut er dies mit französischem Akzent, durch welchen die verwendeten deutschsprachigen Ausdrücke gleichsam deterritorialisiert werden. Aus ‚ich‘ wird ‚ik‘. Das ‚Ich‘ gerät dabei in die Spannung von Schibboleth/Sibboleth. Aber kann ein Spieler – ein Schau*spieler* – nicht auch die Simulation eines inkorporierten Akzents hervorbringen? Gilt Riccauts französischer Akzent tatsächlich als Bürge seiner französischen Abstammung oder simuliert er diese muttersprachliche Inkorporation nicht vielmehr? Indem er mit französischem Akzent spricht, hybridisiert er zwar ‚die reine deutsche Mundart‘. Einher geht damit aber keineswegs schon die Authentifizierung der französischen. Denn ist das Französische als Sprache des Hofes und Hochadels nicht immer auch die Sprache der Verstellung,[50] die Sprache der Simulation? Unter dieser Prämisse löst sich selbst die Unterscheidung von Schibboleth/Sibboleth in ein Spiel auf, welches gleichwohl soziale Wirklichkeiten setzt, indem es sie verhandelbar macht. – Riccauts Sprechweise verkörpert weniger die Bindung an eine muttersprachliche Sozialisation als das Problem des zwischen Simulation und Dissimulation changierenden theatralen Sprechens[51] und macht ihn zur Reflexionsfigur des Schauspiels als Sprechspiel und Sprechhandel.

---

47 Ebd., S. 394.

48 Siehe dazu auch Achim Küpper, „Spiel und Zufall in Gotthold Ephraim Lessings ‚Lustspiel‘ *Minna von Barnhelm*“, in: Luis Gerrekens/Achim Küpper (Hg.), *Der Spieler in der deutschsprachigen Literaturgeschichte*, Würzburg, 2012, S. 41-57.

49 Vgl. zu Bedeutung der hybriden Sprache der Literatur Michail M. Bachtin, „Das Wort im Roman“, in: ders., *Die Ästhetik des Wortes*, hg. von Rainer Grübel, Frankfurt/M., 1979, S. 154-300.

50 Ursula Geitner, *Sprache der Verstellung. Studien zum rhetorischen und anthropologischen Wissen im 17. und 18. Jahrhundert*, Tübingen, 1992, S. 40-50; Gunhild Berg, *Erzählte Menschenkenntnis: Moralische Erzählungen und Verhaltensschriften*, Tübingen, 2006, S. 40 ff.

51 Es zeugt von einem „hohe[n] Maß an Künstlichkeit, durch das die Komödie ihr Wirkungsziel erst erreicht“ (Bernhard Greiner, „Streitkultur des Als Ob: Komödie als transzendentale Bedingung des Streitens in Minna von Barnhelm“, in: Wolfram Mauser/Günter Saße (Hg.), *Streitkultur. Strategien des Überzeugens im Werk Lessings*, Tübingen, 1993, S. 247-258: 257).

Devin Fore

„Aktueller Realismus": Sowjetische Faktografie und die Noetik der Zeitung

Nach der Oktoberrevolution begannen Verben aus der russischen Sprache zu verschwinden. Nicht bestimmte Verben, sondern schlicht alle. Diese Entwicklung war derart verbreitet, dass ein Dichter von so hohem Einfühlungsvermögen und Format wie Ossip Mandel'stam 1931 feststellte: „[I]n der gegenwärtigen Praxis sind Verben aus der Literatur verschwunden."[1] Das Verschwinden des Verbs im Russland der 1920er erinnert uns ganz prinzipiell daran, dass politische Erschütterungen, wie schon Thukydides beschrieben hatte, immer mit Veränderungen der Sprechweisen einhergehen. Dass die bolschewistische Revolution keine Ausnahme war, erkannten die Zeitgenossen sogleich. Grigorii Vinokur, ein zentrales Mitglied der avantgardistischen Gruppe Lef und Sekretär des Moskauer Linguistenkreises, formulierte konzise: „Sogar so zu sprechen, wie man es vor der Revolution tat, ist unmöglich."[2] Es ließe sich tatsächlich eine lange Liste solcher Aussagen von Wissenschaftlern und Linguisten der 1920er Jahre über die Überschneidung von Politik und Sprache erstellen. Die zeitgenössische Forschungsliteratur zu diesem Thema beschränkte sich allerdings größtenteils auf einen einzigen Aspekt des Einflusses der Revolution auf die Sprache: das russische Vokabular.[3] Lexikalische Eingriffe waren selbstverständlich kein unwichtiger Aspekt der Revolutionierung in der Sprache, denn es wurden neue Wörter gebraucht, um die unbekannten Objekte, Ereignisse, Konzepte, sozialen Verhältnisse und politischen Institutionen zu bezeichnen, die von den Bolschewiki ins Leben gerufen worden waren, wie der Linguist Selischew 1928 schrieb: „[D]ie Ereignisse und Umstände der revolutionä-

1 Ossip Mandel'stam, „Zapisi 1931 goda", in: *Voprosy literatury*, 4 (1968), S. 201. Das genaue Datum dieses Eintrags wurde von den Redakteuren von *Sobranie sochinenii* bestritten, die behaupten, er sei in der Mitte der 1930er Jahren geschrieben worden.

2 Grigorii O. Vinokur, „A. Mazon. *Lexique de la guerre et de la revolution en Russie* (Paris, 1920)", in: *Iazyk. Kul'tura. Gumanitarnoe znanie. Nauchnoe nasledie G. O. Vinokura i sovremennost'*, hg. von S. I. Gindin et al., Moskau: Nauchnyi mir, 1999, S. 415.

3 André Mazon, *Lexique de la guerre et de la revolution en Russie*, Paris: Champion, 1920; Roman Jakobsons Rezension von Mazon, „Vliv revoluce na ruský jazyk" [1921], in: *Selected Writings*, Band 9, hg. von Jindřich Toman, Den Haag: Mouton, 1962-, S. 28-60; Sergei I. Kartsevskii, *Iazyk, voina i revoliutsiia*, Berlin: Russkoe universal'noe izd-vo, 1923; Evgenii Polivanov, „Russkii iazyk segodniashchnego dnia", in: *Literatura i marksizm*, (1928), S. 167-180; Afanasii M. Selishchev, *Iazyk revoliutsionnoi epokhi. Iz nabliudenii nad russkim iazykom (1917-1926)* [1928], Moskau: URSS, 2003; Pavel Ia. Chernykh, „Russkii iazyk i revoliutsiia", in: *Sovremennye techeniia v lingvistika*, Irkutsk: Vlast' truda 1929, S. 40-64 und Evgenii Polivanov, „Revolution and the Literary Languages of the USSR" [1931], in: *Selected Works*, hg. von Aleksei A. Leont'ev, übers. von Daniel Armstrong, Den Haag: Mouton, 1974, S. 179-194.

ren Epoche verursachten massive Veränderungen im Bereich der Benennung, der nominativen Aktivität in der Sprache."[4] Ob es die Zunahme an Silbenwörtern, der Zustrom ausländischer Lehnwörter, die Ausbreitung von neuen Akronymen oder die Wanderung von spezialisierten Jargons zwischen sozialen Schichten ist; selbst der flüchtigste Blick auf die russische Sprache nach der Revolution zeigt eine Explosion lexikalischer Erneuerungen. In einem Text von 1921 über die Sprachen der Revolution und den Bürgerkrieg drückt Vinokur, der den Futuristen nahestand, in wenigen Worten aus: „Neue Fakten wurzeln in unserem sprachlichen Bewusstsein so tiefgehend, dass es jetzt schon unmöglich, ja sogar absurd scheint, zu sprechen und zu schreiben, wie wir es vorher getan haben."[5]

Im Gegensatz zu dem großen wissenschaftlichen Interesse an lexikalischen Entwicklungen im postrevolutionären Russland – durchaus verständlich angesichts der unübersichtlichen Menge neuer Wortschöpfungen zu dieser Zeit –, wurden die strukturellen Veränderungen, die auf darunterliegenden Ebenen wie der Syntax und der Grammatik stattfanden, weit weniger in Betracht gezogen.[6] Der folgende Aufsatz untersucht eine dieser Entwicklungen, die in der frühen Sowjetzeit verbreitet war und in jenen tieferen Schichten der Sprache situiert ist: eine Explosion des Gebrauchs von „deverbativen Nomen" (*otglagol'nye sushchestvitel'nye*) und den damit einhergehenden Verlust an „Verbalität" (*glagol'nost'*) schlechthin. Trotz des allgemeinen Mangels an Forschung zu diesem Thema weist das obige Zitat von Mandel'stam darauf hin, dass die Deverbalisierung des Russischen von ihren Nutzerinnen und Nutzern nicht unbemerkt geblieben ist. Tatsächlich stellt sich heraus, dass die Bemerkung, dass „Verben aus der Literatur verschwunden [sind]", am Ende einer nun vergessenen Reihe von hitzigen Debatten über die zunehmende Menge von deverbativen Nomen im Russischen steht. Für die TeilnehmerInnen an diesen Diskussionen war die Wahl zwischen „Der Bolschewist stürmte den Winterpalast" (verbativ) und „Das Stürmen des Winterpalasts durch den Bolschewisten" (deverbativ) mehr als eine Frage der Ausdrucksmittel. Der Unterschied beschränkte sich nicht auf eine stilistische Präferenz, sondern war einer der Weltanschauung.[7]

Der entscheidende Schauplatz, auf dem diese Deverbalisierung registriert wurde, war die Zeitung. Seit Mitte der 1920er erkannten TheoretikerInnen und Linguistinnen bzw. Linguisten, die das entstehende Fach der Zeitungswissenschaft (*gazetovedenie*) begründeten, dass deverbative Konstruktionen ein distinktives syn-

---

4 Selishchev (2003), *Iazyk revoliutsionnoi epokhi*, S. 157.

5 Vinokur (1999), A. Mazon. *Lexique de la guerre et de la revolution en Russie* (Paris, 1920), S. 415.

6 Und aus gutem Grund: Gemäß den Argumenten von Linguistinnen und Linguisten, können lexikalische Erneuerungen von einem neuen Regierungssystem schnell umgesetzt werden, während Veränderungen in den tieferen strukturellen Ebenen der Sprache viel langsamer geschehen. Im Vergleich zu den Veränderungen im Vokabular und im Jargon, die die Oberfläche der historischen und politischen Ereignisse berühren, nimmt die strukturelle Entwicklung der Sprache eine ganz andere Ordnung der Zeit an. Sie entfaltet sich im Laufe vieler Generationen.

7 Wie im Englischen, wird der Gebrauch von Deverbativen im Russischen als stillos angesehen, während die unpersönlichen Konstruktionen im Deutschen tendenziell solchen Nominalisierungen offener gegenüber sind. Vgl. Aleksandr Peshkovskii, „Glagol'nost' kak vyrazitel'noe sredstvo", in: *Sbornik statei*, Moskau: Gos. izd-vo, 1925, S. 141-152.

taktisches Merkmal der sowjetischen Presse wurden. Vinokur war wohl der erste, der diese Entwicklung zur Kenntnis nahm und der, ein Jahr bevor er 1924 die erste formalistische Untersuchung der Zeitungssprache veröffentlichte, einen Aufsatz über die zeitgenössische Sprache schrieb, in dem er nebenbei die „ungewöhnliche Ausbreitung der Nomen auf Kosten der Verben“ und den daraus entstehenden Zustand der Verblosigkeit (*bezglagol'nost'*) vermerkte.[8] Vinokurs Hypothese bestätigte sich im folgendem Jahr, als eine Forschungsgruppe, die damit beauftragt war, das Vokabular unter Soldaten der Roten Armee zu untersuchen, unter anderem einen zunehmenden Gebrauch von Nomen in der Sprache ihrer Versuchspersonen entdeckte. Unter Führung des Moskauer Psycholinguisten Isaak Spiel'rein lieferte die Forschungsgruppe den empirischen Beleg, um die anekdotische Spekulation Vinokurs zu untermauern: Während im Standardgespräch 24 Prozent der verwendeten Wörter Nomen und 20 Prozent Verben waren, erhöhte sich die Häufigkeit der Nomen in der modernen Sprache der Presse auf 37 Prozent und verringerte sich der Gebrauch von Verben auf 16 Prozent.[9] Obwohl Spiel'reins Forschungsgruppe beobachtete, dass diese Tendenz zur Nominalisierung in der Zeitungsreportage viel stärker war als in anderen Sprachformen wie der mündlichen Rede, beobachteten sie dennoch einen Anstieg deverbativer Äußerungsakte im verbalen Sprachgebrauch bestimmter sozialer Schichten.

Spiel'reins Forschung wurde breit rezipiert, gewann die Aufmerksamkeit von Nadescheda Krupskaja, der Partnerin Lenins, und löste eine mehrjährige Debatte im *Zhurnalist* aus, dem Publikationsorgan des Staatlichen Instituts für Journalismus (GIZh). Zumindest am Anfang richteten sich die Bedenken gegen die angeblich verminderte Verständlichkeit einer mit deverbativen Nomen durchsetzten Sprache. Ermutigt durch die posthume Entdeckung und Veröffentlichung einer Anmerkung von Lenin im Jahr 1924, die „die Reinigung der russischen Sprache“ in der Zeitung forderte,[10] argumentierten Gegner der Deverbalisierung, dass das „authentische“ und „lebendige“ Russisch, das von den Bauern oder Bäuerinnen gesprochen werde, mehr aktive Verben verwende, während die StadtbewohnerInnen zu komplizierten Nominalkonstruktionen neigten. In seinem 1930 erschienenen Buch *Die Sprache des Bauernkorrespondenten* wies etwa A. Meromskii darauf hin, dass es auf dem Land wahrscheinlicher sei, der Formulierung „ich mag es, zu lesen“ (*ia interesuius' chitat'*) zu begegnen, während man in der Stadt den gleichen Gedanken tendenziell als „ich mag Lesen“ (*ia interesuius' chteniem*) höre.[11] In der Kampagne gegen deverbative Konstruktionen wiederholten die VerteidigerInnen

---

8 Grigorii Vinokur, „Iazyk NEPa“ [1923], in: *Kul'tura iazyka. Ocherki lingvisticheskoi tekhnologii*, Moskau: Raboknik prosveshcheniia, 1925, S. 69.

9 Isaak N. Shpil'rein/D. I. Reityngbarg/G. O. Netskii, *Iazyk krasnoarmeitsa. Opyt issledovaniia slovaria krasnoarmeitsa moskovskogo garnizona*, Moskau: Gos. izd-vo, 1928, S. 31.

10 Die im Jahr 1919 oder 1920 geschriebene Anmerkung wurde am 3. Dezember 1924 in der *Prawda* veröffentlicht. Zur Rolle der Presse bei der Reinigung des Russischen vgl. Michael S. Gorham, „Mastering the Perverse: State Building and Language ‚Purification‘ in Early Soviet Russia“, in: *Slavic Review* 59, 1 (2000), S. 133-153.

11 A. Meromskii, *Iazyk sel'kora*, Moskau: Federatsiia, 1930, S. 51.

des traditionellen Russisch eine geläufige These von Sprachpuristinnen und -puristen: den Glauben, dass das Verb dem Nomen ontologisch vorausgehe. Auf ähnliche Weise wird der große Vertreter einer „authentischen" deutschen Sprachauffassung, Martin Heidegger, das Verbalsubstantiv als „die leerste Form" behaupten, dass es noch entleerter sei als der Verbalinfinitiv, eine Form, deren Entstehung die erste grammatikalische Abstraktion markiert habe.[12] Laut Heidegger ist das Verb „die Urform des Wortes" und die historische Rückbildung vom konjugierten Verb zum Infinitiv und schließlich zum deverbalisierten Nomen folgt dem Entwicklungsverlauf einer existenziellen Verarmung und zunehmenden Entfernung von der Primärerfahrung.[13]

Die russischen KritikerInnen der verbativen Sprache verknüpften die deverbative Sprache mit dem Bürokratenjargon der Stadttechnokraten. Diese gesellschaftliche Gruppe zeigte eine ausgeprägte Vorliebe für komplizierte „Kanzleilokutionen" (*kantseliarizmy*) ebenso wie für Readymades oder „Verbalklischees" (*rechevye shtampy*), also feststehende syntaktische Sprachblöcke scheinbar ohne semantischen Inhalt.[14] Dies waren die Ausdrucksmittel von gelehrten Städtern wie den Raznochintsi, einer deklassierten Intelligenzija des 19. Jahrhunderts, die, nach Meinung der PuristenInnen, die Kontrolle über die Sowjetpresse ergriffen hatte.[15] Die linguistischen Neigungen von zwei demografischen Gruppen, einer ländlichen und einer städtischen, spiegelten sich in ihren jeweiligen Zeitungen wider: Zeitungen für die Intelligenzija wie die *Prawda* gebrauchten deverbative Nomen fast doppelt so häufig wie Bauernzeitungen wie *Bednota* oder *Krestianskaia gazeta*. Zwei soziale Schichten und zwei Produktionsweisen stießen in den Debatten über Nomen und Verb aufeinander: einerseits die technische Intelligenzija, die in einer entpersönlichten Sprache und mit hochabstrakten Nominalkonstruktionen schrieb, und andererseits ein unvermittelt redender Bauernstand, der aktive Verbalkonstruktionen und Narrative bevorzugte. Einer der Redakteure von *Bednota* schrieb, dass, während die Sprache des Bauernstandes begrifflich von Linien der direkten Kausalität und grammatikalisch von klaren Transitivkonstruktionen (Subjekt – Verb – Objekt) zusammengehalten werde, „das Mitglied der Intelligenzija sich mit gelehrten Überlegungen über das Leben, mit Abstraktionen und indirekten Situationen [*otvlechennymi polozheniiami*] beschäftig[e]"[16]. Anscheinend war diese Erfahrung der Indirektheit und Mittelbarkeit so prägend, die existenzielle Entfremdung so

[12] Martin Heidegger, *Einführung in die Metaphysik*, Frankfurt/M.: Klostermann, 1983, S. 74. Obwohl er mitnichten Sprachpurist war, situiert der sowjetische Linguist Viktor Vinogradow den Infinitiv ebenfalls „am Rande des Verbs". Der Infinitiv ist effektiv ein Verb auf dem Weg zum Nomen. Ders., *Russkii iazyk* [1947], Moskau: Vysshaia shkola, 1972, S. 511.

[13] Heidegger (1983), *Einführung in die* Metaphysik, S. 60.

[14] Zu Vinokur, der Mechanisierung der Sprache und dem verbalen Readymade vgl. Devin Fore, „The Operative Word in Soviet Factography", in: *October*, 118 (2006), S. 95-131.

[15] In seiner Antwort auf die Rede von Gus, „Predmet, zadachi i metody izucheniia gazetnogo iazyka" (1927), erklärte Lewidow: „[H]eute ist die Zeitung in die Hände einer bestimmten kleinen sozialen Gruppe gefallen, die *raznochinnaia Intelligentsia*", in: *Zhurnalist*, 5 (1927), S. 60.

[16] Viacheslav A. Karpinskii, „Chem dolzhen byt' krest'ianskii pisatel'", in: *Krest'ianskii korrespondent. Ego rol', ego rabota*, Moskau: Bednota, 1924, S. 71.

durchschlagend, dass die VerfasserInnen von Briefen an die *Prawda* sogar ihre persönlichen Nachrichten oft in der dritten Person schrieben.[17]

Die Bedenken bezüglich der Ausbreitung der deverbativen Sprache in der Presse erreichten einen Höhepunkt im Jahr 1926 mit der Veröffentlichung von *Die Sprache der Zeitung* von dem Redakteur der *Roten* Presse, Mikhail Gus, und zwei seiner Kollegen. Dieses einflussreiche Buch, aus dem einige Kapitel im *Zhurnalist* neu veröffentlicht wurden, mobilisierte die Forschung Spiel'reins in einem Großangriff auf Vinokur und argumentierte, dass jeglicher logische und linguistische Mangel der Zeitungssprache auf die Erbsünde der deverbalisierten Nomen zurückgeführt werden könne. Durch den Ersatz der Verben durch Nomen habe die Zeitung einen Überschuss an Passivkonstruktionen geschaffen; die Zeitungssprache tendiere folglich zur Tautologie und zum Pleonasmus; sie verursache syntaktische Inversionen und kontraintuitive Wortstellungen; sie begünstige festgelegte syntaktische Readymades anstelle von ausdrucksvoller dynamischer Sprache; und sie bilde ungeschickte neue Komposita, deren Bedeutungen nicht immer klar seien. Das Endergebnis sei nicht das „lebendige Wort", sondern eine ausgedehnte Kanzleisprache, in der schräge Kasus und inhaltslose Phraseologien florierten. Einer der Verbündeten von Gus bemerkte 1930, dass infolge des Gebrauchs deverbativer Konstruktionen, „die aufgehetzte, eigensinnige, stürmische Sprache des Redners auf Veranstaltungen [...] durch die ökonomische Übersichtsdarstellung, den Bericht von Verwaltern samt Zahlen und Diagrammen [ersetzt wird]"[18]. Für Gus und seinen Kreis waren die Dringlichkeit und die Spontanität, die das Russische in den Jahren des Bürgerkriegs ausgezeichnet hatten, in der verkümmerten Sprache der sowjetischen Zeitung verloren gegangen, seitdem diese sich von einem direkten Vermittler des revolutionären Eifers in einen Irrgarten bürokratischen Jargons verwandelt hatte.

Vinokur antwortete auf *Die Sprache der Zeitung* in einem im April des Jahres 1927 an der Staatlichen Akademie für Kunstwissenshaft (GAKhN) gehaltenen Vortrag, der später unter dem Titel „Verb oder Nomen?" veröffentlicht wurde.[19] Darin verwies er auf zahlreiche Fehler in der Position von Gus und dessen Kollegen. Anstelle der groben, grundsätzlichen Entgegensetzung vom Nomen und Verben durch Gus, deckte Vinokur ein breites Spektrum an Unterscheidungen zwischen den beiden auf: Einerseits erinnerte er sein Publikum daran, dass nicht alle deverbativen Nomen im gleichen Maße „nominal" seien, zum Beispiel seien die Nomen „Spielen" (*igranie*) und „Schauen" (*smotrenie*) prozesshafter und „verbaler" als die jeweiligen Dubletten „ein Spiel" (*igra*) und „eine Schau" (*smotr*); umgekehrt habe ein perfektives Verb wie „gehen" (*udmu*), das die geschlossene Totalität der Handlung des Gehens hervorhebe, eine „nominalere" Valenz als sein Gegenstück „ge-

---

17 Irina Lysakova, *Iazyk gazety i tipologiia pressy*, St. Petersburg: Filologicheskii faktultet gos. universiteta, 2005, S. 50.

18 V. A. Kuz'michev, *Pechatnaia agitatsiia i propaganda*, Moskau: Gos. izd-vo, 1930, S. 11.

19 Grigorii Vinokur, „Glagol ili imia?", in: *Russkaia rech'*, 3 (1928), S. 75-93. Er erweitert diesen Text in „Opyt stilisticheskoi interpretatsii", in: *Kul'tura iazyka*, 2. Aufl., Moskau: Federatsiia, 1929, S. 49-84.

hen" (*idti*), das eine iterative, dauerhafte Qualität vermittle.[20] Als Antwort auf die Behauptung von Gus, dass Nominalisierung den Journalisten zwinge, eine vorgefertigte „Kanzleisprache" voller semantisch leerer, lokutiver Readymades zu verwenden, zitierte Vinokur eine Stelle aus der *Abhandlung über die französische Stilistik*,[21] in welcher der Schweizer Linguist Charles Bally ausführt, dass die kulturelle Funktion der Zeitung – Informationen schnell und unverzüglich zu übermitteln – in der Tat am besten durch solche *locutions toutes faites* erfüllt werde. „Bally stellt fest, dass es, wenn das Klischee in der Zeitung nicht überwiegen würde, nicht möglich wäre, in der Zeitung ‚schnell und richtig' zu schreiben."[22] Am umfassendsten jedoch stellt Vinokur den zweifelhaften Gewinn der von Gus vorgeschlagenen Reverbalisierung des Russischen infrage. Auf die Verbreitung der Nominalkonstruktionen in rechtlichen, administrativen und technischen Diskursen verweisend, wirft Vinokur die Frage auf, ob es wünschenswert sei, auf die noetischen und kulturellen Fortschritte, die durch die Nominalisierung ermöglicht würden, zu verzichten. Reverbalisierung wäre katastrophal für „wissenschaftliches Denken" schlechthin, das von Nominalkonstruktionen viel abhängiger sei als die Sprache des „Alltagslebens". Unter Bezugnahme auf die *Philosophy of Grammar* (*Die Philosophie der Grammatik*, 1925) von Otto Jespersen merkte Vinokur an, dass es möglich sei, „Ideen durch Nomen mit größerer Genauigkeit und Angemessenheit auszudrücken als durch bildhaftere Verben."[23] Da Nominalkonstruktionen SprachnutzerInnen „das höhere Leben des Intellekts" zugänglich machten, müsse die Reverbalisierung Russland praktisch ins finstere Mittelalter zurückwerfen.

Die Debatten über die Nominalisierung tobten weiter, obwohl man den von Vinokur und Gus etablierten Positionen wenig Neues hinzufügte.[24] Statt den Streit ins nächste Jahrzehnt zu verfolgen, untersucht dieser Aufsatz daher im Folgenden die poetischen und epistemologischen Dimensionen der zwei Positionen mit Blick auf die Faktografen in Lef, besagte Gruppe futuristischer Dichter, die die Konsequenzen der Deverbalisierung am weitesten getrieben haben. Unter der Führung von Sergei Tret'iakow begab sich diese Gruppe von Wortkünstlern an die vorderste Front der Nominalisierung in Russland. Genetisch gesehen ist das kaum überraschend: Die *Raznochinsti* des 19. Jahrhunderts zu ihren politischen und stilisti-

---

20 Ebd., S. 82.

21 Ebd.

22 Ebd., S. 91.

23 Das Zitat von Jespersen erscheint nur in der revidierten Version, „Opyt stilisticheskoi interpretatsii", S. 78.

24 Im Jahr 1927 erhob eine mit Gus verbundene Arbeitsgruppe eine Studie über den Gebrauch von Verben in der *Prawda*; sie entdeckte, dass während 2.246 Verben in der führenden Zeitung korrekt verwendet wurden, 1.042 „ungerechtfertigterweise" nominalisiert wurden – „mit anderen Worten wurden zum gegenwärtigen Zeitpunkt 36,6 % [Verben] durch deverbative Nomen verdrängt". Mikhail Gus diskutiert diese Forschung in Gus (1927), „Predmet, zadachi i metody izucheniia gazetnogo iazyka", S. 59. Im nächsten Jahr stürzte sich Spiel'rein selbst ins Getümmel; an der Seite von Vinokur ergriff er gegen Gus und jene Kollegen Partei, die seine Forschung in der Kampagne gegen die Nominalisierung als Waffe benutzt hatten.

schen Vorläufern erklärend,[25] pflegte sie eine Leidenschaft für technische Neologismen und szientistische Phraseologismen, die den einst von der radikalen, deklassierten Intelligenzija verwendeten bürokratischen Redewendungen stark ähnelten. Angesichts ihrer Bewunderung der Massenpresse, die sie zum Vorbild einer sowohl industrialisierten als auch kollektiven Sprache machen wollten, konnte es nicht verwundern, dass die Faktografen in ihren Schriften ein zentrales grammatisches Merkmal der Zeitung wie die Deverbalisierung aufnahmen. Hinzu kamen die personalen Verbindungen. Die Faktografen waren regelmäßige Mitarbeiter des *Zhurnalist*, insbesondere Mitte der 1920er Jahre, in dem Moment also, in dem die Debatten über die Zeitung und die Nominalisierung erstmals in dieser Zeitschrift entbrannten.[26] Dass eines der Hauptmitglieder ihrer eigenen Gruppe, der Linguist Vinokur, im Zentrum dieser Auseinandersetzungen stand, lässt es als äußerst unwahrscheinlich erscheinen, dass diese Debatte ihrer Aufmerksamkeit entgangen war.

Aber auch gesetzt den Fall, dass die Verbindung zwischen Faktografie und Nominalisierung den Mitgliedern von Lef selbst verborgen blieb, hatten andere sie bemerkt. Als ein Kritiker im Jahr 1929 über den Gebrauch von Deverbativen in Zeitungs- und Radiosprache schrieb, zitierte er einen Artikel in der *Prawda*, der viele dieser Konstruktionen enthielt und forderte, dass der Text niemals im Radio vorgelesen werden sollte; gelte es doch zu verhindern, dass der „Rundfunkhörer ihn [...] mit Lefistischer Poesie [verwechsele]."[27] In einem 1928 erschienen Aufsatz über Tret'iakow erklärte Il'ia Dukor: Der „Überfluss an deverbativen Nomen ist kein Zufall. Die Objekte sind mit Handlungen gesättigt. Dinge, Leute, Schlagwörter werden aktiviert." Dukor zufolge wurden die einst vom Verb vermittelte Kraft und Handlungsmacht auf das Nomen übertragen und vom Objekt selbst absorbiert. Er stellte fest, dass in den Schriften Tret'iakows sogar Adjektive tendenziell nominalisiert werden.[28] Die gleiche Tendenz zur Nominalisierung prägt das Werk von Majakowski, einem weiteren Mitglied der Gruppe. Wenngleich dieser nicht selbst zu den Faktografen gerechnet werden kann, so experimentierte er doch mit der Ausdrucksweise der Faktografie in Zeitungsepen wie *Khorosho!* (1927). In *Die Sprache des Bauernkorrespondenten* stellte Meromskii fest, dass „der Urbanist Majakowski, indem er die Geschwindigkeit seiner Sprache beschleunigt, aus einem oder zwei Wörtern bestehende Sätze bevorzugt, [die] oft ohne jegliche Verben" auskommen. Solchen „Verlust an Verbalität" verknüpfte er mit der „Sprache unserer Zeitungen".[29] Spätere Untersuchungen bestätigten diese Einsicht. In einem wichtigen

---

25 Chuzhak behauptet, dass die Faktografie von der Raznochintsi abstamme in „Literatura zhiznestroeniia: istoricheskii probeg", in: *Literatura fakta*, hg. von Nikolai Chuzhak, Moskau: Federatsiia, 1929, S. 36 f.

26 Sergei Tret'iakow, Nikolai Chuzhak, Viktor Pertsow, Viktor Shklovskii, Vladimir Majakowski, Grigorii Vinokur, Ossip Brik, Nikolai Aseev und Pavel Neznamov veröffentlichten alle in *Zhurnalist* – mit einer noch größeren Häufigkeit in dem Zeitraum, in dem ihre eigenen Publikationsorgane wie *Lef* (1923-1925) und *Novyi Lef* nicht verfügbar waren (1927-1928).

27 S. Rozval, „O iazyke nashikh gazet", in: *Zhurnalist*, 9 (1929), S. 282.

28 Il'ia Dukor, „Sergei Tret'iakow", in: *Na literaturnom postu*, 18 (1928), S. 46-50.

29 Meromskii (1930), *Iazyk sel'kora*, S. 117.

Text über den „Ideostil" von Majakowski bemerkte der Kritiker Michail Gasparow, dass in frühen Texten wie *Wolke in Hosen* (1914) Verben semantischen Vorrang vor anderen Wortarten haben, diesen aber in den Texten wie *Lenin* (1924) Mitte der 1920er Jahre verlieren, als – unter dem Einfluss der Zeitungssprache – die Häufigkeit und die kreative Energie der Nomen in den Schriften Majakowskis deutlich zunehmen.[30]

Theorie und Praxis der Faktografie beleuchten einige Folgen der Deverbalisierung, angefangen bei der Beschränkung der zeitlichen Dauer. Aktualität wurde in erster Linie in ihrem phänomenalen Sinne verstanden: Nominalisierung beschleunigt das Wort. Unter Rückgriff auf Wilhelm Wundts Forschungen über die Geschwindigkeit der Sprache, bemerkte beispielsweise P. Chernych in „Die russische Sprache und die Revolution" (1929), dass der Gebrauch von deverbativen Nomen die sprachliche Übermittlung von Information beschleunige.[31] Darin unterscheide sich journalistische Sprache grundsätzlich vom narrativen Schreiben, welches außerordentlich viel Zeit sowohl in der Produktion als auch in der Rezeption in Anspruch nehme. Wie die Faktografen nie zu betonen versäumten, dauert es Jahre, Romane zu schreiben; und als Folge dieser beständigen „Verzögerung" (*otstavanie*) neutralisieren sie jene dringenden Angelegenheiten, die ihr Anlass gewesen sind.[32] Solche Verspätung wird nochmals verschärft durch den übermäßigen Zeitaufwand, der notwendig ist, um die Romane zu lesen (ein Lef-Mitglied, Viktor Pertsow, berechnete, dass ein Proletarier bei 1.423 Seiten und 2.520 Wörtern pro Seite, 46 Abende bräuchte, um *Krieg und Frieden* zu lesen).[33] Im Gegensatz dazu zielt die Sprache der Zeitung streng auf Aktualität. Mithilfe von klischeehaften linguistischen Readymades, welche die zum Schreiben erforderliche Zeit redu-

---

30 Mit dieser Wendung werden die Energien der linguistischen Erfindung Majakowskis auf die Nomen ausgerichtet (ein Drittel der Neologismen in *Wolke* sind Nomen, während eine Hälfte der Neologismen in *Lenin* Nomen sind); zwei Drittel der Ellipsen, die in einem Gedicht wie *Lenin* von Majakowski verwendet werden, betreffen die Verben (d. h. die Verben sind im wahrsten Sinne des Wortes verschwunden [396]); die Adverbien, die er erfindet, derivieren zunehmend – gegen die russischen Gesetze verstoßend – von Nomen statt Verben (folglich wird *ogromiv* vom Nomen *grom* statt vom Verb *gromit'* abgeleitet [392]); sogar die Metaphern, die Majakowski in den faktografischen Texten in den 1920er Jahren verwendet, haben eine doppelte Menge an Nomen wie seine Texte aus dem vorigen Jahrzehnt (im Jahr 1914 ist das Verhältnis zwischen auf Nomen basierten Metaphern und auf Prädikaten und Verben basierten Metaphern jeweils 4:2:4, aber im Jahr 1924 verschiebt sich das gleiche Verhältnis zu 6:1:3 [399]). Mikhail L. Gasparow, „Idiostil' Mayakovskogo", in: *Izbrannye trudy*, Band 2, Moskau: Iazyki russkoi kul'tury, 1997, S. 383-415.

31 Chernykh (1929), Russkii iazyk i revoliutsiia, S. 61. Der Dichter Carl Einstein beobachtet im Jahr 1931: „Bei einigen Schriftstellern überrascht die Präferenz für Substantive. Man eilt von Totalisierung zu Totaliltät, die Geschwindigkeit der Summationen. Das Tempo der Vorstellungen ist beschleunigt; die Hauptmotive werden hervorgehoben. Gleichwohl sind diese Substantive keineswegs rationale Begriffe, sondern komprimierte Prozesse; man zerbricht das Gegenständliche; hier eine zeitliche Folge, und stellt die Gegensätze oder Verwandtschaften schroff gegeneinander. Nicht anders als die Teilformen in den kubistischen Bildern." Carl Einstein, *Die Kunst des 20. Jahrhunderts*, 2. Aufl., Leipzig: Reclam, 1988 [1931], S. 117.

32 Boris Kushner, „Prichiny otstavaniia", in: *Krasnaia nov'*, 11 (1930), S. 131-141.

33 Viktor Pertsow, „Ob'em khudozhestvennogo proizvedeniia i biudzhet vremeni russkogo rabochego" [1926], in: *Literatura zavtrashnego dnia*, Moskau: Federatsiia, 1929, S. 117-123.

zieren, sind die Journalistinnen und Journalisten im Stande, „schnell und richtig“ zu schreiben (Bally) und die vorfabrizierten Phraseologismen in kurze Prosaentwürfe zusammenzufügen. Diese Zügigkeit der Textkomposition spiegelt sich auf Seiten der Rezeption in verschiedenen, zeitsparenden typografischen Merkmalen der Zeitung wider: von eindeutigen Schlagzeilen, die den Lesenden ermöglichen, sich schnell auf der Seite zu orientieren, bis zu schmalen Textspalten, die darauf berechnet sind, es dem Auge der Lesenden zu ermöglichen, eine ganze Zeile auf einen Blick wahrzunehmen.[34] Die Geschwindigkeit der Zeitungsmitteilung wird durch ein gewisses Maß an syntaktischer Gespanntheit (*napriazhennost'*) erhöht, das Formen der mündlichen Sprache und narrativer Prosa gleichermaßen fremd ist. In der Syntax der Zeitung nähert sich die Sprache maximaler Prägnanz und Kompaktheit an. Wie beim Telegramm, auf das die Russinnen und Russen oft als generisches Modell verwiesen, ist es das Ziel der Zeitungssprache, die größtmögliche Quantität an Informationen in der kürzest möglichen Folge von Symbolen zu verdichten. Dementsprechend bemerkte Gus, dass mit der deverbativen Sprache „eine ganze Reihe von Behauptungen, von eigenständigen Gedanken, die eigenständige Aussagen über ein und denselben Gegenstand bilden [...] in Eins vereinigt [werden].“[35] Angesichts seiner Vergangenheit als futuristischer Dichter, dessen „Poetik des Slogans“[36] und dessen „‚Verdichtung‘ des Satzes“ in einer „maximal ‚dichten‘ Semantik“[37] resultierten, war Tret'iakow besonders gut vorbereitet, um in dieser kompakten Ausdrucksweise zu kommunizieren. In der Tat schien die Zeitung den Traum der literarischen Moderne von einem unmittelbaren Ausdruck zu verwirklichen. Lange bevor er sich für die Faktografie engagierte, hatte Nikolai Chuzhak die Entstehung der Zeitungssprache in seiner im Jahre 1910 veröffentlichten Forderung nach einer neuen Poesie vorausgesehen, deren „Stil der flüchtigen Einheit des Eindrucks [...] sich von dem alten Stil des ‚Aufeinanderfolgens‘ [*posledovatel'nosti*] [unterscheidet]“.[38] Die Dichte dieses Stils, der, laut Chuzhak, die Gesetze des *Laokoon* von Lessing aufhebe, sei ein einzig der russischen Sprache eigenes grammatikalisches Vermögen. Anders als analytischere Sprachen wie Französisch oder Deutsch, in denen die Wortfolge einen bedeutenden semantischen Wert besitze, enthielten synthetischere Sprachen wie Russisch einen höheren Grad an syntaktischer Flexibilität und seien aus diesem Grund weniger von der verbalen Sequenz und der linearen Verteilung der Informationen abhängig.

34 Vgl. bspw.: Die von Miles Tinker und Donald Patterson in den späten 1920er und 30er Jahren ausgeführten Experimente zur „Lesehygiene [reading hygiene]“ bestätigten, dass die Kürze der Zeilenlänge in Zeitungskolumnen das Verständnis des Textes beschleunigte und die Lesezeit deshalb reduzierte.

35 Gus (1927), Predmet, zadachi i metody izucheniia gazetnogo iazyka, S. 59.

36 Tret'iakow verglich den Slogan mit anderen kurzen, dichten Formen wie dem Epigramm und dem Aphorismus, aber vor allem dem Telegramm und der Zeitung. Sergei Tret'iakow, „Obrabotka lozunga“, in: *Gorn*, 9 (1923), S. 117-122: insbes. 117 f. Viele Kritiker hielten Tret'iakows Arbeit an Slogans für einen Ausdruck seines größten dichterischen Talents.

37 Dukor (1928), Sergei Tret'iakow, S. 48.

38 Nikolai Chuzhak, „Tvorchestvo slova“ [1910], in: *K dialektike iskusstva: Ot realizma do iskusstva, kak odnoi iz proizvodstvennykh form. Teoreticheski-polemicheskie stat'i*, Chita: 1921, S. 14-19.

Für Chuzhak war die russische Sprache also das optimale Labor eines „neuen Stils“, dessen Besonderheit „in Geschwindigkeit, einer Augenblicklichkeit der lebendigen Wahrnehmung [liege], in einer Vernetzung der Eindrücke, die so vollständig ist, dass sie sogar das Zufällige umfasst.“[39]

Der „neue Stil“, von dem Chuzhak 1910 schwärmte, wurde fünfzehn Jahre später in der Sprache der Faktografie verwirklicht. Zurecht beklagten Gus et al., dass die Nominalisierung das „Verschwinden der Zeit und des Aspekts“ zur Folge habe.[40] Während in einer Geschichte die Darstellung von Informationen immer auf die Zeitachse projiziert wird, verdichtet die Zeitung diese aufeinanderfolgenden Momente in einen Zustand der syntaktischen und zeitlichen Gleichzeitigkeit. Dies ist ein Punkt, den Vinokur in seinem 1924 geschriebenen Text „Die Sprache unserer Zeitung“ entwickelt hatte, in dem er die syntaktisch dichte Sprache der Zeitung mit der verlängerten syntagmatischen Abfolge der geschriebenen Erzählung verglich:

> *Aufmerksamkeit für die Syntax* offenbart sich in der systematischen Verteilung der kopulativen Partikel und Wörter auf den ganzen Abschnitt (*perioda*) und ermöglicht es, eine ganze Reihe von Fakten in eine *einzige grammatikalische Kette* zu fügen. Die Darstellung dieser Fakten in typischer *Umgangssprache* – ebenso wie in allen anderen Arten der geschriebenen Sprache außer der der Zeitung – würde eine ganz andere narrative Form aus mehreren unabhängigen Sätzen verlangen. Wenn wir versuchen würden, den eigentlichen Text des (Zeitungs-)Telegramms auf diese Weise zu zerteilen, würden wir damit der Sprache des Telegramms seine grundsätzlichste Eigenschaft rauben und womit wir dann zu tun hätten, wäre kein Telegramm mehr, sondern eine Art historische Erzählung [Herv. i. O.].[41]

Aufgrund seiner äußersten syntaktischen Kompaktheit, so Vinokurs Argument, zieht der Zeitungsartikel die temporale Qualität der Dauer, die für die narrative Darstellung charakteristisch ist, von historischen Ereignissen ab und übermittelt den Lesenden diese Ereignisse praktisch sofort. Als Konsequenz der maximal dichten Syntax wird der Inhalt der telegrafischen Zeitung von den Lesenden als synchron begriffen, während sich ein narratives Werk diachron durch die Folge der Verwandlungen fortschreibt, die sich über die Länge des Textes entfalten. Die syntaktische „Spannung“ zu entschärfen und die elektrische „Spannung“ (*napriazhenie*) in den verdichteten periodischen Sätzen der Zeitung zu entladen, würde die Nachrichten in eine Geschichte umwandeln.

Eine logische Folge der Verkürzung der Zeit in der Zeitung ist der Verzicht auf kausales Denken. Auch hier ist die deverbative Sprache von Vorteil, denn konjugierte Verben situieren eine bestimmte Tat in der Zeit, verankern das Ereignis in festen Koordinaten der Vergangenheit, Gegenwart oder Zukunft. Trotz ihrer vermeintlichen Dynamik erweisen sich Verben in dieser Hinsicht als durchaus sta-

39 Ebd., S. 15-17.

40 Mikhail Gus/Iu. Zagorianskii/N. Kaganovich, *Iazyk gazety*, Moskau: Rabotnik prosveshcheniia, 1926, S. 17.

41 Grigorii O. Vinokur, „Iazyk nashei gazety“, in: *Kul'tura iazyka*, Moskau: Rabotnik prosveshcheniia, 1925, S. 104.

tisch. Sie erfassen die Zeit eindeutig. Im Gegensatz dazu präzisieren deverbative Ausdrücke nicht, wann ein Ereignis im Verhältnis zu anderen Ereignissen stattgefunden hat, sondern schweben stattdessen außerhalb der Zeit, in einem Zustand des ewigen Werdens. Verbal- und Nominalkonstruktionen evozieren deshalb zwei ganz unterschiedliche Bilder der Geschichte, ein geschlossenes und ein offenes. Betrachten wir noch einmal: „Der Bolschewist stürmte den Winterpalast." Dieses Ereignis fand offensichtlich an einem Punkt in der Vergangenheit statt. Nach dem Moment, in dem „der Bolschewist den Winterpalast gestürmt hatte", aber vor der Zeit, in der „der Bolschewist den Winterpalast stürmt", die selbst dem Moment, in dem „der Bolschewist den Winterpalast stürmen wird", vorangeht. Im Unterschied zu allen diesen Beispielen trägt „das Stürmen des Winterpalasts durch den Bolschewisten" keine solche Zeitmarkierung. Ohne ein konjugiertes Verb, das anzeigt, wann das Ereignis stattgefunden hat, behauptet der Satz auch keine zeitliche Sequenz und projiziert keine narrative Einbettung. Wenn, wie Vinokur erklärt, „eine der Eigenschaften des Verbs als eine semantische Kategorie [...] seine *narrative* Funktion [ist] [Herv. i. O.]", dann entspräche der Verlust des Verbs dem Verlust des Narrativs.[42] Aus diesem Grund bemerkte Jespersen (eine von Vinokurs Quellen), dass Deverbative häufig in englischen Konstruktionen verwendet werden, die mit *was auch immer* (*whatever*) oder *wie auch immer* (*however*) beginnen, um einen fortlaufenden Prozess anzuzeigen:

> Die Häufigkeit der verblosen Sätze mit *was auch immer* usw. (was auch immer die Erklärung sei; was auch immer der Ursprung sei; wer auch immer der ursprüngliche Autor sei; wie offensichtlich auch immer der Grund sein mag) ließe sich auch dadurch erklären, dass das flektierte Verb einen Zeitindex hätte, und dass der Satz ohne Verb als undefinierter und allgemeiner wahrgenommen würde und insofern eher in Übereinstimmung mit *immer* [ever] stünde [Herv. i. O.].[43]

Deverbative Konstruktionen sind im wörtlichen Sinne zeitlos. Laut Gus et al. verwandelte die Nominalisierung die russische Sprache in eine Menge „algebraische[r] Formeln". Indem der deverbative Satz, wie sie es formulierten, „eine Handlung durch ein Zeichen der Handlung [ersetzt]"[44], konstituiere er eine elementare Einheit in einem kombinatorischen Diagramm der Handlung, welches – weil es zeitlich unspezifiziert ist – nicht-linear und im Prinzip auch umkehrbar sei wie eine mathematische Formel. Sie beanstandeten, dass die Nominalisierung uns verleite, „das Vorhergehende mit der Zukunft [zu verwechseln]."[45]

---

42 Vinokur (1928), Glagol ili imia?, S. 87.

43 Otto Jespersen, „The Role of the Verb" [1911], in: *Selected Writings*, New York, NY: Routledge, 2010, S. 175.

44 Gus/Zagorianskii/Kaganovich (1926), *Iazyk gazety*, S. 230.

45 Ebd., S. 18. Viel später beklagte eine französische Kritikerin des Sowjetjargons das „Opfern" des Verbs für das Nomen. Trotzdem fügte sie einschränkend hinzu: „[J]edoch sind nicht alle Verben gleich verkleinert. Die, die sich auf *kontinuierliche Prozesse* beziehen, sind widerständiger gegen das sich aufdrängende Nomen. Die Verben, die liquidiert werden, sind tendenziell die, die das Konzept der Zeit und insbesondere die Idee der zeitlichen Sequenz in einen Satz einführen [...] Die meisten Verben drücken das Wahre aus, während Nomen [...] die Oase der leeren Formen [sind]", schrieb Valéry. „So oft wie möglich vermeidet der *Neusprech* die Genauigkeit des Verbs

Für die Faktografen lag der Reiz der Nominalisierung jedoch gerade in dieser Verwirrung von Vergangenheit und Zukunft, der Vermengung der geschichtlichen Vektoren. Indem sie sich vom Verb befreit, befreit sich die zeitgenössische Sprache auch von der Abfolge und dem inhärenten Drang des Narrativen nach Abschluss und Totalisierung. TheoretikerInnen haben stets darauf hingewiesen, dass dieses Verlangen nach Vollendung eines der Erkennungsmerkmale der Erzählung, insbesondere des Romans, sei. Einen Begriff von Aristoteles übernehmend, bezeichnet Roland Barthes dies als den „prohairetischen" Drang der Erzählung, der von der ständigen Erwartung der Lesenden auf einen noch ausstehenden formalen Schluss angeregt ist (Barthes schlussfolgert auf beeindruckende Weise, dass jeder Roman rückwärts gelesen wird, gewissermaßen von dem Punkt seines projizierten Endes her). Dementsprechend verknüpft Peter Brooks den Mechanismus der Handlung und ihr Verlangen, zum Ende zu kommen, mit dem freudschen Todestrieb. Nach Dafürhalten Tret'iakows und seiner Kollegen hatte faktografisches Schreiben solche Vollendung um jeden Preis zu vermeiden. Eine sich ständig verändernde Gegenwart sollte fokussiert werden, statt eine unbekannte Zukunft zu entwerfen. Dem Bekenntnis der Faktografen zur Zeitung entsprachen ihre legendären Angriffe auf den proletarischen Roman, den sie mit Formen der sogenannten „handlungslose[n] Prosa" (*bessiuzhetnaia proza* oder *vnesiuzhetnaia proza*) ersetzen wollten.[46] Das Alltägliche war für sie zwangsläufig sowohl ohne Handlung als auch präsentisch, da es danach verlangte, Ereignisse noch in ihrer Entfaltung darzustellen. Die Zeitung kennt kein Vorher und Nachher, nur eine Gegenwart, die stets in Echtzeit aktualisiert wird. Der tschechische Autor Karel Capek beobachtete 1924:

> Die Welt der Zeitung, wie die der wilden Bestie, existiert ausschließlich in der Gegenwart. Das Bewusstsein der Presse (wenn man von Bewusstsein sprechen kann) ist von der einfachen gegenwärtigen Zeit begrenzt, die sich von der Morgen- zur Abendausgabe erstreckt oder andersherum. Wenn man eine Zeitung liest, die eine Woche alt ist, fühlt man sich als ob man die Seiten der Dalimil-Chronik umblättert: es ist keine Zeitung mehr, sondern ein Denkmal. Das noetische System der Zeitung ist aktueller Realismus: was gerade jetzt ist, existiert; *Extra praesentiam non est existentia: ergo bibamus.*[47]

In Übereinstimmung mit dieser präsentischen Ausrichtung wenden sich die deverbativen Lokutionen der Zeitung aktuellen Ereignissen als Phänomen zu, die noch unvollendet und ergebnislos sind. Im Gegensatz zum Roman, dessen Handlungsbogen eine Totalität der Ereignisse schildert, die einen begrenzten Umfang

---

und entscheidet sich für eine vage Zeitlosigkeit; er weicht sorgsam der Erzählung aus während er die *Bewegung* betont, die allen Sachen immanent ist [Herv. i. O.]". Françoise Thom, *Newspeak. The Language of Soviet Communism*, übers. von Ken Connelly, London: The Claridge Press, 1989, S. 22. Die Debatten über die Nominalisierung in den 1920er Jahren sind Thom nicht bekannt, obwohl sie auf die wichtige Arbeit von Patrick Seriot zum Thema Nominalisierung verweist.

46 Zur handlungslosen Prosa, vgl. Ossip Brik, „Razlozhenie siuzheta", und Viktor Shklovskii, „K tekhnike vneisiuzhetnoi prozy", in: *Literatura fakta* (1929), S. 219-222 und S. 223-227.

47 Karel Čapek, „In Praise of Newspapers" [1924], in: *In Praise of Newspapers and Other Essays on the Margin of Literature*, übers. von M. and R. Weatherall, London: Allen, 1951, S. 9-10. [Von mir korrigierte Übersetzung; D. F.]

hat, sowie einen prohairetischen Prozess, der vollständig ist, bevor er beginnt, suspendiert die Zeitung die eindeutige Auflösung der Erzählung. Die Faktografen glaubten, dass der Roman aufgrund seines formalen Schlusses ungeeignet für die Darstellung der epochalen historischen Veränderungen ihrer Zeit sei. Vielmehr gelte es letztlich, die Geschichte offenzuhalten, um keine vorherbestimmten Schlüsse jener historischen Ereignisse zu beschreiben, die noch im Prozess der Entstehung waren. Die Faktografie sollte das erfassen, was Tret'iakow mit einer bemerkenswert deverbativen Formulierung „das unerhörte Mittendrinstehen im Leben“ nannte. Diese „Literatur des Werdens“ (*literatura stanovleniia*), wie Chuzhak sie nannte, sollte den Anforderungen der Gegenwart „maximale Biegsamkeit“ (*maksimal'naia gibkost'*) und Reaktionsbereitschaft entgegenbringen.

Es verwundert darum nicht, dass keines der berühmten Werke von Tret'iakow einen eigentlich narrativen Schluss hat. Sie brechen einfach auf der letzten Seite ab. Die Sammlung von Kolchos-Skizzen, *Vyzov* (1930), ist der zeitlichen Abfolge der Geschenisse folgend, in drei Abschnitte geteilt: 1928, 1929, 1930. Die offene Struktur der Chronik als eine Form, die von Rezensenten vehement kritisiert wurde, vermeidet den Fallstrick narrativer Vollendung und wiederholt stattdessen an jeder Ecke die Unvorhersehbarkeit dessen, was auf die Genossenschaftsbauern noch zukommt. Tatsächlich erweisen sich jene Arten von Landarbeit, die in *Vyzow* dokumentiert werden, als das ideale Thema einer fortlaufenden und nicht endenden Chronik; denn ihre Abhängigkeit von den wiederkehrenden Zyklen der natürlichen Zeit eliminiert die Möglichkeit eines endgültigen Schlusses. Jede Bepflanzung wird neue Gelegenheiten bieten, jede Ernte neue Herausforderungen. Das Buch ist nie abgeschlossen. Durch die episodische, aber grundsätzlich offene Vorstellung des Lebens in *Vyzov* schildert Tret'iakow „eine dialektisch wahrgenommene Realität, die sich in einem kontinuierlichen Prozess des Werdens befindet“ (*v protsesse nepreryvnogo stanovleniia*).[48] Ein weiteres, genauso berühmtes Buch von Tret'iakow, das Bio-Interview *Den Shi-Khua* (1930), hat ebenfalls kein Ende. In diesem Fall verschwindet die titelgebende Hauptfigur einfach mitten im Interview, so dass Tret'iakow das Buch unabgeschlossen lässt. Noch seltsamer jedoch als das Fehlen des Schlusses ist die generelle Indifferenz des Buches gegenüber zeitlichen Unterscheidungen. Alle Ereignisse, die in diesem Buch geschildert werden, scheinen in der Gegenwart ihrer Darstellung zu koexistieren. Offensichtlich ist dieser Zustand der Gleichzeitigkeit und das Fehlen einer Unterscheidung zeitlicher Schichten sehr ungewöhnlich für ein biografisches Memoire, eine Gattung, die typischerweise im Akt des Rückblickens gründet. Selbst wenn die Lesenden sich in die hintersten Winkel der Erinnerung von Den in China vertiefen, machen ihnen die Sprünge in der Zeit stets die Szene bewusst, in der der Stenograf im Moskau des Jahres 1927 das Diktat von Tret'iakow aufnimmt, die Gegenwart, in der Den und Tret'iakow sich begegnen. Diese Einfaltung der Gegenwart in die Vergangenheit irritiert Georg Lukács sehr, der *Den Shi-Khua* in seiner berühmten Kritik der Faktografie „Reportage oder Gestaltung?“ (1932) aufgreift. Darin verweist der Vertei-

48 Sergei M. Tret'iakov, „Otkuda i kuda“ in: *Lef* 1 (1924), S. 200.

diger des Romans des 19. Jahrhunderts auf eine besondere Szene, in der Den, damals ein fünfjähriger Junge, beschreibt, wie er seinen Vater bei der Belehrung einer Gruppe von Zuhörern über die Dringlichkeit der revolutionären Aktion belauscht. In jenem Abschnitt wendet sich Lukács gegen den Umstand, dass die Rede eine übersichtliche und genaue soziopolitische Analyse der Situation bietet, in der die chinesischen Revolutionäre sich 1907 befanden: Etwas, das ein fünfjähriges Kind niemals in dem Grad der Komplexität hätte begreifen können, in dem es im Buch geschildert wird. Lukács zufolge hätte eine solche Episode, um die zeitliche Integrität der Geschichte zu bewahren, durch die Sicht des Kindes gefiltert werden und somit notwendigerweise weniger komplex sein müssen, als die des erwachsenen Den. Stattdessen spricht der Fünfjährige in *Den Shi-Khua* wie ein reifer Revolutionär, der die Ereignisse im Präteritum mit dem Bewusstsein der Gegenwart verfälscht. Ähnlich wie Gus, der an der Nominalisierung die Verwechslung des „Vorausgehende[n] mit der Zukunft“[49] bemängelt hatte, kritisiert Lukács die Entdifferenzierung des faktografischen Schreibens: der Unmittelbarkeit und der Gegenwart werde dort der Vorzug vor komplexer zeitlicher Schichtung gegeben.

Die deverbative Grammatik schwächt, wie vorher beschrieben, die narrative Abfolge und verschleiert die festgelegten Koordinaten der historischen Zeit. Darüber hinaus überlagert sie Schemata menschlicher Handlungsfähigkeit. Nach der Deverbalisierung stürmen Individuen nicht mehr den Winterpalast, sondern das Stürmen wird von Individuen durchgeführt oder geleitet. In der letzten Formulierung übernimmt das Subjekt eine über die Tat hinausgehende Position. Obwohl es das Stürmen ermöglicht, ist es nicht dessen Autor oder Urheber. Im Russischen wird die grammatikalische Struktur des Satzes dementsprechend komplizierter und verschwommener, weil die einfache Konstruktion mit dem Nominativ und dem Akkusativ durch eine umständlichere Konstruktion ersetzt wird, die schräge Fälle wie den Genitiv und den Instrumental verwendet. Der Gebrauch von Deverbativen in Russland verursachte vor allem eine Explosion des Instrumentals, eines Kasus, der Jakobson zufolge dem Subjekt eine „periphere Stellung“ im Verhältnis zum Verb gewährt. Eine Art grammatikalischen Kopernikanismus vollziehend, verschiebt der Instrumental das Subjekt vom Zentrum des Handlungsuniversums an dessen Rand. Wie Gus et al. formulierten: „Das echte Agens – das Subjekt – wandelt sich zur Ergänzung und wird eine Art Instrument der Handlung.“[50] So wurde von Gus eine zunehmende Tendenz unter Zeitungsleserinnen und -lesern moniert, das logische Subjekt mit dem Objekt eines Satzes zu verwechseln, da der schräge Kasus und das Instrumental ihre Ausbreitung finden. Vielleicht war es die Verschleierung der Handlungsfähigkeit in diesen „unpersönlichen Konstruktionen“ (*beslichnye predlozheniia*), in denen Subjekte und Objekte ständig die Positionen tauschten, die Gus et al. ideologisch am meisten ärgerte. Prinzipiell sollte das revolutionäre Zeitalter – ein Zeitalter des Heldentums und des Muts – „einen Überfluss an Verben haben und zwar *aktive* Formen des Letzteren. Allerdings [sei]

49 Gus/Zagorianskii/Kaganovich (1926), *Iazyk gazety*, S. 18.
50 Ebd., S. 164.

das kaum der Fall. *Inaktive und passive Formen überwiegen gegenüber den Aktiven* [Herv. i. O.]." Die Syntax der sowjetischen Presse zeige zu viele Beispiele, in denen „das Subjekt in Gestalt eines deverbativen Substantivs oder eines abstrakten Konzepts ein aktives Element ist, im Gegensatz zu der Person, die tatsächlich aktiv ist."[51] Das Subjekt ist hier nicht mehr der eindeutige und explizite Urheber eines Ereignisses, sondern stattdessen lose damit verbunden, als dessen Verstärker oder Instrument. „Die konkrete Verbindung im Ausdruck ‚ein Subjekt handelt' wird durch die elliptische Verbindung ‚ein Subjekt hat die Eigenschaft einer Handlung' (*sub'ekt imeet svoistvo deistviia*) ersetzt."[52] Die deverbative Sprache der Faktografie schildert nicht individuelle Heldentaten, sondern unpersönliche Netzwerke der Handlungsfähigkeit, die unter (grammatisch – und für Gus et al., ideologisch) schwachen Subjekten verteilt ist.

Gus et al. kamen vor diesem Hintergrund zu einem seltsamen Schluss über die Sprache der Zeitung: da „erscheint das Verb in der medialen Diathese" (*glagol stoit v srednem zaloge*).[53] Ihre Beobachtung ist umso beeindruckender, da das moderne Russisch, im Gegensatz zu alten Sprachen wie dem Griechischen oder Sanskrit keine mediale Diathese hat, sondern nur das Aktiv und das Passiv kennt. Aber die Verbindung zwischen der Zeitung und der medialen Diathese wirft die Frage auf, warum Russischsprechende der damaligen Zeit ein dringendes und plötzliches Bedürfnis hatten, diese verlorene diathetische Kategorie wiederzubeleben, oder zumindest eine Art expressives Äquivalent dafür zu finden. Die Beantwortung der Frage erfordert das Verständnis von zwei soziotechnischen Dringlichkeiten, die mit der Revolution entstanden. Zunächst war da das Bedürfnis, die Kategorien der Erfahrung umzuorientieren, von einer Ontologie des Seins zu einer funktionalistischen Pragmatik. „Es gibt keine aktiven Charaktere", behauptete Tret'iakow: „Es gibt nur aktive Prozesse."[54] Als Reaktion auf dieses Bedürfnis nach einer Analytik der Handlung und des Prozesses, drückt die mediale Diathese eine Existenzweise aus, die provisorisch und kontextuell entsteht. Der Linguist Émile Benveniste bemerkt, dass aktive Verben „einen Prozess [bezeichnen], der außerhalb des Subjekts vollendet wird", während das Verb der medialen Diathese „einen auf das Subjekt zentrierten Prozess [anzeigt], das Subjekt als innerhalb des Prozesses."[55] Indem das Subjekt handelt, wird es selbst Gegenstand einer Handlung und verwandelt sich reflexiv. Vinokur erfasste diese auf merkwürdige Weise tautologische Struktur der Selbstkonstitution in einem Abschnitt, der die logische Entstehung von deverbativen Nomen in indoeuropäischen Sprachen erklärt als „eine Tätigkeit, die auf die Tätigkeit selbst gerichtet ist, die Letztere als ihr eigenes *Objekt* sieht:

51 Ebd., S. 109 f. Majakowski war besonders geschickt darin, den Instrumental zu verwenden, um eine vage und unspezifische Verbindung zwischen Nomen zu etablieren, eine *relation sans contact*.

52 Gus/Zagorianskii/Kaganovich (1926), *Iazyk gazety*, S. 201.

53 Ebd., S. 164.

54 Sergei Tret'iakow, „Skvoz' neprotertye ochki", in: *Literatura fakta* (1929), S. 232.

55 Émile Benveniste, „Active and Middle Voice in the Verb", in: *Problems in General Linguistics*, übers. von Mary Elizabeth Meek, Coral Gables, FL: University of Miami Press, 1971, S. 145-151: 148.

solcher Art ist der Sinn dieses Prozesses [Herv. i. O.].“[56] In diesem Fall geht das Bewusstsein der Tat nicht voran, sondern entsteht durch sie. In der medialen Diathese hilft eine ontologisch unbestimmte Subjektivität sich selbst und schafft und definiert dabei ihre Umrisse durch Tätigkeiten, Praktiken und Verpflichtungen. Wie Benveniste bemerkt hatte, ist die mediale Diathese deshalb eine wichtige linguistische Ressource „in einer Gesellschaft, in der man sich engagieren muss, um etwas zu erreichen.“[57] Es wäre schwierig, eine kohärentere Charakterisierung der idealen Verhältnisse in der sowjetischen Gesellschaft zu finden. Gemäß Bruno Latour, der die mediale Diathese zur Konzeptionalisierung distributiver Akteur-Netzwerke heranzieht, setzt diese diathetische Kategorie eine „stotternde Version von Kausalität“ voraus, in der das Individuum „eingerichtet ist, einer Kette von Vermittlern zu folgen, von denen keiner die einzige Ursache des nächsten ist, sondern stattdessen jeder Zwischenschritt den nächsten überhaupt erst befähigt, seinerseits zum Anfang einer Handlung zu werden.“[58] Das Subjekt entsteht nicht dadurch, dass es sich behauptet, sondern dadurch, dass es sich in eine „Kaskade“ von Ereignissen einfügt.[59] Im Unterschied zu aktiven und passiven Verben, die sich entweder an den Urheber oder das Objekt der Handlung richten, nimmt die mediale Diathese beide Begriffe in einer hinzukommenden Kette von Operationen auf, denn Benveniste zufolge geht das Bewusstsein in der medialen Diathese dem Verb, das es ausführt, nicht voran. Diese linguistische Konstruktion drückt eine flüchtige Existenz aus, die dem Ereignis innewohnt, statt ihm vorauszugehen. Das Subjekt, das in der medialen Diathese entsteht, bleibt dem Verb immanent, ein kontingentes Wesen, dessen flackernde Existenz von seiner kurzzeitigen Teilnahme an dieser oder jener Tat ermöglicht wird. In dem dynamischen und sich ständig verändernden sozialen Kontext des revolutionären Russlands hatte Handlung Vorrang vor Wesenhaftigkeit. Daher verkündete der Theoretiker der Faktografie, Ossip Brik, dass

> wir die Literatur mit der folgenden Aufgabe betrauen [müssen]: uns nicht Menschen sondern die Tat [*delo*] vorzulegen; nicht Menschen sondern die Tat zu beschreiben; sich nicht für Menschen, sondern für Taten zu interessieren. Der Mensch ist uns wichtig, nicht weil er Gefühle empfindet, sondern wegen der Rolle, die er in der Tat spielt.[60]

Die Verschiebung von einem identitären Verständnis des Selbst (der „Person“) zu einem auf Tätigkeit und Engagement (der „Tat“) basierten Selbst reagierte also auf das Bedürfnis nach kognitiven und ästhetischen Mitteln, die dazu fähig sind, eine, die Pluralität von Subjekten einbeziehende, multinodale Handlung zu konzeptualisieren und zu repräsentieren. Die dringliche Suche nach Methoden der Darstel-

---

56 Vinokur (1928), Glagol ili imia?, S. 81.

57 Benveniste (1971), Active and Middle Voice in the Verb, S. 151.

58 Bruno Latour, „Faktur/Fraktur. Vom Netzwerk zur Bindung“, in: *Bio und Zoë. Die menschliche Natur im Zeitatler ihrer technischen Reproduzierbarkeit*, hg. von Martin G. Weiß, Frankfurt/M.: Suhrkamp, 2009), S. 359-385: 371 f.

59 Ebd., S. 378.

60 Ossip Brik, „Razgrom Fadeeva“, in: *Literatura fakta* (1929), S. 88-93: 96.

lung zerstreuter kollektiver Handlungsfähigkeit war der zweite soziotechnische Zwang, auf den die mediale Diathese reagierte. Brik hatte argumentiert, dass die traditionellen ästhetischen Gattungen wie der Roman und die Malerei der Sache nicht gewachsen seien, weil sie das Individuum von seiner sozialen Gruppe und seiner materiellen Umwelt isolieren und es als eine autonome Einheit hypostasieren. So war die Hauptfigur eines Romans nicht das Abbild einer wirklichen Person, sondern eine literarische Konvention, die dazu diente, die Tätigkeit eines großen Kollektivs in einer einzigen Figur zusammenzufassen: „Das Heldentum ist ein literarisches Ausdrucksmittel, wodurch eine Summe von Taten (Heldentaten) von einem Menschen gefordert wird, obwohl diese Summe tatsächlich das Resultat der Arbeit einer ganzen Reihe von Menschen ist."[61] Nach der Revolution war es an der Zeit, diese Konvention abzulegen. Mit ihrer „stotternden Version von Kausalität" ermöglichte die mediale Diathese der Zeitung, diese Verzerrung zu korrigieren, indem sie die Taten umverteilte, die man im Helden des Romans versammelt hatte.

Die Faktografie erweitert somit das Netzwerk der Handlungsfähigkeit über jene Parameter hinaus, die dem Menschen traditionell zugeschrieben wurden. Das hatte etwa Dukor im Sinn, als er beobachtete, dass „der Überfluss an deverbativen Nomen" in den Schriften von Tret'iakow Gegenstände erzeuge, die „mit Handlung gesättigt" seien. Diese grammatikalische Vorliebe wurde literaturgenerisch ausgearbeitet in der Schreibpraxis, die Tret'iakow 1929 „die Biographie des Dings" taufte, eine Gattung, die „nicht de[n] individuelle[n] Mensch[en], der sich durch ein System der Objekte bewegt, sondern das Objekt, das durch das System der Menschen fortfährt"[62] schildert. Dieser Antiroman sollte ein ganzes Kollektiv in einer ununterbrochenen und kontinuierlichen Kette von Tätigkeiten zusammenbinden, deren Struktur Tret'iakow mit einem Fließband verglich. Weder geht hier die Subjektivität der Tat als deren souveräner Ursache voran, noch ist sie das passive Objekt ihres Zwanges. Stattdessen entsteht sie Benvenistes Darstellung nach, indem sie „sich engagiert". Eine solche Grammatik entwertet die Einbildung heroischer Autonomie. Das Subjekt ist nicht Ursprung der Tat, nicht deren treibende Kraft; es ist stattdessen gewissermaßen der Tat entlang zerstreut. Um zu handeln, muss sich das Subjekt in ein konkretes aber distributives Handlungsfeld einfügen, dessen Gestaltung von sozialen Normen und Verhältnissen, von der physischen Architektur der Dinge und von der operativen Logik vielfältiger Kommunikationstechniken bedingt ist. Wie die Medientheoretikerin und Rechtswissenschaftlerin Cornelia Vismann schreibt, zwingt uns dieses diffuse Schema, die Kategorien der Handlungsfähigkeit und Verantwortlichkeit neu zu konzeptualisieren:

> Anders als bei Aktiv- und Passivbildungen eines Verbs kommt darin zum Ausdruck, dass das handelnde Subjekt (grammatikalisch betrachtet) auf etwas Drittes angewie-

[61] Ossip Brik, „Pochemu ponravilsia *Tsement*", in: *Literatura fakta* (1929), S. 85. Zu den gleichen Verzerrungen in der Malerei vgl. ders., „From the Painting to the Photograph" [1928], in: *Photography in the Modern Era*, hg. von Christopher Phillips, New York, NY: Metropolitan Museum of Art, 1989, S. 227-233.

[62] Sergei Tret'iakov, „Biography of the Object", in: *October*, 118 (2006), S. 57-62: 62.

> sen ist. Weder geht in der medialen Form eine Handlung von jemandem aus und trifft auf etwas, noch verhält es sich genau umgekehrt. […] [Der Begriff des Mediums besagt,] dass es einen Handlungsträger gibt, dem man zwar mangels Personeneigenschaft keine Handlungsfähigkeit im syntaktisch-juristischen Rahmen zugesteht, der aber dennoch etwas tut. Der Umstand, dass bestimmte Handlungen keiner Person zurechenbar sind, gleichwohl aber die Handlung von etwas getragen wird, kommt im Medium zum Ausdruck.[63]

In diesem fortlaufenden Prozess des Werdens gestaltet sich das individuelle Bewusstsein *in medias res*, zwischen den und in den Dingen. Der Protest eines Kritikers von *Vyzow* erfasst diesen mediatischen Zustand genau; Tret'iakow, schrieb er, „ist haltlos in die *Dinge* um sich aufgelöst, oder genauer: Weil der vulgär-empirische Ansatz immer unausweichlich zur Zerstörung der individuellen Perspektive führen wird, ist er in ein *Chaos der Dinge* aufgelöst [Herv. i. O.]."[64] Wie diese letzten Worte andeuten, ist die Existenz der medialen Diathese, die durch Dinge umgeleitet und zwischen ihnen zerstreut ist, verwirrend, chaotisch und ontologisch unrein.

Aus Sicht späterer GegnerInnen des „Neusprechs" (Newspeak) – um auf George Orwells' Neologismus zurückzugreifen, der entweder als Neu-Sprech (New-speak) oder wie hier, als Nachrichten-Sprache (News-speak) verstanden werden kann – musste dieses agentielle Chaos die Subjektfunktion schwächen und somit den Weg für einen Totalitarismus des Denkens bereiten.[65] Um den unpersönlichen Konstruktionen der Zeitung wieder Persönlichkeit zu verleihen und das Subjekt als den emphatischen Ursprung von Sprache und Handlung zu restituieren, musste diesen Kritikerinnen und Kritikern zufolge die kopernikanische Syntax der Zeitung ptolemäisiert werden. Nachrichtensprache sollte durch Romansprache ersetzt werden. Und es waren nicht nur die überzeugten Antisowjets, die zu diesem Schluss kamen. In ihrem Wunsch, Verantwortlichkeit in einer funktional differenzierten Gesellschaft sicherzustellen, beschwören wohlmeinende Progressive bis heute die individuelle Handlungsfähigkeit,[66] obwohl diese anthropomorphe Phan-

---

63 Cornelia Vismann, „Kulturtechniken und Souveränität", in: *Zeitschrift für Medien- und Kulturforschung*, Schwerpunkt Kulturtechnik, 1 (2010), S. 171-181: 172.

64 L. Varpakhovskii, „Sergei Tret'iakow. Vyzov", in: *Literatura i iskusstvo*, 4 (1930), S. 249.

65 Mikhail Heller, *Cogs in the Wheel. The Formation of Soviet Man*, New York, NY: Knopf, 1987 [1985] und Thom (1989), *Newspeak*.

66 John E. Richardson beklagt im Abschnitt „Syntax and Transitivity" seiner Monografie *Analyzing Newspapers: An Approach from Critical Discourse Analysis* (Basingstoke: Palgrave, 2009, S. 56) die Häufigkeit, in der „eine transitive Handlung (treten, stoßen, angreifen, usw.) […] so verwandelt [wird], dass der Handlungsträger [in der Zeitung] gelöscht ist". Als Folge werde „ein aktiver Prozess" in „ein Verhältnis oder einen ‚Stand der Dinge'" verwandelt. Für Richardson besteht die Lösung der Unklarheit der letzten Formulierung darin, die intransitiven Redewendungen in transitive umzuformulieren. Folglich empfiehlt er, dass der Satz „die internationale Wirtschaftsordnung ist in einem Zustand der Veränderung" durch „der IWF verändert die internationale Wirtschaftsordnung" ersetzt wird. Trotzdem müssen wir fragen: Ist letzterer tatsächlich konkreter? Dem IWF diese Handlung zuzuschreiben scheint die Frage der Handlungsfähigkeit kaum zu klären, denn der IWF ist eine Körperschaft ohne individuellen Willen, materiale Substanz oder festgelegte Konturen. (Ebd., S. 56.)

tasie wenig Halt in einer aus kollektiven Taten hergestellten Lebenswelt hat – einer „Gesellschaft, in der man sich engagieren muss, um etwas zu erreichen"[67]. Das Menschliche aus der von Chuzhak sogenannten „Kette der Dinge" (*veshchnaia tsep*[68]) zu extrahieren, mag Differenzierung und Kontur in die flache Ontologie der medialen Diathese einführen; aber das erneuerte Subjekt impliziert damit seinen eigenen philosophischen Trugschluss: Es ist ein metaphysischer Beobachter, der von jeglichem *Mittendrinstehen im Leben* abgeschnitten ist.

Übersetzung Mari Jarris.

---

67 Benveniste (1971), Active and Middle Voice in the Verb, S. 151.

68 Nikolai Chuzhak, „Ot iliuzii k materii", in: *Reviziia levogo fronta*, hg. von Viktor Pertsov, Moskau: Vserossiskii proletkul't, 1925, S. 102-132: 125.

Dorothea Walzer

Politische Groteske – Groteske Realität. Gerichtsreportage und -karikatur

Bilder einer grotesken Realität entwerfen Publizisten und Schriftsteller der 1920er Jahre in ihren Gerichtsreportagen. Für den politischen Journalisten Kurt Tucholsky oder Reporter wie Egon Erwin Kisch, Gabriele Tergit oder Paul Schlesinger, genannt Sling, ebenso wie für die Schriftsteller Joseph Roth und Ernst Ottwalt ist das Gericht der Ort, an dem die gesellschaftliche Wirklichkeit der Zwischenkriegszeit sich in all ihrer Widersprüchlichkeit zeigt und zur Darstellung bringen lässt. Doch damit nicht genug. Vor Gericht kann über den Realitätsgehalt der Darstellung befunden werden. Denn die juristische Frage nach der Wahrheit des Zeugnisses korrespondiert mit einem Unterscheidungsproblem, das die epistemologische Dimension künstlerischer Repräsentation betrifft. Vor Gericht wird deutlich, dass Wissen ohne Macht nicht zu denken ist. Wie das Wesentliche des Ereignisses zu erfassen ist, hängt aber mit dieser Frage zusammen. Nicht von ungefähr nimmt auch der marxistische Theoretiker Georg Lukács im Rahmen seiner Beiträge zur Realismusdebatte an prominenter Stelle auf die Verarbeitung juristischer Fälle Bezug. Mit Blick auf den Gerichtsroman von Ernst Ottwalt[1], dem er ein reportageartiges Vorgehen vorwirft, formuliert Lukács unter dem Titel *Reportage oder Gestaltung?* (1932) eine Kritik des Tatsachenberichts.

Im Folgenden ist ausgehend von Lukács' Text der spezifische Status der Gerichtsreportage in Hinblick auf die Frage nach einer „Wirklichkeit des Realismus" zu untersuchen; das Problem der Typenbildung wird dabei im Mittelpunkt stehen. Durch die Analyse der Gerichtsberichterstattung des Publizisten Tucholsky soll zweitens eine über Lukács hinausgehende Antwort auf dieses Problem formuliert werden. Tucholsky kann die groteske Realität des Justizapparats so treffend beschreiben, weil er seine Typen weniger durch Offenlegung von Fakten, als durch karikierende Überspitzung gewinnt. Geschult an den Karikaturen Honoré Daumiers, der seine Meisterschaft prominent in einer langen Reihe von Gerichtszeichnungen unter Beweis gestellt hatte, gelingt es Tucholsky, ebenso wie seinem Künstlerkollegen Sergej Eisenstein, die Karikatur als intellektuelle Methode zu profilieren. Vor dem Hintergrund wird es drittens um die Schnittmenge von Karikatur und Groteske gehen. Erlaubt es uns die politische Groteske doch, die realismustheoretischen Implikationen des Karikierens in den Blick zu nehmen. Grotesken lassen sich nämlich, wie an dieser Stelle vorauszuschicken ist, einerseits als Reflexion einer spezifisch modernen Macht analysieren; zum anderen prägt sich

1 Ernst Ottwalt, *Denn sie wissen, was sie tun. Ein deutscher Justiz-Roman*, Berlin, 1931.

in ihnen eine genuin moderne Schreibhaltung aus, die – verbunden mit einem von Erich Auerbach ausbuchstabierten Formenkalkül – dem grotesken Realismus eine herausragende Position unter den Realismen sichert.

1. Joseph Roth: Die Wahrheit des Zeugen

Es ist bekannt, dass die kriminalistische Spurensuche zur Metapher eines auf die Wirklichkeit gerichteten schöpferischen Verfahrens werden konnte.[2] Etwa, als bei Robin George Collingwood der Historiker als Detektiv auf- und bei Sigfried Kracauer wieder abtrat[3]; oder aber, als Bertolt Brecht für die Rückkehr zum Kriminalroman plädierte.[4] Weitaus weniger diskutiert, wenn auch nicht minder relevant für realismustheoretische Überlegungen, ist der Topos der Gerichtsverhandlung oder *enquête*, also der Untersuchung juristischer Fälle, der sich in der literarischen oder publizistischen Berichterstattung über diese Fälle reflektiert. Ähnlich wie bei der kriminalistischen Rekonstruktion eines delinquenten Falles, haben wir es auch im Gerichtsprozess mit der Konstruktion und Bewertung eines Bildes zu tun. Hinzu kommt jedoch eine entscheidende Erweiterung. Die juristische Zeugenvernehmung und die Berichterstattung über sie ruft das Problem der Zeugenschaft auf den Plan.[5]

In seiner polemischen Kampfansage „Schluss mit der Neuen Sachlichkeit!"[6] hatte Joseph Roth die überragende Bedeutung der Zeugenschaft in der neusachlichen

---

2 Vgl. hierzu Achim Saupe, *Der Historiker als Detektiv – Der Detektiv als Historiker. Historik, Kriminalistik und der Nationalsozialismus als Kriminalroman*, Bielefeld, 2009.

3 Robin George Collingwood, *Philosophie der Geschichte*, Stuttgart, 1955, insbes S. 243-261; dazu auch: Maria Muhle, „History will repeat itself. Für eine (Medien-)Philosophie des Reenactment", in: Lorenz Engell/Frank Hartmann/Christiane Voss (Hg.), *Körper des Denkens. Neue Positionen der Medienphilosophie*, München, 2013, S. 113-135, insbes. S. 125-128. Siegfried Kracauer, *Der Detektiv-Roman. Ein philosophischer Traktat*, Frankfurt/M., 1979 [1925]; ders., *Geschichte. Vor den letzten Dingen, Schriften. Band 4*, Frankfurt/M., 1971.

4 Bertolt Brecht, *Große kommentierte Berliner und Frankfurter Ausgabe. Schriften 1*, hg. von Werner Hecht, Jan Knopf, Werner Mittenzwei und Klaus-Detlef Müller, Berlin, Weimar, Frankfurt/M., 1992, S. 128-132. Nicht zufällig verdankt sich auch das Realitätsversprechen einer Fotografie, die von jeher – so auch bei den genannten Autoren – als Folie realismustheoretischer Überlegungen affirmiert oder abgewiesen wurde, der Wirkmächtigkeit des Paradigmas der Spur. Von den fotografietheoretischen Anfängen eines Henry Fox Talbot bis hin zu Positionen von Rosalind Krauss, Roland Barthes, Philippe Dubois oder Georges Didi-Huberman wurde das fotografische Medium ganz maßgeblich als Medium der Einschreibung, des Abdrucks und der Spur gelesen. (Peter Geimer, *Theorien der Fotografie. Zur Einführung*, Hamburg, 2009, S. 13-69.)

5 Ein in der Gerichtsuntersuchung angelegter Nexus von Episteme und Zeugenschaft erlaubt es Michel Foucault sogar, die *enquête* als Modell der empirischen Wissenschaften zu präsentieren: „Tatsächlich war die Gerichtsuntersuchung der erste aber grundlegende Ansatz zur Konstituierung der empirischen Wissenschaften; sie war die juristisch-politische Matrix des experimentellen Wissens, das am Ende des Mittelalters plötzlich entriegelt worden ist." (Michel Foucault, *Überwachen und Strafen. Die Geburt des Gefängnisses*, Frankfurt/M., 1994, S. 289.)

6 Joseph Roth, „Schluss mit der ‚Neuen Sachlichkeit'!", in: ders., *Werke 3. Das journalistische Werk. 1929-1939*, hg. von Klaus Westermann, Köln, 1991, S. 153-164. Im Folgenden werden die Seitenzahlen im laufenden Text angegeben.

Berichterstattung nicht nur erkannt, sondern auch der Kritik unterzogen. Er bemängelte, die bezeugende „Auskunft *über* [Herv. i. O.]" etwas könne noch längst nicht das „Ereignis selbst", dessen „innere Wahrheit" oder höhere Wirklichkeit" wiedergeben. (155 f.) Doch während in der Zeugenaussage das „Faktum" und das „Detail" den Inhalt dominiert, sei es im Bericht nur „Rohmaterial" der Gestaltung.[7] (155) Letztere zu vergessen, weigert sich Roth. Um die Faktengläubigkeit an den Pranger zu stellen, kritisiert er die fraglose Anerkennung des Zeugnisses im Bereich der literarischen Produktion:

> Erstaunlich, daß in einer Zeit, in der die einfachen Zeugenaussagen vor Gericht von der modernen medizinischen Wissenschaft mit Recht als unzuverlässig bezeichnet werden, erstaunlich, daß in dieser Zeit die literarische Zeugenaussage gültiger ist als die künstlerische Gestaltung. Man zweifelt an der Zuverlässigkeit des beeideten Zeugen. Aber man verleiht dem geschriebenen Zeugnis die höchste Anerkennung, die es in der Literatur gibt: die der Wahrhaftigkeit. Und wäre noch wenigstens die Kritik mächtig genug, das ‚Dokument' auf seine Echtheit zu prüfen! Nein! (153)

Mit diesem Aufschrei zieht Roth die Maßstäbe der neusachlichen Literatur in Zweifel. Polemisch stellt er die Gleichsetzung von Augenzeuge und Schriftsteller zur Disposition, wenn er erklärt: „Der Autor behauptet, er sei dabeigewesen. Man glaubt ihm: erstens: als wäre er wirklich dabeigewesen; zweitens: als wäre es wichtig, ob er dabeigewesen sei oder nicht." (154) Während man die Wahrheit der Aussage durch Abgleich des Dargestellten mit einer empirischen Realität zu entscheiden hoffe, werde die „Identität von Formlosigkeit und Gehaltlosigkeit" in den meisten Dokumenten schlichtweg übersehen, so lautet der Vorwurf. (164) Die Behauptung, „so ist es eben gewesen" ersetzt demnach die Frage nach der Präzision, der Dichte oder Komplexität der Beschreibung. (163) Gerade in jenem Moment, in dem man die Sprache vergessen mache und die Nuancen als „unsachlich" kritisiere, könne die Sachlichkeit ihren Siegeszug antreten. (164) Dabei ziehe der naive „Respekt vor dem Stoff" eine Reihe von Verwechslungen nach sich: „des Simplen mit dem Unmittelbaren; der Mitteilung mit dem Bericht; des fotografierten Moments mit dem andauernden Leben; der ‚Aufnahme' mit der Realität". (153) Tatsächlich hält die sachliche Beschreibung Roth zufolge keinerlei Unterscheidungsvermögen bereit, wenn sie den wahrscheinlichen Bericht zugunsten einer Auswahl zufälliger Augenzeugenberichte *ad acta* legt:

> Die Aussage des ‚Augenzeugen', der ‚zufällig anwesend war', klärt noch lange nicht über das Ereignis auf, sondern über ihn selbst, seine Anwesenheit, seine Eindrücke, seine Beobachtungen, sein Verhältnis zum Ereignis. Auch die Aussagen mehrerer Augenzeugen, zueinander addiert, ergeben nicht ein Bild vom Ereignis, sondern die Summe ihrer selbst, ihre Eindrücke und so weiter. (154)

---

7 Ironisch bemerkt Roth, der Begriff der ‚Neuen Sachlichkeit' sei einer genuin deutschen Verwechslung von Voraussetzung und Ziel geschuldet: „Es gab nur ein einziges Land, in dem das Wort von der ‚Neuen Sachlichkeit' erfunden werden konnte: Deutschland. Bei uns wurde (wie oft im Lauf der Geschichte) ein Ziel, was bei den andern primäre Voraussetzung war. Wir sind das einzige Volk, dem die Sachlichkeit ‚neu' erscheinen konnte." (Ebd., S. 158.)

Der „Wirklichkeit des Realismus“ von Zeugenaussagen ist, wie Roth klarstellt, nicht die subjektive Einstellung abträglich, sondern die Objektivitätsbehauptung, die darin besteht, seinen eigenen Standpunkt und mithin die Darstellung selbst unsichtbar zu machen: „Der Berichterstatter ist nicht zufällig anwesend, ist nicht unpersönlich. Auch er ist subjektiv. Aber er trägt die Verantwortung für seine Subjektivität.“ (154)

2. Georg Lukács: Kritik der Typen

Ähnlich wie Joseph Roth ruft auch Georg Lukács in seinem Text „Reportage oder Gestaltung?“[8] die Frage nach der Gestaltung auf den Plan. Zwar werde „[d]ie Tatsache, der individuelle Fall in der guten Reportage in voller sinnlicher Nacherlebbarkeit, konkret und individuell dargestellt, zuweilen sogar gestaltet.“ (40) Gleichwohl unterscheide sich die literarische – und das heißt realistische – Gestaltung des Fallbeispiels von der Gestaltung der Reportage, die illustrativ und verallgemeinernd, beweisend und erklärend auf verstandesmäßiger Erschließung basiert und damit einem quasi-wissenschaftlichen Vorgehen folgt:

> Dieser dargestellte, eventuell gestaltete Einzelfall ist aber hier nur Beispiel, Illustration für den allgemeinen, mehr oder weniger wissenschaftlich, jedenfalls aber begrifflich dargelegten, belegten (statistisch unterbauten), mit Verstandesgründen motivierten allgemeinen Zusammenhang. (40)

Sofern die Reportage „nur verstandesgemäß davon überzeugen [will], daß die Folgerungen, die sie aus den Tatsachen zieht, richtig sind“, arbeitet sie – wie die Publizistik überhaupt – „vorwiegend mit den Methoden der Wissenschaft“ (40). Im Beispielgebrauch der Reportage zeige sich wohl am deutlichsten die Subsumption des gestalteten Materials unter wissenschaftlich begründete Argumente und Begriffe; mit der Unterordnung der Form unter festgelegte Schemata geht die Zufälligkeit und Ersetzbarkeit der Beispiele einher:

> Je besser die Reportage ist, d. h. auf je gründlicherem und umfassenderem Studium sie beruht, einen je größeren und besser durchgearbeiteten Tatsachenkomplex sie umfaßt, je klarer sie darstellerisch ihre ‚Beispiele‘ hinstellt, desto stärker tritt zutage, daß die vorgebrachten Beispiele eben nur Beispiele, nur Illustrationen für die erkannten und dargelegten Zusammenhänge sind; desto austauschbarer sind sie mit anderen Beispielen aus dem großen Arsenal von Tatsachen, Beispielen und Illustrationsfällen, die der Verfasser der Reportage beobachtet, gesammelt und systematisiert hat. Sie müssen freilich typische Fälle sein, um die Zusammenhänge, die aus ihnen gezogenen Folgerungen richtig zu unterbauen und zu beleuchten. (40 f.)

Was Lukács als Schematismus des reportierenden Genres kritisiert, findet er in dem Reportage-Roman von Ottwalt wieder: Hier werde ein umfassendes Bild des Justizwesens mit mathematischer Genauigkeit gezeichnet. Klassenjustiz, so die

---

8 Georg Lukács, „Reportage oder Gestaltung?“, in: ders., *Werke. Band 4. Über Realismus I*, Neuwied, Berlin, 1971, S. 35-55. Im Folgenden werden die Seitenzahlen im laufenden Text angegeben.

von Ottwalt zu beweisende These, äußert sich darin, dass das Urteil der Richter von vorneherein bereits feststeht – ganz unabhängig davon, was der Arbeiter vor Gericht sagt oder tut: „Die Komposition ist also bewußt als Rechenexempel gestellt: anfangs die These, dann der Beweis. Oder als Schachaufgabe: Weiß zieht und gibt in drei Zügen matt." (47) Selbst die Entwicklung des Helden ist der arbeitsteiligen Ordnung des Justizwesens angepasst; sie gleicht einer „Schmetterlingssammlung", in der „mit sauberen Inschriften – sauber aufgespießte Exemplare des Staatsanwalts, des höheren Richters, des kapitalistischen Advokaten usw. zu finden sind." (47 f.) Hier ist „jeder Zufall ausgeschaltet"; jene Erfahrungen, die „nicht vom Schema vorgeschrieben wäre[n]" (48), kommen schlicht und ergreifend nicht vor:

> [A]uf der Universität ein Verhältnis mit einem Handwerkermädel, ein bißchen Teilnahme an Arbeitermord gelegentlich des Kapp-Putsches, Typen von Studenten (Korpsbrüder, einen armen Streber, einen reichen Skeptiker); während der Referendarzeit ein Verhältnis mit einer ‚aufgeklärten', ‚linksgerichteten' Jüdin usw.; als Provinzrichter dito mit einer nymphomanischen Aristokratin, Bekanntschaften mit verschiedenen Typen des Junkertums usw. usw. Es ist wirklich alles da, was der vorgeschriebene Inhalt erfordert, alles ist systematisch geordnet, an die notwendige Stelle gesetzt. (49)

Da also das allgemeine Schema sowohl die Form als auch den Inhalt von Ottwalts Reportage-Roman bestimmt und – mangels der immanenten Konstruktion eines wahrscheinlichen Zusammenhangs – den Verweis auf die Empirie als Beweis seiner Wahrhaftigkeit benötigt, verkommt der Einzelfall zum allgemeinen Typus. So wenig die individuelle Seite des gesellschaftlichen Falls, die Besonderheit des Durchschnittsmenschen in dieser Darstellung gewahrt ist, so wenig wird dem entfremdenden Justizapparat eine Perspektive von unten und der kapitalistischen Maschinerie der Klassenkampf entgegengesetzt. Dies aber wäre Lukács zufolge notwendig, um den gesellschaftlichen Prozess unter Bedingungen kapitalistischer Produktion angemessen zu beschreiben statt die in ihm vollzogene Entfremdung einfach zu verdoppeln. Mag es effektvoll und unter Umständen nützlich sein, das Justizwesen als Maschine zu Report zu bringen, welche den Menschen in unmenschlicher Objektivität und Sachlichkeit zertrümmert, so wird der mechanistische Charakter einer solchen Verallgemeinerung der fetischistischen Grundanschauung dort evident, wo der Reportage-Roman ihn zum kompositionellen Prinzip erhebt. Erschöpft er sich darin, das Justizwesen als fertig gefasstes Gebilde zu schildern, dann wird die „Verselbständigung der Produkte der Gesamtentwicklung" (45) verabsolutiert, der Fetischcharakter total:

> Dann ist nämlich das Justizwesen ein fertiges Produkt, nicht Moment eines Prozesses, das selbst prozessiert, sich im Prozeß entwickelt, sich in steter lebendiger Wechselwirkung mit seinen Voraussetzungen und Folgen befindet, stets lebendiges Resultat der (klassenmäßigen) menschlichen Beziehung jener Menschen ist, deren Tätigkeit ihm selbst als Subjekt und Objekt dient. Starr, mechanisch, von ‚eigenen' Gesetzen (im Kreise) bewegt, steht es im Gegenteil unbezwingbar und unüberwindbar allen Einzelmenschen gegenüber, die diese Maschine teils bedienen, und zwar in

> einer Weise, daß sie selbst zu bloßen Räderchen der Maschinerie werden, teils ihr widerstandslos zum Opfer fallen, etwa wie das Korn von der Mühle zermahlen wird. (45)

Für Lukács stellt sich die Frage nach der Wahrheit des Dargestellten also in jenem Moment, in dem die Wirklichkeit als Entfremdete erscheint. Die Justiz als Ausdruck größtmöglicher Objektivierung und Verdinglichung von Subjekten einerseits, als möglicher Anlass des Klassenkampfs andererseits, wird ihm zum Prüfstein des Realitätsgehalts im Reportage-Roman, also der „Reportage als schöpferischer Methode" (46). Mit der Darstellung des Klassenkampfes das Wesentliche des gesellschaftlichen Lebens offenzulegen, ist das erklärte Ziel. (46) Gerade dieses Ziel zu verfehlen, lastet Lukács der publizistischen Reportage und ihrem Entwurf eines Typisch-Allgemeinen an.

Eine Typenbildung anderer Art wird Lukács in Leo Tolstois Roman *Auferstehung* ausmachen. Auch in ihm steht die Wirklichkeit des Justizwesens, wenn auch des russischen, auf dem Spiel; im „Dichterisch-Typischen" (40) eines Tolstoi kann sich das gesellschaftlich Allgemeine jedoch anders als in der Reportage nur im Umweg über das Individuelle und Besondere erweisen: „In der Gestaltung muß das Individuum, das individuelle Schicksal als solches typisch erscheinen, d. h. die klassenmäßigen Züge als individuelle enthalten." (40 f.) Die Notwendigkeit des Beispiels und die Wahrhaftigkeit der Darstellung verdankt sich hier keineswegs dem empirischen Beweis; sie hat sich immanent zu verifizieren. Bereits für Friedrich Engels und Lenin liegt die Klasse des Realismus eines Romans von Tolstoi in der Art und Weise begründet, in der die Notwendigkeit aus dem Zusammenhang selbst erkennbar wird (44); das Typische des Romans erscheint, um einen Begriff von Walter Benjamin zu verwenden, als eine komplexe „Idee"[9], als das, was Marx eine „Einheit des Mannigfaltigen"[10] bezeichnet hat:

> Die konkrete Gesamtheit der dichterischen Gestaltung verträgt nur Individuen und individuelle Schicksale, die in ihrer lebendigen Wechselwirkung einander beleuchten, ergänzen, vervollständigen, verständlich machen, deren individuelle Verknüpftheit miteinander das Ganze typisch macht. (41)

Eine Perspektive ‚von unten' und eine Perspektive ‚von oben' verschränken sich in dieser Wechselbeleuchtung miteinander. Und nur diese demonstrative Bindung der Justizwirklichkeit an einen sie begründenden und rahmenden Klassenkampf, lässt sie von einer „fetischistisch-erstarrte[n] Erscheinungsform" (46) zu einer ‚wirklichen' Darstellung des gesellschaftlichen Prozesses werden.

Statt also wie Ottwalt unter Rückgriff auf empirisches Material die Justizirrtümer, die Willkür der Justiz oder die Klassenjustiz anzuprangern, demonstriert die kleinste Anekdote aus dem individuellen Leben von Tolstois Held den Klassencha-

---

9 Walter Benjamin, *Ursprung des deutschen Trauerspiels*, in: ders., *Gesammelte Schriften. Band I.1*, hg. von Rolf Tiedemann und Hermann Schweppenhäuser, Frankfurt/M., 1991, S. 203-431: 221.

10 Karl Marx, „Einleitung zu den ‚Grundrissen der Kritik der politischen Ökonomie'", in: ders./Friedrich Engels, *Werke. Band 42 [MEW]*, hg. vom Institut für Marxismus-Leninismus beim ZK der SED, Berlin, 1983, S. 15-47: 35.

rakter der Justiz besser als Ottwalts Reportage-Roman es je könnte. Wenn Tolstoi das Engagement einer Aristokratin beschreibt, die sich wegen eines Flirts dazu hinreißen lässt, ihren Mann um Gnade für einen Inhaftierten politischen Gefangenen zu bitten, der dann vom Kommandanten auch umgehend freigelassen werden kann, „so beleuchten diese Zeilen viel besser, schlagender und vernichtender den ganzen Klassencharakter der Justiz, als hundert Seiten von Daten und Reflexionen (mag ihr Dokumentenmaterial noch so authentisch sein)." (49)

3. Nach Daumier: Tucholskys Typen

Kurt Tucholsky, der ursprünglich selbst eine juristische Laufbahn eingeschlagen und sich 1915 zum Dr. iur. promoviert hatte, bevor seine publizistische Karriere als Hausautor der radikaldemokratisch linksgerichteten Wochenzeitschrift *Schaubühne* – später *Weltbühne* – begann,[11] verarbeitet die politische Wirklichkeit seiner Zeit auf der Grundlage seiner Prozessbeobachtungen: indem er zahlreiche Fälle aus dem juristischen Alltag der Weimarer Republik aufnimmt und in kleine Formen gießt, sie wahlweise lyrisch oder reportierend, lehrstückartig oder im Schwank, mit parodistischem Spott, satirischem Witz oder scharfem politischem Angriff behandelt. Als engagierter Schriftsteller und Publizist, der mit seinen Texten in den öffentlichen Diskurs seiner Zeit einzugreifen versucht, arbeitet Tucholsky bevorzugt mit den Mitteln der Karikatur. Die von Lukács für ihre Beliebigkeit und ihre Verallgemeinerung kritisierte Typisierung gewinnt damit eine über den Idealtypus hinausweisende Qualität. Durch das Überzeichnen (*caricare* von beladen, übertreiben[12]) physiognomischer Merkmale fokussiert die Karikatur auf charakteristische und individuelle Züge, die sie auf ein Allgemeines hin überschreitet.[13] Seit ihrem Entstehen auf der Basis von Lithografie und Vervielfältigungstechniken der Presse ist die Karikatur das Medium einer neuen massenmedialen Öffentlichkeit, in der sie die Funktion der Kritik übernimmt.[14] Sie antwortet auf aktuelle Ereignisse, gesellschaftliche Missstände und Problemlagen und wirkt mit ihrer Bildhaftigkeit ganz unmittelbar demonstrativ auf die Gesellschaft ein. Eine Positionierung, die Tucholskys Texten immer wieder den Vorwurf der Tendenzliteratur eingebracht hat, ist mithin weit mehr als nur die Unterordnung des ästhetischen unter das politische Kalkül. Verkürzung, Akzentuierung und Parteilichkeit lassen seine publizistischen Miniaturen zu einer bildhaften, fast plastischen Kunstform werden. „Auf dem Platz des Vorsitzenden saß ein Greis, mit unange-

---

11 Kurt Tucholsky, „Vita Dr. Tucholsky", in: Heinz Ludwig Arnold (Hg.), *Text und Kritik. Kurt Tucholsky. Band 29*, 1971, S. 1-6: 1.

12 Art. „Karikatur", in: *Reallexikon der Deutschen Literaturwissenschaft. Band 2 (H-O)*, hg. von Klaus Weimar, Berlin, New York, NY, 2000, S. 233-237: 234.

13 Ebd., S. 235.

14 Eduard Fuchs, *Die Karikatur der europäischen Völker. Band 1. Vom Altertum bis zur Neuzeit*, Berlin, 1901, S. 19; Walter Benjamin, *Gesammelte Schriften. Band II.1*, hg. von Rolf Tiedemann und Herrmann Schweppenhäuser, Frankfurt/M., 1991, S. 504.

nehm grünlichen Augen, die Hände fielen mir auf, weiche mißgestaltete, kellerkartoffelgroße Greisenfinger."[15] Mit diesen Worten skizziert Tucholsky den vorsitzenden Richter in einem Prozess gegen den Herausgeber der *Weltbühne* Carl von Ossietzky. Letzterer hatte einen von Tucholsky geschriebenen Artikel zu verantworten. Nach der Schilderung der unzeitgemäßen Erscheinung des Richters, hebt er dessen Gestus treffend aus einer Reihe typischer Haltungen heraus:

> Dieser Richter redete ohne Aufhören anderthalb Stunden. Ich hatte so etwas noch nie in Moabit gesehen. Ich kannte den ironischen Richter, den bösen Richter, den gleichgültigen Richter (dieser kam am häufigsten vor), den gereizten Richter, den ritterlichen Richter (dieser am seltensten) – hier war der redende Richter. Er redete, redete und redete.[16]

Was diese Charakterisierung impliziert, ist klar; sofern der redende Richter auf die Staatsanwälte ebenso verzichten kann wie auf die Rechtsanwälte, auf die zu vernehmenden Zeugen oder die Angeklagten, steht von Vorneherein fest, was die Untersuchung ergeben wird. Jede Frage ist in diesem Prozess eine Scheinfrage, die ihre Antwort schon kennt; die dialogische Erörterung des Tatbestands wird zugunsten der fraglosen Monologführung zu den Akten gelegt. Das heißt: „Während die Hauptverhandlung ja grade dazu dienen soll, den Sachverhalt erst aufzuklären, dem Angeklagten Gelegenheit zur Äußerung und Rechtfertigung zu geben – war hier alles fix und fertig."[17] Zuspitzen wird Tucholsky diese Problematik durch einen komischen Vorschlag:

> Wieder fiel mir das von mir so oft vorgeschlagene Postkartensystem ein. Die Kammer schreibt dem Angeklagten eine Postkarte, ungefähr folgenden Inhalts: ‚Sehr geehrter Herr, wir haben Sie heute wegen Diebstahls zu drei Monaten Gefängnis verurteilt. Hochachtend Die Strafkammer.' Da weiß man doch. Der andere Modus lohnt kaum das Fahrgeld.[18]

Tucholskys Charakterisierung des monologisierenden Richters läuft somit auf die Skizze eines Justizapparats hinaus, dessen Gesprächsbereitschaft reine Show ist, weil das Sprechen vor Gericht ganz offensichtlich einem einseitigen Kommunikationsschema folgt. Durch solch eine Beschreibung werden Gemengelage und Interessengegensätze vor Gericht auf die ideologische Ausrichtung der Beteiligten und die damit zusammenhängenden Umstände hin durchsichtig. Gesellschaftliche Bedingungen werden mithin als wahrhaftige Grundlage des Urteilens ausgemacht und die Justiz als Klassenjustiz dargestellt.

Noch im Jahr 1926 orientiert sich Tucholsky mit Beschreibungen wie diesen am Vorbild des wohl größten Karikaturisten des 19. Jahrhunderts, Honoré Daumier, der seine Lithografien seit 1831/1832 vor allem für die Satirezeitschriften *La Caricature* und *Le Charivari* gefertigt hatte. In einer kurzen Rezension über eine Mappe mit vierzig Steindrucken des großen Daumier aus Philipons, die 1913 im Verlag von

---

15 Kurt Tucholsky, „Erinnerung", in: ders., *Politische Justiz*, Reinbek bei Hamburg, 1970, S. 109-113: 110.

16 Ebd.

17 Ebd., S. 112.

18 Ebd.

Erich Baron unter dem Titel *Recht und Gericht* erschienen war, erläutert Tucholsky, worum es ihm später in seiner Gerichtsberichterstattung gehen wird. „Dieser hier gibt viel mehr als das karikierte Gericht", so der Autor bewundernd: „stets geht er über den Einzelfall hinaus. Er gibt, was es schon zu des Aristides Zeiten gegeben hat: die menschlichen Grimassen, die Geste, das Gehaben bei feierlichen Anlässen – alles."[19] Was dieser Künstler Tucholsky zufolge entdeckt, ist die Wirklichkeit einer juristischen Realität, die – wie auch der Verweis auf den griechischen Rhetor nahelegt – in erster Linie theatral, durch Grimassen, Gesten, Gehabe bestimmt ist, während sie ihren gesellschaftlichen Nutzen zwar behauptet, nicht aber erfüllen kann. „[D]en sinnlosen Selbstzweck erkannt" zu haben, „zu dem eine nützliche Institution wie die Verteidigung vor Gericht geworden ist", erlaubt es Daumier, die Theatralität des Geschehens auszustellen, wobei ihm die Unterbrechung vom fundamentalen Prinzip aller Formgebung zum ästhetischen Mittel ihrer Enttarnung wird. Jede Szene ein eingefrorenes Bild, jeder Ablauf eine Folge von Stills wie sie mit fotografischen Mitteln nicht besser einzufangen wäre:

> Wie die Redner zu weiten, vielversprechenden Gesten ausholen, die dann plötzlich in der Luft stehen bleiben – ein Talar flattert noch im Schwunge, eine Hand dreht sich nach außen, und mit hochgezogenen Nasen siehts die Konkurrenz der Anwälte.[20]

Mit diesen Worten skizziert Tucholsky, was sich mit Benjamin als Erarbeitung eines Gestentableaus beschreiben ließe. „Gesten erhalten wir um so mehr, je häufiger wir einen Handelnden unterbrechen"[21], hatte Benjamin in seinem Aufsatz über das Epische Theater von Brecht erklärt und die gesellschaftskritische Fluchtlinie eines solchen Verfahrens herausgestellt. Ihm galt die „Unterbrechung von Abläufen" als eine an der fotografischen Technik geschulte und auf die „Entdeckung der Zustände" angelegte Methode.[22] Doch wo Benjamin die statische, auf Distanzierung ausgehende Funktion einer Unterbrechung des Bewegten unterstreicht, hebt Tucholsky die dynamische Wirkung der gestischen Unterbrechung hervor:

> Diese Gesten sind wohl das beste in der Mappe: weitgeöffnete Münder. Von Angeklagten, entrüstet hochgezogene Schultern derer, die sich für unschuldig halten, eindringlich gespreizte Finger, und hinter allem ein gewisses Augurenlächeln – Kinder! es ist ja alles nicht so schlimm![23]

---

19 Kurt Tucholsky, „Das Barreau", in: ders., *Politische Justiz*, Reinbek bei Hamburg, 1970, S. 10.
20 Ebd.
21 Benjamin (1991), *Gesammelte Schriften. Band II.1*, S. 521.
22 Ebd., S. 522.
23 Tucholsky (1970), Das Barreau, S. 10.

1 – Honoré Daumier, „Ein Triumph des Advokaten"

Dass Daumier wie kein anderer die Eignung der Karikatur als Mittel der Darstellung einer flüchtigen Moderne herausarbeitet, macht sie in Tucholskys Augen so „gut", so wirklich und wahrhaftig. Ähnlich wie sein Kollege Eisenstein unterstreicht er die zum Widerspruch drängende Spannung von Daumiers Figuren. Ihn interessiert der Umstand, dass jede einzelne ihrer Gesten gesellschaftliche Widersprüche verdichtet und zur Darstellung bringt. Was in Tucholskys Erinnerung insistiert, ist eine Art Traumbild (Abb. 1), das die juristische Situation als unaufgelösten Konflikt zwischen den Protagonisten ausstellt:

> Ein Blatt aber verläßt uns nicht mehr. Der Advokat umarmt das angeklagte Täubchen, auf daß die staunenden Geschworenen sehen sollen, welch ein reiner Prachtmensch das sei. Und während er ihn küßt, daß die Brille gerührt von der bewegten Nase rutscht, zieht der andre ganz leise, ganz vorsichtig, dem Verteidiger der Un-

> schuld die Börse aus der Tasche und die grauen Habichtsaugen sind in träumende Weiten gerichtet.[24]

In einer innigen Umarmung, einer stürmischen Handbewegung oder einem Augurenlächeln erfahren die Komplexität, die spannende Dramatik und Überdeterminiertheit von Daumiers Gesten eine konfliktuelle Zuspitzung. Dies aber ist für die oben aufgeworfene Frage nach der realistischen Darstellung von Fällen zentral. Denn Daumiers Typen, so könnte man sagen, bringen weniger einen individuellen als vielmehr einen gesellschaftlichen Charakter zur Darstellung. Zwar verdankte sich die Entstehung der Karikatur ganz maßgeblich ihren Anleihen bei einer physiognomischen Wissenschaft, die das Besondere des Menschen durch eine biologistische Deutung seines psychischen Innenlebens in sein Äußeres zu projizieren suchte. Wo die Karikatur die Bildsprache der Physiognomie übernahm, modifizierte sie gleichwohl das vorgegebene Interpretationsschema. So stürzten sich die Karikaturisten wie Grandville oder Daumier auf Johann Caspar Lavaters Motiv der Tierwerdung des Menschen, um die biologistische Deutung gleichzeitig in eine gesellschaftliche umzumünzen: „Caricature exploited for its own purpose what was here the illustration of a ‚scientific' doctrine. It turns man into an animal."[25] Wie kein anderer erkannte Daumier, dass die Darstellung gesellschaftlicher Zustände nicht den Menschen selbst, sondern menschliche Beziehungen zu ihrem Gegenstand machen musste. Seine Karikaturen zeichnen nicht das beispielhafte Porträt des Angehörigen einer Klasse, sondern das Porträt des Klassengegensatzes selbst. Damit weichen sie von der Beliebigkeit einer am experimentalwissenschaftlichen Modell orientierten, reportierenden Falldarstellung, die Lukács kritisiert hatte, ebenso ab, wie von der organischen Totalität einer realistischen Gestaltung als deren angeblicher Alternative.

In Eisensteins Daumier-Lektüre wird das besonders deutlich. In einer Zeit, in der die radikalen Montageexperimente der 1920er Jahre zunehmend von den Vertretern eines proletarischen Realismus diskreditiert werden, wendet sich dieser Regisseur der Karikatur zu; zahlreiche Abhandlungen zu Daumier, aber auch eine Rücknahme der Montagetechnik zugunsten der Karikatur in Filmen wie *Ivan der Schreckliche* belegen dies.[26] Indem Eisenstein die Karikatur als quasi-filmisches Verfahren interpretiert – Devin Fore hat von einer „structural equivalence"[27] zwischen den Techniken von Karikatur und Montage gesprochen –, gelingt es ihm nämlich, die organische Figuration des sozialistischen Realismus einerseits mit der mechanistisch-experimentellen Montage einer Kunst der Avantgarden andererseits zu vermitteln.[28] Wie Tucholsky begeistert sich auch Eisenstein für Daumiers

---

24 Ebd.

25 E. H. Gombrich/Ernst Kris, „The Principles of Caricature", in: *British Journal of Medical Psychology*, 17 (1938), S. 319-342, online unter: https://gombricharchive.files.wordpress.com/2011/05/showdoc85.pdf, zuletzt aufgerufen am 20.05.2017.

26 Devin Fore, *Realism after Modernism. The Rehumanization of Art and Literature*, Cambridge, MA, 2012, S. 249.

27 Ebd.

28 Ebd.

visuellen Dynamismus, der die Statik geschlossener Figuren aufbricht, um eine Reihe unterschiedlicher – unter Umständen widersprüchlicher – Momente einer Bewegung in einer einzigen Haltung zusammenzuführen. Am Beispiel von Daumiers Ratapoil (Abb. 2) erläutert Eisenstein, wie Daumier eine Sequenz von sechs unterschiedlichen Bewegungen in der Silhouette einer einzigen Figur verdichtet und damit – einer filmischen Sequenz vergleichbar – eine Kette von Ereignissen in ein einziges Bild [*frame*] übersetzt:

> By the law of *pars pro toto* from the position of the foot you mentally extrapolate the attitude which the entire figure should be taking up at that moment. The same applies to the knee, the neck, and the head, so that in effect the figure drawn in this way is interpreted as if it were six successive ‚frames' of the same figure in the various sequential phases of movement.[29]

Während Ratapoil also auf den ersten Blick der Organizität einer realistischen Figurendarstellung zu entsprechen scheint, ist sein Körper tatsächlich vielfach fragmentiert und gebrochen. Anatomisch sind die Positionen von Knie, Nacken, Kopf, Ellenbogen etc., die diese Figur zu einer Einheit zusammenfasst, schlicht nicht kompatibel, so dass sie in eine Gestentafel zerfällt und als zeitliche Sequenz unterschiedlicher Bewegungen interpretiert werden muss. Der Betrachter ist also gezwungen, eine Vielzahl von Haltungen aus Ratapoils Geste herauszulesen: „Ratapoil's individual body is in fact a multiple".[30] Dies gibt einer gegenläufigen Bewegung Raum: Einerseits wird die statische Ganzheit der realistischen Figurendarstellung durch die Stillstellung von Bewegung in eine dynamische Haltung überführt; andererseits lassen die Theatralität, die Plastizität und Bewegtheit von Daumiers Szenen aufgrund ihrer Vieldimensionalität ein Sitten- und Gesellschaftsbild entstehen, welches selbst Klassen- und Interessenkonflikte impliziert. Die individuelle Geste ist hier zu einem sozialen Gestus geworden sowie der individuelle Typ zur gesellschaftlichen Typage.

---

29 Sergei Eisenstein, *Selected Works. Band 2. Towards a Theory of Montage*, hg. von M. Glanny und R. Taylor, London, 1992, S. 111.

30 Fore (2012), *Realism after Modernism*, S. 251.

2 – Honoré Daumier, „Ratapoil reicht seinen Arm der Republik" (1851)

Auch Tucholskys Karikaturen sind montiert; er lässt sie entstehen, indem er Bilder übereinander legt. So etwa, wenn in einem kurzen Gedicht unter dem Titel „Die Objektiven" (1926) der Skattisch mit dem richterlichen Sitzungstisch und der kommunistenfeindliche Stammtischschwatz mit der Abstrafung von Sozialisten durch das Gerichtsurteil enggeführt wird:

Wenn so fünf Männer Sonnabend abends
um einen runden Tisch herum
den Bierskat kloppen – und sie habens
auch niemals über (wegen dumm) –;
wenn sie von Politike brummeln,
im Maule die Zigarrenstummel,
von Hindenburg und Ludendorffen,
und wie wir fast Paris geworfen,
vom Präsidenten in der Stadt,
der keinen Bohrt wie Wilhelm hat;
wenn sie so zwischen As und Trümpfen
– (‚Wer jibt?') – auf Kommunisten schimpfen –
        die Welt ist eine Kinderfibel,
        das Morgenblatt ist ihre Bibel –;
wenn Lehmann ansagt: ‚Knautschke hats!' –:
        Das nennt man einen Stammtischschwatz.

Doch wenn fünf Männer in Talaren
an einem langen Sitzungstisch
ein Menschenkind da im Verfahren
verknacken frisch und künstlerisch –
was sie als Studios schon forcierten,
geführt von ihren Erstchargierten;
was sie als Referendare lernten:
den Glauben an die reich Besternten;
was der Assessor, scheu geduckt,
dem Staatsanwalte abgeguckt –
wenn diese fünf bei den Prozessen
ihr ganzes Leben glatt vergessen,
        weil Orgeschmann und Sozialist
        für das Gericht dasselbe ist!
wenn da was fällt wie'n Donnerkeil –:
        Das nennt man ein Gerichtsurteil.[31]

Wie reaktionär die Richter der Weimarer Republik dem Kaiserreich verhaftet sind, wie streng sie dessen Moral, dessen Wahrheit und Gesetz zur Geltung bringen, stellt Tucholsky auch in anderen Gedichten parodistisch klar. „Im Namen des Volkes –!" wird hier nur zum Schein verhandelt; „So hat die Urteilsformel sich gewandelt. / Doch wird im alten Ungeist fortverhandelt, / ganz wie in jener Kaiserzeit", als es hieß: „Im Namen des Königs –!"[32] Durch den Gleichklang der Strophen werden Kaiserzeit und Republik ineinander montiert, um das Zerrbild einer vom Volk ausgehenden parlamentarischen Demokratie entstehen zu lassen.

Doch nicht allein das Angesicht der Justiz wird bei Tucholsky mit den Mitteln der Montage karikiert und enthüllt; der Autor Tucholsky selbst wird zur montierten, zur dividuierten und karikierten Gestalt, wie sein Umgang mit Pseudonymen

---

[31] Kurt Tucholsky, „Die Objektiven", in: ders., *Politische Justiz*, Reinbek bei Hamburg, 1970, S. 9.

[32] Kurt Tucholsky, „Zu einigen dieser Prozesse", in: ders., *Politische Justiz*, Reinbek bei Hamburg, 1970, S. 11.

zeigt. Tucholsky ist nur einer von vielen: Ignaz Wrobel, Peter Panter, Theobald Tiger und Kaspar Hauser assistieren ihm, wenn es darum geht, publizistisch ein Bild der militärischen, der juristischen und der politischen Welt der Weimarer Republik und ihres proto-faschistischen Wesens zu zeichnen. Um seine Pseudonyme zu prägen, nimmt Tucholsky, wie er in einem Vorwort zu seinem Band *Mit 5 PS*[33] erläutert, jene „Namen der Paradigmata" (655) auf, die einst sein juristischer Repetitor Siegfried Jacobsohn aus Berlin für die „Kasperlebühne seiner ‚Fälle'" (ebd.) erfunden hatte: „Die Personen, an denen er das Bürgerliche Gesetzbuch und die Pfändungsbeschlüsse und die Strafprozeßordnung demonstrierte, hießen nicht A und B, nicht: Erbe und nicht Erblasser", so Tucholskys Erinnerung (ebd.).

> Sie hießen Benno Büffel und Theobald Tiger; Peter Panter und Isidor Iltis und Leopold Löwe und so durchs ganze Alphabet. Seine Alliterationstiere mordeten und stahlen; sie leisteten Bürgschaft und wurden gepfändet; begingen öffentliche Ruhestörung in Idealkonkurrenz mit Abtreibung und benahmen sich überhaupt recht ungebührlich. (Ebd.)

Tucholsky selbst entscheidet sich, „[z]wei dieser Vorbestraften" mit nach Hause zu nehmen: „– und, statt Amtsrichter zu werden, zog ich sie auf." (Ebd.)

Wenn also Tucholsky die paradigmatischen Figurationen seines alten Lehrers „aufzieht", sie animiert und für seine politischen Zwecke einspannt, wenn er sein Lehr- und Kasperltheater in die mediale Öffentlichkeit bringt und es damit einem viel größeren Publikum zugänglich macht, als das Kasperltheater seines juristischen Mentors es je hätte erreichen können, dann hält er diesem Lehrer auf überraschende Weise die Treue. „Der auf dem Titelblatt und: Ignaz Wrobel. Peter Panter. Theobald Tiger. Kaspar Hauser", so erklärt der Autor: „[W]ir sind fünf Finger an einer Hand." (654) Als solches greifen sie ein; ein jeder auf seinem Fachgebiet, als Experte für eine bestimmte Haltung bekannt, auf sie abonniert und authentisch, glaubwürdig in dieser Hinsicht, kurz: als eine Karikatur einer je spezifischen Sprecherposition oder Expertise:

> Wir wollten uns nicht diskreditieren lassen und taten jeder seins. Ich sah mit ihren Augen, und ich sah sie alle fünf: Wrobel, einen essigsauern, bebrillten, blaurasierten Kerl, in der Nähe eines Buckels und roter Haare; Panter, einen beweglichen, kugelrunden, kleinen Mann; Tiger sang nur Verse, waren keine da, schlief er – und nach dem Kriege schlug noch Kaspar Hauser die Augen auf, sah in die Welt und verstand sie nicht. (654 f.)

Abgesehen von dem ganz praktischen Vorteil, den es hat, in einer von Zensur bedrohten Presse unter Pseudonym zu veröffentlichen, antizipiert Tucholsky mit seinen Pseudonymen die Rezeptionshaltung seiner auf fach- und genrespezifische Lektüre getrimmten Leser:

---

33 Kurt Tucholsky, „Start", in: ders., *Gesamtausgabe. Texte und Briefe. Band 9: 1927*, hg. von Antje Bonitz, Dirk Grathoff, Michael Hepp und Gerhard Kraiker, Reinbek bei Hamburg, 1998, S. 654-657. Im Folgenden werden die Seitenzahlen im laufenden Text angegeben.

> Und es war auch nützlich, fünfmal vorhanden zu sein – denn wer glaubt in Deutschland einem politischen Schriftsteller Humor? dem Satiriker Ernst? dem Verspielten Kenntnis des Strafgesetzbuches, dem Städteschilderer lustige Verse? Humor diskreditiert. (654)

Zusammen können Tucholskys „homunculi" dem Leser jedoch problemlos unterschiedliche Perspektiven und Stile erschließen. Als Karikaturen (oder Typen) einer arbeitsteilig differenzierten Welt mit wenigen Handstrichen gezeichnet, prägen Tucholskys Autor-Ichs gemeinsam eine kritische Perspektive aus, die nicht nur komplex, sondern sogar widersprüchlich sein kann: „Eine Fehde zwischen ihnen wäre durchaus möglich. Sie dauert schon siebenunddreißig Jahre." (655)

Was Tucholsky mit dem Auftritt seiner ‚homunculi' inszeniert, ist weniger die Klassifizierung seiner Selbst als schizophrener Fall, als vielmehr die Eröffnung der politischen Bühne seines Schreibens. Allein das montierte Selbst des Autors Tucholsky kann zum Schauplatz eines polyfonen und konfliktgeladenen Sprechens werden. In demselben Maße, in dem die prototypischen Ich-Figurationen Tucholskys miteinander in Dialog treten, sich mitunter widersprechen und auf diese Weise einen vielstimmigen Diskurs – Öffentlichkeit – entstehen lassen, lässt die Sammlung von Fallbeispielen lyrischer und reportierender, humoresker und satirischer, polemischer und fachlich informierter Texte ein komplexes Gesellschaftsbild entstehen. Entscheidend ist aber, dass dabei kein konsensuelles, sondern ein dissensuelles Bild entsteht. Der Typensammler Tucholsky vermeidet es, gesellschaftliche Widersprüche in der von Lukács kritisierten Beliebigkeit von Fällen untergehen zu lassen. Bewertung und kritisches Urteilsvermögen sind seiner Typisierung insofern eingeschrieben, als er jeden Einzelfall als karikierende Zuspitzung eines wesentlichen Zuges innerhalb eines konfliktuellen Feldes entwirft.

Durch solche Zuspitzung kann die Karikatur, wenn wir Theodor W. Adorno glauben, zum Werkzeug einer intellektuellen Tätigkeit werden. Denn Adorno hatte Daumiers Karikaturen als philosophisches Werkzeug verstanden, das „die Hülle der Gleichheit physiognomisch zu durchschlagen" versucht.[34] Das unterscheidende Detail gegenüber der Uniform maßlos herauszutreiben, wie es der physiognomische Blick – und nach seinem Vorbild die Daumier'sche Karikatur – vermag, hat demnach „keine andere Bedeutung als das Besondere im Allgemeinen zu retten".[35] Adornos Einschätzung mag zuerst einmal verwundern, scheint die Karikatur jene Gleichheit, die sie durch Übertreibung durchbricht, doch im gleichen Zuge wieder einzurichten, wenn sie die Normalität des Typus installiert: „[D]enn je weiter eine groteske Nase von der Norm entfernt ist, desto besser wird sie als Nase schlechthin das Typische des benasten Menschen zeigen", bemerkt Adorno selbst.[36] Entscheidend sei aber, dass die in Daumiers Karikaturen projektierte Gleichheit des Normalmenschen oder Typus immer nur als theatrale und komische Geste zu haben

---

34 Adorno an Benjamin, New York, 01. Februar 1939, in: Benjamin (1991), *Gesammelte Schriften. Band 1.3*, S. 1107-1114: 1110 f.

35 Ebd.

36 Ebd., S. 1115.

ist: „Daumiers Gelächter gilt vielmehr der Bürgerklasse; er durchschaut die Gleichheit, mit der sie prunkt: nämlich als die windige égalité, wie sie sich im Beinamen Louis Philippes breitmachte."[37] Keine hundert Jahre später werden Tucholskys publizistische Karikaturen nach dem Vorbild Daumiers eine andere Gerechtigkeit anprangern und verwitzeln: die Gerechtigkeit der Weimarer Republik, die zwar zu fragen vorgab, tatsächlich aber ihre Antworten bereits parat hatte, die dialogisch zu untersuchen behauptete, in Wirklichkeit aber monologisierte, die „im Namen des Volkes" zu richten erklärte, *de facto* aber den Gesetzmäßigkeiten einer Klassenjustiz folgte – durchgesetzt im Korpsgeist derjenigen, die einst im Namen des Kaisers angetreten waren, ihre Normen und Vorstellungen beibehalten hatten und noch in der Zwischenkriegszeit „im Namen des Königs" entschieden. So scharf der politische Publizist Tucholsky diese Justizwirklichkeit anprangerte, so sehr wurde sie von Ignaz Wrobel mit Zynismus gestraft, von Peter Panter spielerisch erkundet, von Kaspar Hauser durch Unverständnis verfremdet und von Theobald Tiger reimend verlacht. Wenn also E. H. Gombrich und Ernst Kris sehr richtig bemerken, dass „caricature, showing more of the essential, is truer than reality itself"[38], dann wäre mit Tucholsky zu ergänzen, dass die Karikatur allein in einem seriellen Format wie der Zeitung eine nicht nur komplexe und dialogische, sondern gleichsam dissensuelle Struktur entwickeln kann, die für diesen Wahrheitsanspruch verantwortlich ist.

4. Politische Groteske – groteske Realität

Seinen Mehrwert gewinnt das karikierende Schreiben, das oben als Typage besonderer Art beschrieben worden ist, in Tucholskys Gerichtsreportagen jedoch nicht allein als intellektuelles Werkzeug eines engagierten Autors. Wenn Tucholsky die Welt als groteske Karikatur darstellt, kommt der Wortsinn von *caricare* – beladen, übertreiben – im mehrfachen Sinne zur Geltung: Übertreibung wird einerseits als Stilmittel einer kritisch verfremdenden Methode und als Haltung eines kritischen, das Wesentliche zur Geltung bringenden Geistes eingesetzt; gleichzeitig ist sie Effekt einer in der Wirklichkeit selbst angelegten Verzerrung: Nicht Gerechtigkeit, sondern die äußerste Verzerrung gerechter Maßstäbe wird in der Rechtspraxis durchgesetzt. An jenem Punkt also, an dem die Karikatur und die Groteske[39] inei-

---

[37] Ebd.

[38] Gombrich/Kris (1938), The Principles of Caricature.

[39] Der Begriff Groteske [*grottesche*], abgeleitet von *grotta*, ‚im Stil der Grottenmalerei' etabliert sich im europäischen Kontext um 1530; er dient zuerst der Beschreibung einer antike Vorbilder imitierenden Malerei, wird dann als Bezeichnung ornamentaler Muster (von Tapeten, Schmuck, Schnitzwerk, Goldarbeiten oder Buchillustrationen) gebraucht und schließlich zunehmend auf die Beschreibung von Schreibstilen, tänzerischen oder künstlerischen Ausdrucksformen wie der Farce, der Komödie, das komische Epos oder den Roman übertragen. Während die Groteske im 15. Jahrhundert das Ornamentale und das Monströse ästhetisch miteinander verschmelzen lässt, zeichnet sich im 18. Jahrhundert eine Ausdifferenzierung zwischen dem Ästhetisch-Erhabenen

nander fallen, erscheint die Realität der beschriebenen Institution und der Gesellschaftsformation, die sie stützt: ihrer Macht- und Herrschaftsverhältnisse.

Schaustück der politischen Groteske eines Gerichtsprozesses ist für Tucholsky „Der Prozess Harden".[40] Als Sohn jüdischer Eltern und Kriegsgegner war Maximilian Harden am 3. Juli 1922 vor seinem Haus in Berlin-Grunewald zum Opfer eines von Anhängern der Freikorps verübten Attentats geworden. Über den darauffolgenden Prozess ist der Prozessbeobachter Tucholsky empört. Grotesk ist nach seiner Schilderung zuerst einmal der Umstand, dass der politische Mord einem klaren Schema folgt: „Der deutsche politische Mord der letzten vier Jahre ist schematisch und straff organisiert. Die Broschüre: ‚Wie werde ich in acht Tagen ein perfekter nationaler Mörder?' sollte nicht auf sich warten lassen."[41] Der Betriebscharakter des Mordens schlägt sich in diesem Schematismus nieder:

> Alles steht von vorneherein fest: Anstiftung durch unbekannte Geldgeber, die Tat (stets von hinten), schludrige Untersuchung, faule Ausreden, ein paar Phrasen, jämmerliches Kneifertum, milde Strafen, Strafaufschub, Vergünstigungen – ‚Weitermachen!'[42]

Unangemessen wie diese politische Normalität, die vor Gericht nicht bestraft, sondern vielmehr begünstigt wird, ist der Modus dieser juristischen Befragung, die sich weniger als Vernehmung, denn als Kaffeeklatsch gestaltet: „Man hatte mit ihnen [den Angeklagten] geplaudert; und nett geplaudert", so die groteske Realität: „Keine Vorhaltungen, keine Bedrängungen, kein böses Wort – nichts."[43] Ebenso vermessen wie diese Verhörsituation ist der Umstand, dass die Angeklagten nicht allein von ihren Anwälten, sondern auch von dem vorsitzenden Richter verteidigt werden, während der Staatsanwalt schlicht nicht existent zu sein scheint: „An seiner Stelle saß ein älterer Herr, der mit leiser Stimme und freundlichen Allüren hier und da vorsichtig in die Verhandlung eingriff. Einmal, stockend: ‚Die Mordtaten, wie ich sie nenne ...'"[44]. So unangemessen diese Behandlung der eines Mordversuchs Bezichtigten und so deutlich ihre Schuld, so willkürlich zuletzt das Urteil: „Es lagen vor: mündliche und schriftliche Geständnisse beider, in denen die Worte ‚Erledigen', ‚Beseitigen' und ‚Töten' klar und deutlich enthalten sind. Zusammen: ein paar Jahre Gefängnis. Der Angeklagte Harden kann gehen."[45]

Fragen wir nach dem Status der Groteske in diesem Bericht über eine Gerichtsverhandlung, so dient sie ganz offensichtlich nicht in erster Linie der kritischen Verfremdung, der Verunglimpfung oder Beleidigung, noch ist sie der Fehlfunktion

---

und dem Niedrig-Fürchterlichen ab. (Art. „Grotesk", in: *Reallexikon der Deutschen Literaturwissenschaft*, hg. von Klaus Weimar, Berlin, New York, NY, 1997, S. 745-751: 746 f.)

40 Kurt Tucholsky, „Der Prozess Harden", in: ders., *Politische Justiz*, Reinbek bei Hamburg, 1970, S. 97-106.

41 Ebd., S. 98.

42 Ebd.

43 Ebd., S. 101.

44 Ebd., S. 102.

45 Ebd., S. 105.

innerhalb des institutionellen Apparats oder einem Unfall in der Geschichte geschuldet. In diesem Gericht ist die Groteske dem Funktionieren der Macht selbst inhärent. Grotesk ist jene Maßstabsverzerrung, die den organisierten Mord rechtfertigt, die Mörder freispricht und das Mordopfer im Laufe des Prozesses zum Angeklagten werden lässt.[46] Als politischer Prognostiker hatte Tucholsky früher und klarsichtiger als die meisten seiner Zeitgenossen die Kontinuitäten erkannt, welche die Justizwirklichkeit der Weimarer Republik mit der Gesetzgebung des Kaiserreichs, aber auch mit der nahenden faschistischen Terrorherrschaft verband. Seine Grotesken der Juristerei zeigen diese Weitsichtigkeit auf frappante Weise. Denn während die Groteske ganz offensichtlich zu den wesentlichen Verfahren der Willkürherrschaft gehört – später haben dies Charlie Chaplin in seinem Film *The Great Dictator* (1940) oder Brecht in seinem Drama *Der Aufstieg des Arturo Ui* (1941) ausgestellt –, ist sie gleichzeitig, wenn auch weniger offensichtlich, der bürokratischen Macht, ihren Verfahren und ihrer Funktionsweise eingeschrieben. Michel Foucault bemerkt dies in Auseinandersetzung mit dem, was er als groteske oder „ubueske" Macht bezeichnet:

> Daß die Verwaltungsmaschine mit ihren unumgänglichen Machteffekten durch die Hände eines mittelmäßigen, untauglichen, dummen, schuppigen, lächerlichen, abgearbeiteten, armen und ohnmächtigen Beamten läuft, all das gehörte zu den wesentlichen Zügen der großen westlichen Bürokratien seit dem 19. Jahrhundert.[47]

Das verwaltungsmäßige Groteske ist bei Honoré de Balzac, Fjodor M. Dostojewski, Georges Courteline und am prominentesten wohl bei Franz Kafka beschrieben worden. Dabei leitet das „Prinzip des fehlenden Grunds", wie Joseph Vogls Kafka-Lektüre beweist, die Komik jener politischen Groteske an, die der Versicherungsangestellte Kafka klarsichtig in den bürokratischen Apparaten am Werke sieht[48]:

> Vom Schrecken heimlicher Folterszenen bis zu kindischen Beamten, vom Schmutz der Kanzleiwelt bis zu atavistischen Machtritualen reicht bei ihm eine Spur, die mit ihrem komischen Element stets das Grundlose, das Willkürliche im Vollzug von Macht und Herrschaft markiert.[49]

---

46 Ihre schärfste Zuspitzung erfährt Tucholskys Schilderung der willkürlichen, politisch aber durchaus motivierten Gerichtsentscheide, durch einen Vergleich der Strafmaße, die für rechte Fememorde auf der einen Seite und linkspolitisch motivierte Morde auf der anderen Seite verhängt wurden: „Für 314 Morde von rechts 31 Jahre 3 Monate Freiheitsstrafe, sowie eine lebenslängliche Festungshaft. Für 13 Morde von links 8 Todesurteile, 176 Jahre 10 Monate Freiheitsstrafe. / Das ist alles Mögliche. Justiz ist das nicht. / Ganz klar wird das, wenn wir das Schicksal der beiden Umsturzversuche: Kapps und der münchner Kommunisten vergleichen, zweier Versuche, die sich juristisch in nichts unterscheiden: / Die Kommunisten haben für ihren Hochverrat 519 Jahre 9 Monate Freiheitsstrafe erhalten. Eine Todesstrafe hat man vollstreckt. / Die Kapp-Leute sind frei ausgegangen." (Kurt Tucholsky, „Das Buch von der deutschen Schande", in: ders., *Politische Justiz*, Reinbek bei Hamburg, 1970, S. 85-90: 89.)

47 Michel Foucault, *Die Anormalen*, Frankfurt/M., 2013, S. 29.

48 Joseph Vogl, „Kafkas Komik", in: *Kontinent Kafka. Mosse-Lectures an der Humboldt-Universität zu Berlin*, Berlin, 2006, S. 73-88: 86.

49 Ebd.

Insofern das Lächerliche und Bizarre, das Clowneske und das Liederliche, der Blödsinn oder die schlichte Gemeinheit die Verteilung von Willküreffekten in den Organisationstypen moderner Institutionen anzeigen, sei das Groteske, so Vogls Fazit, „zu einer Kategorie der historisch-politischen Analyse" geworden.[50] Dies hat Kafka ebenso wie der Kafka-Fan Tucholsky verstanden.[51] Kaum weniger aussichts- und grundlos, kaum weniger brutal und komisch als die Lage des Angeklagten K. in Kafkas *Prozess* ist die Lage des Angeklagten Autors Tucholsky in einer Verhandlung, in der er sich selbst zusammen mit dem Herausgeber der *Weltbühne* Ossietzky wegen einer längst korrigierten Fehldarstellung verantworten und gegen den Vorwurf der Beleidigung verteidigen muss:

> Vor der Tür des Verhandlungszimmers stand der Gerichtsdiener. Er sah nach der Uhr, es war fünf Minuten vor Beginn unserer Sache. ‚Ihr Anwalt noch nich da?' fragte er uns. Nein, der war noch nicht da. ‚Na, is ejal!' sagte der Engel des Gerichts. ‚Der kann Ihnen ooch nich helfen!'.[52]

In Tucholskys Schilderung fungiert die Groteske also nicht allein als Zeichen der Entfremdung, als die sie so häufig – prominent etwa von Wolfgang Kayser[53] – gelesen wurde, sondern als Signum moderner Macht wie sie von Benjamin in seinem Essay „Zur Kritik der Gewalt" geschildert wurde: Es ist die Wirklichkeit eines juristischen Apparats, in dem die rechterhaltende von einer rechtsetzenden Macht abhängt, hier wird die Einschreibung des mythischen Grundes in das moderne Rechtssystem inszeniert.[54] Die Groteske wäre vor diesem Hintergrund ganz im Sinne Carl Einsteins als eine Form des „mythischen Realismus" zu beschreiben.[55]

Wie in diesem Punkt Rechtskunde und Formkunde miteinander kulminieren, ist leicht verständlich: In der Groteske wird die *ent*staltende Macht der Phantasie, wie Benjamin an anderer Stelle bemerkt hatte, durch eine Macht ersetzt, die „zerstörend überstaltet": „Die Groteske ist eine Grenzform im Bereich der Phantasie, sie steht, wo diese an ihrer äußersten Grenze wieder Gestaltung zu werden sucht."[56] Der visuelle Dynamismus, den sowohl Eisenstein als auch Tucholsky an Daumier so bewundert hatten, stellt sich nunmehr als ein dem modernen Denken

---

50 Ebd.

51 Anton Häflinger, *Kurt Tucholsky als Kulturkritiker*, Dissertation vorgelegt an der Universität Freiburg in der Schweiz, Juni 1971, S. 131.

52 Tucholsky (1970), Erinnerung, S. 110.

53 Wolfgang Kayser, *Das Groteske*, Oldenburg, Hamburg, 1957, S. 198.

54 In Benjamins Überlegungen zur „Kritik der Gewalt" heißt es: „[W]ie der Ausgang, so verweist auch der Ursprung jeden Vertrages auf Gewalt. Sie braucht als rechtsetzende zwar nicht unmittelbar in ihm gegenwärtig zu sein, aber vertreten ist sie in ihm, sofern die Macht, welche den Rechtsvertrag garantiert, ihrerseits gewaltsamen Ursprungs ist, wenn sie nicht eben in jenem Vertrag selbst durch Gewalt rechtmäßig eingesetzt wird. Schwindet das Bewußtsein von der latenten Anwesenheit der Gewalt in einem Rechtsinstitut, so verfällt es." (Walter Benjamin, „Zur Kritik der Gewalt", in: ders., *Gesammelte Schriften. Band II.1*, hg. von Rolf Tiedemann und Hermann Schweppenhäuser, Frankfurt/M., 1991, S. 179-203: 190.)

55 Vgl. Fore (2012), *Realism after Modernism*, S. 233.

56 Walter Benjamin, „Zur Ästhetik", in: ders., *Gesammelte Schriften. Band VI.*, hg. von Rolf Tiedemann und Hermann Schweppenhäuser, Frankfurt/M., 1991, S. 109-130: 115.

inhärentes, ihm entspringendes und nach seinem Vorbild geprägtes Formprinzip dar.

Wenden wir uns mit Auerbach an einen jener Autoren, die der Groteske eine hervorragende Position in ihren realismustheoretischen Auseinandersetzungen eingeräumt haben, so bestätigt sich diese Einschätzung. Wie Auerbach mit Blick auf Michail Michailowitsch Bachtin erläutert, erlaubt es die der Groteske eigene Poetik der „Stilmischung"[57], unterschiedlichste Perspektiven miteinander zu verbinden und die kleine Welt „in Pantagruels Mund" in einer Komplexität zu beschreiben, die der Realität der wirklichen Welt entspricht: „[S]o daß die ganze Maschinerie der ungeheuren Proportionen und der kühnen Entdeckungsreisen nur in Gang gesetzt worden zu sein scheint, um uns einen Bauern aus der Touraine beim Kohlpflanzen vorzuführen."[58] Auerbach attestiert Bachtins Grotesken einen gelehrten Ernst, der in einer „mit allen Möglichkeiten schwangeren, jedes wirkliche und überwirkliche Experiment wagenden Entdeckerfreude"[59] liegt. Und was könnte der flüchtigen Moderne angemessener sein als eine solchermaßen experimentelle Haltung, die er in dem darauffolgenden Kapitel bei dem paradigmatischen Autor eines erprobenden Schreibens, nämlich Michel de Montaigne, ausmachen wird? „Mimesis besteht eben", wie Friedrich Balke es formuliert hat, „in dieser Erzeugung einer ‚monströsen' Unähnlichkeit innerhalb der Ähnlichkeit".[60]

Es verwundert nicht, dass Auerbach den grotesken Realismus zwar als modernes, nicht aber als epochenspezifisches Phänomen interpretiert. Für ihn ist dieser Realismus eine dem modernen Denken entsprechende „Schreibhaltung"[61], deren figurative Voraussetzung er einige Jahre vorher in seinem „Figura"-Aufsatz erläutert hat.[62] Es handelt sich um eine Figuration, welche die geschlossene Figur aufschließt, indem sie den Text, die Plastik oder andere Figuren an eine Figuraldeutung bindet und somit die Präsenz des Präsentierten auf eine kommende Gemeinschaft bezieht[63]:

> In der figuralen Interpretation verkörpert die Figur nicht allein sich selbst und ihre eigene gegenwärtige Realität, sondern zugleich eine Person, eine Auffassung oder ein Ereignis, das erst in der Zukunft eintritt. Die *figura* ist ‚hier und jetzt' zugleich aber auch ‚noch nicht'. Sie zeigt deshalb eine Offenheit – die Möglichkeit einer Verände-

---

57 Erich Auerbach, *Mimesis. Dargestellte Wirklichkeit in der abendländischen Literatur*, Bern, München, 1946, S. 258.

58 Ebd.

59 Ebd., S. 270.

60 Friedrich Balke, „Mimesis und Figura. Erich Auerbachs niederer Materialismus", in: ders./Hanna Engelmeier (Hg.), *Mimesis und Figura*, Paderborn, 2016, S. 13-89: 43.

61 Galili Shahar, „Auerbachs Narben. Der Monotheismus und die Frage der Literatur", in: Nicolas Berg/Dieter Burdorf (Hg.), *Textgelehrte: Literaturwissenschaft und literarisches Wissen im Umkreis der Kritischen Theorie*, Göttingen, 2014, S. 329-353: 335.

62 Ebd., S. 333; vgl. Friedrich Balke/Hanna Engelmeier, „Vorbemerkung", in: dies. (Hg.), *Mimesis und Figura*, Paderborn, 2016, S. 7-13.

63 Balke (2016), Mimesis und Figura, S. 21.

> rung in der Zeit, die Möglichkeit des Werdens, in dem das Selbst zum Anderen wird. Die Gegenwart bleibt hier ‚offen und fraglich' und ‚weist auf etwas noch Verhülltes'.[64]

Gerade weil „*figura* […] sinnlicher und beweglicher als *forma*"[65] ist, kann Auerbach sie zur Prägung eines neuen und flexibleren Formbegriffs heranziehen. Die Groteske entwirft er als Repräsentationsmodus, der einem solchen Formbegriff – mit den vormals beschriebenen Mitteln der Stilmischung und der deformierenden Transposition einer Gestalt in eine andere – Rechnung trägt. Den Fluchtpunkt der viel beschworenen „Kombination von Heterogenitäten"[66] in der Groteske bildet somit ein Gestaltwandel, ein Exzess der Lächerlichkeit, eine Metamorphose, die auch Tucholsky und Eisenstein an Daumiers Karikaturen so fasziniert hatte: „Just as the grotesque showcases Phaeton's sisters being changed into trees or Actaeon becoming a stag, caricature turns an envious man into an owl or a king into a pear."[67] Was Karikatur und Groteske verbindet, ist die Freisetzung jenes unheimlichen Moments, „when objects suddenly twist themselves into other shapes", um fortan „on the threshold of two meanings" zu stehen.[68] Es geht also um das, was Eisenstein in seinen Überlegungen *On Disney* als eine „transformation of stable forms into forms of mobility"[69] bezeichnet, bei den großen Karikaturisten des 19. Jahrhunderts bewundert, und in seinen Filmgrotesken realisiert hat; es geht um ein Aufschließen der geschlossenen Figur und um eine Dynamisierung des Statischen, die er als ein Echo des prä-logischen Affekts und des mythischen Denkens in der formalen Logik und dem ‚logical case' verstanden wissen wollte[70]. Und es bleibt zu fragen, ob die Groteske, indem sie ein Modell der Figuration liefert, zu einer Art Metarealismus avanciert.

Nun wäre es übertrieben, Tucholskys publizistische Versuche über das Gericht, seine epischen Verse und Reportagen, seinen komödiantischen Schwank und sein strenges Lehrgedicht, seine bösen Satiren und politischen Aufrufe als eine Stilmischung zu beschreiben, wie sie uns aus dem grotesken Realismus eines Dante, Bachtin oder Montaigne bekannt ist. Mit der publizistischen Verbreitung seiner Texte scheint Tucholsky gleichwohl ein Medium gefunden zu haben, mit dessen Hilfe er Multiperspektivität und Akzentverschiebung in ein ästhetisches und poli-

---

64 Galili Shahar, „Auerbachs Narben. Der Monotheismus und die Frage der Literatur", in: Nicolas Berg/Dieter Burdorf (Hg.), *Textgelehrte: Literaturwissenschaft und literarisches Wissen im Umkreis der Kritischen Theorie*, Göttingen, 2014, S. 329-353: 333.

65 Erich Auerbach, „Figura", Neuedition des Textes von 1938, in: Friedrich Balke/Hanna Engelmeier (Hg.), *Mimesis und Figura*, Paderborn, 2016, S. 121-189: 126.

66 Art. „Grotesk" (1997), S. 745.

67 Virginia E. Swain, *Grotesque Figure. Baudelaire, Rousseau, and the Aesthetics of Modernity*, Baltimore, MD, London, S. 77.

68 Werner Hofmann, *Caricature from Leonardo to Picasso*, New York, NY, 1957, S. 28. Auf diese Schnittmenge machen auch Gombrich und Kris aufmerksam: „It is obvious how near the caricaturist's work of transformation comes to the grotesque-maker's task. The Rabelais woodcuts transformed implements into human beings. The Carracci transformed the portraits of their friends into pots, lanterns or barrels." (Gombrich/Kris (1938), The Principles of Caricature.)

69 Sergej Eisenstein, *On Disney*, hg. von Jay Leyda, Calcutta, 1986, S. 21.

70 Ebd., S. 23.

tisches Programm überführen kann. Während er sich selbst in ein montiertes Wesen, in ein Konglomerat von Typen oder Pseudonymen verwandeln muss, um ein Bild der grotesken Gerichtswirklichkeit der 1920er Jahre zu zeichnen, so hat er mit der Zeitung das ideale Publikationsorgan für sein Vorhaben gefunden: es besetzt den Ort, an dem öffentliche Debatten ausgetragen werden, an dem der hohe auf den niederen Stil trifft und die Akzente aneinanderprallen, an dem die Kunst in das Leben eingreifen und der Publizist zum engagierten Autor werden kann.

Ich möchte abschließend auf einen Aspekt von Tucholskys Typen zu sprechen kommen, der uns bisher entgangen ist. Denn das Motiv der grotesken Verwandlung findet sich in seinen ‚homunculi' parodistisch gewendet. Mit Theobald Tiger und Peter Panter hat Tucholsky zwei seiner vier Pseudonyme als Mischwesen zwischen Mensch und Tier entworfen, während er mit Kaspar Hauser das Paradigma eines Geschöpfes gewählt hat, das – weder Mensch noch Tier – der symbolischen Ordnung fremd ist. Ob Ignaz Wrobel in Anlehnung an ein Fabelwesen mit menschlichen Zügen entstanden ist, muss zwar dahingestellt bleiben. So zynisch wie der aggressive kleine Mäuserich Ignatz, der als steinewerfender Liebling von „Krazy Kat" aus Herrimans gleichnamigem Comicstrip seit 1913 in den Vereinigten Staaten Furore macht, ist Ignaz jedoch allemal. Dass Tucholskys Typen den Menschen nicht einer ersten, sondern einer zweiten Natur anverwandeln, legt bereits die Rede von seinen ‚homunculi' nah. So bezeichnet der Homunculus (von lateinisch ‚Menschlein') einen künstlich geschaffenen Menschen. Der alchemistischen Theoriebildung des Spätmittelalters entsprungen, erscheint dieser dämonische Helfer magischer Praktiken in der Literatur nicht selten als Sinnbild der Ambivalenz einer technischen Moderne.

Wie vermittelt die Verwandlung des Menschen in den grotesken Typus ist, zeigt sich auch in einer Karikatur von John Heartfield (Abb. 3), die sich in Tucholskys Band *Deutschland, Deutschland über alles!* findet. In ihm hatte Tucholsky Gedichte und Artikel versammelt, die er, inspiriert von Heartfields Fotomontagen, für die *Arbeiter Illustrierte Zeitung* geschrieben hatte. Während Tucholskys Text „Deutsche Richter" eine Typenbeschreibung des deutschen Richters abgibt, die sich als Generalabrechnung mit der grotesken Klassenjustiz der Weimarer Republik liest, stellt sich Heartfields Richterkarikatur in mehrfacher Hinsicht als Reflexion auf das karikierende Verfahren dar: Ein der Richterrobe einmontierter Paragrafenleib veranschaulicht, wie sich der lebendige menschliche Leib in einen Korpus aus (Schrift-)Typen verwandelt. Heartfields Richter als Paragrafenmonster zu interpretieren, das Kopf und Hand in den Dienst des Gesetzestextes stellt, ist naheliegend. Gehen wir jedoch der Bedeutung des Paragrafen als Schrifttypus nach, dann lässt sich Heartfields Entwurf als Karikatur eines Verfahrens lesen, in dem der Körper buchstäblich zum Typus wird, also als Karikatur des Karikierens selbst. Zum-Typus-Werden impliziert dabei nicht allein, dass sich das karikierende Verfahren – wie oben mit Eisenstein beschrieben – der Montagetechnik bedient; es zeigt auch, dass sich die Karikatur als eine „Mischgattung" bestimmen lässt, deren Lebendigkeit der Spannung zwischen Wort und Bild entspringt.[71] Und es verdeutlicht drittens, dass die Karikatur ihre demonstrative Schlagfertigkeit und ihre soziale Tragweite durch ihren Witz gewinnt. Witz stellt sich dort ein, wo das Spiel der Bilder durch ein Wortspiel supplementiert wird, das die karikierte Gestalt zum Symbol werden lässt.

3 – John Heartfield, „Ich kenne nur Paragraphen"

Bereits die Wirksamkeit des königlichen Birnenkopfes von Louis-Philippe, die – von Charles Philipon für die von ihm herausgegebene Zeitschrift *La Caricature* entworfen und von Daumier umgesetzt – zu einem der beliebtesten Motive der Karikaturisten des 19. Jahrhunderts werden sollte, verdankte sich einer doppelten Bedeutung; denn im Pariser Slang bedeutete ‚poire'/‚Birne' dasselbe wie ‚Dummkopf'. Als solches wurde die Birne zum Schlagwort, zum Symbol im Kampf des französischen Volks für ihre Freiheit.[72] Sowohl die Überdeterminiertheit des König-

[71] Art. „Karikatur" (2000), S. 235.
[72] Gombrich/Kris (1938), The Principles of Caricature.

lichen Birnenkopfes von Philipon als auch die Doppeldeutigkeit des von Heartfield entworfenen richterlichen Paragrafen-/Typenkopfes lassen die Karikatur zu einem „graphischen Witz“[73] werden. Dessen soziale Funktion verdankt sich jedoch, wie wir gesehen haben, nicht allein dem Umstand, dass der Witz mit der „komische[n] Entlastung“[74] eine sozial anerkannte Form von Regression und Aggression realisiert, sondern auch der Transformation des individuellen in einen sozialen Typus, welche die Typologie des sozialen Lebens offenlegt. „Hier ist gelacht worden, wenn andere gedonnert haben“[75], fasst Tucholsky treffend die antifaschistische Haltung der Mitarbeiter und Leser der *Weltbühne* zusammen – eine Haltung, die den Gegner so sehr reizte, dass er Herausgeber und Mitarbeiter mit immer neuen Anklagen überzog.

73 Ebd.

74 Art. „Karikatur“ (2000), S. 234.

75 Kurt Tucholsky, „Für Carl v. Ossietzky“, in: ders., *Politische Justiz*, Reinbek bei Hamburg, 1970, S. 106-109: 108.

Ulrich Plass

Nach Lukács: Realistische Schreibweisen in Krachts *Imperium* und Sebalds *Die Ringe des Saturn*

In einem Brief an Georg Lukács im Juni 1938 kritisiert Anna Seghers die in der Moskauer Exilzeitschrift *Das Wort* geführte Debatte über expressionistische Kunst. Ausgangspunkt dieser Debatte war eine marxistische Kritik am Expressionismus als Symptom der Krise des Kapitalismus und der „Lösung" dieser Krise durch den Faschismus. Seghers bemängelt, dass die Begrifflichkeit von Realität und Realismus unscharf bleibe:

> In Eurer Diskussion wird die ganze Terminologie sehr verschieden und oft ungenau gebraucht. Es geht unter anderem durcheinander: Realismus *heute* oder Realismus *überhaupt*, also Richtung auf die der jeweiligen Zeit erreichbarste höchstmögliche Realität. [Herv. i. O.][1]

Lukács reagiert auf diesen Einwand, indem er unterstreicht, dass die zwei Aspekte nicht getrennt werden können: Was Realismus als ein *bestimmtes historisches* Phänomen heute sei, das könne nur beurteilt werden, wenn ein normativer „Realismus überhaupt" zum objektiven Maßstab genommen werde.[2] Anders gesagt, von Realismus in *geschichtlicher* Unterscheidung zu Modernismus (oder Post-Modernismus) kann eigentlich nur dann gesprochen werden, wenn gleichzeitig die *strukturelle* Möglichkeit von Realismus mitreflektiert wird. Folgerichtig begreift Lukács in seiner Antwort auf Seghers Realismus als eine künstlerische Darstellungsform, die daran zu messen sei, inwieweit eine bestimmte historische Realität überhaupt den jeweiligen historischen Subjekten kognitiv und empirisch zugänglich ist.[3] Für Lukács ist Wirklichkeit ein objektiver geschichtlicher Prozess, den der Künstler nur dann darzustellen vermag, wenn er seine Gesetze und Tendenzen erfasst.[4] Und weil nach Lukács' marxistischer Auffassung die Tendenz der Wirklichkeit der Kapital-Logik permanenter und grenzenloser Akkumulation gehorcht,

---

1 „Ein Briefwechsel zwischen Anna Seghers und Georg Lukács", in: *Die Expressionismusdebatte. Materialien zu einer marxistischen Realismuskonzeption*, hg. von Hans-Jürgen Schmitt, Frankfurt/M., 1973, S. 264-301: 269.

2 Vgl. ebd., S. 284.

3 Vgl. z. B. ebd., S. 276-281.

4 Der Frage nach dem Wissen und der Gestaltungsfähigkeit des Künstlers nachzugehen, würde den Rahmen dieses Beitrags sprengen. Bemerkt sei daher nur, dass Lukács sich bei der Artikulation dieses Verhältnisses schnell in einer Zirkellogik verfängt und es daher unklar bleibt, ob das Wissen der Gestaltung vorausgeht oder ob das Wissen sich erst aus der Gestaltung ergibt. Lukács artikuliert, ohne es so zu nennen, eine Antinomie von Erkenntnis und Darstellung, die laut Jameson jeden Realismus strukturiert. Vgl. Fredric Jameson, *The Antinomies of Realism*, London, New York, NY, 2013, S. 5 f.

ist auch die Kunst Teil einer kapitalistischen Realität, die, wie es im *Kommunistischen Manifest* heißt, „sich eine Welt nach ihrem eigenen Bilde schafft", eine Welt, in der ein „allseitiger Verkehr [und] eine allseitige Abhängigkeit der Nationen voneinander"[5] herrschen.

„Realismus heute" bedeutet, so meine These, dass sich mit dem seit dem Ende des sozialistischen Blocks verstärkten Augenmerk auf die Unhintergehbarkeit des globalen Kapitalismus die Frage nach dem „Realismus überhaupt" in transnational perspektivierte, literarische Erzählformen eingeschrieben hat. Meine zwei Beispiele für realistische Schreibweisen in der Postmoderne sind Christian Krachts *Imperium* und W. G. Sebalds *Die Ringe des Saturn*, die ich im theoretischen Rahmen der Auseinandersetzung über Expressionismus und Realismus zwischen Bloch und Lukács lesen werde.

1.

Die analytische Begrifflichkeit der Expressionismusdebatte entstammt der marxistischen Epistemologie von Lukács' *Geschichte und Klassenbewußtsein*, einem Werk, welches das Problem der Darstellbarkeit von Wirklichkeit in den Mittelpunkt rückt. Auf Grundlage der dialektischen Unterscheidung von Wesen und Erscheinung formuliert Lukács eine Theorie der Unerkennbarkeit der kapitalistischen Wirklichkeit: Die ihr eigentümlichen widersprüchlichen Prozesse erscheinen im Bewusstsein der Menschen nur als unvermittelte und verdinglichte Gegensätze. In seinen Schriften zum Realismus nimmt Lukács diese Epistemologie wieder auf. So bemerkt er in seinem wichtigsten Beitrag zur Expressionismusdebatte, der programmatischen Schrift „Es geht um den Realismus": „Und jeder Marxist weiß, daß die grundlegenden ökonomischen Kategorien des Kapitalismus sich in den Köpfen der Menschen *unmittelbar stets verkehrt widerspiegeln.* [Herv. i. O.]"[6] Die Wirklichkeit des Realismus lässt sich für Lukács allein durch marxistische Kategorien wie Warenform, Tausch, Ausbeutung usw. adäquat erfassen. Sie ist zunächst nur theoretisch zugänglich. In der unmittelbaren nicht-theoretischen Wahrnehmung hingegen erscheint ihr Wesen verkehrt; ein Umstand, den Lukács vorwiegend mit ästhetischen Metaphern wie Verzerrung und Zerrissenheit bezeichnet. Aufgabe realistischer Darstellungsweisen ist für ihn, die Erscheinung der Realität – von Bloch als „Oberfläche" beschrieben – so zu gestalten, dass in der gestalteten Form mehr als nur die bloße Oberfläche anschaulich wird. Realistische Darstellung zielt demnach auf Entzerrung oder, wie es in Lukács' später Ästhetik heißt, Defetischisierung.[7]

5 Karl Marx/Friedrich Engels, *Werke*, Band 4, Berlin, 1959, S. 466.

6 Georg Lukács, „Es geht um den Realismus", in: *Die Expressionismusdebatte. Materialien zu einer marxistischen Realismuskonzeption*, hg. von Hans-Jürgen Schmitt, Frankfurt/M., 1973, S. 192-230: 197.

7 Georg Lukács, *Die Eigenart des Ästhetischen*, Band 1, Berlin, Weimar, 1981, S. 660-739.

Realismus und Krise gehören zusammen, weil in der Krise die wesenhafte Widersprüchlichkeit der kapitalistischen Wirklichkeit im systemischen, strukturellen Zusammenhang erkennbar – und damit darstellbar wird. Jedoch nur, wenn dieser Zusammenhang künstlerisch gestaltet wird; die Wahrnehmung bedarf also der vermittelnden Darstellung. An sich, in seiner Unmittelbarkeit, erscheint der Zusammenhang nur als Zerrissenheit und die Krise wird als unerklärbare Katastrophe erfahren. Daher bemerkt Lukács über die verkehrte Widerspiegelung des Kapitalismus ferner:

> Das heißt in unserem Fall so viel, daß die in der Unmittelbarkeit des kapitalistischen Lebens befangenen Menschen zur Zeit des sogenannten normalen Funktionierens des Kapitalismus (Etappe der verselbständigten Momente) eine Einheit erleben und denken, zur Zeit der Krise (Herstellung der Einheit der verselbständigten Momente) jedoch die Zerrissenheit als Erlebnis ansehen. Infolge der allgemeinen Krise des kapitalistischen Systems verfestigt sich dieses letztere Erlebnis in sehr breiten Kreisen jener, die sich zu den Phänomenen unmittelbar erlebend verhalten.[8]

Lukács gesteht ein, dass die Beziehung von Krise und Literatur nicht selbstverständlich ist. Denn die Krise enthüllt nicht einfach, wie Lukács bemerkt, Marx zitierend, „die Einheit der gegeneinander verselbständigten Momente“[9]: Diese Einheit bleibt auch in der Krise unlesbar, und so sind die Reaktionen auf Krisensituationen fast immer politisch partikularistisch und imaginieren falsche Kausalitäten wie etwa Komplotte geheimer Cliquen. Gerade Krisensituationen führen zu paranoischen Reaktionen, also zu irrationalen Techniken der Erfassung von Totalität. In der Krise wird ein Anspruch sichtbar, den der Lukács'sche Realismus zu erfüllen sucht: nämlich zu zeigen, wie die Einheit des kapitalistischen Systems mit der Erscheinung seiner Zerrissenheit zusammenhängt. Für Lukács besteht die Leistung des Realismus deshalb nicht darin, die Totalität des Systems als solche zu zeigen – dieses kann nur vermittelt und abstrakt, also durch Begriff anstatt durch Narration, geleistet werden; es ist eine Sache der Theorie, nicht der Literatur. Vielmehr zielt eine realistische Darstellung darauf, den *Zusammenhang* von gesellschaftlichem Wesen und Erscheinung *zu gestalten*. Daraus erklärt sich auch Lukács' Kritik an der Montage: Diese nimmt ein Stück Wirklichkeit unmittelbar, montiert es in den Text, gestaltet es aber nicht. Daher missverstehen Expressionismus und Surrealismus, wie Lukács meint, die vorgefundene empirische Wirklichkeit, die doch nur Erscheinung ist, als Wesen.[10] Ernst Bloch, der Verteidiger des Expressionismus und Antipode von Lukács in dieser Debatte, muss sich daher den Vorwurf des Vulgärmaterialismus gefallen lassen:

> Blochs Fehler liegt bloß darin, daß er diesen Bewußtheitszustand [der inneren Zerrissenheit der Protagonisten von Thomas Mann und James Joyce; U. P.] unmittelbar und vorbehaltlos mit der Wirklichkeit selbst, das in diesem Bewußtsein vorhandene Bild in seiner ganzen Verzerrtheit mit der Sache selbst identifiziert, statt durch Ver-

---

8 Ebd., S. 197.

9 Karl Marx/Friedrich Engels, *Werke*, Band 26.2: *Theorien über den Mehrwert*, Berlin, 1967, S. 501.

10 Ebd., S. 199.

> gleich des Bildes mit der Wirklichkeit das Wesen, die Ursachen, die Vermittlungen etc. des verzerrten Bildes konkret aufzudecken.[11]

Dem Zusammenhang kommt man dadurch auf die Spur, dass Ursachen und Vermittlungen geradezu detektivisch aufgedeckt werden. Literarischer Realismus ist eine Form des gesellschaftlichen Wissens, wie es sich im Handeln einzelner Figuren, also im Prozess literarischer Narration, manifestiert. Lukács unterstreicht, dass Thomas Mann

> genau weiß, *wer* Christian Buddenbrock, *wer* Tonio Kröger, *wer* Hans Castorp, Settembrini oder Naphta ist. Er braucht es nicht im Sinne einer abstrakt-wissenschaftlichen sozialen Analyse zu wissen: hier mag er sich irren, so wie vor ihm auch Balzac, Dickens oder L. Tolstoi geirrt haben – er weiß es aber im Sinne des schaffenden Realisten; er weiß, wie Denken und Empfinden aus dem gesellschaftlichen Sein herauswachsen, wie Erlebnisse und Empfindungen Teile eines Gesamtkomplexes der Wirklichkeit sind. Dabei zeigt er als Realist, *wohin* dieser Teil im Gesamtkomplex des Lebens gehört, *woher* er aus dem gesellschaftlichen Leben kommt, *wohin* er geht, usw. [Herv. i. O.][12]

Das realistische Wissen ist ein schaffendes, es ist, wie Lukács im selben Aufsatz schreibt, „harte Arbeit". Die wissende Darstellung, die aus solch harter Arbeit gewonnen wird, beschreibt er wiederholt mit den räumlichen Metaphern der Tiefe, Breite und Verschlungenheit. Doch es ist nicht allein ein Mehr an Komplexität, das für Lukács die realistische von der expressionistischen Darstellung unterscheidet; die Oberflächlichkeit der letzteren impliziert auch eine zeitliche Flüchtigkeit. Sie erfüllt und erschöpft sich im Jetzt des Augenblicks. Der Realismus hingegen stellt historische Zusammenhänge her, nicht nur mit Vergangenem: Weil er Tendenzen aufspürt, hat er auch eine prophetische Dimension. Gleichzeitig muss Lukács aber betonen, dass das prophetische Wissen des Realismus kein visionäres ist, sondern eines der Darstellung, sofern es dieser gelingt, die vom Alltagsbewusstsein unbemerkten Bewegungen und Prozesse der Wirklichkeit hervortreten zu lassen. Lukács macht sich zum Fürsprecher einer realistischen Schreibpraxis, die Abbildung (Mimesis) und Gestaltung (Konstruktion) zusammenfügt. Er unternimmt dies, indem er die Abbildung verzeitlicht und die Konstruktion mehrdimensional verräumlicht: Abgebildet werden also Prozesse im Hinblick auf Ursprung (Vergangenheit) und Tendenz (Zukunft), gestaltet werden Zusammenhänge im Hinblick auf anschauliche Vermittlung von Wesen (unsichtbar) und Erscheinung (sichtbar). Erreicht wird dies nicht dadurch, dass *ein* korrekter Zusammenhang dargestellt wird, sondern dass eine *Vielheit* von Zusammenhängen narrativ (also zeitintensiv und zeitextensiv) konstruktiv gestaltet wird. All dies geschieht nicht aufgrund vorgegebener ästhetischer Normen der Schönheit oder Plastizität, sondern allein nach der epistemologischen Maßgabe, dass „vielfältiger, reicher, verschlungener" auch „schlauer" bedeutet.[13]

---

11 Ebd.
12 Ebd., S. 201.
13 Ebd., S. 205.

Lukács' Kritik an der avantgardistischen Ästhetik ist daher, genau genommen, keine ästhetische, sondern eine erkenntniskritische. Weil Expressionismus und Surrealismus bei der Gestaltung der Oberfläche stehenbleiben und somit die Erscheinung der Wirklichkeit mit der Wirklichkeit überhaupt verwechseln, produzieren sie eine rein ästhetische, eine historisch und gesellschaftlich blinde Anschauung. Die Haltung avantgardistischer Künstler beschreibt Lukács als eine reaktive; sie rührt aus einem Mangel an Denk- und Gestaltungs*arbeit*. Salopp gesagt, Lukács argumentiert eigentlich ganz im Sinne einer protestantischen Arbeitsethik, wonach die Wurzel des avantgardistischen Übels in der Scheu ihrer Protagonisten vor „harter Arbeit"[14] liegt. Bloch scheint etwas von diesem Lukács'schen Ressentiment gegen den Ästhetizismus der Moderne zu ahnen, wenn er in Bezug auf Joyce bemerkt: „[D]ie Worte sind arbeitslos geworden."[15] In seiner direkten Replik auf Lukács' Essay „Größe und Verfall des Expressionismus" wird Bloch deutlicher. So schreibt er: „Überall sonst [außer in Lukács' Polemik gegen Mörike; U. P.] ist hier Klassik das Gesunde, Romantik das Kranke, Expressionismus das Allerkrankste, und dieses nicht nur wegen des unzerfallenen, objektiven Realismus, der der Klassik eignet." Bei dieser polemischen Feststellung aber belässt es Bloch: „Es ist hier nicht der Ort, auf diesen Punkt einzugehen: gerade wegen seiner Wichtigkeit erforderte er die gründlichste Behandlung, doch müßten dazu alle Probleme der dialektisch-materialistischen Abbildlehre zur Sprache kommen."[16]

Bloch hat gegenüber Lukács, so scheint mir, zumindest instinktiv recht: Lukács' Vorwurf an die Avantgarde, sie verfahre irrational, verkennt die der kapitalistischen Vernunft eigene Unvernunft. Die zyklischen Krisen sind möglicherweise nicht nur Manifestationen periodischer Überproduktion, Fall der Profitrate (usw.) und entsprechender Readjustierung des Weltsystems; sie verschärfen sich und führen den Kapitalismus an eine strukturell unüberschreitbare Grenze, jenseits derer die Möglichkeiten zur Produktion des Mehrwerts immer geringer werden. Die Kritische Theorie der Frankfurter Schule, die mit Bloch und Lukács immerhin mittelbar verbunden war, bestand darauf, dass die Totalität des Kapitalismus eine antagonistische ist, dass seine Rationalität im Kern irrational und (selbst-)zerstörerisch ist. Dies erlaubt die Überlegung, ob der literarische Realismus nach Lukács nicht trotz, sondern aufgrund seiner Annäherung an Techniken der literarischen Avantgarde *überhaupt realistisch wird*. Dieser Überlegung möchte ich nun anhand zweier Beispiele kursorisch nachspüren.

---

14 Ebd., S. 203. Zu realistischem Schreiben als intellektueller Arbeit vgl. ebd., S. 278.

15 Ernst Bloch, *Erbschaft dieser Zeit*, in: *Werkausgabe*, Band 4, Frankfurt/M., 1985, S. 130 (zit. in Lukács (1973), Es geht um den Realismus, S. 200).

16 Ernst Bloch, „Diskussionen über Expressionismus", in: *Die Expressionismusdebatte. Materialien zu einer marxistischen Realismuskonzeption*, hg. von Hans-Jürgen Schmitt, Frankfurt/M., 1973, S. 180-191: 186.

2.

Lukács beschreibt den Realismus emphatisch als „künstlerische Dialektik von Wesen und Erscheinung“[17]. Nicht zu Unrecht wird die sogenannte postmoderne Literatur oft unter dem Gesichtspunkt einer Ästhetik der Oberfläche behandelt[18], obwohl eine solche Zuschreibung genauso klischeehaft ist wie eine Definition des Realismus als Ästhetik der Tiefe. Dass der Widerspruch der theoretischen Positionen von Bloch und Lukács sich in die narrativen Praktiken der Gegenwartsliteratur eingeschrieben hat, belegt Christian Krachts Roman *Imperium*, der in mindestens dreifacher Hinsicht als metafiktional – d. h. als Literatur, die ihre eigene Theorie reflektiert – beschrieben werden kann: 1) Er zitiert die exotistischen Narrative der Machtphantasien des deutschen Kolonialismus und der mit ihm verwobenen Aussteigersubkulturen; 2) er vergleicht die Fiktionskraft der Literatur mit der des Films; 3) er reflektiert die Debatte zwischen Realismus und Modernismus und damit auch seine eigene Funktion als vermeintlich postmoderner Roman.[19] Metafiktional ist Krachts Verfahren nicht nur insofern, als sein Roman dokumentarisch belegte und frei erfundene Personen und Begebenheiten ineinander verflechtet, sondern vor allem insofern die Fiktionalität des Verfahrens selbst zum Gegenstand des Erzählens wird. Dies geschieht auf nonchalante Weise; der Erzähler gleicht einem Unterhalter, der nur das zum Ausdruck bringt, was sich ohne weitere Umstände ausdrücken lässt. Er befindet sich im sicheren Fahrwasser des *commercial realism*, einer Erzähltechnik, die sich am Comic und am Film orientiert und sozusagen nur das zu erzählen versucht, was in ein *panel* oder einen *frame* passt. Indem der Erzähler gelegentlich darauf hinweist, dass es auch ein außerhalb des Rahmens Liegendes gibt, das nicht erzählt wird, rückt Realismus nicht als Leistung des Erzählens in den Blick, sondern als *Problem*: Was bedeutet es, eine geschichtliche Realität mit Mitteln zu erzählen, die ihr nicht angemessen sind?

Die Skepsis des Erzählers gegenüber dem eigenen Vermögen drückt sich zunächst – besonders im Vergleich zu den Allmachtsphantasien, in die der verstörte Protagonist August Engelhardt unwiderruflich abdriftet – in einer gewissen Genügsamkeit aus: Operiert wird mit durchgängig konventionellen formalen Mitteln. Nichts an seiner Erzählweise weist den Erzähler als Avantgardisten aus, und sein eher heiterer Plauderton bedient sich sowohl bei Fontane und Thomas Mann als auch beim Jugendroman. Die dargestellte Wirklichkeit von *Imperium* ist nicht, wie es eine Lukács'sche Poetik verlangen würde, die gesellschaftliche Realität der Geschichte des deutschen Kolonialismus im Zeitalter des Imperialismus, sondern die diskursive Realität der Literatur- und Mediengeschichte, die eine Rückkehr zu realistischen Erzählverfahren nur in Form des Pastiche erlaubt. Der Realismus von

---

17 Lukács (1973), Es geht um den Realismus, S. 205.

18 Spezifisch zur Ästhetik der Oberfläche bei Kracht ist Frank Finlay, „'Surface is an Illusion but so is Depth'. The Novels of Christian Kracht“, in: *German Life and Letters* 66, 2 (2013), S. 213-231.

19 Vgl. Robin Hauenstein, *Historiographische Metafiktionen. Ransmayr, Sebald, Kracht, Beyer*, Würzburg, 2014, S. 120-151.

Imperium ist also einer der *Theorie* des Realismus. Vor realistischen Erzählern wie Conrad, Dickens, Thomas Mann, Hoffmann, Büchner, Keller und Poe lüpft der Erzähler den Hut.[20] Doch anstatt sich die Erzählverfahren des 19. Jahrhunderts als Parodie oder Pastiche anzueignen, geht die Erzählung von *Imperium* an manchen Stellen noch einen weiteren Schritt zurück, zur *Chronik*: „[I]n diese Zeit fällt diese Chronik“[21].

Es gibt in den Kalendergeschichten Johann Peter Hebels eine Form des chronistischen Erzählens, die von Autoren wie Kafka und Canetti als eine besonders meisterhafte Form der gerafften Darstellung von Zeitverläufen geschätzt wurde. In seinem „Erzähler“-Aufsatz unterscheidet Benjamin den Chronisten als „Geschichts-Erzähler“ vom Historiker als „Geschichts-Schreiber“:

> Der Chronist ist der Geschichts-Erzähler. Man denke an die Hebel-Stelle zurück, die durchaus den Tonfall der Chronik hat, und ermesse ohne Mühe den Unterschied zwischen dem, der Geschichte schreibt, dem Historiker, und dem, der sie erzählt, dem Chronisten. Der Historiker ist gehalten, die Vorfälle, mit denen er es zu tun hat, auf die eine oder andere Art zu erklären; er kann sich unter keinen Umständen damit begnügen, sie als Musterstücke des Weltlaufs herzuzeigen. Genau das aber tut der Chronist.[22]

Es ist wohl kaum verfehlt, im Duktus des Erzählers von *Imperium* Anklänge des rheinländischen Hausfreundes zu hören, gerade in den diskursiven Passagen, in denen den Lesern erläutert wird, was es mit der Wirklichkeit der Moderne auf sich habe:

> So sah die Besitznahme der Insel Kabakon durch unseren Freund ganz unterschiedlich aus, je nachdem von welcher Warte aus man das Szenario betrachtete und wer man tatsächlich war. Diese Splitterung der Realität in verschiedene Teile war indes eines der Hauptmerkmale jener Zeit, in der Engelhardts Geschichte spielt. Die Moderne war nämlich angebrochen, die Dichter schrieben plötzlich atomisierte Zeilen; grelle, für ungeschulte Ohren lediglich atonal klingende Musik wurde vor kopfschüttelndem Publikum uraufgeführt, auf Tonträger gepreßt und reproduziert, von der Erfindung des Kinematographen ganz zu schweigen, der unsere Wirklichkeit exakt so dinglich machen konnte, wie sie geschah, zeitlich kongruent, als sei es möglich, ein Stück aus der Gegenwart herauszuschneiden und sie für alle Ewigkeiten als bewegtes Bild zwischen den Perforationen eines Zelluloidstreifens zu konservieren.[23]

Der Erzähler spricht hier nicht – und auch nicht anderswo im Roman – von *der* Geschichte überhaupt. Geschichte gibt es nur im Besonderen, etwa als die Geschichte Engelhardts, die zwar einerseits repräsentativ sein soll, sich aber andererseits in der episodischen Darstellung kurioser Ereignisse und Augenblicke erschöpft. Festhalten lässt sich nicht Geschichte, sondern *Zeit*: ein Stück Gegenwart auf dem Träger Zelluloid. Die Chronik, deren Form *Imperium* nachahmt, leistet

---

20 Vgl. Christian Kracht, *Imperium*, Frankfurt/M., 2012, S. 59, S. 74, S. 84, S. 131 und S. 158.

21 Ebd., S. 18.

22 Walter Benjamin, „Der Erzähler“, in: *Gesammelte Schriften*, Band II.2, hg. von Rolf Tiedemann und Hermann Schweppenhäuser, Frankfurt/M., 1991, S. 438-465: 451.

23 Kracht (2012), *Imperium*, S. 66 f.

das Aneinanderreihen von punktueller Zeit, von Gegenwarten. Im historischen Ganzen jedoch entzieht sich die Realität; von ihr sind nur Splitter zu haben. Mit dem Ausdruck der „Splitterung" zitiert Krachts Erzähler das zentrale Anliegen der Expressionismusdebatte, nämlich ob die als „gesplittert" erscheinende Wirklichkeit zugleich als in sich zusammenhängend künstlerisch erfasst werden kann. An die Stelle der Totalität der kapitalistischen Geschichte, die Lukács als Darstellungsziel realistischen Erzählens postuliert, tritt in *Imperium* die Totalität der Zeit als Raum. Mit dem Wort „Imperium" ist darum nur vordergründig die Machtphantasie eines deutschen Imperiums gemeint, das sich erst im Kolonialismus, dann im Dritten Reich zu verwirklichen suchte. Diese reale Geschichte ist lediglich Staffage dafür, worum es in Krachts Chronik eigentlich geht: Um die Darstellung von verselbstständigter und verdinglichter Zeit. In einer anderen diskursiven Passage erläutert der Erzähler-Chronist:

> Die vorherrschende Ansicht, die Zeit sei ein unaufhaltsamer Strom, in dem alles seinen präzisen Anfang habe und seinen klar definierten Verlauf, hat sich auch in Slütters Denken festgesetzt; dabei ist es, wie ihm in manchen luziden Momenten gewahr wird, eher so, daß das Ende sehr wohl feststeht, nicht aber das immerwährende Präsens, welches einen dorthin zu führen weiß. Das perfide, unfaßbare Jetzt mäandert, einem ektoplasmischen Wabern gleich, aus allen Ecken und Enden und fließt unkontrollierbar wie ein Gas in sämtliche Richtungen des Daseins, dabei die unwiderrufliche Einzigartigkeit jedes seiner Augenblicke außer Acht lassend, so auch den Folgenden.[24]

Als „immerwährende[s] Präsens" bleibt Zeit reine Gegenwartsform, ohne Richtung, ohne Tendenz, und eignet sich damit narrativ vor allem, wie Fredric Jameson beobachtet[25], zur Darstellung von szenischem Geschehen. Die Rolle des Erzählers in *Imperium* besteht daher nicht selten im Ordnen und Erläutern szenischer Momente. Diese nehmen jedoch nie überhand, wie, um ein Beispiel Jamesons zu zitieren, die „immense two-hundred-page lunches in Proust"[26], sondern tauchen überhaupt nur als Produkt der metafiktionalen Rahmung technologisch gestalteter Zeit auf. Daher ist es nicht verwunderlich, dass der Roman mit einer Hommage an das filmische Erzählen und seine Kraft schließt, weltumspannende Jetztzeit zu produzieren und projizieren:

> [E]s rattert der Projektor, nein, es flirren Hunderte Projektoren und werfen ihre von wild tanzenden Staubpartikeln begleiteten Lichtnadeln auf Hunderte Leinwände, in Cincinnati, Los Angeles, Chicago, Miami, San Francisco, Boston, auf denen sich ein weißes Dampfpostschiff unter langen weißen Wolken durch einen endlosen Ozean begibt. Die Kamera fährt nah heran, ein Tuten, die Schiffsglocke läutet zu Mittag, und ein dunkelhäutiger Statist (der im Film nicht wieder auftaucht) schreitet sanft-

24 Ebd., S. 201.
25 Jameson (2013), *The Antinomies of Realism*, S. 25.
26 Ebd.

füßig und leise das Oberdeck ab, um jene Passagiere mit behutsamem Schulterdruck aufzuwecken, die gleich nach dem üppigen Frühstück wieder eingeschlafen waren.[27]

Krachts Roman endet damit, dass er die vielfache, gleichzeitige Vorführung seiner Verfilmung imaginiert: Die Geschichte beginnt noch einmal, aber dieses Mal als Film. Damit thematisiert *Imperium*, wie auch schon an anderen Stellen, die ihm eigene Erzähltechnik der Herausstellung des Rahmens. Zum *Hollywood realism* des *continuity editing*, dessen oberstes Gebot das Verschwinden der Apparatur ist, lenkt Krachts Erzähler – in bester Manier eines Brecht'schen oder Godard'schen kritischen Realismus – an entscheidenden Stellen den Blick auf die Apparatur des Erzählens. Besonders deutlich wird dies am Ende des zweiten Kapitels:

> Und dort, im Abteil sitzend (der Nachmittag senkte sich nun, Preußischblau eingefärbt und süßlich duftend, gegen den frühen Abend hin), die Schulter an einen Mitreisenden gelehnt, den Rücken an die Holzbank gedrückt, die Augen geschlossen, dafür die wirren langen Haare offen, die Reisetasche vorn an seinen Bauch gepreßt, beginnt plötzlich der Kinematograph zu rattern: Ein Zahnrad greift nicht mehr ins andere, die dort vorne auf dem weißen Leintuch projizierten, bewegten Bilder beschleunigen sich wirr, ja sie laufen für einen kurzen Augenblick nicht mehr vorwärts, wie vom Schöpfer ad aeternitatem vorgesehen, sondern holpern, zucken, jagen rückwärts [...].[28]

Mit der Aussage „dort vorne auf dem weißen Leintuch" deutet der Erzähler auf außerhalb des Erzählrahmens Liegendes: den Kinematografen, die Leinwand, den Kinosaal. Der Gestus ist einer des metafiktionalen Aufzeigens der Konstruiertheit des Erzählten. Dies erinnert an die Technik des Comics, den Rahmen des Panels zu durchbrechen und dadurch sowohl die Fiktion als Fiktion sichtbar zu machen und die chronologische Abfolge des Erzählten rekursiv zu einer Schleife zu verknüpfen.

Nun ist dies nicht nur eine formale Spielerei, sondern auch mit dem Inhalt des Erzählten verknüpft: nämlich dem Wahn des Protagonisten, der sich durch den alleinigen Konsum von Kokosnüssen den Zwängen des technologischen Fortschritts zu entziehen sucht. Doch führt der Entzug zur Regression und schließlich zur Auto-Anthropophagie Engelhardts. Dies ist die tragikomische Konsequenz eines Erzählverfahrens, das sich der Realität durch Rekursivität zu versichern sucht. Der durch Mangelernährung kranke Engelhardt findet die ultimative Bestätigung, dass er überhaupt noch existiert, im Verspeisen des eigenen Körpers. Seine monomanische, selbstzerstörerische Fixierung auf die Kokosnuss als Mittel zur Befreiung von allen Übeln der Moderne repräsentiert nicht nur das wahnhaft monokausale Denken aller Erweckungs-und Reformbewegungen und die ihnen eigene Mischung von (idealistischer) Erlösungsphantasie und (praktischer) Mehrwertaneignung; er allegorisiert auch den puristischen deutschen Machtwahn des Strebens nach Lebensraum und Reinigung der Rasse von „unnatürlichen", „unreinen" Anteilen. Dass Krachts Erzähler selbst mit rassistischen und sexistischen Kli-

---

[27] Kracht (2012), *Imperium*, S. 241 f.

[28] Ebd., S. 47.

schees operiert, disqualifiziert den Roman als ernst zu nehmende Kritik[29] am latenten Fortbestehen deutscher Kolonialphantasien. Zur Verteidigung von Krachts Erzähler kann man allerdings anmerken, dass die Verwendung exotistischer und rassistischer Stereotype ganz genretypisch einem Abenteuerroman oder einem *Tim und Struppi*-Comic[30] gleicht. Metafiktional gewendet sollte man hierbei eher nicht von der bloßen Reproduktion eines Klischees sprechen, sondern von seiner Verdoppelung: Schon der erste Satz ist ja das Klischee eines Klischees (worauf die filmische Wiederholung dieses Klischees am Ende des Buchs nachdrücklich verweist).

Die Erzähltechniken metafiktionaler Distanzierung, die wiederholt auf eine Positionierung des Erzählers außerhalb des Rahmens des Erzählten hindeuten, erzeugen eine vertrauliche Ironie, die auf provinzielle Leser setzt, die einerseits Vergnügen daran finden, nach Art des rheinländischen Hausfreundes über die Ereignisse an fernen Gestaden unterrichtet zu werden, andererseits aber bereits historisch unterrichtet sind, der Instruktion also eigentlich nicht mehr bedürfen. Diesen Lesern beispielsweise muss nicht mehr erläutert werden, dass die Spinnerei des Protagonisten keineswegs harmlos ist und dass der deutsche Kolonialismus nur das Vorspiel zu viel Schlimmerem war, was mit der narrativen Geste eines „Etc." kurz angedeutet wird: „Komödiantisch wäre es wohl anzusehen, wenn da nicht unvorstellbare Grausamkeit folgen würde: Gebeine, Excreta, Rauch."[31] Dass Krieg und Massenvernichtung hier nur stichwortartig katalogisiert werden, deutet darauf hin, dass dieses ausgesparte historisch Reale, dessen Name unausgesprochen bleibt, so etwas wie den traumatischen Kern des Erzählten bildet. Dieses Reale lässt sich nicht komödiantisch darstellen; Engelhardts Leben hingegen schon. Man kann also, leicht schematisch, das Verhältnis des Erzählten zu dem in der Erzählung nur Angedeuteten so fassen: *Imperium* erzählt die deutsche Geschichte des 20. Jahrhunderts von ihren Rändern her; und zwar 1) zeitlich: als das politische Streben nach einem Imperium, das teleologisch den rassistischen Eroberungskrieg der Nazis präfiguriert; 2) räumlich: als Verwirklichung totalitärer Machtphantasien an der Peripherie der sogenannten zivilisierten (d. h. von Europa dominierten und ausgebeuteten) Welt; 3) narrativ-formal: als komödiantische, ironische, metafiktionale Distanzierung vom traumatischen Realen der Geschichte.

Lukács setzt den Anspruch auf Totalität als für realistisches Schreiben wesentlich: Es geht um die narrative Gestaltung von Zusammenhängen, um Konkretisierung von Wirklichkeit gerade wo sie, wie etwa der Kapital-Fetisch von „Geld heckendes Geld", abstrakt ist.[32] Diesem realistischen Anspruch widersetzt sich *Imperium* auf fast schon ostentative Weise, indem beispielsweise der Zusammenhang von (ver-

29 Vgl. Claudia Breger, „Transnationalism, Colonial Loops, and the Vicissitudes of Cosmopolitan Affect: Christian Kracht's *Imperium* and Teju Cole's *Open City*", in: *Transnationalism in Contemporary German-Language Literature*, hg. von Elisabeth Herrmann, Carrie Smith-Prei und Stuart Taberner, Rochester, NY, 2015, S. 106-124.

30 Vgl. dazu Finlay (2013), ‚Surface Is an Illusion', S. 228.

31 Kracht (2012), *Imperium*, S. 79.

32 Lukács (1973), Es geht um den Realismus, S. 204.

meintlicher) Idylle und Gewalt zwar thematisiert, aber nicht erzählt wird: Das, was für Lukács überhaupt erst eine realistische Schreibweise ausmacht, erscheint in *Imperium* nur ausgespart, als jäher Sprung und Ellipse. So erwähnt der Erzähler die Ermordung des einer Vergewaltigung schuldigen Heinrich Aueckens erst, nachdem sie geschehen ist: „Wir sehen Aueckens erst tot wieder, bäuchlings und nackt am Boden liegend, mit zerschmettertem Schädel, etwas Gehirnmasse ist ausgetreten."[33] Über den eigentlichen Tathergang und die Täterschaft schweigt der Erzähler. Stattdessen beschränkt sich seine Mitteilung auf die forensische Feststellung, der Tod sei durch einen harten Gegenstand zustande gekommen:

> Ob Engelhardt dem Antisemiten [Aueckens] selbst eine Kokosnuß auf den Kopf schlug oder ob Aueckens, im selben Palmenhain wandelnd, in dem er den jungen Makeli geschändet, zufällig von einer herabfallenden Frucht erschlagen wurde oder ob die Hand des Eingeborenenjungen aus Notwehr einen Stein erhoben hat, verschwindet im Nebel der erzählerischen Unsicherheit. Sicher ist nur die Tatsache, daß der Helgoländer durch den Aufprall eines harten, runden Gegenstandes aus dieser Welt nach Ultima Thule gelangte, vom sonnenbeschienenen Palmenstrand hinüber in das kalte, finstere Eisreich.[34]

Der „Nebel der erzählerischen Unsicherheit" gleicht jenem Nebel, der im Film zum Einsatz kommt, wenn das Budget nicht für realistisch wirkende Kulissen gereicht hat. Der Nebel verdeckt den Apparat; und gleichzeitig weist sein Auftauchen darauf hin, dass etwas versteckt wird. Es sind in *Imperium* immer wieder diese metafiktionalen rekursiven Augenblicke, die die Frage, was eigentlich eine realistische Darstellung wäre, hervortreten lassen. Gleichzeitig aber dienen diese Augenblicke geradezu als Vorwand dafür, die Kompetenz des Erzählers zu überhöhen und ihn mit sozusagen imperialer Macht schalten und walten zu lassen, wie etwa zu Beginn des fünften Kapitels:

> Da wir uns nun bemüht haben, von der Vergangenheit unseres armen Freundes zu erzählen, werden wir im Folgenden also, einem ausdauernden und stolzen Seevogel gleich, dem das Überfliegen der Zeitzonen unseres Erdenballs vollends konsequenzlos erscheint, ja diese weder wahrnimmt noch darüber reflektiert, einige Jährchen überspringen und August Engelhardt dort wieder aufsuchen, wo wir ihn vor einigen Seiten verlassen haben; splitternackt am Strande spazierend, an seinem eigenen Strand wohlgemerkt, sich hier und da bückend, ein besonders reizvolles Muschelexemplar auflesend und es in einen Sammelkorb aus Bast gleiten lassend, den er zu diesem Zweck über die Schulter geworfen hat.[35]

Der eigentlich durch und durch sentimentalische Erzähler beruft sich hier auf das Vorrecht der epischen Naivität, die zwingende Kontinuität der Zeit zu überspringen. Dies erlaubt ihm eine metanarrative Reflexion über die Formbarkeit und Relativität von Zeit sowie einen Hinweis auf die Zeitgenossenschaft von Engelhardt und Einstein, dessen Dissertation „wenige Jahre später nicht nur das gesam-

---

33 Kracht (2012), *Imperium*, S. 129.

34 Ebd., S. 129 f.

35 Ebd., S. 93.

te bisherige Wissen der Menschheit auf den Kopf stellen würde, sondern gewissermaßen die Warte, von der aus man die Welt und dieses Wissen wahrnahm, auch die Zeit“[36]. Das Wissen der Moderne widersetzt sich der Ur-Form des Erzählens, der epischen Einheit von Zeitlauf und menschlicher Erfahrung. Mit dem Hinweis auf die Relativität der Zeit weiß Krachts Erzähler sich in guter literarischer Gesellschaft. Das Problem des Realismus im 20. Jahrhundert ist eines des erzählerischen Standpunktes: der tendenziellen Ununterscheidbarkeit von Realien und Bildern, von Außen- und Innenraum. Krachts Ästhetik der Oberfläche bezieht sich auf diese Einsicht in die strukturelle Krise des Erzählens einer „zersplitterten“ Wirklichkeit. Fern liegt ihm dabei allerdings der Lukács'sche Anspruch, diese Oberfläche auf ein vermeintliches Wesen hin zu durchdringen. Viel eher im Sinne einer Lukács'schen „Gesinnung zur Totalität“[37] verfährt W. G. Sebald, dessen theoretisch und narrativ hoch ambitionierter Reisebericht *Die Ringe des Saturn* hier sehr gerafft als Beleg dafür angeführt werden soll, wie gerade durch eine Fokussierung auf das Partikulare Verknüpfungen hergestellt werden können, anhand derer jene Zusammenhänge zwischen Zentrum und Peripherie, die in *Imperium* nur ironisch-elliptisch angedeutet werden, *als* Zusammenhänge in Erscheinung treten.

3.

Sebalds Reisebericht ist in weiten Teilen eine Hommage an Thomas Browne[38] und, obgleich weniger direkt, an Walter Benjamin.[39] Der Ich-Erzähler entdeckt, wie sich gerade durch ein Betrachten des Entlegenen, Veralteten und Beschädigten Zusammenhänge erschließen, die eine den Globus umspannende Perspektive auf die Geschichte des Kolonialismus und sein Nach- und Weiterleben eröffnet. Während Krachts Erzähler durch die Figur der Ironie die Referenzialität des Erzählten infrage stellt und das Begehren des Lesers nach einem sinnstiftenden Zusammenhang durch die Belustigung über den Kokosnuss-Wahn des tragikomischen Protagonisten unterläuft, stützt sich Sebalds Erzähler auf die Allegorie, die in seinen Händen zu einer Trope der Lesbarkeit von zeitlich und räumlich Zerstreutem wird.[40] Anders gesagt, wo die Kracht'sche Ironie die Gefahr der Bedeutungsinflation am Verfremdungseffekt des erscheinenden Erzählapparates scheitern lässt, da praktiziert Sebalds Allegorie genau das Gegenteil, nämlich eine intentionale Inflation der Referenzialität. Der Unterschied drückt sich in den Erzählfiguren aus: Krachts sanguiner Erzähler agiert stets distanziert von der Monomanie und Paranoia Engelhardts; Sebalds melancholischer Erzähler verfährt monomanisch und paranoisch,

36 Ebd., S. 95.

37 Georg Lukács, *Die Theorie des Romans. Ein geschichtsphilosophischer Versuch über die Formen der großen Epik*, München, 1994, S. 47.

38 Dazu insbesondere Carol Jacobs, *Sebald's Vision*, New York, NY, 2015, S. 54-62.

39 Vgl. Eric Santner, *On Creaturely Life: Rilke, Benjamin, Sebald*, Chicago, IL, 2006.

40 Vgl. Bianca Theisen, „A Natural History of Destruction: W.G. Sebald's *The Rings of Saturn*“, in: *MLN* 121 (2006), S. 563-581: 578.

jedes Zeichen, das er wahrnimmt, hat die Gewalt eines realen Referenten. Die Landschaft der Grafschaft Suffolk, die er durchwandert, ist durchzogen von der Schrift der Geschichte – eine nicht von Geschichte geprägte Natur gibt es überhaupt nicht, insofern sich dem saturnischen Blick, auf den der Titel anspielt, die Landschaft nie im Lichte der Erlösung, sondern immer nur im Lichte der Gewalt der Geschichte darbietet, wie es Benjamin im *Ursprung des deutschen Trauerspiels* ausdrückt:

> Während im Symbol mit der Verklärung des Unterganges das transfigurierte Antlitz der Natur im Lichte der Erlösung flüchtig sich offenbart, liegt in der Allegorie die facies hippocratica der Geschichte als erstarrte Urlandschaft dem Betrachter vor Augen. Die Geschichte in allem was sie Unzeitiges, Leidvolles, Verfehltes von Beginn an hat, prägt sich in einem Antlitz – nein in einem Totenkopfe aus.[41]

In seiner Vorrede betont Benjamin die Verwandtschaft von Barock und künstlerischer Moderne. Barock und Expressionismus seien beide Ausdruck eines unbedingten Kunstwollens als Antwort auf den Verfall geschlossener Formen in der Wahrnehmung und Darstellung von Wirklichkeit:

> Immer ist diese Gewaltsamkeit [der literarischen Darstellung; U. P.] Kennzeichen einer Produktion, in welcher ein geformter Ausdruck wahrhaften Gehalts kaum dem Konflikt entbundener Kräfte abzuringen ist. In solcher Zerrissenheit spiegelt die Gegenwart gewisse Seiten der barocken Geistesverfassung bis in die Einzelheiten der Kunstübung.[42]

Was in Benjamins Habilitationsschrift 1925 noch in erster Linie eine Krise von Kunst, Kultur und Gesellschaft war, das ist in der Expressionismusdebatte ein Jahrzehnt später eine Krise von Kunst, Politik und Kapitalismus. In seiner Kritik am Expressionismus bemängelt Lukács vor allem, dass es den expressionistischen Künstlern am tiefer gehenden Verständnis der Ökonomie fehle. Die Wirklichkeit erscheine ihnen als Chaos, als etwas Irrationales, dem die Kunst ihrerseits nur mit Irrationalismus, mit Gefühlen und Leidenschaften, entgegentreten kann: „Sie stehen in einer romantischen Opposition zum Kapitalismus, jedoch von einer rein ideologischen Seite her, die Einsicht in seine ökonomische Gesetzmäßigkeit nicht einmal suchend."[43] Kracht zeichnet seinen Helden Engelhardt ganz ähnlich: Als romantischen Verweigerer, der am Ende genau dem faschistischen Irrsinn verfällt, dessen Vorstufen er zu entkommen suchte. Der Erzähler behauptet sogar unumwunden eine Parallele zwischen dem Romantiker Engelhardt und dem Romantiker Hitler.[44]

Eine solche telelogische Verbindung von Faschismus und romantischem Protest liegt den *Ringen des Saturn* fern, denn Sebalds Text geht es um die Zeitgenos-

---

41 Walter Benjamin, *Ursprung des deutschen Trauerspiels*, in: *Gesammelte Schriften*, Band I.1, hg. von Rolf Tiedemann und Hermann Schweppenhäuser, Frankfurt/M., 1991, S. 203-430: 343.

42 Ebd., S. 236.

43 Georg Lukács, „‚Größe und Verfall' des Expressionismus", in: *Essays über Realismus*, Neuwied, Berlin, 1971, S. 109-149: 138.

44 Kracht (2012), *Imperium*, S. 18 f.

senschaft von Barock und post-kolonialer Gegenwart Groß-Britanniens am Ende des 20. Jahrhunderts. Verglichen mit der kurzen Episode des deutschen Kolonialismus garantieren allein die ungeheure Ausdehnung und Dauer des britischen Imperiums die Bedingungen einer tragischen Fallhöhe im Kontrast zwischen globaler Machtfülle und lokalem Verfall. Sebalds Erzähler bemüht sich das, was ihm auf seiner Wanderschaft begegnet, als historisch Gewordenes zu begreifen, und sein Begehren nach einem Wissen des Zusammenhangs treibt seine Gedanken und Studien durch die Geschichte und um den Erdball. Dies geschieht, indem er das Schicksal von Figuren wie Roger Casement und Joseph Conrad nachzeichnet, aber auch, indem er versucht, die Geschichte des Kapitalismus als Geschichte bestimmter Waren zu verstehen: des Zuckers, des Holzes, des Herings und der Seide. Während in Krachts *Imperium* die Warenförmigkeit der Kokosnuss – ihr Anbau, ihre Ernte, ihre Verarbeitung, ihre Vermarktung, ihr Vertrieb, ihr Konsum – als ganz und gar unproblematisch behandelt wird, kann sich Sebalds Erzähler nicht helfen: Er totalisiert die einzelne Ware, sieht sie synekdochisch in einem verhängnisvollen Zusammenhang der Ausbeutung und Zerstörung von natürlichen Ressourcen ebenso wie von menschlicher Arbeitskraft. Nicht Menschen, sondern Waren sind die Agenten, die Zentrum und Peripherie miteinander verknüpfen und so den Kapitalismus als ein Weltsystem etablieren, das sich in der Grafschaft Suffolk einem Mikrokosmos ähnlich widerspiegelt. Die Küste entlang, durch verfallene Herrensitze und deindustrialierte Ortschaften wandernd, erfasst der Erzähler die Widersprüche der post-kolonialen Realität von der Peripherie des Zentrums her, als wäre es möglich, gleichzeitig innerhalb wie auch außerhalb des durchwanderten und dadurch erfahrenen Raumes zu sein. Während in *Imperium* der verfremdende Verweis auf die Rahmung des Erzählten als Ausweichen vor der Verantwortung dem Erzählten gegenüber dient, offenbaren sich dem melancholischen Blick von Sebalds Erzähler immer neue Rahmungen und Verschachtelungen. Dieses Prinzip einer sich vom jeweiligen partikularen Standort aus konzentrisch – aber auch exzentrisch – bis ins potenziell Unendliche fortsetzenden Rahmenstruktur wird gleich am Anfang der Erzählung eingeführt.

Sebalds Reisebericht beginnt 1992 im Krankenhaus von Norwich, ein Jahr nach der „Wallfahrt" durch Suffolk, die nun auf den folgenden Seiten des Buchs narrativ wiederholt wird. Im Krankenhaus jedoch ergeht es dem erschöpften Patienten wie Kafkas Handlungsreisenden Gregor Samsa, als er sich in ein ungeheures Ungeziefer verwandelt findet: Der Blick aus dem Fenster zeigt eine grau verschwommene, kaum zu entziffernde Welt. Aber der Blick aus dem Fenster wird nicht nur erzählt, sondern auch gezeigt, in Form der Reproduktion einer Schwarz-Weiß-Fotografie. Auf ihr ist ein Fenster zu sehen, umrahmt von einer dunklen Wand. Durchs Fenster sind Himmel und Wolken zu sehen, die Fensterscheibe selbst ist mit einem Gitternetz versehen. Die Fotografie unterstreicht die Geometrie von Rechteck und Rahmung. Die Erzählung wiederum bildet den Rahmen der Fotografie, sowohl grafisch als auch inhaltlich:

> Genau entsinne ich mich noch, wie ich, gleich nach der Einlieferung, in meinem im achten Stockwerk des Krankenhauses gelegenen Zimmer überwältigt wurde von der Vorstellung, die in Suffolk im Vorsommer durchwanderten Weiten seien nun endgültig zusammengeschrumpft auf einen einzigen blinden und tauben Punkt. Tatsächlich war von meiner Bettstatt aus von der Welt nichts anderes mehr sichtbar als das farblose Stück Himmel im Rahmen des Fensters.[45]

Das Zusammenschrumpfen der Welt auf einen blinden Punkt ist jedoch nicht nur Symptom des Zusammenbruchs. Es wird auch zum Ausgangspunkt einer Methode, von einer unscheinbaren Einzelheit ausgehend aufs Ganze zu kommen. Dies erläutert der Erzähler am Beispiel seiner verstorbenen Kollegin Janine Dakyns, einer Romanistin, die eine „stets vom obskuren Detail, nie vom Offenkundigen ausgehende, gewissermaßen private Wissenschaft von der französischen Romanliteratur des 19. Jahrhunderts entwickelt“[46]. An dieser Methode orientiert sich auch der Erzähler der *Ringe des Saturn*, und der Reisebericht steht damit am Anfang ganz im Zeichen des Realismus des 19. Jahrhunderts, insbesondere seines Repräsentanten Gustave Flaubert, in dessen Werk Janine Dakyns das Motiv des Sandes hervorhebt: „In einem Sandkorn im Saum eines Winterkleides der Emma Bovary, sagte Janine, hat Flaubert die ganze Sahara gesehen, und jedes Stäubchen wog für ihn soviel wie das Atlasgebirge.“[47] Eine solchermaßen synekdochische Weltwahrnehmung, in der das kleinste Detail von gleicher Bedeutung ist wie das große Ganze, macht sich auch der Erzähler zu eigen, allerdings nicht mit Verweis auf Flaubert, sondern auf die barocke Gelehrtenprosa Brownes, die er so beschreibt:

> [W]enn er, mitsamt seiner Fracht, auf den Kreisen seiner Prosa höher und höher getragen wird wie ein Segler auf den warmen Strömungen der Luft, dann ergreift selbst den heutigen Leser noch ein Gefühl der Levitation. Je mehr die Entfernung wächst, desto klarer wird die Sicht. Mit der größtmöglichen Deutlichkeit erblickt man die winzigsten Details. Es ist, als schaute man zugleich durch ein umgekehrtes Fernrohr und durch ein Mikroskop.[48]

In dieser Dialektik von Nähe und Distanz, von Wirklichkeit und Unwirklichkeit gewahrt der Erzähler sowohl die realen, unmittelbar offenbaren, zerstörerischen Folgen, die dem Ort Lowestoft unter „dem realen Kapitalismus […] der Ära der Baronin Thatcher“[49] widerfahren sind, als auch die Übertragung realer Erfahrungen in Traumbilder: „Wahrscheinlich sind es verschüttete Erinnerungen, die die eigenartige Überwirklichkeit dessen erzeugen, was man im Traum sieht.“[50] *Die Ringe des Saturn* ist durchsetzt von solchen Bildern, in denen das historisch Reale als traumhaft erscheint. Die Möglichkeit realistischen Schreibens beruht auf der Möglichkeit eines konstruktiven Erinnerns, denn Geschichte an sich ist abstrakt, bilderlos. Dies wird besonders deutlich im achten Kapitel, in dem der Erzähler

---

45 W. G. Sebald, *Die Ringe des Saturn. Eine englische Wallfahrt*, Frankfurt/M., 1997, S. 12.

46 Ebd., S. 16.

47 Ebd., S. 17.

48 Ebd., S. 30.

49 Ebd., S. 56.

50 Ebd., S. 98.

einen holländischen Geschäftsmann über die Geschichte des Zuckerrohranbaus und Zuckerhandels und die damit zusammenhängende ungeheure Kapitalakkumulation dozieren lässt:

> Das im 18. und 19. Jahrhundert durch verschiedene Formen der Sklavenwirtschaft akkumulierte Kapital, sagte de Jong, läuft nach wie vor um, trägt Zins und Zinseszins, vermehrt und vervielfacht sich und treibt aus eigener Kraft andauernd neue Blüten. Eines der probatesten Mittel zur Legitimierung solchen Geldes ist von jeher die Förderung der Kunst, der Ankauf und das Zurschaustellen von Kunstgegenständen und, wie heute zu beobachten ist, das immer weiter fortschreitende, beinahe schon lachhafte Höhertreiben der Preise auf den großen Auktionen, sagte de Jong.[51]

Die fortdauernde Vermehrung des auf Zwangsarbeit beruhenden Kapitals und die weitere Kapitalisierung von Kunst: Dies ist, das macht die Erzählung deutlich, der objektive Wahnsinn der Logik des Kapitals. Der Fetisch des „Geld heckenden Geldes" verbirgt die reale Arbeit, die den Mehrwert geschaffen hat. Die Kehrseite des Reichtums der niederländischen Zuckerdynastien ist nicht nur die Ausbeutung der Arbeit in den Anbauländern der globalen Peripherie; zur Totalität des Systems zählt auch das Verschwinden der Arbeit in den globalen Zentren, wie in dem Ort Lowestoft, wo der Erzähler kein „Ende der stetig fortschreitenden Verelendung"[52] abzusehen vermag. Verglichen mit diesem Wahnsinn ist die von Monomanie bis zu einem geradezu paranoischen Beziehungswahn changierende Melancholie des Erzählers und seiner Figuren sekundär. Mehr noch, die allegorische Methode dieser Melancholie hat nichts Romantisches, sondern ist, um noch einmal Lukács' Replik auf Bloch zu zitieren, „harte Arbeit". Mit touristischer Muße hat die Wanderung des Erzählers durch Suffolk wenig gemein. Die Schreibarbeit, die diese Wanderung nachzuzeichnen sucht, tendiert zur Totalität vermöge der Versenkung ins scheinbar Partikulare, das sich immer wieder als Typisches entpuppt. Die episodische und degressive Komposition des Reiseberichts bietet eine Oberflächenerscheinung der Zerstückelung. Als Ganzes zusammengehalten wird dieses Gebilde jedoch durch das alles überlagernde Motiv historischer Vergänglichkeit und Zerstörung. Allerdings wird zugleich deutlich gemacht, dass dieses Kompositionsprinzip ein hoch künstlerisches ist, das aus dem barocken Denken auf die Gegenwart übertragen wird. Darstellbar ist der post-koloniale Kapitalismus, das scheint die implizite These von Sebalds Reisebericht zu sein, nur durch allegorische Entrückung in einen anderen Bedeutungsrahmen. Damit ist der Erzählrahmen, anders als bei Kracht, weniger ein Mittel zur ironischen Metafiktion als eher ein Mittel zur Ermöglichung der Darstellung von Geschichte. Erst als allegorisch verfahrende Fiktion wird die objektiv ins Abstrakte tendierende Geschichte von Ausbeutung und Akkumulation als konkrete Gewalt erfahrbar und erzählbar.

---

[51] Ebd., S. 230 f.

[52] Ebd., S. 57.

Jenny Nachtigall

Realism after Fetishism, or What is the Realism that We Need in a Time of Catastrophe?

Almost a century ago Walter Benjamin wrote about Paul Klee's *Angelus Novus* (1920) as an allegory of catastrophe, indeed of progress as a site of catastrophe. In the aftermath of multiple crises and the consolidation of National Socialism as the power to be, for Benjamin art seemed to have turned into a witness rather than a force within history. In the ninth of his "Thesis on the Concept of History" (1939) he commented on Klee's drawing: "This is how the angel of history must look. His face is turned toward the past. Where a chain of events appears before us, he sees one single catastrophe, which keeps piling wreckage upon wreckage and hurls it at his feet."[1]

Whilst the "wreckages" of today are different ones, Benjamin's evocation of a non-linear image of catastrophe as a kind of dumpster of time has some resonance with the catastrophic temporalities of the present. They materialise in financialised capital and its digital infrastructure. Although frequently understood as an entirely new order,[2] from outsourcing production to the global South that provides the human hardware that keeps the system running, to the austerity measures in the global North, feudalisms and (Post-)Fordisms persist amidst financialisation, are endemic to it. If this proliferation of different temporalities is catastrophic, it is not in the sense of an end time scenario of apocalypse for, as Benjamin reminds us, the "tradition of the oppressed teaches us that the 'emergency situation' in which we live is the rule."[3]

Benjamin's contemporary Rosa Luxemburg – and after her Gilles Deleuze and Félix Guattari amongst others – have analysed this situation and the non-linear temporality that it obeys as sustaining a process of accumulation by dispossession

---

1 Walter Benjamin, "Theses on the Concept of History", in: *Selected Writings, Volume 4: 1938-1940*, Cambridge, MA, London, pp. 389-400: here p. 392. On the contemporary moment see Lazzarato: "From one financial crisis to the next, we have now entered a period of permanent crisis, which we shall call 'catastrophe' to refer to the discontinuity of the concept of crisis itself." Maurizio Lazzarato, *The Making of the Indebted Man. An Essay on the Neoliberal Condition*, New York, NY, 2012, pp. 123-124.

2 An order which appears to have dispensed with the human subject as intermediary in the production of surplus value, accruing value 'immaterially' and autonomously (e.g. through algorithmic procedures like high-frequency-trading). Yet while the ideological position of labour as a binding nucleus of subjectivisation has vanished, the function of labour power certainly has not. See Lazzarato (2012), *The Making of the Indebted Man.*

3 Benjamin (1939), Theses on the Concept of History, p. 392.

that is ongoing.[4] Stressing that Marx's notion of "so-called primitive accumulation" implies the continuity of capitalist exploitation as well as the "origin narratives" that mask it, the notion of progress is suspended. Or, to return, to Benjamin's allegorical phrasing:

> [A] storm is blowing from Paradise and has got caught in his wings; it is so strong that the angel can no longer close them. The storm drives him irresistibly into the future to which his back is turned, while the pile of debris before him grows toward the sky. What we call progress is *this* storm [emphasis in the original].[5]

Recently Benjamin's reading of Klee's *Angelus Novus* was at the centre of an art world skirmish where two opposing views on the significance of the figure as much as on the question of realism clashed. I would like to take them as an entry point into the question that shall concern me in the following: What kind of realism do we need in a state of catastrophe and what role may art have to play in it? Although neither of the conflicting positions allows for a sufficient response, they are instructive as problems. The first one revived a traditional, Lukácsian notion of realism that is based on a reflection theory of art. The second one was informed by an anti-Marxist (and anti-poststructuralist) philosophical trend going by the name of speculative realism.[6] The philosophical notion of realism on which the latter relies, is, of course, of an entirely different order than the realism over which Georg Lukács fought with Ernst Bloch amongst others in the 1930s. The nature of that debate revolved around the political function of the aesthetic; it was riven not least by conflicting conceptions of capitalism and by how to fight fascism on the terrain of culture (a point to which I shall return).[7] Moving diachronically between these different 'realism debates', will put the political implications of speculative realism into perspective. Although it initially evolved as a purely academic project

---

4 In Marx's own revision of Adam Smiths's notion of "original accumulation", "so-called primitive accumulation" defined the founding myth of political economy, where the capitalist is said to have accumulated the first wealth through saving, while the proletariat was spend everything "and more" until only her own labour-time remained. Karl Marx, *Capital. A Critique of Political Economy. Volume 1*, trans. by Ben Fowkes, London, 1990, p. 873. See Gilles Deleuze and Félix Guattari, *Anti-Oedipus*, New York, NY, 2009, p. 225 and Rosa Luxemburg, *Die Akkumulation des Kapitals oder was die Epigonen aus der Marxschen Theorie gemacht haben: Eine Antikritik*, Leipzig, 1921. See also Jason Read, "Primitive Accumulation: The Aleatory Foundation of Capitalism", in: *Rethinking Marxism* 14, 2 (2002), pp. 24-49.

5 Benjamin (1939), Theses on the Concept of History, p. 392.

6 Although by no means homogenous, what unites speculative realism's various subdivisions and offshoots – including new materialism, object-oriented ontology and accelerationism – is a shared repudiation of continental philosophy's tenacious vice of "correlationism" and a return to the traditions of (fundamental) ontology and (pre-critical) rationalism.

7 As Rodney Livingstone noted on the exchange between Lukács and Bloch: "Driven by the 'impressionistic' character of Bloch's defence to emphasise the unity of the social whole, Lukács failed to register its essential point: that this unity was irreducibly contradictory. In this way, an opportunity to debate the problems of the artistic presentation of contradiction – the absent context of Bloch's remarks on montage, and a stubborn crux in Lukács's realist aesthetics – was missed." See Rodney Livingstone, "Presentation 1", in: *Aesthetics and Politics*, trans. and ed. by Ronald Taylor, London, 2007, pp. 9-15: here p. 14.

it certainly has political implications that become not least tangible in its 'second-hand' appearances within contemporary art and theory.[8] More specifically, what will concern me are some post-digital theories and practices that have mobilised the lessons of speculative realism for staking out a realist ontology of art that is driven by an occlusion of history from temporality and of contradiction from form. As a symptom of contemporary capitalism and its origin narratives, this phenomenon is remarkable and I will spend some time discussing it. It has no consequences, however, for an understanding of realism in art that moves beyond a positivism of the given. For that I will draw on another reading of Klee, namely by critic, art historian and political activist Carl Einstein. Returning to the political ontology of realism that Einstein developed in the 1920s and 30s (in part vis-à-vis Klee's work), opens onto a problem that seems particularly urgent within today's catastrophe and to which speculative realism is structurally blind: the role that obscured histories, "fictions", fetishism and myth have to play in realism.[9]

1. From the Angel to the Cloud

The 2015 iteration of the Venice Biennale, titled "All the World's Futures" had placed Benjamin's allegory of catastrophe at the centre of its curatorial concept, where it was called upon as an epistemological figure for representing history and grasping the present. Benjamin, "compels us to revision (sic!) the representational capacity of art", we are told and thus provokes the question as to how "the current disquiet of our time be properly grasped, made comprehensible, examined, and articulated?"[10] Although the Biennale's broader conceptual framework employs Bruno Latour's thing theory – following which "catastrophe" seems to turn into one of the many "fascinating subject matter[s]" that artists ought to depict as the "present 'state of things'" – the understanding of realism underlying its version of Benjamin is basically Lukácsian.[11] It is rooted in art's capacity of *representing reali-*

---

8 From the Documenta (13), an exhibition series programmed around speculative realism at the Museum Fridericianum in Kassel to various smaller gallery exhibitions, this in fact genuinely philosophical realism has had an intense, if brief, afterlife in the field of contemporary art. See for instance Carolyn Christov-Bakargiev, "Der Tanz war sehr frenetisch, rege, rasselnd, klingend, rollend, verdreht und dauerte eine lange Zeit", 2012 (Press Release Documenta (13): http://www3.documenta.de/fileadmin/press/for_the_press/press_kit/de/4_An_Essay_by_Carolyn.pdf) (retrieved 26/3/2017) and the series of exhibitions that Susanne Pfeffer curated at Fridericianum, Kassel: "Speculations on Anonymous Materials" (2013), "Nature after Nature" (2014) and "Inhuman" (2015).

9 In my thinking on Einstein in this essay I am indebted to Anselm Franke and Tom Holert, who plan an exhibition around Einstein's work at Haus der Kulturen der Welt, Berlin.

10 Okwui Enwezor, "All the World's Futures", http://www.labiennale.org/en/art/archive/56th-exhibition/enwezor/ (retrieved 16/3/2017).

11 In the 1930s Lukács has formulated art's obligation to realism at the case of literature as follows: "If literature is a particular form by means of which objective reality is reflected, then it becomes of crucial importance for it to grasp that reality as it truly is, and not merely to confine itself to reproducing whatever manifests itself immediately and on the surface." Georg Lukács, "Realism in the

ty for the subject, i.e. in documenting and articulating aspects of reality in order to make them "graspable" and "comprehensible" to us.[12] Yet divorced from the philosophical-political premises that – regardless of how problematic themselves – galvanised Lukács's staunch defence of art's obligation to realist representation, it remains uncertain why it is exactly that art should have epistemological priority in comprehending reality (rather than political theory, for instance).

For the "realist" vanguard of contemporary art, however, the problem with the Biennale's reading of Benjamin's allegory was situated elsewhere: it did not pertain to how it was put to use, but to the fact *that* it was used in the first place. Understood as "one of the central philosophical allegories of twentieth century leftist thought",[13] Benjamin's angel of history is dismissed as a ghost from a (Marxist) past that finally needs to be put to rest. It apparently still haunts the art world as the spectre of a left-wing-melancholic future angst and science-phobia that forecloses an engagement with the future, which is determined as the foremost terrain of art's tasks in the present. Accordingly, curator Mohammad Salemy calls for an "Art After the Machines", one that – schooled in the lessons of speculative realism and cybernetics – will enable art's "extraction from its history and ontology", a "separation that only loosens its ties to its human past so it can invent today its machinic future."[14] Robin Mackay, editor of *Collapse* (one of speculative realism's discursive mouthpieces) approaches artworks as "technologies of the future"[15] and Suhail Malik emphatically demands a realist refashioning of art as a "rational exercise" of contingency.[16] The relentless orientation towards the future and the cybernetically inflected understanding of present-day digital technology as the matrix of contemporaneity are two sides of the same coin that aim to redeem art from the clutches of the 'angel of history'. Rather than an aberration of the original premises of speculative realism, however, the figure of this coin should be taken as the adjustment of its conceptions of history and science to a digital present. In this sense speculative realism's most prominent intervention, Quentin Meillassoux's infamous indictment against "correlationism" – i.e. the structural anthropomorphism that is said to mar the post-Kantian view of the world – is only of secondary importance. More pertinent is its cumbersome bedrock of "non-correlationist" thought, which is to say, the hypothesis of "ancestral statements" or the so-called "arche-fossil":

Balance", in: *Aesthetics and Politics*, trans. and ed. by Ronald Taylor, London, 2007, pp. 28-59: here p. 33.

12 Enwezor (2015), All the World's Futures.

13 Mohammad Salemy, "Between Angelus Novus & the Mechanical Turk" (response to Julieta Aranda and Ana Teixeira Pinto, "Turk, Toaster, Task Rabbit"), http://conversations.e-flux.com/t/superconversations-day-6-mohammad-salemy-responds-to-julieta-aranda-and-ana-teixeira-pinto-turk-toaster-task-rabbit/1639 (retrieved 19/3/2017).

14 Mohammad Salemy, "Art after the Machines", in: *e-flux journal*, 65 (May-August 2015), p. 6, http://supercommunity-pdf.e-flux.com/pdf/supercommunity/article_1178.pdf (retrieved 26/3/2017).

15 Robin Mackay, "Introduction: Three Figures of Contigency", in: Robin Mackay (ed.), *The Medium of Contingency*, Falmouth, 2011, pp. 1-8.

16 Suhail Malik, "Reason to Destroy Contemporary Art", in: Amy Christoph Cox/Jenny Jaskey/Suhail Mailk (eds.), *Realism, Materialism, Art*, Berlin, 2015, pp. 185-192.

statements that experimental science produces today concerning "objects" that are anterior to the human species and thus to thought. In Meillassoux's frame it is specifically the "arche-fossil" that disarms correlationism by allowing access to a world beyond the limitations of humanity, that however, is thinkable, i.e. mathematisable with the (discursive) instruments of science. It "is the enigma which we must confront", he writes, "mathematics' ability to discourse about the great outdoors; to discourse about a past where both humanity and life are absent".[17]

A specific conception of science is consequently the lynchpin of this realism (and as I will show, it equally defines the art that takes up its "challenge"). As a number of critics have pointed out, this is also its most glaring blind spot. From Alenka Zupančič's psychoanalytic perspective, speculative realism succumbs to idealism (in which discourse has no consequences),[18] whereas from Alexander Galloway's media-theoretical view it accedes to capitalism.[19] Historicising Meillassoux's understanding of mathematics as entry point into the absolute, Galloway has pointed out that today, in the age of the algorithm, the logic of the mathematical discipline (e.g. in the form of computer science and cybernetics) converges with the logic of the capitalist mode of production. Hence, "pure math makes claims about the world and extracts value from it."[20]

What appears as a liability in Galloway's perspective, manifests as an asset for the spokesmen of speculation in contemporary art: Here it is precisely the proximity between financial and philosophical (as well as artistic) speculation that underpins the relevance of the new realism. Whereas Meillassoux still mused about how Stéphane Mallarmé's *Un coup de Dés jamais n'abolira le Hasard* – homologous to mathematics – opens onto the radical contingency of hyper-chaos,[21] his advocates in contemporary art and theory seem to have given these modernist proclivities a decisively contemporary turn. As a "medium of contingency" contemporary art is said to converge with the contingency of finance.[22]

---

17 Quentin Meillassoux, *After Finitude. An Essay on the Necessity of Contingency*, New York, NY, 2008, p. 26.

18 Alenka Zupančič, "Realism in Psychoanalysis", in: Lorenzo Chiesa (ed.), *Lacan and Philosophy: The New Generation*, Melbourne, 2014, pp. 21-33: esp. pp. 27 f. and p. 32.

19 Following Frank Kuhne, these charges can be said to converge given that the structure of capital is "necessarily idealist", see Frank Kuhne, *Begriff und Zitat bei Marx. Die idealistische Struktur des Kapitals und ihre nicht-idealistische Darstellung bei Marx*, Lüneburg, 1995.

20 Alexander Galloway, "The Poverty of Philosophy: Realism and Post-Fordism", in: *Critical Inquiry* 39, 2 (Winter 2013), pp. 347-366: here pp. 358 f.

21 A space where "there is no reason for anything to be or remain the way it is; everything must, without reason, be able not to be and/or be able to be other than it is." Meillassoux (2008), *After Finitude*, p. 60. Alenka Zupančič has called this absolutation of contingency an idealism that installs a "God of atheists". Zupančič (2014), Realism in Psychoanalysis, p. 23. For an incisive reading of Meillassoux's *Le nombre et la sirène: un déchiffrage du Coup de dés de Mallarmé*, Paris, 2011 see Svenja Bromberg, "The Anti-Political Aesthetics of Objects and Worlds Beyond", in: *Mutamute*, July 2013, http://www.metamute.org/editorial/articles/anti-political-aesthetics-objects-and-worlds-beyond (retrieved 18/3/2017).

22 See for instance Suhail Malik/Gerald Nestler, "Introduction: Art and Finance", in: *Finance and Society* 2, 2 (2016), pp. 94-95; here p. 94.

Consequently, for Malik and Co. both art as we know it and Marxism as an epistemo-political framework for understanding capitalism are rendered obsolete by financialised capitalism and its digital infrastructure.[23] Both are hopelessly anachronistic, incurably "analogue", in a world that is ruled by code. Or, to remain in the picture: For the pioneers of art's digital futurity the place once occupied by the 'angel of history' is now taken by the cloud, that mighty digital structure that knows all your data, personal contacts, images and whatever else you upload when you connect to the holy/digital spirit. Given that digitality is the meta-medium of the present, being the medium of finance, everyday communication, and cultural production,[24] art, too, ought to free itself from the prison house of an artistic medium ontology and remake itself on the model of the derivative, a commodity that accrues value by deferral, banking on the future.[25]

In its 'hard' version this command yields the production of "Art as a Sublime Asset", to quote the apposite title of *Real Flow's* prospectus. *Real Flow* is a group that consists of artists and theorists Diann Bauer, Victoria Ivanova, Christopher Kulendran-Thomas and Malik himself and aims at "re-engineering the artwork's commodity form" by integrating art into "its diverse channels of exhibition, circulation, and marketization".[26] In practice such mimicry of the value form results in the sale of artworks as financial instruments, in which its tradable elements can be purchased separately from its exhibitionary components (i.e. the objects themselves, monochrome airbrushed canvases covered with *Real Flow* logos). In its 'soft' version it results in a mimicry of an everyday life that is permeated by value, for which the last Berlin Biennale (2016) can be taken as a case in point. Curated by the New York based collective *DIS* (Lauren Boyle, Solomon Chase, Marco Roso, and David Toro), the Biennale showcased a generalised aesthetics in the age of the algorithm. Across Airbnb-styled installations, trade fair information booths, workout zones and juice bars the dissolution of the boundaries between artistic form and the commodified forms of digital media was omnipresent. Not despite but because of its rhetoric of futurity and radical rupture, projects like *DIS* and *Real Flow* turn out strikingly modern, presenting post-digital art as a kind of financial-

---

23 That is to say, Marxism is redundant due to the supposed obsolescence of labour-power within capital's 'immaterial' financialised modes of reproduction. See for instance Suhail Malik, "The Ontology of Finance", in: *Collapse*, 8 (December 2014), pp. 629-812 and "Reason to Destroy Contemporary Art". I will return to the latter.

24 See Kerstin Stakemeier, "Krise und Materialität in der Kunst. Über Formwerdung und Digitalität", in: Kerstin Stakemeier/Susanne Witzgall (eds.), *Macht des Materials – Politik der Materialität*, Zurich, 2014, pp. 184-198.

25 On the derivative as vital for financialised capital as contemporary technology of power see Spyros Lapatsioras/John Milios/Dimitris P. Sotiropoulos, *A Political Economy of Contemporary Capitalism and its Crisis. Demystifying Finance*, London, New York, NY, 2013.

26 Real Flow, "Art Is the Sublime Asset", in: *prospectus*, 1 (March 2015), p. 3, http://diannbauer.net/#/real-flow/ (p. 5) (retrieved 18/3/2017). For another reading of *Real Flow* see Sven Lütticken, "The Coming Exception. Art and the Crisis of Value", in: *New Left Review*, 99 (May-June 2016), pp. 111-136: here p. 126.

ised productivism that has failed to emancipate itself from the narratives of progress at the heart of its initial iterations.[27]

Take Boris Arvatov characterisation of Russian productivism as an "art that is right down to the last detail contemporary, urban, industrial, 'americanized'", aiming at the "transformation of art in its entirety into the organisation of the material culture of society."[28] But if for Arvatov the demand of the productivist artists to replace the engineers and the designers was contingent on the post-revolutionary hopes of a communist society to come, the horizon of *DIS*'s "neo-productivist" techno-utopia is an exaggerated version of the present. In a text on "Styles and Customs in the 2020s", for instance, the globalised digital culture of the future is said to close the "infamous 'gap' between art and life [...] after over a century of separation. There are no more 'artists,' 'interior designers,' or 'PR agents,' there are simply operators within culture."[29] The productivists' projected suspension of difference (between artistic and social forms, artists and engineers) today returns as the "flat ontology" of universal exchangeability. The approximation between the artistic and the economic that pertains to this development, to be sure, is not a moral problem (e.g. the loss of art's modern autonomy and critical distance in rampant complicity). It is rather a problem of form that is stripped of its contradictions (rather than its autonomy) and of history subjected to the progressivism of a cybernetic utopia.

As Benjamin already knew, however, history does not progress in a straight line, sublating its previous iterations into a higher order (and one should add, neither does form). It is traversed by the unresolved contradictions of the past, of 'angels of history', if you will, that do not dissolve in even the most speculative of clouds. 'Mythic' remainders nestle also in the austere formulas of systems theory. Unlike the speculative realists of today, historians and philosophers of science have been long aware of the fact that mathematical logic cannot fully rid itself of the 'mythic'. Refuting Norbert Wiener's triumphant claim that cybernetics has finally settled the old fight between mechanism and vitalism, Georges Canguilhem, for example, insisted on the recurrence of vitalist figures, of anachronistic motives, images and theorems that reach into "the night and the drives and dreams".[30] In the heyday of cybernetics John Cohen in turn, presented a richly illustrated history of robotics that traces its roots to the long tradition of speaking figures and golems, whose

---

27 See also Benjamin Noys's critique of accelerationism – one of speculative realism's offshoots – and its debts to Futurism's utopian project of mastering the forces of production, which returns today as a (nostalgic) attempt to move beyond the constrictions of labour. Benjamin Noys, *Malign Velocities. Acceleration and Capitalism*, Winchester, 2014, p. 16.

28 Boris Arvatov, "Kunst und Produktion in der Geschichte der Arbeiterbewegung" (1926), in: *Kunst und Produktion*, ed. and trans. by Hans Günther and Karla Hielscher, Hamburg, 1972, pp. 37-51: here p. 48.

29 DIS, "Styles and Customs in the 2020s", in: *e-flux journal* (June 2015), http://supercommunity.e-flux.com/texts/styles-and-customs-in-the-2020s/ (retrieved 19/3/2017).

30 Canguilhem quoted in Thomas Brandstetter, "Vom Nachleben in der Wissenschaftsgeschichte", in: *Zeitschrift für Medienwissenschaft*, 1 (2009), pp. 74-80: here p. 75.

"magic" has been merely displaced.[31] And, more recently, Anselm Franke has suggested that cybernetics inherited the "modern bewilderment over the 'being-in-communication' of so-called primitive societies [...]. This is the backdrop against which one can understand Marshall McLuhan's insistence that in the information age humanity would go 'tribal' again."[32]

It is precisely by seeking to expel such "historical" clutter that the new realism comes into view as an anachronism itself, and thus as a tangible symptom not only of crisis, but of catastrophe as the breakdown of temporal order. In her critique of the ontological turn – and speculative realism certainly falls under this label – Jordana Rosenberg has proposed that we should understand such symptom of untimeliness through a primitivism/futurity figuration that is endemic to the current stage of primitive accumulation and the origin narratives that accompany it. Its "time is not historical time, but rather the fungible contradictoriness of narrative."[33] Following Rosenberg, the frenzy of claiming an uncharted terrain of thought (via philosophical/financial speculation's radical contingency) and the urge towards objects in themselves "calls to mind any number of New-World-style fantasies about locations unmediated by social order." The ontological turn thus updates a primitivist paradigm "that hinges on a violent erasure of the social: the conjuring of a realm – an 'ancestral realm' – that exists in the present, but in parallax to historical time. A terra nullius of the theoretical landscape."[34] If for speculative realism the narrative logic of primitive accumulation consists in the primordial rocks of pre-history and the radical contingency of speculation that converge in the figure of the "great outdoors", for its artistic counterparts this manifests as the return of the modern, of the very figures, tropes and conceptions that their prerogative of contemporaneity so urgently seeks to disavow.

2. Real "Fictions": Myth, Fetishism, and Realism

In the 1930s Benjamin's contemporary Ernst Bloch described the persistence of anachronistic temporalities as non-contemporaneous contradictions. In contrast to Lukács – his nemesis in the realism debates of the 1930s – Bloch stressed the unevenness of capitalism (rather its totalising character), defined by a "polyrhythmic and multi-spatial" logic in which "not even [...] the obsolete forms of production and exchange, have passed away, let alone their ideological super-

31 See Brandstetter (2009), Vom Nachleben, p. 80 and John Cohen, *Golem und Roboter. Über künstliche Menschen*, Frankfurt/M., 1968.

32 Anselm Franke, "Emancipatory Mimesis", in: *Metropolis M* (2016), http://www.metropolism.com/en/opinion/29012_emancipatory_mimesis (retrieved 26/3/2017).

33 Jordana Rosenberg, "The Molecularization of Sexuality: On Some Primitivisms of the Present", in: *Theory & Event* 17, 2 (2014), p. 7. As Rosenberg further specifies the figuration of primitiveness as the verso face of millennialism defines the relation between settler-colonialism and financialisation as the two levers of the primitive accumulation of the present, both as the actual process of dispossession and as a narrative logics that obeys a dual temporality.

34 Ibid., p. 2.

structures, let alone genuine contents of not yet defined Irratio."[35] Bloch's reflections on capitalism's multi-temporality and spatiality were embedded in a theory of non-contemporaneity that took National Socialism as its point of departure. But whereas in the Artwork Essay Benjamin emphasises the novelty of fascism – of *how* it organised the masses through technology – Bloch's focus lies on *where* fascism filled a void, addressed a lack:[36] in contrast to Marxism the Nazis were able to tap into the non-contemporaneous contradictions that traversed the present – "the unfulfilled fairytale of the good old times, the unsolved myth of dark ancient being or of nature" – and to bind them into a cultural synthesis based on blood and soil.[37] Thus, by drawing attention to the "unclaimed heritage of Münzer, Medieval mysticism, Nietzsche and Lebensphilosophie", Anson Rabinbach observed, "Bloch's theory is also an indictment of the Left for abandoning the terrain of fantasy to fascist colonization."[38]

Carl Einstein shared the urgency of reclaiming the terrain of the "irrational" and it not least informed his notion of realism.[39] Like Bloch, who wrote one of the first positive reviews of Einstein's 1915 study on African sculpture,[40] he distinguished his approach from orthodox Marxism since, unlike the latter, he "attribute[d] to the new myths the strongest reality."[41] In the 1920s and early 30s Einstein developed a political ontology of realism that rested on a radically contemporary and outspokenly political conception of myth. For him myth did not signify "conservation of the past, but revolt against the given".[42] The understanding of realism that followed from this was consequently not to be mistaken with "imitation or representation" of reality, but instead aimed at "the new creation of something that's concretely real [Wirkliches]".[43]

The art of Paul Klee served as exemplary for Einstein's notion of activated realism and its production of the real. And like Benjamin's reading of Klee, his was premised on a non-linear concept of time. In his essay on the artist from the third edition of his major survey on contemporary art, *Die Kunst des 20. Jahrhunderts*

---

35 Ernst Bloch, *Heritage of Our Times* (1934), trans. by Neville and Stephen Plaice, Berkeley and Los Angeles, CA, 1991, p. 62.

36 See Anson Rabinbach, "Unclaimed Heritage: Ernst Bloch's Heritage of Our Times and the Theory of Fascism", in: *New German Critique*, 11 (1977), pp. 5-21.

37 Bloch (1991), *Heritage of Our Times*, p. 112.

38 Rabinbach (1977), Unclaimed Heritage, p. 19

39 The connection between Bloch and Einstein has been also made by Devin Fore in his incisive reading of Einstein's unfinished autobiography (*Bebuquin II*) as a "necrologue of the ego". See Devin Fore, *Realism after Modernism. The Rehumanization of Art and Literature*, Cambridge, MA, London, 2012, p. 233.

40 See David Pan, "The Struggle for Myth in the Nazi Period: Alfred Baeumler, Ernst Bloch, and Carl Einstein", in: *South Atlantic Review* 65, 1 (2000), pp. 41-57: here p. 44.

41 Carl Einstein, "Georges Braque" (1934), in: *Werke. Berliner Ausgabe. Volume 3*, ed. by Hermann Haarmann and Klaus Siebenhaar, Berlin, 1996, pp. 251-516: here p. 280.

42 Carl Einstein, "Paul Klee" (1931), in: *Werke. Berliner Ausgabe. Volume 3*, ed. by Hermann Haarmann and Klaus Siebenhaar, Berlin, 1996, pp. 259-269: here p. 262.

43 Ibid., the translation is taken from Sebastian Zeidler, *Form as Revolt. Carl Einstein and the Ground of Art*, Ithaca, NY, 2016, p. 223.

(1931) Einstein espoused a view that will be familiar to readers of the "Thesis on the Concept of History":

> History is constructed from that which is contemporary and the selection of that which is past depends on its contemporary significance. This fact explains the continuous transformation of conceptions of history; at the same time it refutes the possibility of an objective historiography. It thus explains contemporary art's approximation to the primitive [die Primitive].[44]

However, unlike for Benjamin in the late 1930s in the beginning of the decade, the possibility of activating non-contemporaneous contradictions, and in particular myth, was not yet fully eclipsed.[45] Art was one terrain, although not the only one, on which such activation could be actualised. Klee's work did precisely this, and most importantly, it did so on the level of form:

> Reason imposes on man an idiotic monotony of existence and of the gestalts, of which he will at best produce variations or rearrangements; this is a fatal limitation. In earlier times, myths had served as a means of defense against such gestalt monotony; gestalt formation was not a matter of aesthetics but of religion [...]. This same impulse is at work today in the experiments with new gestalt relations; the fundamental drama of metamorphosis, of gestalt transformation, is being played out anew. That's easily possible in an image, for every form can signify a tremendous number of things.[46]

In his recent in-depth study of Einstein's specific mode of realism as a formalism, Sebastian Zeidler has made the intriguing argument that "the fundamental drama of metamorphosis", or what he calls "metamorphotic revolt", is a synonym for Einstein's understanding of myth. It encompassed a multiplicity of diverging practices that were engaged in the production of the real as revolt: "Tattoo, scientific hypothesis, sexual deviancy, totemist rituals, and Greek cosmogonies are all mythic practices insofar as they are all revolts against the given."[47] In this sense Klee's work actualised metamorphotic revolt through their perpetual oscillation between the fixing and the unfixing of forms: One sees this for instance in *Angelus Novus* (1920), where the diagrammatic structure that defines the angel's erect posture starts to fray into the dynamic lines of the figure's curly hair, becoming arrested again in the crystalline forms of its hands and further pared down in the reduced tripartite form of its feet; or even more so when, in the *Ventriloquist and Crier in the Moor* (1923) form wavers between the stabilisation of the grid and the amorphous contour of the figure placed upon it (and the doubling of this tension within the figure itself, in whose gridded core a plethora of fantastical figures circulates).

---

44 Ibid., p. 261.

45 Einstein's understanding of myth and of realism is admittedly more complex than I am able to convey in the frame of this article. I here focus on the aspect that strikes me as a productive counter-model to contemporary ontologies of realism. For the shifting significations of myth, e.g. from a marker of collectivity to one of individualism see Zeidler (2016), *Form as Revolt*, pp. 250 f.

46 Einstein (1996), Paul Klee, pp. 263 f. The translation is taken from Zeidler (2016), *Form as Revolt*, p. 209.

47 Ibid., p. 218.

For Einstein the "ungrounding" that animates Klee's work figured as homologous to other mythic practice, from the tattoo (a revolt against the biologically defined surface of the body) to the scientific hypothesis (a revolt against verifiability).[48]

The political ontology of such realism as metarmorphotic revolt hinged on a specific reading of vitalism and left-wing Nietzscheanism that – if Einstein had the time to assemble all his material – might have resulted in what Zeidler calls a "kind of *Thousand Plateaus* of the 1930s".[49] Considering that Gilles Deleuze's and Felix Guattari's magnum opus was indebted to Nietzsche as much as to Marx, however, it is interesting to note that Einstein's approach to form equally resonates with Marx's "formalism" (whether intended or not).

For Einstein, as mentioned above, myth did not simply figure as "illusion" or as fiction in the common sense but as a generative structure that was productive of the real.[50] His realism could be thus also understood as a productivism that, on account of the political shifts of the 1930s, dispensed with the centrality of work. In the face of the aborted or failed revolutions in Europe and the Soviet Union, succeeded by fascism's own brand of collectivity, the function of work as a binding nucleus of subjectivisation and collectivisation lost increasingly its political purchase and legitimacy. Instead of filling this (still) vacant position of collective practice with the universality of the value form (as characteristic for productivism's 'realist' returns in the present), Einstein's interest was not in the latter's monetary functions but in the 'mythic' logic through which form operates. Hence, despite the different ways in which Marx's notion of fetishism and Einstein's notion of myth were put to work by their respective authors, they converge at least on one point: Marx equally conceived of fetishism as productive of the real. His description of value as a dynamism of form in the third volume of *Capital* is illuminating in this respect:

> Taking the social capital as a whole, one part of this is always on the market as a commodity, waiting to pass over into money [...] [A]nother part is on the market as

48 See ibid., p. 216. In this respect it is worth considering that Einstein's transversal notion of form resonated not only diachronically with the aesthetics of Félix Guattari (see in particular his essay "The New Aesthetic Paradigm", in: *Chaosmosis. An Eethico-Aeshetic Paradigm*, trans. by Paul Bains and Julian Pefanis, Bloomington, IN, 1995, pp. 98-118). It also shared a lot with the socially expanded formalism that was contemporaneous to him, ranging from Czech structuralist Jan Mukařovský, Poetists Karel Teige and Bedřich Václavek, to particularly Lu Märten in Germany. A self-taught heterodox Marxist art historian, writer, feminist and theoretician, Märten developed a radically de-hierarchised and non-disciplinary theory and history of form that was indebted to the Arts and Crafts and *Lebensreform* movements as much as to Marx's *Capital*. See in particular her major work Lu Märten, *Wesen und Veränderung der Formen/Künste. Resultate historisch-materialistischer Untersuchengen*, Frankfurt/M., 1924. I engage with Märten's socially expanded formalism in more detail in my thesis *Beyond Modernism. Berlin Dada and Form as Contradiction*, University College London, 2016.

49 Zeidler (2016), *Form as Revolt*, pp. 210 f. and p. 216.

50 Ibid., p. 214.

> money, waiting to pass over into commodities. Capital is always involved in this movement of transition, this *metamorphosis of form* [emphasis J. N.].[51]

For Marx then capital as a "metamorphosis of form" enacts a kind of "vitalism of form" that defines precisely its fetish character, which is to say, the idea of the self-generation of value (the notorious „Geld heckendes Geld", money-breeding money).[52] The fetish of value consists in the fact that it is produced presumably in an immaculate way, so to speak, i.e., without any exploitation involved, but also without any contradiction on the level of the form. At the highest level of the fetishisation of value capital thus appears as a vital, self-reproducing force, an automatic subject that by "virtue of being value has acquired the occult ability to add value to itself. It brings forth living offspring, or at least lays golden eggs."[53] To say that this logic is fetishistic, however, does not mean that it is a fiction as opposed to objective economic 'facts'. It is a *real*, or *objective* fiction (not a subjective illusion) in the sense that it is constitutive of reality under capitalism. It does not simply distort social reality but 'produces' it *in* this and *through* this distortion.

Unlike orthodox Marxists, however, who tended to focus on the economic register of Marx's understanding of capital, Einstein's own take on the 'metamorphosis of form' could be seen as invested in the productivity of its 'mythic' register. Following Zeidler's argument that his politics was not one of resistance (that occupies a reality in order to destabilise it from within) but one of displacement (which displaces a reality with a counter-reality),[54] metamorphotic revolt opens onto a realism that does not consist of a fetishistic mimicry of the value form as it characterises contemporary ontologies of realism in art. Rather Einstein's understanding of form as revolt can be understood to mobilise the fetish (capital's "vitalism of form") itself as a mythic intensity to counter, i.e. to displace the mythic intensity of the value form.[55] Consequently, in Einstein's political ontology of realism, myth figured as praxis that aimed at the production of counter-realities, not in the sense of an escapism or a transgression but in the sense of a displacement, a torsion in reality in which its familiar terms are ungrounded by another one.[56]

This realism, too, was deemed 'corrective' to Marxism, but not because it was not scientific enough (one of speculative realism's charges) but because it was too scientific. At a time when fascism was retrieving past myths as a fixed set of racial

51 Karl Marx, *Capital. A Critique of Political Economy. Volume 3*, trans. by David Fernbach, New York, NY, 1993, p. 379.

52 For my discussion of fetishism and vitalism I draw on Samo Tomšič, *The Capitalist Unconscious: Marx and Lacan*, London, 2015, pp. 35-37 and p. 158.

53 Marx (1990), *Capital. Volume 1*, p. 255.

54 Zeidler (2016), *Form as Revolt*, p. 220.

55 On such logic of displacement or "competition" as the task of a militant poetry, see Sean Bonney, "Further Notes on Militant Poetics", in: *All This Burning Earth. Selected Writings of Sean Bonney*, 2016, p. 51, http://ill-will-editions.tumblr.com/post/141051275164/all-this-burning-earth-selected-writings-of-sean (retrieved 18/3/2017).

56 This practice could be seen in dialogue with psychoanalytic notion of the real, which, as Zupančič has argued, is not so much understood performatively but as a cut into reality (which in Einstein's terms would be revolt). See Zupančič (2014), Realism, pp. 30 f.

ties, social customs and iconographies, Einstein insisted that "society is not only determined by economic powers but equally by social myth" and that it is the latter's energies and binding forces that need to be reclaimed for a political ontology of realism.[57] His interest in social myths revolved around forms of animism, perversion and hallucination but so did Marx's understanding of the fetish of capital as the most enduring and 'productive' of 'social myths'.[58]

Especially today, when a bleak re-enchantment of the present and a new 'anti-realist' discourse (a discourse of so-called 'alternative facts') has taken hold of media and politics, it is worth taking a step back and reconsidering whether we really need more rationality, to work harder on getting the facts right and adhere to our faltering notions of knowledge as disillusionment. Doing so seems to fall prey to what Alenka Zupančič, following Lacan, calls geometric vision: "[W]e can see all there is to see except that which constitutes the field of vision by falling out of it." In order to see that fallen out element, Zupančič writes, it is futile to look "at things directly and realistically". Instead we have to look elsewhere, namely at the fictions that structure our social interactions.[59] Although Zupančič's psychoanalytic notion of fiction, Marx's notion of fetish and Einstein's myth all operate in different historical and epistemological domains, they intersect in the 'realism' they attribute to that which is commonly deemed irrational, illusory or a psychological 'surplus'. They are, so to speak, allies in 'metamorphotic revolt', to put it in Einstein's terms. Perhaps it is time to return to this kind of realism and retrieve the terrain of fiction, of myth and the fetish from the wastebasket of discarded ideas. Perhaps this is the realism that we need, as opposed to the latest attempts of reviving a facticity and temporality drained of history and of contradictions.

57 Einstein (1996), Georges Braque, p. 280.

58 Einstein's focus on anachronisms is consequently not be mistaken with an attempt to salvage the energies of the outmoded in order to secure art's modernist autonomy (speculative realism's charge against art history *in toto*). Given that his formalism was radically transversal, the energies of the outmoded that he discerned in works of modern art (amongst others) are not exterior to the commodity but indeed at its very core. Ironically, his realism thus turns out to be less "modernist" than its speculative variant in the present.

59 Alenka Zupančič, "'You'd Have to Be Stupid Not to See That'", in: *Parallax* 22, 4 (2016), pp. 413-425: here pp. 420 f.

Joseph Vogl

Das Reale und das Allzumenschliche

Je häufiger man Vokabeln wie ,wirklich' oder ,real' hört, desto mehr stellt sich der Verdacht ein, dass etwas in der Wirklichkeit nicht stimmt, und die hohe Dichte von zirkulierenden Real-Signifikanten lässt auf einige Turbulenzen im Wirklichkeitssinn schließen. Das verhält sich wohl wie bei den Spekulationen und Krisen in der Finanzindustrie: Angesichts ungedeckter Schulden auf den Finanzmärkten können noch die schmutzigen Posten der sogenannten Realwirtschaft geradezu idyllisch oder attraktiv erscheinen.

Es könnte also sein, dass das, was sich seit einiger Zeit ,Realismus' oder ,Spekulativer Realismus' nennt und Anspruch auf eine neue Sparte im philosophischen Fach erhebt, nicht nur ein jüngstes Krisensymptom darstellt, sondern überdies mit einer Art Deckungsproblem operiert. Das jedenfalls scheint in seine Kardinalthesen eingebaut, in Thesen, an denen unterschiedliche Programme und Autoren wenigstens vorübergehend aufeinandertreffen.

Es handelt sich um ein zweiteiliges Thesenprofil. Der eine Teil zieht die Konsequenzen aus einigen philosophischen Dogmen seit Kant und meint schlicht, dass es eine Welt oder eine Wirklichkeit da draußen gibt, die sich ungerührt, indifferent, selbstgenügsam, souverän und in völliger Unabhängigkeit von Denkprozessen und Begriffen behauptet. Was dort passiert, hängt nicht von Subjekten, Hirnen und Mentaloperationen ab; was dort existiert, verfügt über Qualitäten, die für uns unspürbar und undenkbar bleiben. Es manifestiert sich darin ein unhintergehbarer Bruch zwischen Denken und Sein.

Andererseits – und das ist der zweite Teil – muss gerade darum dieses Draußen, diese unzugängliche Welt an sich, als fixer Referenzpunkt angesehen werden, als etwas, woran sich jeder philosophische Zweifel bricht. Es taucht in naturwissenschaftlichen Aussagen auf, es zeigt sich in Sätzen wie „vor 13,5 Milliarden Jahren entstand das Universum", „vor 3,5 Milliarden Jahren das irdische Leben". Und gerade weil dort draußen (und vor aller Menschenzeit) dies oder das geschah, weil dort dieses oder jenes geschehen konnte (oder auch nicht), muss es – wie Quentin Meillassoux sagt – als ein Reservoir „ewiger Wahrheiten" erscheinen.[1] Weil es ein menschenfreies Geschehen gibt, von dem man weiß, dass es so oder so – und also kontingenterweise – passiert, darf es Anspruch auf den Charakter des Absoluten erheben: Es besteht kein Zweifel, dass irgendetwas ohne uns geschah oder geschieht.

---

1 Quentin Meillassoux, „Metaphysik, Spekulation, Korrelation", in: Armen Avanessian (Hg.), *Realismus Jetzt. Spekulative Philosophie und Metaphysik für das 21. Jahrhundert*, Berlin, 2013, S. 23-56: 23.

Das hat – kurz gesagt – drei Konsequenzen. Es bedeutet erstens, dass alle unsere Begriffe, Erzählungen und Bewertungen angesichts dieses großen Draußenseins kollabieren. Das betrifft noch jene schwierigen Versuche, mit denen man Weltverhältnisse und die Grenzen des Erkennens zu kontrollieren glaubte: Auch die Transzendentalien, auch die Anschauungsformen, Kategorien und Aprioris des Denkens können unter dieser Perspektive selbst nur kontingent, also haltlos erscheinen und belegen allenfalls eine narzisstische Denkverwicklung der Subjekte mit sich selbst. Umgekehrt und zweitens hat das Denken darum neue spekulative Freiheiten gewonnen; so wenig die Welt erdenklich ist, so sehr fordert sie das Denken zum Fabulieren, Phantasieren, Fingieren auf. Jeder Welt-Denk-Versuch ist zwangsläufig spekulativ. Wie einmal der literarische Realismus des 19. Jahrhunderts die literarische Phantastik ermöglichte, begründet der jetzige spekulative Realismus eine philosophische Fantasy.

All das ist aber – drittens – nur möglich, weil mit dem Realen da draußen ein neuer Angelpunkt, ein neuer Wertmaßstab gesetzt werden konnte: Alle Konstruktionen und Konstruktivismen, alle Selbstreferenzen und Sprachspiele werden durch die Vertikalachse des Real-Absoluten oder Absolut-Realen befestigt oder eben gedeckt. Die Spekulation hat – wenn man so will – ihren Anker in einer Art philosophischen Goldstandards gefunden. Gegen die Relativismen im Denken wird somit auf die Restauration einer alten philosophischen Ordnung gesetzt, es wird (wie Ray Brassier etwa schreibt) auf die Hoffnung gesetzt, dass mit den erprobten Dualismen wie Bedeutung und Sein, Erkennen und Fühlen, Begriff und Gegenstand die ungetrübte Vernunft von Neuem die Regierung übernimmt.[2]

So kurz und korrupt dieses philosophische Szenario hier skizziert wurde und obgleich sich zuweilen der Eindruck aufdrängt, dass in diesen Entwürfen mehr Antworten gegeben als Fragen gestellt werden, bieten sie doch einige Wendungen, mit denen unsere Zeit in Gedanken gefasst ist. Es liegen hier ein paar Problemfiguren vor, die die Frage betreffen, was Denken heute bedeutet. Einige Probleme aus dieser Liste anzusprechen und zugleich ein paar Seitenbemerkungen zum spekulativen Realismus zu machen, ist demnach angebracht.

Eine erste Frage, eine erste Problemfigur betrifft – naturgemäß – das Verhältnis von „Denken und Draußen". Auch wenn man im Umkreis des neuen Realismus zuweilen darüber klagt, dass der Philosophie das Außen verloren gegangen sei, ist es doch unübersehbar, wie man seit geraumer Zeit im Außen des Denkens einen kardinalen philosophischen Vorwurf reklamierte. Schon Heidegger hat den denkerischen Auftrag im Verhältnis von Denken und Undenkbarem lokalisiert. In seinem Aufsatz „Was heißt Denken?" wurde der Philosophie nicht nur eine konstitutive Anfangslosigkeit zugesprochen und das „Bedenkliche" als das dem Denken immer Entzogene markiert. Vielmehr noch hat er die bloße abstrakte Möglichkeit

2 Vgl. Ray Brassier, „Begriffe und Gegenstände", in: Armen Avanessian (Hg.), *Realismus Jetzt. Spekulative Philosophie und Metaphysik für das 21. Jahrhundert*, Berlin, 2013, S. 137-182: 182.

des Denkens als die Möglichkeit dessen gefasst, dass „wir noch nicht denken".[3] Wie das Denken damit aus jeder Übung des Wissens ausgeschlossen bleibt, so wird es umgekehrt zum Problem eines prekären Akts, der sich nicht in den Formen des Nachahmens, des Reproduzierens, des Ähnlichen und Analogen fassen lässt. Der neue Realismus teilt offenbar diese Intuition, deren schärfste Formulierung man dann bei Gilles Deleuze finden kann. Demnach kommt das Denken nicht in einer Vermittlung zwischen Wissen und Nicht-Wissen voran, und sei es in einem unendlichen Prozess. Es gibt keine Analogie, keine Isomorphie, keine natürliche Neigung und keine *philia* zwischen Denken und Draußen;[4] und es kann sein, schreiben Gilles Deleuze und Félix Guattari, „dass an diese Welt, an dieses Leben zu glauben unsere schwierigste Aufgabe geworden ist"[5].

Es steht also nicht weniger als die Art der Begegnung zwischen Denken und Sein auf dem Spiel, und hier deutet sich allerdings eine fundamentale Abzweigung an. Auf der einen Seite geht es im sogenannten Realismus darum, einen philosophischen Diskurs zu begründen, der zu denken vermag, was da ist, wo es kein Denken gibt. Damit wird nicht nur ein Dualismus befestigt, der Denken als Bewusstsein, Bewusstsein als menschliches Bewusstsein konsolidiert und nur dem Außen die Position eines ersten Prinzips, den Posten einer absolut notwendigen Kontingenz verschafft. Vielmehr wird das Verhältnis von Denken und Draußen als ein Repräsentationsproblem gefasst: Das unrepräsentierbare Außen erhält in den Propositionen der Wissenschaft seinen Ort oder seine Referenz. Was nicht gedacht werden kann, wird als Außen des Denkens repräsentiert.

Demgegenüber handelt es sich bei Deleuze um eine Begegnungsform, die alle Merkmale des Gewaltsamen besitzt. Hier zerbricht ein dogmatisches Bild des Denkens, das sich auf die Innerlichkeit des Bewusstseins beruft. In der Begegnung zwischen Denken und Draußen eskaliert selbst ein kontingentes Geschehen, das Denken „kennt kein anderes Abenteuer als das Unwillkürliche"[6], und das Außen des Denkens wird als Gewalt, Zwang, Notstand im Denken manifest. Am Anfang des Denkens steht also nicht ein aporetischer Außenbezug, sondern ein Denken, das sich selbst im Außenkontakt fremd geworden ist. „Am Anfang des Denkens", schreibt Deleuze, „steht der Einbruch, die Gewalt, der Feind, und nichts setzt die Philosophie voraus, alles beginnt mit einer Misosophie."[7] Dem Repräsentationsverhältnis steht also ein Wirkungs- oder Aktionsverhältnis gegenüber.

Das führt unmittelbar zu einer zweiten Problemfigur, zu einer Sache, die ich gerne als Frage nach dem „Idiotischen im Denken" adressieren möchte. Im Unterschied zum neuen Realismus muss nämlich die Relation zwischen Denken und Draußen nicht unbedingt als Exklusionsrelation aufgefasst werden. Vielmehr wur-

---

3 Martin Heidegger, „Was heißt Denken?" [1952], in: *Martin Heidegger Gesamtausgabe, I. Abteilung: Veröffentlichte Schriften 1910-1976, Band 7: Vorträge und Aufsätze (1936-1953)*, hg. von Friedrich-Wilhelm von Herrmann, Frankfurt/M., 2002, S. 127-143: 130-132.

4 Gilles Deleuze, *Differenz und Wiederholung*, München, 1992, S. 188.

5 Gilles Deleuze/Félix Guattari, *Was ist Philosophie?*, Frankfurt/M., 2000, S. 85.

6 Deleuze (1992), *Differenz und Wiederholung*, S. 189.

7 Ebd., S. 181.

de gerade von Autoren wie Maurice Blanchot, Gilles Deleuze oder Michel Foucault der Vorschlag gemacht, die Naht zwischen Denken und Ungedachtem als Einschluss des Außen im Denken und somit als Ende der Repräsentation zu denken. Dies hat einige Konsequenzen für das Bild, das sich das Denken von sich selbst macht und dabei – wenn man so will – einem zerbrochenen Spiegel begegnet. Das bedeutet einerseits, dass das moderne *cogito* einer mehrfachen Gewalt ausgesetzt ist, die mit dem Einbruch von Außenwelt und Endlichkeit die Selbstgewissheit des Bewusstseins und die Willkürlichkeit seiner Akte unterbricht. Foucault hat das als die Entdeckung jener uneinholbaren Mächte des Außen beschrieben, als das Auftauchen der Mächte von Leben, Arbeit, Sprache, die den Menschen zu seiner eigenen empirisch-transzendentalen Verdoppelung auftreiben und verhindern, dass sich das „Ich denke" in einem „Ich bin" wiederfinden kann.[8] Keine Innerlichkeit, kein Bewusstsein, sondern ein Denken des Außen, das in der Selbstgegenwart des Denkens nur Alterität, die größtmögliche Entfernung des Denkens zu sich selbst erkennt.

Andererseits ist damit die Frage verbunden, die Deleuze und Guattari einmal stellen: „Welche Gewalt muß auf das Denken einwirken, damit wir zum Denken fähig werden [...]?"[9] Das Denken geht aus einem Undenkbaren hervor; dieses lässt sich aber nicht nur als bloße Negation, als faktisches Hindernis, als Irrtum, Täuschung oder Illusion bannen. Es hat vielmehr den Charakter einer konstitutiven Ohnmacht angenommen, die sich als äußerstes Außen im Innern des Denkens positiviert. Das moderne Denken hat damit seine eigenen Missgeschicke oder Verfallenheiten, und das problematische Schaubild dessen, was Denken heißt, wird man weniger in einem *Discours de la méthode* oder in einer *Kritik* finden. Eher stehen dafür die Anstrengungen Daniel Paul Schrebers oder Antonin Artauds oder jene Archive bereit, die die Psychiatrie angelegt hat: Stereotypien, ein endloses Wiederkäuen, ein Azephales im Denken oder schlicht die Unfähigkeit, irgendeinen Gedanken zu haben.[10] Mitten im Denken breitet sich also etwas Nicht-Menschliches, Bestialisches oder Idiotisches aus. In der Athletik des Denkens zerbricht die erbauliche Gleichung von Mensch, Subjekt und Bewusstsein; und der Appell an ein denkendes Vermögen wird von einem Transzendental-Werden von Dummheit oder Idiotie heimgesucht.

Daran schießt sich eine dritte Problemfigur an, die systematischen Charakter besitzt. Wenn nämlich der Bruch zwischen Denken und Sein stets die Frage nach Grenzen und Transgressionen, nach der Begründung des einen im anderen stellt, so steht dabei die Aufteilung jener Kontinente auf dem Spiel, die man das Empirische und das Transzendentale genannt hat. Und hier läuft die moderne Philosophie einen Scheideweg entlang, der nicht nur unterschiedliche philosophische Stile, sondern intellektuelle Unvereinbarkeiten hervorgebracht hat. Das eine Ende

---

8 Vgl. Michel Foucault, *Die Ordnung der Dinge. Eine Archäologie der Humanwissenschaften*, Frankfurt/M., 1974, insb. S. 389-396.

9 Deleuze/Guattari (2000), *Was ist Philosophie?*, S. 64.

10 Deleuze (1992), *Differenz und Wiederholung*, S. 191.

wird von der jüngsten spekulativen Lösung reklamiert. Hier wird, wenn ich richtig sehe, das Gebiet des Transzendentalen durch ein empirisches Feld begrenzt, das nicht durch mögliche Erfahrungen, sondern durch ein notwendiges Nichts an Erfahrung ausgezeichnet ist. Das wäre das, was Meillassoux das Anzestrale genannt hat: das Gebiet jener vormenschlichen Daten und Fakten, die mit den Formeln der Wissenschaft in unserer Erfahrungswelt aufschlagen, hier aber nur die transzendentale Unmöglichkeit empirischer Erfahrung anzeigen.[11] Was draußen geschah oder geschieht, wird für uns niemals Gegenstand möglicher Erfahrung gewesen sein können. Im Anzestralen hat das Transzendentale sozusagen eine empirische Schlagfertigkeit erhalten. Anders gesagt: Das Subjekt möglicher Erfahrung (oder der Rekognition) bleibt unbehelligt, muss sich aber – zugunsten seiner Letztbegründung im Realen – mit Löchern unmöglicher Erfahrung abfinden.

Einen entgegengesetzten Weg nimmt Deleuze, einen Weg, der die Frage nach spekulativer Gründung meidet und dennoch an der Unähnlichkeit zwischen dem Empirischen und dem Transzendentalen festhält. Das empirische Feld ist hier nicht jenes Milieu, in dem man vom Mannigfaltigen zum Anschauungsobjekt, vom Sinnlichen zum Intelligiblen aufsteigt; es ist nicht das Feld der Rekognition. Vielmehr geht es um ein empirisches Feld vor jeder Empirie, in dem das Sinnliche weder an Objekten noch für ein Subjekt gegeben ist. Die Bedingung ist hier nicht weiter gefasst als das Bedingte; und was Deleuze „transzendentalen Empirismus" nennt, fragt nicht nach den Bedingungen möglicher Erfahrung, sondern nach der realen Voraussetzung aktueller Erfahrung. Deleuze sagt:

> Es gibt etwas in der Welt, das zum Denken nötigt. Dieses Etwas ist Gegenstand einer fundamentalen *Begegnung*, und nicht einer Rekognition. [...] Wir fragen etwa: Was nötigt die Sinnlichkeit dazu, zu empfinden? Und was kann nur empfunden werden? Und ist zugleich das Nicht-Sinnliche? [Herv. i. O.][12]

Was zur Empfindung nötigt und was an der Empfindung wiederum zum Denken nötigt – dies führt bei Deleuze zu einer differenziellen Theorie der Vermögen, die nicht in der Form des Gemeinsinns zusammenarbeiten. Sie befördern eine zustoßende Intensität: von etwas, das nur empfunden werden kann und vom empirischen Standpunkt aus zugleich unsinnlich bleibt, zu etwas, das gedacht werden muss und zugleich undenkbar ist.[13] Der Grund des Denkens liegt also weder im Subjekt noch draußen, sondern in jenem empirisch-transzendentalen Immanenzfeld, in dem Denken und Sein verwickelt sind, bevor sie sich zu Subjekt- und Objektwelten entwickeln. Hier kehrt die Beziehung, die das Denken zum Außen unterhält, im Denken selbst wieder. Und das wäre die Unvereinbarkeit: Dem metaphysischen Versuch, das Außen als Absolutes zu denken, stehen die Beschwernisse gegenüber, die man mit einem Denken der Immanenz auf sich nimmt.

---

11 Vgl. Quentin Meillassoux, *Nach der Endlichkeit: Versuch über die Notwendigkeit der Kontingenz* (*Subjektile*), Zürich, Berlin, 2008, S. 13-46.

12 Deleuze (1992), *Differenz und Wiederholung*, S. 182 und S. 186.

13 Ebd., S. 181-184.

Wenn es schließlich stimmt, dass sich im neuen Realismus eine Wendung von der Epistemologie zur Ontologie vollzog, so lässt sich darin eine vierte und letzte Problemfigur ausmachen: mit der Frage nämlich, auf welche Seinsweisen man sich dabei bezieht. Und hier überrascht zunächst eine eigentümliche Fraglosigkeit, die manche Spielarten des Realismus bestimmt. So ist etwa bei Meillassoux das Gewicht des Realseins nicht nur in den entrückten Bezirk des Anzestralen verlegt, dessen Existenz nur die Inexistenz des Menschen aussagen kann. Seine Aktivitäten bleiben zudem darauf beschränkt, in Gestalt von wissenschaftlichen Propositionen in die Menschenwelt zu geraten, in Sätzen also, die allenfalls Interpretationen verlangen.[14] Das äußerste Reale ist wohl vorhanden, bleibt aber aktiv nur für sich selbst.

Demgegenüber könnte man hier – wenigstens kurz – an Heideggers Zeug-Analyse erinnern, die sich ja als ontologische Schlüsselszene verstehen lässt. Demnach ist das Vorhandensein der Dinge kein bloßes Gegebensein, sondern das Resultat eines Prozesses, in dem sich ihr Zeugcharakter, ihr unbemerktes Zuhandensein verflüchtigt und in der Unzuhandenheit den Modus des Widerstands, der Auffälligkeit, der Aufsässigkeit gewinnt. Gerade in ihrer Vorhandenheit hat die Dingwelt tückischen und rebellischen Charakter. Sie ist vorhanden nur, weil sie sich beim Zugriff in Fernstlage versetzt. Und wenn dabei (nach Heidegger) das Dasein in seiner ontischen Benommenheit, in seinem vertrauten In-der-Welt-Sein aufgestört wird, so bedeutet das zugleich, dass die Welt-Dinge eben niemals ungerührt und abgeschieden existierten. Sie sind vielmehr die Produktivkräfte des Daseins selbst. Die vorhandenen Dinge sind defektes Zeug und erinnern daran, dass auch die Subjekte nur im Handgemenge mit den Dingen hervorgebracht werden.[15] Das Reale wäre demnach nicht draußen, es schließt vielmehr auch jene Produkte und Produktionen ein, die sich in den Subjekten selbst verkörpern. Anders gesagt: die Qualität der ontologischen Frage entscheidet sich daran, ob und wie sie sich auf Gegebenheiten oder Gemachtheiten bezieht.

Das wären also einige Fragen, die mit der Aktualität des spekulativen Realismus gegeben sind: die Art der Begegnung zwischen Denken und Sein; die Frage nach jenen Ohnmachten, die das Denken in sich selbst hervorbringt; die Art und Weise, wie sich die Gebiete des Empirischen und des Transzendentalen verteilen; und die Frage nach jener Ereignishaftigkeit, die in der Seinsweise selbst wirkt.

Wahrscheinlich liegt, um damit zum Schluss zu kommen, die Gegenwart des neuen Realismus in der Vergegenwärtigung einer Frage, die der modernen Philosophie anhaftet und die sie nicht loswerden kann: die Frage nach einem Denken der Kontingenz. Dabei geht es nicht zuletzt darum, dass gerade ein Denken der Kontingenz nicht von Entscheidungsfragen erlöst werden kann; es bleibt von einer dezisiven, dezisionistischen Anspannung geprägt. Hier scheiden sich allerdings die Denkwege unwiderruflich und ein letztes Mal. Der eine, dogmatische Weg folgt einer Eschatologie des Realen und nimmt mit seiner Entscheidung für die Univer-

---

[14] Vgl. Meillassoux (2008), *Nach der Endlichkeit*, S. 23-28.

[15] Martin Heidegger, *Sein und Zeit*, Tübingen, 1967, S. 68-76.

salität des Kontingenten in Kauf, dass das Unentscheidbare entsorgt und nur in den Sätzen der Wissenschaft immer neu entschieden wird. Der andere, kritische Weg ist sozusagen heillos und findet im Denken der Kontingenz nur den kontingenten, d. h. beschränkten Ort seines historischen Seins. Die Endlichkeit des Allzumenschlichen wird im Menschen selbst aufgesucht: mit der Frage nach den positiven Beschränkungen dessen, was Ereignisse der Universalisierbarkeit ermöglicht. Das Denken der Kontingenz erhebt hier Anspruch auf Unerlösbarkeit; es kümmert sich um den Ort und die Wirksamkeit singulärer, d. h. kontingenter Daten in dem, was sich als universal, notwendig und verpflichtend manifestiert.

Samo Tomšič

Das unmögliche Reale der Mathematik: Koyré und Lacan

1. Polemik

Die ungewöhnliche Definition des Realen als Unmöglichem ist wohl Jacques Lacans bekanntester Beitrag zu epistemologischen Debatten. Dabei vergisst man oft, dass die Formel aus Alexandre Koyrés historischer Epistemologie übernommen wurde, in der sie das Reale der Mathematik und der Geometrie bezeichnet, d. h. Objekte, für die es in der Erfahrungswelt keine gegenständlichen Entsprechungen gibt und die vielmehr als Idealisierungen von Form und Erfahrung, als Konstruktionen oder Fiktionen aufgefasst werden müssen. In *empirischer* Hinsicht ist das Reale der Mathematik und Geometrie also unmöglich, weil es nicht auf die gleiche Art und Weise existieren kann wie die Objekte der Erfahrung. Andererseits scheint Unmöglichkeit die falsche *logische* Modalität für die Beschreibung von diesen epistemischen Objekten zu sein. Man müsste sie vielmehr als notwendig bezeichnen, da die Mathematik und die Geometrie immer danach streben, ihre Realitäten durch eine Reihe stabiler und unveränderlicher Gesetze zu begründen. In dieser Hinsicht hat die Auffassung des Realen als Unmöglichem keinen Sinn. Aber Koyré und Lacan zielen offensichtlich auf eine dritte Möglichkeit.

Bei seiner Rückkehr zu Freud bezog sich Lacan auf Koyrés Epistemologie, um die Beziehung zwischen Wissenschaft und Psychoanalyse neu zu durchdenken. Im Unterschied zu Freud, der sein ganzes Leben lang positivistische Wissenschaftsideale verfolgte, kehrte Lacan die Perspektive um: „Es bleibt also die Frage, die unser Projekt radikal macht: der Übergang von: *Ist die Psychoanalyse eine Wissenschaft?* zu: *Was ist Wissenschaft, die auch die Psychoanalyse umfasst?* [Herv. i. O.]“[1] Die Radikalität der Psychoanalyse besteht also in ihren subversiven Konsequenzen für die Auffassung der Wissenschaftlichkeit überhaupt und somit in ihrer Herausforderung der vorherrschenden Wissenschaftsgeschichten und -theorien. In dieser Hinsicht wurde Koyrés historische Epistemologie (zu der Lacan zwar eine dialektisch-materialistische Umkehrung beisteuerte) zum Hauptverbündeten der Psychoanalyse.

Koyrés Zentralthema ist bekanntlich der Übergang von der vormodernen (aristotelischen und ptolemäischen) zur klassischen (galiläischen und newtonschen) Physik. Im Vordergrund steht die Rolle der Formalisierung und des mathemati-

---

1 Jacques Lacan, *Autres écrits*, Paris, 2001, S. 187. „Permanente donc restait la question qui fait notre projet radical: celle qui va de: *la psychanalyse est-elle une science?* à: *qu'est-ce qu'une science qui inclut la psychanalyse?*“

schen Realismus (den Koyré mit dem Platonismus gleichsetzt) in der Theoretisierung und Mobilisierung des Realen[2], die Verankerung des wissenschaftlichen Experiments zwischen mathematischer ‚Idealisierung' und ‚empirischer' Erfahrung. Koyrés Versuch, die moderne wissenschaftliche Revolution als metaphysische und nicht als anti-metaphysische oder anti-philosophische Revolution im Wissen zu denken, umfasst eine offene Polemik gegen Heideggers pessimistische Vision der ontologischen Konsequenzen der modernen Wissenschaft. Denn Heidegger zufolge stellt die Anwendung der *mathesis* und der Technik auf die physische, biologische und menschliche Realität eine ontologische Gefahr dar und verschärft das Vergessen der ursprünglichen Frage nach dem Sein. Koyré polemisiert auch gegen die logisch-positivistischen Epistemologien, in denen die Bestrebungen der modernen Wissenschaft auf einen naiven Empirismus heruntergebrochen sind. In diesem Rahmen wird das Reale vom Empirischen nicht unterschieden und die mathematische Sprache beschreibt eine stabile, funktionierende und notwendige Realität, den genauen Gegensatz zu dem, worauf Koyrés Verbindung des Realen mit dem Unmöglichen zielt.

Koyrés Position in der Wissenschaftsgeschichte ist als strukturalistisch zu bezeichnen. Diese Bezeichnung mag nicht selbstverständlich sein, findet jedoch eine eigentümliche biografische Unterstützung in der Tatsache, dass es gerade Koyré war, der Claude Lévi-Strauss mit Roman Jakobson in New York bekanntmachte.[3] Diese anekdotische ‚Urszene' des Strukturalismus betrifft also drei Kerndisziplinen: die Linguistik, Anthropologie und Wissenschaftsgeschichte. Es ist durchaus symptomatisch, dass Koyré in dem strukturalistischen Familienporträt bis heute nicht vorkommt, obwohl ein Großteil der französischen Strukturalisten seine Wissenschaftslehre übernommen hat. Die strukturalistische Bewegung entstand jedoch in einem breiteren Rahmen, der schon vor dem Zweiten Weltkrieg von der formalistischen Linie in der französischen Philosophie (Léon Brunschvicg, Jean Cavaillès, Albert Lautman und das mathematische Autorenkollektiv Nicholas Bourbaki) umrissen wurde.[4] Diese theoretische Richtung erneuerte Platons mathematischen Realismus und affirmierte die Dimension des Werdens und die Praxis des Experimentierens in der Mathematik. Der moderne Platonismus behauptete den realen Status der mathematischen Strukturen und die Autonomie der mathematischen Sprache unter Berücksichtigung der historischen Dynamik des mathematischen Feldes und der immanenten Instabilität mathematischer

---

2 Die „Mobilisierung des Realen" verweist auf Heideggers *Herausfordern*, die Isolierung einer ‚Surplus-Realität' innerhalb der Erscheinungswelt oder der phänomenalen Realität. Siehe Martin Heidegger, *Vorträge und Aufsätze*, Stuttgart, 2004 [1954], insb. S. 18 f.

3 Siehe Gérard Jorland, *La science dans la philosophie*, Paris, 1981, S. 23. Auch wenn diese Tatsache Koyré noch nicht zu einem *godfather* des Strukturalismus macht, ist zu berücksichtigen, dass sein Werk nach 1945 den Strukturbegriff in großem Maße anwendet.

4 Cavaillès beschrieb die konfliktvolle Situation in der Philosophie mit folgenden Worten: „Es ist nicht die Philosophie des Bewusstseins, sondern die Philosophie des Konzepts, die eine Wissenschaftsdoktrin beisteuern kann. [Ce n'est pas une philosophie de la conscience mais une philosophie du concept qui peut donner une doctrine de la science.]" Jean Cavaillès, *Oeuvres complètes de philosophie des sciences*, Paris, 1994, S. 560.

Strukturen. In direkter Kontinuität zu dieser Ausrichtung erhob Koyré einen doppelten Einspruch gegen das logisch-positivistische Forschungsprogramm: einerseits gegen dessen Behauptung, die Philosophie von metaphysischen ‚Spekulationen' auf den scheinbar soliden Grund logischer Gesetze und objektiver Erfahrung zu bringen; und andererseits gegen dessen theoretisch schwache Auffassung der Wissenschaftlichkeit, die das Streben nach Erkenntnissen mit der Idee des Fortschritts zusammenbringt (Fortschritt des Bewusstseins, unterstützt durch ein akkumulatives Wissensregime, sind dabei zwei Schlüsselelemente der ‚positivistischen' Weltanschauung).[5]

Im Gegensatz zur Hegemonie des logischen Positivismus und Empirismus schlägt Koyré eine Lektüre des wissenschaftlichen Werdens vor, die die lineare geschichtliche Entwicklung konsequent ablehnt. Denn die Annahme einer solchen Entwicklung riskiert bekanntlich, die wissenschaftlichen Ereignisse in einen teleologischen Horizont zu stellen. Darüber hinaus setzt die Annahme einer kontinuierlichen Entfaltung der Wissenschaft den Wissenschaftler als ein „Subjekt, dem man unterstellt, zu wissen" (Lacan) voraus: ein Subjekt also, das die Konsistenz der wissenschaftlichen Erkenntnis ermöglicht und die adäquate Beziehung zwischen dem Empirischen und dem Experimentellen garantiert.[6] Für Koyré ist die epistemische Situation wesentlich komplexer: Das Subjekt der Wissenschaft (obwohl Koyré den Begriff meidet, aber darin besteht Lacans Ergänzung seiner Epistemologie) ist eine nicht-psychologische Entität, die sich auf keine existierenden Individuen reduzieren lässt. Das Subjekt der Wissenschaft manifestiert sich weniger in der positiven Figur des *savant* (des Wissenschaftlers bzw. des Wissenden) als in den Lücken und Kämpfen, Sackgassen und Irrtümern, die die Konstruktion einer wissenschaftlichen Theorie begleiten und der ideologischen Fabel vom epistemischen Fortschritt eine dezentrierte, instabile und konfliktvolle Struktur der Wissenschaft gegenüberstellen. Die moderne Wissenschaft „sprang nicht sofort in ihrer Endform, wie die Athene vom Haupte des Zeus, von Descartes oder Galileis Denken", die wissenschaftliche Revolution ist ein Werden, „in dem der menschliche Geist hartnäckig auf dieselben Probleme, die gleichen Einwände und Schwierigkeiten stößt und langsam und mühsam die Instrumente schmiedet, die es ihm ermöglichen, sie zu überwinden"[7]. Kritisch dabei ist, dass dieses Werden in keiner Weise

---

5 Dabei spielt die Auffassung des Empirismus als ultimativer Aufruf zur Faktizität eine Hauptrolle. Aber zu welcher Faktizität? Denn mit der klassischen Wissenschaft lösen sich alle angeblich festen empirischen Tatsachen in mathematische Erfahrung auf. Letztere ist materiell, ohne dafür auch noch sinnlich zu sein (siehe Jean-Claude Milner, *Constats*, Paris, 2002, S. 117). Für den modernen Platonismus bleibt die mathematische Sprache weiterhin das privilegierte Beispiel von abstrakter Materie ohne sinnliche Qualitäten.

6 Wer mit Lacans Diskurstheorie vertraut ist, wird darin die linke Seite des Universitätsdiskurses wiedererkennen: S_2 (Wissen) nimmt die Stelle eines angeblich autonomen Agens ein, aber diese Autonomie und Neutralität des Wissens wird von S_1 (Herr-Signifikant), d. h. von der Funktion der Autorität unterstützt.

7 Alexandre Koyré, *Études galiléennes*, Paris, 1966, S. 164 f.: „[Le principe d'inertie] n'est pas sorti tout fait, comme Athéna de la tête de Zeus, de la pensée de Descartes ou de Galilée. [H]istoire dans laquelle on voit l'esprit humain aborder obstinément les mêmes problèmes, se heurter inlassable-

überdeterminiert oder auf einen Punkt der Schließung gerichtet ist. Der Prozess ist konstitutiv offen, nicht-endlich und umfasst neben der Wissensproduktion auch die Produktion von Irrtümern und Sackgassen. Die moderne Wissenschaft ist daher ein epistemisches *panta rhei*, das sich durch den mathematischen logos an das Reale hält – und nur in dieser Hinsicht kann sie überhaupt als „Wissenschaft vom Realen" (Koyré) bezeichnet werden.

Im Gegensatz zu progressistischen Erkenntnistheorien setzt Koyré auf den dialektischen Kern der modernen Wissenschaft, worin sich ihr immanentes Werden widerspiegelt, sowie auf das Insistieren der metaphysischen Spekulationen im Herzen der Experimentalwissenschaften, die Dialektik von Wissen und Nicht-Wissen, von Lösung und Irrtum, von Schein und Realem. Die philosophische Orientierung der Wissenschaft enthüllt sich als inhärenter Bestandteil der Wissenschaft, als ihre notwendige Ausdrucksweise und nicht als zufälliges Nebenprodukt. Das Philosophische und das Wissenschaftliche begegnen sich im Experimentieren. Letzteres richtet das Denken auf ein Merkmal des Realen, das dem stabilisierenden Regime der logischen Notwendigkeit widersteht. In diesem Rahmen wird die Unmöglichkeit, und nicht die Notwendigkeit, endlich zum privilegierten Zeichen des rationalen, dialektischen und materialistischen Charakter des Realen.

Das Beharren der modernen Wissenschaft im philosophischen Horizont erreicht seinen Höhepunkt im Streit zwischen der formalistischen und der empiristischen Auffassung der Wissenschaftlichkeit. Dieser Konflikt zeigt, dass beide Wissenschaftsdoktrinen den Gegensatz zwischen dem Platonismus (mathematischen Realismus) und dem Aristotelismus (empiristischen Idealismus) weiterführen. Koyrés Hauptthese zufolge ist die von Galilei initiierte und von Newton vorübergehend stabilisierte, wissenschaftliche Revolution eine systematische Rückkehr zu Platon; Koyré spricht sogar vom „experimentellen Beweis der platonischen Lehre"[8]. Natürlich war dieser Sieg kein vollständiger, da die empiristische Tendenz ihre Hegemonie erneuerte und eine nicht-dialektische Auffassung des Realen sowie eine normative Vision der Wissenschaft aufzwang, aus der jede Spur von Dialektik und Negativität (in erster Linie der Negativität des *unmöglichen* Realen) eliminiert war.

2. Von der Sprache des Realen zum Realen der Sprache

Experimentieren bedeutet methodische Befragung der Natur, eine Befragung, die eine *Sprache* voraussetzt und impliziert, in der die Fragen zu formulieren sind, und ein Wörterbuch, das uns die Antworten lesbar und interpretierbar werden lässt. Für Galilei waren das bekanntlich Kurven, Kreise und Dreiecke: die mathematische, oder noch genauer, die *geometrische Sprache* – nicht die Sprache des gesunden Menschenverstandes oder die der reinen Symbole – in der die Natur anzusprechen war,

ment aux mêmes objection, aux mêmes difficultés, et se forger lentement et péniblement l'instrument qui lui permettra de les surmonter."

8 Alexandre Koyré, *Leonardo, Galilei, Pascal*, Frankfurt/M., 1998, S. 113.

> um Antwort zu erhalten. Die Wahl der Sprache, die Entscheidung, sie zu benutzen, konnte aber doch nicht durch jene Erfahrung bestimmt werden, die mit Hilfe dieser erst möglich wurde. [Herv. i. O.][9]

Entgegen einer weit verbreiteten Überzeugung, haben Beobachtung und Erfahrung die frühneuzeitliche Wissenschaft nicht im Wesentlichen begründet, sondern stellten vielmehr ein Hindernis für ihre Konstitution dar. Die vormoderne Wissenschaft kannte keinen Unterschied zwischen Realität und Realem, Erscheinung und Struktur, Erfahrung und Experiment; sie fokussierte sich auf die Beschreibung des Sublunaren und die Geometrisierung des Supralunaren und sah ihre Hauptaufgabe darin, „die Erscheinungen zu retten"[10]. Aristoteles, *der* Philosoph des gesunden Menschenverstands, gilt nicht zufällig als Begründer der vormodernen Wissenschaft und der epistemologischen Ausrichtung, die die Wissenschaft auf die Beschreibung der sinnlichen Erfahrung und auf die Bestimmung der notwendigen Gesetze der Erscheinungswelt beschränkt. Das Reale wird dabei als notwendig und regelmäßig aufgefasst. Aus diesem Grund bleibt die aristotelische Wissenschaft – in epistemo-politischer Übereinstimmung mit dem Diskurs des Herren – eine Wissenschaft des Herren:

> Der Herrendiskurs z. B. zielt darauf, dass die Dinge im Gleichschritt mit der Welt marschieren. Aber das ist gar nicht das Gleiche wie das Reale, denn das Reale ist genau das, was nicht geht, was diesem Konvoi im Wege steht – noch mehr, es ist, was nicht aufhört, sich zu wiederholen, um diesen Marsch zu verhindern. Ich sagte es zuerst in dieser Form – das Reale ist, was immer an denselben Ort zurückkehrt. Die Betonung liegt auf *Rückkehr*. Es ist der Ort, an dem es sich befindet, der Ort des Scheins. [Herv. i. O.][11]

Die Wiederholung des Realen, die das regelmäßige Funktionieren der Realität sabotiert, findet *im* Schein statt. Das Reale ist daher ein immanentes Hindernis und stellt keine ‚andere' Realität dar, die fundamentaler wäre als die phänomenale Realität. Was Lacan als Schein beschreibt ist real, aber mit einer immanenten ontologischen Sackgasse, die verhindert, dass eine geschlossene Ordnung gebildet wird, die auf unveränderlichen, stabilen und notwendigen Gesetzen beruht.[12]

---

9 Ebd., S. 90. [Modifizierte Übersetzung; S. T.]

10 Siehe Pierre Duhem, *Sauver les apparances*, Paris, 2003 [1908]. Für Duhem folgt die moderne Wissenschaft weiterhin dieser Ausrichtung.

11 Jacques Lacan, „La troisième", in: *La cause freudienne*, 79 (2011), S. 15 f. „Le discours du maître, par exemple, sa fin, c'est que les choses aillent au pas de tout le monde. Eh bien, ça, ce n'est pas du tout la même chose que le réel, parce que le réel, justement, c'est ce qui ne va pas, ce qui se met en croix dans ce charroi – bien plus, ce qui ne cesse pas de se répéter pour entraver cette marche. Je l'ai dit d'abord sous cette forme – le réel est ce qui revient toujours à la même place. L'accent est à mettre sur *revient*. C'est la place qu'il découvre, la place du semblant [Herv. i. O.]."

12 Aus demselben Grund hat Lacan jeden Vergleich von seinem Begriff des Realen mit dem kantischen Ding an sich zurückgewiesen: „Aber das ist überhaupt nicht kantisch. Ich weise sogar darauf hin. Wenn es einen Begriff des Realen gibt, ist er äußerst komplex, und insofern ist er nicht greifbar, nicht greifbar auf eine Weise, die daraus ein Ganzes machen würde." Jacques Lacan, *Der Triumph der Religion*, Berlin, Wien, 2006, S. 85. Daran anschließend insistiert Lacan, dass das Reale auf kontingenten, dynamischen Gesetzen beruht: „Doch ist absolut nicht einzusehen, warum das Reale nicht ein Gesetz zulassen sollte, das sich bewegt." Ebd., S. 86.

Während die vormoderne Wissenschaft sich bemühte, das Reale zu totalisieren, fokussiert die moderne Wissenschaft auf die symptomatischen Verzerrungen in der phänomenalen Realität und verwirft dadurch die Auffassung des Realen als Notwendigem, d. h. als etwas, das sich als *automaton* wiederholt, immer wieder an denselben Ort des Scheins zurückkehrt. Bezeichnete für ‚die Alten' der Schein die Stabilität und Notwendigkeit des Realen, verbinden ‚die Modernen' das Reale mit dem, was im Weg steht: ein ontologisches Hindernis, das eine andere Modalität des Funktionierens nachweist, nämlich des *Dis*-Funktionierens, die Aristoteles in der Wiederholung, die er als *tyché* bezeichnete, detektierte. Letzteres bestimmt Lacan als die Wiederholung, die immanent den „Konvoi" hemmt, d. h., sie verhindert die Strukturierung der Realität durch Verankerung in zwei zentralen *semblants*, Stabilität und Notwendigkeit (für Aristoteles sind das auch die Hauptmerkmale des antiken Herren). Das unmögliche Reale ist also keine gesonderte Realität, sondern ein Schnitt im Schein, der die empirische Realität kennzeichnet, eine instabile Struktur, die in Bezug auf die angenommene Notwendigkeit des Scheins als unmöglich zu fassen ist.

Die Frage nach dem Realen ist eng mit der wissenschaftlichen Wahl der Sprache verbunden. Im Kern der modernen Wissenschaft findet man keine Sprache des gesunden Menschenverstandes, keine sinnvolle und bedeutungsvolle menschliche Sprache, sondern das Reale der Sprache, das in der Mathematik und Geometrie exemplarisch wird, eine Sprache ohne Sinn und Bedeutung, die aber weiterhin eine Sprachform bleibt – *die* Form, die den Sackgassen des Realen entspricht und die stabilisierende Funktion des Herren ausschließt. Daraus folgt, dass die wissenschaftliche Moderne weniger in der Überschneidung oder adäquaten Beziehung zwischen dem Schein und dem Realen wurzelt als in der Koinzidenz zwischen dem Realen der Erscheinungen und dem Realen der Sprache: eine Begegnung zweier Unmöglichkeiten, wodurch die Rolle der menschlichen Erfahrung in der Begründung der Wissenschaften an Bedeutung verliert. Anders gesagt, was zusammenfällt, sind zwei Nicht-Übereinstimmungen oder Nicht-Beziehungen, die der Sprache mit sich selbst und die der Realität mit sich selbst; beide folgen aus der Tatsache, dass es sich um nicht-totalisierbare dynamische Ordnungen handelt (die die vormoderne Wissenschaft vergeblich zu totalisieren und stabilisieren versuchte). Die mehr oder weniger explizite Entdeckung der modernen Wissenschaft besteht darin, dass weder Realität noch Sprache in einer überdeterminierten und notwendigen Weise funktionieren und dass die Begegnung zweier Unmöglichkeiten, der linguistischen und der ontologischen, einen ungeahnten epistemischen Horizont eröffnet. Nicht nur die menschliche Erfahrung, sondern auch der Akzent auf der Sprache des gesunden Menschenverstands war ein zentrales Hindernis bei der modernen Neubegründung der Wissenschaft und bei der Einführung eines dialektischen Begriffs des Realen.

Koyrés Unterscheidung von Erfahrung und Experiment ist hier von entscheidender Bedeutung und steht in engem Zusammenhang mit der Wahl der Sprache. Es geht um die Gegenüberstellung der ‚natürlichen Sprache', d. h. der Menschensprache, in der die aristotelische Wissenschaft versucht, die Naturerscheinungen aufrechtzuerhalten und Totalität, Stabilität und Notwendigkeit ins Reale einzuführen, und der ‚Sprache der Natur', d. h. der unpersönlichen, ent-psychologisierten und spekulativen Sprache des mathematisch begründeten Experimentierens, die gleichzeitig als Verwirklichung der Autonomie, die der Menschensprache innewohnt, aufzufassen ist.[13] Die Wahl der Sprache enthält also eine Wahl des Realen der Sprache gegen den Schein der Sprache, die Anerkennung eines immanenten Kurzschlusses des Scheins durch die Mathematik und durch die Autonomie des Signifikanten überhaupt. Mit dieser diskursiven Neuorientierung verwarf die moderne Wissenschaft den aristotelischen Primat des *automaton* und führte *tyché* in die Wissenschaft ein. Dabei verwarf sie auch die zentrale epistemische Position des sinnlichen Bewusstseins: „Mathematik ist Wissenschaft ohne Bewusstsein".[14] Diese Verwerfung bedeutet jedoch nicht, dass die Mathematik subjektlos ist, sondern dass das Subjekt der Mathematik (bzw. das Subjekt der Wissenschaft) mit dem Subjekt des Unbewussten gleichzusetzen ist: dezentralisiertes Denken, das von seinen psychologischen Trägern abgelöst ist. Auf diese Weise legte die moderne Wissenschaft die epistemischen Grundlagen, die Freud ermöglichten, das Reale des Denkens im Begriff des Unbewussten zu isolieren.

Die Opposition ‚Erfahrung – Experiment' entspricht also der Opposition ‚natürliche Sprache – Sprache der Natur' sowie der Opposition ‚Interpretation – Formalisierung':

> Galilei [...] weiß, daß die Erfahrung – oder wenn ich mir erlauben darf, hier den lateinischen Terminus des *experimentum* dem der gemeinen *experience*, welche nichts als Beobachtung ist, entgegenzusetzen –, daß also das *experimentum* vorbereitet werden muß, daß dies eine Frage ist, die der Natur gestellt wird, in einer ganz speziellen Sprache, jener der Geometrie und Mathematik; er weiß, daß es nicht genügt, das, was der Fall ist, das, was sich normaler- und natürlicherweise unseren Augen darbietet, zu beobachten; daß man wissen muß, wie die Frage zu formulieren und wie darüber hinaus die Antwort zu entziffern und zu begreifen ist: wie also auf das *experimentum* die strikten Gesetze der Meßkunst und der mathematischen Interpretation anzuwenden sind. [...] Galileis Instrumente [...] waren Instrumente im strengsten Sinn des Begriffs: Sie waren Inkarnationen der Theorie.[15]

Die moderne Wissenschaft endet nicht bei der Frage nach dem Sein, das auf der Ebene des Scheins verharrt (und vielleicht hat dieser Aspekt des Galileismus Heidegger am meisten skandalisiert). Die Problematik des Seins ist nicht radikal genug, um

---

13 Lacan begründete seine Lehre in der Verbindung von beiden oben erwähnten Aspekten und zeigte dadurch, dass der Signifikant im selben Rahmen wie die Formalsprachen und unterschiedliche Geometrien zu begreifen ist: „Die Linguistik, mit Saussure und dem Prager Kreis, richtet sich ein von einem Schnitt her, der die Barre ist, gesetzt zwischen den Signifikanten und das Signifikat, auf daß hier die Differenz vorwiege, aus der der Signifikant sich konstituiert absolut, doch ebenso effektiv sich ordnet aus einer Autonomie, die in nichts den Effekten von Krystall nachsteht." Jacques Lacan, *Television, Radiophonie*, Berlin, 1988, S. 7. D. h., dass man die (strukturale) Linguistik der Mathematik und der Geometrie beifügen muss, um die erweiterte epistemische Plattform der wissenschaftlichen Moderne zu denken.

14 Lacan (2001), *Autres écrits*, S. 453. „[L]a mathématique est la science sans conscience".

15 Koyré (1998), *Leonardo, Galilei, Pascal*, S. 67 f.

die Welt der Erscheinungen zu hinterfragen. Es ist das heraklitische Werden, das allmählich ins Zentrum des neuen Wissensregimes rückt. Dabei handelt es sich um das Problem der Instabilität im Sein, um die Verflechtung von Sein und Nicht-Sein bzw. um die Erschütterung des Scheins durch etwas, das weder Sein noch Nicht-Sein darstellt, sondern als Nicht-Realisiertes im Rahmen der Realität insistiert und die treibende Kraft des nicht-teleologischen Werdens der Realität repräsentiert. Das wissenschaftliche Experiment demonstriert in der Welt die Dynamik des Realen. In der Experimentalwissenschaft bestimmt die Mathematik die Struktur und den Umfang der Forschung[16] und ermöglicht gleichzeitig, das Unmögliche in der Realität zu mobilisieren. Anders gesagt, die experimentelle Methode konkretisiert die Tatsache, dass ein Diskurs reale Konsequenzen hervorbringen kann.[17]

Für die klassische und moderne Wissenschaft ist die Mathematik die Realisierung des Symbolischen; sie demonstriert die Einschließung des Symbolischen ins Reale. Natürlich kann diese Einschließung nur unter der Bedingung erkannt werden, dass die Sprache von ihren menschlichen Nutzern abgelöst wird. Aber diese Ablösung impliziert, dass der Wissenschaftler weder ein psychologisches Individuum noch ein Subjekt des Wissens ist. Der Wissenschaftler ist unbewusst (genauso wie Lacan zufolge Gott, und vielleicht ist der Wissenschaftler tatsächlich ein moderner Ersatz für den toten Gott, der in seinem Beruf ebenso experimentell vorgeht wie Gott im Augenblick der Schöpfung). Die klassische Wissenschaft impliziert eine Emanzipation der Sprache, indem sie den mathematischen Realismus affirmiert. Daraus folgt, dass das Experiment streng genommen eine unmenschliche Erfahrung ist, die in ihrem eigenartigen empirischen Charakter (insofern sie wissenschaftliche Hypothesen durch die künstlich erzeugten empirischen Bedingungen verifiziert oder falsifiziert) unvermeidlich den diskursiven Apparat in seiner Autonomie voraussetzt. Das gleiche gilt für die Technologie, die eine weitere Art der Realisierung oder Materialisierung mathematisierter Theorien darstellt. Um an Koyrés anschaulichstes Beispiel zu erinnern[18]: Ein Objekt wie das Teleskop ist durch die Optik bedingt, die selbst die moderne Geometrisierung des Raums voraussetzt und, so könnte man sagen, den Blick vom Auge ablöst; ein Apparat, der das Sehen in seiner Autonomie verkörpert. Lacans Auffassung des Blicks als Objekt *a* geht hier nur einen Schritt weiter.

Im Gegensatz zu logischem Positivismus und Empirismus, die weiterhin auf den gesunden Menschenverstand bauen und in dieser Hinsicht die aristotelische Wissenschaftslehre bis weit in die Moderne hinein fortsetzen, finden wir im Kern der modernen Naturwissenschaft kein notwendiges, in der natürlichen Sprache beschriebenes empirisches Reales, sondern ein unmögliches Reales, demonstriert in der formalen Sprache und verifiziert durch Experimentieren. Kurz, wir finden eine dialektische und materialistische Sprachform (Mathematik als Realisierung

16 Die poetische Sprache ist eine weitere Form des Experimentierens und eine weitere Konkretisierung des Realen der Sprache. Ein solches Experimentieren kommt zum Punkt im Unbewussten, das der freudsche Name für das Reale des Denkens ist.

17 Siehe Jacques Lacan, *Le Séminaire, livre XVI, D'un Autre à l'autre,* Paris, 2006, S. 33.

18 Siehe Alexandre Koyré, *Études d'histoire de la pensée philosophique*, Paris, 1961, S. 311-329.

der Autonomie der Sprache) und Erfahrungsform (Experiment, das der Autonomie der Sprache entspricht).

Mit dem dezentralisierenden Effekt der Mathematik ist der Niedergang der Kosmologie verbunden, die bekanntlich ihr privilegiertes Objekt verlor, den Kosmos, verstanden als eine geschlossene und lückenfreie Welt. Die moderne Dezentralisierung des Wissens und die Verschiebung von der Notwendigkeit zur Unmöglichkeit des Realen bedeuten offensichtlich nicht, dass das Reale nicht mehr als rational begriffen wird, sondern nur, dass die Ordnung des Seins und die logische Notwendigkeit keine privilegierten Zeichen der Rationalität des Realen sind.[19] Die Rationalität des mathematischen Realen unterscheidet sich von der Rationalität des gesunden Menschenverstandes, und während sich die vormoderne Wissenschaft durch das Imaginäre der korrekten Formen dem Realen annäherte (daher der Diskurs über Totalität, Harmonie und Schönheit, der aus der Kosmologie sozusagen eine Kosmetik des Realen macht), begegnet die moderne Wissenschaft dem Realen ausschließlich durch den symbolischen Apparat (Kalkül und Technik) und schafft somit den vormodernen qualitativen Gegensatz von korrekten und inkorrekten Formen als unbegründet und nicht-wissenschaftlich ab. Eine weitere entscheidende Konsequenz der Wahl, der zufolge die dialektische und spekulative Sprache der Formalisierung und nicht länger die nicht-dialektische und logisch normalisierte Sprache des gesunden Menschenverstandes als Sprache des Realen aufzufassen ist, besteht in der Unterscheidung von Bewusstsein und Subjektivität. An dieser Stelle erweitert Lacan den Umfang von Koyrés Epistemologie durch die These, dass „das Subjekt, mit dem die Psychoanalyse operiert, nur das Subjekt der Wissenschaft sein kann“[20].

3. Mathematischer Realismus und dialektischer Materialismus

Mit der Entscheidung für die autonome und gegen die menschliche Sprache führte die wissenschaftliche Moderne zu einer „Verwerfung des Menschen“[21] im Bereich des Wissens und forderte somit die aristotelischen Grundlagen der Wissenschaft heraus. Im 20. Jahrhundert erwies die strukturalistische Bewegung, dass diese Verwerfung eine homologe Ablehnung des Aristotelismus im Bereich der ‚menschlichen Objekte‘ (sprachliche, soziale und subjektive Realität) impliziert. Weiter gefasst hat die moderne epistemische Entwicklung in den Geisteswissenschaften drei radikale Projekte hervorgebracht, die letztlich eine Synthese in Lacans theoretischen Bemühungen gefunden haben: die strukturale Linguistik, die Kritik der

---

19 Daraus kann man die drei negativen Eigenschaften des Realen deduzieren: Abwesenheit eines Gesetzes, Verwerfung des Sinns und Fragmentierung. Auch das bedeutet nicht, dass das Reale nicht strukturiert ist; das Nicht-All (*pas-tout*) ist der lacansche Begriff für die Struktur des Realen als Unmöglichen. Siehe Jacques Lacan, *Le Séminaire, livre XXIII, Le sinthome*, Paris, 2005, Vorlesung IV, VIII und IX.

20 Jacques Lacan, *Schriften II*, Berlin, 1986, S. 236.

21 Jorland (1981), *La science dans la philosophie*, S. 147.

politischen Ökonomie und schließlich die Psychoanalyse, die ihr gemeinsames Objekt in dem finden, was man als das Reale des Symbolischen bezeichnen könnte. „Die Struktur ist also real. Das wird überhaupt durch die Konvergenz mit einer Unmöglichkeit bestimmt. Dadurch ist sie real."[22] Lacans Aussage (die offensichtlich nur im Universum der modernen Wissenschaft sinnvoll ist) gilt für jede Struktur, nicht nur für die linguistische (die Verkettung von reinen Differenzen, d. h. von strukturiertem Nichts); man kann hier nochmals die These wiederholen, dass jede Begegnung zwischen dem Diskurs und dem Realen eine Konvergenz zweier unmöglicher Strukturen darstellt.

Die Verwerfung des Menschen vervollständigt sich mit der Psychoanalyse, die das Unbewusste als eine Wissensform auffasst: dezentralisiertes „Wissen, das sich nicht weiß"[23], was auch eine geeignete Definition von wissenschaftlichem Wissen wäre. In ihrer Endphase nimmt die moderne wissenschaftliche Revolution das Denken überhaupt (d. h. Denken ohne Qualitäten) zum Objekt und subvertiert somit die vorherrschenden philosophischen, soziologischen und psychologischen Auffassungen der Subjektivität: Das Ego ist kein reales Zentrum des mentalen Mikrokosmos, sondern eine manipulierbare imaginäre *Projektion*; folglich gibt es keinen mentalen Mikro*kosmos*, der einem objektiven Makro*kosmos* gegenüberstünde. Die Problematik der Entfremdung bringt diese Dezentralisierung auf den Punkt: Lacans Aussagen wie ‚das Unbewusste ist draußen', ‚der Mensch denkt mit seinem Objekt' oder ‚Struktur ist real' thematisieren dieselbe topologische Problematik, nämlich dass mit der Affirmation des mathematischen Realismus die Begründer der modernen Wissenschaft „die ganze Struktur unserer Intelligenz umbauen mussten"[24].

Der Kern des psychoanalytischen Beitrags zur Epistemologie besteht im Versuch, eine Orientierung auszuarbeiten, die sowohl kritisch als auch materialistisch ist. Diese Tendenz steht im Mittelpunkt von Lacans radikalisiertem Koyréianismus, der drei philosophische Aussagen verbindet: ‚das Reale ist ideal' (Platon), ‚das Reale ist rational' (Hegel) und schließlich ‚das Reale ist unmöglich' (Koyré). Die letzte Aussage gibt den beiden anderen eine materialistische Wendung, indem sie ein Konzept des Realen einführt, das auf drei negativen Eigenschaften basiert: instabile Gesetzmäßigkeit, Verwerfung des Sinns und Nicht-Totalisierbarkeit. Mit der Affirmation des mathematischen Realismus und der strukturellen Instabilität

---

22 Lacan (2006), *D'un Autre à l'autre*, S. 30. „La structure, c'est donc réel. Ça se détermine en général par convergence vers une impossibilité. C'est par ça que c'est réel."

23 Jacques Lacan, *Encore*, Berlin, 1991, S. 103.

24 Koyré (1998), *Leonardo, Galilei, Pascal*, S. 92. [Korrigierte Übersetzung; S. T.] Die Abschaffung der Seele, die mit der modernen Aktualisierung des mathematischen Realismus verbunden werden kann, hat tatsächlich die räumliche Auffassung des Denkens umgestaltet und den Denkraum überhaupt umstrukturiert. Aber man brauchte Jahrhunderte, bevor eine systematische Theorie der Dezentralisierung des Denkens ausgearbeitet wurde. Der kartesianische Übergang von *cogito* zu *res cogitans* hat schließlich das Denken neu zentralisiert und es war nur der freudsche Übergang von denkender *Substanz* zum psychischen *Apparat*, der diese kartesianische Neusubstanzialisierung des Denkens herausforderte und seine Verdichtung im bewussten Sitz der epistemischen Gewissheit hinterfragte.

umreißen Koyré und Lacan einen breiteren historischen Rahmen, der von Heraklit und Platon (im Gegensatz zu Parmenides und Aristoteles) über Descartes und Hegel (im Gegensatz zu Hume und Kant) bis hin zu Koyré und Lacan selbst (im Gegensatz zu Popper und Wittgenstein) reicht.

Koyrés Kritik des empiristischen Reduktionismus greift in einen materialistischen Streit ein, der dem philosophischen Konflikt von Idealismus vs. Materialismus, den Konflikt von empirischem Materialismus vs. dialektischem Materialismus beiseite stellt. Wie schon anfangs erwähnt, hat die von Koyré und Lacan verfolgte Epistemologie einen wichtigen Vorläufer in Cavaillès' Philosophie der Mathematik, die von einer eigentümlichen „Umkehrung des Platonismus" (Deleuze) ausgeht. Während für Deleuze die Umkehrung darin besteht, sich auf das niedrigste Seiende zu konzentrieren (das Simulakrum, ein paradoxes Seiendes ohne ein adäquates Modell in der Ideenwelt), subvertiert Cavaillès' philosophischer Ansatz den Platonismus auf dem Terrain der mathematischen Objekte selbst, ohne dafür Platons mathematischen Realismus zu negieren. Für Cavaillès ist die Mathematik ein autonomes Werden, eine instabile historische Struktur, die sich auf nichts anderes außerhalb ihrer selbst reduzieren lässt. Darüber hinaus ist Geschichtlichkeit der Mathematik durch ihre internen Krisen und Destabilisierungen eingeschrieben:

> [E]very definition, within a given epoch, is relative to that epoch – that is to say, to the history that gives rise to it. There is no eternal definition. To speak of mathematics is always to remake mathematics. This becoming seems to be autonomous; it seems possible for the epistemologist to find beneath the historical accidents a necessary consecution: the notions introduced were necessitated by the solution to a problem – and by virtue of their sole presence amongst the notions that already existed, they pose, in their turn, new problems. There really is a becoming: the mathematician embarks upon an adventure which can be arrested only arbitrarily, every moment of which endows it with a radical novelty.[25]

Cavaillès argumentiert, „we can perceive necessities beneath the sequence of notions and procedures", aber diese Notwendigkeit wird von Kontingenz durchlaufen und konstituiert sich nur retroaktiv. Man könnte sagen, dass die mathematischen Objekte und Prinzipien vorübergehende Stabilisierungen von kontinuierlichen Prozessen sind, deren Ergebnis stets unvorhersehbar bleibt. Diese dynamische Komponente macht aus der Mathematik eine dialektische Wissenschaft (das Werden ist „the fundamental dialectic of mathematics") und eine Experimentalwissenschaft („the activity of mathematicians is an experimental activity"). Diese Kombination von Dialektik und Experiment bzw. die Auffassung des Experiments als einer dialektischen Praxis liegt im Kern der materialistischen Orientierung der Epistemologie und ermöglicht es, das Experimentieren auf geisteswissenschaftliche Disziplinen auszudehnen – und in letzter Instanz auf den Diskurs schlechthin

[25] Jean Cavaillès/Albert Lautman, „Mathematical Thought", online unter: www.urbanomic.com, zuletzt aufgerufen am 14.11.2016. Alle Zitate entstammen dieser Quelle.

(das Unbewusste demonstriert ein fortlaufendes Experimentieren in der Sprache überhaupt).

Wie gesagt, hat Lacan die Autonomie der Mathematik entscheidend auf den Begriff des Diskurses erweitert. Somit begegnet die linguistische Struktur *qua* Instabilität der Dynamik des Realen, die in den drei angeführten negativen Merkmalen zusammengefasst wird.[26] So wie die klassische Wissenschaft die Teilung in die mathematische und physische, supralunare und sublunare Sphäre abschaffte, muss die Frage nach dem Realen so formuliert werden, dass sie das Reale der Sprache mitumfasst: „Sagen wir, dass es im Prinzip von nichts anderem wert ist zu sprechen, als vom Realen, in dem der Diskurs selbst Konsequenzen hat."[27] Durch die Realisierung des Symbolischen aufgrund der Affirmation seiner absoluten Autonomie führt die Wissenschaft zu einer systematischen Ablehnung des philosophischen Idealismus. Die klassische Physik konnte also mit den vormodernen Fetischisierungen der Natur brechen (aus dieser Hinsicht führen die New-Age-Obskurantismen und einige ökologische Ideologien die vormoderne Naturauffassung wieder ein), indem sie anfing, die Natur mit dem entpsychologisierten Diskurs und nicht länger mit einem (philosophischen) Liebesdiskurs zu behandeln:

> [F]ür die Physik lohnt es sich etwas zu sagen, nämlich dass der Diskurs darin Konsequenzen hat, während, wie jeder weiß, in der Natur kein Diskurs irgendeine Konsequenz hat, und darum liebt man sie so sehr. Ein Naturphilosoph zu sein galt noch nie als ein Zertifikat des Materialismus oder der Wissenschaftlichkeit.[28]

Dabei begegnet man erneut der Frage nach der wissenschaftlichen Wahl der Sprache; in Lacans Sprache übersetzt, lautet Koyrés These, dass der Platoniker insistiert, der Diskurs habe Konsequenzen im Realen, während der Aristoteliker (Liebes-)Lust aus einer vorausgesetzten natürlichen Ordnung schöpft, in der Diskurse angeblich keine Konsequenzen haben.

Es gibt eine letzte Problematik, die zu einer materialistischen und dialektischen Perspektive auf moderne Wissenschaft nötigt, nämlich die Leere. Sie ist die Triebkraft der modernen Geometrisierung des Raumes und bedingt die Abschaffung des sphärischen Modells der Realität (Kosmos) und des Denkens (Seele). Wie Koyré schreibt,

> in der Leere (d. h. im Raum der euklidischen Geometrie) gibt es keine privilegierten Orte oder Richtungen. [...] [E]in Körper in der Leere weiß nicht, wohin er gehen soll, hat keinen Grund, sich in eine bestimmte Richtung zu bewegen und hat demnach

---

[26] Siehe Fußnote 19.

[27] Lacan (2006), *Le Séminaire, livre XVI, D'un Autre à l'autre*, S. 31. „Disons que, dans le principe, ce n'est pas la peine de parler d'autre chose que du réel dans lequel le discours lui-même a des conséquences."

[28] Ebd., S. 33. „[L]a physique vaut qu'on en dise quelque chose, que le discours y a des conséquences, tandis que, comme chacun sait, aucun discours n'en a aucune dans la nature, et, c'est même pourquoi on l'aime tant. Être philosophe de la nature n'a jamais passé en aucun temps pour un certificat de matérialisme, de scientificité non plus." Siehe auch Alenka Zupančič, „Realism in Psychoanalysis", in: Lorenzo Chiesa (Hg.), *Lacan and Philosophy: The New Generation*, Melbourne, 2014, S. 21-33.

> überhaupt keinen Grund sich zu bewegen. [...] [Ni]icht nur gibt es keine natürlichen Plätze, es gibt gar keine Plätze mehr.[29]

Die moderne Geometrisierung des Raumes und die damit einhergehende Abschaffung der Teilung auf die supralunare und sublunare Sphäre lassen jedoch Raum für blinde Flecken, die am deutlichsten bei Descartes zu erkennen sind, dessen Geometrie und Philosophie in einer Verwerfung der Temporalität münden. Descartes ersetzt dabei die Idee eines mathematischen und ontologischen Werdens durch die traditionelle Seinsfrage, bzw. dynamische durch statische Struktur:

> Kartesianische Bewegung [...] ist eine Bewegung des Geometers, die Bewegung geometrischer Entitäten: die Bewegung eines Punktes, der eine gerade Linie zieht, die Bewegung einer Linie, die einen Kreis beschreibt. Aber Bewegungen wie diese haben im Gegensatz zu physikalischen Bewegungen keine Geschwindigkeit und finden nicht in der Zeit statt. Durchgehende Geometrisierung – die Ursünde des kartesianischen Denkens – führt zum Atemporalen: der Raum bleibt erhalten, aber die Zeit wird beseitigt. Es löst das reale Sein im Geometrischen auf. Aber das Reale nimmt Rache.[30]

Diese ‚Rache des Realen' zeigte sich in der Ablösung des mathematischen Realismus von seiner statischen kartesischen Variante, die in einer scheinbar extravaganten Kombination von Platonismus und Atomismus mündete. Dabei wurde eine wahrhaft materialistische Mathematik der Leere eingeführt. Mit der atomistischen Komponente lässt sich der dynamische Charakter des Raumes vollständig affirmieren und die Folgen der kartesischen Verwerfung der Temporalität neutralisieren: „Die Revolution im XVII. Jahrhundert, die ich einst Platons Rache nannte, war tatsächlich der Effekt eines Bündnisses, Platon mit Demokrit."[31] Es war Newton, der diese philosophische und wissenschaftliche Synthese vollzog: „For him, just as for Boyle, the book of nature is written in corpuscular characters and words. But, just as for Galileo and Descartes, it is a purely mathematical syntax that binds them together and gives its meaning to the text of the book."[32] Newtons Lösung kehrt also zu *zwei* Entitäten zurück, die Aristoteles dermaßen empörten, dass er ihnen keinen realen Status anerkennen wollte: Demokrits Atom und Platons Idee.

---

29 Koyré (1966), *Études galiléennes*, S. 23: „[D]ans le vide (c'est à dire, dans l'espace de la géométrie euclidienne), il n'y a ni lieux ni directions privilégiés. [...] [U]n corps, dans le vide, ne saurait où aller, n'aurait pas de raison de se mouvoir dans une direction plutôt que dans une autre, et donc de se mouvoir du tout. [...] [D]ans le vide, en effet, non seulement il n'y a pas de lieux naturels, il n'y a même pas de lieux du tout."

30 Ebd., S. 131: „Le mouvement cartésien [...] est le mouvement des géomètres. Et des êtres géométriques: le mouvement du point qui trace une ligne droite, le mouvement d'une droite qui décrit un cercle. . . . Mais ces mouvements-là, à l'encontre des mouvements physiques, n'ont pas de vitesse, et ne se font pas dans le temps. La géométrisation à outrance – ce péché originel de la pensée cartésienne – aboutit à l'intemporel: elle garde l'espace, elle élimine le temps. Elle dissout l'être réel dans le géométrique. Mais le réel se venge."

31 Koyré (1961), *Études d'histoire de la pensée philosophique*, S. 239. „La révolution du XVIIe siècle, que j'ai appelée jadis ‚la revanche de Platon' a été, en fait, l'effet d'une alliance. De celle de Platon avec Démocrite."

32 Alexandre Koyré, *Newtonian Studies*, London, 1965, S. 12.

Die klassische Wissenschaft mag zwar für den Triumph von Platon über Aristoteles stehen, aber dieser Triumph konnte nur auf dem Hintergrund der Synthese von Platonismus und Atomismus stattfinden, also unter der Voraussetzung der epistemischen und philosophischen Vereinigung von Dialektik und Materialismus. In der Überwindung des Dualismus von Form und Materie bzw. von Mathematischem und Materiellem findet man ein Bemühen, den Zwischenraum oder die Verflechtung zwischen dem Diskurs und dem Realen zu denken. Auf diese ontologische Grauzone zwischen dem Symbolischen und dem Realen zielt auch der Begriff der Struktur *qua* Instabilität. Was daraus folgt, ist ein dynamischer Platonismus bzw. dialektischer Materialismus, der die verschobene Perspektive auf die Mathematik umfasst, die Cavaillès so passend formulierte, als er von ihrem singulären Werden sprach. Mathematik fällt offensichtlich als erste in diese ontologische Grauzone zwischen dem Symbolischen und dem Realen. Als ein nichtteleologischer Prozess der Strukturierung und Umstrukturierung stehen ihre Sprache und Objekte sowohl für die absolute Autonomie des Symbolischen als auch für eine Dynamik des Realen. Schließlich ist es die Einsicht, dass eine beliebige Struktur nur real wird, insofern sie instabil, d. h. unmöglich ist, die Dialektik und Materialismus zusammenführt.

Die materialistische Umkehrung des Platonismus vollzieht sich also durch die Temporalisierung der Mathematik: „Mathematical entities have to be, in some sense, brought nearer to physics, subjected to motion, and viewed not in their ‚being' but in their ‚becoming' or in their ‚flux'"[33] Es war der Atomismus, der verhinderte, dass die moderne Wissenschaft in einen idealistischen Realismus überging (worauf Platons Philosophie allzu oft reduziert wird). Atomismus garantiert aber nur einen Gesichtspunkt der korrekten materialistischen Orientierung. Die andere Seite wird durch das Mathem gestützt, welches verhindert, dass der Atomismus in einen vulgären Materialismus abgleitet (worauf er seit Aristoteles reduziert wurde). Der wahrhaft revolutionäre Materialismus (Materialismus des Unmöglichen) besteht nun in der scheinbar bizarren Synthese des mathematischen und atomistischen Objekts.

In dieser Synthese von Demokrit und Platon kann die Wissenschaft schließlich als Kampfplatz, nicht nur zwischen Empirismus und Idealismus, sondern zwischen vulgärem Materialismus und dialektischem Materialismus aufgefasst werden. Somit verändert die moderne wissenschaftliche Revolution nachträglich den Sinn des Streits, der die Philosophie inaugurierte: Der aristotelische Empirismus ist in Wirklichkeit ein maskierter Idealismus und Platons Idealismus ein dialektischer Materialismus. Dieser Streit animiert noch heute die Wissenschaft, die Philosophie und das Denken schlechthin. Er markiert auch den Punkt, an dem die epistemologischen Fragen von politischen Fragen nicht mehr zu trennen sind. Lacan hat in seiner Lehre am deutlichsten demonstriert, dass der dialektische Materialismus direkt in den mathematischen Realismus der modernen Wissenschaft eingeschrieben ist und eine Orientierung im Denken darstellt, die synchron

---

33 Ebd., S. 10.

mit den emanzipatorischen Potenzialen der wissenschaftlichen Moderne verläuft. Projekte wie die Kritik der politischen Ökonomie oder die Psychoanalyse können daher als Sammelorte dieses Potenzials betrachtet werden, wobei auch sie nicht immun gegen interne Konflikte sind. Im Gegenteil: dem Scheitern ausgesetzt, machen sie den konfliktuösen Charakter der modernen Wissenschaft vollkommen sichtbar.

Abbildungsnachweise

Volker Pantenburg

Abb. 1 und 2: *Barque sortant du port*, Regie: Auguste und Louis Lumière. DVD Screenshot: *The Movies Begin: a Treasury of Eearly Cinema 1894-1913. Vol. 2: The European Pioneers*, New York, NY, 2002.

Abb. 3 und 4: *Der Mann mit der Kamera*, Regie: Dziga Vertov. DVD Screenshot: *L'homme à la caméra*, Paris, 2004.

Abb. 5 und 6: *Umberto D.*, Regie: Vittorio de Sica. DVD Screenshot, New York, NY, 2003.

Abb. 7 und 8: *Leviathan*, Regie: Lucien Castaing-Taylor und Véréna Paravel. DVD Screenshot, London, 2013.

Abb. 9 und 10: *Manakamana*, Regie: Stephanie Spray und Pacho Velez. DVD Screenshot, London, 2015.

Dorothea Walzer

Abb. 1: Honoré Daumier, „Ein Triumph des Advokaten", in: *Recht und Gericht: vierzig Steindrucke, 1808-1879*, Berlin, 1918-1919, 14 Seiten, No. 42.

Abb. 2: Honoré Daumier, „Ratapoil reicht seinen Arm der Republik" (1851), in: *Caricatures. Spott und Humor in Frankreich von 1700 bis in die Gegenwart*, Katalog, hg. von Gisela Vetter-Liebenow, Hannover: Wilhelm Busch – Deutsches Museum für Karikatur und Zeichenkunst 2016.

Abb. 3: John Heartfield, „Ich kenne nur Paragraphen", in: Kurt Tucholsky, *Deutschland, Deutschland über alles. Ein Bilderbuch von Kurt Tucholsky und vielen Fotografen*, montiert von John Heartfield, Reinbek bei Hamburg, 1980 [1929], S. 163.

Über die Autorinnen und Autoren

Friedrich Balke lehrt Medienwissenschaft mit dem Schwerpunkt bilddokumentarische Medien an der Ruhr-Universität Bochum.

Christian Begemann lehrt Neuere deutsche Literatur an der Ludwig-Maximilians-Universität München.

Natalie Binczek lehrt Theorie und Geschichte literarischer Kommunikation und ihrer Medien an der Ruhr-Universität Bochum.

Till Breyer lehrt Neugermanistik an der Ruhr-Universität Bochum.

Devin Fore lehrt Germanistik und Kunstgeschichte an der Princeton University.

Hal Foster lehrt Kunstgeschichte an der Princeton University.

Niklaus Largier lehrt Germanistik und vergleichende Literaturwissenschaft an der University of California, Berkeley.

Maria Muhle lehrt Philosophie und Ästhetische Theorie an der Akademie der Bildenden Künste München.

Jenny Nachtigall lehrt Ästhetik und Kunsttheorie an der Akademie der Bildenden Künste München.

Volker Pantenburg lehrt Filmwissenschaft an der Freien Universität Berlin.

Ulrich Plass lehrt deutsche Literatur an der Wesleyan University.

Elisabeth Strowick lehrt Neuere deutsche Literatur und Literaturtheorie an der New York University.

Chenxi Tang lehrt Neuere deutsche Literatur an der University of California, Berkeley.

Veronika Thanner lehrt Neuere deutsche Literatur an der Humboldt-Universität Berlin.

Samo Tomšič forscht im Exzellenzcluster „Bild – Wissen – Gestaltung“ der Humboldt-Universität Berlin.

ULRIKE VEDDER lehrt Neuere deutsche Literatur und Geschlechterforschung an der Humboldt-Universität Berlin.

JOSEPH VOGL lehrt Literatur-, Kultur- und Medienwissenschaft an der Humboldt-Universität Berlin.

DOROTHEA WALZER lehrt Theorie und Geschichte literarischer Kommunikation und ihrer Medien an der Ruhr-Universität Bochum.